Excel® 2007 Bible

Excel® 2007 Bible

John Walkenbach

Wiley Publishing, Inc.

Excel® 2007 Bible

Published by
Wiley Publishing, Inc.
10475 Crosspoint Boulevard
Indianapolis, IN 46256
www.wiley.com

Copyright © 2007 by Wiley Publishing, Inc., Indianapolis, Indiana

Published simultaneously in Canada

Library of Congress Control Number: 2006934841

ISBN-13: 978-0-470-04403-2
ISBN-10: 0-470-04403-9

Manufactured in the United States of America

10 9 8 7

1B/QY/RS/QW/IN

About the Author

John Walkenbach is a bestselling Excel author and has published more than 50 spreadsheet books. He lives amid the saguaros, javelinas, and gila monsters in Southern Arizona. For more information, Google him.

*This one's for Pamn, who pretty much
left me alone while I was writing it.*

Credits

Acquisitions Manager
Gregory S. Croy

Project Editor
Kelly Ewing

Technical Editor
Doug Sahlin

Editorial Manager
Jodi Jensen

Vice President & Executive Group Publisher
Richard Swadley

Vice President and Publisher
Andy Cummings

Editorial Director
Mary C. Corder

Project Coordinator
Erin Smith

Graphics and Production Specialists
Beth Brooks
Carrie A. Foster
Joyce Haughey
Jennifer Mayberry
Barbara Moore
Lynsey Osborn
Heather Pope
Ronald Terry

Quality Control Technicians
Laura Albert
Jessica Kramer
Christine Pingleton
Brian H. Walls

Media Development Project Supervisor
Laura Moss

Media Development Specialist
Steve Kudirka

Proofreading and Indexing
Techbooks

Contents at a Glance

Contents at a Glance

Contents

Contents

Contents

Contents

Contents

Part III: Creating Charts and Graphics   349

Chapter 19: Getting Started Making Charts 351

Contents

Part IV: Using Advanced Excel Features   459

Chapter 23: Customizing the Quick Access Toolbar 461

Chapter 24: Using Custom Number Formats 465

Chapter 25: Using Data Validation 481

Contents

Contents

Chapter 32: Making Your Worksheets Error-Free 551

Part V: Analyzing Data with Excel   573

Chapter 33: Using Microsoft Query with External Database Files 575

Contents

Part VI: Programming Excel with VBA   679

Chapter 39: Introducing Visual Basic for Applications 681

Contents

Contents

Acknowledgments

Writing *Excel 2007 Bible* was one of my most challenging projects. Never before has an Excel upgrade incorporated so many new features and changes. Thanks to the brilliant people at Microsoft for the hard work it took to get this product out the door at Redmond, and onto my hard drive. I can't say that I agree with all of their user interface decisions, but I have no doubt that this is the best version of Excel ever. It's always a pleasure to deal with **Greg Croy**, acquisitions editor. I've worked with Greg for many years, and I appreciate all he does to get my books to market in a timely manner. And a special thank-you to **Kelly Ewing**, project editor for this book. She and the other talented people behind the scenes did an incredible job of converting my sloppy and often incomprehensible Word files into real book pages that actually make sense.

A few other people also deserve thanks. First of all, I'd like to acknowledge **Mark Tedeschi**, who was the first to request. I must also thank **~Q~** for opening my eyes to new possibilities for the oft-neglected tilde. And I thank **Michael D. Bono** for his life-long guidance and sound hypocritical stance on key issues.

It is with deepest humility that I thank **Anagram**, a longtime contributor to banjo, biplane, biker, and binary appreciation societies around the world. When I grow up, I want to be just like her. And, to keep it in the family, a special thanks to **Bisbonian**, who introduced me to the art of flailing the banjo and took me on an awesome biplane ride over Bisbee, Arizona.

A few random pages of this book (towards the back) are dedicated to young **MacDonald** — the one without the farm. Thanks to **Satyrsong** and **MK**, for sushi and steaming up my glasses. Just as **Joe Blow** taught me the true meaning of Swiss cheese, **Keveena** taught me the meaning of bhroondaglog (and I'm truly grateful for that). And my gratitude even extends to **Michael R. Bernstein**, who taught me everything I know about Hannukwanzaamas.

Very special thanks go out to my long-time friend **Wendy Lauver**, a dedicated fan, an occasional pivot table princess, and a self-described charting hag. She's one of the few people in this modern world who deserves an exclamation point after her name. Here's to you, **Wendy!**

A special acknowledgment goes out to **Margie Corbett**, for encouraging her husband to pursue his Excel obsession, and for allowing him to buy this book with his own money. I'd also like to thank **Gerard Gibbons**, who simply wants to confuse his wife by having his name appear in an Excel book. I'd be remiss if I didn't thank **Curtis Curtington** for being meshugeh ahf toit. Oh, and for the underpants.

A special thanks to **Stephen**, from Kennesaw State University, for his commitment to raising the quality of education in our great country. I'd also like to thank the always deft **Biff**, for answering thousands of Excel questions in the Microsoft newsgroups so I could spend my time writing this book. And thanks to **Brent Nichols**, who took the time to explain to me the difference between Excel and axles. Now, looking under my car isn't so perplexing. Thanks, **Mr. Ed**, for siring the love of my life.

I'm down on my knees when I thank **Spirit Mountain** for providing the inspiration to complete this book. And I'm grateful to **RickHap**, for donating Faith Mountain to my charity fundraiser for Whole Wheat Radio. And, of course, special thanks to **Cindy in Wasilla** for helping me with the decorating plan for a very special Kinkade Christmas. And while I'm on the subject, thanks to **Jim Kloss**, for his successful effort to make Whole Wheat Radio so bad that I had no desire to tune in and get distracted while writing this book. On a similar note, I'm grateful to **Esther Golton**, for not releasing her long-awaited CD while I was working on this book. It's likely that I'll be able to use this same acknowledgment when I write the *Excel 2010 Bible*.

I don't really want to, but legal pressure forces me to acknowledge the contributions of **Toad**, whose life I saved during the war — and then lived to regret it. I also thank **Mrs. Toad**, not because she actually did anything, but because it's very unlikely that she will be mentioned in any other Excel 2007 books, and she might buy a copy if she sees her name here.

I'd also like to acknowledge **Alison Young**, for being generally awesome. **Zach Fraile** also deserves special recognition for his key role in seeing me through the early stages of ribbon UI crisis. Thanks also go out to **Mark Coles,** who showed his wife how to do a household budget in Excel, rather than writing it like a story in Notepad. And, of course, I'd like to thank **Joe Bardi** for being Joe Bardi. But not as much as I'd like to thank **Joshua O'Keefe**, who really knows how to move sides of beef.

I bow down to **12-Stringer**, whose proclivity, propensity, and capacity for single malt Scotch rivals my own, and whose flummoxing right-hand technique on 12-string guitar was so flabbergasting that I was inspired to devote life to learning an instrument with seven fewer strings.

This book, of course, never would have come to fruition without the awesome Austin music from **Casey**. I'd like to thank **The One True Dan Tripp** for agreeing to buy this book because his name is in this section. I'm certain I should thank **mare**, but I can't find the note that explains what I have to thank him/her/it for. In any case, thanks! And that also goes to **moioci**, for general intrepidity. Thanks are also due to **The Necklace Lady** for making sure everyone can hang their name badge on a sparkle — something that's vitally important in this day and age.

I also appreciate **Mr. Mike**, for teaching me to play chess. His crushing victory over his 7-year old opponent was truly inspirational. I would also like to thank **Victor Conte** and his peeps at BALCO. And special thanks to **Dan** and **Spencer** for remaining faithful to the Padres, even when they shouldn't have been.

It would be a grievous error to overlook **Andrew Methmann**, who has several J-Walk books floating around his office, and has promised to add to the collection if he finds his name here. I hereby dedicate 11.5 pages of this book to **Kirk**. In this world woven of illusions and insubstantial impressions, I always wonder how he can stand me and my books — and, of course, the blog.

I'd like to inform **Mary** — who keeps telling me that putting things/people in boxes is wrong, wrong, wrong — to go soak her head. Putting things in boxes is what Excel is about. So there. Now, back to the acknowledgments. I thank **Tina**, for her desire to get a raise by learning all she can about Excel, and for dazzling her boss and coworkers with material that she lifts directly from my books. And I must mention **Raymond Allan**, one of thousands of people who can't remember the password for Power Utility Pak and apologize to me via e-mail.

Thanks to **Ruth Maher** in Ireland, who figured out the secret to using Excel. She always takes her Excel with a full pint of Guinness. I must also thank **Soren Bo Christensen** from Denmark, for being the only Dane interested in Excel 2007 (or so he claims). But most of all, I thank **Gareth Forster** in England, for being over there and not here. And least but certainly not last, I pay tribute to **Lindsay**, for his riveting links and his unflappable insistence on bifurcating them. I almost forgot. Thanks to **Miss Cellania** for being so miscellaneous.

I would especially like to thank **Terry Davies**, for pointing out the similarities between Excel and the *Daily Telegraph* Cryptic Crossword. I still can't do the crossword, but I *can* type letters into cells — which is almost as gratifying. I'm also thankful to **Vilhjálmur Helgason**, for not changing his name to **William Tell**. My buddy **Sol** also deserves some credit. He's the guy who scours the Internets to find all the stuff that may or may not interest you — and he sends it to me.

At least nine pages of this book are dedicated to **Eenie Meenie**, who just keeps hanging around. I'd like to thank **Jordon Kalilich** for being so incredibly thankable, and **Mikey McGrinder** for being **Guitarded**. But most of all, I'm grateful to **cyberhobo** for his respectful silence. I would also like to acknowledge **Granny Dee**. When she purchases her copy of the *Excel 2007 Bible*, it's very likely that she will own more copies than the Vatican Library.

This book wouldn't be the book it is if it weren't for **danielo**, whose favorite answer is usually found in cell G16. Thanks also go out to **Aníbal Fraquelli**, because he teaches that there's more to life than cells (a concept that continues to be debated in academic circles). Many thanks to **Don Frickson**, for his help with the past pluperfect tense, an archaic but surprisingly useful literary device. And special thanks go out to **Guy** and **Bob**, for making 2006 the "Year of the Banjo" — even if **Candy** insists that they still can't play very well. Hopefully, this book will set them on a more productive path to 5-string nirvana.

In the nonhuman realm, a bark out goes to **Tootsie**, the best darn chocolate Cocker Spaniel living in California. And thanks to **Jean.** I hereby offer my official apology for running over her dog and blaming it on the neighbors. I'm also grateful to **Rex.** He doesn't understand most of the words in my books, but he *does* enjoy entering formulas in cell K9.

A big thanks to **Dave Green**, for *not* contributing to this book. Without his interference, I was able to complete it on time with only a few dozen major rewrites. I send a round-about circular thanks to **Andrew Reynolds**, who often insists on reinventing the wheel.

I'd also like to thank five of **Dave Brett's** seven personalities for their valuable assistance (the other two are Access mavens). And I simply must acknowledge **Nazire** because she has an uncanny ability to interpret my crystal clear instructions without even trying very hard. I also appreciate **Alexis Cole**, who insists on spending his birthday working on very clunky macros. A big thanks is due **Charles Chickering**, for plagiarizing my code to help the multitudes on the public newsgroups.

I truly admire **Stuart O'Brien**, for all the long hours, hard work, and Herculean effort he put into writing his own acknowledgment. And thanks to **Lewis Johnson**, for giving me my big break — both times. Special thanks to **Mike C**, for thoughtfully stroking his beard and looking intelligent while reading my books in public places (that sort of thing *really* helps sales). And equally special thanks to **Jan Chan**, for demonstrating his semi-amazing Reverse Tsil Tnemgdelwonkca formula.

For the first time, I'd like to publicly acknowledge **Dustin Spicuzza**, for showing me how much fun exploding billboards can be. Also, thanks to **Joel Schultz** for using my book in all of his Excel classes, and for being a genius in general. I'd like to give a special thanks to **Roger Martin**, for his suggestion to use numbered pages. If only I'd learned that trick sooner in my career!

I must acknowledge **Artoch**, for his tireless efforts with the Reckoning. This book would have two fewer sentences if it weren't for him. And I extend special thanks to **Tobias H. Schmidbauer**, for thinking that my blog had a connection with The Tonight Show. How could I forget **Greg P. in Fairfield**? He showed me that Excel is much easier when you use both hands.

Acknowledgments

I'll always be thankful to **Champthom**, for waking up at 5 a.m. on those cold Saturday mornings to take me to skating practice. And, of course, I must thank my **grandma** for giving me the genetic gift of fidgeting. I'd also like to thank my mother and **Anne Kulak**, both of whom where equally important in making me who I am today.

My thanks to **Tank**, for doing the thankless job of giving thanks at my Thanksgiving dinner. And I have undying gratitude to **John Owen**, who stopped me from hearing the voices — at least for a while. Oh, and I'm really grateful for **Fred**, for not commenting much.

I'll always be grateful for the culinary contributions of **Jon Anderson**, who showed me how to use conditional formatting to make a delicious cheese spread. And I would like to give a special thanks to **Adam Poranski**, for truly teaching me to appreciate Stamen. More thanks are due to **Heidi Buckner**. Because of her constant praise of Microsoft Word, I was forced to write this book out of spite. Also thank-worthy is **ElMoney**, who continued to contribute to my blog even after she became famous. And I'm especially grateful to **Rory**, for not being a troll.

A warm thank-you to **Danille Bouchonnet**, for spreading on the lotion after that mishap in the tanning booth. And thanks to **pat...** who introduced me to some innovative uses of the ellipsis. Thanks go out to **fancypants...** for being inspired by the following to learn Excel the J-Walk way: **Victor Torres**, **Doug Durdan**, **Tony Williamson**, **Avalon**, **Lori**, **Eden**, **Cardi**, **Ricardo Dittmer**, **Jeremy Mathis**, **Dan and Angie McKenzie**, **Di Hogg**, **Roger Holmes**, **Katarina Kotulakova**, and (last, but least) **Phil Borkstrom**.

I'm much obliged to **Claire Summers**, a friend of mine who uses Excel a lot in her work, even though she doesn't really need to. Special thanks to **Art C**, who taught me everything I know about Excel — but unfortunately not everything *he* knows about Excel. I'd also like to thank **Big Leather Dave**, for teaching me how to hit without hurting and hurt without hitting, skills that come in handy several times a week.

I can't thank **Evan** and **Robyn C.** enough. I admire that fact that they use their Excel powers only for good purposes. I'm also grateful to **Rich** (aka **shades**), who is old, slow, and confused — which makes me feel young, fast, and alert. And a very special thanks to **Tombraider**. In my time of need, he was the only one who knew the Hungarian phrase for "But officer, the llama was on fire when I got here." I'm also indebted to **Rufus** for accepting that extra cash I had lying around without making a big deal of it.

I checked my "Excel can do anything" files, and remembered **Guy**, who deserves thanks for helping me modify the wiring in my '51 NoCaster using a circuit design created in an Excel worksheet (no macros). I would also like to thank the **Gideon Society**. It may be a baseless rumor, but I've heard that they will be bundling a copy of this book along with the standard fare they supply to hotel and motel rooms everywhere. And, of course, I'd like to acknowledge **Mike Hiscock**. He's just this guy I know.

I'm also appreciative of **Sheldon Reynolds**. Even though he's not the guitarist Sheldon Reynolds from Earth Wind and Fire, he made me laugh once (or maybe I'm thinking of someone else). And a very extra super-special thanks to **ClownPie**. His love of pie taught me that there's only one thing in this world to live for. Unfortunately, the love of his life generates a #NAME error in Excel. The correct spelling is PI().

And a special word up to **Jack Faley**, for pointing out that I forgot to carry the zero on page 582. Because of his observation, this book is now certified error-free. I'd also like to thank **Wilma Compton**, for being the only 17-year-old regular reader of the J-Walk Blog. But that's just because her dad reads Excel books. And I'd really like to thank **Quasimike** Why? Falettinme Be Mice Elf Agin.

I'm left with no choice but to express my heartfelt gratitude to **Fine-line**, whose incalculable ignorance of Excel assures me gainful employment well into my twilight years. And if I spoke Spanish, I'd say *gracias* to **Rob Richard and Rubberband** for rockin' the house. On a related note, many thanks **Left Hand Green** for rocking my face off.

I may be faceless, but I'm still grateful to **Grant Willson** and **William Strunk Jr.** for the loan of several semi-colons (I'll return them when I'm finished, I promise). And I must acknowledge **Jerry Przygocki** for teaching me to paint, and for showing me that a working class hero is something to be. Special thanks to **Jonco**, who created a workbook that will ultimately assist me in the search for the real killers. I would also like to thank **Josh Voog**, for his half-hearted commitment to average, everyday mediocrity. And still more thanks to **Zack Barresse**, who is mostly unhelpful, but is often good for some comic relief, a sturdy smile, and forced laughter.

I should probably thank **Ross Mclean**, but I don't think I will. But I *will* give a "shout out" (as the kids say) to **Doug Glancy**, who is fairly tall. And I must mention **Richard Schollar**, who was absolutely no help whatsoever in the production of this book. Thanks are truly due to **Dan Maxey**, who reads my blog with amusement almost every day. And thanks to **Renee Fabry**, for... Well, you know.

I may be stretching it, but I'm grateful to Abu Ja'far Muhammad ibn Musa al-Khwarizmi (c.778 - c.850), who created the Arabic number system that powers Excel. I must also acknowledge **Ian Huitson**, for being the first person to produce a Mandelbrot in Excel, complete with graphical output and not a single statement of VBA code. He deserves almost as much thanks as **Graham Long**, who actually taught me everything I know.

Kudos to **Sally I. Villarreal** (for valuable assistance), to **Philip A. DiStefano** (for no specific reason), and to **Nate Roth** (who reminds me that even pirates need a little R & R). A belated thanks to **Allan Moore**, for his lack of contributions to this book and all of my previous books. And thanks to **John Pritzlaff**, for the same reason. I'd also like to express my heartfealt thanks to **Neal Eiserman** for correcting the spelling erors in this book.

If I had a Hallmark thank-you card, I'd send it without a stamp to **Jonathan Caws-Elwitt**, because he prematurely said, "You're welcome." I owe him one. I also owe one to **Russel Maxwell**, for teaching me the true meaning of life, and without whose help this book would be very one-dimensional. Warm and almost-sincere thanks to **Steven Nelson**, for buying several of my books over the years (at discount prices). Without his personal support, I might not have been able to write this edition. **Yvette**, I will always remember our time at the River Walk, Viva Le Tour! I also thank **Blayne Rutledge**, for his unparalleled involvement and keen perception of all things perceptible. And, of course, I would be remiss if I didn't acknowledge **ac** for her... well... knowledge.

My prayers were answered by the tireless efforts of **BobOldSchoolBolin**, who gave me the faith to accept that Excel is just a spreadsheet program and not Satan's Soul Stealer. I give praise to **Barry of Maryland**, for spreading the four gospels of Excel: Pivot Tables, Functions, Charting and VBA — all in accordance with the J-Walk Bible.

And here's to the dazzling **Janessa Allen** — the loveliest programmer in Royal Oak, Michigan. And special recognition goes to **AnnMarie Johnson**, for her longstanding membership in my fan club (to make up for her husband's recognition as such on the LoTR DVD). Thanks to **Jim Westrich** for sending me a copy of his innovative Excel Origami project. Sadly, this project has folded, but a documentary will soon be released on Paper View. And I'll never forget **Chip Gorman**, for showing me a great little VBA trick to calculate pi to the last digit. His tip on squaring the circle is also worth mentioning, but I won't.

A special thanks is extended to **Oscar Binley**, whose obsession with tennis balls led me to uncover a hitherto unexplored aspect of VBA. And I can't overlook **LinDee Kangas**, who first opened my eyes to the power of VLOOKUP. I offer a most sincere thank-you to the sometimes irascible **Steve**. Finalizing this edition of the book would not have been possible in the absence of his advice that the anagram of my name is "belch no jaw hank". And this is my long-overdue thanks to **Jonathan (Ozzy) Osborne**, whose contribution to the spin-cycle of my washing machine defies words, thoughts, and most nonmundane feelings.

Acknowledgments

I almost forgot to thank the following: **Leandro Castillo** (for unleashing Custom Lists), **Pete Dozier** (my VBA Jedi Master), and **Thomasina Campbell** (who believed in me when I didn't believe in me). Oh, and thanks are due to **Jennifer Irving**, for her outstanding contributions to the field of font color management (despite my suggestions to try colors other than pink, dark pink, and baby pink).

My undying gratitude goes out to **John Leo**, who taught me the four key elements of financial modeling in Excel: Simplicity, flexibility, elegance, and (most importantly) Alt-Tab. Thank to **Ike Gerardo**, who sleeps better at night after he realized that when you have the solution, it's better to give than to receive. A big thanks to **Ray Lee**, who pointed out that financial modeling has nothing to do with fashion (which certainly opened the door to some new formulas). I'm equally grateful to **Xcelion**, who demonstrated that using the SUM function is indeed more efficient than using a hand-held calculator and typing the result in a cell. Who'd a thunk?

If I live to be 50, I'll never forget **Joan Perry**, who walked from coast to coast in support of this book (and no, I won't reimburse her for the shoes). And I must acknowledge **Malicious Earn**, who will be buying this book to see whether he actually got acknowledged. I am eternally grateful to **TimS**, who dutifully patrols the bookstores, straightens up the Excel section, and then hides the non-Walkenbach Excel books in the Stephen King section. And I must certainly acknowledge **Woody**, whom everyone expected would be the last one to be acknowledged.

And finally, I *really and truly* thank the readers of the J-Walk Blog and the Daily Dose of Excel for helping me write what is perhaps the longest Acknowledgments section in the nearly 200-year history of Wiley Publishing.

Introduction

Thanks for purchasing the *Excel 2007 Bible.* For the first time in many years, Excel users finally have some significant new features to get excited about. And if you're just starting with Excel, you'll be glad to know that Excel 2007 is the easiest version ever.

My goal in writing this book is to share with you some of what I know about Excel, and in the process, make you more efficient on the job. The book contains everything that you need to know to learn the basics of Excel and then move on to more advanced topics at your own pace. You'll find many useful examples and lots of tips and tricks that I've accumulated over the years.

As a Microsoft MVP, I was fortunate to get access to early versions of Excel 2007, long before the beta versions were made public. So I'd been working with Excel 2007 for well over a year before it was finally released. It took me a while to get used to the new user interface, but once I passed that hurdle, I was convinced that this version of Excel is the best ever.

Is This Book for You?

The *Bible* series from Wiley Publishing, Inc. is designed for beginning, intermediate, and advanced users. This book covers all the essential components of Excel and provides clear and practical examples that you can adapt to your own needs.

In this book, I've tried to maintain a good balance between the basics that every Excel user needs to know and the more complex topics that will appeal to power users. I've used Excel for nearly 20 years, and I realize that almost everyone still has something to learn (including myself). My goal is to make that learning an enjoyable process.

Software Versions

This book was written for Excel 2007 for Windows. No exceptions. If you're using an older version of Excel, I suggest that you put down this book immediately and find a book that's appropriate for your version of Excel. The changes in Excel 2007 are so extensive that you'll probably be hopelessly confused if you use an earlier version.

Conventions This Book Uses

Take a minute to scan this section to learn some of the typographical and organizational conventions that this book uses.

Excel commands

Excel 2007 features a brand new "menu-less" user interface. In place of a menu system, Excel uses a context-sensitive Ribbon system. The words along the top (such as Home, Insert, Page Layout, and so on) are known as *tabs*. Click a tab, and the Ribbon displays the commands for the selected tab. Each command has a name, which is (usually) displayed next to or below the icon. The commands are arranged in groups, and the group name appears at the bottom of the Ribbon.

The convention I use is to indicate the tab name, followed by the group name, followed by the command name. So, the command used to toggle word wrap within a cell is indicated as:

```
Home@@-->Alignment@@-->Wrap Text
```

You'll learn more about using the new Ribbon user interface in Chapter 1.

Filenames, named ranges, and your input

Input that you make from the keyboard appears in **bold**. Named ranges appear in a monospace `font`. Lengthy input usually appears on a separate line. For example, I may instruct you to enter a formula such as the following:

```
="Part Name: " &VLOOKUP(PartNumber,PartList,2)
```

Key names

Names of the keys on your keyboard appear in normal type. When two keys should be pressed simultaneously, they're connected with a plus sign, like this: "Press Ctrl+C to copy the selected cells." Here are the key names as I refer to them throughout the book:

Alt	down arrow	Num Lock	right arrow
Backspace	End	Pause	Scroll Lock
Caps Lock	Home	PgDn	Shift
Ctrl	Insert	PgUp	Tab
Delete	left arrow	Print Screen	up arrow

Functions

Excel's built-in worksheet functions appear in uppercase, like this: "Enter a SUM formula in cell C20."

Mouse conventions

You'll come across some of the following mouse-related terms, all standard fare:

- **Mouse pointer:** The small graphic figure that moves on-screen when you move your mouse. The mouse pointer is usually an arrow, but it changes shape when you move to certain areas of the screen or when you're performing certain actions.

- **Point:** Move the mouse so that the mouse pointer is on a specific item: for example, "Point to the Save button on the toolbar."

- **Press:** Press the left mouse button once and keep it pressed. Normally, this is used when dragging.
- **Click:** Press the left mouse button once and release it immediately.
- **Right-click:** Press the right mouse button once and release it immediately. The right mouse button is used in Excel to pop up shortcut menus that are appropriate for whatever is currently selected.
- **Double-click:** Press the left mouse button twice in rapid succession.
- **Drag:** Press the left mouse button and keep it pressed while you move the mouse. Dragging is often used to select a range of cells or to change the size of an object.

What the Icons Mean

Throughout the book, you'll see special graphic symbols, or icons, in the left margin. These call your attention to points that are particularly important or relevant to a specific group of readers. The icons in this book are as follows:

 This icon signals the fact that something is important or worth noting. Notes may alert you to a concept that helps you master the task at hand, or they may denote something that is fundamental to understanding subsequent material.

 This icon marks a more efficient way of doing something that may not be obvious.

This icon marks a more efficient way of doing something that may not be obvious.

I use this symbol when a possibility exists that the operation I'm describing may cause problems if you're not careful.

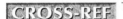 This icon indicates that a related topic is discussed elsewhere in the book.

 This icon indicates that a related example or file is available on the companion CD-ROM.

This icon indicates a feature that is new to Excel 2007.

How This Book Is Organized

Notice that the book is divided into six main parts, followed by four appendixes.

Part I: Getting Started with Excel: This part consists of ten chapters that provide background about Excel. These chapters are considered required reading for Excel newcomers, but even experienced users will probably find some new information here.

Part II: Working with Formulas and Functions: The chapters in Part II cover everything that you need to know to become proficient with performing calculations in Excel.

Part III: Creating Charts and Graphics: The chapters in Part III describe how to create effective charts. In addition, you'll find a chapter on the new conditional formatting features, and a chapter on graphics — including the new SmartArt.

Part IV: Using Advanced Excel Features: This part consists of ten chapters that deal with topics that are sometimes considered advanced. However, many beginning and intermediate users may find this information useful as well.

Part V: Analyzing Data with Excel: Data analysis is the focus of the chapters in Part IV. Users of all levels will find some of these chapters of interest.

Part VI: Programming Excel with VBA: Part VI is for those who want to customize Excel for their own use or who are designing workbooks or add-ins that are to be used by others. It starts with an introduction to recording macros and VBA programming and then provides coverage of UserForms, add-ins, and events.

Appendixes: The book has four appendixes that cover Excel worksheet functions, the contents of the book's CD-ROM, other Excel resources, and Excel shortcut keys.

How to Use This Book

Although you're certainly free to do so, I didn't write this book with the intention that you would read it cover to cover. Rather, it's a reference book that you can consult when:

- You're stuck while trying to do something.
- You need to do something that you've never done.
- You have some time on your hands, and you're interested in learning something new about Excel.

The index is comprehensive, and each chapter typically focuses on a single broad topic. If you're just starting out with Excel, I recommend that you read the first few chapters to gain a basic understanding of the product and then do some experimenting on your own. After you become familiar with Excel's environment, you can refer to the chapters that interest you most. Some users, however, may prefer to follow the chapters in order.

Don't be discouraged if some of the material is over your head. Most users get by just fine by using only a small subset of Excel's total capabilities. In fact, the 80/20 rule applies here: 80 percent of Excel users use only 20 percent of its features. However, using only 20 percent of Excel's features still gives you *lots* of power at your fingertips.

What's on the Companion CD

This book contains many examples, and the workbooks for those examples are available on the companion CD-ROM, arranged in directories that correspond to the chapters. Refer to Appendix B for a complete list of the files.

In addition, the CD-ROM contains an electronic version of this book. It's a searchable PDF file that's a perfect companion for your notebook computer when you take your next cross-country flight.

Part I

Getting Started with Excel

The chapters in this part are intended to provide essential background information for working with Excel. Here, you'll see how to make use of the basic features that are required for every Excel user. If you've used Excel (or even a different spreadsheet program) in the past, much of this information may seem like review. Even so, it's possible that you'll find quite a few tricks and techniques.

Chapter 1

Introducing Excel

This chapter serves as an introductory overview of Excel 2007. If you're already familiar with a previous version of Excel, reading this chapter is still a good idea. Excel 2007 is different from every previous version — *very* different.

What Is Excel Good For?

Excel, as you probably know, is the world's most widely-used spreadsheet program, and is part of the Microsoft Office suite. Other spreadsheet programs are available, but Excel is by far the most popular and has become the world standard.

Much of the appeal of Excel is due to the fact that it's so versatile. Excel's forte, of course, is performing numerical calculations, but Excel is also very useful for non-numerical applications. Here are just a few of the uses for Excel:

- **Number crunching:** Create budgets, analyze survey results, and perform just about any type of financial analysis you can think of.
- **Creating charts:** Create a wide variety of highly customizable charts.
- **Organizing lists:** Use the row-and-column layout to store lists efficiently.
- **Accessing other data:** Import data from a wide variety of sources.
- **Creating graphics and diagrams:** Use Shapes and the new SmartArt to create professional-looking diagrams.
- **Automating complex tasks:** Perform a tedious task with a single mouse click with Excel's macro capabilities.

IN THIS CHAPTER

Understanding what Excel is used for

Learning the parts of Excel's window

Introducing the Ribbon user interface, shortcut menus, and dialog boxes

Navigating Excel worksheets

Introducing Excel with a quick hands-on session

Understanding Workbooks and Worksheets

The work you do in Excel is performed in a workbook file, which appears in its own window. You can have as many workbooks open as you need. By default, Excel 2007 workbooks use an XLSX file extension.

Each *workbook* is comprised of one or more worksheets, and each *worksheet* is made up of individual *cells*. Each cell contains a value, a formula, or text. A worksheet also has an invisible *draw layer*, which holds charts, images, and diagrams. Each worksheet in a workbook is accessible by clicking the *tab* at the bottom of the workbook window. In addition, workbooks can store chart sheets. A *chart sheet* displays a single chart and is also accessible by clicking a tab.

Newcomers to Excel are often intimidated by all the different elements that appear within Excel's window. Once you become familiar with the various parts, it all starts to make sense.

Figure 1.1 shows you the more important bits and pieces of Excel. As you look at the figure, refer to Table 1.1 for a brief explanation of the items shown in the figure.

TABLE 1.1

Parts of the Excel Screen That You Need to Know

Name	Description
Active cell indicator	This dark outline indicates the currently active cell (one of the 17,179,869,184 cells on each worksheet).
Application close button	Clicking this button closes Excel.
Window close button	Clicking this button closes the active workbook window.
Column letters	Letters range from A to IXFD — one for each of the 16,384 columns in the worksheet. You can click a column heading to select an entire column of cells.
Office button	This button leads to lots of options for working with your document, or Excel in general.
Formula bar	When you enter information or formulas into Excel, they appear in this line.
Horizontal scrollbar	Enables you to scroll the sheet horizontally.
Maximize/Restore button	Clicking this button increases the workbook window's size to fill Excel's complete workspace. If the window is already maximized, clicking this button "unmaximizes" Excel's window so that it no longer fills the entire screen.
Minimize application button	Clicking this button minimizes Excel's window.
Minimize window button	Clicking this button minimizes the workbook window.
Name box	Displays the active cell address or the name of the selected cell, range, or object.
Page view buttons	Change the way the worksheet is displayed by clicking one of these buttons.
Quick Access Toolbar	A toolbar that you customize to hold commonly-used commands
Ribbon	The main location to find Excel's commands. Clicking an item in the Tab list changes the ribbon that's displayed.
Row numbers	Numbers range from 1 to 1,048,576 — one for each row in the worksheet. You can click a row number to select an entire row of cells.
Sheet tabs	Each of these notebook-like tabs represents a different sheet in the workbook. A workbook can have any number of sheets, and each sheet has its name displayed in a sheet tab. By default, each new workbook that you create contains three sheets. Add a new sheet by clicking the Insert Worksheet button (which is displayed after the last sheet tab).

Name	Description
Sheet tab scroll buttons	These buttons let you scroll the sheet tabs to display tabs that aren't visible.
Status bar	This bar displays various messages as well as the status of the Num Lock, Caps Lock, and Scroll Lock keys on your keyboard. It also shows summary information about the range of cells that is selected. Right-click the status bar to change the information that's displayed
Tab list	Commands that display a different ribbon, similar to a menu.
Title bar	All Windows programs have a title bar, which displays the name of the program and the name of the current workbook and also holds some control buttons that you can use to modify the window.
Vertical scrollbar	Lets you scroll the sheet vertically.
Zoom control	A scroller that lets you zoom your worksheet in and out.

FIGURE 1.1

The Excel screen has many useful elements that you will use often.

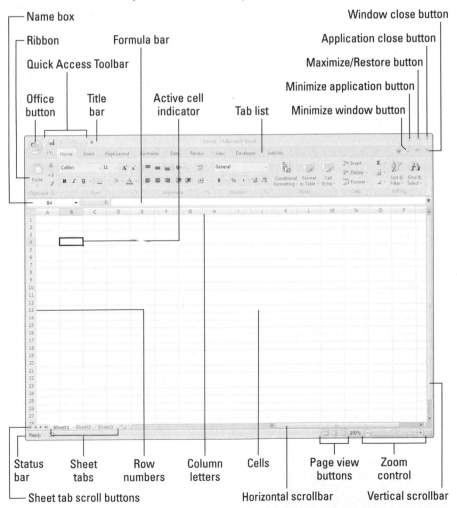

Moving Around a Worksheet

This section describes various ways to navigate through the cells in a worksheet. Every worksheet consists of rows (numbered 1 through 1,048,576) and columns (labeled A through XFD). After column Z comes column AA, which is followed by AB, AC, and so on. After column AZ comes BA, BB, and so on. After column ZZ is AAA, AAB, and so on.

The intersection of a row and a column is a single cell. At any given time, one cell is the *active cell*. You can identify the active cell by its darker border, as shown in Figure 1.2. Its *address* (its column letter and row number) appears in the Name box. Depending on the technique that you use to navigate through a workbook, you may or may not change the active cell when you navigate.

Notice that the row and column headings of the active cell appear in different colors to make it easier to identify the row and column of the active cell.

FIGURE 1.2

The active cell is the cell with the dark border — in this case, cell C8.

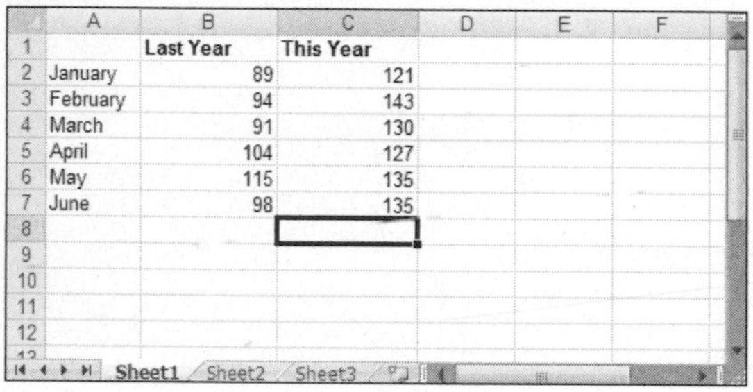

	A	B	C	D	E	F	
1		Last Year	This Year				
2	January	89	121				
3	February	94	143				
4	March	91	130				
5	April	104	127				
6	May	115	135				
7	June	98	135				
8							
9							
10							
11							
12							

Sheet1 / Sheet2 / Sheet3

Navigating with your keyboard

As you probably already know, you can use the standard navigational keys on your keyboard to move around a worksheet. These keys work just as you'd expect: The down arrow moves the active cell down one row, the right arrow moves it one column to the right, and so on. PgUp and PgDn move the active cell up or down one full window. (The actual number of rows moved depends on the number of rows displayed in the window.)

TIP You can use the keyboard to scroll through the worksheet without changing the active cell by turning on Scroll Lock, which is useful if you need to view another area of your worksheet and then quickly return to your original location. Just press Scroll Lock and use the direction keys to scroll through the worksheet. When you want to return to the original position (the active cell), press Ctrl+Backspace. Then, press Scroll Lock again to turn it off. When Scroll Lock is turned on, Excel displays Scroll Lock in the status bar at the bottom of the window.

The Num Lock key on your keyboard controls how the keys on the numeric keypad behave. When Num Lock is on, Excel displays Num Lock in the status bar, and the keys on your numeric keypad generate numbers. Most keyboards have a separate set of navigational (arrow) keys located to the left of the numeric keypad. The state of the Num Lock key doesn't affect these keys.

Table 1.2 summarizes all the worksheet movement keys available in Excel.

TABLE 1.2

Excel's Worksheet Movement Keys

Key	Action
Up arrow	Moves the active cell up one row.
Down arrow	Moves the active cell down one row.
Left arrow of Shift+Tab	Moves the active cell one column to the left.
Right arrow or Tab	Moves the active cell one column to the right.
PgUp	Moves the active cell up one screen.
PgDn	Moves the active cell down one screen.
Alt+PgDn	Moves the active cell right one screen.
Alt+PgUp	Moves the active cell left one screen.
Ctrl+Backspace	Scrolls the screen so that the active cell is visible.
Up arrow*	Scrolls the screen up one row (active cell does not change).
Down arrow*	Scrolls the screen down one row (active cell does not change).
Left arrow*	Scrolls the screen left one column (active cell does not change).
Right arrow*	Scrolls the screen right one column (active cell does not change).

* With Scroll Lock on

Navigating with your mouse

To change the active cell by using the mouse, click another cell; it becomes the active cell. If the cell that you want to activate isn't visible in the workbook window, you can use the scrollbars to scroll the window in any direction. To scroll one cell, click either of the arrows on the scrollbar. To scroll by a complete screen, click either side of the scrollbar's scroll box. You also can drag the scroll box for faster scrolling.

TIP If your mouse has a wheel on it, you can use the mouse wheel to scroll vertically. Also, if you click the wheel and move the mouse in any direction, the worksheet scrolls automatically in that direction. The more you move the mouse, the faster the scrolling.

Press Ctrl while you use the mouse wheel to zoom the worksheet. If you prefer to use the mouse wheel to zoom the worksheet without pressing Ctrl, choose Office ➪ Excel Options and select the Advanced section. Place a check mark next to the Zoom On Roll With Intellimouse check box.

Using the scrollbars or scrolling with your mouse doesn't change the active cell. It simply scrolls the worksheet. To change the active cell, you must click a new cell after scrolling.

Introducing the Ribbon

The most dramatic change in Office 2007 is the new user interface. Traditional menus and toolbars are gone, and they've been replaced with the Ribbon. Office 2007 is the first software in history to use this new interface, and it remains to be seen whether it will catch on and replace traditional menus and toolbars.

Ribbon tabs

The commands available in the Ribbon vary, depending upon which tab is selected. The Ribbon is arranged into groups of related commands. Here's a quick overview of Excel's tabs.

- **Home:** You'll probably spend most of your time with the Home tab selected. This tab contains the basic Clipboard commands, formatting commands, style commands, commands to insert and delete rows or columns, plus an assortment of worksheet editing commands

- **Insert:** Select this tab when you need to insert something in a worksheet — a table, a diagram, a chart, a symbol, and so on.

- **Page Layout:** This tab contains commands that affect the overall appearance of your worksheet, including settings that deal with printing.

- **Formulas:** Use this tab to insert a formula, name a range, access the formula auditing tools, or control how Excel performs calculations.

- **Data:** Excel's data-related commands are on this tab.

- **Review:** This tab contains tools to check spelling, translate words, add comments, or protect sheets.

- **View:** The View tab contains commands that control various aspects of how a sheet is viewed. Some commands on this tab are also available in the status bar.

- **Developer:** This tab isn't visible by default. It contains commands that are useful for programmers. To display the Developer tab, choose Office ➪ Excel Options and then select Popular. Place a check mark next to Show Developer Tab In The Ribbon.

- **Add-Ins:** This tab is visible only if you've loaded a workbook or add-in that customizes the menu or toolbars. Because menus and toolbars are no longer available in Excel 2007, these customizations appear in the Add-Ins tab.

The appearance of the commands on the ribbon varies, depending on the width of Excel window. When the window is too narrow to display everything, the commands adapt and may seem to be missing. But the commands are still available. Figure 1.3 shows the Home tab of the Ribbon with all controls fully visible. Figure 1.4 shows the Ribbon when Excel's window is made more narrow. Notice that some of the descriptive text is gone, but the icons remain. Figure 1.5 shows the extreme case when the window is made very narrow. Some groups display a single icon. However, if you click the icon, all the group commands are available to you.

FIGURE 1.3

The Home tab of the Ribbon.

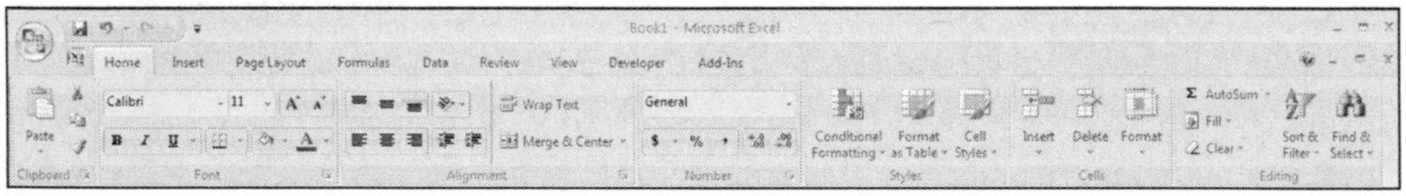

The Home tab when Excel's window is made narrower.

The Home tab when Excel's window is made very narrow.

> **TIP** If you would like to hide the Ribbon to increase your worksheet view, just double-click any of the tabs. The Ribbon goes away, and you're able to see about five additional rows of your worksheet. When you need to use the Ribbon again, just click a tab, and it comes back temporarily. To keep the ribbon turned on, double-click a tab. You can also press Ctrl+F1 to toggle the Ribbon display on and off.

Contextual tabs

In addition to the standard tabs, Excel 2007 also includes *contextual tabs*. Whenever an object (such as a chart, a table, or a SmartArt diagram) is selected, specific tools for working with that object are made available in the Ribbon.

Figure 1.6 shows the contextual tab that appears when a chart is selected. In this case, it has three contextual tabs: Design, Layout, and Format. Notice that the contextual tabs contain a description (Chart Tools) in Excel's title bar. When contextual tabs appear, you can, of course, continue to use all the other tabs.

FIGURE 1.6

When you select an object, contextual tabs contain tools for working with that object.

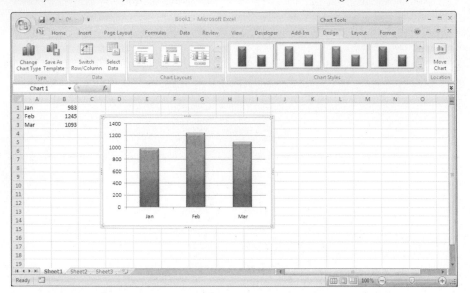

Types of commands on the Ribbon

When you hover your mouse pointer over a Ribbon command, you'll see a pop-up box that contains the command's name, and a brief description. For the most part, the commands in the Ribbon work just as you would expect them to. You do encounter several different styles of commands on the Ribbon:

- **Simple buttons:** Click the button, and it does its thing. An example of a simple button is the Increase Font Size button in the Font group of the Home tab. Some buttons perform the action immediately; others display a dialog box so that you can enter additional information. Button controls may or may not be accompanied by text.

- **Toggle buttons:** A toggle button is clickable and also conveys some type of information by displaying two different colors. An example is the Bold button in the Font group of the Home tab. If the active cell is not bold, the Bold button displays in its normal color. But if the active cell is already bold, the Bold button displays a different background color. If you click this button, it toggles the Bold attribute for the selection.

- **Simple drop-downs:** If the Ribbon command has a small downward pointing arrow, then the command is a drop-down. Click it, and additional commands appear below it. An example of a simple drop-down is The Conditional Formatting command in the Styles group of the Home Tab. When you click this control, you see several options related to conditional formatting.

- **Split buttons:** A split button control combines a one-click button with a drop-down. If you click the button part, the command is executed. If you click the drop-down part (a down-pointing arrowhead), you choose from a list of related commands. You can identify a split button command because it displays in two colors when you hover the mouse over it. An example of a split button is the Merge & Center command in the Alignment group of the Home tab (see Figure 1.7). Clicking the left part of this control merges and centers the selected cells. If you click the arrow part of the control (on the right), you get a list of commands related to merging cells.

- **Check boxes:** A check box control turns something on or off. An example is the Gridlines control in the Show/Hide group of the View tab. When the Gridlines check box is checked, the sheet displays gridlines. When the control isn't checked, the sheet gridlines don't appear.

- **Spinners:** Excel's Ribbon has only one spinner control. It's in the Scale To Fit group of the Page Layout tab. Click the top part of the spinner to increase the value; click the bottom part of the spinner to decrease the value.

Some of the Ribbon groups contain a small icon on the right side, known as a *dialog launcher.* For example, if you examine the Home ⇨ Alignment group, you see this icon (refer to Figure 1.8). Click it, and Excel displays the Format Cells dialog box, with the Alignment tab pre-selected. The dialog launchers generally provide options that aren't available in the Ribbon.

FIGURE 1.7

The Merge & Center command is a split button control.

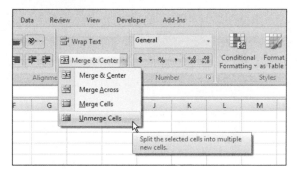

FIGURE 1.8

Some of the Ribbon groups contain a small icon on the right side, known as a *dialog launcher.*

Accessing the Ribbon using your keyboard

At first glance, you may think that the Ribbon is completely mouse-centric. After all, none of the commands have the traditional underline letter to indicate the Alt+keystrokes. But in fact, the Ribbon is *very* keyboard friendly. The trick is to press the Alt key to display the pop-up *keytips.* Each Ribbon control has a letter (or series of letters) that you type to issue the command.

 **TIP** You don't need to hold down the Alt key as you type the keytip letters.

Changing Your Mind

You can reverse just about every action in Excel by using the Undo command, located in the Quick Access Toolbar. Click Undo (or press Ctrl+Z) after issuing a command in error, and it's as if you never issued the command. You can reverse the effects of the last 100 actions that you performed by executing Undo more than once.

If you click the arrow on the right side of the Undo button, you see a description of the action that you can reverse. If you click an item in that list, that action and all the subsequent actions will be undone.

You can't reverse every action, however. Generally, anything that you do using the Office button can't be undone. For example, if you save a file and realize that you've overwritten a good copy with a bad one, you're just out of luck.

The Repeat button, also in the Quick Access Toolbar, performs in the opposite direction of the Undo button: Repeat re-issues commands that have been undone. If nothing has been undone, then you can use the Repeat button (or Ctrl+Y) to repeat the last command that you performed. For example if you applied a particular style to a cell (by choosing Home ⇨ Styles ⇨ Cell Styles), you can activate another cell and press Ctrl+Y to repeat the command.

Figure 1.9 shows how the Home tab looks after I hit the Alt key to display the keytips. If you press one of the keytips, the screen then displays more keytips. For example, to use the keyboard to align the cell contents to the left, press Alt, followed by H (for Home) and then AL (for Align Left). If you're a keyboard fan (like me), it takes just a few times before you memorize the keystrokes required for commands that you use frequently.

FIGURE 1.9

Pressing Alt displays the keytips.

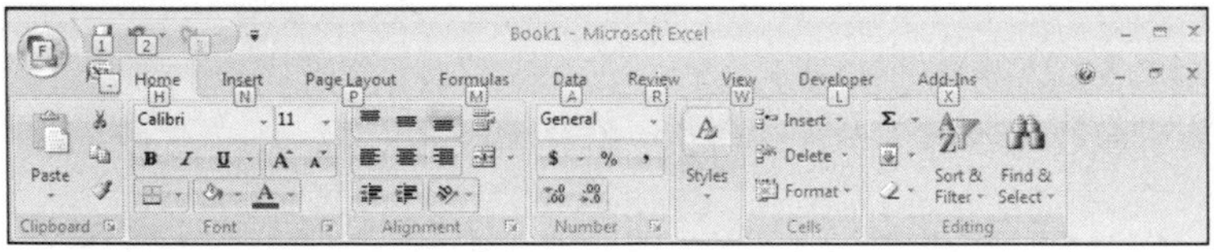

After you press Alt, you can also use the left and right arrow keys to scroll through the tabs. When you reach the proper tab, press down arrow to enter the Ribbon. Then use left and right arrow keys to scroll through the Ribbon commands. When you reach the command you need, press Enter to execute it. This method isn't as efficient as using the keytips, but it's a quick way to take a look at the commands available.

Using the shortcut menus

In addition to the Ribbon, Excel features a slew of shortcut menus, which you access by right-clicking just about anything within Excel. Shortcut menus don't contain every relevant command, just those that are most commonly used for whatever is selected.

As an example, Figure 1.10 shows the shortcut menu that appears when you right-click a cell. The shortcut menu appears at the mouse-pointer position, which makes selecting a command fast and efficient. The shortcut menu that appears depends on what you're doing at the time. For example, if you're working with a chart, the right-click shortcut menu contains commands that are pertinent to what is selected.

FIGURE 1.10

Click the right mouse button to display a shortcut menu with the commands that you're most likely to use.

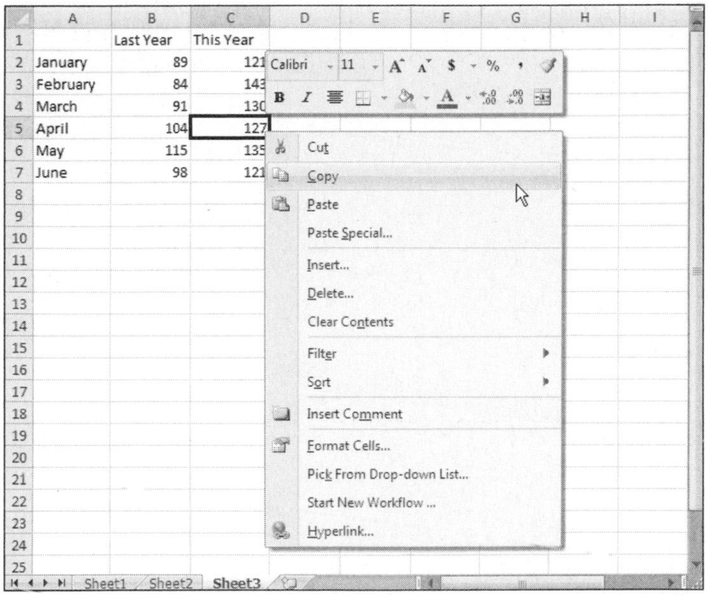

	A	B	C	D	E	F	G	H	I
1		Last Year	This Year						
2	January	89	121						
3	February	84	143						
4	March	91	130						
5	April	104	127						
6	May	115	135						
7	June	98	121						

Calibri ~ 11 ~ A˘ A˘ $ ~ % , ✧
B I ≣ ⊞ ~ ◇ ~ A ~ ⁺⁰₀ ⁰⁰₀ ⊞

- ✂ Cut
- ⧉ Copy
- ▣ Paste
- Paste Special...
- Insert...
- Delete...
- Clear Contents
- Filter ▶
- Sort ▶
- 🗐 Insert Comment
- 🖅 Format Cells...
- Pick From Drop-down List...
- Start New Workflow...
- 🌐 Hyperlink...

The box above the shortcut menu is known as the Mini toolbar and contains commonly used tools from the Home tab. The Mini toolbar was designed to reduce the distance your mouse has to travel around the screen. Just right-click, and common formatting tools are within an inch from your mouse pointer. The Mini toolbar is particularly useful when a tab other than Home is displayed. If you use a tool on the Mini toolbar, then the toolbar remains displayed in case you want to perform other formatting on the selection.

 **TIP** If you find the Mini toolbar too distracting, you can turn if off. Choose Office ⇨ Excel Options. Click the Popular tab and remove the check mark from Show Mini Toolbar On Selection.

Customizing your Quick Access Toolbar

In previous versions of Excel, end users were free to customize their menus and toolbars. Things have changed in Excel 2007. Now, the only end user customization option is the Quick Access Toolbar (QAT). Normally, the QAT appears on the left side of the title bar. Alternatively, you can display the QAT below the ribbon. Right-click the QAT and select Show Quick Access Toolbar Below Ribbon.

By default, the QAT contains three tools: Save, Undo, and Repeat. You can, of course, customize the QAT by adding other commands that you use often. To add a command from the Ribbon to your QAT, right-click the command and choose Add To Quick Access Toolbar. If you click the downward-pointing arrow to the right of the QAT, you see a drop-down menu with some additional commands that you might want to place in your QAT.

Excel has commands that aren't available in the Ribbon. In most cases, the only way to access these commands is to add them to your QAT. Figure 1.11 shows the Customization section of the Excel Options dialog box. This section is your one-stop shop for QAT customization. A quick way to display this dialog box is to right-click the QAT and choose Customize Quick Access Toolbar.

FIGURE 1.11

Add new icons to your QAT by using the Customization section of the Excel Options dialog box.

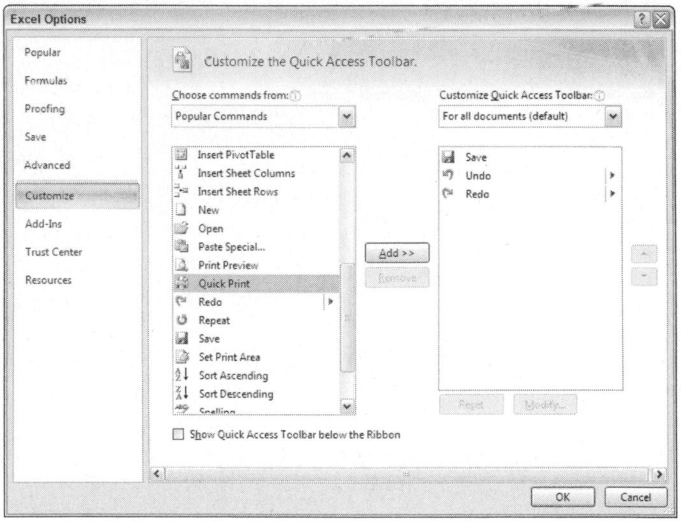

CROSS-REF   Refer to Chapter 23 for more information about customizing your QAT.

Working with Dialog Boxes

Many Excel commands display a dialog box, which is simply a way of getting more information from you. For example, if you choose Review ⇨ Changes ⇨ Protect Sheet, Excel can't carry out the command until you tell it what parts of the sheet you want to protect. Therefore, it displays the Protect Sheet dialog box, shown in Figure 1.12.

FIGURE 1.12

Excel uses a dialog box to get additional information about a command.

The Excel dialog boxes vary in how they work. Excel uses two types of dialog boxes:

- **Normal dialog box:** A *modal* dialog box, which takes the focus away from the spreadsheet. When this type of dialog box is displayed, you can't do anything in the worksheet until you dismiss the dialog box. Clicking the OK button performs the specified actions, and clicking Cancel (or pressing Esc) closes the dialog box without taking any action. Most Excel dialog boxes are of this type.

- **Stay-on-top dialog box:** A *modeless* dialog box, which works in a manner similar to a toolbar. When a modeless dialog box is displayed, you can continue working in Excel, and the dialog box remains open. Changes made in a modeless dialog box take effect immediately. For example, if you're applying formatting to a chart, changes you make in the Format dialog box appear in the chart as soon as you make them. Modeless dialog boxes have a Close button instead of an OK button.

Most people find working with dialog boxes to be quite straightforward and natural. If you've used other programs, you'll feel right at home. You can manipulate the controls either with your mouse or directly from the keyboard.

Navigating dialog boxes

Navigating dialog boxes is generally very easy—you simply click the control you want to activate.

Although dialog boxes were designed with mouse users in mind, you can also use the keyboard. Every dialog box control has text associated with it, and this text always has one underlined letter (a *hot key* or *accelerator key*). You can access the control from the keyboard by pressing the Alt key and then the underlined letter. You also can use Tab to cycle through all the controls on a dialog box. Shift+Tab cycles through the controls in reverse order.

 When a control is selected, it appears with a darker outline. You can use the spacebar to activate a selected control.

Using tabbed dialog boxes

Many of Excel's dialog boxes are "tabbed" dialog boxes. A *tabbed dialog box* includes notebook-like tabs, each of which is associated with a different panel.

When you click a tab, the dialog box changes to display a new panel containing a new set of controls. The Format Cells dialog box is a good example. This dialog box is shown in Figure 1.13; it has six tabs, which makes it functionally equivalent to six different dialog boxes.

FIGURE 1.13

Use the dialog box tabs to select different functional areas in the dialog box.

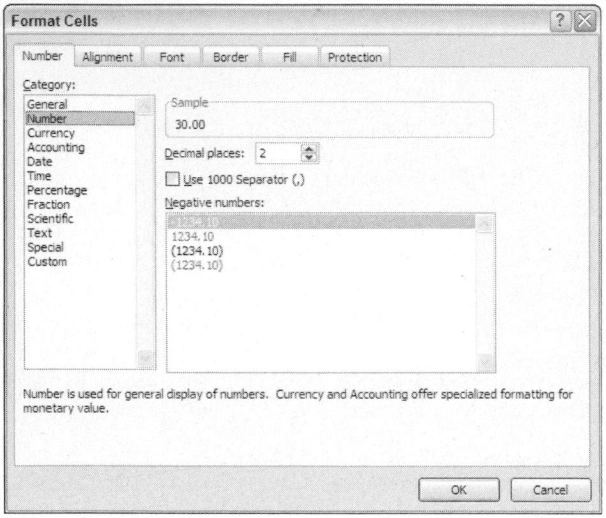

Format Cells	? X
Number Alignment Font Border Fill Protection	

Category:
General
Number
Currency
Accounting
Date
Time
Percentage
Fraction
Scientific
Text
Special
Custom

Sample
30.00

Decimal places: 2

☐ Use 1000 Separator (,)

Negative numbers:

-1234.10
1234.10
(1234.10)
(1234.10)

Number is used for general display of numbers. Currency and Accounting offer specialized formatting for monetary value.

OK   Cancel

Tabbed dialog boxes are quite convenient because you can make several changes in a single dialog box. After you make all your setting changes, click OK or press Enter.

TIP To select a tab by using the keyboard, use Ctrl+PgUp or Ctrl+PgDn, or simply press the first letter of the tab that you want to activate.

Excel 2007 introduced a new style of modeless tabbed dialog box in which the tabs are on the left, rather than across the top. An example is shown in Figure 1.14. To select a tab using the keyboard, use the up and down arrow keys and then press Tab to access the controls.

FIGURE 1.14

A "new style" tabbed dialog box with tabs on the left.

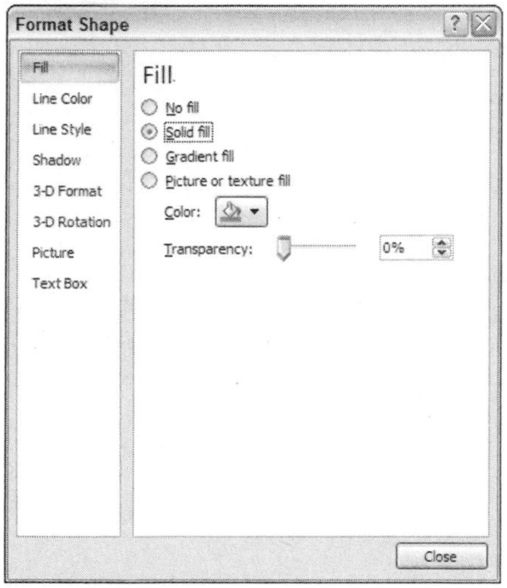

Using the Taskbar

The final user interface element that I discuss is the taskbar. The taskbar appears automatically in response to several commands. For example, if you want to insert a clip art image, choose Insert ⇨ Illustrations ⇨ Clip Art. Excel responds by displaying the Clip Art Task bar, shown in Figure 1.15. The taskbar is similar to a dialog box, except that you can keep it visible as long as you like. There's no OK button. When you're finished using a Task bar, click the Close button in the upper right corner. By default, the taskbar is docked on the right side of the Excel window, but you can drag it anywhere you like.

FIGURE 1.15

The Clip Art taskbar.

Creating Your First Excel Worksheet
==

This section presents an introductory hands-on session with Excel. If you haven't used Excel, you may want to follow along on your computer to get a feel for how this software works.

In this example, you create a simple monthly sales projection table along with a chart.

Getting started on your worksheet

Start Excel and make sure that you have an empty workbook displayed. To create a new, blank workbook, press Ctrl+N.

The sales projection will consist of two columns of information. Column A will contain the month names, and column B will store the projected sales numbers. You start by entering some descriptive titles into the worksheet. Here's how to begin:

1. **Move the cell pointer to cell A1 by using the direction keys.** The Name box displays the cell's address.

2. **Enter** Month **into cell A1.** Just type the text and then press Enter. Depending on your setup, Excel either moves the cell pointer to a different cell, or the pointer remains in cell A1.

3. **Move the cell pointer to B1, type** Projected Sales, **and press Enter.**

Filling in the month names

In this step, you enter the month names in column A.

1. **Move the cell pointer to A2 and type** Jan **(an abbreviation for January).** At this point, you can enter the other month name abbreviations manually, but we'll let Excel do some of the work by taking advantage of the AutoFill feature.

2. **Make sure that cell A2 is selected.** Notice that the active cell is displayed with a heavy outline. At the bottom-right corner of the outline, you'll see a small square known as the *fill handle*. Move your mouse pointer over the fill handle, click, and drag down until you've highlighted from A2 down to A13.

3. **Release the mouse button, and Excel will automatically fill in the month names.**

Your worksheet should resemble the one shown in Figure 1.16.

FIGURE 1.16

Your worksheet, after entering the column headings and month names.

	A	B	C	D	E	F	G	H	I
1	Month	Projected Sales							
2	Jan								
3	Feb								
4	Mar								
5	Apr								
6	May								
7	Jun								
8	Jul								
9	Aug								
10	Sep								
11	Oct								
12	Nov								
13	Dec								
14									
15									

Sheet1 / Sheet2 / Sheet3

Entering the sales data

Next, you provide the sales projection numbers in column B. Assume that January's sales are projected to be $50,000, and that sales will increase by 3.5 percent in each of the subsequent months.

1. **Move the cell pointer to B2 and type** 50000, **the projected sales for January.**

2. **To enter a formula to calculate the projected sales for February, move to cell B3 and enter the following:** =B2*103.5%. When you press Enter, the cell will display 51750. The formula returns the contents of cell B2, multiplied by 103.5%. In other words, February sales are projected to be 3.5% greater than January sales.

3. **The projected sales for subsequent months will use a similar formula**. But rather than retype the formula for each cell in column B, once again take advantage of the AutoFill feature. Make sure that cell B3 is selected. Click the cell's fill handle, drag down to cell B13, and release the mouse button.

At this point, your worksheet should resemble the one shown in Figure 1.17. Keep in mind that, except for cell B2, the values in column B are calculated with formulas. To demonstrate, try changing the projected sales value for the initial month, January (in cell B2). You'll find that the formulas recalculate and return different values. But these formulas all depend on the initial value in cell B2.

FIGURE 1.17

Your worksheet, after creating the formulas.

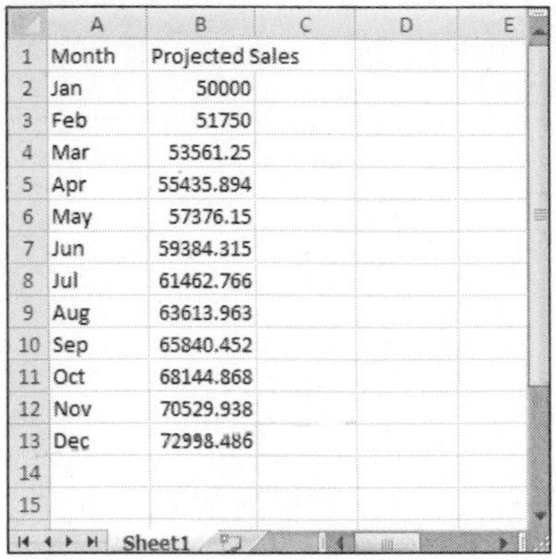

	A	B	C	D	E
1	Month	Projected Sales			
2	Jan	50000			
3	Feb	51750			
4	Mar	53561.25			
5	Apr	55435.894			
6	May	57376.15			
7	Jun	59384.315			
8	Jul	61462.766			
9	Aug	63613.963			
10	Sep	65840.452			
11	Oct	68144.868			
12	Nov	70529.938			
13	Dec	72998.486			
14					
15					

Sheet1

Formatting the numbers

The values in the worksheet are difficult to read because they aren't formatted. In this step, you apply a number format to make the numbers easier to read and more consistent in appearance:

1. **Select the numbers by clicking cell B2 and dragging down to cell B13.**
2. **Choose Home ➪ Number, click the drop-down Number Format control (it initially displays General), and select Currency from the list.** The numbers now display with a currency symbol and two decimal places. Much better!

Making your worksheet look a bit fancier

At this point, you have a functional worksheet — but it could use some help in the appearance department. Converting this range to an "official" (and attractive) Excel table is a snap:

1. **Move to any cell within the range.**
2. **Choose Insert ➪ Tables ➪ Table.** Excel displays its Create Table dialog box to make sure that it guessed the range properly.
3. **Click OK to close the Create Table dialog box.** Excel applies its default table formatting and also displays its Table Tools ➪ Design contextual tab. Your screen should look like Figure 1.18.

FIGURE 1.18

Your worksheet, after converting the range to a table.

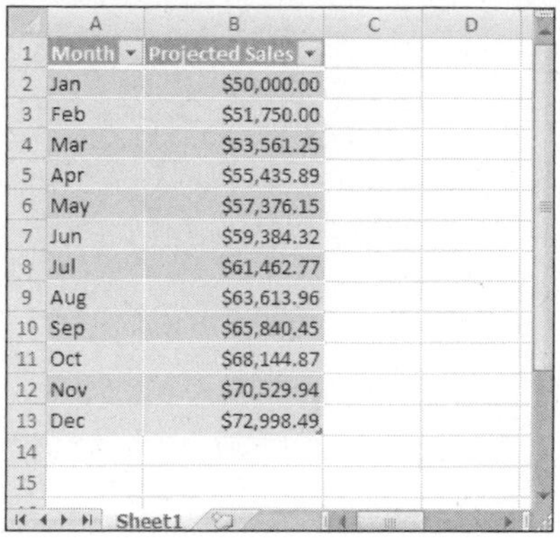

	A	B	C	D
1	Month	Projected Sales		
2	Jan	$50,000.00		
3	Feb	$51,750.00		
4	Mar	$53,561.25		
5	Apr	$55,435.89		
6	May	$57,376.15		
7	Jun	$59,384.32		
8	Jul	$61,462.77		
9	Aug	$63,613.96		
10	Sep	$65,840.45		
11	Oct	$68,144.87		
12	Nov	$70,529.94		
13	Dec	$72,998.49		
14				
15				

Sheet1

4. **If you don't like the default table style, just select another one from the Table Tools ⇨ Design ⇨ Table Styles group.** Notice that you can get a preview of different table styles by moving your mouse over the ribbon. When you find one you like, click it, and style will be applied to your table.

Summing the values

The worksheet displays the monthly projected sales, but what about the total sales for the year? Because this range is a table, it's simple:

1. **Activate any cell in the table**
2. **Choose Table Tools ⇨ Design ⇨ Table Style Options ⇨ Totals Row.** Excel automatically adds a new row to the bottom of your table, including a formula that calculated the total of the Projected Sales column.
3. **If you'd prefer to see a different summary formula (for example, average), click cell B14 and choose a different summary formula from the drop-down list.**

Creating a chart

How about a chart that shows the projected sales for each month?

1. **Activate any cell in the table.**
2. **Choose Insert ⇨ Charts ⇨ Column and then select one of the 2-D column chart types.** Excel inserts the chart in the center of your screen.
3. **To move the chart to another location, click its border and drag it.**
4. **To change the appearance and style of the chart, use the commands in the Chart Tools context tab.**

Figure 1.19 shows the worksheet after creating the chart. Your chart may look different, depending on the chart layout or style you selected.

The table and chart.

This workbook is available on the companion CD-ROM. The filename is table and chart.xlsx.

Printing your worksheet

Printing your worksheet is very easy (assuming that you have a printer attached and that it works properly).

1. **First, make sure that the chart isn't selected.** If a chart is selected, it will print on a page by itself. To deselect the chart, just press Esc or click any cell.

2. **To make use of Excel's handy new page layout view, click the Page Layout View button on the right side of the status bar.** Excel will then display the worksheet page by page (see Figure 1.20) so that you can easily see how your printed output will look. For example, you can tell immediately if the chart is too wide to fit on one page. If the chart is too wide, click and drag its lower right corner to resize it.

FIGURE 1.20

Viewing the worksheet in Page Layout mode.

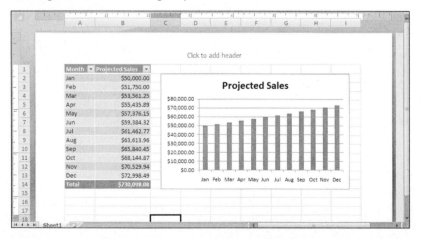

3. **When you're ready to print, choose Office ⇨ Print ⇨ Quick Print**

The worksheet is printed using the default settings.

Saving your workbook

Until now, everything that you've done has occurred in your computer's memory. If the power should fail, all may be lost — unless Excel's AutoRecover feature happened to kick in. It's time to save your work to a file on your hard drive.

1. **Click the Save button on the Quick Access Toolbar.** (This button looks like an old-fashioned floppy disk.) Because the workbook hasn't been saved yet and still has its default name, Excel responds with the Save As dialog box.

2. **In the box labeled File Name, enter a name such as Monthly Sales Projection, and then click Save or press Enter.** Excel saves the workbook as a file. The workbook remains open so that you can work with it some more.

NOTE By default, Excel saves a copy of your work automatically every ten minutes. To adjust this setting (or turn if off), use the Save tab of the Excel Options dialog box. To display this dialog box, choose File ⇨ Excel Options. However, you should never rely on Excel's AutoRecover feature. Saving your work frequently is a good idea.

If you've followed along, you may have realized that creating this workbook was not at all difficult. But, of course, you've barely scratched the surface. The remainder of this book will cover these tasks (and many, many more) in much greater detail.

Chapter 2

What's New in Excel 2007?

I f you've used a previous version of Excel, this chapter is for you. Here you'll find a quick overview of what's new and what's changed in Excel 2007.

IN THIS CHAPTER

The new features in Excel 2007

A New User Interface

The first thing you notice about Excel 2007 is its new look. The time-honored menu-and-toolbar user interface has been scrapped and replaced with a new "tab-and-ribbon" interface. Although the new interface kind of resembles menus and toolbars, you'll find that it's radically different.

Long-time Excel users have probably noticed that, with each new version, the menu system has gotten increasingly complicated. In addition, the number of toolbars had become almost overwhelming. After all, every new feature must have a way to be accessed. In the past, access meant adding more items to the menus and building new toolbars. The Microsoft designers set out to solve the problem, and the new Ribbon interface is their solution.

Time will tell how users will accept the new Ribbon interface. As I write this book, the reaction can best be described as "mixed." As with anything new, some people love it, others hate it.

CROSS-REF Chapter 1 contains more information about the new Ribbon interface, including a description of its components.

I think many experienced Excel users will suffer from a mild case of bewilderment as they realize that all their familiar command sequences no longer work. Beginning users, on the other hand, will be able to get up to speed much more quickly because they won't be overwhelmed with irrelevant menus and toolbars.

Other elements that comprise the new look include

- **Six new modern-looking fonts:** The default workbook font is now 11-point Calibri, which, I think, is much more readable than the old 10-point Arial, especially in smaller sizes.

- **Quick Access Toolbar:** A personal toolbar, to which you can add commands that you use regularly. This toolbar is the only part of the Excel 2007 interface that the user can customize.

- **The Mini toolbar:** A new addition to the right-click menu. This toolbar contains commonly-used formatting icons, displayed near your mouse pointer for quick access.

Larger Worksheets

Over the years, perhaps the most common complaint about Excel was the size of a worksheet. Users who required more rows or columns were simply out of luck. Microsoft finally responded, and Excel 2007 has upped the ante significantly. A worksheet now has 1,048,576 rows and 16,384 columns, which works out to more than 17 billion cells — almost three cells for every man, woman, and child on the planet. Stated differently, an Excel 2007 worksheet has more than 1,000 times as many cells as an Excel 2003 worksheet.

NOTE   Having more rows and columns doesn't mean that you can actually use them all. If you attempted to fill up all cells in a worksheet, you would soon run out of memory. The advantage to having more rows and columns is the flexibility it provides.

In addition to a larger worksheet grid, Excel 2007 has also increased some other limits that have frustrated users. Table 2.1 summarizes some of these changes.

TABLE 2.1

By the Numbers: Excel 2003 versus Excel 2007

	Excel 2003	Excel 2007
Number of rows	65,536	1,048,576
Number of columns	256	16,384
Amount of memory used	1 Gbytes	Maximum allowed by Windows
Number of colors	56	4.3 billion
Number of conditional formats per cell	3	Unlimited
Number of levels of sorting	3	64
Number of levels of undo	16	100
Number of items shown in the Auto-Filter dropdown	1,000	10,000
The total number of characters that can display in a cell	1,000	32,000
Number of unique styles in a workbook	4,000	64,000
Maximum number of characters in a formula	1,000	8,000
Number of levels of nesting in a formula	7	64
Maximum number of function arguments	30	255

New File Formats

Over the years, Excel's XLS file format has become an industry standard. Excel 2007 still supports that format, but it now uses new default "open" file formats that are based on XML (Extensible Markup Language).

CROSS-REF Find out more about the new Excel file formats in Chapter 9.

For compatibility, Excel 2007 still supports the old file formats so that you can continue to share your work with those who haven't upgraded to Excel 2007.

Worksheet Tables

Excel, of course, has always been able to deal with tables. A *table* is just a rectangular range of cells that (usually) contains column headers. The designers of Excel 2007 realized that such tables are widely used in Excel, and they've taken the concept to a new level. Working with tables is easier than ever.

Once you designate a particular range to be a table (using the Insert ➪ Tables ➪ Table command), Excel provides you with some very efficient tools that work with the table. For example:

- You can apply attractive formatting with a single click.
- You can easily insert summary formulas in the table's total row.
- If each cell in a column contains the same formula, you can edit one of the formulas, and the others change automatically.
- You can easily toggle the display of the table's the header row and totals row.
- Removing duplicate entries is easy.
- Autofiltering and sorting options have been expanded.
- If you create a chart from a table, the chart will always reflect the data in the table — even if you add new rows.
- If you scroll a table downwards so that the header row is no longer visible, the column headers now display where the worksheet column letters would be.

Figure 2.1 shows a table in a worksheet.

Working with tables of data has never been easier.

	A	B	C	D	E	F	G
3		State	July 2005 Population	July 2004 Population	Change	Pct Change	
4		Alabama	4,557,808	4,525,375	32,433	0.71%	
5		Alaska	663,661	657,755	5,906	0.89%	
6		Arizona	5,939,292	5,739,879	199,413	3.36%	
7		Arkansas	2,779,154	2,750,000	29,154	1.05%	
8		California	36,132,147	35,842,038	290,109	0.80%	
9		Colorado	4,665,177	4,601,821	63,356	1.36%	
10		Connecticut	3,510,297	3,498,966	11,331	0.32%	
11		Delaware	843,524	830,069	13,455	1.60%	
12		District of Columbia	550,521	554,239	-3,718	-0.68%	
13		Florida	17,789,864	17,385,430	404,434	2.27%	
14		Georgia	9,072,576	8,918,129	154,447	1.70%	
15		Hawaii	1,275,194	1,262,124	13,070	1.02%	
16		Idaho	1,429,096	1,395,140	33,956	2.38%	
17		Illinois	12,763,371	12,712,016	51,355	0.40%	
18		Indiana	6,271,973	6,226,537	45,436	0.72%	
19		Iowa	2,966,334	2,952,904	13,430	0.45%	
20		Kansas	2,744,687	2,733,697	10,990	0.40%	
21		Kentucky	4,173,405	4,141,835	31,570	0.76%	
22		Louisiana	4,523,628	4,506,685	16,943	0.37%	
23		Maine	1,321,505	1,314,985	6,520	0.49%	
24		Maryland	5,600,388	5,561,332	39,056	0.70%	
25		Massachusetts	6,398,743	6,407,382	-8,639	-0.14%	
26		Michigan	10,120,860	10,104,206	16,654	0.16%	
27		Minnesota	5,132,799	5,096,546	36,253	0.71%	
28		Mississippi	2,921,088	2,900,768	20,320	0.70%	
29		Missouri	5,800,310	5,759,532	40,778	0.70%	
30		Montana	935,670	926,920	8,750	0.94%	
31		Nebraska	1,758,787	1,747,704	11,083	0.63%	
32		Nevada	2,414,807	2,332,898	81,909	3.39%	

NST03

Styles and Themes

I've see thousands of Excel workbooks over the years. A good proportion of them can best be described as "ugly." You can find lots of exceptions, but numbers people generally aren't very good with graphic design. Worksheets with gaudy colors and unreadable blue-on-green text are common.

Excel has always supported named styles, which can be applied to cells and ranges. Excel 2007 brings this feature to the forefront by providing a good assortment of predefined styles, easily accessible by choosing Home ➪ Styles ➪ Cell Styles.

With the introduction of document themes, Excel 2007 makes it easy to create good-looking worksheets. A theme consists of a color palette, font set, and effects. You now have one-click access to a gallery of professionally-designed themes that can dramatically change the look of your entire spreadsheet — almost always for the better. Access the theme gallery by choosing Page Layout ➪ Themes ➪ Themes. And yes. You can still create ugly Excel documents if you try hard enough.

CROSS-REF Learn more about styles and themes in Chapter 7.

Better Looking Charts

There is both good news and bad news relating to the charting features in Excel 2007. First the bad news: Excel 2007 offers no new chart types, and many of the long-time chart-related feature requests have been ignored by Microsoft. The good news? Excel charts now look better than ever. For the first time, you can honestly use the term "boardroom quality" to describe Excel charts.

CROSS-REF   I discuss charts in Chapters 19 and 20.

Page Layout View

As an option, you can display your worksheet as a series of pages. This new Page Layout view ensures no surprises when it's time to print your work. Even better, the Page Layout view includes "click and type" page headers and footers — which is much more intuitive than the old method. Unlike the standard print preview, Page Layout view is fully functional in terms of spreadsheet editing.

Figure 2.2 shows a spreadsheet displayed in Page Layout view. The display is zoomed out to show multiple pages.

FIGURE 2.2

Excel's new Page Layout view makes it easy to see how your printed work will appear.

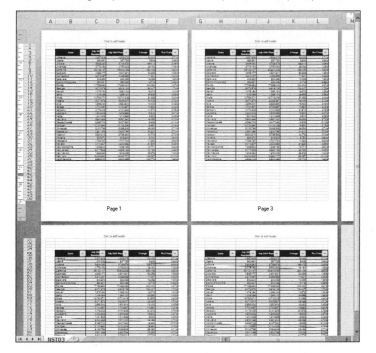

Enhanced Conditional Formatting

Conditional formatting refers to the ability to format a cell based on its value. Conditional formatting makes it easy to highlight certain values so that they stand out visually. For example, you may set up conditional formatting so that if a formula returns a negative value, the cell background displays green.

In the past, a cell could have at most three conditions applied. With Excel 2007, a you can format a cell based on an unlimited number of conditions. But that's the least of the improvements. Excel 2007 provides a number of new data visualizations: data bars, color scales, and icon sets. Figure 2.3 shows an example of a range that uses conditional formatting to display data bars directly in the cells. The size of each data bar is proportional to the value in the cell.

FIGURE 2.3

Data bars are just one of the new conditional formatting options.

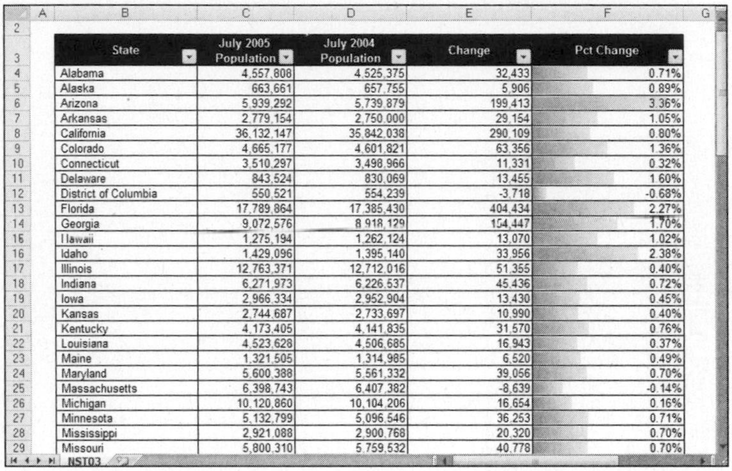

State	July 2005 Population	July 2004 Population	Change	Pct Change
Alabama	4,557,808	4,525,375	32,433	0.71%
Alaska	663,661	657,755	5,906	0.89%
Arizona	5,939,292	5,739,879	199,413	3.36%
Arkansas	2,779,154	2,750,000	29,154	1.05%
California	36,132,147	35,842,038	290,109	0.80%
Colorado	4,665,177	4,601,821	63,356	1.36%
Connecticut	3,510,297	3,498,966	11,331	0.32%
Delaware	843,524	830,069	13,455	1.60%
District of Columbia	550,521	554,239	-3,718	-0.68%
Florida	17,789,864	17,385,430	404,434	2.27%
Georgia	9,072,576	8,918,129	154,447	1.70%
Hawaii	1,275,194	1,262,124	13,070	1.02%
Idaho	1,429,096	1,395,140	33,956	2.38%
Illinois	12,763,371	12,712,016	51,355	0.40%
Indiana	6,271,973	6,226,537	45,436	0.72%
Iowa	2,966,334	2,952,904	13,430	0.45%
Kansas	2,744,687	2,733,697	10,990	0.40%
Kentucky	4,173,405	4,141,835	31,570	0.76%
Louisiana	4,523,628	4,506,685	16,943	0.37%
Maine	1,321,505	1,314,985	6,520	0.49%
Maryland	5,600,388	5,561,332	39,056	0.70%
Massachusetts	6,398,743	6,407,382	-8,639	-0.14%
Michigan	10,120,860	10,104,206	16,654	0.16%
Minnesota	5,132,799	5,096,546	36,253	0.71%
Mississippi	2,921,088	2,900,768	20,320	0.70%
Missouri	5,800,310	5,759,532	40,778	0.70%

Excel 2007 includes quite a few other improvements to conditional formatting. In general, conditional formatting is much more flexible, easier to set up, and relies less on creating custom formulas to define the formatting rules.

CROSS-REF Chapters 8 and 21 cover conditional formatting.

Consolidated Options

In the past, Excel provided far too many dialog boxes to set various options. In Excel 2007, most dialog boxes have been consolidated into a massive Excel Options dialog box (see Figure 2.4). To display this dialog box, choose File ➪ Excel Options.

The options are grouped into tabs, which you select on the left. Locating some of the options still isn't easy, but the new implementation is much better than it used to be. The Excel Options dialog box is also resizable — just click and drag the lower right corner to change the size.

FIGURE 2.4

The newly designed Excel Options dialog box.

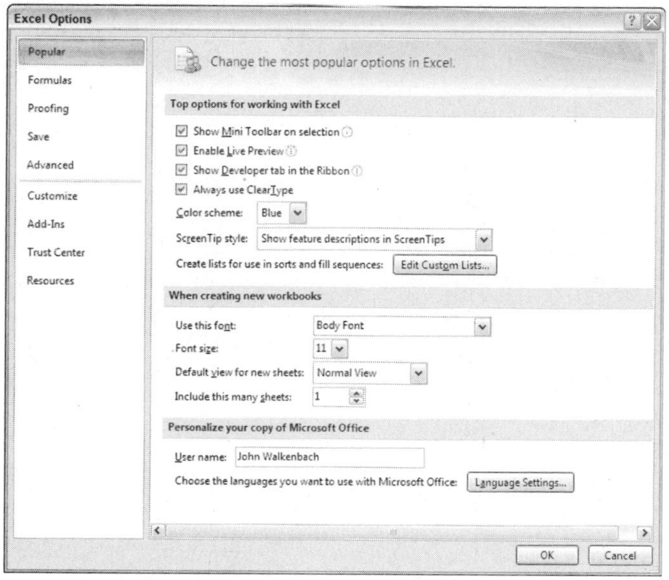

SmartArt

Excel 2007 still includes a wide assortment of Shapes that you can use to create visual diagrams, such as flow charts, org charts, or diagrams that depict relationships. But the new SmartArt feature is a much better tool for such tasks. You can quickly add shadows, reflection, glow, and other special effects.

Figure 2.5 shows two SmartArt diagrams. The diagram on the left is the original, and the one on the right is the same diagram after a single mouse click that changed the layout and style.

FIGURE 2.5

Diagrams created with SmartArt.

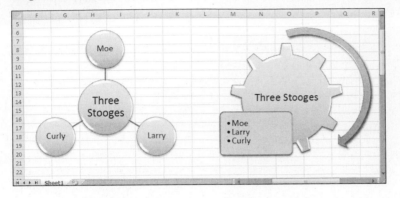

> **CROSS-REF**   Refer to Chapter 22 for more information about SmartArt.

Formula AutoComplete

Entering formulas in Excel 2007 can be a bit less cumbersome, thanks to the new Formula AutoComplete feature. When you begin typing a formula, Excel displays a continually updated drop-down list of matching items (see Figure 2.6), including a description of each item. When you see the item you want, press Tab to enter it into your formula. The items in this list consist of functions, defined names, and table references.

FIGURE 2.6

The Formula Autocomplete feature can speed up formula entry.

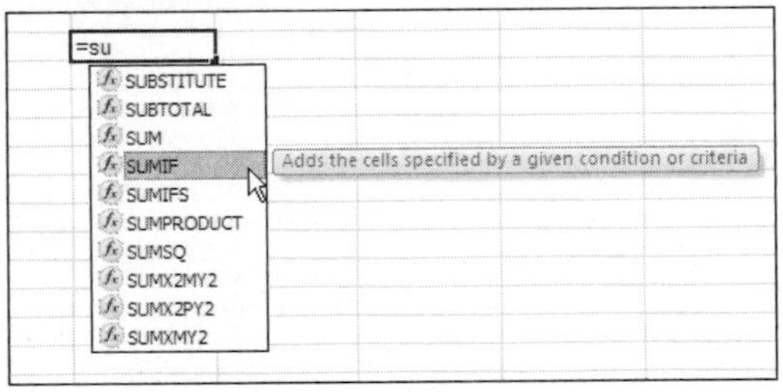

> **CROSS-REF**   Refer to Chapter 11 for more information about Formula AutoComplete.

Collaboration Features

Excel Services is new server technology that ships with Office 12. It's part of the Microsoft Office Share Point Server product. Excel Services supports loading, calculating, and rendering Excel spreadsheets on servers.

If your company is set up with Excel Services, you can use Excel 2007 to collaborate with your coworkers efficiently and present data to those who don't use Excel.

> **NOTE** Using the new Excel Services-based collaboration features is very specific to your organization. Consequently, these features are not covered in this book.

Compatibility Checker

Given all the new features in Excel 2007, you may be hesitant to share a workbook with others who use an earlier version of Excel. To find out how your workbook will function with previous versions, use the compatibility checker. Choose Office ➪ Prepare ➪ Run Compatibility Checker. Figure 2.7 shows an example.

FIGURE 2.7

Use the Compatibility Checker if you plan to share your workbooks with people who use an earlier version of Excel.

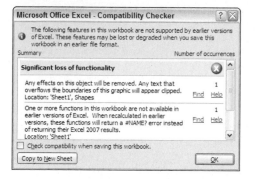

Improved Pivot Tables

Excel's pivot table feature is probably one of its most underutilized features. A *pivot table* can turn a large range of raw data into a useful interactive summary table with only a few mouse clicks. Microsoft hopes to make this feature more accessible by improving just about every aspect of pivot tables in Excel 2007.

One other thing worth noting: Charts created from pivot tables (*pivot charts*) now retain their formatting when they're updated. This loss of formatting had been a frustration for hundreds of thousands of users, and Microsoft finally did something about it.

> **CROSS-REF** See Chapters 34 and 35 for more information about pivot tables.

New Worksheet Functions

Excel 2007 has five new worksheet functions, described in Table 2.2.

New Worksheet Functions

Function	Use
IFERROR	Returns a value you specify if a formula evaluates to an error; otherwise, returns the result of the formula.
AVERAGEIF	Calculates a conditional average (similar to SUMIF and COUNTIF).
AVERAGEIFS	Calculates a conditional average using multiple criteria.
SUMIFS	Calculates a conditional sum using multiple criteria.
COUNTIFS	Calculates a conditional COUNT using multiple criteria.

In addition, 39 worksheet functions that used to require the Analysis Toolpak add-in are now built-in.

Excel 2007 also includes seven new CUBE functions that retrieve data from SQL Server Analysis Services.

CROSS-REF Chapter 11 covers formulas and functions.

Other New Features

Other new features in Excel 2007 worth noting are

- **Trust Center:** Protecting yourself from malicious macros is a bit easier with Excel 2007. For example, you can disable all macros, except those in workbooks that are stored in trusted locations on your computer.

- **PDF add-in:** You can create an industry-standard Adobe PDF file directly from Excel using an add-in available from Microsoft.

- **Improved zooming:** Use the zoomer control on the right side of the status bar to quickly zoom in or zoom out on your worksheet.

- **More control over the status bar:** You can now control the type of information that appears in the status bar.

- **Color Schemes:** Change the appearance of Excel by applying one of three color schemes that ship with Excel (Blue, Silver, or Black).

- **Resizable formula bar:** When editing lengthy formulas, you can increase the height of the formula bar so that it doesn't obscure your worksheet. Just click and drag on the bottom border of the formula bar.

- **Lots of new templates:** Why reinvent the wheel? Choose Office ➪ New, and you can choose from a variety of templates. One of them may be exactly (or at least close to) what you need.

Chapter 3

Entering and Editing Worksheet Data

This chapter describes what you need to know about entering, using, and modifying data in your worksheets. As you see, Excel doesn't treat all data equally. Therefore, you need to learn about the various types of data that you can use in an Excel worksheet.

Exploring the Types of Data You Can Use

An Excel workbook can hold any number of worksheets, and each worksheet is made up of more than 17 billion cells. A cell can hold any of three basic types of data:

- Numerical values
- Text
- Formulas

A worksheet can also hold charts, diagrams, pictures, buttons, and other objects. These objects aren't contained in cells. Rather, they reside on the worksheet's *draw layer,* which is an invisible layer on top of each worksheet.

CROSS-REF Chapter 18 discusses some of the items you can place on the draw layer

About numerical values

Numerical values represent a quantity of some type: sales amounts, number of employees, atomic weights, test scores, and so on. Values also can be dates (such as Feb-26-2007) or times (such as 3:24 a.m.).

CROSS-REF Excel can display values in many different formats. Later in this chapter, you see how different format options can affect the display of numerical values (see "Applying Number Formatting").

IN THIS CHAPTER

Understanding the types of data you can use

Entering text and values into your worksheets

Entering dates and times into your worksheets

Modifying and editing information

Using built-in number formats

Excel's Numerical Limitations

You may be curious about the types of values that Excel can handle. In other words, how large can numbers be? And how accurate are large numbers?

Excel's numbers are precise up to 15 digits. For example, if you enter a large value, such as 123,456,789,123,456,789 (18 digits), Excel actually stores it with only 15 digits of precision. This 18-digit number displays as 123,456,789,123,456,000. This precision may seem quite limiting, but in practice, it rarely causes any problems.

One situation in which the 15-digit accuracy can cause a problem is when entering credit-card numbers. Most credit-card numbers are 16 digits long. But Excel can handle only 15 digits, so it will substitute a zero for the last credit-card digit. Even worse, you may not even realize that Excel made the card number invalid. The solution? Enter the credit-card numbers as text. The easiest way is to preformat the cell as Text (choose Home ➪ Number and choose Text from the drop-down Number Format list). Or you can precede the credit-card number with an apostrophe. Either method prevents Excel from interpreting the entry as a number.

Here are some of Excel's other numerical limits:

Largest positive number: 9.9E+307

Smallest negative number: −9.9E+307

Smallest positive number: 1E−307

Largest negative number: −1E−307

These numbers are expressed in scientific notation. For example, the largest positive number is "9.9 times 10 to the 307th power." (In other words, 99 followed by 306 zeros.) But keep in mind that this number has only 15 digits of accuracy.

About text entries

Most worksheets also include text in their cells. You can insert text to serve as labels for values, headings for columns, or instructions about the worksheet. Text is often used to clarify what the values in a worksheet mean.

Text that begins with a number is still considered text. For example, if you type **12 Employees** into a cell, Excel considers the entry to be text rather than a value. Consequently, you can't use this cell for numeric calculations. If you need to indicate that the number 12 refers to employees, enter **12** into a cell and type **Employees** into the cell to the right.

About formulas

Formulas are what make a spreadsheet a spreadsheet. Excel enables you to enter powerful formulas that use the values (or even text) in cells to calculate a result. When you enter a formula into a cell, the formula's result appears in the cell. If you change any of the values used by a formula, the formula recalculates and shows the new result.

Formulas can be simple mathematical expressions, or they can use some of the powerful functions that are built into Excel. Figure 3.1 shows an Excel worksheet set up to calculate a monthly loan payment. The worksheet contains values, text, and formulas. The cells in column A contain text. Column B contains four values and two formulas. The formulas are in cells B6 and B10. Column D, for reference, shows the actual contents of the cells in column B.

ON the CD-ROM This workbook, named **loan payment calculator.xlsx**, is available on the companion CD-ROM.

FIGURE 3.1

You can use values, text, and formulas to create useful Excel worksheets.

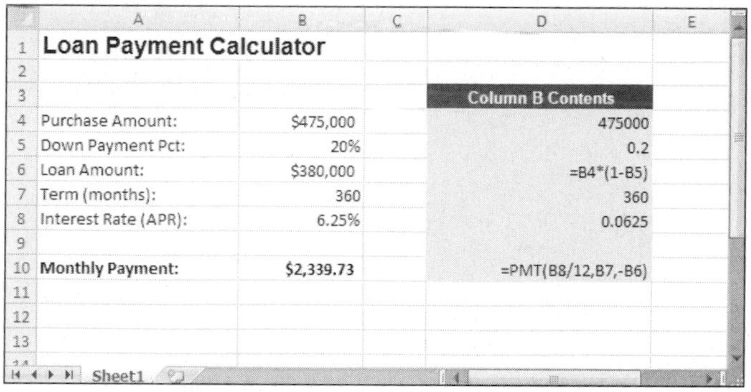

	A	B	C	D	E
1	**Loan Payment Calculator**				
2					
3				Column B Contents	
4	Purchase Amount:	$475,000		475000	
5	Down Payment Pct:	20%		0.2	
6	Loan Amount:	$380,000		=B4*(1-B5)	
7	Term (months):	360		360	
8	Interest Rate (APR):	6.25%		0.0625	
9					
10	**Monthly Payment:**	$2,339.73		=PMT(B8/12,B7,-B6)	
11					
12					
13					

Sheet1

CROSS-REF You can find out much more about formulas in Part II.

Entering Text and Values into Your Worksheets

To enter a numerical value into a cell, move the cell pointer to the appropriate cell, type the value, and then press Enter or one of the arrow keys. The value is displayed in the cell and also appears in Excel's Formula bar when the cell is active. You can include decimal points and currency symbols when entering values, along with plus signs, minus signs, and commas. If you precede a value with a minus sign or enclose it in parentheses, Excel considers it to be a negative number.

Entering text into a cell is just as easy as entering a value: Activate the cell, type the text, and then press Enter or an arrow key. A cell can contain a maximum of about 32,000 characters — more than enough to hold a typical chapter in this book. Even though a cell can hold a huge number of characters, you'll find that it's not possible to actually display all these characters.

TIP If you type an exceptionally long text entry into a cell, the Formula bar may not show all the text. To display more of the text in the Formula bar, click the bottom of the Formula bar and drag down to increase the height (see Figure 3.2).

FIGURE 3.2

The Formula bar, expanded in height to show more information in the cell.

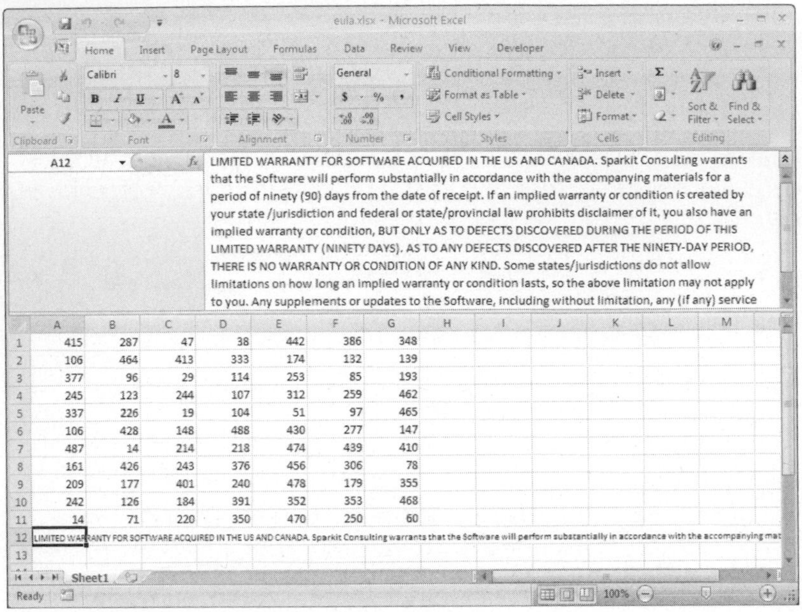

What happens when you enter text that's longer than its column's current width? If the cells to the immediate right are blank, Excel displays the text in its entirety, appearing to spill the entry into adjacent cells. If an adjacent cell isn't blank, Excel displays as much of the text as possible. (The full text is contained in the cell; it's just not displayed.) If you need to display a long text string in a cell that's adjacent to a nonblank cell, you can take one of several actions:

- Edit your text to make it shorter.
- Increase the width of the column.
- Use a smaller font.
- Wrap the text within the cell so that it occupies more than one line. Choose Home ➪ Alignment ➪ Wrap Text to toggle wrapping on and off for the selected cell or range.

Entering Dates and Times into Your Worksheets

Excel treats dates and times as special types of numeric values. Typically, these values are formatted so that they appear as dates or times because we humans find it far easier to understand these values when they appear in the correct format. If you work with dates and times, you need to understand Excel's date and time system.

Entering date values

Excel handles dates by using a serial number system. The earliest date that Excel understands is January 1, 1900. This date has a serial number of 1. January 2, 1900, has a serial number of 2, and so on. This system makes it easy to deal with dates in formulas. For example, you can enter a formula to calculate the number of days between two dates.

Most of the time, you don't have to be concerned with Excel's serial number date system. You can simply enter a date in a familiar date format, and Excel takes care of the details behind the scenes.

For example, if you need to enter June 1, 2007, you can simply enter the date by typing **June 1, 2007** (or use any of several different date formats). Excel interprets your entry and stores the value 39234, which is the date serial number for that date.

NOTE The date examples in this book use the U.S. English system. Depending on your regional settings, entering a date in a format (such as June 1, 2007) may be interpreted as text rather than a date. In such a case, you need to enter the date in a format that corresponds to your regional date settings — for example, 1 June, 2007.

CROSS-REF For more information about working with dates and times, refer to Chapter 13.

Entering time values

When you work with times, you simply extend Excel's date serial number system to include decimals. In other words, Excel works with times by using fractional days. For example, the date serial number for June 1, 2007, is 39234. Noon on June 1, 2007 (halfway through the day), is represented internally as 39234.5 because the time fraction is simply added to the date serial number to get the full date/time serial number.

Again, you normally don't have to be concerned with these serial numbers (or fractional serial numbers, for times). Just enter the time into a cell in a recognized format.

CROSS-REF Refer to Chapter 13 for more information about working with time values.

Modifying Cell Contents

After you enter a value or text into a cell, you can modify it in several ways:

- Erase the cell's contents
- Replace the cell's contents with something else
- Edit the cell's contents

Erasing the contents of a cell

To erase the contents of a cell, just click the cell and press Delete. To erase more than one cell, select all the cells that you want to erase and then press Delete. Pressing Delete removes the cell's contents but doesn't remove any formatting (such as bold, italic, or a different number format) that you may have applied to the cell.

For more control over what gets deleted, you can choose Home ⇨ Editing ⇨ Clear. This command's drop-down list has four choices:

- **Clear All:** Clears everything from the cell.
- **Clear Formats:** Clears only the formatting and leaves the value, text, or formula.
- **Clear Contents:** Clears only the cell's contents and leaves the formatting.
- **Clear Comments:** Clears the comment (if one exists) attached to the cell.

NOTE   Clearing formats doesn't clear the background colors in a range that has been designated as a table, unless you've replace the table style background colors manually.

Replacing the contents of a cell

To replace the contents of a cell with something else, just activate the cell and type your new entry, which replaces the previous contents. Any formatting that you previously applied to the cell remains in place and is applied to the new content.

TIP   You can also replace cell contents by dragging and dropping or by pasting data from the Clipboard. In both cases, the cell formatting will be replaced by the format of the new data. To avoid pasting formatting, choose Home ⇨ Clipboard ⇨ Paste and select Formulas or Paste Values.

Editing the contents of a cell

If the cell contains only a few characters, replacing its contents by typing new data usually is easiest. But if the cell contains lengthy text or a complex formula and you need to make only a slight modification, you probably want to edit the cell rather than re-enter information.

When you want to edit the contents of a cell, you can use one of the following ways to enter cell-edit mode:

- **Double-clicking the cell** enables you to edit the cell contents directly in the cell.
- **Selecting the cell and pressing F2** enables you to edit the cell contents directly in the cell.
- **Selecting the cell that you want to edit and then clicking inside the Formula bar** enables you to edit the cell contents in the Formula bar.

You can use whichever method you prefer. Some people find editing directly in the cell easier; others prefer to use the Formula bar to edit a cell.

NOTE   The Advanced tab of the Excel Options dialog box contains a section called Editing Options. These settings affect how editing works. (To access this dialog box, choose Office ⇨ Excel Options.) If the option labeled Allow Editing Directly In Cells isn't enabled, you aren't able to edit a cell by double-clicking. In addition, pressing F2 allows you to edit the cell in the Formula bar (not directly in the cell).

All these methods cause Excel to go into *edit mode*. (The word Edit appears at the left side of the status bar at the bottom of the screen.) When Excel is in edit mode, the Formula bar displays two new icons: the X and Check Mark (see Figure 3.3). Clicking the X icon cancels editing, without changing the cell's contents. (Pressing Esc has the same effect.) Clicking the Check Mark icon completes the editing and enters the modified contents into the cell. (Pressing Enter has the same effect.)

FIGURE 3.3

While editing a cell, the Formula bar displays two new icons.

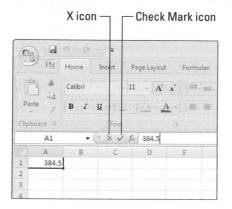

When you begin editing a cell, the insertion point appears as a vertical bar, and you can move the insertion point by using the arrow keys. Use Home to move the insertion point to the beginning of the cell and use End to move the insertion point to the end. You can add new characters at the location of the insertion point. To select multiple characters, press Shift while you use the arrow keys. You also can use the mouse to select characters while you're editing a cell. Just click and drag the mouse pointer over the characters that you want to select.

Learning some handy data-entry techniques

You can simplify the process of entering information into your Excel worksheets and make your work go quite a bit faster by using a number of useful tricks, described in the following sections.

Automatically moving the cell pointer after entering data

By default, Excel automatically moves the cell pointer to the next cell down when you press the Enter key after entering data into a cell. To change this setting, choose Office ➪ Excel Options and click the Advanced tab (see Figure 3.4). The check box that controls this behavior is labeled After Pressing Enter, Move Selection. You can also specify the direction in which the cell pointer moves (down, left, up, or right).

Your choice is completely a matter of personal preference. I prefer to keep this option turned off. When entering data, I use the arrow keys rather than the Enter key (see the next section).

FIGURE 3.4

You can use the Advanced tab in the Excel Options dialog box to select a number of helpful input option settings.

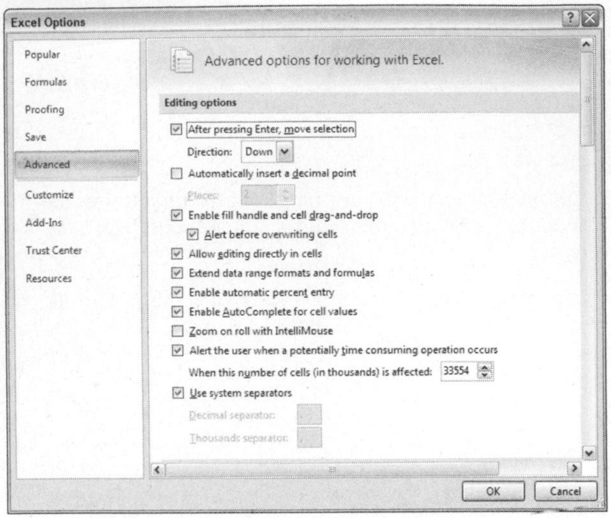

Using arrow keys instead of pressing Enter

Instead of pressing the Enter key when you're finished making a cell entry, you also can use any of the direction keys to complete the entry. Not surprisingly, these direction keys send you in the direction that you indicate. For example, if you're entering data in a row, press the right-arrow (→) key rather than Enter. The other arrow keys work as expected, and you can even use PgUp and PgDn.

Selecting a range of input cells before entering data

Here's a tip that most Excel users don't know about: When a range of cells is selected, Excel automatically moves the cell pointer to the next cell in the range when you press Enter. If the selection consists of multiple rows, Excel moves down the column; when it reaches the end of the selection in the column, it moves to the first selected cell in the next column.

To skip a cell, just press Enter without entering anything. To go backward, press Shift+Enter. If you prefer to enter the data by rows rather than by columns, press Tab rather than Enter.

Using Ctrl+Enter to place information into multiple cells simultaneously

If you need to enter the same data into multiple cells, Excel offers a handy shortcut. Select all the cells that you want to contain the data, enter the value, text, or formula, and then press Ctrl+Enter. The same information is inserted into each cell in the selection.

Entering decimal points automatically

If you need to enter lots of numbers with a fixed number of decimal places, Excel has a useful tool that works like some adding machines. Access the Excel Options dialog box and click the Advanced tab. Select the check box Automatically Insert A Decimal Point and make sure that the Places box is set for the correct number of decimal places for the data you need to enter.

When this option is set, Excel supplies the decimal points for you automatically. For example, if you've specified two decimal places, entering **12345** into a cell is interpreted as 123.45. To restore things to normal, just uncheck the Automatically Insert a Decimal Point check box in the Excel Options dialog box. Changing this setting doesn't affect any values that you have already entered.

CAUTION The fixed-decimal-places option is a global setting and applies to all workbooks (not just the active workbook). If you forget that this option is turned on, you can easily end up entering incorrect values — or some major confusion if someone else uses your computer.

Using AutoFill to enter a series of values

Excel's AutoFill feature makes inserting a series of values or text items in a range of cells easy. It uses the AutoFill handle (the small box at the lower right of the active cell). You can drag the AutoFill handle to copy the cell or automatically complete a series.

If you drag the AutoFill handle while you press the right mouse button, Excel displays a shortcut menu with additional fill options.

Figure 3.5 shows an example. I entered 1 into cell A1 and 3 into cell A2. Then I selected both cells and dragged the fill handle down to create a linear series of odd numbers.

FIGURE 3.5

This series was created using AutoFill.

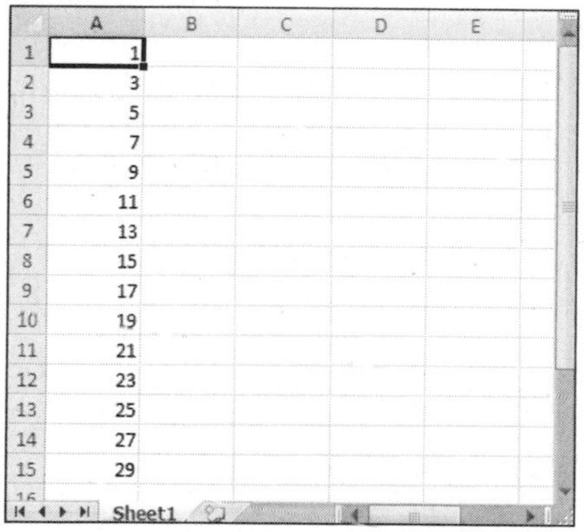

Using AutoComplete to automate data entry

Excel's AutoComplete feature makes entering the same text into multiple cells easy. With AutoComplete, you type the first few letters of a text entry into a cell, and Excel automatically completes the entry based on other entries that you've already made in the column. Besides reducing typing, this feature also ensures that your entries are spelled correctly and are consistent.

Here's how it works. Suppose that you're entering product information in a column. One of your products is named Widgets. The first time that you enter Widgets into a cell, Excel remembers it. Later, when you start typing Widgets in that same column, Excel recognizes it by the first few letters and finishes typing it for you. Just press Enter, and you're done. It also changes the case of letters for you automatically. If you start entering widget (with a lowercase w) in the second entry, Excel makes the w uppercase to be consistent with the previous entry in the column.

TIP You also can access a mouse-oriented version of AutoComplete by right-clicking the cell and selecting Pick From Drop-Down List from the shortcut menu. Excel then displays a drop-down box that has all the entries in the current column, and you just click the one that you want.

Keep in mind that AutoComplete works only within a contiguous column of cells. If you have a blank row, for example, AutoComplete identifies only the cell contents below the blank row.

If you find the AutoComplete feature distracting, you can turn it off by using the Advanced tab of the Excel Options dialog box. Remove the check mark from the check box labeled Enable AutoComplete For Cell Values.

Forcing text to appear on a new line within a cell

If you have lengthy text in a cell, you can force Excel to display it in multiple lines within the cell. Use Alt+Enter to start a new line in a cell.

NOTE When you add a line break, Excel automatically changes the cell's format to Wrap Text. But unlike normal text wrap, your manual line break forces Excel to break the text at a specific place within the text, which gives you more precise control over the appearance of the text than if you rely on automatic text wrapping.

TIP To remove a manual line break, edit the cell and press Delete when the insertion point is located at the end of the line that contains the manual line break. You won't see any symbol to indicate the position of the manual line break, but the text that follows it will move up when the line break is deleted.

Using AutoCorrect for shorthand data entry

You can use Excel's AutoCorrect feature to create shortcuts for commonly used words or phrases. For example, if you work for a company named Consolidated Data Processing Corporation, you can create an AutoCorrect entry for an abbreviation, such as cdp. Then, whenever you type cdp, Excel automatically changes it to Consolidated Data Processing Corporation.

Excel includes quite a few built-in AutoCorrect terms (mostly common misspellings), and you can add your own. To set up your custom AutoCorrect entries, access the Excel Options dialog box (choose Office ➪ Excel Options) and click the Proofing tab. Then click the AutoCorrect Options button to display the AutoCorrect dialog box. In the dialog box, click the AutoCorrect tab, check the option labeled Replace Text As You Type, and then enter your custom entries. (Figure 3.6 shows an example.) You can set up as many custom entries as you like. Just be careful not to use an abbreviation that might appear normally in your text.

FIGURE 3.6

AutoCorrect allows you to create shorthand abbreviations for text you enter often.

> **TIP**   Excel shares your AutoCorrect list with other Office applications. For example, any AutoCorrect entries you created in Word also work in Excel.

Entering numbers with fractions

To enter a fractional value into a cell, leave a space between the whole number and the fraction. For example, to enter 6⅞, enter **6 7/8** and then press Enter. When you select the cell, 6.875 appears in the Formula bar, and the cell entry appears as a fraction. If you have a fraction only (for example, ⅛), you must enter a zero first, like this: **0 1/8** — otherwise, Excel will likely assume that you're entering a date. When you select the cell and look at the Formula bar, you see 0.125. In the cell, you see ⅛.

Simplifying data entry by using a form

Many people use Excel to manage lists in which the information is arranged in rows. Excel offers a simple way to work with this type of data through the use of a data entry form that Excel can create automatically. This data form works with either a normal range of data, or with a range that has been designated as a table (choosing Insert ⇨ Tables ⇨ Table). Figure 3.7 shows an example.

FIGURE 3.7

Excel's built-in data form can simplify many data-entry tasks.

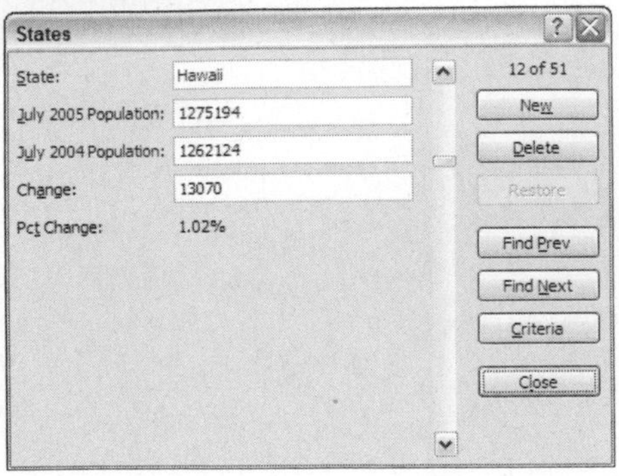

Unfortunately, the command to access the data form is not in the Ribbon. To use the data form, you must add it to your Quick Access Toolbar (QAT):

1. **Right-click the QAT and select Customize Quick Access Toolbar.** The Customize panel of the Excel Options dialog box appears.
2. **In the Choose Commands From drop-down list, select Commands Not In The Ribbon.**
3. **In the list box on the left, select Form**
4. **Click the Add button to add the selected command to your QAT.**
5. **Click OK to close the Excel Options dialog box.**

After performing these steps, a new icon appears on your QAT.

To use a data entry form, you must arrange your data so that Excel can recognize it as a table. Start by entering headings for the columns in the first row of your data entry range. Select any cell in the table and click the Form button on your QAT. Excel then displays a dialog box customized to your data. You can use Tab to move between the text boxes and supply information. If a cell contains a formula, the formula result appears as text (not as an edit box). In other words, you can't modify formulas using the data entry form.

When you complete the data form, click the New button. Excel enters the data into a row in the worksheet and clears the dialog box for the next row of data.

Entering the current date or time into a cell

If you need to date-stamp or time-stamp your worksheet, Excel provides two shortcut keys that do this task for you:

- **Current date:** Ctrl+; (semicolon)
- **Current time:** Ctrl+Shift+; (semicolon)

NOTE When you use either of these shortcuts to enter a date or time into your worksheet, Excel enters a static value into the worksheet. In other words, the date or time entered doesn't change when the worksheet is recalculated. In most cases, this setup is probably what you want, but you should be aware of this limitation. If you want the date or time display to update, use one of these formulas:

```
=TODAY()
=NOW()
```

Applying Number Formatting

Number formatting refers to the process of changing the appearance of values contained in cells. Excel provides a wide variety of number formatting options. In the following sections, you see how to use many of Excel's formatting options to quickly improve the appearance of your worksheets.

> **TIP**
>
> Remember that the formatting you apply works with the selected cell or cells. Therefore, you need to select the cell (or range of cells) before applying the formatting. Also remember that changing the number format does not affect the underlying value. Number formatting affects only the appearance.

Improving readability by formatting numbers

Values that you enter into cells normally are unformatted. In other words, they simply consist of a string of numerals. Typically, you want to format the numbers so that they're easier to read or are more consistent in terms of the number of decimal places shown.

Figure 3.8 shows a worksheet that has two columns of values. The first column consists of unformatted values. The cells in the second column are formatted to make the values easier to read. The third column describes the type of formatting applied.

> **ON the CD-ROM**
>
> This workbook is available on the companion CD-ROM. The file is named **number formatting.xlsx.**

FIGURE 3.8

Use numeric formatting to make it easier to understand what the values in the worksheet represent.

	A	B	C	D
1				
2	Unformatted	Formatted	Type	
3	1200	$1,200.00	Currency	
4	0.231	23.1%	Percentage	
5	2/3/2008	2/3/2008	Short Date	
6	2/3/2008	Sunday, February 03, 2008	Long Date	
7	123439832	123,439,832.00	Accounting	
8	5559832	555-9832	Phone Number	
9	434988723	434-98-8723	Social Security Number	
10	0.552	1:14:53 PM	Time	
11	0.25	1/4	Fraction	
12	12332354090	1.23E+10	Scientific	
13				
14				

> **TIP**
>
> If you move the cell pointer to a cell that has a formatted value, the Formula bar displays the value in its unformatted state because the formatting affects only how the value appears in the cell — not the actual value contained in the cell.

Using automatic number formatting

Excel is smart enough to perform some formatting for you automatically. For example, if you enter 12.2% into a cell, Excel knows that you want to use a percentage format and applies it for you automatically. If you use commas to separate thousands (such as 123,456), Excel applies comma formatting for you. And if you precede your value with a dollar sign, the cell is formatted for currency (assuming that the dollar sign is your system currency symbol).

TIP A handy default feature in Excel makes entering percentage values into cells easier. If a cell is formatted to display as a percent, you can simply enter a normal value (for example 12.5 for 12.5%). If this feature isn't working (or if you prefer to enter the actual value for percents), access the Excel Options dialog box and click the Advanced tab. In the Editing Options section, locate the check box labeled Enable Automatic Percent Entry, and remove the check mark.

Formatting numbers by using the Ribbon

The Home ➪ Number group in the Ribbon contains controls that let you quickly apply common number formats (see Figure 3.9).

FIGURE 3.9

You can find number formatting commands in the Number group of the Home tab.

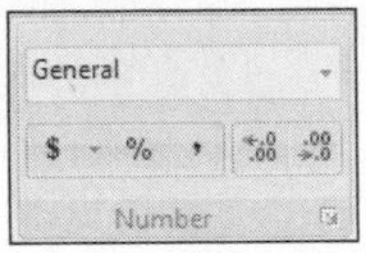

The Number Format drop-down list contains 11 common number formats. Additional options include an Accounting Number Format drop-down list (to select a currency format), plus a Percent Style and a Comma Style button. In addition, the group contains a button to increase the number of decimal places, and another to decrease the number of decimal places.

When you select one of these controls, the active cell takes on the specified number format. You also can select a range of cells (or even an entire row or column) before clicking these buttons. If you select more than one cell, Excel applies the number format to all the selected cells.

Using shortcut keys to format numbers

Another way to apply number formatting is to use shortcut keys. Table 3.1 summarizes the shortcut-key combinations that you can use to apply common number formatting to the selected cells or range. Notice that these Ctrl+Shift characters are all located together, in the upper left part of your keyboard.

TABLE 3.1

Number-Formatting Keyboard Shortcuts

Key Combination	Formatting Applied
Ctrl+Shift+~	General number format (that is, unformatted values)
Ctrl+Shift+$	Currency format with two decimal places (negative numbers appear in parentheses)
Ctrl+Shift+%	Percentage format, with no decimal places
Ctrl+Shift+^	Scientific notation number format, with two decimal places
Ctrl+Shift+#	Date format with the day, month, and year
Ctrl+Shift+@	Time format with the hour, minute, and AM or PM
Ctrl+Shift+!	Two decimal places, thousands separator, and a hyphen for negative values

Formatting numbers using the Format Cells dialog box

In most cases, the number formats that are accessible from the Number group on the Home tab are just fine. Sometimes, however, you want more control over how your values appear. Excel offers a great deal of control over number formats through the use of the Format Cells dialog box, shown in Figure 3.10. For formatting numbers, you need to use the Number tab.

FIGURE 3.10

When you need more control over number formats, use the Number tab of the Format Cells dialog box.

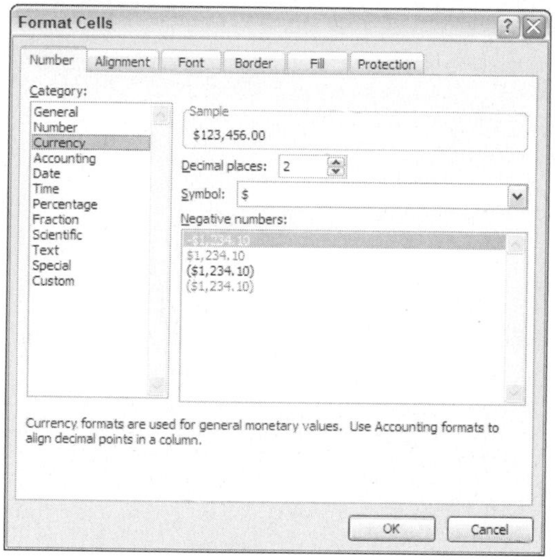

You can bring up the Format Cells dialog box in several ways. Start by selecting the cell or cells that you want to format and then do the following:

- Choose Home ➪ Number and click the small dialog launcher icon.
- Choose Home ➪ Number, click the Number Format drop-down list, and select More Number Formats from the drop-down list.
- Right-click and choose Format Cells from the shortcut menu.
- Press the Ctrl+1 shortcut key.

The Number tab of the Format Cells dialog box displays 12 categories of number formats from which to choose. When you select a category from the list box, the right side of the tab changes to display the appropriate options.

The Number category has three options that you can control: the number of decimal places displayed, whether to use a thousand separator, and how you want negative numbers displayed. Notice that the Negative Numbers list box has four choices (two of which display negative values in red), and the choices change depending on the number of decimal places and whether you choose to separate thousands.

When Numbers Appear to Add Up Incorrectly

Applying a number format to a cell doesn't change the value — only how the value appears in the worksheet. For example, if a cell contains 0.874543, you may format it to appear as 87%. If that cell is used in a formula, the formula uses the full value (0.874543), not the displayed value (87%).

In some situations, formatting may cause Excel to display calculation results that appear incorrect, such as when totaling numbers with decimal places. For example, if values are formatted to display two decimal places, you may not see the actual numbers used in the calculations. But because Excel uses the full precision of the values in its formula, the sum of the two values may appear to be incorrect.

Several solutions to this problem are available. You can format the cells to display more decimal places. You can use the ROUND function on individual numbers and specify the number of decimal places Excel should round to. Or you can instruct Excel to change the worksheet values to match their displayed format. To do so, access the Excel Options dialog box and click the Advanced tab. Check the Set Precision As Displayed check box (which is located in the section named When Calculating This Workbook).

The top of the tab displays a sample of how the active cell will appear with the selected number format (visible only if a cell with a value is selected). After you make your choices, click OK to apply the number format to all the selected cells.

CAUTION   Selecting the Precision As Displayed option changes the numbers in your worksheets to permanently match their appearance onscreen. This setting applies to all sheets in the active workbook. Most of the time, this option is *not* what you want. Make sure that you understand the consequences of using the Set Precision As Displayed option.

CROSS-REF   Chapter 11 discusses ROUND and other built-in functions.

The following are the number-format categories, along with some general comments:

- **General:** The default format; it displays numbers as integers, as decimals, or in scientific notation if the value is too wide to fit in the cell.

- **Number:** Enables you to specify the number of decimal places, whether to use a comma to separate thousands, and how to display negative numbers (with a minus sign, in red, in parentheses, or in red and in parentheses).

- **Currency:** Enables you to specify the number of decimal places, whether to use a currency symbol, and how to display negative numbers (with a minus sign, in red, in parentheses, or in red and in parentheses). This format always uses a comma to separate thousands.

- **Accounting:** Differs from the Currency format in that the currency symbols always line up vertically.

- **Date:** Enables you to choose from several different date formats.

- **Time:** Enables you to choose from several different time formats.

- **Percentage:** Enables you to choose the number of decimal places and always displays a percent sign.

- **Fraction:** Enables you to choose from among nine fraction formats.
- **Scientific:** Displays numbers in exponential notation (with an E): 2.00E+05 = 200,000; 2.05E+05 = 205,000. You can choose the number of decimal places to display to the left of E.
- **Text:** When applied to a value, causes Excel to treat the value as text (even if it looks like a number). This feature is useful for such items as part numbers.
- **Special:** Contains four additional number formats (Zip Code, Zip Code +4, Phone Number, and Social Security Number).
- **Custom:** Enables you to define custom number formats that aren't included in any other category.

> **TIP** If a cell displays a series of hash marks (such as ########), it usually means that the column isn't wide enough to display the value in the number format that you selected. Either make the column wider or change the number format.

Adding your own custom number formats

Sometimes you may want to display numerical values in a format that isn't included in any of the other categories. If so, the answer is to create your own custom format.

> **CROSS-REF** Excel provides you with a great deal of flexibility in creating number formats — so much so that I've devoted an entire chapter (Chapter 24) to this topic.

Chapter 4

Essential Worksheet Operations

This chapter covers some basic information regarding workbooks, worksheets, and windows. You discover tips and techniques to help you take control of your worksheets. The result? You'll be a more efficient Excel user.

Learning the Fundamentals of Excel Worksheets

In Excel, each file is called a *workbook,* and each workbook can contain one or more *worksheets.* You may find it helpful to think of an Excel workbook as a notebook and worksheets as pages in the notebook. As with a notebook, you can view a particular sheet, add new sheets, remove sheets, and copy sheets.

The following sections describe the operations that you can perform with worksheets.

Working with Excel's windows

An Excel workbook file can hold any number of sheets, and these sheets can be either worksheets (sheets consisting of rows and columns) or *chart sheets* (sheets that hold a single chart). A worksheet is what people usually think of when they think of a spreadsheet. You can open as many Excel workbooks as necessary at the same time.

Figure 4.1 shows Excel with four workbooks open, each in a separate window. One of the windows is minimized and appears near the lower-left corner of the screen. (When a workbook is minimized, only its title bar is visible.) Worksheet windows can overlap, and the title bar of one window is a different color. That's the window that contains the active workbook.

FIGURE 4.1

You can open several Excel workbooks at the same time.

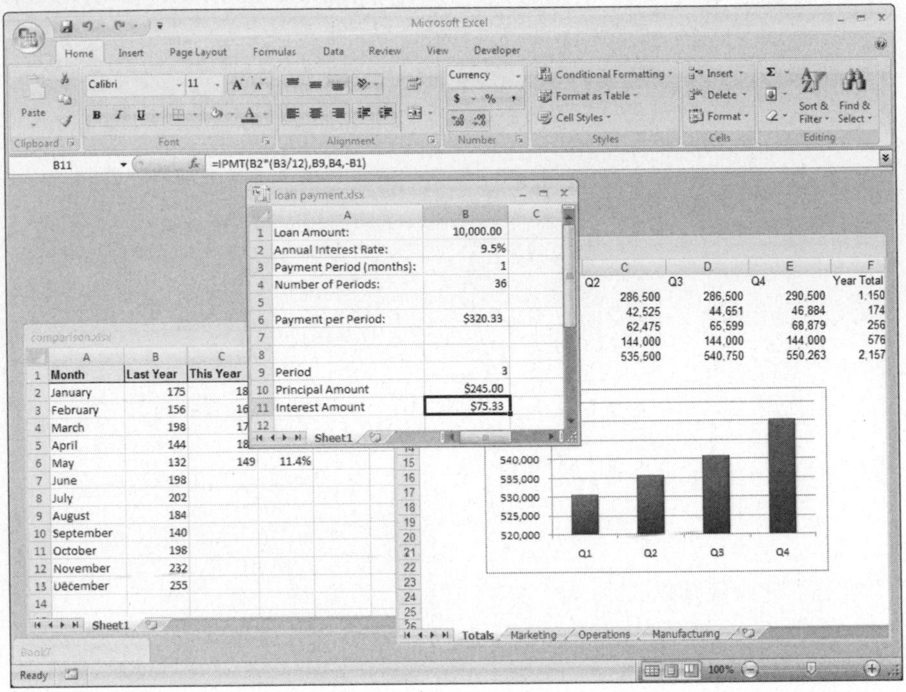

The workbook windows that Excel uses work much like the windows in any other Windows program. Each window has three buttons at the right side of its title bar. From left to right, they are Minimize, Maximize (or Restore), and Close. When a workbook window is maximized, the three buttons appear directly below Excel's title bar.

Excel's windows can be in one of the following states:

- **Maximized:** Fills Excel's entire workspace. A maximized window doesn't have a title bar, and the workbook's name appears in Excel's title bar. To maximize a window, click its Maximize button.

- **Minimized:** Appears as a small window with only a title bar. To minimize a window, click its Minimize button.

- **Restored:** A nonmaximized size. To restore a maximized or minimized window, click its Restore button.

If you work with more than one workbook simultaneously (which is quite common), you have to know how to move, resize, and switch among the workbook windows.

Moving and resizing windows

To move a window, make sure that it's not maximized. Then click and drag its title bar with your mouse.

To resize a window, click and drag any of its borders until it's the size that you want it to be. When you position the mouse pointer on a window's border, the mouse pointer changes to a double-sided arrow, which lets you know that you can now click and drag to resize the window. To resize a window horizontally and vertically at the same time, click and drag any of its corners.

> **NOTE**   You can't move or resize a workbook window if it's maximized. You can move a minimized window, but doing so has no effect on its position when it's subsequently restored.

If you want all your workbook windows to be visible (that is, not obscured by another window), you can move and resize the windows manually, or you can let Excel do it for you. Choosing View ➪ Window ➪ Arrange All displays the Arrange Windows dialog box, shown in Figure 4.2. This dialog box has four window-arrangement options. Just select the one that you want and click OK. Windows that are minimized aren't affected by this comment.

FIGURE 4.2

Use the Arrange Windows dialog box to quickly arrange all open workbook windows.

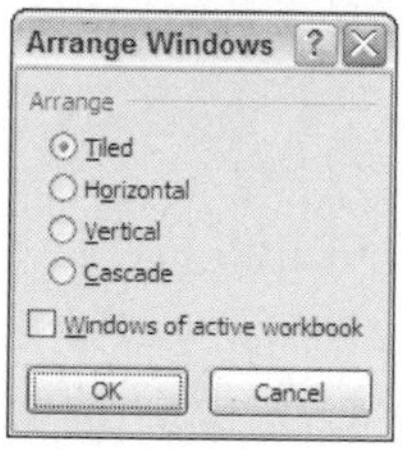

Switching among windows

At any given time, one (and only one) workbook window is the active window. The active window accepts your input and is the window on which your commands work. The active window's title bar is a different color, and the window appears at the top of the stack of windows. To work in a different window, you need to make that window active. You can make a different window the active workbook in several ways:

- Click another window, if it's visible. The window you click moves to the top and becomes the active window. This method isn't possible if the current window is maximized.

- Press Ctrl+Tab (or Ctrl+F6) to cycle through all open windows until the window that you want to work with appears on top as the active window. Shift+Ctrl+Tab (or Shift+Ctrl+F6) cycles through the windows in the opposite direction.

- Choose View ➪ Window ➪ Switch Windows and select the window that you want from the drop-down list (the active window has a check mark next to it). This menu can display up to nine windows. If you have more than nine workbook windows open, choose More Windows (which appears below the nine window names).

- Click the icon for the window in the Windows taskbar. This technique is available only if the Show All Windows In The Taskbar option is turned on. You can control this setting in the Advanced tab of the Excel Options dialog box (in the Display section).

> **TIP** Most people prefer to do most of their work with maximized workbook windows, which enables you to see more cells and eliminates the distraction of other workbook windows getting in the way. At times, however, viewing multiple windows is preferred. For example, displaying two windows is more efficient if you need to compare information in two workbooks or if you need to copy data from one workbook to another.

When you maximize one window, all the other windows are maximized, too (even though you don't see them). Therefore, if the active window is maximized and you activate a different window, the new active window is also maximized.

> **TIP** You also can display a single workbook in more than one window. For example, if you have a workbook with two worksheets, you may want to display each worksheet in a separate window in order to compare the two sheets. All the window-manipulation procedures described previously still apply. Choose View ➪ Window ➪ New Window to open an additional window in the active workbook.

Closing windows

If you have multiple windows open, you may want to close those windows that you no longer need. Excel offers several ways to close the active window:

- Choose Office ➪ Close.
- Click the Close button (the *X* icon) on the workbook window's title bar. If the workbook window is maximized, its title bar is not visible, so its Close button appears directly below Excel's Close button.
- Press Ctrl+W.

When you close a workbook window, Excel checks whether you have made any changes since the last time you saved the file. If not, the window closes without a prompt from Excel. If you've made any changes, Excel prompts you to save the file before it closes the window.

Activating a worksheet

At any given time, one workbook is the active workbook, and one sheet is the active sheet in the active workbook. To activate a different sheet, just click its sheet tab, located at the bottom of the workbook window. You also can use the following shortcut keys to activate a different sheet:

- **Ctrl+PgUp:** Activates the previous sheet, if one exists
- **Ctrl+PgDn:** Activates the next sheet, if one exists

If your workbook has many sheets, all its tabs may not be visible. Use the tab-scrolling controls (see Figure 4.3) to scroll the sheet tabs. The sheet tabs share space with the worksheet's horizontal scroll bar. You also can drag the tab split control to display more or fewer tabs. Dragging the tab split control simultaneously changes the number of tabs and the size of the horizontal scroll bar.

> **TIP** When you right-click any of the tab-scrolling controls, Excel displays a list of all sheets in the workbook. You can quickly activate a sheet by selecting it from the list.

FIGURE 4.3

Use the tab controls to activate a different worksheet or to see additional worksheet tabs.

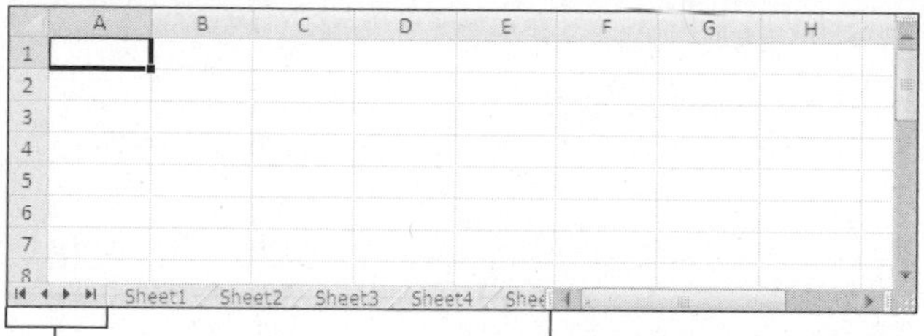

Tab scrolling controls   Tab split control

Adding a new worksheet to your workbook

Worksheets can be an excellent organizational tool. Instead of placing everything on a single worksheet, you can use additional worksheets in a workbook to separate various workbook elements logically. For example, if you have several products whose sales you track individually, you may want to assign each product to its own worksheet and then use another worksheet to consolidate your results.

The following are three ways to add a new worksheet to a workbook:

- Click the Insert Worksheet control, which is located to the right of the last sheet tab. This method inserts the new sheet after the last sheet in the workbook.
- Press Shift+F11. This method inserts the new sheet before the active sheet.
- Right-click a sheet tab, choose Insert from the shortcut menu, and click the General tab of the Insert dialog box. Then select click the Worksheet icon and click OK. This method inserts the new sheet before the active sheet.

Deleting a worksheet you no longer need

If you no longer need a worksheet, or if you want to get rid of an empty worksheet in a workbook, you can delete it in either of two ways:

- Right-click the sheet tab and choose Delete from the shortcut menu.
- Choose Home ➪ Cells ➪ Delete Sheet. If the worksheet contains any data, Excel asks you to confirm that you want to delete the sheet. If you've never used the worksheet, Excel deletes it immediately without asking for confirmation.

> **TIP** You can delete multiple sheets with a single command by selecting the sheets that you want to delete. To select multiple sheets, press Ctrl while you click the sheet tabs that you want to delete. To select a group of contiguous sheets, click the first sheet tab, press Shift, and then click the last sheet tab. Then use either method to delete the selected sheets.

> **CAUTION** When you delete a worksheet, it's gone for good. Deleting a worksheet is one of the few operations in Excel that can't be undone.

Changing the Number of Sheets in Your Workbooks

By default, Excel automatically creates three worksheets in each new workbook. You can change this default behavior. For example, I prefer to start each new workbook with a single worksheet. After all, you can easily add new sheets if and when they're needed. To change the default number of worksheets:

1. **Choose Office ⇨ Excel Options to display the Excel Options dialog box.**
2. **In the Excel Options dialog box, click the Popular tab.**
3. **Change the value for the Include This Many Sheets setting and click OK.**

Making this change affects all new workbooks but has no effect on existing workbooks.

Changing the name of a worksheet

The default names Excel uses for worksheets — Sheet1, Sheet2, and so on — aren't very descriptive. If you don't change the worksheet names, remembering where to find things in multiple-sheet workbooks can be a bit difficult. That's why providing more meaningful names for your worksheets is often a good idea.

To change a sheet's name, double-click the sheet tab. Excel highlights the name on the sheet tab so that you can edit the name or replace it with a new name.

Sheet names can be up to 31 characters, and spaces are allowed. However, you can't use the following characters in sheet names:

:   colon

/   slash

\   backslash

?   question mark

*   asterisk

Keep in mind that a longer worksheet name results in a wider tab, which takes up more space on-screen. Therefore, if you use lengthy sheet names, you won't be able to see very many sheet tabs without scrolling the tab list.

Changing a sheet tab's color

Excel allows you to change the color of your worksheet tabs. For example, you may prefer to color-code the sheet tabs to make identifying the worksheet's contents easier.

To change the color of a sheet tab, right-click the tab and choose Tab Color. Then select the color from the color selector box.

Rearranging your worksheets

You may want to rearrange the order of worksheets in a workbook. If you have a separate worksheet for each sales region, for example, arranging the worksheets in alphabetical order or by total sales may be helpful. You may want to move a worksheet from one workbook to another. (To move a worksheet to a different workbook, both workbooks must be open.) You can also create copies of worksheets.

You can move or copy a worksheet in the following ways:

■ Right-click the sheet tab and choose Move or Copy to display the Move or Copy dialog box (see Figure 4.4). Use this dialog box to specify the operation and the location for the sheet.

■ To move a worksheet, click the worksheet tab and drag it to its desired location (either in the same workbook or in a different workbook). When you drag, the mouse pointer changes to a small sheet, and a small arrow guides you.

■ To copy a worksheet, click the worksheet tab, and press Ctrl while dragging the tab to its desired location (either in the same workbook or in a different workbook). When you drag, the mouse pointer changes to a small sheet with a plus sign on it.

TIP You can move or copy multiple sheets simultaneously. First select the sheets by clicking their sheet tabs while holding down the Ctrl key. Then you can move or copy the set of sheets by using the preceding methods.

FIGURE 4.4

Use the Move or Copy dialog box to move or copy worksheets in the same or another workbook.

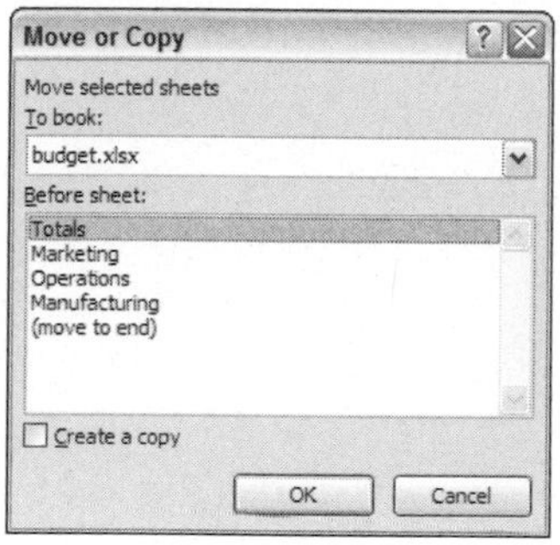

If you move or copy a worksheet to a workbook that already has a sheet with the same name, Excel changes the name to make it unique. For example, Sheet1 becomes Sheet1 (2).

NOTE When you move or copy a worksheet to a different workbook, any defined names and custom formats also get copied to the new workbook.

Hiding and unhiding a worksheet

In some situations, you may want to hide one or more worksheets. Hiding a sheet may be useful if you don't want others to see it or if you just want to get it out of the way. When a sheet is hidden, its sheet tab is also hidden. You can't hide all the sheets in a workbook, so at least one sheet must remain visible.

To hide a worksheet, right-click its sheet tab and choose Hide. The active worksheet (or selected worksheets) will be hidden from view.

To unhide a hidden worksheet, right-click any sheet tab and choose Unhide. Excel opens its Unhide dialog box that lists all hidden sheets. Choose the sheet that you want to redisplay and click OK. You can't select multiple sheets from this dialog box, so you need to repeat the command for each sheet that you want to unhide.

Preventing Sheet Actions

To prevent others from unhiding hidden sheets, inserting new sheets, renaming sheets, copying sheets, or deleting sheets, protect the workbook's structure:

1. **Choose Review ⇨ Changes ⇨ Protect Workbook.**
2. **In the Protect Workbook dialog box, click the Structure option.**
3. **Provide a password, if you like.**

After performing these steps, several commands will no longer be available when you right-click a sheet tab: Insert, Delete, Rename, Move or Copy, Hide, and Unhide. Be aware, however, that this is a very weak security measure. Cracking Excel's protection features is relatively easy.

You can also make a sheet "very hidden." A sheet that is very hidden doesn't appear in the Unhide dialog box. To make a sheet very hidden:

1. **Activate the worksheet.**
2. **Choose Developer ⇨ Controls ⇨ Properties.** The Properties dialog box, shown in the following figure, appears. (If the Developer tab isn't available, you can turn it on using the Popular tab of the Excel Options dialog box.)
3. **In the Properties box, select the Visible option and choose 2 - xlSheetVeryHidden.**

After performing these steps, the worksheet is hidden and doesn't appear in the Unhide dialog box.

Be careful! After you make a sheet very hidden, you can't use the Properties box to unhide it because you aren't able to select the sheet! In fact, the only way to unhide such a sheet is to use a VBA macro. (See Part VI for more information about VBA.) For example, this VBA statement unhides Sheet1 in the active workbook:

```
ActiveWorkbook.Worksheets("Sheet1").Visible = True
```

Controlling the Worksheet View

As you add more information to a worksheet, you may find that navigating and locating what you want gets more difficult. Excel includes a few options that enable you to view your sheet, and sometimes multiple sheets, more efficiently. This section discusses a few additional worksheet options at your disposal.

Zooming in or out for a better view

Normally, everything you see on-screen is displayed at 100 percent. You can change the *zoom percentage* from 10 percent (very tiny) to 400 percent (huge). Using a small zoom percentage can help you to get a bird's-eye view of your worksheet to see how it's laid out. Zooming in is useful if your eyesight isn't quite what it used to be and you have trouble deciphering tiny type. Zooming doesn't change the font size, so it has no effect on printed output.

CROSS-REF Excel contains separate options for changing the size of your printed output. (Use the controls in the Page Layout ⇨ Scale To Fit ribbon group.) See Chapter 10 for details.

Figure 4.5 shows a window zoomed to 10 percent and a window zoomed to 400 percent.

FIGURE 4.5

You can zoom in or out for a better view of your worksheets.

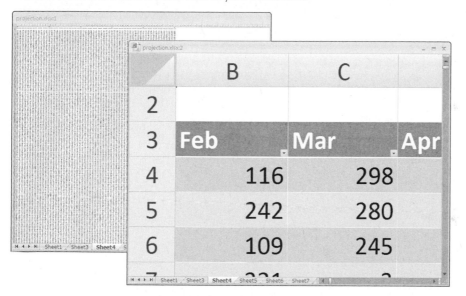

You can easily change the zoom factor of the active worksheet by using the Zoom slider located on the right side of the status bar. Click and drag the slider, and your screen transforms instantly.

Another way to zoom is to choose View ⇨ Zoom ⇨ Zoom, which displays a dialog box. Choosing View ⇨ Zoom ⇨ Zoom To Selection zooms the worksheet to display only the selected cells (useful if you want to view only a particular range).

TIP Zooming affects only the active worksheet, so you can use different zoom factors for different worksheets. Also, if you have a worksheet displayed in two different windows, you can set a different zoom factor for each of the windows.

CROSS-REF If your worksheet uses named ranges (see Chapter 5), zooming your worksheet to 39 percent or less displays the name of the range overlaid on the cells. Viewing named ranges in this manner is useful for getting an overview of how a worksheet is laid out.

Viewing a worksheet in multiple windows

Sometimes, you may want to view two different parts of a worksheet simultaneously — perhaps to make referencing a distant cell in a formula easier. Or you may want to examine more than one sheet in the same workbook simultaneously. You can accomplish either of these actions by opening a new view to the workbook, using one or more additional windows.

To create and display a new view of the active workbook, choose View ➪ Window ➪ New Window.

Excel displays a new window for the active workbook, similar to the one shown in Figure 4.6. In this case, each window shows a different worksheet in the workbook. Notice the text in the windows' title bars: `climate data.xls:1` and `climate data.xls:2`. To help you keep track of the windows, Excel appends a colon and a number to each window.

TIP If the workbook is maximized when you create a new window, you may not even notice that Excel has created the new window; but if you look at the Excel title bar, you'll see that the workbook title now has `:2` appended to the name. Choose View ➪ Window ➪ Arrange and choose one of the Arrange options in the Arrange Windows dialog box to display the open windows. If you select the Windows Of Active Workbook check box, only the windows of the active workbook are arranged.

FIGURE 4.6

Use multiple windows to view different sections of a workbook at the same time.

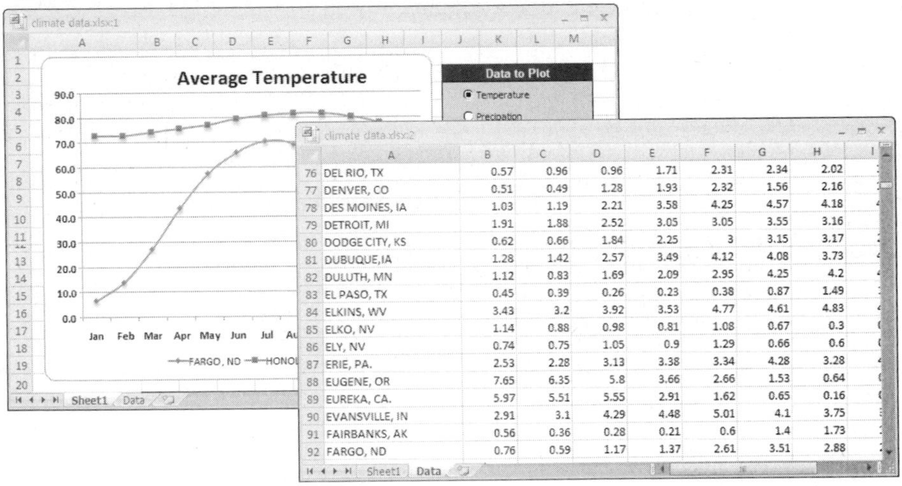

A single workbook can have as many views (that is, separate windows) as you want. Each window is independent of the others. In other words, scrolling to a new location in one window doesn't cause scrolling in the other window(s).

You can close these additional windows when you no longer need them. For example, clicking the Close button on the active window's title bar closes the active window but doesn't close the other windows for the workbook.

> **TIP** Multiple windows make copying or moving information from one worksheet to another easier. You can use Excel's drag-and-drop procedures to copy or move ranges.

Comparing sheets side by side

In some situations, you may want to compare two worksheets that are in different windows. The View Side By Side feature makes this task a bit easier.

First, make sure that the two sheets are displayed in separate windows. (The sheets can be in the same workbook or in different workbooks.) If you want to compare two sheets in the same workbook, choose View ➪ Window ➪ New Window to create a new window for the active workbook. Activate the first window; then choose View ➪ Window ➪ View Side by Side. If more than two windows are open, you see a dialog box that lets you select the window for the comparison. The two windows appear next to each other.

When using the Compare Side by Side feature, scrolling in one of the windows also scrolls the other window. If, for some reason, you don't want this simultaneous scrolling, choose View ➪ Window ➪ Synchronous Scrolling (which is a toggle). If you have rearranged or moved the windows, choose View ➪ Window ➪ Reset Window Position to restore the windows to the initial side-by-side arrangement. To turn off the side-by-side viewing, choose View ➪ Window ➪ View Side by Side again.

Keep in mind that this feature is for manual comparison only. Unfortunately, Excel doesn't provide a way to show you the differences between two sheets.

Splitting the worksheet window into panes

If you prefer not to clutter your screen with additional windows, Excel provides another option for viewing multiple parts of the same worksheet. Choosing View ➪ Window ➪ Split splits the active worksheet into two or four separate panes. The split occurs at the location of the cell pointer. If the cell pointer is in row 1 or column A, this command results in a 2-pane split. Otherwise, it gives you four panes. You can use the mouse to drag the individual panes to resize them.

Figure 4.7 shows a worksheet split into two panes. Notice that row numbers aren't continuous. In other words, splitting panes enables you to display in a single window widely separated areas of a worksheet. To remove the split panes, choose View ➪ Window ➪ Split again.

FIGURE 4.7

You can split the worksheet window into two or four panes to view different areas of the worksheet at the same time.

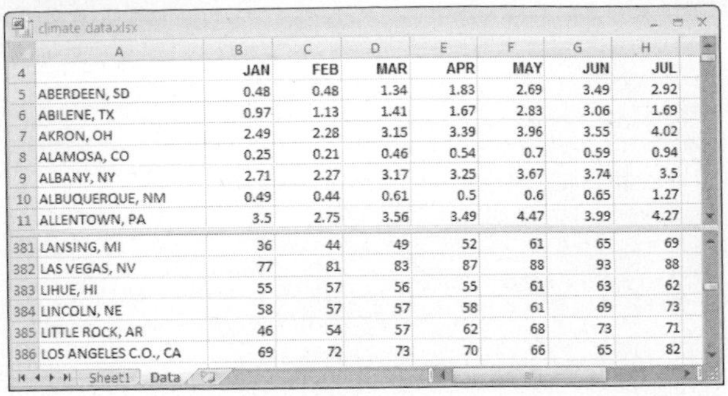

	A	B	C	D	E	F	G	H
4		JAN	FEB	MAR	APR	MAY	JUN	JUL
5	ABERDEEN, SD	0.48	0.48	1.34	1.83	2.69	3.49	2.92
6	ABILENE, TX	0.97	1.13	1.41	1.67	2.83	3.06	1.69
7	AKRON, OH	2.49	2.28	3.15	3.39	3.96	3.55	4.02
8	ALAMOSA, CO	0.25	0.21	0.46	0.54	0.7	0.59	0.94
9	ALBANY, NY	2.71	2.27	3.17	3.25	3.67	3.74	3.5
10	ALBUQUERQUE, NM	0.49	0.44	0.61	0.5	0.6	0.65	1.27
11	ALLENTOWN, PA	3.5	2.75	3.56	3.49	4.47	3.99	4.27
381	LANSING, MI	36	44	49	52	61	65	69
382	LAS VEGAS, NV	77	81	83	87	88	93	88
383	LIHUE, HI	55	57	56	55	61	63	62
384	LINCOLN, NE	58	57	57	58	61	69	73
385	LITTLE ROCK, AR	46	54	57	62	68	73	71
386	LOS ANGELES C.O., CA	69	72	73	70	66	65	82

Another way to split and unsplit panes is to drag either the vertical or horizontal split bar. These bars are the small rectangles that normally appear just above the top of the vertical scroll bar and just to the right of the horizontal scroll bar. When you move the mouse pointer over a split bar, the mouse pointer changes to a pair of parallel lines with arrows pointing outward from each line. To remove split panes by using the mouse, drag the pane separator all the way to the edge of the window or just double-click it.

Keeping the titles in view by freezing panes

If you set up a worksheet with row or column headings, these headings will not be visible when you scroll down or to the right.. Excel provides a handy solution to this problem: freezing panes. Freezing panes keeps the headings visible while you're scrolling through the worksheet.

To freeze panes, start by moving the cell pointer to the cell below the row that you want to remain visible as you scroll vertically, and to the right of the column that you want to remain visible as you scroll horizontally. Then, choose View ⇨ Window ⇨ Freeze Panes and select the Freeze Panes option from the drop-down list. Excel inserts dark lines to indicate the frozen rows and columns. The frozen row and column remain visible as you scroll throughout the worksheet. To remove the frozen panes, choose View ⇨ Window ⇨ Freeze Panes, and select the Unfreeze Panes option from the drop-down list.

Figure 4.8 shows a worksheet with frozen panes. In this case, rows 1:3 and column A are frozen in place. This technique allows you to scroll down and to the right to locate some information while keeping the column titles and the column A entries visible.

NEW FEATURE The vast majority of the time, you'll want to freeze either the first row or the first column. Excel 2007 makes it a bit easier. The View ⇨ Window ⇨ Freeze Panes drop-down list has two additional options: Freeze Top Row and Freeze First Column. Using these commands eliminates the need to position the cell pointer before freezing panes.

NEW FEATURE If you have designated a range to be a table (by choosing Insert ⇨ Tables ⇨ Table), you may not even need to freeze panes. When you scroll down, Excel displays the table column headings in place of the column letters. Figure 4.9 shows an example. The table headings replace the column letters only when a cell within the table is selected.

FIGURE 4.8

By freezing certain columns and rows, they remain visible while you scroll the worksheet.

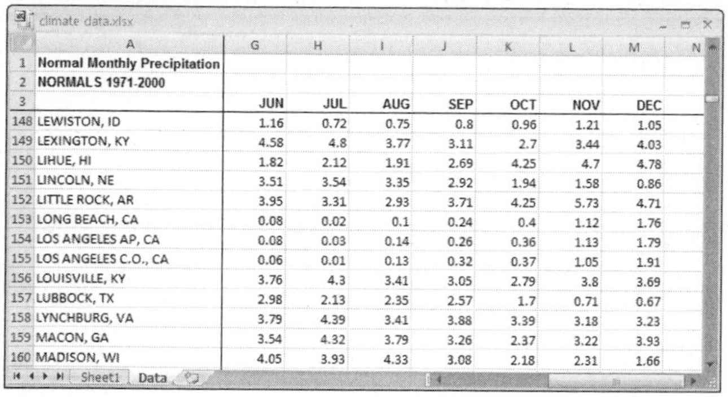

	G	H	I	J	K	L	M
1 Normal Monthly Precipitation							
2 NORMALS 1971-2000							
3	JUN	JUL	AUG	SEP	OCT	NOV	DEC
148 LEWISTON, ID	1.16	0.72	0.75	0.8	0.96	1.21	1.05
149 LEXINGTON, KY	4.58	4.8	3.77	3.11	2.7	3.44	4.03
150 LIHUE, HI	1.82	2.12	1.91	2.69	4.25	4.7	4.78
151 LINCOLN, NE	3.51	3.54	3.35	2.92	1.94	1.58	0.86
152 LITTLE ROCK, AR	3.95	3.31	2.93	3.71	4.25	5.73	4.71
153 LONG BEACH, CA	0.08	0.02	0.1	0.24	0.4	1.12	1.76
154 LOS ANGELES AP, CA	0.08	0.03	0.14	0.26	0.36	1.13	1.79
155 LOS ANGELES C.O., CA	0.06	0.01	0.13	0.32	0.37	1.05	1.91
156 LOUISVILLE, KY	3.76	4.3	3.41	3.05	2.79	3.8	3.69
157 LUBBOCK, TX	2.98	2.13	2.35	2.57	1.7	0.71	0.67
158 LYNCHBURG, VA	3.79	4.39	3.41	3.88	3.39	3.18	3.23
159 MACON, GA	3.54	4.32	3.79	3.26	2.37	3.22	3.93
160 MADISON, WI	4.05	3.93	4.33	3.08	2.18	2.31	1.66

climate data.xlsx   Sheet1   Data

FIGURE 4.9

When using a table, scrolling down displays the table headings where the column letters normally appear.

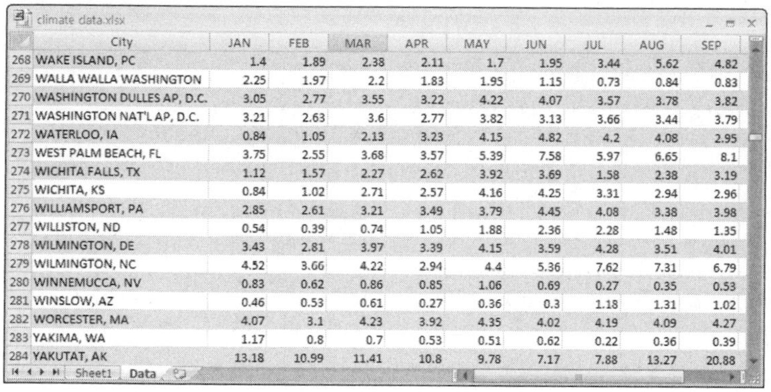

City	JAN	FEB	MAR	APR	MAY	JUN	JUL	AUG	SEP
268 WAKE ISLAND, PC	1.4	1.89	2.38	2.11	1.7	1.95	3.44	5.62	4.82
269 WALLA WALLA WASHINGTON	2.25	1.97	2.2	1.83	1.95	1.15	0.73	0.84	0.83
270 WASHINGTON DULLES AP, D.C.	3.05	2.77	3.55	3.22	4.22	4.07	3.57	3.78	3.82
271 WASHINGTON NAT'L AP, D.C.	3.21	2.63	3.6	2.77	3.82	3.13	3.66	3.44	3.79
272 WATERLOO, IA	0.84	1.05	2.13	3.23	4.15	4.82	4.2	4.08	2.95
273 WEST PALM BEACH, FL	3.75	2.55	3.68	3.57	5.39	7.58	5.97	6.65	8.1
274 WICHITA FALLS, TX	1.12	1.57	2.27	2.62	3.92	3.69	1.58	2.38	3.19
275 WICHITA, KS	0.84	1.02	2.71	2.57	4.16	4.25	3.31	2.94	2.96
276 WILLIAMSPORT, PA	2.85	2.61	3.21	3.49	3.79	4.45	4.08	3.38	3.98
277 WILLISTON, ND	0.54	0.39	0.74	1.05	1.88	2.36	2.28	1.48	1.35
278 WILMINGTON, DE	3.43	2.81	3.97	3.39	4.15	3.59	4.28	3.51	4.01
279 WILMINGTON, NC	4.52	3.66	4.22	2.94	4.4	5.36	7.62	7.31	6.79
280 WINNEMUCCA, NV	0.83	0.62	0.86	0.85	1.06	0.69	0.27	0.35	0.53
281 WINSLOW, AZ	0.46	0.53	0.61	0.27	0.36	0.3	1.18	1.31	1.02
282 WORCESTER, MA	4.07	3.1	4.23	3.92	4.35	4.02	4.19	4.09	4.27
283 YAKIMA, WA	1.17	0.8	0.7	0.53	0.51	0.62	0.22	0.36	0.39
284 YAKUTAT, AK	13.18	10.99	11.41	10.8	9.78	7.17	7.88	13.27	20.88

climate data.xlsx   Sheet1   Data

Monitoring cells with a Watch Window

In some situations, you may want to monitor the value in a particular cell as you work. As you scroll throughout the worksheet, that cell may disappear from view. A feature known as Watch Window can help. A *Watch Window* displays the value of any number of cells in a handy window that's always visible.

To display the Watch Window, choose Formulas ➪ Formula Auditing ➪ Watch Window. The Watch Window appears in the task pane, but you can also drag it and make it float over the worksheet.

To add a cell to watch, click Add Watch and specify the cell that you want to watch. The Watch Window displays the value in that cell. You can add any number of cells to the Watch Window, and you can move the window to any convenient location. Figure 4.10 shows the Watch Window monitoring four cells.

TIP   Double-click a cell in the Watch Window to immediately jump to that cell.

FIGURE 4.10

Use the Watch Window to monitor the value in one or more cells.

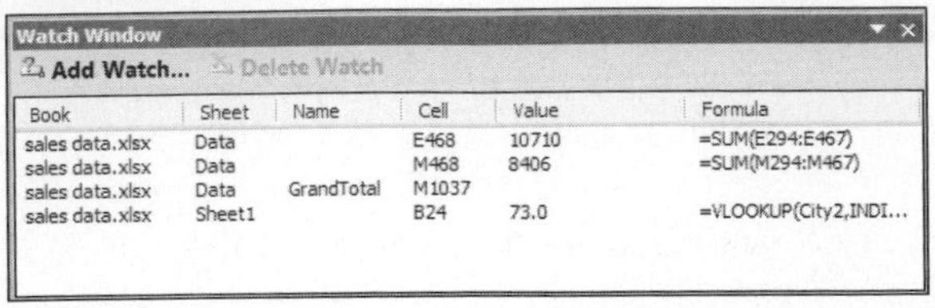

Book	Sheet	Name	Cell	Value	Formula
sales data.xlsx	Data		E468	10710	=SUM(E294:E467)
sales data.xlsx	Data		M468	8406	=SUM(M294:M467)
sales data.xlsx	Data	GrandTotal	M1037		
sales data.xlsx	Sheet1		B24	73.0	=VLOOKUP(City2,INDI...

Working with Rows and Columns

This section discusses worksheet operations that involve rows and columns. Rows and columns make up an Excel worksheet. Every worksheet has exactly 1,048,576 rows and 16,384 columns, and these values can't be changed.

> **NOTE** If you open a workbook that was created in a previous version of Excel, the workbook is opened in "compatibility mode." These workbooks have 65,536 rows and 256 columns. To increase the number of rows and columns, save the workbook as an Excel 2007 XLSX file and then reopen it.

Inserting rows and columns

Although the number of rows and columns in a worksheet is fixed, you can still insert and delete rows and columns if you need to make room for additional information. These operations don't change the number of rows or columns. Rather, inserting a new row moves down the other rows to accommodate the new row. The last row is simply removed from the worksheet if it's empty. Inserting a new column shifts the columns to the right, and the last column is removed if it's empty.

> **NOTE** If the last row isn't empty, you can't insert a new row. Similarly, if the last column contains information, Excel doesn't let you insert a new column. Attempting to add a row or column displays the dialog box shown in Figure 4.11.

FIGURE 4.11

You can't add a new row or column if it causes nonblank cells to move off the worksheet.

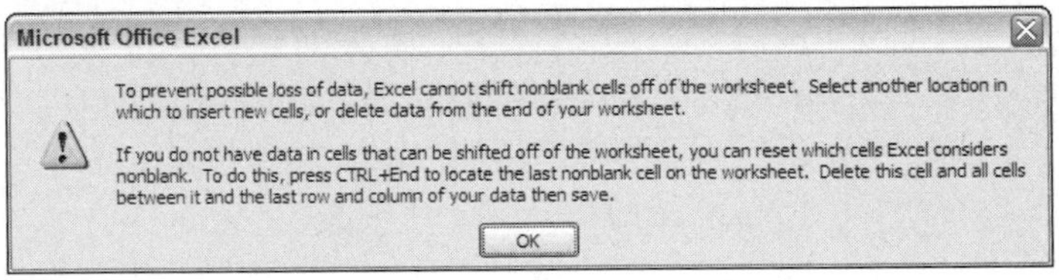

Microsoft Office Excel

To prevent possible loss of data, Excel cannot shift nonblank cells off of the worksheet. Select another location in which to insert new cells, or delete data from the end of your worksheet.

If you do not have data in cells that can be shifted off of the worksheet, you can reset which cells Excel considers nonblank. To do this, press CTRL+End to locate the last nonblank cell on the worksheet. Delete this cell and all cells between it and the last row and column of your data then save.

[OK]

To insert a new row or rows, you can use any of these techniques:

- Select an entire row or multiple rows by clicking the row numbers in the worksheet border. Right-click and choose Insert from the shortcut menu.

- Move the cell pointer to the row that you want to insert and then choose Home ➪ Cells ➪ Insert ➪ Insert Sheet Rows. If you select multiple cells in the column, Excel inserts additional rows that correspond to the number of cells selected in the column and moves the rows below the insertion down.

The procedures for inserting a new column or columns is similar, but you choose Home ➪ Cells ➪ Insert ➪ Insert Sheet Columns.

You also can insert cells, rather than just rows or columns. Select the range into which you want to add new cells and then choose Home ➪ Cells ➪ Insert ➪ Insert Cells (or right-click the selection and choose Insert). To insert cells, the existing cells must be shifted to the right or shifted down. Therefore, Excel displays the Insert dialog box shown in Figure 4.12 so that you can specify the direction in which you want to shift the cells.

FIGURE 4.12

You can insert partial rows or columns by using the Insert dialog box.

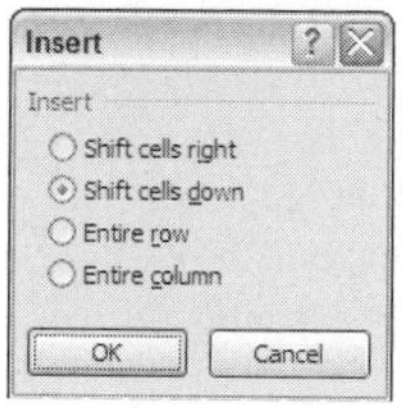

Deleting rows and columns

You may also want to delete rows or columns in a worksheet. For example, your sheet may contain old data that is no longer needed.

To delete a row or rows, use either of these methods:

- Select an entire row or multiple rows by clicking the row numbers in the worksheet border. Right-click and choose Delete from the shortcut menu.

- Move the cell pointer to the row that you want to delete and then choose Home ➪ Cells ➪ Delete Sheet Rows. If you select multiple cells in the column, Excel deletes all rows in the selection.

Deleting columns works in a similar way. If you discover that you accidentally deleted a row or column, select Undo from the Quick Access Toolbar (or press Ctrl+Z) to undo the action.

Hiding rows and columns

In some cases, you may want to hide particular rows or columns. Hiding rows and columns may be useful if you don't want users to see particular information or if you need to print a report that summarizes the information in the worksheet without showing all the details.

CROSS-REF Chapter 26 discusses another way to summarize worksheet data without showing all the details — outlining.

To hide rows or columns in your worksheet, select the row or rows that you want to hide by clicking in the row or column header. Then right-click and choose Hide from the shortcut menu. Or, you can use the commands on the Home ➪ Cells ➪ Format drop-down list.

TIP You also can drag the row or column's border to hide the row or column. You must drag the border in the row or column heading. Drag the bottom border of a row upward or the border of a column to the left.

A hidden row is actually a row with its height set to zero. Similarly, a hidden column has a column width of zero. When you use the arrow keys to move the cell pointer, cells in hidden rows or columns are skipped. In other words, you can't use the arrow keys to move to a cell in a hidden row or column.

Unhiding a hidden row or column can be a bit tricky because selecting a row or column that's hidden is difficult. The solution is to select the columns or rows that are adjacent to the hidden column or row. (Select at least one column or row on either side.) Then right-click and choose Unhide. For example, if column G is hidden, select columns F and H.

Another method is to choose Home ➪ Find & Select ➪ Go To (or its F5 equivalent) to select a cell in a hidden row or column. For example, if column A is hidden, you can press F5 and specify cell A1 (or any other cell in column A) to move the cell pointer to the hidden column. Then you can choose Home ➪ Cells ➪ Format ➪ Hide & Unhide ➪ Unhide Columns.

Changing column widths and row heights

Often, you'll want to change the width of a column or the height of a row. For example, you can make columns narrower to accommodate more information on a printed page. Or you may want to increase row height to create a "double-spaced" effect.

Excel provides several different ways to change the widths of columns and the height of rows.

Changing column widths

Column width is measured in terms of the number of characters of a *fixed pitch font* that will fit into the cell's width. By default, each column's width is 8.43 units, which equates to 64 pixels.

TIP If hash symbols (#) fill a cell that contains a numerical value, the column isn't wide enough to accommodate the information in the cell. Widen the column to solve the problem.

Before you change the column width, you can select multiple columns so that the width will be the same for all selected columns. To select multiple columns, either click and drag in the column border or press Ctrl while you select individual columns. To select all columns, click the button where the row and column headers intersect (or press Ctrl+A). You can change columns widths by using any of the following techniques.

- Drag the right-column border with the mouse until the column is the desired width.
- Choose Home ➪ Cells ➪ Format ➪ Column Width and enter a value in the Column Width dialog box.

- Choose Home ➪ Cells ➪ Format ➪ AutoFit Column Width to adjust the width of the selected column so that the widest entry in the column fits. Rather than selecting an entire column, you can just select cells in the column, and the column is adjusted based on the widest entry in your selection.

- Double-click the right border of a column header to set the column width automatically to the widest entry in the column.

TIP To change the default width of all columns, choose Home ➪ Cells ➪ Format ➪ Column ➪ Default Width. This command displays a dialog box into which you enter the new default column width. All columns that haven't been previously adjusted take on the new column width.

CAUTION After you manually adjust a column's width, Excel will no longer automatically adjust the column to accommodate longer numerical entries.

Changing row heights

Row height is measured in points (a standard unit of measurement in the printing trade — 72 points is equal to 1 inch). The default row height using the default font is 15 points, or 20 pixels.

The default row height can vary, depending on the font defined in the Normal style. In addition, Excel automatically adjusts row heights to accommodate the tallest font in the row. So, if you change the font size of a cell to 20 points, for example, Excel makes the column taller so that the entire text is visible.

You can set the row height manually, however, by using any of the following techniques. As with columns, you can select multiple rows.

- Drag the lower row border with the mouse until the row is the desired height.

- Choose Home ➪ Cells ➪ Format ➪ Row Height and enter a value (in points) in the Row Height dialog box.

- Double-click the bottom border of a row to set the row height automatically to the tallest entry in the row. You also can choose Home ➪ Cells ➪ Format ➪ Autofit Row Height for this task.

Changing the row height is useful for spacing out rows and is almost always preferable to inserting empty rows between lines of data.

Working with Cells and Ranges

M ost of the work you do in Excel involves cells and ranges.
Understanding how best to manipulate cells and ranges will save you
time and effort. This chapter discusses a variety of techniques that you
can use to help increase your efficiency.

Understanding Cells and Ranges

A *cell* is a single element in a worksheet that can hold a value, some text, or a formula. A cell is identified by its *address,* which consists of its column letter and
row number. For example, cell D12 is the cell in the fourth column and the
twelfth row.

A group of cells is called a *range.* You designate a range address by specifying its
upper-left cell address and its lower-right cell address, separated by a colon.

Here are some examples of range addresses:

C24	A range that consists of a single cell.
A1:B1	Two cells that occupy one row and two columns.
A1:A100	100 cells in column A.
A1:D4	16 cells (four rows by four columns).
C1:C1048576	An entire column of cells; this range also can be expressed as C:C.
A6:XFD6	An entire row of cells; this range also can be expressed as 6:6.
A1:XFD1048576	All cells in a worksheet.

IN THIS CHAPTER

Understanding Excel's cells and ranges

Selecting cells and ranges

Copying or moving ranges

Using names to work with ranges

Adding comments to cells

Selecting ranges

To perform an operation on a range of cells in a worksheet, you must first select the range. For example, if you want to make the text bold for a range of cells, you must select the range and then choose Home ➪ Font ➪ Bold (or press Ctrl+B).

When you select a range, the cells appear highlighted. The exception is the active cell, which remains its normal color. Figure 5.1 shows an example of a selected range (B4:C11) in a worksheet. Cell B4, the active cell, is selected but not highlighted.

FIGURE 5.1

When you select a range, it appears highlighted, but the active cell within the range is not highlighted.

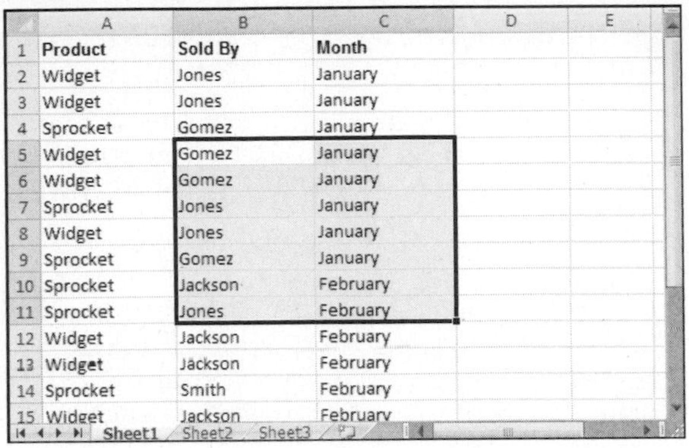

You can select a range in several ways:

- Press the left mouse button and drag, highlighting the range. If you drag to the end of the screen, the worksheet will scroll.
- Press the Shift key while you use the direction keys to select a range.
- Press F8 and then move the cell pointer with the direction keys to highlight the range. Press F8 again to return the direction keys to normal movement.
- Type the cell or range address into the Name box and press Enter. Excel selects the cell or range that you specified.
- Choose Home ➪ Editing ➪ Find & Select ➪ Go To (or press F5) and enter a range's address manually into the Go To dialog box. When you click OK, Excel selects the cells in the range that you specified.

TIP As you're selecting a range, Excel displays the number of rows and columns in your selection in the Name box (located on the left side of the Formula bar). As soon as you finish the selection, the Name box reverts to showing the address of the active cell.

Selecting complete rows and columns

Often, you'll need to select an entire row or column. For example, you may want to apply the same numeric format or the same alignment options to an entire row or column. You can select entire rows and columns in much the same manner as you select ranges:

- Click the row or column border to select a single row or column.
- To select multiple adjacent rows or columns, click a row or column border and drag to highlight additional rows or columns.
- To select multiple (nonadjacent) rows or columns, press Ctrl while you click the row or column borders that you want.
- Press Ctrl+spacebar to select a column. The column of the active cell (or columns of the selected cells) is highlighted.
- Press Shift+spacebar to select a row. The row of the active cell (or rows of the selected cells) is highlighted.

TIP **Press Ctrl+A to select all cells in the worksheet, which is the same as selecting all rows and all columns. You can also click the area at the intersection of the row and column borders to select all cells.**

Selecting noncontiguous ranges

Most of the time, the ranges that you select are *contiguous* — a single rectangle of cells. Excel also enables you to work with *noncontiguous ranges,* which consist of two or more ranges (or single cells) that aren't next to each other. Selecting noncontiguous ranges is also known as a *multiple selection. If* you want to apply the same formatting to cells in different areas of your worksheet, one approach is to make a multiple selection. When the appropriate cells or ranges are selected, the formatting that you select is applied to them all. Figure 5.2 shows a noncontiguous range selected in a worksheet. (Three ranges are selected.)

FIGURE 5.2

Excel enables you to select noncontiguous ranges.

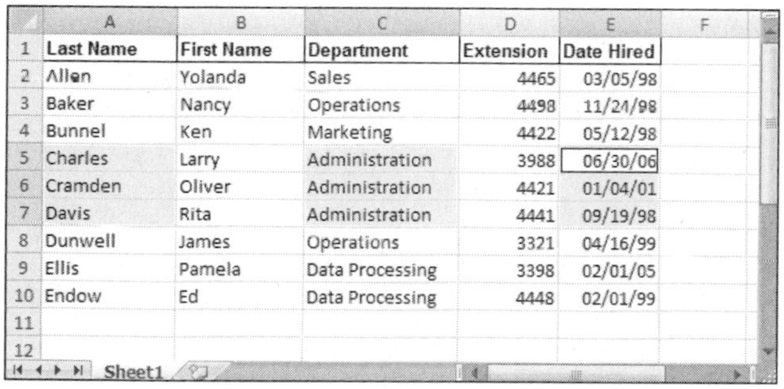

	A	B	C	D	E	F
1	Last Name	First Name	Department	Extension	Date Hired	
2	Allen	Yolanda	Sales	4465	03/05/98	
3	Baker	Nancy	Operations	4498	11/24/98	
4	Bunnel	Ken	Marketing	4422	05/12/98	
5	Charles	Larry	Administration	3988	06/30/06	
6	Cramden	Oliver	Administration	4421	01/04/01	
7	Davis	Rita	Administration	4441	09/19/98	
8	Dunwell	James	Operations	3321	04/16/99	
9	Ellis	Pamela	Data Processing	3398	02/01/05	
10	Endow	Ed	Data Processing	4448	02/01/99	
11						
12						

You can select a noncontiguous range in several ways:

- Select the first range (or cell). Then press Ctrl as you click and drag the mouse to highlight additional cells or ranges.

- From the keyboard, select a range as described previously (using F8 or the Shift key). Then press Shift+F8 to select another range without canceling the previous range selections.

- Enter the range (or cell) address in the Name box and press Enter. Separate each range address with a comma.

- Choose Home ➪ Editing ➪ Find & Select ➪ Go To (or press F5) to display the Go To dialog box. Enter the range (or cell) address in the Reference box and separate each range address with a comma. Click OK, and Excel selects the ranges.

> **NOTE**   Noncontiguous ranges differ from contiguous ranges in several important ways. **One obvious difference is that you can't use drag-and-drop methods to move or copy noncontiguous ranges.**

Selecting multisheet ranges

In addition to two-dimensional ranges on a single worksheet, ranges can extend across multiple worksheets to be three-dimensional ranges.

Suppose that you have a workbook set up to track budgets. A common approach is to use a separate worksheet for each department, making it easy to organize the data. You can click a sheet tab to view the information for a particular department.

Figure 5.3 shows a simplified example. The workbook has four sheets, named Totals, Marketing, Operations, and Manufacturing. The sheets are laid out identically. The only difference is the values. The Totals sheet contains formulas that compute the sum of the corresponding items in the three departmental worksheets.

FIGURE 5.3

The worksheets in this workbook are laid out identically.

	A	B	C	D	E	F	
1	Budget Summary						
2							
3		Q1	Q2	Q3	Q4	Year Total	
4	Salaries	286,500	286,500	286,500	290,500	1,150,000	
5	Travel	40,500	42,525	44,651	46,884	174,560	
6	Supplies	59,500	62,475	65,599	68,879	256,452	
7	Facility	144,000	144,000	144,000	144,000	576,000	
8	Total	530,500	535,500	540,750	550,263	2,157,013	
9							
10							
11							

H ◄ ► H   Totals / Marketing / Operations / Manufacturing

> **ON the CD-ROM**   This workbook, named **budget.xlsx**, is available on the companion CD-ROM.

Assume that you want to apply formatting to the sheets — for example, make the column headings bold with background shading. One (not so efficient) approach is simply to format the cells in each worksheet separately. A better technique is to select a multisheet range and format the cells in all the sheets simultaneously. The following is a step-by-step example of multisheet formatting, using the workbook shown in Figure 5.3.

1. **Activate the Totals worksheet by clicking its tab.**
2. **Select the range B3:F3.**
3. **Press Shift and click the sheet tab labeled Manufacturing.** This step selects all worksheets between the active worksheet (Totals) and the sheet tab that you click — in essence, a three-dimensional range of cells (see Figure 5.4). Notice that the workbook window's title bar displays [Group] to remind you that you've selected a group of sheets and that you're in Group edit mode.

FIGURE 5.4

In Group mode, you can work with a three-dimensional range of cells that extend across multiple worksheets.

	A	B	C	D	E	F	
1	Budget Summary						
2							
3		Q1	Q2	Q3	Q4	Year Total	
4	Salaries	286,500	286,500	286,500	290,500	1,150,000	
5	Travel	40,500	42,525	44,651	46,884	174,560	
6	Supplies	59,500	62,475	65,599	68,879	256,452	
7	Facility	144,000	144,000	144,000	144,000	576,000	
8	Total	530,500	535,500	540,750	550,263	2,157,013	
9							
10							
11							

budget.xlsx [Group]

Totals / Marketing / Operations / Manufacturing

---

4. **Choose Home ⇨ Font ⇨ Bold and then choose Home ⇨ Font ⇨ Fill Color to apply a colored background.**
5. **Click one of the other sheet tabs.** This step selects the sheet and also cancels Group mode; [Group] is no longer displayed in the title bar. Excel applies the formatting to the selected range across the selected sheets.

When a workbook is in Group mode, any changes that you make to cells in one worksheet also apply to all the other grouped worksheets. You can use this to your advantage when you want to set up a group of identical worksheets because any labels, data, formatting, or formulas you enter are automatically added to the same cells in all the grouped worksheets.

 **NOTE** When Excel is in Group mode, some commands are "grayed out" and can't be used. In the preceding example, you can't convert all these ranges to tables by choosing Insert ⇨ Tables ⇨ Table.

In general, selecting a multisheet range is a simple two-step process: Select the range in one sheet and then select the worksheets to include in the range. To select a group of contiguous worksheets, you can press Shift and click the sheet tab of the last worksheet that you want to include in the selection. To select individual worksheets, press Ctrl and click the sheet tab of each worksheet that you want to select. If all the worksheets in a workbook aren't laid out the same, you can skip the sheets that you don't want to format. When you make the selection, the sheet tabs of the selected sheets appear with a white background, and Excel displays [Group] in the title bar.

TIP To select all sheets in a workbook, right-click any sheet tab and choose Select All Sheets from the shortcut menu.

Selecting special types of cells

As you use Excel, you may need to locate specific types of cells in your worksheets. For example, wouldn't it be handy to be able to locate every cell that contains a formula — or perhaps all the cells whose value depends on the current cell? Excel provides an easy way to locate these and many other special types of cells. Simply choose Home ➪ Select & Find ➪ Go To Special to display the Go To Special dialog box, shown in Figure 5.5.

FIGURE 5.5

Use the Go To Special dialog box to select specific types of cells.

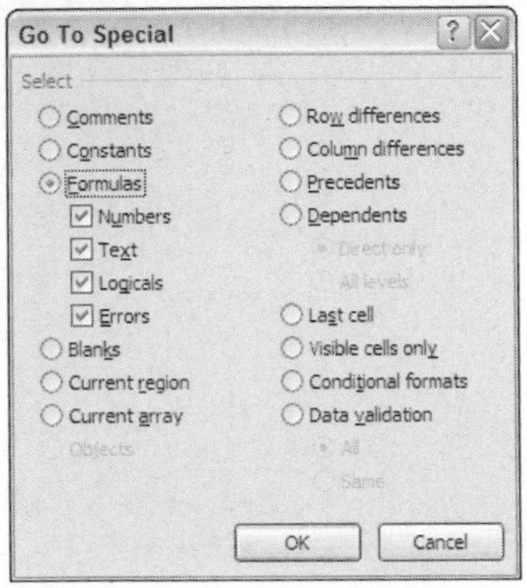

After you make your choice in the dialog box, Excel selects the qualifying subset of cells in the current selection. Usually, this subset of cells is a multiple selection. If no cells qualify, Excel lets you know with the message No cells were found.

TIP If you bring up the Go To Special dialog box with only one cell selected, Excel bases its selection on the entire used area of the worksheet. Otherwise, the selection is based on the selected range.

Table 5.1 offers a description of the options available in the Go To Special dialog box. Some of the options are very useful.

TABLE 5.1

Go To Special Options

Option	What It Does
Comments	Selects only the cells that contain a cell comment.
Constants	Selects all nonempty cells that don't contain formulas. Use the check boxes under the Formulas option to choose which types of nonformula cells to include.
Formulas	Selects cells that contain formulas. Qualify this by selecting the type of result: numbers, text, logical values (TRUE or FALSE), or errors.
Blanks	Selects all empty cells.

Option	What It Does
Current Region	Selects a rectangular range of cells around the active cell. This range is determined by surrounding blank rows and columns. You can also the use Ctrl+Shift+* shortcut key combination.
Current Array	Selects the entire array. See Chapter 17 for more information about arrays.
Objects	Selects all graphic objects on the worksheet.
Row Differences	Analyzes the selection and selects cells that are different from other cells in each row.
Column Differences	Analyzes the selection and selects the cells that are different from other cells in each column.
Precedents	Selects cells that are referred to in the formulas in the active cell or selection (limited to the active sheet). You can select either direct precedents or precedents at any level.
Dependents	Selects cells with formulas that refer to the active cell or selection (limited to the active sheet). You can select either direct dependents or dependents at any level.
Last Cell	Selects the bottom-right cell in the worksheet that contains data or formatting.
Visible Cells Only	Selects only visible cells in the selection. This option is useful when dealing with outlines or a filtered table.
Conditional Formats	Selects cells that have a conditional format applied (by choosing Home ➪ Styles ➪ Conditional Formatting).
Data Validation	Selects cells that are set up for data-entry validation (by choosing Data ➪ Date Tools ➪ Data Validation). The All option selects all such cells. The Same option selects only the cells that have the same validation rules as the active cell.

> **TIP**
>
> When you select an option in the Go To Special dialog box, be sure to note which suboptions become available. For example, when you select Constants, the suboptions under Formulas become available to help you further refine the results. Likewise, the suboptions under Dependents also apply to Precedents, and those under Data Validation also apply to Conditional formats.

Selecting cells by searching

Another way to select cells is to use Excel's Home ➪ Editing ➪ Find & Select ➪ Find command (or press Ctrl+F), which allows you to select cells by their contents. The Find And Replace dialog box is shown in Figure 5.6. This figure shows additional options that are available when you click the Options button.

FIGURE 5.6

The Find And Replace dialog box, with its options displayed.

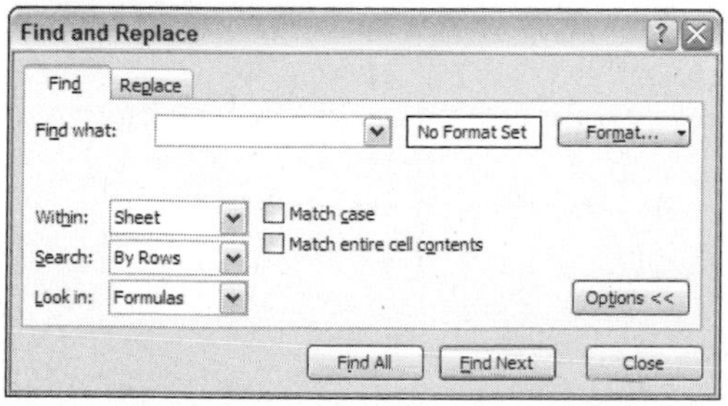

Enter the text that you're looking for; then click Find All. The dialog box expands to display all the cells that match your search criteria. For example, Figure 5.7 shows the dialog box after Excel has located all cells that contain the text Tucson. You can click an item in the list, and the screen will scroll so that you can view the cell in context. To select all the cells in the list, first select any single item in the list. Then press Ctrl+A to select them all.

FIGURE 5.7

The Find And Replace dialog box, with its results listed.

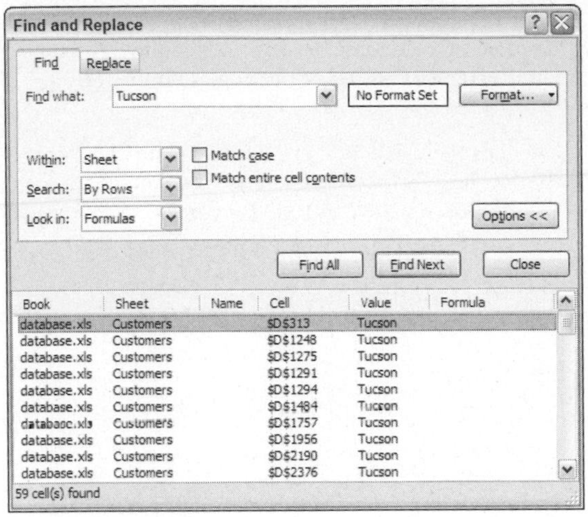

Note that the Find and Replace dialog box allows you to return to the worksheet without dismissing the dialog box.

Copying or Moving Ranges

As you create a worksheet, you may find it necessary to copy or move information from one location to another. Excel makes copying or moving ranges of cells easy. Here are some common things you might do:

- Copy a cell to another cell.
- Copy a cell to a range of cells. The source cell is copied to every cell in the destination range.
- Copy a range to another range. Both ranges must be the same size.
- Move a range of cells to another location.

The primary difference between copying and moving a range is the effect of the operation on the source range. When you copy a range, the source range is unaffected. When you move a range, the contents are removed from the source range.

NOTE Copying a cell normally copies the cell's contents, any formatting that is applied to the original cell (including conditional formatting and data validation), and the cell comment (if it has one). When you copy a cell that contains a formula, the cell references in the copied formulas are changed automatically to be relative to their new destination.

Copying or moving consists of two steps (although shortcut methods do exist):

1. **Select the cell or range to copy (the source range) and copy it to the Clipboard.** To move the range instead of copying it, cut the range rather than copying it.

2. **Move the cell pointer to the range that will hold the copy (the destination range) and paste the Clipboard contents.**

CAUTION When you paste information, Excel overwrites any cells that get in the way without warning you. If you find that pasting overwrote some essential cells, choose Undo from the Quick Access Toolbar (or press Ctrl+Z).

NOTE When you copy a cell or range, Excel surrounds the copied area with an animated border (sometimes referred to as "marching ants"). As long as that border remains animated, the copied information is available for pasting. If you press Esc to cancel the animated border, Excel removes the information from the Clipboard.

Because copying (or moving) is used so often, Excel provides many different methods. I discuss each method in the following sections. Copying and moving are similar operations, so I point out only important differences between the two.

Copying by using Ribbon commands

Choosing Home ➪ Clipboard ➪ Copy transfers a copy of the selected cell or range to the Windows Clipboard and the Office Clipboard. After performing the copy part of this operation, select the cell that will hold the copy and choose Home ➪ Clipboard ➪ Paste.

Rather than using Home ➪ Clipboard ➪ Paste, you can just activate the destination cell and press Enter. If you use this technique, Excel removes the copied information from the Clipboard so that it can't be pasted again.

NOTE If you click the Copy button more than once before you click the Paste button, Excel may automatically display the Office Clipboard task bar. To prevent this task bar from appearing, click the Options button at the bottom and then remove the check mark from Show Office Clipboard Automatically.

If you're copying a range, you don't need to select an entire same-sized range before you click the Paste button. You need only activate the upper-left cell in the destination range.

Copying by using shortcut menu commands

If you prefer, you can use the following shortcut menu commands for copying and pasting:

■ Right-click the range and choose Copy (or Cut) from the shortcut menu to copy the selected cells to the Clipboard.

■ Right-click and choose Paste from the shortcut menu that appears to paste the Clipboard contents to the selected cell or range.

Rather than using Paste, you can just activate the destination cell and press Enter. If you use this technique, Excel removes the copied information from the Clipboard so that it can't be pasted again.

Understanding the Office Clipboard

Whenever you cut or copy information from a Windows program, Windows stores the information on the Windows Clipboard, which is an area of your computer's memory. Each time that you cut or copy information, Windows replaces the information previously stored on the Clipboard with the new information that you cut or copied. The Windows Clipboard can store data in a variety of formats. Because Windows manages information on the Clipboard, it can be pasted to other Windows applications, regardless of where it originated.

Office has its own Clipboard, the Office Clipboard, which is available only in Office programs. Whenever you cut or copy information in an Office program, such as Excel, the program places the information on both the Windows Clipboard and the Office Clipboard. However, the program treats information on the Office Clipboard differently than it treats information on the Windows Clipboard. Instead of replacing information on the Office Clipboard, the program appends the information to the Office Clipboard. With multiple items stored on the Clipboard, you can then paste the items either individually or as a group.

Find out more about this feature in "Using the Office Clipboard to paste," later in this chapter.

Copying by using shortcut keys

The copy and paste operations also have shortcut keys associated with them:

- Ctrl+C copies the selected cells to both the Windows and Office Clipboards.
- Ctrl+X cuts the selected cells to both the Windows and Office Clipboards.
- Ctrl+V pastes the Windows Clipboard contents to the selected cell or range.

TIP Most other Windows applications also use these shortcut keys.

Copying or moving by using drag-and-drop

Excel also enables you to copy or move a cell or range by dragging. Be aware, however, that dragging and dropping does not place any information on either the Windows Clipboard or the Office Clipboard.

NOTE The drag-and-drop method of moving does offer one advantage over the cut-and-paste method — Excel warns you if a drag-and-drop move operation will overwrite existing cell contents. However, you do *not* get a warning if a drag-and-drop copy operation will overwrite existing cell contents.

To copy using drag-and-drop, select the cell or range that you want to copy and then press Ctrl and move the mouse to one of the selection's borders (the mouse pointer is augmented with a small plus sign). Then, simply drag the selection to its new location while you continue to press the Ctrl key. The original selection remains behind, and Excel makes a new copy when you release the mouse button. To move a range using drag-and-drop, don't press Ctrl while dragging the border.

TIP If the mouse pointer doesn't turn into an arrow when you point to the border of a cell or range, you need to make a change to your settings. Access the Excel Options dialog box, click the Advanced tab, and place a check mark on the option labeled Enable Fill Handle And Cell Drag-And-Drop.

Using Smart Tags When Inserting and Pasting

Some cell and range operations — specifically inserting, pasting, and filling cells by dragging — result in the display of a Smart Tag. A *Smart Tag* is a small square that, when clicked, presents you with options. For example, if you copy a range and then paste it to a different location, a Smart Tag appears at the lower-right of the pasted range. Click the Smart Tag, and you see the options shown in the following figure. These options enable you to specify how the data should be pasted. In this case, using the Smart Tag is an alternative to using options in the Paste Special dialog box.

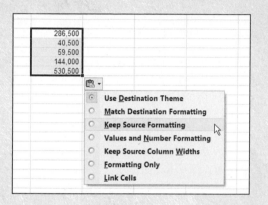

Some users find these Smart Tags helpful, while others think that they're annoying. (Count me in the latter group.) To turn off these Smart Tags, choose Office ➪ Excel Options and click the Advanced tab. Remove the check mark from the two options labeled Show Paste Options Buttons and Show Insert Options Buttons.

Copying to adjacent cells

Often, you'll find that you need to copy a cell to an adjacent cell or range. This type of copying is quite common when working with formulas. For example, if you're working on a budget, you might create a formula to add the values in column B. You can use the same formula to add the values in the other columns. Rather than re-enter the formula, you can copy it to the adjacent cells.

Excel provides additional options for copying to adjacent cells. To use these commands, select the cell that you're copying and the cells that you're copying to. Then issue the appropriate command from the following list for one-step copying:

- Home ➪ Editing ➪ Fill ➪ Down (or Ctrl+D) copies the cell to the selected range below.
- Home ➪ Editing ➪ Fill ➪ Right (or Ctrl+R) copies the cell to the selected range to the right.
- Home ➪ Editing ➪ Fill ➪ Up copies the cell to the selected range above.
- Home ➪ Editing ➪ Fill ➪ Left copies the cell to the selected range to the left.

None of these commands places information on either the Windows Clipboard or the Office Clipboard.

> **TIP** You also can use AutoFill to copy to adjacent cells by dragging the selection's *fill handle* (the small square in the bottom-right corner of the selected cell or range). Excel copies the original selection to the cells that you highlight while dragging. For more control over the AutoFill operation, drag the fill handle with the right mouse button, and you'll get a shortcut menu with additional options.

Copying a range to other sheets

You can use the copy procedures described previously to copy a cell or range to another worksheet, even if the worksheet is in a different workbook. You must, of course, activate the other worksheet before you select the location to which you want to copy.

Excel offers a quicker way to copy a cell or range and paste it to other worksheets in the same workbook. Start by selecting the range to copy. Then, press Ctrl and click the sheet tabs for the worksheets to which you want to copy the information. (Excel displays [Group] in the workbook's title bar.) Choose Home ⇨ Editing ⇨ Fill ⇨ Across Worksheets, and a dialog box appears to ask you what you want to copy (All, Contents, or Formats). Make your choice and then click OK. Excel copies the selected range to the selected worksheets; the new copy occupies the same cells in the selected worksheets as the original occupies in the initial worksheet.

> **CAUTION** Be careful with the Home ⇨ Editing ⇨ Fill ⇨ Across Worksheets command because Excel doesn't warn you when the destination cells contain information. You can quickly overwrite lots of cells with this command and not even realize it.

Using the Office Clipboard to paste

Whenever you cut or copy information in an Office program, such as Excel, you can place the data on both the Windows Clipboard and the Office Clipboard. When you copy information to the Office Clipboard, you append the information to the Office Clipboard instead of replacing what is already there. With multiple items stored on the Office Clipboard, you can then paste the items either individually or as a group.

To use the Office Clipboard, you first need to open it. Use the dialog launcher on the bottom right of the Home ⇨ Clipboard group to toggle the Clipboard task pane on and off.

> **TIP** To make the Clipboard task pane open automatically, click the Options button near the bottom of the task pane and choose the Show Office Clipboard Automatically option.

After you open the Clipboard task pane, select the first cell or range that you want to copy to the Office Clipboard and copy it by using any of the preceding techniques. Repeat this process, selecting the next cell or range that you want to copy. As soon as you copy the information, the Office Clipboard task pane shows you the number of items that you've copied and a brief description (it will hold up to 24 items). Figure 5.8 shows the Office Clipboard with five copied items.

FIGURE 5.8

Use the Clipboard task pane to copy and paste multiple items.

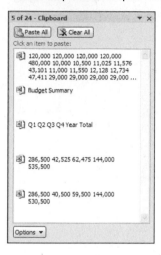

When you're ready to paste information, select the cell into which you want to paste information. To paste an individual item, click it in the Clipboard task pane. To paste all the items that you've copied, click the Paste All button.

You can clear the contents of the Office Clipboard by clicking the Clear All button.

The following items about the Office Clipboard and its functioning are worth noting:

- Excel pastes the contents of the Windows Clipboard when you paste either by choosing Home ⇨ Clipboard ⇨ Paste, by pressing Ctrl+V, or by right-clicking to choose Paste from the shortcut menu.

- The last item that you cut or copied appears on both the Office Clipboard and the Windows Clipboard.

- Pasting from the Office Clipboard also places that item on the Windows Clipboard. If you choose Paste All from the Office Clipboard toolbar, you paste all items stored on the Office Clipboard onto the Windows Clipboard as a single item.

- Clearing the Office Clipboard also clears the Windows Clipboard.

WARNING The Office Clipboard, however, has a serious problem that makes it virtually worthless for Excel users: If you copy a range that contains formulas, the formulas are not transferred when you paste to a different range. Only the values are pasted. Furthermore, Excel doesn't even warn you about this fact.

Pasting in special ways

You may not always want to copy everything from the source range to the destination range. For example, you may want to copy only the formula results rather than the formulas themselves. Or you may want to copy the number formats from one range to another without overwriting any existing data or formulas.

To control what is copied into the destination range, choose Home ➪ Clipboard ➪ Paste and use the drop-down menu shown in Figure 5.9. Options are

- **Paste:** Pastes the cell's contents, formats, and data validation from the Windows Clipboard.
- **Formulas:** Pastes formulas, but not formatting.
- **Paste Values:** Pastes the results of formulas. The destination for the copy can be a new range or the original range. In the latter case, Excel replaces the original formulas with their current values.
- **No Borders:** Pastes everything except any borders that appear in the source range.
- **Transpose:** Changes the orientation of the copied range. Rows become columns, and columns become rows. Any formulas in the copied range are adjusted so that they work properly when transposed.
- **Paste Link:** Creates formulas in the destination range that refer to the cells in the copied range.
- **Paste Special:** Displays the Paste Special dialog box (described in the next section)
- **Paste As Hyperlink:** Creates a clickable hyperlink to the copied cell or range, which can be in the same workbook or in a different workbook. The Paste As Hyperlink command is not available if the workbook has not been saved.
- **As Picture:** Pastes the copied information as a picture. If you use the Paste Picture Link option, Excel creates a "live" picture that is updated if the source range is changed.

FIGURE 5.9

Excel offers several pasting options.

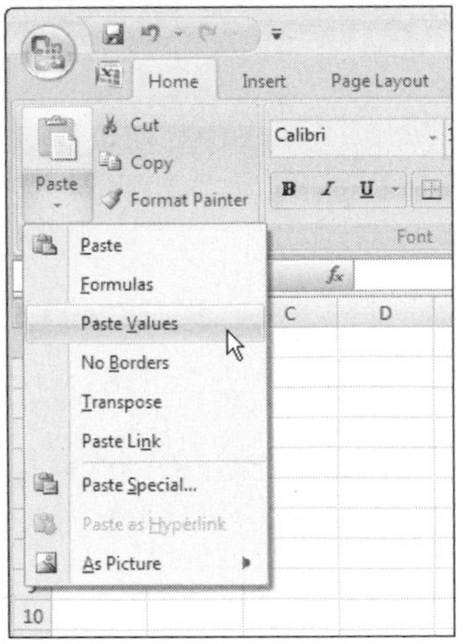

Using the Paste Special Dialog box

For maximum flexibility in what gets pasted, choose Home ⇨ Clipboard ⇨ Paste ⇨ Paste Special to display the Paste Special dialog box (see Figure 5.10). You can also right-click and select Paste Special to display this dialog box. This dialog box has several options, which I explain in the following list.

 NOTE　Excel actually has several different Paste Special dialog boxes. The one displayed depends on what's copied. This section describes the Paste Special dialog box that appears when a range or cell has been copied.

FIGURE 5.10

The Paste Special dialog box.

Paste Special	? ☒
Paste	
⊙ All	○ All using Source theme
○ Formulas	○ All except borders
○ Values	○ Column widths
○ Formats	○ Formulas and number formats
○ Comments	○ Values and number formats
○ Validation	
Operation	
⊙ None	○ Multiply
○ Add	○ Divide
○ Subtract	
☐ Skip blanks	☐ Transpose
Paste Link	OK　Cancel

TIP　For the Paste Special command to be available, you need to copy a cell or range. (Choosing Home ⇨ Clipboard ⇨ Cut doesn't work.)

- **All:** Pastes the cell's contents, formats, and data validation from the Windows Clipboard.
- **Formulas:** Pastes values and formulas, with no formatting.
- **Values:** Pastes values and the results of formulas (no formatting). The destination for the copy can be a new range or the original range. In the latter case, Excel replaces the original formulas with their current values.
- **Formats:** Copies only the formatting.
- **Comments:** Copies only the cell comments from a cell or range. This option doesn't copy cell contents or formatting.
- **Validation:** Copies the validation criteria so the same data validation will apply. Data validation is applied by choosing Data ⇨ Data Tools ⇨ Data Validation.
- **All Using Source Theme:** Pastes everything, but uses the formatting from the document theme of the source. This option is relevant only if you're pasting information from a different workbook, and the workbook uses a different document theme than the active workbook.
- **All Except Borders:** Pastes everything except borders that appear in the source range.
- **Column Widths:** Pastes only column width information.

- **Formulas And Number Formats:** Pastes all values, formulas and number formats (but no other formatting).
- **Values And Number Formats:** Pastes all values and numeric formats, but not the formulas themselves.

In addition, the Paste Special dialog box enables you to perform other operations, described in the following sections.

Performing mathematical operations without formulas

The option buttons in the Operation section of the Paste Special dialog box let you perform an arithmetic operation. For example, you can copy a range to another range and select the Multiply operation. Excel multiplies the corresponding values in the source range and the destination range and replaces the destination range with the new values.

This feature also works with a single copied cell, pasted to a range. Assume that you have a range of values, and you want to increase each value by 5 percent. Enter **105%** into any blank cell and copy that cell to the Clipboard. Then select the range of values and bring up the Paste Special dialog box. Select the Multiply option, and each value in the range is multiplied by 105 percent.

> **WARNING** If the destination range contains formulas, the formulas are also modified. In many cases, this is *not* what you want.

Skipping blanks when pasting

The Skip Blanks option in the Paste Special dialog box prevents Excel from overwriting cell contents in your paste area with blank cells from the copied range. This option is useful if you're copying a range to another area but don't want the blank cells in the copied range to overwrite existing data.

Transposing a range

The Transpose option in the Paste Special dialog box changes the orientation of the copied range. Rows become columns, and columns become rows. Any formulas in the copied range are adjusted so that they work properly when transposed. Note that you can use this check box with the other options in the Paste Special dialog box. Figure 5.11 shows an example of a horizontal range (A1:F1) that was transposed to a vertical range (A3:A8).

FIGURE 5.11

Transposing a range changes the orientation as the information is pasted into the worksheet.

> **TIP** If you click the Paste Link button in the Paste Special dialog box, you create formulas that link to the source range. As a result, the destination range automatically reflects changes in the source range.

Using Names to Work with Ranges

Dealing with cryptic cell and range addresses can sometimes be confusing. (This confusion becomes even more apparent when you deal with formulas, which I cover in Chapter 11.) Fortunately, Excel allows you to assign descriptive names to cells and ranges. For example, you can give a cell a name such as Interest_Rate, or you can name a range JulySales. Working with these names (rather than cell or range addresses) has several advantages:

- A meaningful range name (such as Total_Income)) is much easier to remember than a cell address (such as AC21).

- Entering a name is less error-prone than entering a cell or range address.

- You can quickly move to areas of your worksheet either by using the Name box, located at the left side of the Formula bar (click the arrow to drop down a list of defined names) or by choosing Home ➪ Editing ➪ Find & Select ➪ Go To (or F5) and specifying the range name.

- Creating formulas is easier. You can paste a cell or range name into a formula by using Formula Autocomplete, a new feature in Excel 2007.

- Names make your formulas more understandable and easier to use. A formula such as =Income — Taxes is more intuitive than =D20 — D40.

Creating range names in your workbooks

Excel provides several different methods that you can use to create range names. Before you begin, however, you should be aware of some important rules about what is acceptable:

- Names can't contain any spaces. You may want to use an underscore character to simulate a space (such as Annual_Total).

- You can use any combination of letters and numbers, but the name must begin with a letter. A name can't begin with a number (such as 3rdQuarter) or look like a cell reference (such as QTR3). If these are desirable names, you can precede the name with underscore: _3rd Quarter and _QTR3.

- Symbols, except for underscores and periods, aren't allowed.

- Names are limited to 255 characters, but it's a good practice to keep names as short as possible yet still meaningful and understandable.

Excel also uses a few names internally for its own use. Although you can create names that override Excel's internal names, you should avoid doing so. To be on the safe side, avoid using the following for names: Print_Area, Print_Titles, Consolidate_Area, and Sheet_Title.

Using the New Name dialog box

To create a range name, start by selecting the cell or range that you want to name. Then, choose Formulas ➪ Defined Names ➪ Define Name. Excel displays the New Name dialog box, shown in Figure 5.12. Note that this is a resizable dialog box. Click and drag a border to change the dimensions.

FIGURE 5.12

Create names for cells or ranges by using the New Name dialog box.

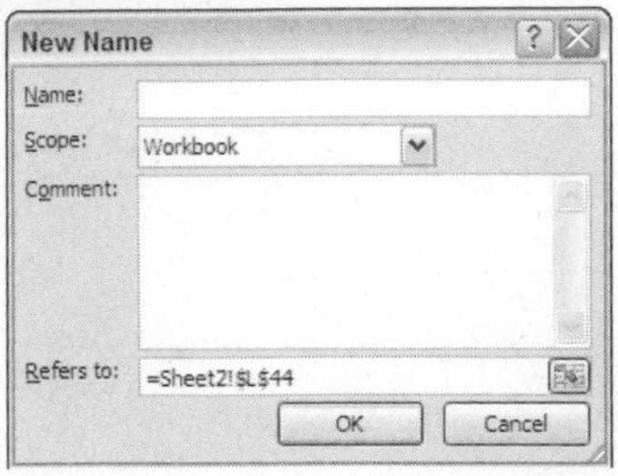

Type a name in the box labeled Name (or use the name that Excel proposes, if any). The selected cell or range address appears in the box labeled Refers To. Use the Scope drop-down to indicate the scope for the name. The scope indicates where the name will be valid, and it's either the entire workbook, or a particular sheet. If you like, you can add a comment that describes the named range or cell. Click OK to add the name to your workbook and close the dialog box.

Using the Name box

A faster way to create a name is to use the Name box (to the left of the Formula bar). Select the cell or range to name, click the Name box, and type the name. Press Enter to create the name. (You must press Enter to actually record the name; if you type a name and then click in the worksheet, Excel doesn't create the name.) If a name already exists, you can't use the Name box to change the range to which that name refers. Attempting to do so simply selects the range.

The Name box is a drop-down list and shows all names in the workbook. To choose a named cell or range, click the Name box and choose the name. The name appears in the Name box, and Excel selects the named cell or range in the worksheet.

Using the Create Names From Selection dialog box

You may have a worksheet that contains text that you want to use for names for adjacent cells or ranges. For example, you may want to use the text in column A to create names for the corresponding values in column B. Excel makes this task easy to do.

To create names by using adjacent text, start by selecting the name text and the cells that you want to name. (These items can be individual cells or ranges of cells.) The names must be adjacent to the cells that you're naming. (A multiple selection is allowed.) Then, choose Formulas ➪ Defined Names ➪ Create From Selection. Excel displays the Create Names From Selection dialog box, shown in Figure 5.13. The check marks in this dialog box are based on Excel's analysis of the selected range. For example, if Excel finds text in the first row of the selection, it proposes that you create names based on the top row. If Excel didn't guess correctly, you can change the check boxes. Click OK, and Excel creates the names.

NOTE If the text contained in a cell would result in an invalid name, Excel modifies the name to make it valid. For example, if a cell contains the text Net Income (which is invalid for a name because it contains a space), Excel converts the space to an underscore character. If Excel encounters a value or a numeric formula where text should be, however, it doesn't convert it to a valid name. It simply doesn't create a name — and does not inform you of that fact.

FIGURE 5.13

Use the Create Names From Selection dialog box to name cells using labels that appear in the worksheet.

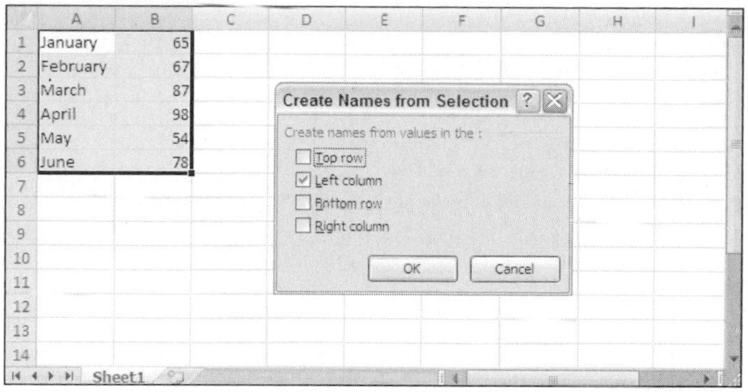

CAUTION If the upper-left cell of the selection contains text and you choose the Top Row and Left Column options, Excel uses that text for the name of the entire data excluding the top row and left column. So, before you accept the names that Excel creates, take a minute to make sure that they refer to the correct ranges. If Excel creates a names that is incorrect, you can delete or modify it by using the Name Manager (described next).

Managing Names

A workbook can have any number of names. If you have many names, you should know about the Name Manager, shown in Figure 5.14.

FIGURE 5.14

The Name Manager is new in Excel 2007.

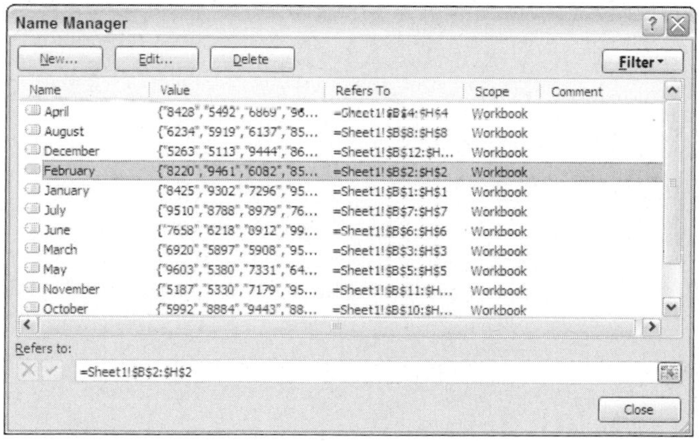

NEW FEATURE The Name Manager is a new feature in Excel 2007.

The Name Manager appears when you choose Formulas ➪ Defined Names ➪ Name Manager (or press Ctrl+F3). The Name Manager has the following features:

- **Displays information about each name in the workbook.** You can resize the Name Manager dialog box and widen the columns to show more information. You can also click a column heading to sort the information by the column.

- **Allows you to filter the displayed names.** Clicking the Filter button lets you show only those names that meet a certain criteria. For example, you can view only the worksheet level names.

- **Provides quick access to the New Name dialog box.** Click the New button to create a new name without closing the Name Manager.

- **Lets you edit names.** To edit a name, select it in the list and then click the Edit button. You can change the name or the Refers To range or edit the comment.

- **Lets you quickly delete unneeded names.** To delete a name, select it in the list and click Delete.

CAUTION Be extra careful when deleting names. If the name is used in a formula, deleting the name causes the formula to become invalid. (It displays #NAME?.) However, deleting a name can be undone, so if you find that formulas return #NAME? after you delete a name, choose Undo from the Quick Access Toolbar (or press Ctrl+Z) to get the name back.

If you delete the rows or columns that contain named cells or ranges, the names contain an invalid reference. For example, if cell A1 on Sheet1 is named Interest and you delete row 1 or column A, the name Interest then refers to =Sheet1!#REF! (that is, to an erroneous reference). If you use Interest in a formula, the formula displays #REF.

TIP The Name Manager is useful, but it has a shortcoming: It doesn't let you display the list of names in a worksheet range so you can view or print them. Such a feat is possible, but you need to look beyond the Name Manager.

To create a list of names in a worksheet, first move the cell pointer to an empty area of your worksheet — the list is created at the active cell position and overwrites any information at that location. Press F3 to display the Paste Name dialog box, which lists all the defined names. Then click the Paste List button. Excel creates a list of all names in the workbook and their corresponding addresses.

Adding Comments to Cells

Documentation that explains certain elements in the worksheet can often be helpful. One way document your work is to add comments to cells. This feature is useful when you need to describe a particular value or explain how a formula works.

To add a comment to a cell, select the cell and then choose Review ➪ Comments ➪ New Comment. Alternative, you can right-click the cell and choose Insert Comment from the shortcut menu. Excel inserts a comment that points to the active cell. Initially, the comment consists of your name. Enter the text for the cell comment and then click anywhere in the worksheet to hide the comment. You can change the size of the comment by clicking and dragging any of its borders. Figure 5.15 shows a cell with a comment.

FIGURE 5.15

You can add comments to cells to help clarify important items in your worksheets.

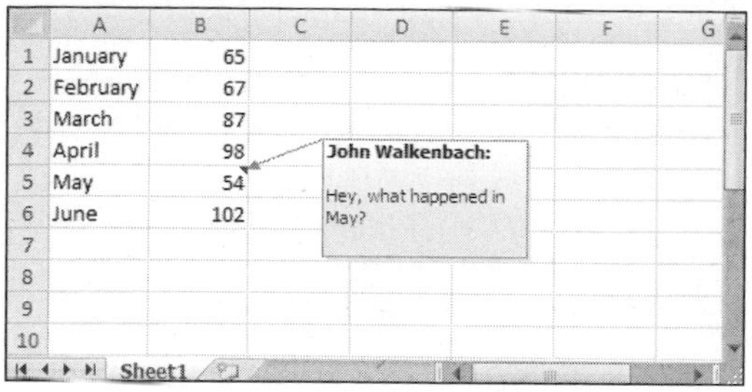

	A	B	C	D	E	F	G
1	January	65					
2	February	67					
3	March	87					
4	April	98		**John Walkenbach:**			
5	May	54					
6	June	102		Hey, what happened in May?			
7							
8							
9							
10							

Sheet1

Cells that have a comment display a small red triangle in the upper-right corner. When you move the mouse pointer over a cell that contains a comment, the comment becomes visible.

 You can control how comments are displayed. Access the Advanced tab of the Excel Options dialog box. In the Display section, an option lets you turn off the comment indicators if you like.

Formatting comments

If you don't like the default look of cell comments, use the Home ➪ Font and Home ➪ Alignment groups to make changes to the comment's appearance.

For even more formatting options, right-click the comment's border and choose Format Comment from the shortcut menu. Excel responds by displaying the Format Comment dialog box, which allows you to change many aspects of its appearance.

 You can also display an image inside of a comment. Select the Colors and Lines tab in the Format Comment dialog box. Click the Color drop-down list and select Fill Effects. In the Fill Effects dialog box, click the Picture tab and then click the Select Picture Button to specify a graphics file. Figure 5.16 shows a comment that contains a picture.

FIGURE 5.16

This comment contains a graphic image.

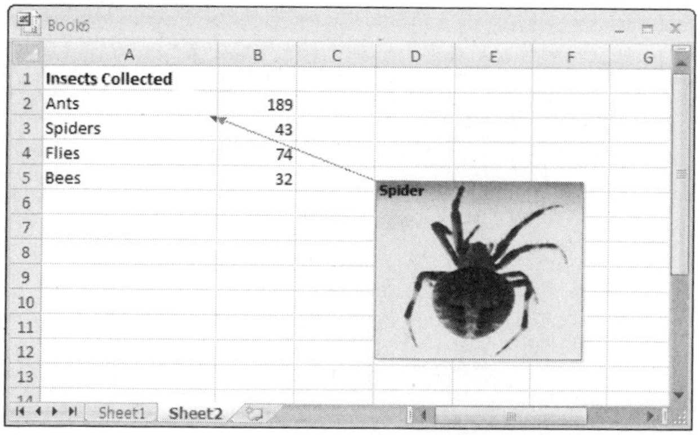

	A	B	C	D	E	F	G
1	**Insects Collected**						
2	Ants	189					
3	Spiders	43					
4	Flies	74					
5	Bees	32		Spider			
6							
7							
8							
9							
10							
11							
12							
13							

Sheet1   Sheet2

An Alternative to Cell Comments

You can make use of Excel's Data Validation feature to add a different type of comment to a cell. This type of comment appears automatically when the cell is selected. Follow these steps:

1. **Select the cell that will contain the comment.**
2. **Choose Data ➪ Data Tools ➪ Data Validation to display the Data Validation dialog box.**
3. **In the Data Validation dialog box, click the Input Message tab.**
4. **Make sure that the Show Input Message When Cell Is Selected check box is checked.**
5. **Type your comment in the Input Message box.**
6. **As an option, type a title in the Title box.** (This text will appear in bold at the top of the message.)
7. **Click OK to close the Data Validation dialog box.**

After performing these steps, the message appears when the cell is activated, and it disappears when any other cell is activated.

Note that this message isn't a "real" comment. For example, a cell that contains this type of message doesn't display a comment indicator, and it's not affect by any of the commands used to work with cell comments. In addition, you can't format these messages in any way.

Changing a comment's shape

Normally, a cell comment is rectangular, but they don't have to be. To change the shape of a cell comment, add a command to your Quick Access Toolbar (QAT):

1. **Right-click the QAT and select Customize Quick Access Toolbar.** The Customization section of the Excel Options dialog box appears.
2. **In the drop-down list labeled Choose Commands From, select Drawing Tools | Format Tab.**
3. **In the list on the left, select Change Shape and click the Add button.**
4. **Click OK to close the Excel Options dialog box.**

After performing these steps, your QAT has a new Change Shape icon.

To change the shape of a comment, make sure that it's visible (right-click the cell and select Show/Hide Comments). Then click the comment's border to select it as a Shape (or, Ctrl+click the comment to select it as a Shape). Click the Change Shape button on the QAT and choose a new shape for the comment. Figure 5.17 shows a cell comments with a nonstandard shape.

FIGURE 5.17

Cell comments don't have to be rectangles.

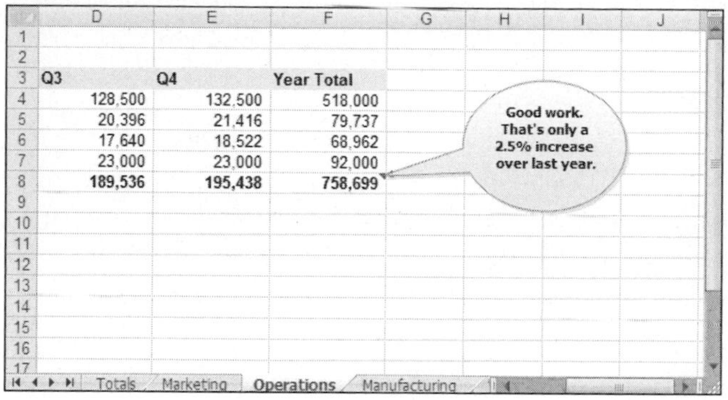

Reading comments

To read all of the comments in a workbook, choose Review ➪ Comments ➪ Next. Click this command repeatedly to cycle through all the comments in a workbook. Choose Review ➪ Comments ➪ Previous to view the comments in reverse order.

Hiding and showing comments

If you want all cell comments to be visible (regardless of the location of the cell pointer), choose Review ➪ Comments ➪ Show All Comments. This command is a toggle; select it again to hide all cell comments. To toggle the display of an individual comments, select its cell and then choose Review ➪ Comments ➪ Show/Hide Comment.

Editing comments

To edit a comment, activate the cell, right-click, and then choose Edit Comment from the shortcut menu. When you've made your changes, click any cell.

Deleting comments

To delete a cell comment, activate the cell that contains the comment and then choose Review ➪ Comments ➪ Delete. Or, right-click and then choose Delete Comment from the shortcut menu.

Chapter 6

Introducing Tables

One of the most significant new features in Excel 2007 is tables. A *table* is a rectangular range of data that usually has a row of text headings to describe the contents of each column. Excel, of course, has always supported tables. But the new implementation makes common tasks much easier — and a lot better looking. More importantly, the new table features may help eliminate some common errors.

This chapter is a basic introduction to the new table features. As always, I urge you to just dig in and experiment with the various table-related commands. You may be surprised at what you can accomplish with just a few mouse clicks.

What Is a Table?

A *table* is simply a rectangular range of structured data. Each row in the table corresponds to a single entity. For example, a row can contain information about a customer, a bank transaction, an employee, a product, and so on. Each column contains a specific piece of information. For example, if each row contains information about an employee, the columns can contain data such as name, employee number, hire date, salary, department, and so on. Tables typically have a header row at the top that describes the information contained in each column.

So far, I've said nothing new. Every previous version of Excel is able to work with this type of table. The magic happens when you tell Excel to convert a range of data into an "official" table. You do this by selecting any cell within the range and then choosing Insert ⇨ Tables ⇨ Table.

When you explicitly identify a range as a table, Excel can respond more intelligently to the actions you perform with that range. For example, if you create a chart from a table, the chart will expand automatically as you add new rows to the table.

IN THIS CHAPTER

Understanding how a table differs from a normal range

Working with tables

Using the Totals Row

Removing duplicate rows from a table

Sorting and filtering a table

Excel 2003 introduced a rudimentary version of the table feature. In that version, tables were known as *lists*. The implementation in Excel 2007 is much better.

Figure 6.1 shows a range of data that has not yet been converted to a table. Notice that this range corresponds to the description I provide earlier: It's a range of structured data with column headers. In this example, each row contains information about a single real estate listing. The range has 10 columns and 125 rows of data (plus a descriptive header row).

FIGURE 6.1

This range of data is a good candidate for a table.

	Agent	Date Listed	Area	List Price	Bedrooms	Baths	SqFt	Type	Pool	Sold
1	Agent	Date Listed	Area	List Price	Bedrooms	Baths	SqFt	Type	Pool	Sold
2	Lang	10/18/2007	S. County	$360,000	3	2.5	2,330	Single Family	FALSE	FALSE
3	Romero	1/28/2007	N. County	$369,900	4	3	1,988	Condo	FALSE	TRUE
4	Robinson	1/25/2007	Central	$375,000	4	3	2,368	Single Family	TRUE	TRUE
5	Shasta	9/16/2007	S. County	$205,500	4	2.5	2,036	Condo	FALSE	TRUE
6	Robinson	9/4/2007	Central	$239,900	4	3	2,278	Single Family	FALSE	FALSE
7	Peterson	4/15/2007	N. County	$259,900	4	3	1,734	Condo	FALSE	TRUE
8	Lang	8/23/2007	N. County	$264,900	3	2.5	2,062	Condo	FALSE	FALSE
9	Romero	4/4/2007	N. County	$799,000	6	5	4,800	Single Family	FALSE	FALSE
10	Robinson	8/28/2007	S. County	$300,000	4	3	2,650	Condo	FALSE	FALSE
11	Adams	5/24/2007	N. County	$349,000	4	2.5	2,730	Condo	TRUE	TRUE
12	Jenkins	4/11/2007	Central	$319,000	4	2	1,690	Condo	TRUE	FALSE
13	Romero	8/3/2007	N. County	$359,900	3	2	2,198	Condo	TRUE	FALSE
14	Hamilton	8/29/2007	Central	$225,911	4	3	2,285	Single Family	TRUE	FALSE
15	Lang	7/22/2007	N. County	$349,000	4	3	8,930	Single Family	TRUE	FALSE
16	Randolph	9/3/2007	Central	$149,900	2	1	1,234	Single Family	FALSE	FALSE
17	Daily	2/20/2007	Central	$354,000	4	2	2,088	Single Family	FALSE	FALSE
18	Peterson	3/14/2007	Central	$364,900	4	2.5	2,507	Single Family	FALSE	FALSE
19	Peterson	4/7/2007	N. County	$309,900	5	3	2,447	Condo	TRUE	FALSE
20	Adams	7/19/2007	Central	$268,500	4	2.5	1,911	Single Family	FALSE	FALSE
21	Lang	10/14/2007	Central	$243,000	4	2.5	1,914	Single Family	FALSE	FALSE
22	Peterson	2/27/2007	S. County	$269,900	4	2.5	1,911	Single Family	FALSE	FALSE
23	Adams	6/6/2007	N. County	$379,900	3	2.5	2,468	Condo	FALSE	FALSE

Figure 6.2 shows the range after I converted it to a table by choosing Insert ➪ Tables ➪ Table.

FIGURE 6.2

An Excel table.

	Agent	Date Listed	Area	List Price	Bedrooms	Baths	SqFt	Type	Pool	Sold
2	Lang	10/18/2007	S. County	$360,000	3	2.5	2,330	Single Family	FALSE	FALSE
3	Romero	1/28/2007	N. County	$369,900	4	3	1,988	Condo	FALSE	TRUE
4	Robinson	1/25/2007	Central	$375,000	4	3	2,368	Single Family	TRUE	TRUE
5	Shasta	9/16/2007	S. County	$205,500	4	2.5	2,036	Condo	FALSE	TRUE
6	Robinson	9/4/2007	Central	$239,900	4	3	2,278	Single Family	FALSE	FALSE
7	Peterson	4/15/2007	N. County	$259,900	4	3	1,734	Condo	FALSE	TRUE
8	Lang	8/23/2007	N. County	$264,900	3	2.5	2,062	Condo	FALSE	FALSE
9	Romero	4/4/2007	N. County	$799,000	6	5	4,800	Single Family	FALSE	FALSE
10	Robinson	8/28/2007	S. County	$300,000	4	3	2,650	Condo	FALSE	FALSE
11	Adams	5/24/2007	N. County	$349,000	4	2.5	2,730	Condo	TRUE	TRUE
12	Jenkins	4/11/2007	Central	$319,000	4	2	1,690	Condo	TRUE	FALSE
13	Romero	8/3/2007	N. County	$359,900	3	2	2,198	Condo	TRUE	FALSE
14	Hamilton	8/29/2007	Central	$225,911	4	3	2,285	Single Family	TRUE	FALSE
15	Lang	7/22/2007	N. County	$349,000	4	3	8,930	Single Family	TRUE	FALSE
16	Randolph	9/3/2007	Central	$149,900	2	1	1,234	Single Family	FALSE	FALSE
17	Daily	2/20/2007	Central	$354,000	4	2	2,088	Single Family	FALSE	FALSE
18	Peterson	3/14/2007	Central	$364,900	4	2.5	2,507	Single Family	FALSE	FALSE
19	Peterson	4/7/2007	N. County	$309,900	5	3	2,447	Condo	TRUE	FALSE
20	Adams	7/19/2007	Central	$268,500	4	2.5	1,911	Single Family	FALSE	FALSE
21	Lang	10/14/2007	Central	$243,000	4	2.5	1,914	Single Family	FALSE	FALSE
22	Peterson	2/27/2007	S. County	$269,900	4	2.5	1,911	Single Family	FALSE	FALSE
23	Adams	6/6/2007	N. County	$379,900	3	2.5	2,468	Condo	FALSE	FALSE

ON the CD-ROM If you'd like to practice working with tables, the workbook shown here is available on the CD-ROM. The file is named real estate table.xlsx.

What's the difference between a standard range and table?

- Activating any cell in the table gives you access to a new Table Tools context tab on the Ribbon (see Figure 6.3).
- The cells contain background color and text color formatting. This formatting is optional.
- Each column header contains a drop-down list, which you can use to sort the data or filter the table to hide specific rows.
- If you scroll the sheet down so that the header row disappears, the table headers replace the column letters in the worksheet header.
- Tables support calculated columns. A single formula in a column is automatically propagated to all cells in the column. (See Chapter 11.)
- Tables support structured references. Rather than using cell references, formulas can use table names and column headers. (See Chapter 11.)
- The lower-right corner of the lower-right cell contains a small control that you can click and drag to extend the table's size, either horizontally (add more columns) or vertically (add more rows).
- Excel is able to remove duplicate rows automatically.
- Selecting rows and columns within the table is simplified.

FIGURE 6.3

When you select a cell in a table, you can use the commands located on the Table Tools ➪ Design tab.

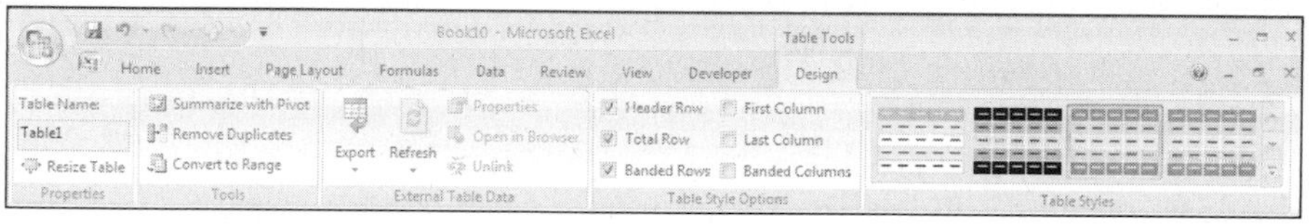

Creating a Table

Most of the time, you'll create a table from an existing range of data. But Excel also allows you to create a table from an empty range so that you can fill in the details later. The following instructions assume that you already have a range of data that's suitable for a table.

1. **First, make sure that the range doesn't contain any completely blank rows or columns.**
2. **Activate any cell within the range.**
3. **Choose Insert ➪ Tables ➪ Table (or press Ctrl+T).** Excel responds with its Create Table dialog box, shown in Figure 6.4. Excel tries to guess the range, and whether the table has a header row. Most of the time, it guesses correctly. If not, make your corrections before you click OK.

FIGURE 6.4

Use the Create Table dialog box to verify that Excel guessed the table dimensions correctly.

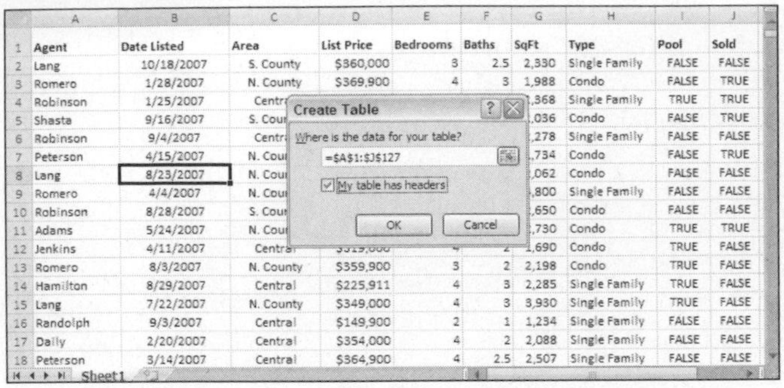

The range is converted to a table (using the default table style), and the Table ➪ Tools ➪ Design tab of the Ribbon appears.

NOTE Excel may guess the table's dimensions incorrectly if the table isn't separated from other information by at least one empty row or column. If Excel guesses incorrectly, just specify the exact range for the table in the Create Table dialog box. Or, click Cancel and rearrange your worksheet such that the table is separated from your other data by at least one blank row or column.

Changing the Look of a Table

When you create a table, Excel applies the default table style. The actual appearance depends on which document theme is used in the workbook. If you prefer a different look, you can easily change the entire look of the table.

Select any cell in the table and choose Table Tools ➪ Design ➪ Table Styles. The Ribbon shows one row of styles, but if you click the bottom of the scrollbar to the right, the table styles group expands, as shown in Figure 6.5. The styles are grouped into three categories: Light, Medium, and Dark. Notice that you get a "live" preview as you move your mouse among the styles. When you see one you like, just click to make it permanent.

For a different set of color choices, choose Page Layout ➪ Themes ➪ Themes to select a different document theme. For more information about themes, refer to Chapter 7.

FIGURE 6.5

Excel offers many different table styles.

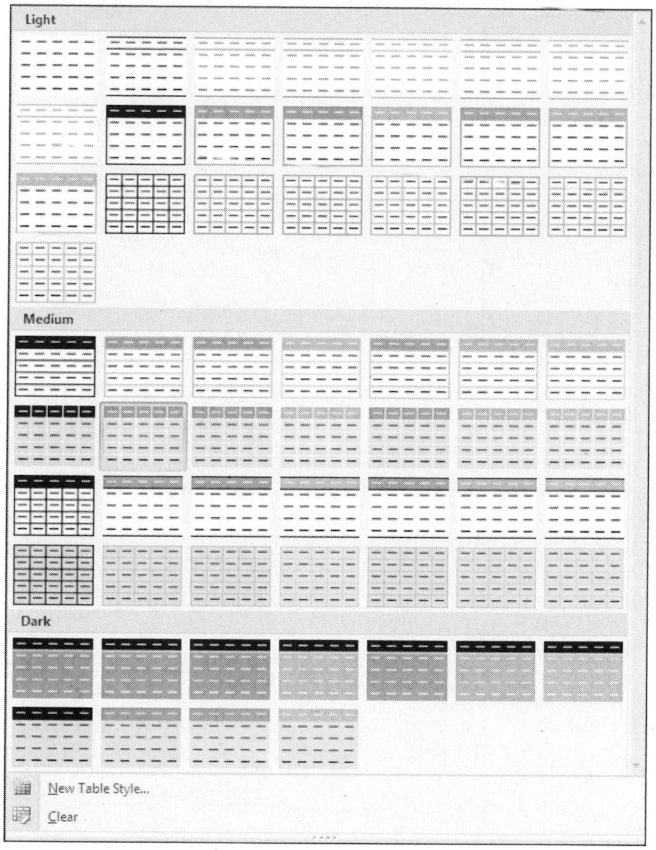

If applying table styles isn't working, it's probably because the range was already formatted before you converted it to a table. Table formatting doesn't override normal formatting. To clear the existing background fill colors, select the entire table and choose Home ➪ Font ➪ Fill Color ➪ No Fill. To clear the existing font colors, choose Home ➪ Font ➪ Font Color ➪ Automatic. After you issue these commands, the table styles should work as expected.

If you'd like to create a custom table style, choose Table Tools ➪ Design ➪ Table Styles ➪ New Table Style to display the New Table Quick Style dialog box shown in Figure 6.6. You can customize any or all of the 13 table elements. Select an element from the list, click Format, and specify the formatting for that element. When you're finished, give the new style a name and click OK. Your custom table style will appear in the Table Styles gallery in the Custom category. Unfortunately, custom table styles are available only in the workbook in which they were created.

 **TIP** If you would like to make changes to an existing table style, locate it in the Ribbon and right-click. Choose Duplicate from the shortcut menu. Excel displays the Modify Table Quick Style dialog box with all of the settings from the specified table style. Make your changes, give it a new name, and click OK to save it as a custom table style.

FIGURE 6.6

Use this dialog box to create a new table style.

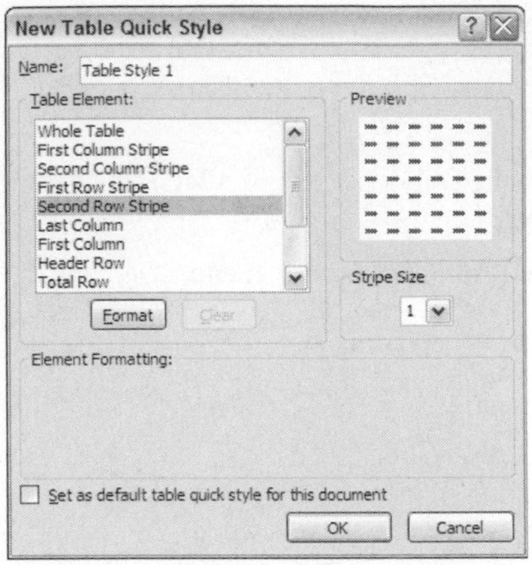

Working with Tables

This section describes some common actions you'll take with tables.

Navigating in a table

Selecting cells in a table works just like selecting cells in a normal range. One difference is when you use the Tab key. Pressing Tab moves to the cell to the right, and when you reach the last column, pressing Tab again moves to the first cell in the next row.

Selecting parts of a table

When you move your mouse around in a table, you may notice that the pointer changes shapes. These shapes help you select various parts of the table.

- **To select an entire column:** Move the mouse to the top of a cell in the header row, and the mouse pointer changes to a down-pointing arrow. Click to select the data in the column. Click a second time to select the entire table column (including the header). You can also press Ctrl+Space (once or twice) to select a column.

- **To select an entire row:** Move the mouse to the left of a cell in the first column, and the mouse pointer changes to a right-pointing arrow. Click to select the entire table row. You can also press Shift+Space to select a table row.

100

- **To select the entire table:** Move the mouse to the upper-left part of the upper-left cell. When the mouse pointer turns into a diagonal arrow, click to select the data area of the table. Click a second time to select the entire table (including the Header Row and the Totals Row). You can also press Ctrl+A (once or twice) to select the entire table.

> **TIP** Right-clicking a cell in a table displays several selection options in the shortcut menu.

Adding new rows or columns

To add a new column to the end of a table, just active a cell in the column to the right of the table and start entering the data. Excel automatically extends the table horizontally. Similarly, if you enter data in the row below a table, Excel extends the table vertically to include the new row.

> **NOTE** An exception to automatically extending tables is when the table is displaying a Totals Row. If you enter data below the Totals Row, the table will not be extended.

To add rows or columns within the table, right-click and choose Insert from the shortcut menu. The Insert shortcut menu command displays additional menu items:

- Table Columns To The Left
- Table Columns To The Right
- Table Rows Above
- Table Rows Below

> **TIP** When the cell pointer is in the bottom-right cell of a table, pressing Tab inserts a new row at the bottom.

When you move your mouse to the resize handle at bottom-right cell of a table, the mouse pointer turns into a diagonal line with two arrow heads. Click and drag down to add more rows to the table. Click and drag to the right to add more columns.

When you insert a new column, the Header Row displays a generic description, such as Column 1, Column 2, and so on. Normally, you'll want to change these names to more descriptive labels.

Deleting rows or columns

To delete a row (or column) in a table, select any cell in the row (or column) to be deleted. If you want to delete multiple rows or columns, select them all. Then right-click and choose Delete ⇨ Table Rows (or Delete ⇨ Table Columns).

Moving a table

To move a table to a new location in the same worksheet, move the mouse pointer to any of its borders. When the mouse pointer turns into a cross with four arrows, click and drag the table to its new location.

To move a table to a different worksheet (in the same workbook or in a different workbook):

1. **Press Alt+A *twice* to select the entire table.**
2. **Press Ctrl+X to cut the selected cells.**
3. **Activate the new worksheet and select the upper-left cell for the table.**
4. **Press Ctrl+V to paste the table.**

Excel Remembers

When you do something with a complete column in a table, Excel remembers that and extends that "something" to all new entries added to that column. For example, if you apply currency formatting to a column and then add a new row, Excel applies currency formatting to the new value in that column.

The same thing applies to other operations, such as conditional formatting, cell protection, data validation, and so on. And if you create a chart using the data in a table, the chart will be extended automatically if you add new data to the table. Those who have used a previous version of Excel will appreciate this feature the most.

Setting table options

The Table Tools ➪ Design ➪ Table Style Options group contains several check boxes that determine whether various elements of the table are displayed, and whether some formatting options are in effect:

- **Header Row:** Toggles the display of the Header Row.
- **Totals Row:** Toggles the display of the Totals Row.
- **First Column:** Toggles special formatting for the first column.
- **Last Column:** Toggles special formatting for the last column.
- **Banded Rows:** Toggles the display of banded (alternating color) rows.
- **Banded Columns:** Toggles the display of banded (alternating color) columns.

Working with the Total Row

The Total Row in a table contains formulas that summarize the information in the columns. Normally, the Total Row isn't turned on. To display the Total Row, choose Table Tools ➪ Design ➪ Table Style Options and put a check mark next to Total Row.

By default, the Total Rows display the sum of the values in a column of numbers. In many cases, you'll want a different type of summary formula. When you select a cell in the Total Row, a drop-down arrow appears, and you can select from a number of other summary formulas (see Figure 6.7):

- None: No formula
- Average: Displays the average of the numbers in the column
- Count: Displays the number of entries in the column (blank cells are not counted)
- Count Numbers: Displays the number of numeric values in the column (blank cells, text cells, and error cells are not counted).
- Max: Displays the maximum value in the column
- Min: Displays the minimum value in the column
- Sum: Displays the sum of the values in the column

■ StdDev: Displays the standard deviation of the values in the column. Standard deviation is a statistical measure of how "spread out" the values are.

■ Var: Displays the variance of the values in the column. Variance is another statistical measure of how "spread out" the values are.

■ More Functions: Displays the Insert Function dialog box so that you can select a function that isn't in the list.

FIGURE 6.7

Several types of summary formulas are available for the Totals Row.

	Agent	Date Listed	Area	List Price	Bedrooms	Baths	SqFt	Type	Pool	Sold
117	Jenkins	4/22/2007	N. County	$238,000	4	2.5	1,590	Condo	FALSE	TRUE
118	Romero	8/26/2007	S. County	$229,500	3	2	1,694	Single Family	FALSE	FALSE
119	Peterson	6/26/2007	S. County	$225,000	4	3	2,018	Single Family	TRUE	FALSE
120	Barnes	3/14/2007	N. County	$264,900	3	3	2,495	Condo	FALSE	FALSE
121	Daily	10/3/2007	Central	$340,000	4	2.5	2,517	Condo	FALSE	FALSE
122	Bennet	5/12/2007	Central	$229,500	4	3	2,041	Single Family	FALSE	TRUE
123	Shasta	5/19/2007	Central	$335,000	3	2.5	2,000	Single Family	TRUE	TRUE
124	Barnes	6/26/2007	N. County	$355,000	4	2.5	2,647	Condo	TRUE	FALSE
125	Randolph	4/24/2007	N. County	$405,000	2	3	2,444	Single Family	TRUE	TRUE
126	Bennet	5/9/2007	Central	$549,000	4	3	1,940	Single Family	TRUE	FALSE
127	Total			$308,037	3.648	2.634	2,226 ▾			
128							None			
129							Average			
130							Count			
131							Count Numbe			
132							Max			
133							Min			
134							Sum			
135							StdDev			
							Var			
							More Function			

H ◀ ▶ H Sheet1

 **WARNING** If you have a formula that refers to a value in the Total Row of a table, the formula returns an error if you hide the Total Row. But if you make the Total Row visible again, the formula works as it should.

CROSS-REF For more information about formulas, including the use of formulas in a table column, refer to Chapter 11.

Removing duplicate rows from a table

If you have a table that contains duplicate items, you may want to eliminate the duplicates. In the past, removing duplicate data was essentially a manual task. But Excel 2007 makes it very easy if the data is in a table.

Start by selecting any cell in your table. Then choose Table Tools ➪ Design ➪ Remove Duplicates. Excel responds with the dialog box shown in Figure 6.8. The dialog box lists all the columns in your table. Place a check mark next to the columns that you want to be included in the duplicate search. Most of the time, you'll want to select all the columns, which is the default. Click OK, and Excel weeds out the duplicate rows and displays a message that tells you how many duplicates it removed.

Removing duplicate rows from a table is easy.

WARNING It's important to understand that duplicate values are determined by the value *displayed* in the cell — not necessarily the value *stored* in the cell. For example, assume that two cells contain the same date. One of the dates is formatted to display as 5/15/2007, and the other is formatted to display as May 15, 2007. When removing duplicates, Excel considers these dates to be different.

Sorting and filtering a table

The Header Row of a table contains a drop-down arrow that, when clicked, displays sorting and filtering options (see Figure 6.9).

Each column in a table contains sorting and filtering option.

Sorting a table

Sorting a table rearranges the rows based on the contents of a particular column. You may want to sort a table to put names in alphabetical order. Or, maybe you want to sort your sales staff by the totals sales made.

To sort a table by a particular column, click the drop-down in the column header and choose one of the sort commands. The exact command varies, depending on the type of data in the column.

You can also select Sort By Color, to sort the rows based on the background or text color of the data. This option is relevant only if you've overridden the table style colors with custom colors.

NOTE When a column is sorted, the drop-down in the header row displays a different graphic to remind you that the table is sorted by that column.

You can sort on any number of columns. The trick is to sort the least significant column first and then proceed until the most significant column is sorted lasted. For example, in the real estate table, you may want the list to be sorted by agent. And within each agent's group, the rows should be sorted by area. And within each area, the rows should be sorted by list price. For this type of sort, first sort by the List Price column, then sort by the Area column, and then sort by the Agent column. Figure 6.10 shows the table sorted in this manner.

FIGURE 6.10

A table, after performing a 3-column sort.

	A	B	C	D	E	F	G	H	I	J
1	Agent	Date Listed	Area	List Price	Bedrooms	Baths	SqFt	Type	Pool	Sold
2	Adams	10/9/2007	Central	$199,000	3	2.5	1,510	Condo	FALSE	FALS
3	Adams	8/19/2007	Central	$214,500	4	2.5	1,862	Single Family	TRUE	FALS
4	Adams	4/28/2007	Central	$265,000	4	3	1,905	Single Family	FALSE	FALS
5	Adams	7/19/2007	Central	$268,500	4	2.5	1,911	Single Family	FALSE	FALS
6	Adams	2/6/2007	Central	$273,500	2	2	1,552	Single Family	TRUE	TRU
7	Adams	8/1/2007	Central	$309,950	4	3	2,800	Single Family	FALSE	FALS
8	Adams	1/15/2007	Central	$325,000	3	2.5	1,752	Single Family	FALSE	TRU
9	Adams	4/15/2007	N. County	$339,900	3	2	1,828	Single Family	TRUE	TRU
10	Adams	5/24/2007	N. County	$349,000	4	2.5	2,730	Condo	TRUE	TRU
11	Adams	2/8/2007	N. County	$379,000	3	3	2,354	Condo	FALSE	TRU
12	Adams	6/6/2007	N. County	$379,900	3	2.5	2,468	Condo	FALSE	FALS
13	Adams	4/21/2007	S. County	$208,750	4	3	2,207	Single Family	TRUE	TRU
14	Barnes	9/27/2007	N. County	$239,900	4	3	2,041	Condo	FALSE	FALS
15	Barnes	3/14/2007	N. County	$264,900	3	3	2,495	Condo	FALSE	FALS
16	Barnes	3/7/2007	N. County	$299,000	3	2	2,050	Condo	FALSE	FALS
17	Barnes	8/10/2007	N. County	$345,000	4	3	2,388	Condo	TRUE	TRU
18	Barnes	3/22/2007	N. County	$350,000	3	2.5	1,991	Condo	FALSE	TRU
19	Barnes	6/26/2007	N. County	$355,000	4	2.5	2,647	Condo	FALSE	FALS
20	Barnes	6/26/2007	S. County	$208,750	4	2	1,800	Single Family	FALSE	FALS
21	Bennet	5/12/2007	Central	$229,500	4	3	2,041	Single Family	FALSE	TRU
22	Bennet	5/9/2007	Central	$549,000	4	3	1,940	Single Family	TRUE	FALS
23	Bennet	7/1/2007	N. County	$229,500	6	3	2,700	Single Family	TRUE	FALS
24	Bennet	4/21/2007	N. County	$229,900	3	3	2,266	Condo	FALSE	FALS
25	Bennet	5/27/2007	N. County	$229,900	4	3	2,041	Condo	FALSE	FALS
26	Bennet	6/26/2007	S. County	$229,900	3	2.5	1,580	Single Family	FALSE	FALS
27	Chung	7/8/2007	Central	$236,900	3	2	1,700	Single Family	FALSE	FALS
28	Chung	8/27/2007	Central	$339,900	4	2	2,238	Single Family	FALSE	FALS

Another way of performing a multiple-column sort is to use the Sort dialog box. To display this dialog box, choose Home ➪ Editing ➪ Sort & Filter ➪ Custom Sort. Or, right-click any cell in the table and choose Sort ➪ Custom Sort from the shortcut menu.

In the Sort dialog box, use the drop-down lists to specify the first search specifications. Note that the searching is opposite of what I described in the previous paragraph. In this example, you start with Agent. Then, click the Add Level button to insert another set of search controls. In this new set of controls, specify the sort specifications for the Area column. Then, add another level and enter the specifications for the List Price column. Figure 6.11 shows the dialog box after entering the specifications for the three-column sort. This technique produces exactly the same sort as described in the previous paragraph.

FIGURE 6.11

Using the Sort dialog box to specify a three-column sort.

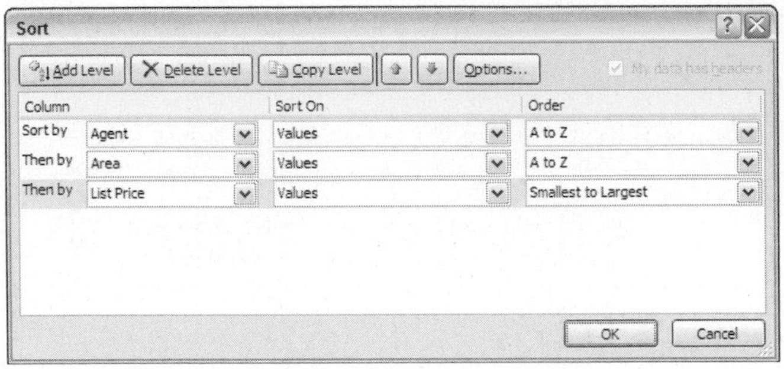

Filtering a table

Filtering a table refers to displaying only the rows that meet certain conditions. (The other rows are hidden.)

Using the real estate table, assume that you're only interested in the data for the N. Country area. Click the drop-down in the Area Row Header and remove the check mark from Select All, which unselects everything. Then, place a check mark next to N. County and click OK. The table, shown in Figure 6.12, is now filtered to display only the listings in the N. County area. Notice that some of the row numbers are missing; these rows contain the filtered (hidden) data.

Also notice that the drop-down arrow in the Area column now shows a different graphic — an icon that indicates the column is filtered.

FIGURE 6.12

This table is filtered to show only the information for N. County.

	A	B	C	D	E	F	G	H	I	J
1	Agent	Date Listed	Area	List Price	Bedrooms	Baths	SqFt	Type	Pool	Sold
9	Jenkins	1/29/2007	N. County	$1,200,500	5	5	4,696	Single Family	TRUE	FALSE
10	Romero	4/4/2007	N. County	$799,000	6	5	4,800	Single Family	FALSE	FALSE
11	Hamilton	2/24/2007	N. County	$425,900	5	3	2,414	Single Family	TRUE	FALSE
12	Randolph	4/24/2007	N. County	$405,000	2	3	2,444	Single Family	TRUE	TRUE
14	Shasta	3/24/2007	N. County	$398,000	4	2.5	2,620	Single Family	FALSE	FALSE
15	Kelly	6/9/2007	N. County	$389,500	4	2	1,971	Single Family	FALSE	FALSE
16	Shasta	8/17/2007	N. County	$389,000	4	3	3,109	Single Family	FALSE	FALSE
17	Adams	6/6/2007	N. County	$379,900	3	2.5	2,468	Condo	FALSE	FALSE
18	Adams	2/8/2007	N. County	$379,000	3	3	2,354	Condo	FALSE	TRUE
19	Robinson	3/30/2007	N. County	$379,000	4	3	3,000	Single Family	TRUE	TRUE
23	Shasta	7/15/2007	N. County	$374,900	4	3	3,927	Single Family	FALSE	FALSE
24	Lang	5/3/2007	N. County	$369,900	3	2.5	2,030	Condo	TRUE	FALSE
25	Romero	1/28/2007	N. County	$369,900	4	3	1,988	Condo	FALSE	TRUE
44	Shasta	7/23/2007	N. County	$369,900	5	3	2,477	Single Family	FALSE	FALSE
47	Robinson	5/14/2007	N. County	$359,900	3	3	1,839	Condo	FALSE	TRUE
48	Romero	8/3/2007	N. County	$359,900	3	2	2,198	Condo	TRUE	FALSE
49	Lang	6/23/2007	N. County	$359,000	3	2.5	2,210	Single Family	FALSE	FALSE
50	Barnes	6/26/2007	N. County	$355,000	4	2.5	2,647	Condo	TRUE	FALSE
56	Barnes	3/22/2007	N. County	$350,000	3	2.5	1,991	Condo	FALSE	TRUE
62	Jenkins	5/1/2007	N. County	$349,900	4	3	2,290	Single Family	TRUE	TRUE
63	Shasta	10/2/2007	N. County	$349,000	3	2.5	1,727	Condo	TRUE	TRUE

You can filter by multiple values — for example, filter the table to show only N. Country and Central.

You can filter a table using any number of columns. For example, you may want to see only the N. County listings in which the Type is Single Family. Just repeat the operation using the Type column. All tables then display only the rows in which the Area is N. County and the Type is Single Family.

For additional filtering options, select Text Filters (or Number Filters, if the column contains values). The options are fairly self-explanatory, and you have a great deal of flexibility in displaying only the rows that you're interested in.

In addition, you can right-click a cell and use the Filter command on the shortcut menu. This menu item leads to several additional filtering options.

NOTE As you may expect, the Total Row is updated to show the total only for the visible rows.

Why you copy data from a filtered table, only the visible data is copied. In other words, rows that are hidden by filtering don't get copied. This filtering makes it very easy to copy a subset of a larger table and paste it to another area of your worksheet. Keep in mind that the pasted data is not a table — it's just a normal range.

To remove filtering for a column, click the drop-down in the Row Header and select Clear Filter. If you've filtered using multiple columns, it may be faster to remove all filters by choosing Home ➪ Editing ➪ Sort & Filter ➪ Clear.

Converting a table back to a range

If you need to convert a table back to a normal range, just select a cell in the table and choose Table Tools ➪ Design ➪ Tools ➪ Convert To Range. The table style formatting remains intact, but the range no longer functions as a table.

Chapter 7

Worksheet Formatting

ormatting your worksheet is like the icing on a cake — it may not be
absolutely necessary, but it can make the end product a lot more attractive.
In an Excel worksheet, formatting can also make it easier for others to
understand the worksheet's purpose.

Stylistic formatting isn't essential for every workbook that you develop —
especially if it is for your own use only. On the other hand, it takes only a few
moments to apply some simple formatting, and, once applied, the formatting will
remain in place without further effort on your part.

In Chapter 6, I show how easy it is to apply formatting to a table. The information in this chapter applies to normal ranges. I show you how to work with the
Excel formatting tools: fonts, colors, and styles, such as bold and italic. I also
cover custom styles that you can create to make formatting large amounts of
material in a similar way easier.

IN THIS CHAPTER

**Understanding how formatting
can improve your worksheets**

**Getting to know the formatting
tools**

**Using formatting in your
worksheets**

**Using named styles for easier
formatting**

**Understanding document
themes**

Getting to Know the Formatting Tools

Figure 7.1 shows how even simple formatting can significantly improve a worksheet's readability.

ON the CD-ROM This workbook is available on the companion CD-ROM. The
file is named **loan payments.xlsx.**

FIGURE 7.1

In just a few minutes, some simple formatting can greatly improve the appearance of your worksheets.

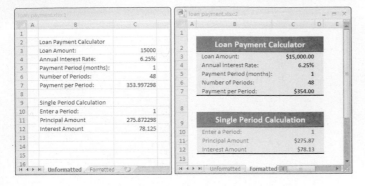

Excel's formatting tools are available in three locations:

- In the Home tab of the Ribbon
- In the Mini toolbar that appears when you right-click a range or a cell
- In the Format Cells dialog box

In addition, many of the common formatting commands have keyboard shortcuts that you can use.

CROSS-REF   Excel provides another way to format cells based on the cell's contents. Chapter 8 discusses conditional formatting.

Using the Formatting Tools in the Home Tab

The Home tab of the Ribbon provides quick access to the most commonly used formatting options. Start by selecting the cell or range; then use the appropriate tool in the Font, Alignment, or Number groups.

Using these tools is very intuitive, and the best way to familiarize yourself with them is to experiment. Enter some data, select some cells, and then click the controls to change the appearance. Note that some of these controls are actually drop-down lists. Click the small arrow on the button, and the button expands to display your choices.

Using the Mini toolbar

When you right-click a cell or a range selection, you get a shortcut menu. In addition, a mini toolbar appears above the shortcut menu. Figure 7.2 shows how this toolbar looks.

The Mini toolbar contains controls for common formatting:

- Font
- Font Size
- Increase Font
- Decrease Font
- Accounting Number Format

- Percent Style
- Comma Style
- Format Painter
- Bold
- Italic
- Center
- Borders
- Fill Color
- Font Color
- Increase Decimal
- Decrease Decimal
- Merge And Center

If you use a tool on the Mini toolbar, the shortcut menu disappears, but the toolbar remains visible so you can apply other formatting if you like. Also, notice that the Mini toolbar gradually fades away if you move the mouse pointer away from it. To hide the Mini toolbar, just click in any cell.

TIP   If you find the Mini toolbar distracting, you can turn it off in the Popular tab of the Excel Options dialog box.

FIGURE 7.2

The Mini toolbar appears above the right-click shortcut menu.

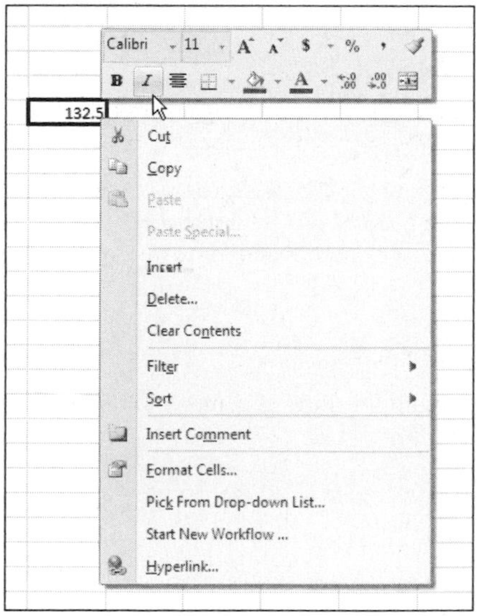

Using the Format Cells dialog box

The formatting controls available on the Home tab of the Ribbon are sufficient most of the time, but some types of formatting require that you use the Format Cells dialog box. This tabbed dialog box lets you apply nearly any type of stylistic formatting, as well as number formatting. The formats that you choose in the Format Cells dialog box apply to the cells that you have selected at the time. Later sections in this chapter cover the tabs of the Format Cells dialog box.

NOTE When you use the Format Cells dialog box, you don't see the effects of your formatting choices until you click OK.

After selecting the cell or range to format, you can display the Format Cells dialog box by using any of the following methods:

- Press Ctrl+1.
- Click the dialog box launcher in Home ➪ Font, Home ➪ Alignment, or Home ➪ Number. The dialog box launcher is the small downward-pointing arrow icon displayed to the right of the group name in the Ribbon. When you display the Format Cells dialog box using a dialog box launcher, the dialog box is displayed with the appropriate tab visible.
- Right-click the selected cell or range and choose Format Cells from the shortcut menu.
- Click the More command in some of the drop-down controls in the Ribbon. For example, the Home ➪ Font ➪ Border ➪ More Borders drop-down includes an item named More Borders.

The Format Cells dialog box contains six tabs: Number, Alignment, Font, Border, Patterns, and Protection. The following sections contain more information about the formatting options available in this dialog box.

Using Formatting in Your Worksheets

Applying stylistic formatting to Excel worksheets is not an exact science. People have varying opinions about what constitutes a good-looking worksheet. Therefore, the following sections focus on the mechanics. It's up to you to choose the formatting options that are most appropriate.

NEW FEATURE Excel 2007's new document themes feature attempts to assist nondesigners in creating attractive worksheets. I discuss Excel 2007 themes later in this chapter. See "Understanding Document Themes."

Using different fonts

You can use different fonts, sizes, or text attributes in your worksheets to make various parts, such as the headers for a table, stand out. You also can adjust the font size. For example, using a smaller font will allow more information on a single page.

By default, Excel 2007 uses the 11-point Calibri font. A *font* is described by its typeface (Calibri, Cambria, Arial, Times New Roman, Courier New, and so on), as well as by its size, measured in points. (Seventy-two points equal one inch.) Excel's row height, by default, is 15 points. Therefore, 11-point type entered into a 15-point rows leaves a small amount of blank space between the characters in adjacent rows.

TIP If you have not manually changed a row's height, Excel automatically adjusts the row height based on the tallest text that you enter into the row.

Updating Old Fonts

Office 2007 includes several new fonts, and the default font has been changed for all the Office applications. In the past, Excel's default font was 10-point Arial. In Excel 2007, the default font for the Office theme is 11-point Calibri. Most people will agree that Calibri is much easier to read, and it gives the worksheet a more modern appearance.

If you use Excel 2007 to open a workbook created in a previous version, the default font will not be changed, even if you apply a document style (by choosing Page Layout ➪ Themes ➪ Themes). But here's an easy way to update the fonts in a workbook that was created using an older version of Excel:

1. **Press Ctrl+N to open a new, empty workbook.** The new workbook will use the default document theme.
2. **Open your old workbook file.**
3. **Choose Home ➪ Styles ➪ Cell Styles ➪ Merge Styles.** Excel displays its Merge Styles dialog box.
4. **In the Merge Styles dialog box, select the new workbook that you created in Step 1.**
5. **Click OK.**
6. **Click Yes in response to Excel's question regarding merging styles that have the same name.**

This technique changes the font and size for all unformatted cells. If you've applied font formatting to some cells (for example, made them bold), the font for those cells will not be changed (but you can change the font manually). If you don't like the new look of your workbook, just close the workbook without saving the changes.

TIP If you plan to distribute a workbook to other users, you should stick with the standard fonts that are included with Windows or Microsoft Office. If you open a workbook and your system doesn't have the font with which the workbook was created, Windows attempts to use a similar font. Sometimes this attempt works OK, and sometimes it doesn't.

Use the Font and Font Size tools in the Home tab of the Ribbon (or in the Mini toolbar) to change the font or size for selected cells.

You also can use the Font tab in the Format Cells dialog box to choose fonts, as shown in Figure 7.3. This tab enables you to control several other font attributes that aren't available elsewhere. Besides choosing the font, you can change the font style (bold, italic), underlining, color, and effects (strikethrough, superscript, or subscript). If you click the check box labeled Normal Font, Excel displays the selections for the font defined for the Normal style. I discuss styles later in this chapter. See "Using Named Styles for Easier Formatting."

Figure 7.4 shows several different examples of font formatting. In this figure, the gridlines were turned off to make seeing the underlining easier. Notice, in the figure, that Excel provides four different underlining styles. In the two non-accounting underline styles, only the cell contents are underlined. In the two accounting underline styles, the entire width of the cells is always underlined.

FIGURE 7.3

The Font tab of the Format Cells dialog box gives you many additional font attribute options.

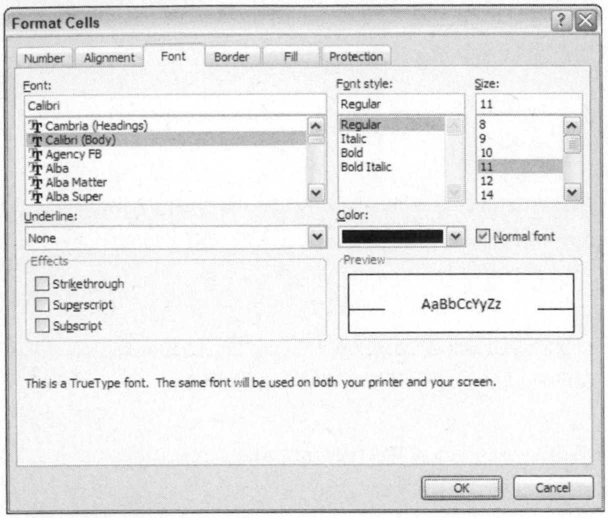

FIGURE 7.4

You can choose many different font-formatting options for your worksheets.

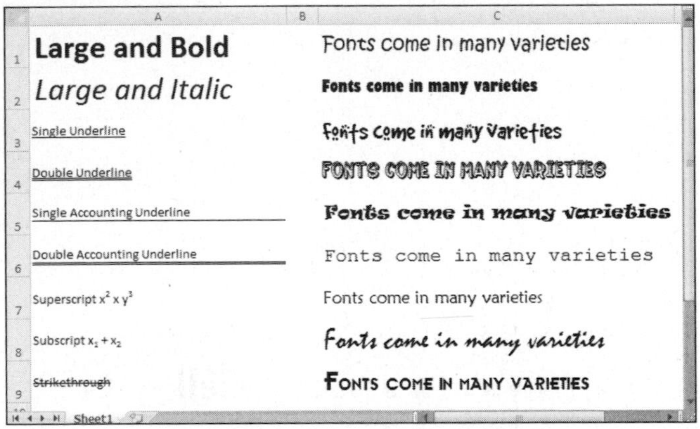

If you prefer to keep your hands on the keyboard, you can use the following shortcut keys to format a selected range quickly:

- **Ctrl+B:** Bold
- **Ctrl+I:** Italic

- **Ctrl+U**: Underline
- **Ctrl+5**: Strikethrough

These shortcut keys act as a toggle. For example, you can turn bold on and off by repeatedly pressing Ctrl+B.

Changing text alignment

The contents of a cell can be aligned horizontally and vertically. By default, Excel aligns numbers to the right and text to the left. All cells use bottom alignment, by default.

Overriding these defaults is a simple matter. The most commonly used alignment commands are in the Home ⇨ Alignment group of the Ribbon. Use the Alignment tab of the Format Cells dialog box for even more options (see Figure 7.5).

FIGURE 7.5

The full range of alignment options are available in the Alignment tab of the Format Cells dialog box.

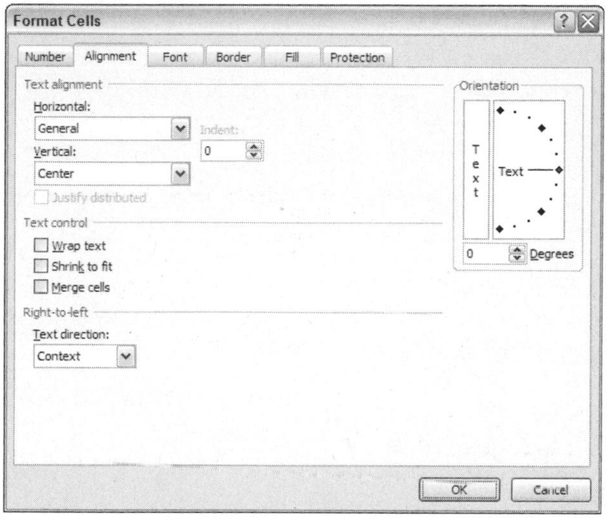

Using Multiple Formatting Styles in a Single Cell

If a cell contains text, Excel also enables you to format individual characters in the cell. To do so, switch to Edit mode (double-click the cell) and then select the characters that you want to format. You can select characters either by dragging the mouse over them or by pressing the Shift key as you press the left- or right-arrow key.

When you've selected the characters for format, use any of the standard formatting techniques. The changes apply only to the selected characters in the cell. This technique doesn't work with cells that contain values or formulas.

Choosing horizontal alignment options

The horizontal alignment options control the way the cell contents are distributed across the width of the cell (or cells). The horizontal alignment options available in the Format Cells dialog box are

- **General:** Aligns numbers to the right, aligns text to the left, and centers logical and error values. This option is the default alignment.
- **Left:** Aligns the cell contents to the left side of the cell. If the text is wider than the cell, the text spills over to the cell to the right. If the cell to the right isn't empty, the text is truncated and not completely visible. Also available on the Ribbon.
- **Center:** Centers the cell contents in the cell. If the text is wider than the cell, the text spills over to cells on either side if they're empty. If the adjacent cells aren't empty, the text is truncated and not completely visible. Also available on the Ribbon.
- **Right:** Aligns the cell contents to the right side of the cell. If the text is wider than the cell, the text spills over to the cell to the left. If the cell to the left isn't empty, the text is truncated and not completely visible. Also available on the Ribbon.
- **Fill:** Repeats the contents of the cell until the cell's width is filled. If cells to the right also are formatted with Fill alignment, they also are filled.
- **Justify:** Justifies the text to the left and right of the cell. This option is applicable only if the cell is formatted as wrapped text and uses more than one line.
- **Center across selection:** Centers the text over the selected columns. This option is useful for precisely centering a heading over a number of columns.
- **Distributed:** Distributes the text evenly across the selected column.

NOTE If you choose Left, Right, or Distributed, you can also adjust the Indent setting, which adds space between the cell border and the text.

Choosing vertical alignment options

The vertical alignment options typically aren't used as often as the horizontal alignment options. In fact, these settings are useful only if you've adjusted row heights so that they're considerably taller than normal.

The vertical alignment options available in the Format Cells dialog box are

- **Top:** Aligns the cell contents to the top of the cell. Also available on the Ribbon.
- **Center:** Centers the cell contents vertically in the cell. Also available on the Ribbon.
- **Bottom:** Aligns the cell contents to the bottom of the cell. Also available on the Ribbon.
- **Justify:** Justifies the text vertically in the cell; this option is applicable only if the cell is formatted as wrapped text and uses more than one line.
- **Distributed:** Distributes the text evenly vertically in the cell.

Wrapping or shrinking text to fit the cell

If you have text that is too wide to fit the column width but don't want that text to spill over into adjacent cells, you can use either the Wrap Text option or the Shrink To Fit option to accommodate that text. The Wrap Text control is also available on the Ribbon.

The Wrap Text option displays the text on multiple lines in the cell, if necessary. Use this option to display lengthy headings without having to make the columns too wide, and without reducing the size of the text.

The Shrink To Fit option reduces the size of the text so that it fits into the cell without spilling over to the next cell. Usually, it's easier to make this adjustment manually.

NOTE **If you apply Wrap Text formatting to a cell, you can't use the Shrink To Fit formatting.**

Merging worksheet cells to create additional text space

Excel also enables you to merge two or more cells. When you merge cells, you don't combine the contents of cells. Rather, you combine a group of cells into a single cell that occupies the same space. The worksheet shown in Figure 7.6 contains four sets of merged cells. For example, range C2:I2 has been merged into a single cell, and so has range J2:P2. In addition, ranges B4:B8 and B9:B13 have also been merged. In the latter two cases, the text direction has been changed (see "Displaying text at an angle," later in this chapter).

FIGURE 7.6

Merge worksheet cells to make them act as if they were a single cell.

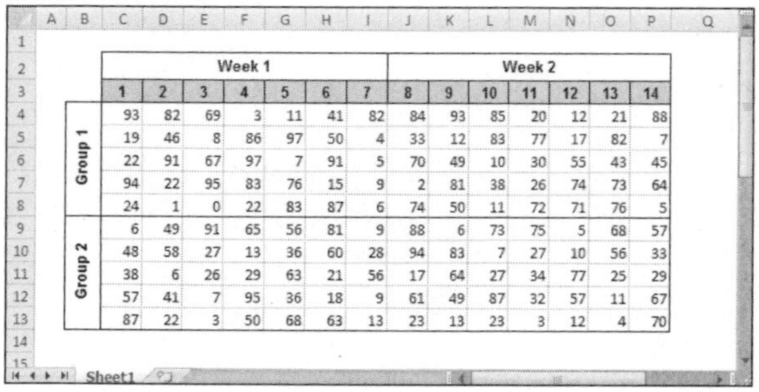

	Week 1							Week 2						
	1	2	3	4	5	6	7	8	9	10	11	12	13	14
Group 1	93	82	69	3	11	41	82	84	93	85	20	12	21	88
	19	46	8	86	97	50	4	33	12	83	77	17	82	7
	22	91	67	97	7	91	5	70	49	10	30	55	43	45
	94	22	95	83	76	15	9	2	81	38	26	74	73	64
	24	1	0	22	83	87	6	74	50	11	72	71	76	5
Group 2	6	49	91	65	56	81	9	88	6	73	75	5	68	57
	48	58	27	13	36	60	28	94	83	7	27	10	56	33
	38	6	26	29	63	21	56	17	64	27	34	77	25	29
	57	41	7	95	36	18	9	61	49	87	32	57	11	67
	87	22	3	50	68	63	13	23	13	23	3	12	4	70

You can merge any number of cells occupying any number of rows and columns. In fact, you can merge all 17,179,869,184 cells in a worksheet into a single cell. However, the range that you intend to merge should be empty except for the upper-left cell. If any of the other cells that you intend to merge are not empty, Excel displays a warning. If you continue, all the data (except in the upper-left cell) will be deleted. To avoid deleting data, click Cancel in response to the warning.

You can use the Alignment tab in the Format Cells dialog box to merge cells, but using the Merge And Center control on the Ribbon (or on the Mini toolbar) is simpler. To merge cells, select the cells that you want to merge and then click the Merge And Center button. This button acts as a toggle. To unmerge cells, select the merged cells and click the Merge And Center button again.

After you've merged cells, you can change the alignment to something other than Center.

Displaying text at an angle

In some cases, you may want to create more visual impact by displaying text at an angle within a cell. You can display text horizontally, vertically, or at an angle between 90 degrees up and 90 degrees down.

The Home ➪ Alignment ➪ Orientation drop-down lets you apply the most common text angles. But for more control, use the Alignment tab of the Format Cells dialog box. In the Format Cells dialog box, use the Degrees spinner control — or just drag the pointer in the gauge. You can specify a text angle between –90 and +90 degrees.

Figure 7.7 shows an example of text displayed at a 45-degree angle.

> **NOTE** Often, rotated text may look a bit distorted on-screen, but the printed output is usually of much better quality.

FIGURE 7.7

Rotate text for additional visual impact.

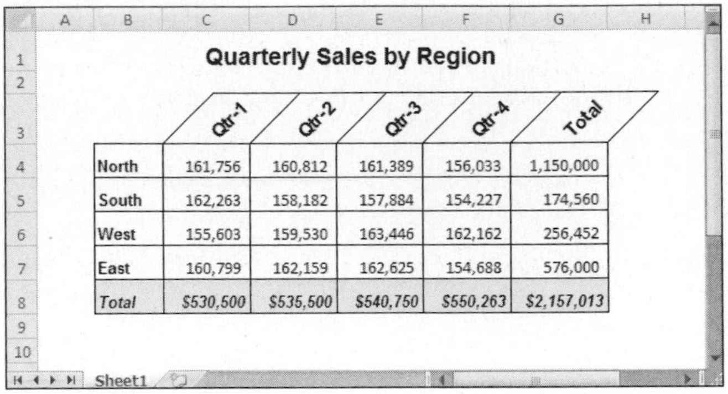

	Qtr-1	Qtr-2	Qtr-3	Qtr-4	Total
Quarterly Sales by Region					
North	161,756	160,812	161,389	156,033	1,150,000
South	162,263	158,182	157,884	154,227	174,560
West	155,603	159,530	163,446	162,162	256,452
East	160,799	162,159	162,625	154,688	576,000
Total	*$530,500*	*$535,500*	*$540,750*	*$550,263*	*$2,157,013*

Controlling the text direction

Not all languages use the same character direction. Although most Western languages read left to right, some other languages are read right to left. You can use the Text Direction option to select the appropriate setting for the language you use. This command is available only in the Alignment tab of the Format Cells dialog box.

Don't confuse the Text Direction setting with the Orientation setting (discussed in the previous section). Changing the text orientation is common. Changing the text direction is used only in very specific situations.

> **NOTE** Changing the Text Direction setting won't have any effect unless you have the proper language drivers installed on your system. For example, you must install Japanese language support from the Office CD-ROM to use right-to-left text direction Japanese characters.

Using colors and shading

Excel provides the tools to create some very colorful worksheets. You can change the color of the text or add colors to the backgrounds of the worksheet cells.

> **NEW FEATURE** Previous versions of Excel could use no more than 56 colors in a workbook. Excel 2007 allows a virtually unlimited number of colors.

You control the color of the cell's text by choosing Home ➪ Font ➪ Font Color. Control the cell's background color by choosing Home ➪ Font ➪ Fill Color. Both of these color controls are also available on the Mini toolbar, which appears when you right-click a cell or range.

Using Colors with Table Styles

In Chapter 6, I discussed the new table feature in Excel 2007. One advantage to using tables is that it's very easy to apply table styles. You can change the look of your table with a single mouse click.

It's important to understand how table styles work with existing formatting. A simple rule is that applying a style to a table doesn't override existing formatting. For example, assume that you have a range of data that uses yellow as the background color for the cells. When you convert that range to a table (by choosing Insert ➪ Tables ➪ Table), the default table style (alternating row colors) isn't visible. Rather, the table will display the previously applied yellow background.

In order to make table styles visible with this table, you need to remove the manually-applied background cell colors. Select the entire table and then choose Home ➪ Font ➪ Fill Color ➪ No Fill.

You can apply any type of formatting to a table, and that formatting will override the table style formatting. For example, you may want to make a particular cell stand out by using a different fill color.

TIP To hide the contents of a cell, make the background color the same as the font text color. The cell contents are still visible in the Formula bar when you select the cell. Keep in mind, however, that some printers may override this setting, and the text may be visible when printed.

Even though you have access to an unlimited number of colors, you might want to stick with the 60 theme colors displayed in the various color selection controls. In other words, avoid using the More Color option, which lets you select a color. Why? First of all, those 60 colors were chosen because they "go together" well. Another reason involves document themes. If you switch to a different document theme for your workbook, nontheme colors aren't changed. In some cases, the result may be less than pleasing, aesthetically. See "Understanding Document Themes," later in this chapter, for more information about themes.

Adding borders and lines

Borders (and lines within the borders) are another visual enhancement that you can add around groups of cells. Borders are often used to group a range of similar cells or to delineate rows or columns. Excel offers 13 preset styles of borders, as you can see in the Home ➪ Font ➪ Border drop-down list shown in Figure 7.8. This control works with the selected cell or range and enables you to specify which, if any, border style to use for each border of the selection.

You may prefer to draw borders rather than select a preset border style. To do so, use the Draw Border or Draw Border Grid command on the Home ➪ Font ➪ Border drop-down list. Selecting either of these commands lets you create borders by dragging your mouse. Use the Line Color or Line Style commands to change the color or style. When you're finished drawing borders, press Esc to cancel the border drawing mode.

Another way to apply borders is to use the Border tab of the Format Cells dialog box, which is shown in Figure 7.9. One way to display this dialog box is to select More Borders from the Border drop-down list.

FIGURE 7.8

Use the Border drop-down list to add lines around worksheet cells.

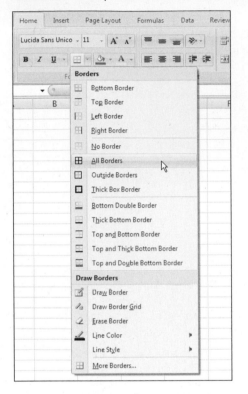

Before you display the Format Cells dialog box, select the cell or range to which you want to add borders. First, choose a line style and then choose the border position for the line style by clicking one of the Border icons (these icons are toggles).

Notice that the Border tab has three preset icons, which can save you some clicking. If you want to remove all borders from the selection, click None. To put an outline around the selection, click Outline. To put borders inside the selection, click Inside.

Excel displays the selected border style in the dialog box (there is no live preview). You can choose different styles for different border positions; you can also choose a color for the border. Using this dialog box may require some experimentation, but you'll get the hang of it.

When you apply diagonal lines to a cell or range, the selection looks like it has been crossed out.

TIP   If you use border formatting in your worksheet, you may want to turn off the grid display in order to make the borders more pronounced. Choose View ➪ Show/Hide ➪ Gridlines to toggle the gridline display.

FIGURE 7.9

Use the Border tab of the Format Cells dialog box for more control over cell borders.

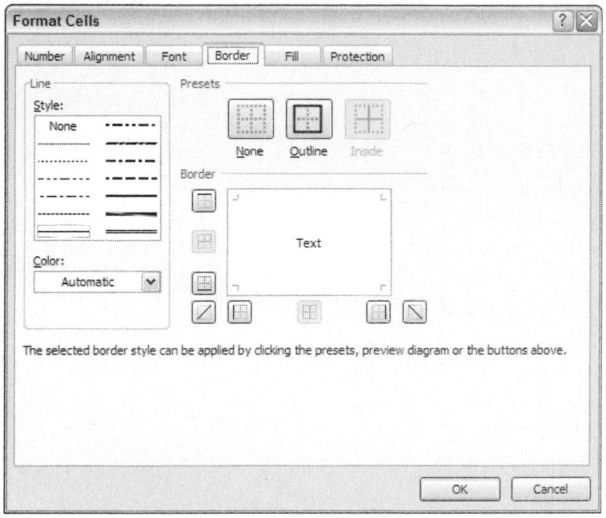

Adding a background image to a worksheet

Excel also enables you to choose a graphics file to serve as a background for a worksheet. This effect is similar to the wallpaper that you may display on your Windows desktop or as a background for a Web page.

To add a background to a worksheet, choose Page Layout ⇨ Page Setup ⇨ Background. Excel displays a dialog box that enables you to select a graphics file (all common graphic file formats are supported). When you locate a file, click Insert. Excel tiles the graphic across your worksheet. Some images are specifically designed to be tiled, such as the one shown in Figure 7.10. This type of image is often used for Web page backgrounds, and it creates a seamless background.

You also want to turn off the gridline display because the gridlines show through the graphic. Some backgrounds make viewing text difficult, so you may want to use a solid background color for cells that contain text.

Keep in mind that using a background image will increase the size of your workbook. This may be a consideration if you plan to e-mail the workbook to others.

> **NOTE** The graphic background on a worksheet is for on-screen display only — it isn't printed when you print the worksheet.

Copying Formats by Painting

Perhaps the quickest way to copy the formats from one cell to another cell or range is to use the Format Painter button (the button with the paintbrush image) in the Home ⇨ Clipboard group.

Start by selecting the cell or range that has the formatting attributes you want to copy. Then click the Format Painter button. Notice that the mouse pointer changes to include a paintbrush. Next, select the cells to which you want to apply the formats. Release the mouse button, and Excel applies the same set of formatting options that were in the original range.

If you double-click the Format Painter button, you can paint multiple areas of the worksheet with the same formats. Excel applies the formats that you copy to each cell or range that you select. To get out of Paint mode, click the Format Painter button again (or press Esc).

FIGURE 7.10

You can add almost any image file as a worksheet background image.

Using Named Styles for Easier Formatting

One of the most underutilized features in Excel is named styles. Named styles make it very easy to apply a set of predefined formatting options to a cell or range. In addition to saving time, using named styles also helps to ensure a consistent look.

A style can consist of settings for up to six different attributes:

- Number format
- Font (type, size, and color)
- Alignment (vertical and horizontal)
- Borders

- Pattern
- Protection (locked and hidden)

The real power of styles is apparent when you change a component of a style. All cells that use that named style automatically incorporate the change. Suppose that you apply a particular style to a dozen cells scattered throughout your worksheet. Later, you realize that these cells should have a font size of 14 points rather than 12 points. Rather than change each cell, simply edit the style. All cells with that particular style change automatically.

Applying styles

The designers of Excel 2007 have revamped this underutilized feature significantly and Excel now includes a good selection of predefined named styles. Figure 7.11 shows the effect of choosing Home ➪ Styles ➪ Cell Styles. Note that this display is a "live preview" — as you move your mouse over the style choices, the selected cell or range temporarily displays the style. When you see a style you like, click it to apply the style to the selection.

FIGURE 7.11

Excel 2007 displays samples of available cell styles.

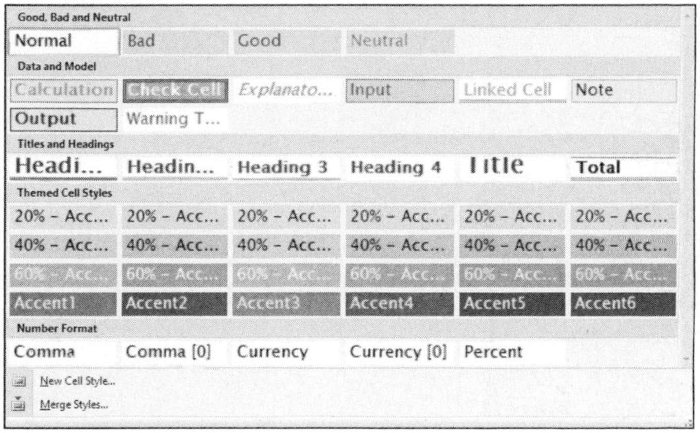

NOTE By default, all cells use the Normal style.

After you apply a style to a cell, you can apply additional formatting to it by using any formatting method discussed in this chapter. Formatting modifications that you make to the cell don't affect other cells that use the same style.

You have quite a bit of control over styles. In fact, you can do any of the following:

- Modify an existing style
- Create a new style
- Merge styles from another workbook into the active workbook.

The following sections describe these procedures.

Modifying an existing style

To change an existing style, choose Home ➪ Styles ➪ Cell Styles. Right-click the style you want to modify and choose Modify from the shortcut menu. Excel displays the Style dialog box, shown in Figure 7.12. In this example, the Style dialog box shows the settings for the Office them Normal style — which is the default style for all cells. (The style definitions vary, depending on which document theme is active.)

Here's a quick example of how you can use styles to change the default font used throughout your workbook.

1. **Choose Home ➪ Styles ➪ Cell Styles.** Excels displays the list of style for the active workbook.
2. **Right-click Normal and select Modify.** Excel displays the Style dialog box, with the current settings for the Normal style.
3. **Click the Format button.** Excel displays the Format Cells dialog box.
4. **Click the Font tab and choose the font and size that you want as the default.**
5. **Click OK to return to the Style dialog box.**
6. **Click OK again to close the Style dialog box.**

The font for all cells that use the Normal style changes to the font that you specified. You can change any formatting attributes for any style.

FIGURE 7.12

Use the Style dialog box to modify named styles.

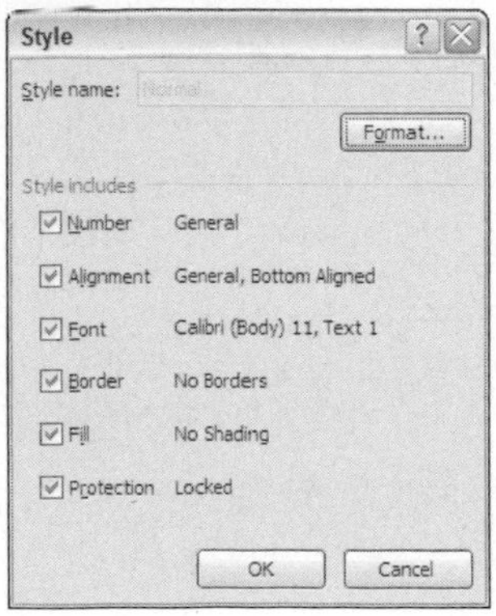

Creating new styles

In addition to using Excel's built-in styles, you can create your own styles. This flexibility can be quite handy because it enables you to apply your favorite formatting options very quickly and consistently.

To create a new style, follow these steps:

1. **Select a cell and apply all the formatting that you want to include in the new style.** You can use any of the formatting that is available in the Format Cells dialog box.

2. **After you format the cell to your liking, choose Home ⇨ Styles ⇨ Cell Styles, and choose New Cell Style.** Excel displays its Style dialog box, along with a proposed generic name for the style. Note that Excel displays the words By Example to indicate that it's basing the style on the current cell.

3. **Enter a new style name in the Style Name box.** The check boxes display the current formats for the cell. By default, all check boxes are checked.

4. **If you don't want the style to include one or more format categories, remove the check(s) from the appropriate box(es).**

5. **Click OK to create the style and to close the dialog box.**

After you perform these steps, the new custom style will be available when you choose Home ⇨ Styles ⇨ Cell Styles. Custom styles are available only in the workbook in which they were created. To copy your custom styles, see the section that follows.

NOTE The Protection option in the Styles dialog box controls whether users will be able to modify cells for the selected style. This option is effective only if you've also turned on worksheet protection, by choosing Review ⇨ Changes ⇨ Protect Sheet.

Merging styles from other workbooks

It's important to understand that custom styles are stored with the workbook in which they were created. If you've created some custom styles, you probably don't want to go through all the work to create copies of those styles in each new Excel workbook. A better approach is to merge the styles from a workbook in which you previously created them.

To merge styles from another workbook, open both the workbook that contains the styles that you want to merge and the workbook into which you want to merge styles. From the workbook into which you want to merge styles, choose Home ⇨ Styles ⇨ Cell Styles and choose Merge Styles. Excel displays the Merge Styles dialog box that shows a list of all open workbooks. Select the workbook that contains the styles you want to merge and click OK. Excel copies styles from the workbook that you selected into the active workbook.

TIP You may want to create a master workbook that contains all your custom styles so that you always know which workbook to merge styles from.

Controlling styles with templates

When you start Excel, it loads with several default settings, including the settings for stylistic formatting. If you spend a lot of time changing the default elements, you should know about templates.

Here's an example. You may prefer to use 10-point Calibri rather than 11-point Calibri as the default font. And maybe you prefer Wrap Text to be the default setting for alignment. Templates provide an easy way to change defaults.

The trick is to create a workbook with the Normal style modified to the way that you want it. Then, save the workbook as a template in your XLStart folder. After doing so, you choose Office ➪ New to display a dialog box from which you can choose the template for the new workbook. Template files also can store other named styles, providing you with an excellent way to give your workbooks a consistent look.

CROSS-REF Chapter 9 discusses templates in detail.

Understanding Document Themes

In an effort to help users create more professional-looking documents, the Office 2007 designers incorporated a concept known as *document themes*. Using themes is an easy (and almost foolproof) way to specify the colors, fonts, and a variety of graphic effects in a document. And best of all, changing the entire look of your document is a breeze. A few mouse clicks is all it takes to apply a different theme and change the look of your workbook.

Importantly, the concept of themes is incorporated into other Office 2007 apps. Therefore, a company can easily create a standard look and feel for all its documents.

NOTE Themes don't override specific formatting that you apply. For example, assume that you apply the Accent 1 named style to a range. Then you use the Fill Color control to change the background color of that range. If you change to a different theme, the manually applied fill color will not be modified. Bottom line? If you plan to take advantage of themes, stick with default formatting choices.

Figure 7.13 shows a worksheet that contains a SmartArt diagram, a table, a chart, and range formatted using the Heading 1 named style. These items all use the default formatting, which is known as Office Theme.

FIGURE 7.13

The elements in this worksheet use default formatting.

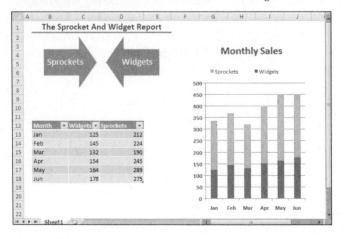

Figure 7.14 shows the same worksheet after applying a different document theme. The different theme changed the fonts, colors (which may not be apparent in the figure), and the graphic effects for the SmartArt diagram.

ON the CD-ROM If you'd like to experiment with using various themes, the workbook shown in Figure 7.14 and 7.15 is available on the companion CD-ROM. The file is named **theme examples.xlsx**.

FIGURE 7.14

The worksheet, after applying a different theme.

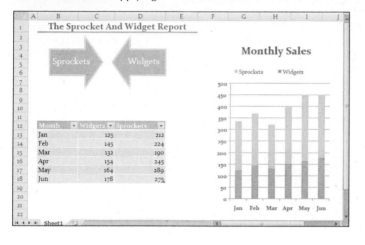

Applying a theme

Figure 7.15 shows the theme choices that appear when you choose Page ➪ Layout ➪ Themes. This display is a live preview. As you move your mouse over the theme choices, the active worksheet displays the theme. When you see a theme you like, click it to apply the theme to all worksheets in the workbook.

NOTE A theme applies to the entire workbook. It's not possible to use different themes on different worksheets within a workbook.

Excel's built-in theme choices.

When you specify a particular theme, the gallery choices for various elements reflect the new theme. For example, the chart styles that you can choose from vary, depending on which theme is active.

Because themes use different fonts and font sizes, changing to a different theme may affect the layout of your worksheet. For example, after applying a new theme, a worksheet that printed on a single page may spill over to a second page. Therefore, you may need to make some adjustments after you apply a new theme.

Customizing a theme

Notice that the Page Layout ➪ Themes group contains three other controls: Colors, Fonts, and Effects. You can use these controls to change just one of the three components of a theme. For example, if you like the Urban theme, but would prefer different fonts, apply the Urban theme and then specify your preferred font set by using the Page Layout ➪ Themes ➪ Font control.

Each theme uses two fonts (one for headers, and one for the body), and in some cases, these two fonts are the same. If none of the theme choices is suitable, choose Page Layout ➪ Themes ➪ Font ➪ Create New Theme Fonts to specify the two fonts you prefer (see Figure 7.16).

FIGURE 7.16

Use this dialog box to specify two fonts for a theme.

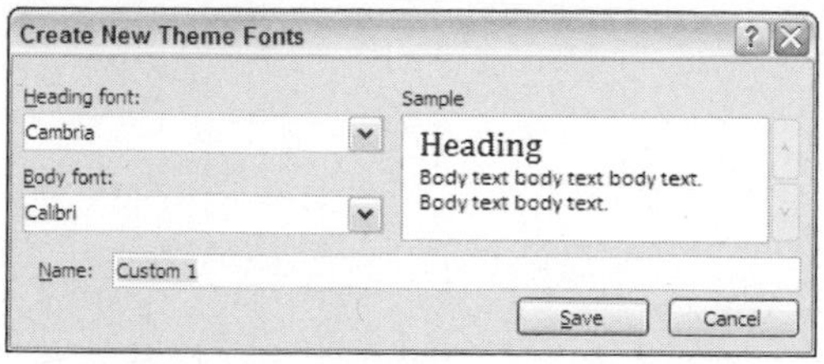

TIP When you use the Home ⇨ Fonts ⇨ Font control, the two fonts from the current theme are listed first in the drop-down list.

Use the Page Layout ⇨ Themes ⇨ Colors control to select a different set of colors. And, if you're so inclined, you can even create a custom set of colors by choosing Page Layout ⇨ Themes ⇨ Colors ⇨ Create Theme Colors. This command displays the dialog box shown in Figure 7.17. Note that each theme consists of 12 colors. Four of the colors are for text and backgrounds, six are for accents, and two are for hyperlinks. As you specify different colors, the preview panel in the dialog box updates.

NOTE Theme effects operate on graphic elements, such as SmartArt, Shapes, and charts. You can't customize theme effects.

If you've customized a theme using different fonts or colors, you can save the new theme by choosing Page Layout ⇨ Themes ⇨ Save Current Theme. Your customized themes appear in the theme list in the Custom category. Other Office 2007 applications, such as Word and PowerPoint, can use these theme files.

FIGURE 7.17

If you're feeling creative, you can specify a set of custom colors for a theme.

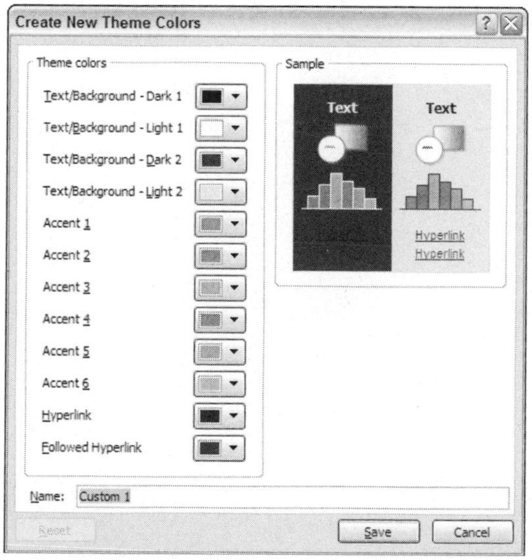

Chapter 8

Understanding Excel's Files

Excel, of course, uses files to store its workbooks. This chapter discusses how Excel uses files and provides an overview of the various types of files.

It also discusses the new Excel 2007 file formats and describes how to determine what (if anything) will be lost if you save your workbook in an earlier file format.

Excel File Operations

This section describes the operations that you perform with workbook files: opening, saving, closing, deleting, and so on.

As you read through this section, remember that you can have any number of workbooks open simultaneously, and that only one workbook is the active workbook at any given time. The workbook's name appears in its title bar (or in the Excel title bar if the workbook is maximized).

Creating a new workbook

When you start Excel normally, it automatically creates a new (empty) workbook called Book1. This workbook exists only in memory and has not been saved to disk. By default, this workbook consists of three worksheets named Sheet1, Sheet2, and Sheet3. If you're starting a new project from scratch, you can use this blank workbook.

IN THIS CHAPTER

Creating a new workbook

Opening an existing workbook

Saving and closing workbooks

Sharing workbooks with those who use an older version of Excel

Excel provides two ways to create a new workbook:

- Choose Office ➪ New (which opens the New Workbook dialog box (see Figure 8.1). This dialog box lets you create a blank workbook, a workbook based on a template, or a workbook based on an existing workbook. To create a new blank workbook, select Blank Workbook and click Create.

- Press the Ctrl+N shortcut key combination. This method is the fastest way to start a new workbook because it bypasses the New Workbook dialog box.

FIGURE 8.1

The New Workbook dialog box enables you to create a new workbook.

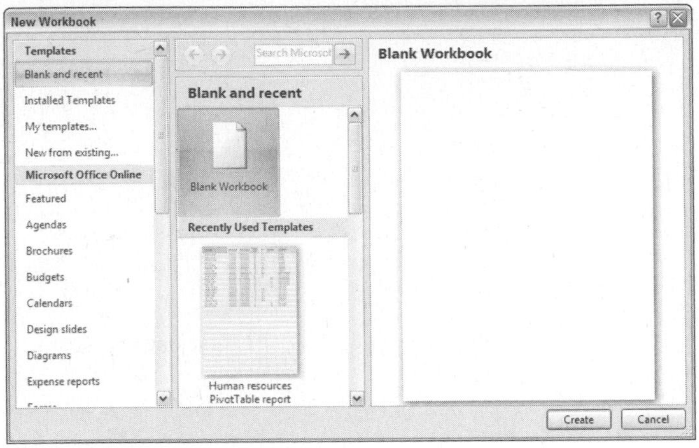

CROSS-REF Refer to Chapter 9 for more information about using and creating templates.

Opening an existing workbook

Following are some of the ways to open a workbook saved on your hard drive:

- Click the Office button and select the file you want from the Recent Documents list. Only the most recently used files are listed. You can specify the number of files to display (maximum of 50) in Advanced section of the Excel Options dialog box.

- Locate the Excel workbook file using a Windows Explorer file list. Just double-click the filename (or icon), and the workbook opens in Excel. If Excel is not running, Windows automatically starts Excel and loads the workbook file.

- Choose Office ➪ Open to display the Open dialog box.

- Press the Ctrl+O shortcut key combination to display the Open dialog box.

The Open dialog box is shown in Figure 8.2. Note that this dialog box is resizable. To make it larger or smaller, click the lower-right corner and drag.

Starting Excel Without an Empty Workbook

If you prefer to avoid the empty workbook displayed when Excel starts up, you can do so by editing the command line that is used to start Excel. You need to create a new shortcut to excel.exe and then modify the properties:

1. **Use Windows Explorer and locate the excel.exe program. The default location is**

   ```
   C:\Program Files\Microsoft Office\OFFICE12\
   ```

2. **Press the right mouse button, drag the excel.exe filename to your desktop, and release the mouse button.** When you release the right mouse button, you'll see a shortcut menu.

3. **Choose Create Shortcut Here.** Windows creates a new shortcut icon on your desktop.

4. **Right-click the shortcut icon and choose Properties.**

5. **In the Properties dialog box, click the Shortcut tab.**

6. **Edit the Target field by adding a space, followed by /e, to the end.** For example:

   ```
   "C:\Program Files\Microsoft Office\OFFICE12\EXCEL.EXE" /e
   ```

7. **Specify a Shortcut Key, if desired. If you provide a shortcut key, you can use that keystroke combination to start or active Excel.**

8. **Click OK.**

After making that change, Excel doesn't display an empty workbook when you start it by clicking that shortcut icon. In addition, you won't see the normal "splash" screen.

FIGURE 8.2

Use the Open dialog box to open any of your Excel workbook files.

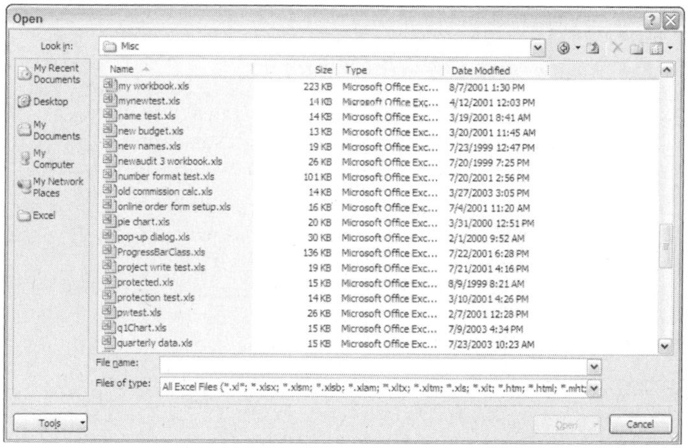

To open a workbook from the Open dialog box, you must provide two pieces of information: the name of the workbook file (specified in the File Name field) and its folder (specified in the Look In field).

Once you've located and selected the file, click Open, and the file opens. You also can just double-click the filename to open it.

Notice that the Open button is actually a drop-down list. Click the arrow, and you see the additional options:

- **Open:** Opens the file normally.
- **Open Read-Only:** Opens the selected file in read-only mode. When a file is opened in this mode, you can't save changes to the original filename.
- **Open as Copy:** Opens a copy of the selected file. If the file is named `budget.xlsx`, the workbook that opens is named `Copy(1)budget.xlsx`
- **Open in Browser:** Opens the file in your default Web browser. If the file can't be opened in a browser, this option is grayed out.
- **Open and Repair:** Attempts to open a file that may be damaged and recover information contained in it.

> **TIP** You can hold down the Ctrl key and select multiple workbooks. When you click Open, all the selected workbook files open.

Right-clicking a filename in the Open dialog box displays a shortcut menu with many extra Windows commands. For example, you can copy the file, delete it, rename it, modify its properties, and so on.

Selecting a different location

The Look In field at the top of the Open dialog box is actually a drop-down list. Click the arrow, and the box expands to show your folders. You can select a different drive or directory from this list.

To move up one level in the folder hierarchy, click the Up One Level (Alt+2) icon to the right of the Look In box.

Using the My Places bar

The left side of the Open dialog box is known as the My Places bar, and it contains a list of shortcuts to folders. To add a new folder to the My Places bar, activate the folder in the Open dialog box, then right-click the My Places bar, and click the Add option. It's a good idea to customize the My Places bar by adding shortcuts to folders that you use frequently.

Right-click any of the My Places items, and you'll have some additional options that enable you to rearrange the items, rename them, delete them, or change the icon size.

Filtering filenames

At the bottom of the Open dialog box is a drop-down list labeled Files Of Type. When the Open dialog box is displayed, it shows All Excel Files (and a long list of file extensions). The Open dialog box displays only the files that match the extensions. In other words, you see only standard Excel files.

If you want to open a file of a different type, click the arrow in the drop-down list and select the file type that you want to open. This changes the filtering and displays only files of the type that you specify.

You can also type a filter directly in the File Name box. For example, typing the following will display only files that have an XLSX extension (press Tab after typing the filter): ***.xlsx**

Choosing your file display preferences

The Open dialog box can display your workbook filenames in several different styles. You control the style by clicking the Views icon and then selecting from the drop-down list (see Figure 8.3). The style that you choose is entirely up to you.

FIGURE 8.3

Use the Views icon to specify how you'd like the filenames displayed.

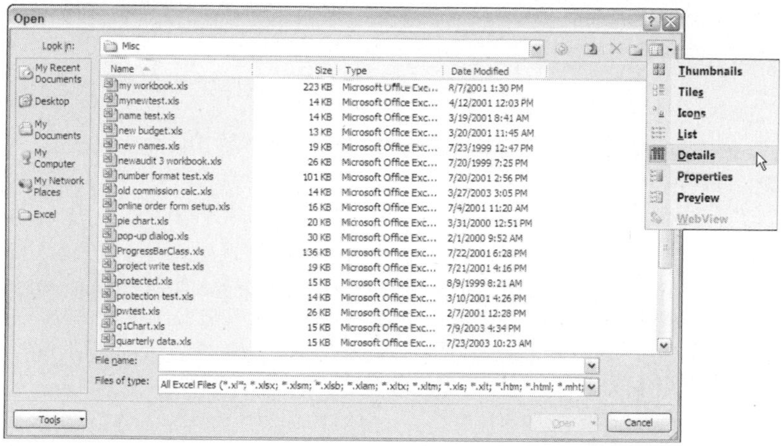

TIP When you click the Office button, each file in the recent file list displays a pushpin icon. If you click the icon, that file is "pinned" to the list and will always appear. This handy feature ensures that commonly used files always appear on the recent file list — even if you haven't opened the file recently.

Opening Workbooks Automatically

Many people work on the same workbooks each day. If this describes you, you'll be happy to know that you can have Excel open specific workbook files automatically whenever you start Excel.

The XLStart folder is located within your Excel document folder. For example, the path may be

`C:\Documents and Settings\<username>\Application Data\Microsoft\Excel\XLStart`

Another XLStart folder may be located here:

`C:\Program Files\Microsoft Office\Office12\XLStart`

Any workbook files (excluding template files) stored in either of these XLStart folders open automatically when Excel starts. If one or more files open automatically from an XLStart folder, Excel won't start up with a blank workbook.

You can specify an alternate startup folder in addition to the XLStart folder. Choose Office ➪ Excel Options and select the Advanced tab. Scroll down to the General section and enter a new folder name in the field labeled At Startup, Open All Files In. After you do that, when you start Excel, it automatically opens all workbook files in both the XLStart folders and the alternate folder that you specified.

Saving a Workbook

When you're working on a workbook, it's vulnerable to day-ruining events, such as power failures and system crashes. Therefore, you should save your work often. Saving a file takes only a few seconds, but re-creating hours of lost work takes many hours.

Excel provides four ways to save your workbook:

- Choose Office ⇨ Save.
- Click the Save icon on the Quick Access Toolbar.
- Press the Ctrl+S shortcut key combination.
- Press the Shift+F12 shortcut key combination.

If your workbook has already been saved, it's saved again using the same filename.

CAUTION   Remember that saving a file overwrites the previous version of the file on your hard drive. If you open a workbook and then completely mess it up, don't save the file! Instead, close the workbook without saving it and then reopen the good copy on your hard drive.

If you want to save the workbook to a new file, choose Office ⇨ Save As (or press F12).

If your workbook has never been saved, its title bar displays a default name, such as Book1 or Book2. Although Excel allows you to use these generic workbook names for filenames, you'll be better off using more descriptive filenames. Therefore, the first time that you save a new workbook, Excel displays the Save As dialog box to let you provide a more meaningful name.

The Save As dialog box is similar to the Open dialog box. Again, you need to specify two pieces of information: the workbook's name and the folder in which to store it. If you want to save the file to a different folder, select the desired folder in the Save In field. If you want to create a new folder, click the Create New Folder icon in the Save As dialog box. The new folder is created within the folder that's displayed in the Save In field.

After you select the folder, enter the filename in the File Name field. You don't need to specify a file extension — Excel adds it automatically, based on the file type specified in the Save As Type field. By default, files are saved in the standard Excel file format, which uses an `.xlst` file extension.

TIP   To change the default file format for saving files, access the Excel Options dialog box. Click the Save tab and change the setting for the Save Files In This Format option.

If a file with the same name already exists in the folder that you specify, Excel asks whether you want to overwrite that file with the new file. Be careful: You can't recover the previous file after you overwrite it.

Using AutoRecover

The Excel AutoRecover feature automatically saves a backup copy of your work at a predetermined time interval. This feature can be a lifesaver if Excel crashes or you experience a power outage. You can turn this feature on and off and also specify the save time interval in the Save tab of the Excel Options dialog box. The default AutoRecover interval is 10 minutes.

Keep in mind that AutoRecover does not overwrite your actual file. Rather, it saves a *copy* of the file. Therefore, you should continue to save your work at frequent intervals, even if AutoRecover is turned on.

When you restart Excel after it crashes, you see a list of documents that were open at the time of the crash. You can then choose to open the original version or the AutoRecovered version.

Filenaming Rules

The Excel workbook files are subject to the same rules that apply to other Windows files. A filename can be up to 255 characters, including spaces. This length enables you to give meaningful names to your files. You can't, however, use any of the following characters in your filenames:

\ (backslash)

? (question mark)

: (colon)

* (asterisk)

" (quote)

< (less than)

> (greater than)

| (vertical bar)

You can use uppercase and lowercase letters in your names to improve readability. The filenames aren't case sensitive — My 2007 Budget.xlsx and MY 2007 BUDGET.xlsx are equivalent names.

Specifying a password

In some cases, you may want to specify a password for your workbook. When a user attempts to open a password-protected workbook, a password must be entered before the file is opened.

For some reason, it seems that Microsoft wants to keep the password-protection feature a secret. Password-protecting a workbook isn't at all obvious. Here's how to do it.

1. Choose Office ➪ Save As to display the Save As dialog box.
2. In the Save As dialog box, click the drop-down button labeled Tools
3. In the Tools drop-down list, select General Options to display the General Options dialog box, shown in Figure 8.4.
4. Type the password to open and click OK. You're asked to re-enter the password.
5. When you return to the Save As dialog box, click the Save button to save the file.

> **CAUTION** Passwords can be up to 15 characters long and are case sensitive. Be careful with this option because it is impossible to open the workbook (using normal methods) if you forget the password. Also, remember that Excel passwords can be cracked, so it's not a perfect security measure.

> **CROSS-REF** For additional security, you may prefer to encrypt your workbook. See "Encrypting a document," later in this chapter.

The General Options dialog box has a few other features.

- **Always Create Backup:** If this option is checked, the existing version of the workbook is renamed before the workbook is saved. The new filename will be named "Backup of xxx.xlk," where xxx represents the original filename. Creating a backup enables you to go back to the previously saved version of your workbook.

- **Password To Modify:** This option enables you to specify a password that will be required before changes to the workbook can be saved under the same filename. Use this option if you want to make sure that changes aren't made to the original version of the workbook.

■ **Read-Only Recommended:** If this option is checked, Excel presents a dialog box suggesting that the file be opened as read-only. This is just a gentle suggestion. The person opening the file can override this suggestion if he or she likes.

This difficult-to-find dialog box is where you specify a password for your workbook.

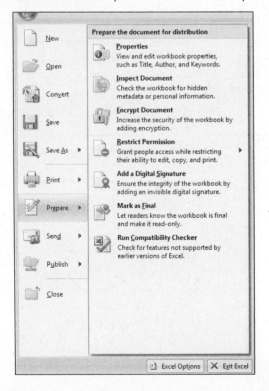

Other workbook options

Choose Office ➪ Prepare, and you'll find still more file-related options, as shown in Figure 8.5. These options, described in the following sections, may be useful if you plan to distribute your workbook to others.

Choose Office ➪ Prepare for some additional options.

Setting workbook properties

The Office ➪ Prepare ➪ Properties command adds a new panel directly below the Ribbon. As you can see in Figure 8.6, Excel is able to store some additional "metadata" about the file. This information includes such items as the author, title, subject, and so on.

Use the Properties panel to store additional information about your workbook.

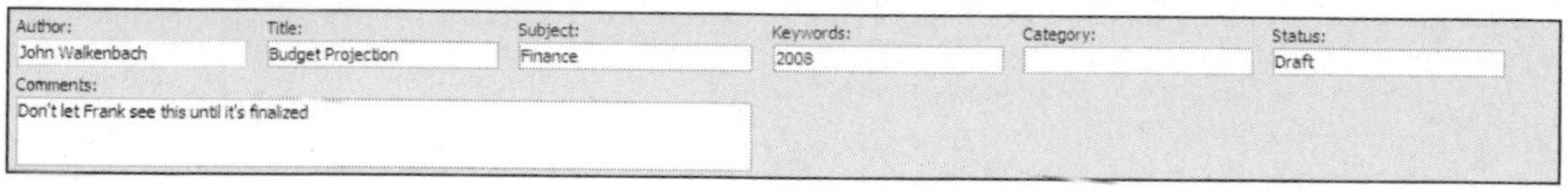

This file information can be useful if you remember to enter the data. For example, when you use the Open dialog box, you can specify Properties as your Views option. Then, the dialog box displays the metadata when you select a file (see Figure 8.7).

If you click the drop-down in the Properties title bar, you can choose Advanced, which displays the Properties dialog box. This dialog box has five tabs:

- **General:** Displays general information about the file — its name, size, location, date created, and so on. You can't change any of the information in this panel.

- **Summary:** Contains nine fields of information that you can enter and modify. Some of these fields are the same as those in the Properties panel.

- **Statistics:** Shows additional information about the file and can't be changed.

- **Contents:** Displays the names of the sheets in the workbook, as well as the named ranges.

- **Custom:** This tab enables you to store, in a sort of database, a variety of information about the file. For example, if the workbook deals with a client named Smith and Jones Corp., you can keep track of this bit of information and use it to help locate the file later.

FIGURE 8.7

You can view workbook properties in the Open dialog box.

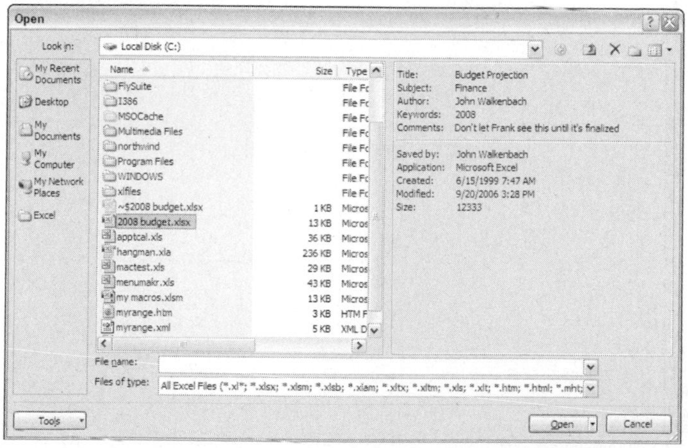

Inspecting a document

The Office ➪ Prepare ➪ Inspect Document command displays the Document Inspector dialog box. This feature can alert you to some potentially private information that may be contained in your workbook — perhaps information that's contained in hidden rows or columns or hidden worksheets.

If you plan on making a workbook available to a large audience, it's an excellent idea to use the Document Inspector for a final check.

Encrypting a document

Earlier in this chapter, in "Specifying a password," I described how to set a password for a workbook. To provide a higher level of security, you may prefer to encrypt your workbook using Office ➪ Prepare ➪ Encrypt Document. When you choose this command, you'll be prompted for a password, which you must enter twice.

Restricting permissions

Excel supports *Information Rights Management (IRM)*, which allows you to restrict access to workbooks in order to prevent sensitive information from being printed, forwarded, or copied.

This feature, accessed by using Office ➪ Prepare ➪ Restrict Permission, is fairly complex and requires additional software. Consult the Help system for additional details.

Adding a digital signature

The Office ➪ Prepare ➪ Add A Digital Signature command allows you to "sign" a workbook.

CROSS-REF   Refer to Chapter 31 for more information about digital signatures.

Marking a document final

Choose Office ➪ Prepare ➪ Mark As Final to mark a workbook as finalized. A finalized document is marked read-only, and you can't edit or modify it. When you open a finalized document, the status bar displays an additional icon, and all editing command are disabled.

Checking compatibility

When you save a workbook using an older file format, Excel displays its very helpful Compatibility Checker dialog box, shown in Figure 8.8. You can also display this dialog box at any time by choosing Office ➪ Prepare ➪ Run Compatibility Checker.

It's important to understand the limitations regarding version compatibility. Even though your colleague is able to open your file, there is no guarantee that everything will function correctly or look the same. You can't expect features that are new to Excel 2007 to work in earlier versions. For example, you'll find that a SmartArt diagram is converted to a picture, table formatting is lost, and charts may look different. In addition, formulas that use any of the new worksheet functions will return an error.

The Compatibility Checker identifies the elements of your workbook that will result in loss of functionality or fidelity (cosmetics). To display the Compatibility Checker results in a more readable format, click Copy To New Sheet.

For more information about file compatibility, see "Excel File Compatibility," later in this chapter.

FIGURE 8.8

The Compatibility Checker dialog box informs you of potential incompatibilities.

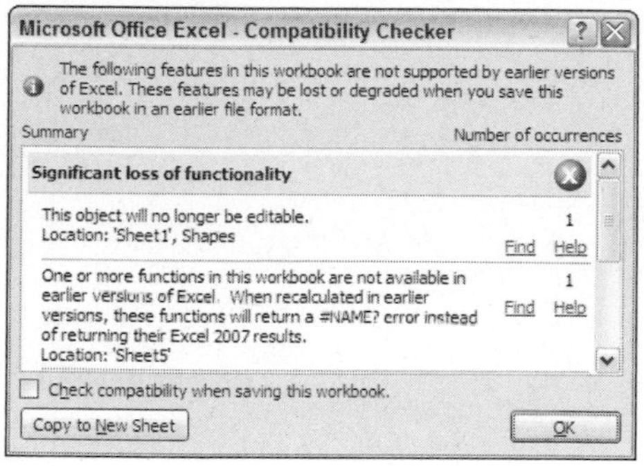

Closing workbooks

After you're finished with a workbook, you should close it to free the memory that it uses. You can close a workbook by using any of the following methods:

- Choose Office ➪ Close.
- Click the Close button (the X) in the workbook's title bar.
- Double-click the Excel icon on the left side of the workbook's title bar.
- Press the Ctrl+F4 shortcut key.
- Press the Ctrl+W shortcut key.

If you've made any changes to your workbook since it was last saved, Excel asks whether you want to save the changes to the workbook before closing it.

Safeguarding your work

Nothing is worse than spending hours creating a complicated Excel workbook only to have it destroyed by a power failure, a hard-drive crash, or even human error. Fortunately, protecting yourself from these disasters is not a difficult task.

Earlier in the chapter, I discussed the AutoRecover feature that makes Excel save a backup copy of your workbook at regular intervals (see "Using AutoRecover"). I also mentioned the Always Create Backup option in the General Options dialog box. These are good ideas, but they certainly aren't the only backup protection you should use. If a file is truly important, you need to take extra steps to ensure its safety. The following backup options help ensure the safety of individual files:

- **Keep a backup copy of the file on the same drive.** Essentially what happens when you select the Always Create A Backup option when you save a workbook file. Although this option offers some protection if you make a mess of the worksheet, it won't do you any good if the entire hard drive crashes.

- **Keep a backup copy on a different hard drive.** Assumes, of course, that your system has more than one hard drive. This option offers more protection than the preceding method, because the likelihood that both hard drives will fail is remote. If the entire system is destroyed or stolen, however, you're out of luck.

- **Keep a backup copy on a network server.** Assumes that your system is connected to a server on which you can write files. This method is fairly safe. If the network server is located in the same building, however, you're at risk if the entire building burns down or is otherwise destroyed.

- **Keep a backup copy on a removable medium.** The safest method. Using a removable medium, such as a CD-ROM, enables you to physically take the backup to another location. So, if your system (or the entire building) is damaged, your backup copy remains intact.

Excel File Compatibility

Perhaps one of the most confusing aspects of Excel is the nearly overwhelming number of files formats that it can read and write. With the introduction of Excel 2007, things got even more confusing because it has quite a few new files formats.

NOTE   Excel 2007 can open all files created with earlier versions of Excel.

Recognizing the Excel 2007 file formats

Excel's new file formats are

- XLSX: A workbook file that does not contain macros
- XLSM: A workbook file that contains macros
- XLTX: A workbook template file that does not contain macros
- XLTM: A workbook template file that contains macros
- XLSA: An add-in file
- XLSB: A binary file similar to the old XLS format but able to accommodate the new features
- XLSK: A backup file

With the exception of XLSB, these are all "open" XLM files, which means that other applications are able to read and write these types of files.

TIP   The XML files are actually zip-compressed text files. If you rename one of these files to have a ZIP extension, then you'll be able to examine the contents using any of several zip file utilities — including the zip file support built into Windows.

The Office 2007 Compatibility Pack

Normally, those who use an earlier version of Excel can't open workbooks saved in the new Excel 2007 file formats. But, fortunately, Microsoft has released a free Compatibility Pack for Office 2003 and Office XP.

If an Office 2003 or Office XP user installs the Compatibility Pack, they will be able to open files created in Office 2007 and also save files in Office 2007 format. The Office programs that are affected are Excel, Word, and PowerPoint.

To download the Compatibility Pak, search the Web for *Office 2007 Compatibility Pack.*

Saving a file for use with an older version of Excel

To save a file for use with an older version of Excel, choose Office ⇨ Save As and select one of the following from the Save As Type drop-down:

- **Excel 97-2003 Workbook (*.xls):** If the file will be used by someone who has Excel 97, Excel 2000, Excel 2002, or Excel 2003.

- **Microsoft Excel 5.0/95 Workbook (*.xls):** If the file will be used by someone who has Excel 5 or Excel 95.

NOTE   If the workbook will be used by someone who has installed the Office 2007 Compatibility Pack, you don't need to save it using an earlier file format (see "The Office 2007 Compatibility Pack" sidebar for details).

Using and Creating Templates

A *template* is essentially a model that serves as the basis for something else. An Excel template is a workbook that's used to create other workbooks. This chapter discusses some of the templates included with Excel and also describes how to create your own template files. Creating a template takes some time, but in the long run, doing so may save you a lot of work.

IN THIS CHAPTER

Understanding Excel's templates

Working with the default templates

Creating custom templates

Exploring Excel Templates

The best way to become familiar with Excel template files is to jump in and try a few. Most versions of Excel include template files, but Excel 2007 gives you quick access to hundreds of such files.

Viewing templates

To explore the Excel templates, choose Office ➪ New to display the New Workbook dialog box. The templates listed in the New Workbook dialog box are in three categories:

- Those installed on your hard drive (Template Categories ➪ Installed Templates)
- Those that you can download from Microsoft Office Online
- Those that you've created (Template Categories ➪ Featuring ➪ My Templates)

In addition, the right side of the dialog box displays a list of templates that you've used recently.

The Microsoft Office Online section contains a number of categories, and some categories have subcategories. Click a category (or subcategory), and you'll see the available templates. Use the View button to change how the templates are displayed (either thumbnails or details). Either view shows a preview of them template in the right panel. Figure 9.1 shows templates available in the Invoices category.

FIGURE 9.1

FIGURE 9.1

Templates that you can use for invoices.

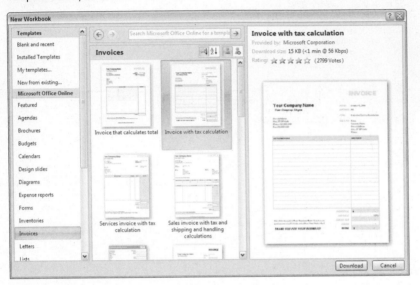

NOTE Microsoft Office Online has a wide variety of templates, and some are better than others. If you download a few duds, don't give up. Even though a template may not be perfect, you can often modify a template to meet your needs. Modifying an existing template is often easier than creating a workbook from scratch.

Creating a workbook from a template

To create a workbook based on a template, just select the template and click Download. Depending on the size of the file and the speed of your Internet connection, it can take anywhere from a few seconds to a minute or more. What you do next depends on the template. Every template is different, but most are self-explanatory. Some workbooks require customization. Just replace the generic information with your own information.

Figure 9.2 shows a workbook that's based on an invoice template.

NOTE It's important to understand that you're not working with the template file. Rather, you're working with a workbook that was created from the template file. If you make any changes, you're not changing the template — you're changing the workbook that's based on the template. After you download a template from Microsoft Office Online, that template is available in the My Templates category in the New Workbook dialog box, so you don't need to redownload it if you want to re-use the template.

This particular workbook has a few simple formulas that perform calculations using the data that you enter. Figure 9.3 shows the workbook after you enter data. Notice that formulas calculate the subtotal, sales tax, and total.

FIGURE 9.2

A workbook created from an invoice template downloaded from Microsoft Office Online.

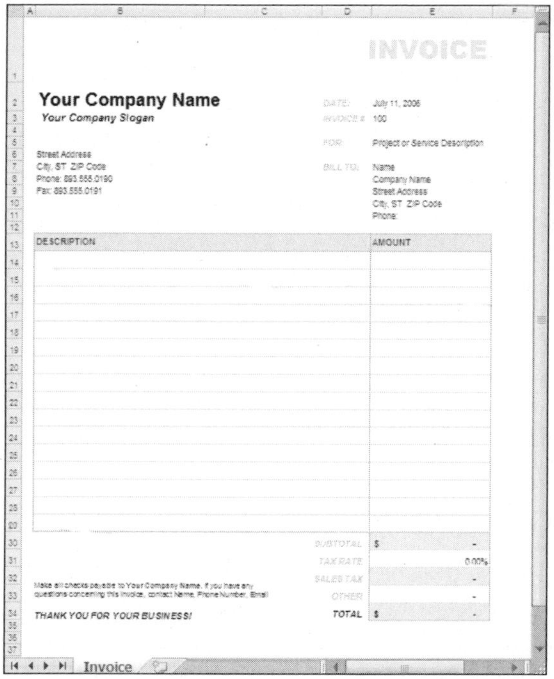

If you want to save the workbook, click the Save button. Excel proposes a named based on the template's name, but you can use any name you like.

FIGURE 9.3

The workbook, after entering some information.

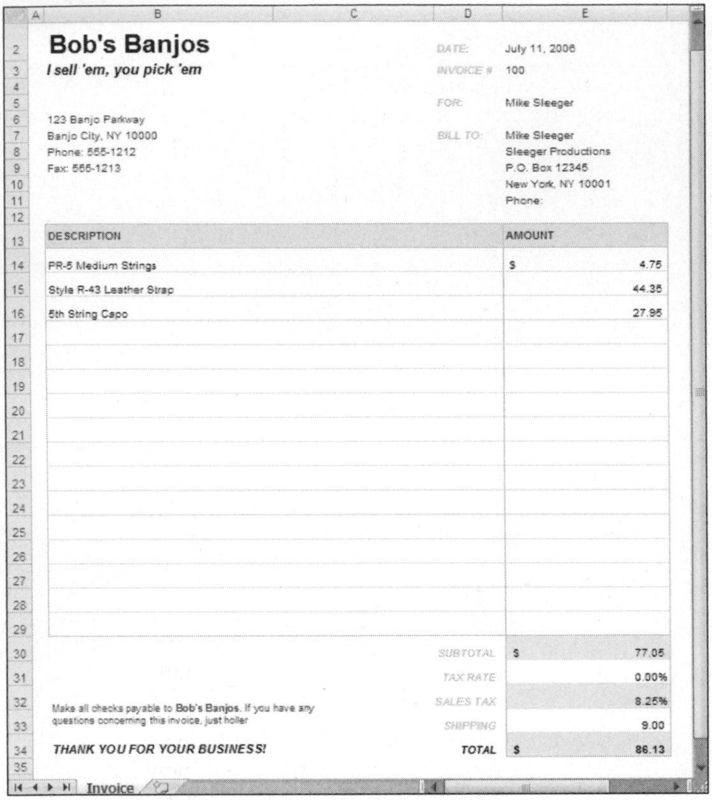

Modifying a template

A template file is just like a workbook file. As such, you can open a template file, make changes to it, and then resave the template file. To open a template, choose Office ➪ Open (not File ➪ New) and locate the template file (it will probably have an XLTX or XLT extension). Template files, by default, are stored in:

```
C:\Documents and Settings\<user name>\Application Data\Microsoft\
Templates
```

When you open a XLST (or *.XLT) template file, you are opening the actual file — you are *not* creating a workbook from the template file.

Looking at the invoice template shown earlier in this chapter, you may want to modify it so that it shows your company information and uses your actual sales tax rate. Then, when you use that template in the future, the workbook created from it will already be customized.

To create a workbook from a modified template, you must select the template from the My Templates section in the New Workbook dialog box. Clicking My Templates displays the New dialog box shown in Figure 9.4. Just select the template and click OK.

The New dialog box displays downloaded templates stored on your hard drive.

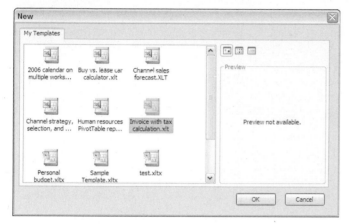

Understanding Custom Excel Templates

So far, this chapter has focused on templates that were created by others. The remainder of the chapter deals with *custom templates* — templates that you create.

Why create custom templates? The main reason is to make your job easier. For example, you may always like to use a particular header or footer on your printouts. Consequently, the first time that you print a worksheet, you need to spend time entering the header and footer information. Although it isn't a lot of work, wouldn't it be easier if Excel simply remembered your favorite page settings and used them automatically?

The solution is to modify the template that Excel uses to create new workbooks. In this case, you modify the template file by inserting your header into the template. Save the template file using a special name, and then every new workbook that you create has your customized page settings.

Excel supports three types of templates, which I discuss in the following sections:

- **The default workbook template:** Used as the basis for new workbooks.
- **The default worksheet template:** Used as the basis for new worksheets inserted into a workbook.
- **Custom workbook templates:** Usually, these ready-to-run workbooks include formulas, but they can be as simple or as complex as you like. Typically, these templates are set up so that a user can simply plug in values and get immediate results. The Microsoft Office Online templates (discussed earlier in this chapter) are examples of this type of template.

Working with the default templates

The term *default template* may be a little misleading. If you haven't created your own template files to control the default settings, Excel uses its own internal settings — not an actual template file. In other words, Excel uses your template files to set the defaults for new workbooks or worksheets, if these files exist. But if you haven't created these files, Excel is perfectly happy to use its own settings.

Using the workbook template to change workbook defaults

Every new workbook that you create starts out with some default settings. For example, the workbook has three worksheets, the worksheets have gridlines, text appears in the fonts specified by the default document template. columns are 8.43 units wide, and so on. If you're not happy with any of the default workbook settings, you can change them.

Making changes to Excel's default workbook is fairly easy to do, and it can save you lots of time in the long run. Here's how you change Excel's workbook defaults:

1. **Open a new workbook.**

2. **Add or delete sheets to give the workbook the number of worksheets that you want.**

3. **Make any other changes that you want to make, which can include column widths, named styles, page setup options, and many of the settings that are available in the Excel Options dialog box.** To change the default formatting for cells, choose Home ➪ Styles ➪ Cell Styles and then modify the settings for the Normal style. For example, you can change the default font, size, or number format.

4. **When your workbook is set up to your liking, choose Office ➪ Save As.**

5. **In the Save As dialog box, select Template (*.xltx) from the box labeled Save As Type.** If your template contains any VBA macros, select Excel Macro-Enabled Template (*.xltm).

6. **Enter book for the filename.**

> **CAUTION**   Excel will offer a name such as Book1.xltx. **You must change this name to** book.xltx **(or** book.xltm**) if you want Excel to use your template to set the workbook defaults.**

7. **Save the file in your \XLStart folder (not in your \Templates folder).**

> **TIP**   The \XLStart folder may be located in either of these directories:
> ```
> C:\Documents and Settings\<username>\Application Data\
> Microsoft\Excel\XLStart
> C:\Program Files\Microsoft Office\Office12\XLStart
> ```

8. **Close the file.**

After you perform the preceding steps, the new default workbook is based on the book.xltx (or book.xltm) workbook template. You can create a workbook based on your template by using any of these methods:

- Press Ctrl+N.
- Open Excel without first selecting a workbook to open.
- Choose Office ➪ New and choose Blank Workbook.

> **CAUTION**   If you insert a new worksheet into a workbook that's based on the book.xlxt template, the new worksheet will *not* use the customized settings specified in the template. Therefore, you may also want to create a *sheet.xltx* template (described in the next section), which controls the settings for new worksheets.

If you ever want to revert to the standard default workbook, just delete the **book.xltx** file.

Using the worksheet template to change worksheet defaults

When you insert a new worksheet into a workbook, Excel uses its built-in worksheet defaults for the worksheet. These default settings include items such as column width, row height, and so on.

If you don't like the default settings for a new worksheet, you can change them by following these steps:

1. **Start with a new workbook and delete all the sheets except one.**
2. **Make any changes that you want to make, which can include column widths, named styles, page setup options, and many of the settings that are available in the Excel Options dialog box.**
3. **When your workbook is set up to your liking, choose Office ⇨ Save As.**
4. **In the Save As dialog box, select Template (*.xltx) from the Save As Type box.**
5. **Enter** sheet.xltx **for the filename.**
6. **Save the file in your \XLStart folder (not in your \Templates folder).**
7. **Close the file.**
8. **Close and restart Excel.**

After performing these steps, all new worksheets that you insert by using any of these methods will be formatted like your `sheet.xltx` template:

- Clicking the Insert Worksheet button (next the last sheet tab)
- Choosing Home ⇨ Cells ⇨ Insert ⇨ Insert Sheet
- Pressing Shift+F11
- Right-clicking a sheet tab, choosing Insert from the shortcut menu, and choosing the Worksheet icon in the Insert dialog box.

Editing your templates

After you create your `book.xltx` or `sheet.xltx` templates, you may discover that you need to change them. You can open the template files and edit them just like any other workbook. After you make your changes, save the file, and close it.

Resetting the default workbook and worksheet settings

If you create a `book.xltx` or `sheet.xltx` file and then decide that you would rather use the standard default settings, simply delete the `book.xltx` or `sheet.xltx` template file — depending on whether you want to use the standard workbook or worksheet defaults — from the XLStart folder. Excel then uses its built-in default settings for new workbooks or worksheets.

TIP You can also rename or move the template files if you'd like to keep them for future use.

Creating custom templates

The `book.xltx` and `sheet.xltx` templates discussed in the preceding section are two special types of templates that determine default settings for new workbooks and new worksheets. This section discusses other types of templates, referred to as *workbook templates,* which are simply workbooks that you set up as the basis for new workbooks or worksheets.

Creating a workbook template can eliminate repeating work. Assume that you create a monthly sales report that consists of your company's sales by region, plus several summary calculations and charts. You can create a template file that consists of everything except the input values. Then, when it's time to create your report, you can open a workbook based on the template, fill in the blanks, and be finished.

> **NOTE**   You could, of course, just use the previous month's workbook and save it with a different name. This is prone to errors, however, because you easily can forget to use the Save As command and accidentally overwrite the previous month's file. Another option is to use the New From Existing option in the New Workbook dialog box. This command creates a new workbook from an existing one, but gives a different name to ensure that the old file is not overwritten.

When you create a workbook that's based on a template, the default workbook name is the template name with a number appended. For example, if you create a new workbook based on a template named `Sales Report.xltx`, the workbook's default name is `Sales Report1.xlsx`. The first time that you save a workbook that is created from a template, Excel displays its Save As dialog box so that you can give the template a new name if you want to.

A *custom template* is essentially a normal workbook, and it can use any Excel feature, such as charts, formulas, and macros. Usually, a template is set up so that the user can enter values and get immediate results. In other words, most templates include everything but the data, which is entered by the user.

> **NOTE**   If your template contains macros, it must be saved as an Excel Macro-Enabled Template, with an `XLTM` extension.

Saving your custom templates

To save a workbook as a template, choose Office ➪ Save As and select Template (*.xltx) from the drop-down list labeled Save As Type. If the workbook contains any VBA macros, select Excel Macro-Enabled

---

Locking Formula Cells in a Template File

If novices will use the template, you might consider locking all the formula cells to make sure that the formulas aren't deleted or modified.

1. **Press F5 to display the Go To dialog box.**
2. **Click the Special button to display the Go To Special dialog box.**
3. **Select Constants and click OK.** This step selects all of the nonformula cells.
4. **Right-click any one of the selected cells and choose Format Cells from the shortcut menu.** The Format Cells dialog box appears.
5. **In the Format Cells dialog box, click the Protection tab.**
6. **Remove the check mark from the Locked check box.**
7. **Click OK to close the Format Cells dialog box.**
8. **Choose Review ➪ Changes ➪ Protect Sheet to display the Protect Sheet dialog box.**
9. **Specify a password if you like and click OK.**

After you perform these steps, you can't modify the formula cells — unless the sheet is unprotected.

Template (*.xltm). Save the template in your Templates folder — which Excel automatically suggests — or a folder within that Templates folder.

If you later discover that you want to modify the template, choose Office ⇨ Open to open and edit the template.

Ideas for creating templates

This section provides a few ideas that may spark your imagination for creating templates. The following is a partial list of the settings that you can adjust and use in your custom templates:

- **Multiple formatted worksheets:** You can, for example, create a workbook template that has two worksheets — one formatted to print in landscape mode and one formatted to print in portrait mode.

- **Style:** The best approach is to choose Home ⇨ Styles ⇨ Cell Styles and modify the attributes of the Normal style. For example, you can change the font or size, the alignment, and so on.

- **Custom number formats:** If you create number formats that you use frequently, you can store them in a template.

- **Column widths and row heights:** You may prefer that columns be wider or narrower, or you may want the rows to be taller.

- **Print settings:** Change these settings in the Page Layout tab. You can adjust the page orientation, paper size, margins, and several other attributes.

- **Header and footer:** Use Page Layout View, and enter a custom header or footer.

- **Sheet settings:** These options are in the View ⇨ Show/Hide group. They include gridlines, automatic page break display, and row and column headings.

You can, of course, also create complete workbooks and save them as templates. For example, if you frequently need to produce a specific report, you may want to create a template that has everything for the report except for the data you need to enter. By saving your master copy as a template, you're less likely to overwrite the original file when you save the file after entering your data.

Chapter 10

Printing Your Work

espite predications of the "paperless office," reports printed on paper remain commonplace, and they will be around for a long time. Many of the worksheets that you develop with Excel can easily serve as printed reports. You'll find that printing from Excel is quite easy and that you can generate attractive, well-formatted reports with minimal effort. In addition, Excel has many options that provide you with a great deal of control over the printed page so that you can make your printed reports even better. These options are explained in this chapter.

IN THIS CHAPTER

One-click printing

Changing your worksheet view

Adjusting your print settings for better results

Preventing some cells from being printed

Using Custom Views

Printing with One Click

If you simply want to print a copy of a worksheet with no fuss and bother, use Excel's Quick Print option. One way to access this command is to choose Office ➪ Print ➪ Quick Print. But if you like the idea of one-click printing, take a few seconds to add a new button to your Quick Access Toolbar (QAT):

1. **Click the downward-point arrow to the right of the QAT, which displays a menu.**
2. **Choose Quick Print from the menu.** Excel adds the Quick Print icon to your QAT.

Clicking the Quick Print button prints the current worksheet on the currently selected printer, using the default print settings. If you've changed any of the default print settings, Excel uses the new settings; otherwise, it uses the following default settings:

- Prints the active worksheet (or all selected worksheets), including any embedded charts or objects.
- Prints one copy.
- Prints the entire worksheet.

- Prints in portrait mode.

- Doesn't scale the printed output.

- Uses letter-size paper with .75-inch margins for the top and bottom and .70-inch margins for the left and right margins (for the U.S. version).

- Prints with no headers or footers.

- Doesn't print cell comments.

- Print with no cell gridlines.

- For wide worksheets that span multiple pages, prints down and then over.

NOTE   When you print a worksheet, Excel prints only the active area of the worksheet. In other words, it won't print all 17 billion cells—just those that have data in them. If the worksheet contains any embedded charts or other graphic objects (such as SmartArt or Shapes), they're also printed.

TIP   To quickly determine the active area of the worksheet, press Ctrl+End to move to the last active cell in the worksheet. The active area is between cell A1 and the last active cell. You may notice that Ctrl+End isn't always accurate. For example, if you've deleted some rows, Ctrl+End will take you to the last row that you deleted. However, when the sheet is printed, the active area is reset, so the empty rows are not printed.

Using Print Preview

Excel's Print Preview feature displays a worksheet exactly as it will be printed. To use Print Preview, choose File ⇨ Print ⇨ Print Preview. Excel displays the first page of your printed output. To view subsequent pages, choose Print Preview ⇨ Preview ⇨ Next Page (or, use the vertical scrollbar).

For easier access to Print Preview add a button to your Quick Access Toolbar (QAT) :

1. **Click the downward-point arrow to the right of the QAT, which displays a menu.**

2. **Choose Print Preview from the menu.** Excel adds the Quick Print icon to your QAT.

The Ribbon displayed in the Print Preview window has a few other commands that you can use while previewing your output. For example, choose Print Preview ⇨ Preview ⇨ Show Margins to display margins. Excel adds markers to the preview that indicate column borders and margins. You can drag the column or margin markers to make changes that appear on-screen.

Print Preview is certainly useful, but you may prefer to use the new Page Layout View introduced in Excel 2007. to preview your output (see "Changing Your Page View"). The Print Preview feature remains, but it probably won't get much usage.

Changing Your Page View

One of the slickest new features in Excel 2007 is Page Layout View, which shows your worksheet divided up into pages. In other words, you're able to visualize your printed output as you work.

Page Layout View is one of three worksheet views, which are controlled by the three icons in the right side of the status bar. These views are also available in the View ➪ Workbook Views group of the Ribbon. The three view options are

- **Normal View:** The default view of the worksheet. This view may or may not show page breaks.
- **Page Layout View:** A view that shows individual pages.
- **Page Break Preview:** A view that lets you manually adjust the page breaks.

Just click one of the icons to change the view. You can also use the Zoom slider to change the magnification from 10% (a very tiny bird's eye view) to 400% (very large, for showing fine detail).

The following sections describe how these views can help with printing.

Normal View

Most of the time when you work in Excel, you'll use Normal View. Normal View displays page breaks in the worksheet. The page breaks are indicated by horizontal and vertical dotted lines. These page break lines adjust automatically if you change the page orientation, add or delete rows or columns, change row heights, change column widths, and so on. For example, if you find that your printed output is too wide to fit on a single page, you can adjust the column widths (keeping an eye on the page-break display) until the columns are narrow enough to print on one page.

NOTE Page breaks aren't displayed until you print (or preview) the worksheet at least one time.

TIP If you'd prefer not to see the page break display in Normal View mode, choose Office ➪ Excel Options and select the Advanced tab. Scroll down the section titled Display Options For This Worksheet and remove the check mark from Show Page Breaks. This setting applies only to the active worksheet. Unfortunately, the option to turn off page break display is not in the Ribbon, and it's not even available for inclusion on the Quick Access Toolbar.

Figure 10.1 shows a worksheet in Normal View mode, zoomed out to show multiple pages. Notice the dotted lines that indicate page breaks.

FIGURE 10.1

In Normal View mode, dotted lines indicate page breaks.

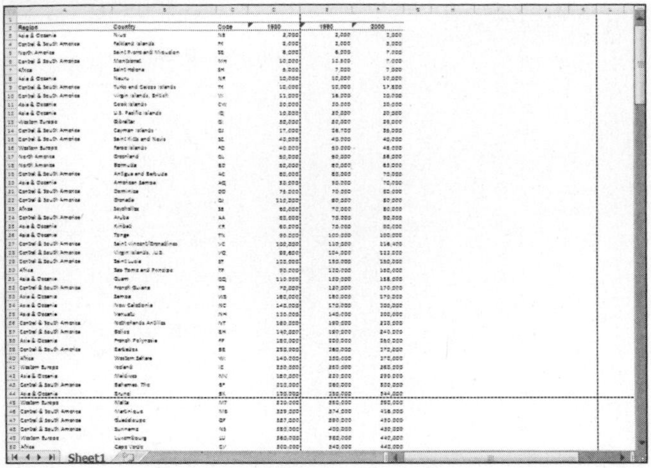

Page Layout View

Page Layout View is the ultimate print preview. Unlike the old print preview, this mode is not a view only mode. You have complete access to all Excel commands. In fact, you can use Page Layout View all the time if you like.

Figure 10.2 shows a worksheet in Page Layout View, zoomed out to show multiple pages. Notice that The page header and footer (if any) appear on each page, giving you a true preview of the printed output.

TIP   If you move the mouse to the corner of a page while in Page Layout View, you can click to hide the white space in the margins. Doing so gives you all the advantages of Page Layout View, but you can see more information on screen because the unused margin space is hidden.

FIGURE 10.2

In Page Layout View, the worksheet resembles printed pages.

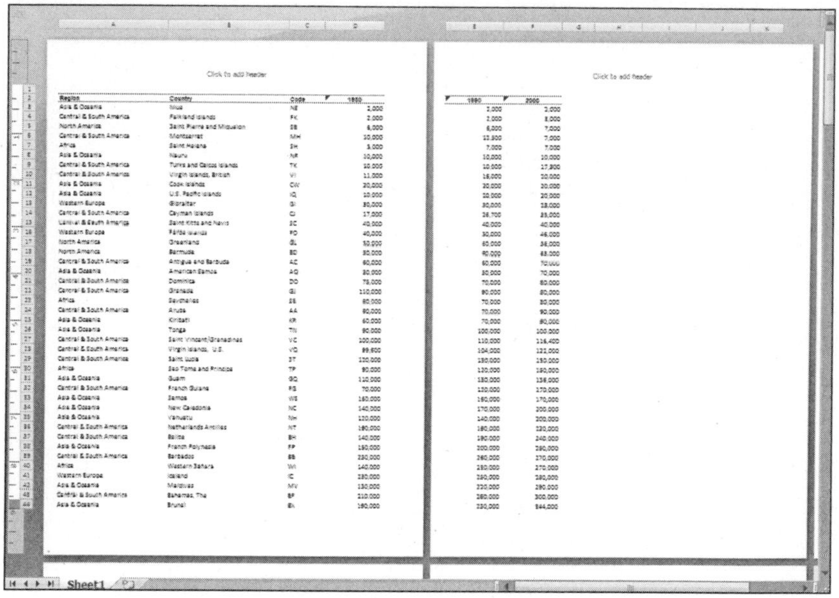

Page Break Preview

Page Break Preview displays the worksheet and shows where the page breaks occur. Figure 10.3 shows an example. This view mode is different from Normal View mode with page breaks turned on. The key difference is that you can drag the page breaks. Unlike Page Layout View, Page Break Preview does not display headers and footers.

When you enter Page Break Preview mode, Excel performs the following:

- Changes the zoom factor so that you can see more of the worksheet.
- Displays the page numbers overlaid on the pages.
- Displays the current print range with a white background; nonprinting data appears with a gray background.
- Displays all page breaks as draggable dashed lines.

When you change the page breaks by dragging, Excel automatically adjusts the scaling so that the information fits on the pages, per your specifications.

> **TIP** In Page Break Preview mode, you still have access to all of Excel's commands. You can change the zoom factor if you find the text to be too small.

To exit Page Break Preview mode, just click one of the other View icons in the status bar.

FIGURE 10.3

Page Break Preview mode gives you a bird's-eye view of your worksheet and shows exactly where the page breaks occur.

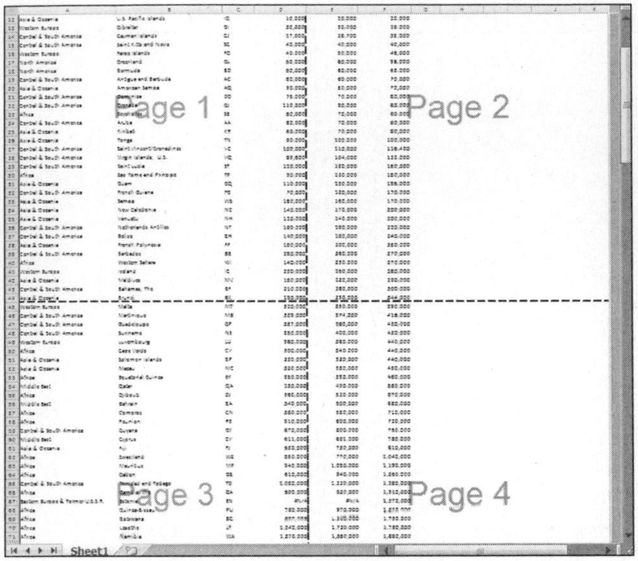

Adjusting Common Page Setup Settings

Simply clicking the Quick Print button (or choosing Office ➪ Print ➪ Quick Print) may produce acceptable results in many cases, but a little tweaking of the print settings can often improve your printed reports. You can make the most common print adjustments directly from the Page Layout tab of the Ribbon.

Adjusting the page margins

Margins are the unprinted areas along the sides, top, and bottom of a printed page. Excel provides four "quick margin" settings, and you can also specify the exact margin size you require. All printed pages have the same margins. You can't specify different margins for different pages.

If you're in Page Layout View, a ruler is displayed above the column header and to the left of the row header. Use your mouse to drag the margins in the ruler. Excel adjusts the page display immediately. Use the horizontal ruler to adjust the left and right margins and use the vertical ruler to adjust the top and bottom margins. See Figure 10.4.

If you use the Page Layout ➪ Page Setup ➪ Margins drop-down list, you can select either Normal, Wide, or Narrow (or the last-used custom margin settings). If none of these settings does the job, choose Custom Margins, which displays the Margins tab of the Page Setup dialog box, shown in Figure 10.5.

To change a margin, click the appropriate spinner (or you can enter a value directly). The margin settings that you specify in the Page Setup dialog box will then be available in the Page Layout ➪ Page Setup ➪ Margins drop-down list, referred to as Last Custom Setting.

 The Preview box in the center of the dialog box is a bit deceiving because it doesn't really show you how your changes look in relation to the page; rather, it displays a darker line to let you know which margin you're adjusting.

FIGURE 10.4

Use your mouse to adjust the margins in Page Layout View.

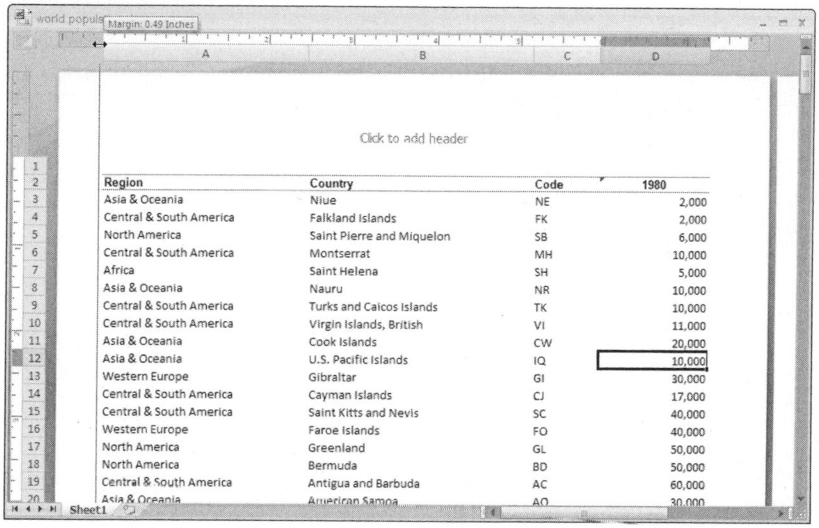

	A	B	C	D
		Click to add header		
2	Region	Country	Code	1980
3	Asia & Oceania	Niue	NE	2,000
4	Central & South America	Falkland Islands	FK	2,000
5	North America	Saint Pierre and Miquelon	SB	6,000
6	Central & South America	Montserrat	MH	10,000
7	Africa	Saint Helena	SH	5,000
8	Asia & Oceania	Nauru	NR	10,000
9	Central & South America	Turks and Caicos Islands	TK	10,000
10	Central & South America	Virgin Islands, British	VI	11,000
11	Asia & Oceania	Cook Islands	CW	20,000
12	Asia & Oceania	U.S. Pacific Islands	IQ	10,000
13	Western Europe	Gibraltar	GI	30,000
14	Central & South America	Cayman Islands	CJ	17,000
15	Central & South America	Saint Kitts and Nevis	SC	40,000
16	Western Europe	Faroe Islands	FO	40,000
17	North America	Greenland	GL	50,000
18	North America	Bermuda	BD	50,000
19	Central & South America	Antigua and Barbuda	AC	60,000
20	Asia & Oceania	American Samoa	AQ	30,000

FIGURE 10.5

The Margins tab of the Page Setup dialog box.

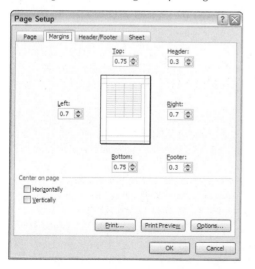

In addition to the page margins, you can adjust the distance of the header from the top of the page and the distance of the footer from the bottom of the page. These settings should be less than the corresponding margin; otherwise, the header or footer may overlap with the printed output.

Normally, Excel aligns the printed page at the top and left margins. If you want the output to be centered vertically or horizontally, check the appropriate check box in the section of the Margins tab labeled Center On Page.

Changing the page orientation

Page orientation refers to the way in which the output is printed on the page. Choose Page Layout ⇨ Page Setup ⇨ Orientation ⇨ Portrait to print tall pages (the default) or Page Layout ⇨ Page Setup ⇨ Orientation ⇨ Landscape to print wide pages. Landscape orientation is useful when you have a wide range that doesn't fit on a vertically oriented page.

If you change the orientation, the on-screen page breaks adjust automatically to accommodate the new paper orientation.

Specifying the paper size

Use the Page Layout ⇨ Page Setup ⇨ Size control to specify the size of the paper you are using.

NOTE   Excel displays a variety of paper sizes, but your printer may not be capable of using them.

Specifying the print area

By default, Excel prints the entire used range of a worksheet. In some cases, you may want to print only part of the worksheet. To do so, select the range to print and then choose Page Layout ⇨ Page Setup ⇨ Print Area ⇨ Set Print Area.

NOTE   If you're working in Page Layout View, the print area is enclosed in dashed lines.

If you specify a print area for a worksheet, Excel automatically give the print area a name: `Print_Area`.

Understanding page breaks

If you print lengthy reports, controlling where pages break is often important. For example, you normally wouldn't want a row to print on a page by itself. Fortunately, Excel gives you precise control over page breaks.

Excel handles page breaks automatically, but sometimes you may want to "force" a page break — either a vertical or a horizontal one — so that the report prints the way you want it to. For example, if your worksheet consists of several distinct sections, you may want to print each section on a separate sheet of paper.

Inserting a page break

To insert a horizontal page-break line, move the cell pointer to the cell that will begin the new page, but make sure that you place the pointer in column A; otherwise, you'll insert a vertical page break *and* a horizontal page break. For example, if you want row 14 to be the first row of a new page, select cell A14. Then choose Page Layout ⇨ Page Setup ⇨ Breaks ⇨ Insert Page Break.

NOTE   Page breaks are visualized differently, depending on which View mode you're using. See "Changing Your Page View," earlier in this chapter.

To insert a vertical page-break line, move the cell pointer to the cell that will begin the new page, but in this case, make sure that you place the pointer in row 1. Choose Page Layout ➪ Page Setup ➪ Breaks ➪ Insert Page Break to create the page break.

Removing page breaks you've added

To remove a manual page break, move the cell pointer to the first row beneath (or the first column to the right) of the manual page break and then choose Page Layout ➪ Page Setup ➪ Breaks ➪ Remove Page Break.

To remove all manual page breaks in the worksheet, choose Page Layout ➪ Page Setup ➪ Breaks ➪ Reset All Page Breaks.

Using a background image

Would you like to have a background image on your printouts? Unfortunately, you can't. You may have noticed the Page Layout ➪ Page Setup ➪ Background command. This button displays a dialog box that lets you select an image to display as a background. Placing this control among the other print-related commands is very misleading. Background images placed on a worksheet are never printed.

> **TIP** In lieu of a background image, you can insert a Shape, WordArt, or a picture on your worksheet and then adjust its transparency. Then copy the image to all printed pages. Alternatively, you can insert an object in a page header or footer. See the sidebar titled, "Inserting a Watermark."

Inserting a Watermark

A *watermark* is an image (or text) that appears on each printed page. A watermark can be a faint company logo, or a word such as DRAFT. Excel doesn't have an official command to print a watermark, but you can add a watermark by inserting a picture in the page header or footer. Here's how to do it.

1. **Locate an image on your hard drive that you want to use for the watermark.**
2. **Choose View ➪ Workbook Views ➪ Page Layout View.**
3. **Click the center section of the header.**
4. **Choose Header & Footer Tools ➪ Header & Footer Elements ➪ Picture.**
5. **Using the Insert Picture dialog box, locate the image from Step 1.**
6. **Click outside of the header to see your image.**
7. **To center the image in the middle of the page, click the center section of the header and add some carriage returns before the** `&[Picture]` **code.** You'll need to experiment to determine the number of carriage returns.
8. **If you need to adjust the image (for example, make it lighter), click the center section of the header and then choose Header & Footer Tools ➪ Header & Footer Elements ➪ Format Picture.** Use the Image controls in the Picture tab of the Format Picture dialog box to adjust the image. You may need to experiment with the settings to make sure that the worksheet text is legible.

continued

---

continued

The accompanying figure shows an example of a header image (a globe) used as a watermark. You can do a similar thing with text, of course.

Printing row and column titles

If your worksheet is set up with titles in the first row and descriptive names in the first column, it can be difficult to identify data that appears on printed pages where those titles do not appear. To resolve this problem, you can choose to print selected rows or columns as titles on each page of the printout.

CROSS-REF Row and column titles serve pretty much the same purpose on a printout as frozen panes do in navigating within a worksheet. See Chapter 4 for more information on freezing panes. Keep in mind, however, that these features are independent of each other. In other words, freezing panes does not affect the printed output.

CAUTION Don't confuse print titles with headers; these are two different concepts. *Headers* appear at the top of each page and contain information, such as the worksheet name, date, or page number. Row and column titles describe the data being printed, such as field names in a database table or list.

You can specify particular rows to repeat at the top of every printed page or particular columns to repeat at the left of every printed page. To do so, choose Page Layout ➪ Page Setup ➪ Print Titles. Excel displays the Sheet tab of the Page Setup dialog box, shown in Figure 10.6.

FIGURE 10.6

Use the Sheet tab of the Page Setup dialog box to specify rows or columns that will appear on each printed page.

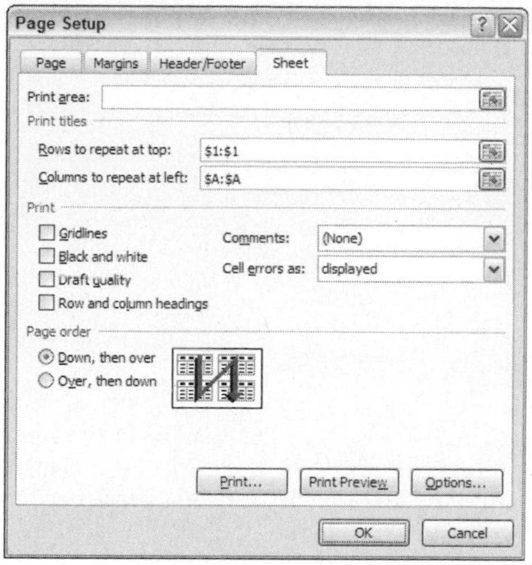

Activate the appropriate box and then select the rows or columns in the worksheet. Or you can enter these references manually. For example, to specify rows 1 and 2 as repeating rows, enter **1:2**.

NOTE When you specify row and column titles and use Page Layout View, these titles will repeat on every page (just as when the document is printed). However, the cells used in the title can be selected only on the page in which they first appear.

Scaling printed output

In some cases, you may need to force your printed output to fit on a specific number of pages. You can do so by enlarging or reducing the size. To enter a scaling factor, use the Page Layout ➪ Scale To Fit ➪ Scale control. You can scale the output from 10% up to 400%. To return to normal scaling, enter 100%.

To force Excel to print using a specific number of pages, choose Page ➪ Layout ➪ Width And Page ➪ Layout ➪ Height. When you change either one of these settings, the corresponding scale factor is displayed in the Scale control.

Excel doesn't care about legibility, however. It will gladly scale your output to be so small that no one can read it.

Printing cell gridlines

Normally, cell gridlines aren't printed. If you want your printout to include the gridlines, choose Page Layout ➪ Sheet Options ➪ Gridlines ➪ Print.

Printing row and column headers

Normally, the row and column headers for a worksheet are not printed. If you want your printout to include these items, choose Page Layout ➪ Sheet Options ➪ Headings ➪ Print.

Adding a Header or Footer to Your Reports

A *header* is information that appears at the top of each printed page. A *footer* is information that appears at the bottom of each printed page. By default, new workbooks do not have any headers or footers.

You can specify headers and footers by using the Header/Footer tab of the Page Setup dialog box. But this task is much easier if you switch to Page Layout View, where you can click the section labeled Click To Add Header or Click To Add Footer.

NOTE **If you're working in Normal view, you can choose Insert ➪ Header & Footer. Excel switches to Page Layout View and activates the center section of the page header.**

You can then type the information and apply any type of formatting you like. Note that headers and footers consist of three sections: left, center, and right. For example, you can create a header that prints your name at the left margin, the worksheet name centered in the header, and the page number at the right margin.

When you activate the header or footer section in Page Layout View, the Ribbon displays a new context tab called Header & Footer Tools ➪ Design. Use the controls in this tab to work with headers and footers.

Selecting a predefined header or footer

You can choose from a number of predefined headers or footers by using either of the two drop-down lists in the Header & Footer Tools ➪ Design ➪ Header & Footer group. Notice that some items in these lists consist of multiple parts, separated by a comma. Each part goes into one of the three header or footer sections (left, center, or right). Figure 10.7 shows an example of a header that uses all three sections.

FIGURE 10.7

This three-part header is one of Excel's predefined headers.

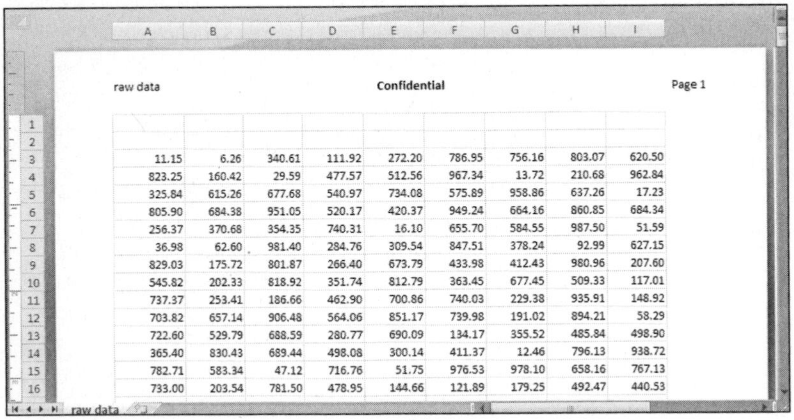

	A	B	C	D	E	F	G	H	I
1									
2									
3	11.15	6.26	340.61	111.92	272.20	786.95	756.16	803.07	620.50
4	823.25	160.42	29.59	477.57	512.56	967.34	13.72	210.68	962.84
5	325.84	615.26	677.68	540.97	734.08	575.89	958.86	637.26	17.23
6	805.90	684.38	951.05	520.17	420.37	949.24	664.16	860.85	684.34
7	256.37	370.68	354.35	740.31	16.10	655.70	584.55	987.50	51.59
8	36.98	62.60	981.40	284.76	309.54	847.51	378.24	92.99	627.15
9	829.03	175.72	801.87	266.40	673.79	433.98	412.43	980.96	207.60
10	545.82	202.33	818.92	351.74	812.79	363.45	677.45	509.33	117.01
11	737.37	253.41	186.66	462.90	700.86	740.03	229.38	935.91	148.92
12	703.82	657.14	906.48	564.06	851.17	739.98	191.02	894.21	58.29
13	722.60	529.79	688.59	280.77	690.09	134.17	355.52	485.84	498.90
14	365.40	830.43	689.44	498.08	300.14	411.37	12.46	796.13	938.72
15	782.71	583.34	47.12	716.76	51.75	976.53	978.10	658.16	767.13
16	733.00	203.54	781.50	478.95	144.66	121.89	179.25	492.47	440.53

Understanding header and footer element codes

When a header or footer section is activated, you can type whatever text you like into the section. Or, to insert variable information, you can insert any of several element codes by clicking a button in the Header & Footer Tools ➪ Design ➪ Header & Footer Elements group.

For example, to insert the current date, click the Current Date button. Each of these buttons inserts a code into the selected section. Table 10.1 lists the buttons and their functions.

TABLE 10.1

Header & Footer Buttons and Their Functions

Button	Code	Function
Page Number	&[Page]	Displays the page number
Number of Pages	&[Pages]	Displays the total number of pages to be printed
Current Date	&[Date]	Displays the current date
Current Time	&[Time]	Displays the current time
File Path	&[Path]&[File]	Displays the workbook's complete path and filename
File Name	&[File]	Displays the workbook name
Sheet Name	&[Tab]	Displays the sheet's name
Picture	Not applicable	Enables you to add a picture
Format Picture	Not applicable	Enables you to change the picture's settings

You can combine text and codes and insert as many codes as you like into each section.

NOTE If the text that you enter uses an ampersand (&), you must enter the ampersand twice (because Excel uses an ampersand to signal a code). For example, to enter the text Research & Development into a section of a header or footer, enter Research && Development.

You also can use different fonts and sizes in your headers and footers. Just select the text that you want to change and then use the formatting tools in the Home ➪ Font group. Or use the controls on the Mini toolbar, which appears automatically when you select the text. If you don't change the font, Excel uses the font defined for the Normal style.

TIP You can use as many lines as you like. Press Enter to force a line break for multiline headers or footers. If you use multiline headers or footers, you may need to adjust the top or bottom margin so the text won't overlap with the worksheet data. See "Adjusting the page margins," earlier in this chapter.

Unfortunately, you can't print the contents of a specific cell in a header or footer. For example, you may want Excel to use the contents of cell A1 as part of a header. To do so, you need to enter the cell's contents manually — or write a macro to perform this operation.

Other header and footer options

The Header & Footer ⇨ Design ⇨ Options group contains controls that let you specify other options:

- **Different First Page:** If checked, you can specify a different header/footer for the first printed page.

- **Different Odd & Even Pages:** If checked, you can specify a different header/footer for odd and even pages.

- **Scale With Document:** If checked, the font size in the header and footer will be sized accordingly if the document is scaled when printed.

- **Align With Page Margins:** If checked, the left header and footer will be aligned with the left margin, and the right header and footer will be aligned with the right margin.

Adjusting the Settings in the Print Dialog Box

Additional print settings are available in the Print dialog box. To display the Print dialog box, select Office ⇨ Print (or press Ctrl+P). Use this dialog box to select which printer you wish to use, to choose what part of the worksheet you want to print, to specify the number of copies you want, and to access the properties settings for your printer. After you select your print settings, click OK in the Print dialog box to print your work.

 **TIP** Clicking OK in the Print dialog box without adjusting any settings is the equivalent of clicking Excel's Quick Print button.

Figure 10.8 shows the Print dialog box; the following sections describe the settings in this dialog box.

FIGURE 10.8

Use the Print dialog box to select a printer or choose what will print.

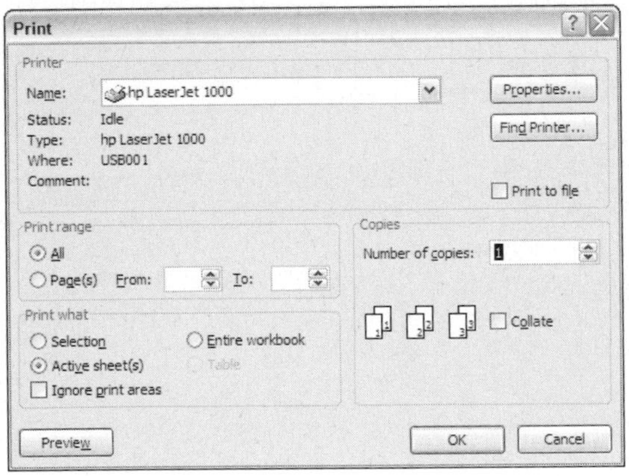

Choosing your printer

The Printer section of the Print dialog box enables you to choose which printer you want to use as well as to access the settings that are specific to the selected printer.

Make sure that you have selected the correct printer (applicable only if you have access to more than one printer). You select the printer from the Name drop-down list. This section of the dialog box also lists information about the selected printer, such as its status and where it's connected.

NOTE If you want to adjust the printer's settings, click the Properties button to display a property box for the selected printer. The exact dialog box that you see depends on the printer. The Properties dialog box lets you adjust printer-specific settings, such as the print quality and the paper source. In most cases, you won't have to change any of these settings, but if you're having print-related problems, you may want to check the settings.

Specifying what you want to print

Sometimes you may want to print only a part of the worksheet rather than the entire active area. Or you may want to reprint selected pages of a report without printing all the pages. You can make both of these types of selections in the Print dialog box, too (see Figure 10.8).

The Print What section of the Print dialog box lets you specify what to print. You have several options:

- **Selection:** Prints only the range that you selected before choosing Office ⇨ Print.
- **Active Sheet(s):** Prints the active sheet or sheets that you selected. (This option is the default.) You can select multiple sheets to print by pressing Ctrl and clicking the sheet tabs. If you select multiple sheets, Excel begins printing each sheet on a new page.
- **Entire Workbook:** Prints the entire workbook, including chart sheets.
- **Table:** Enabled only if the cell pointer is within a table when the Print dialog box is displayed. If selected, only the table will be printed.

TIP You can also choose Page Layout ⇨ Page Setup ⇨ Print Area ⇨ Set Print Area to specify the range or ranges to print. Before you choose this command, select the range or ranges that you want to print. To clear the print area, choose Page Layout ⇨ Page Setup ⇨ Print Area ⇨ Clear Print Area. To override the print area, select the Ignore Print Areas check box in the Print dialog box.

If your printed output uses multiple pages, you can select which pages to print by indicating the number of the first and last pages to print in the Print Range section of the Print dialog box. You can either use the spinner controls or type the page numbers in the edit boxes.

Printing multiple copies of a report

The Copies section of the Print dialog box lets you specify the number of copies to print. Simply enter the number of copies you want and then click OK to print them.

TIP If you're printing multiple copies of a report, make certain that the Collate check box is selected. If you choose this option, Excel prints the pages in order for each set of output. If you're printing only one page, Excel ignores the Collate setting.

Preventing Certain Cells from Being Printed

If your worksheet contains confidential information, you may want to print the worksheet but not the confidential parts. You can use several techniques to prevent certain parts of a worksheet from printing:

- When you hide rows or columns, the hidden rows aren't printed. Use the Home ➪ Cells ➪ Format drop-down list to hide the selected rows or columns.

- You can hide cells or ranges by making the text color the same color as the background color. Be aware, however, that this method may not work for all printers.

- You can hide cells by using a custom number format that consists of three semicolons (;;;). See Chapter 24 for more information about using custom number formats.

- You can mask off a confidential area of a worksheet by covering it with a rectangle Shape. Choose Insert ➪ Illustrations ➪ Shapes and click the Rectangle Shape. You'll probably want to adjust the fill color to match the cell background and remove the border.

If you find that you must regularly hide data before you print certain reports, consider using the Custom Views feature, discussed later in this chapter (see "Creating Custom View of Your Worksheet"). This feature allows you to create a named view that doesn't show the confidential information.

Preventing Objects from being Printed

To prevent objects on the worksheet (such as charts, Shapes, and SmartArt) from being printed, you need to access the Size And Properties dialog box for the object (see Figure 10.9):

1. **Right-click the object and select Size And Properties from the shortcut menu.** Excel displays the Size And Properties dialog box.

2. **In the Size And Properties dialog box, select the Properties tab.**

3. **Remove the check mark from the check box labeled Print Object.**

NOTE   The shortcut menu that appears when you right-click a chart does not display the Size And Properties menu item. To access the Size And Properties dialog box for a chart, click the dialog box launcher in the Chart Tools ➪ Format ➪ Size group.

Use the Size And Properties dialog box to prevent objects from printing.

Creating Custom Views of Your Worksheet

If you need to create several different printed reports from the same Excel workbook, setting up the specific settings for each report can be a tedious job.

For example, you may need to print a full report in landscape mode for your boss. Another department may require a simplified report using the same data, but with some hidden columns in portrait mode. You can simplify the process by creating custom named views of your worksheets that include the proper settings for each report.

The Custom View feature enables you to give names to various views of your worksheet, and you can quickly switch among these named views. A *view* includes settings for the following:

- Print settings, as specified in the Page Layout ➪ Page Setup, Page Layout ➪ Scale To Fit, and Page ➪ Page Setup ➪ Sheet Options groups.
- Hidden rows and columns
- The worksheet view (Normal, Page Layout View, Page Break Preview)
- Selected cells and ranges
- The active cell
- The zoom factor
- Window sizes and positions
- Frozen panes

If you find that you're constantly fiddling with these settings and then changing them back, using named views can save you lots of effort.

CAUTION Unfortunately, the Custom View feature does not work if the workbook contains at least one table. When a workbook that contains a table is active, the Custom View command is grayed out. This limitation severely limits the usefulness of the Custom View feature.

To create a named view, begin by setting up the view settings the way you want them (for example, hide some columns). Then choose View ➪ Workbook Views ➪ Custom Views to display the Custom Views dialog box. Click the Add button and provide a descriptive name in the Add View dialog box that appears (see Figure 10.10). You can also specify what to include in the view by using the two check boxes. For example, if you don't want the view to include print settings, remove the check mark from Print Settings. Click OK to save the named view.

FIGURE 10.10

Use the Add View dialog box to create a named view.

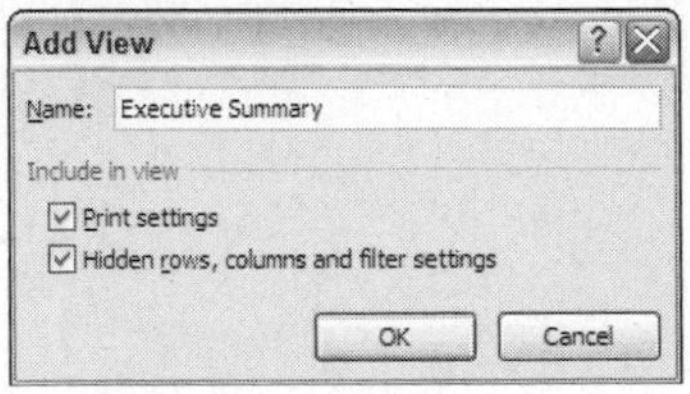

The Custom Views dialog box displays a list of all named views. To select a particular view, just select it from the list and click the Show button. To delete a named view from the list, click the Delete button.

Part II

Working with Formulas and Functions

Formulas and worksheet functions are essential to manipulating data and obtaining useful information from your Excel workbooks. The chapters in this part present a wide variety of formula examples that use many of Excel's functions. Two of the chapters are devoted to array formulas. These chapters are intended primarily for advanced users who need to perform calculations that may otherwise be impossible.

Chapter 11

Introducing Formulas and Functions

Formulas are what make a spreadsheet program so useful. If it weren't for formulas, a spreadsheet would simply be a glorified word-processing document that has great support for tabular information. You use formulas in your Excel worksheets to calculate results from the data stored in the worksheet. When data changes, those formulas calculate updated results with no extra effort on your part. This chapter introduces formulas and functions and helps you get up to speed with this important element.

Understanding Formula Basics

A formula is entered into a cell. It performs a calculation of some type and returns a result, which is displayed in the cell. Formulas use a variety of operators and worksheet functions to work with values and text. The values and text used in formulas can be located in other cells, which makes changing data easy and gives worksheets their dynamic nature. For example, you can see multiple scenarios quickly by changing the data in a worksheet and letting your formulas do the work.

A formula can consist of any of these elements:

- Mathematical operators, such as + (for addition) and * (for multiplication)
- Cell references (including named cells and ranges)
- Values or text
- Worksheet functions (such as SUM or AVERAGE)

NEW FEATURE When you're working with a table, a new feature in Excel 2007 enables you to create formulas that use column names from the table — which can make your formulas much easier to read. I discuss table formulas later in this chapter. (See "Using Formulas In Tables.")

IN THIS CHAPTER

Understanding formula basics

Entering formulas and functions into your worksheets

Understanding how to use references in formulas

Correcting common formula errors

Using advanced naming techniques

Tips for working with formulas

After you enter a formula, the cell displays the calculated result of the formula. The formula itself appears in the Formula bar when you select the cell, however.

Following are a few examples of formulas:

=150*.05	Multiplies 150 times 0.05. This formula uses only values and isn't all that useful because it always returns the same result. You may as well just enter the value 7.5 into the cell.
=A1+A2	Adds the values in cells A1 and A2.
=Income-Expenses	Subtracts the value in the cell named Expenses from the value in the cell named Income.
=SUM(A1:A12)	Adds the values in the range A1:A12.
=A1=C12	Compares cell A1 with cell C12. If they are identical, the formula returns TRUE; otherwise it returns FALSE.

> **NOTE** Formulas always begin with the equal sign so that Excel can distinguish them from text.

Using operators in formulas

Excel lets you use a variety of *operators* in your formulas. Operators are symbols that indicate the type of mathematical operation you want the formula to perform. Table 11.1 lists the operators that Excel recognizes. In addition to these, Excel has many built-in functions that enable you to perform additional calculations.

TABLE 11.1

Operators Used in Formulas

Operator	Name
+	Addition
–	Subtraction
*	Multiplication
/	Division
^	Exponentiation
&	Concatenation
=	Logical comparison (equal to)
>	Logical comparison (greater than)
<	Logical comparison (less than)
>=	Logical comparison (greater than or equal to)
<=	Logical comparison (less than or equal to)
<>	Logical comparison (not equal to)

You can, of course, use as many operators as you need to perform the desired calculation.

Following are some examples of formulas that use various operators.

Formula	What It Does
=`"Part-"&"23A"`	Joins (concatenates) the two text strings to produce Part-23A.
=`A1&A2`	Concatenates the contents of cell A1 with cell A2. Concatenation works with values as well as text. If cell A1 contains `123` and cell A2 contains `456`, this formula would return the value `123456`.
=`6^3`	Raises 6 to the third power (216).
=`216^(1/3)`	Returns the cube root of 216 (6).
=`A1<A2`	Returns TRUE if the value in cell A1 is less than the value in cell A2. Otherwise, it returns FALSE. Logical-comparison operators also work with text. If A1 contained `Bill` and A2 contained `Julia`, the formula would return TRUE, because `Bill` comes before `Julia` in alphabetical order.
=`A1<=A2`	Returns TRUE if the value in cell A1 is less than or equal to the value in cell A2. Otherwise, it returns FALSE.
=`A1<>A2`	Returns TRUE if the value in cell A1 isn't equal to the value in cell A2. Otherwise, it returns FALSE.

Understanding operator precedence in formulas

When Excel calculates the value of a formula, it uses certain rules to determine the order in which the various parts of the formula are calculated. You need to understand these rules if you want your formulas to produce the desired results.

Table 11.2 lists the Excel operator precedence. This table shows that exponentiation has the highest precedence (it's performed first) and logical comparisons have the lowest precedence (they're performed last).

TABLE 11.2

Operator Precedence in Excel Formulas

Symbol	Operator	Precedence
^	Exponentiation	1
*	Multiplication	2
/	Division	2
+	Addition	3
−	Subtraction	3
&	Concatenation	4
=	Equal to	5
<	Less than	5
>	Greater than	5

You can use parentheses to override the Excel's built-in order of precedence. Expressions within parentheses are always evaluated first.

The following formula uses parentheses to control the order in which the calculations occur. In this case, cell B3 is subtracted from cell B2 and the result is multiplied by cell B4:

    =(B2-B3)*B4

If you enter the formula without the parentheses, Excel computes a different answer. Because multiplication has a higher precedence, cell B3 is multiplied by cell B4. Then this result is subtracted from cell B2, which isn't what was intended.

The formula without parentheses looks like this:

    =B2-B3*B4

It's a good idea to use parentheses even when they aren't strictly necessary. Doing so helps to clarify what the formula is intended to do. For example, the following formula makes it perfectly clear that B3 should be multiplied by B4, and the result subtracted from cell B2. Without the parentheses, you would need to remember Excel's order of precedence.

    =B2-(B3*B4)

You can also *nest* parentheses within formulas — that is, put them inside other parentheses. If you do so, Excel evaluates the most deeply nested expressions first — and then works its way out. Here's an example of a formula that uses nested parentheses:

    =((B2*C2)+(B3*C3)+(B4*C4))*B6

This formula has four sets of parentheses — three sets are nested inside the fourth set. Excel evaluates each nested set of parentheses and then sums the three results. This result is then multiplied by the value in B6.

Although the preceding formula uses four sets of parentheses, only the outer set is really necessary. If you understand operator precedence, it should be clear that you can rewrite this formula as:

    =(B2*C2+B3*C3+B4*C4)*B6

Again, using the extra parentheses makes the calculation much clearer.

Every left parenthesis, of course, must have a matching right parenthesis. If you have many levels of nested parentheses, keeping them straight can sometimes be difficult. If the parentheses don't match, Excel displays a message explaining the problem — and won't let you enter the formula.

In some cases, if your formula contains mismatched parentheses, Excel may propose a correction to your formula. Figure 11.1 shows an example of the Formula AutoCorrect feature. You may be tempted simply to accept the proposed correction, but be careful — in many cases, the proposed formula, although syntactically correct, isn't the formula you intended, and it will produce an incorrect result.

FIGURE 11.1

Excel's Formula AutoCorrect feature often suggests a correction to an erroneous formula.

> **TIP** Excel lends a hand in helping you match parentheses. When the insertion point moves over a parenthesis while you're editing a cell, Excel momentarily bolds it — and does the same with its matching parenthesis.

Using functions in your formulas

Most formulas you create use worksheet functions. These functions enable you to greatly enhance the power of your formulas and perform calculations that are difficult (or even impossible) if you use only the operators discussed previously. For example, you can use the TAN function to calculate the tangent of an angle. You can't do this calculation by using only the mathematical operators.

Examples of formulas that use functions

A worksheet function can simplify a formula significantly. To calculate the average of the values in 10 cells (A1:A10) without using a function, you'd have to construct a formula like this:

    =(A1+A2+A3+A4+A5+A6+A7+A8+A9+A10)/10

Not very pretty, is it? Even worse, you would need to edit this formula if you added another cell to the range. Fortunately, you can replace this formula with a much simpler one that uses one of Excel's built-in worksheet functions:

    =AVERAGE(A1:A10)

The following formula demonstrates how using a function can enable you to perform calculations that would not be possible otherwise. If (for example) you need to determine the largest value in a range, a formula can't tell you the answer without using a function. Here's a simple formula that returns the largest value in the range A1:D100:

    =MAX(A1:D100)

Functions also can sometimes eliminate manual editing. Assume that you have a worksheet that contains 1,000 names in cells A1:A1000, and all names appear in all-capital letters. Your boss sees the listing and informs you that the names will be mail-merged with a form letter — so all uppercase is not acceptable; for example, JOHN F. SMITH must appear as John F. Smith. You *could* spend the next several hours re-entering the list — or you could use a formula such as the following, which uses a function to convert the text in cell A1 to the proper case:

    =PROPER(A1)

Enter this formula once in cell B1 and then copy it down to the next 999 rows. Then select B1:B1000 and use Home ⇨ Clipboard ⇨ Copy to copy the range. Next, with B1:B1000 still selected, use Home ⇨ Clipboard ⇨ Paste Values to convert the formulas to values. Delete the original column, and you've just accomplished several hours of work in less than a minute.

New Functions in Excel 2007

Excel 2007 contains five new functions:

- IFERROR — Used to check for an error, and display a message or perform a different calculation.
- AVERAGEIF @md Used to calculate a conditional average (similar to SUMIF and COUNTIF).
- AVERAGEIFS — Used to calculate a conditional average using multiple criteria.
- SUMIFS — Used to calculate a conditional sum using multiple criteria.
- COUNTIFS — Used to calculate a conditional COUNT using multiple criteria.

In addition, worksheet functions that formerly required the Analysis ToolPak add-in (which is shipped with Excel) are now built into Excel. So you have access to dozens of additional functions without installing the add-in.

These new functions are described in detail in the Excel Help, and I present examples in later chapters.

Keep in mind that if you use any of these new functions, you will not be able to share your workbook with someone who uses an earlier version of Excel.

One last example should convince you of the power of functions. Suppose you have a worksheet that calculates sales commissions. If the salesperson sold more than $100,000 of product, the commission rate is 7.5 percent; otherwise the commission rate is 5.0 percent. Without using a function, you would have to create two different formulas and make sure that you used the correct formula for each sales amount. A better solution is to write a formula that uses the IF function to ensure that you calculate the correct commission, regardless of sales amount:

```
=IF(A1<100000,A1*5%,A1*7.5%)
```

This formula performs some simple decision-making. The formula checks the value of cell A1. If this value is less than 100,000, the formula returns cell A1 multiplied by 5 percent. Otherwise it returns what's in cell A1, multiplied by 7.5 percent.

Function arguments

In the preceding examples, you may have noticed that all the functions used parentheses. The information inside the parentheses is called the *list of arguments*.

Functions vary in how they use arguments. Depending on what it has to do, a function may use

- No arguments
- One argument
- A fixed number of arguments
- An indeterminate number of arguments
- Optional arguments

An example of a function that doesn't use an argument is the NOW function, which returns the current date and time. Even if a function doesn't use an argument, you must still provide a set of empty parentheses, like this:

```
=NOW()
```

If a function uses more than one argument, you must separate each argument with a comma. The examples at the beginning of the chapter used cell references for arguments. Excel is quite flexible when it comes to function arguments, however. An argument can consist of a cell reference, literal values, literal text strings, expressions, and even other functions.

NOTE A comma is the list-separator character for the U.S. version of Excel. Some other versions may use a semicolon. The list separator is a Windows setting, which can be adjusted in the Windows Control Panel (the Regional and Language Options dialog box).

More about functions

All told, Excel includes 340 functions. And if that's not enough, you can purchase additional specialized functions from third-party suppliers — and even create your own custom functions (by using VBA) if you're so inclined.

Some users feel a bit overwhelmed by the sheer number of functions, but you'll probably find that you use only a dozen or so on a regular basis. And as you'll see, Excel's Insert Function dialog box (described later in this chapter) makes it easy to locate and insert a function, even if it's not one that you use frequently.

CROSS-REF You'll find many examples of Excel's built-in functions in Chapters 12 through 18. Appendix A contains a complete listing of Excel's worksheet functions, with a brief description of each. Chapter 40 covers the basics of creating custom functions with VBA.

Entering Formulas into Your Worksheets

As I mentioned earlier, a formula must begin with an equal sign to inform Excel that the cell contains a formula rather than text. Excel provides two ways to enter a formula into a cell: manually or by pointing to cell references. The following sections discuss each way in detail.

NEW FEATURE Excel 2007 provides additional assistance when you create formulas by displaying a drop-down list that contains function names and range names. The items displayed in the list are determined by what you've already typed. For example, if you're entering a formula and type the letter T, you'll see the drop-down list shown in Figure 11.2. If you type an additional letter, the list is shortened to show only the matching functions. To have Excel *autocomplete* an entry in that list, use the arrow keys to highlight the entry, and then press Tab. Notice that highlighting a function in the list also displays a brief description of the function. See the sidebar "Using Formula Autocomplete" for an example of how this new feature works.

FIGURE 11.2

Excel 2007 displays a drop-down list when you enter a formula.

Using Formula Autocomplete

The Formula Autocomplete feature in Excel 2007 makes entering formulas easier than ever. Here's a quick walk-through that demonstrates how it works. The goal is to create a formula that uses the SUBTOTAL function to calculate the average value in a range named TestScores.

1. **Activate an empty cell and type an equal sign (=) to signal the start of a formula.**

2. **Type the letter S, and you'll get a list of functions and names that begin with S.** This feature is not case-sensitive, so you can use either uppercase or lowercase characters.

3. **Type the second letter,** U. The list is filtered to show only functions and names that begin with *SU*, as shown in the first figure.

4. SUBTOTAL **is second on the list, so use the Down Arrow to highlight the function and press Tab.** Excel adds the opening parenthesis and displays another list that contains options for the first argument for SUBTOTAL, as shown in the second figure.

5. **Use the Down Arrow to select** AVERAGE **and press Tab.** Excel inserts 101, the code for calculating the average.

6. **Type a comma to separate the next argument.**

7. **Type a T, and you get a list of functions and names that begin with** *T*. **You're looking for** TestScores, **so narrow it down a bit by typing the second character (e).**

8. **Highlight** TestScores **and press Tab.**

9. **Finally, type a closing parenthesis and press Enter.**

Formula Autocomplete includes the following items (and each type is identified by a separate icon):

- Excel built-in functions
- User defined functions (Functions defined by the user through VBA or other methods)
- Defined Names (named using the Formulas ➪ Defined Names ➪ Define Name command).
- Enumerated Arguments (only a few functions use such arguments, and SUBTOTAL is one of them)
- Table structure references (used to identify portions of a table)

Entering formulas manually

Entering a formula manually involves, well, entering a formula manually. In a selected cell, you simply type an equal sign (=) followed by the formula. As you type, the characters appear in the cell and in the Formula bar. You can, of course, use all the normal editing keys when entering a formula.

Entering formulas by pointing

Even though you can enter formulas by typing in the entire formula, Excel provides another method of entering formulas that is generally easier, faster, and less error-prone. This method still involves some manual typing, but you can simply point to the cell references instead of typing their values manually. For example, to enter the formula =A1+A2 into cell A3, follow these steps:

1. **Move the cell pointer to cell A3.**
2. **Type an equal sign (=) to begin the formula.** Notice that Excel displays Enter in the status bar (bottom left of your screen).
3. **Press the up arrow twice.** As you press this key, Excel displays a faint moving border around cell A1, and the cell reference appears in cell A3 and in the Formula bar. In addition, Excel displays Point in the status bar.
4. **Type a plus sign (+). A solid-color border replaces the faint border, and Enter reappears in the status bar.**
5. **Press the up arrow again, which puts the moving border around cell A2, and adds that cell address to the formula.**
6. **Press Enter to end the formula.**

TIP   You can also point to the data cells by using your mouse.

Pasting range names into formulas

If your formula uses named cells or ranges, you can either type the name in place of the address or choose the name from a list and have Excel insert the name for you automatically. Two ways to insert a name into a formula are available:

- **Select the name from the drop-down list:** To use this method, you must know at least the first character of the name. When you're entering the formula, type the first character and then select the name from the drop-down list.
- **Press F3:** This key displays the Paste Name dialog box. Select the name from the list and click OK (or just double-click the name). Excel will enter the name into your formula. If no names are defined, pressing F3 has no effect.

183

Figure 11.3 shows an example. The worksheet contains two defined names: Expenses and Sales. The Paste Name dialog box is being used to insert a name (Sales) into the formula being entered in cell B11.

CROSS-REF   Refer to Chapter 5 for information about defining names.

Inserting functions into formulas

The easiest way to enter a function into a formula is to use the drop-down list that Excel displays while you type a formula. In order to use this method, however, you must know at least the first character of the function's name.

Another way to insert a function is to use the Function Library group on the Formulas tab (see Figure 11.4). This is especially useful if you can't remember which function you need. Click the function category (Financial, Logical, Text, etc.) and you'll get a list of the function in that category. Click the function you want, and Excel displays its Function Arguments dialog box. This is where you enter the function's arguments. In addition, you can click the Help On This Function link to learn more about the selected function.

FIGURE 11.3

You can use the Paste Name dialog box to quickly enter a defined name into a formula.

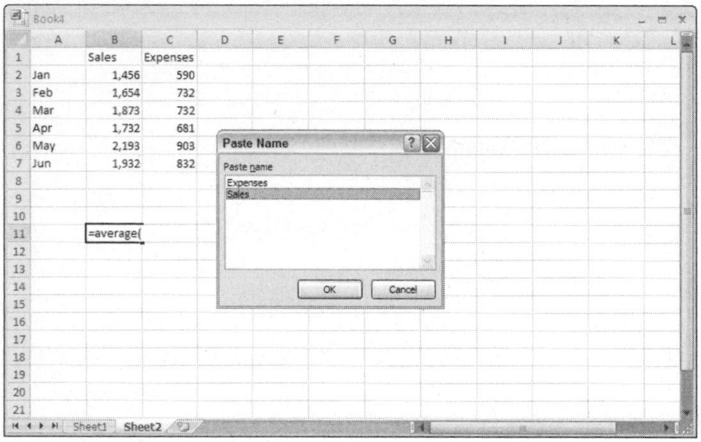

FIGURE 11.4

You can insert a function by selecting it from one of the function categories.

Yet another way to insert a function into a formula is to use Excel's Insert Function dialog box (see Figure 11.5). You can access this dialog box in several ways:

- By using the Formulas ⇨ Function Library ⇨ Insert Function command.
- By clicking the Insert Function icon, which is directly to the left of the Formula bar. This button displays ƒx.
- By pressing Shift+F3.

FIGURE 11.5

The Insert Function dialog box.

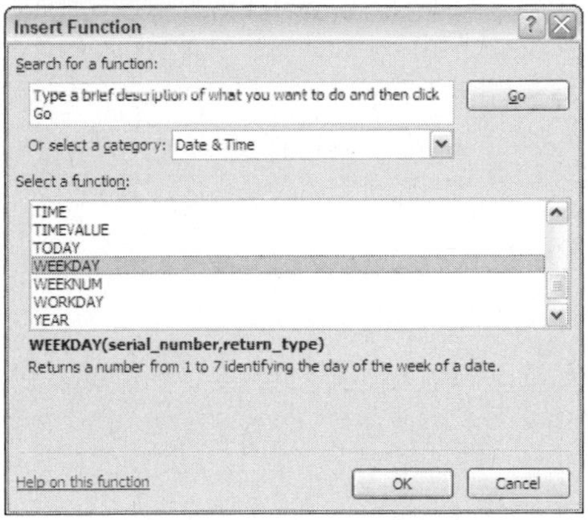

The Insert Function dialog box shows a drop-down list of function categories. Select a category, and the functions in that category are displayed in the list box. To access a function that you've used recently, select Most Recently Used from the drop-down list.

If you're not sure which function you need, you can search for the appropriate function by using the Search For A Function box at the top of the dialog box. Enter your search terms, click Go, and you'll get a list of relevant functions. When you select a function in the Select A Function list box, Excel displays the function (and its argument names) in the dialog box along with a brief description of what the function does.

When you locate the function you want to use, highlight it and click OK. Excel then displays its Function Arguments dialog box, as shown in Figure 11.6. Use this dialog box to specify the arguments for the function. The dialog box will vary, depending on the function you're inserting, and it will show one text box for each of the function's arguments. To use a cell or range reference as an argument, you can enter the address manually or click inside the argument box and then select (that is, point to) the cell or range in the sheet). After you've specified all the function arguments, click OK.

FIGURE 11.6

The Function Arguments dialog box.

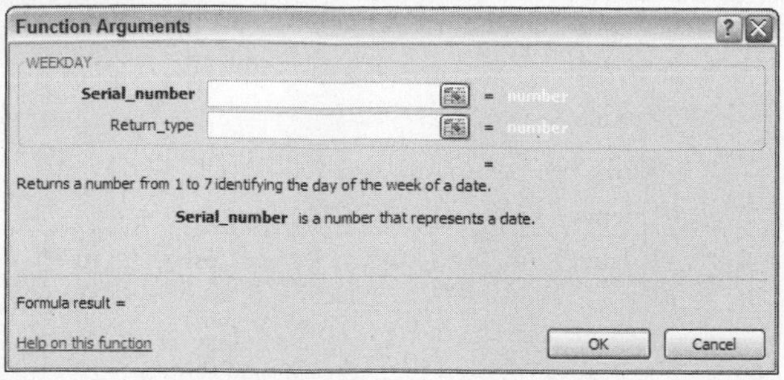

> **TIP**   Yet another way to insert a function while you're entering a formula is to use the Function List
> to the left of the Formula bar. When you are entering or editing a formula, the space normally
> occupied by the Name box displays a list of the functions you've used most recently. After you select a func-
> tion from this list, Excel displays the Function Arguments dialog box.

Function entry tips

Following are some additional tips to keep in mind when you use the Insert Function dialog box to enter functions:

- You can use the Insert Function dialog box to insert a function into an existing formula. Just edit the formula and move the insertion point to the location at which you want to insert the function. Then open the Insert Function dialog box (using any of the methods described above) and select the function.

- You can also use the Function Arguments dialog box to modify the arguments for a function in an existing formula. Click the function in the Formula bar and then click the Insert Function button (the fx button, to the left of the Formula bar).

- If you change your mind about entering a function, click the Cancel button.

- How many boxes you see in the Function Arguments dialog box depends on the number of arguments used in the function you selected. If a function uses no arguments, you won't see any boxes. If the function uses a variable number of arguments (such as the AVERAGE function), Excel adds a new box every time you enter an optional argument.

- As you provide arguments in the Function Argument dialog box, the value of each argument is displayed to the right of each box.

- A few functions, such as INDEX, have more than one form. If you choose such a function, Excel displays another dialog box that lets you choose which form you want to use.

- As you become familiar with the functions, you can bypass the Insert Function dialog box and enter the function directly. Excel prompts you with argument names as you enter the function.

Editing Formulas

After you've entered a formula, you can (of course) edit that formula. You may need to edit a formula if you make some changes to your worksheet and then have to adjust the formula to accommodate the changes. Or the formula may return an error value, in which case you edit the formula to correct the error.

The following are some of the ways to get into cell edit mode:

- Double-click the cell, which enables you to edit the cell contents directly in the cell.
- Press F2, which enables you to edit the cell contents directly in the cell.
- Select the cell that you want to edit, and then click in the Formula bar. This enables you to edit the cell contents in the Formula bar.
- If the cell contains a formula that returns an error, Excel will display a small triangle in the upper-left corner of the cell. Activate the cell, and you'll see a Smart Tag. Click the Smart Tag, and you can choose one of the options for correcting the error. (The options will vary according to the type of error in the cell.)

TIP You can control whether Excel displays these formula-error-checking Smart Tags in the Formulas section of the Excel Options dialog box. To display this dialog box, select Office ⇨ Excel Options. If you remove the check mark from Enable Background Error Checking, Excel no longer displays these Smart Tags.

While you're editing a formula, you can select multiple characters either by dragging the mouse cursor over them or by pressing Shift while you use the direction keys.

TIP If you have a formula that you can't seem to edit correctly, you can convert the formula to text and tackle it again later. To convert a formula to text, just remove the initial equal sign (=). When you're ready to try again, type the initial equal sign to convert the cell contents back to a formula.

Using Cell References in Formulas

Most formulas you create include references to cells or ranges. These references enable your formulas to work dynamically with the data contained in those cells or ranges rather than being restricted to fixed values. For example, if your formula refers to cell A1 and you change the value contained in A1, the formula result changes to reflect the new value. If you didn't use references in your formulas, you would need to edit the formulas themselves in order to change the values used in the formulas.

Using relative, absolute, and mixed references

When you use a cell (or range) reference in a formula, you can use three types of references:

- **Relative:** The row and column references can change when you copy the formula to another cell because the references are actually offsets from the current row and column.
- **Absolute:** The row and column references do not change when you copy the formula because the reference is to an actual cell address.
- **Mixed:** Either the row or column reference is relative, and the other is absolute.

An absolute reference uses two dollar signs in its address: one for the column letter and one for the row number (for example, $A$5). Excel also allows mixed references in which only one of the address parts is absolute (for example, $A4 or A$4).

By default, Excel creates relative cell references in formulas. The distinction becomes apparent when you copy a formula to another cell.

Figure 11.7 shows a simple worksheet. The formula in cell D2, which multiplies the quantity by the price, is

    =B2*C2

This formula uses relative cell references. Therefore, when the formula is copied to the cells below it, the references adjust in a relative manner. For example, the formula in cell D3 is

    =B3*C3

FIGURE 11.7

Copying a formula that contains relative references.

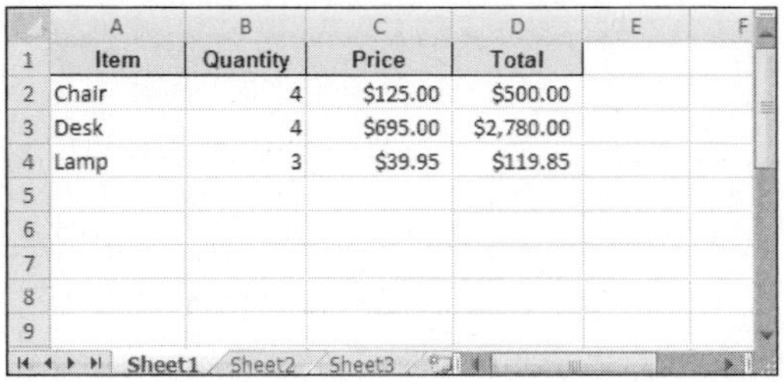

	A	B	C	D	E	F
1	Item	Quantity	Price	Total		
2	Chair	4	$125.00	$500.00		
3	Desk	4	$695.00	$2,780.00		
4	Lamp	3	$39.95	$119.85		
5						
6						
7						
8						
9						

Sheet1 Sheet2 Sheet3

But what if the cell references in D2 contained absolute references, like this?

    =$B$2*$C$2

In this case, copying the formula to the cells below would produce incorrect results. The formula in cell D3 would be exactly the same as the formula in cell D2.

Now I'll extend the example to calculate sales tax, which is stored in cell B7 (see Figure 11.8). In this situation, the formula in cell D2 is

    =B2*C2*$B$7

The quantity is multiplied by the price, and the result is multiplied by the sales-tax rate stored in cell B7. Notice that the reference to B7 is an absolute reference. When the formula in D2 is copied to the cells below it, cell D3 will contain this formula:

    =B3*C3*$B$7

Here, the references to cells B2 and C2 were adjusted, but the reference to cell B7 was not — which is exactly what I want.

FIGURE 11.8

Formula references to the sales tax cell should be absolute.

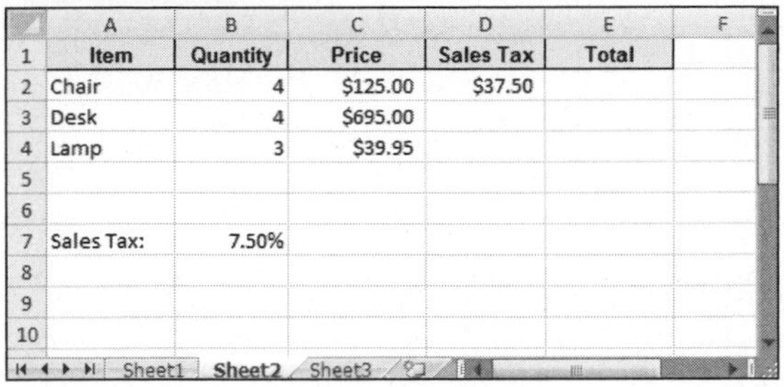

	A	B	C	D	E	F
1	**Item**	**Quantity**	**Price**	**Sales Tax**	**Total**	
2	Chair	4	$125.00	$37.50		
3	Desk	4	$695.00			
4	Lamp	3	$39.95			
5						
6						
7	Sales Tax:	7.50%				
8						
9						
10						

Figure 11.9 demonstrates the use of mixed references. The formulas in the C3:F7 range calculate the area for various lengths and widths. The formula in cell C3 is

    =$B3*C$2

FIGURE 11.9

Using mixed cell references.

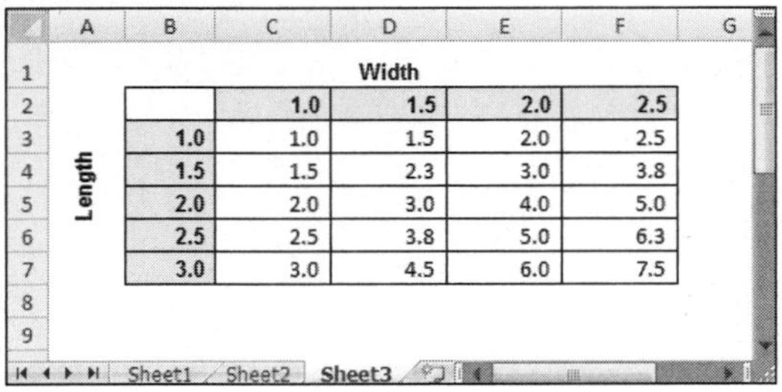

	A	B	C	D	E	F	G
1				**Width**			
2			1.0	1.5	2.0	2.5	
3		1.0	1.0	1.5	2.0	2.5	
4	Length	1.5	1.5	2.3	3.0	3.8	
5		2.0	2.0	3.0	4.0	5.0	
6		2.5	2.5	3.8	5.0	6.3	
7		3.0	3.0	4.5	6.0	7.5	
8							
9							

Notice that both cell references are mixed. The reference to cell B3 uses an absolute reference for the column ($B), and the reference to cell C2 uses an absolute reference for the row ($2). As a result, this formula can be copied down and across, and the calculations will be correct. For example, the formula in cell F7 is

    =$B7*F$2

If C3 used either absolute or relative references, copying the formula would produce incorrect results.

ON the CD-ROM The workbook that demonstrates the various types of references is available on the companion CD-ROM. The file is named **cell references.xlsx.**

NOTE When you cut and paste a formula (move it to another location), the cell references in the formula aren't adjusted. Again, this is usually what you want to happen. When you move a formula, you generally want it to continue to refer to the original cells.

Changing the types of your references

You can enter nonrelative references (that is, absolute or mixed) manually by inserting dollar signs in the appropriate positions of the cell address. Or you can use a handy shortcut: the F4 key. When you've entered a cell reference (by typing it or by pointing), you can press F4 repeatedly to have Excel cycle through all four reference types.

For example, if you enter **=A1** to start a formula, pressing F4 converts the cell reference to =$A$1. Pressing F4 again converts it to =A$1. Pressing it again displays =$A1. Pressing it one more time returns to the original =A1. Keep pressing F4 until Excel displays the type of reference that you want.

NOTE When you name a cell or range, Excel (by default) uses an absolute reference for the name. For example, if you give the name SalesForecast to A1:A12, the Refers To box in the New Name dialog box lists the reference as $A$1:$A$12. This is almost always what you want. If you copy a cell that has a named reference in its formula, the copied formula contains a reference to the original name.

Referencing cells outside the worksheet

Formulas can also refer to cells in other worksheets — and the worksheets don't even have to be in the same workbook. Excel uses a special type of notation to handle these types of references.

Referencing cells in other worksheets

To use a reference to a cell in another worksheet in the same workbook, use this format:

> *SheetName*!*CellAddress*

In other words, precede the cell address with the worksheet name, followed by an exclamation point. Here's an example of a formula that uses a cell on the Sheet2 worksheet:

> =A1*Sheet2!A1

This formula multiplies the value in cell A1 on the current worksheet by the value in cell A1 on Sheet2.

TIP If the worksheet name in the reference includes one or more spaces, you must enclose it in single quotation marks. (Excel does that automatically if you use the point-and-click method.) For example, here's a formula that refers to a cell on a sheet named All Depts:

> =A1*'All Depts'! A1

Referencing cells in other workbooks

To refer to a cell in a different workbook, use this format:

> =[*WorkbookName*]*SheetName*!*CellAddress*

In this case, the workbook name (in square brackets), the worksheet name, and an exclamation point precede the cell address. The following is an example of a formula that uses a cell reference in the Sheet1 worksheet in a workbook named Budget:

> =[Budget.xlsx]Sheet1!A1

If the workbook name in the reference includes one or more spaces, you must enclose it (and the sheet name) in single quotation marks. For example, here's a formula that refers to a cell on Sheet1 in a workbook named Budget For 2008:

```
=A1*'[Budget For 2008.xlsx]Sheet1'!A1
```

When a formula refers to cells in a different workbook, the other workbook doesn't have to be open. If the workbook is closed, however, you must add the complete path to the reference so that Excel can find it. Here's an example:

```
=A1*'C:\My Documents\[Budget For 2008.xlsx]Sheet1'!A1
```

A linked file can also reside on another system that's accessible on your corporate network. The formula below, for example, refers to a cell in a workbook in the files directory of a computer named DataServer.

```
='\\DataServer\files\[budget.xlsx]Sheet1'!$D$7
```

CROSS-REF Refer to Chapter 27 for more information about linking workbooks.

TIP To create formulas that refer to cells not in the current worksheet, point to the cells rather than entering their references manually. Excel takes care of the details regarding the workbook and worksheet references. The workbook you're referencing in your formula must be open if you're going to use the pointing method.

NOTE If you point to a different worksheet or workbook when creating a formula, you'll notice that Excel always inserts absolute cell references. Therefore, if you plan to copy the formula to other cells, make sure that you change the cell references to relative before you copy.

Using Formulas In Tables

One of the most significant new features in Excel 2007 is its support for tables. In this section I describe how formulas work with tables.

CROSS-REF See Chapter 6 for an introduction to the new table features.

Summarizing data in a table

Figure 11.10 shows a simple table with three columns. I entered the data, and then converted the range to a table by choosing Insert ➪ Tables ➪ Table. Note that I didn't define any names, but the table is named Table1 by default.

FIGURE 11.10

A simple table with three columns.

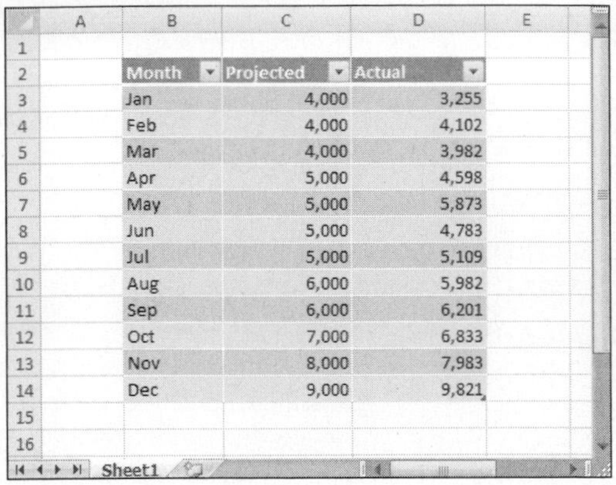

Month	Projected	Actual
Jan	4,000	3,255
Feb	4,000	4,102
Mar	4,000	3,982
Apr	5,000	4,598
May	5,000	5,873
Jun	5,000	4,783
Jul	5,000	5,109
Aug	6,000	5,982
Sep	6,000	6,201
Oct	7,000	6,833
Nov	8,000	7,983
Dec	9,000	9,821

ON the CD-ROM **This workbook is available on the companion CD-ROM. It is named table formulas.xlsx.**

If you'd like to calculate the total projected and total actual sales, you don't even need to write a formula. Simply click a button to add a row of summary formulas to the table:

1. **Activate any cell in the table.**
2. **Place a check mark next to Table Tools ➪ Design ➪ Table Style Options ➪ Total Row.**
3. **Activate a cell in the Total Row and use the drop-down list to select the type of summary formula to use (see Figure 11.11).** For example, to calculate the sum of the Actual column, select `SUM` from the drop-down list in cell D15. Excel creates this formula:

   ```
   =SUBTOTAL(109,[Actual])
   ```

For the `SUBTOTAL` function, 109 is an enumerated argument that represents `SUM`. The second argument for the `SUBTOTAL` function is the column name, in square brackets. Using the column name within brackets is a new way to create "structured" references within a table. (I discuss this further in an upcoming section, "Referencing data in a table.")

FIGURE 11.11

A drop-down list enables you to select a summary formula for a table column.

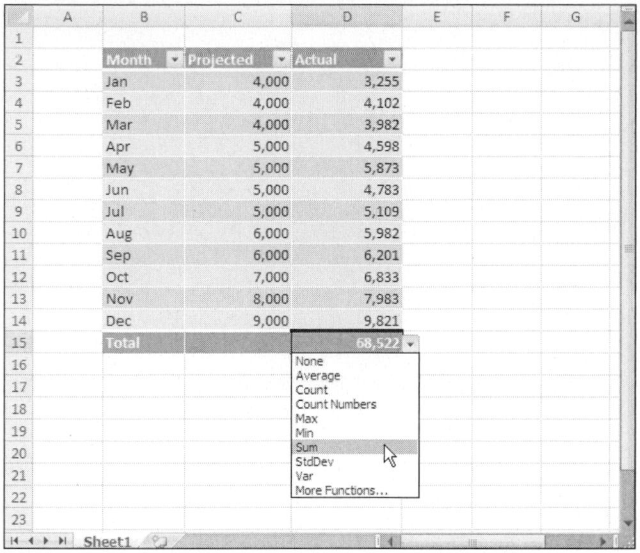

> **NOTE** You can toggle the Total Row display on and off by using Table Tools ⇨ Design ⇨ Table Style Options ⇨ Total Row. If you turn it off, the summary options you selected will be remembered when you turn it back on.

Using formulas within a table

In many cases, you'll want to use formulas within a table. For example, in the table shown in Figure 11.11, you may want a column that shows the difference between the Actual and Projected amounts. As you'll see, Excel 2007 makes this very easy.

1. **Activate cell E2 and type** Difference **for the column header.** Excel automatically expands the table for you.

2. **Next move to cell E3 and type an equal sign to signify the beginning of a formula.**

3. **Press the left arrow key.** Excel displays [Actual], which is the column heading, in the Formula bar.

4. **Type a minus sign and then press left arrow twice.** Excel displays [Projected] in your formula.

5. **Press Enter to end the formula. Excel copies the formula to all rows in the table.**

Figure 11.12 shows the table with the new column.

FIGURE 11.12

The Difference column contains a formula.

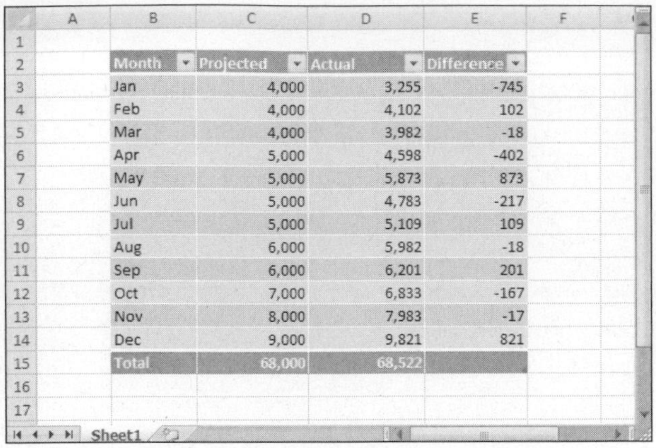

Month	Projected	Actual	Difference
Jan	4,000	3,255	-745
Feb	4,000	4,102	102
Mar	4,000	3,982	-18
Apr	5,000	4,598	-402
May	5,000	5,873	873
Jun	5,000	4,783	-217
Jul	5,000	5,109	109
Aug	6,000	5,982	-18
Sep	6,000	6,201	201
Oct	7,000	6,833	-167
Nov	8,000	7,983	-17
Dec	9,000	9,821	821
Total	68,000	68,522	

If you examine the table, you'll find this formula for all cells in the `Difference` column:

```
=[Actual]-[Projected]
```

Although the formula was entered into the first row of the table, that's not necessary. Any time a formula is entered into an empty table column, it will automatically fill all the cells in that column. And if you need to edit the formula, Excel will automatically copy the edited formula to the other cells in the column.

The steps listed above used the pointing technique to create the formula. Alternatively, you could have entered it manually using standard cell references. For example, you could have entered the following formula in cell E3:

```
=D3-C3
```

If you type the cell references, Excel will still copy the formula to the other cells automatically.

One thing should be clear, however, about formulas that use the column headers: They are much easier to understand.

Referencing data in a table

Excel 2007 adds some news ways to refer to data that's contained in a table by using the table name and column headers. There is no need to create names for these items. The table itself has a name (for example, `Table1`), and you can refer to data within the table by using column headers.

You can, of course, use standard cell references to refer to data in a table, but the new method has a distinct advantage: The names adjust automatically if the table size changes by adding or deleting rows.

Refer to the table shown in Figure 11.11. This table was given the name `Table1` when it was created. To calculate the sum of all the data in the table, use this formula:

```
=SUM(Table1)
```

This formula will always return the sum of all the data, even if rows or columns are added or deleted. And if you change the name of Table1, Excel will adjust formulas that refer to that table automatically. For example, if you renamed `Table1` to be `AnnualData` (by using the Name Manager), the preceding formula would be changed to:

    =SUM(AnnualData)

Most of the time, you'll want to refer to a specific column in the table. The following formula returns the sum of the data in the `Actual` column:

    =SUM(Table1[Actual])

Notice that the column name is enclosed in square brackets. Again, the formula adjusts automatically if you change the text in the column heading.

Even better, Excel provides some helpful assistance when you create a formula that refers to data within a table. Figure 11.13 shows the formula `autocomplete` helping to create a formula by showing a list of the elements in the table.

FIGURE 11.13

The formula `autocomplete` feature is useful when creating a formula that refers to data in a table.

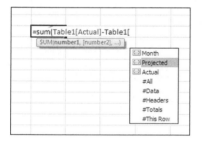

Correcting Common Formula Errors

Sometimes, when you enter a formula, Excel displays a value that begins with a hash mark (#). This is a signal that the formula is returning an error value. You have to correct the formula (or correct a cell that the formula references) to get rid of the error display.

> **TIP**   If the entire cell is filled with hash-mark characters, this means that the column isn't wide enough to display the value. You can either widen the column or change the number format of the cell.

In some cases, Excel won't even let you enter an erroneous formula. For example, the following formula is missing the closing parenthesis:

    =A1*(B1+C2

If you attempt to enter this formula, Excel informs you that you have unmatched parentheses, and it proposes a correction. Often, the proposed correction is accurate, but you can't count on it.

Table 11.3 lists the types of error values that may appear in a cell that has a formula. Formulas may return an error value if a cell to which they refer has an error value. This is known as the *ripple effect* — a single error value can make its way into lots of other cells that contain formulas that depend on that one cell.

TABLE 11.3

Excel Error Values

Error Value	Explanation
#DIV/0!	The formula is trying to divide by zero. This also occurs when the formula attempts to divide by what's in a cell that is empty (that is, by nothing).
#NAME?	The formula uses a name that Excel doesn't recognize. This can happen if you delete a name that's used in the formula or if you have unmatched quotes when using text.
#N/A	The formula is referring (directly or indirectly) to a cell that uses the NA function to signal that data is not available. Some functions (for example, VLOOKUP) can also return #N/A.
#NULL!	The formula uses an intersection of two ranges that don't intersect. (This concept is described later in the chapter.)
#NUM!	A problem with a value exists; for example, you specified a negative number where a positive number is expected.
#REF!	The formula refers to a cell that isn't valid. This can happen if the cell has been deleted from the worksheet.
#VALUE!	The formula includes an argument or operand of the wrong type. An *operand* is a value or cell reference that a formula uses to calculate a result.

Handling circular references

When you're entering formulas, you may occasionally see a Circular Reference Warning message, shown in Figure 11.14, indicating that the formula you just entered will result in a *circular reference*. A circular reference occurs when a formula refers to its own value — either directly or indirectly. For example, you create a circular reference if you enter **=A1+A2+A3** into cell A3 because the formula in cell A3 refers to cell A3. Every time the formula in A3 is calculated, it must be calculated again because A3 has changed. The calculation could go on forever.

FIGURE 11.14

If you see this warning, you know that the formula you entered will result in a circular reference.

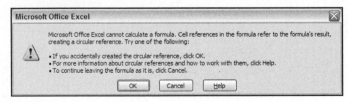

When you get the circular reference message after entering a formula, Excel gives you two options:

- Click OK, and Excel displays a Help screen that tells you more about circular references.
- Click Cancel to enter the formula as is.

Regardless of which option you choose, Excel displays a message in the left side of the status bar to remind you that a circular reference exists.

WARNING Excel won't tell you about a circular reference if the Enable Interative Calculationsetting is in effect. You can check this setting in the Formulas section of the Excel Options dialog box. (To display this dialog box, select Office ➪ Excel Options.) If Enable Interative Calculation is turned on, Excel performs the circular calculation exactly the number of times specified in the `Maximum Iterations` field (or until the value changes by less than 0.001 or whatever value is in the `Maximum Change` field). In a few situations, you may use a circular reference intentionally. In these cases, the Enable Interative Calculation setting must be on. However, it's best to keep this setting turned off so you're warned of circular references. Usually a circular reference indicates an error that you must correct.

Usually, a circular reference is quite obvious — easy to identify and correct. But when a circular reference is indirect — as when a formula refers to another formula that refers to yet another formula that refers back to the original formula — it may require a bit of detective work to get to the problem.

ON the CD-ROM The companion CD-ROM contains a workbook that demonstrates an intentional circular reference. This file is named **circular reference.xlsx**.

Intentional Circular References

You can sometimes use a circular reference to your advantage. For example, suppose a company has a policy of contributing 5 percent of its net profit to charity. The contribution itself, however, is considered an expense — and is therefore subtracted from the net profit figure. This produces a circular reference (see the accompanying figure).

The `Contributions` cell contains the following formula:

```
=5%*Net_Profit
```

The `Net Profit` cell contains the following formula:

```
=Gross_Income-Expenses-Contributions
```

	A	B	C	D	E	F
1	Gross Income	600,000				
2	Expenses	225,000				
3	Contributions	17,857	Should be 5% of Net Profits			
4	Net Profit	357,143	Gross Profits - Expenses - Contributions			
5						
6						
7						

Sheet1

These formulas produce a resolvable circular reference. If the Enable Iterative Calculation setting is on, Excel keeps calculating until the `Contributions` value is, indeed, 5 percent of `Net Profit`. In other words, the result becomes increasingly accurate until it converges on the final solution.

Specifying when formulas are calculated

You've probably noticed that Excel calculates the formulas in your worksheet immediately. If you change any cells that the formula uses, Excel displays the formula's new result with no effort on your part. All this happens when Excel's Calculation mode is set to Automatic. In Automatic Calculation mode (which is the default mode), Excel follows these rules when it calculates your worksheet:

- When you make a change — enter or edit data or formulas, for example — Excel calculates immediately those formulas that depend on new or edited data.

- If Excel is in the middle of a lengthy calculation, it temporarily suspends the calculation when you need to perform other worksheet tasks; it resumes calculating when you're finished with your other worksheet tasks.

- Formulas are evaluated in a natural sequence. In other words, if a formula in cell D12 depends on the result of a formula in cell D11, Excel calculates cell D11 before calculating D12.

Sometimes, however, you may want to control when Excel calculates formulas. For example, if you create a worksheet with thousands of complex formulas, you'll find that processing can slow to a snail's pace while Excel does its thing. In such a case, set Excel's calculation mode to Manual — which you can do by choosing Formulas ➪ Calculation ➪ Calculation Options ➪ Manual (see Figure 11.15)

FIGURE 11.15

You can control when Excel calculates formulas.

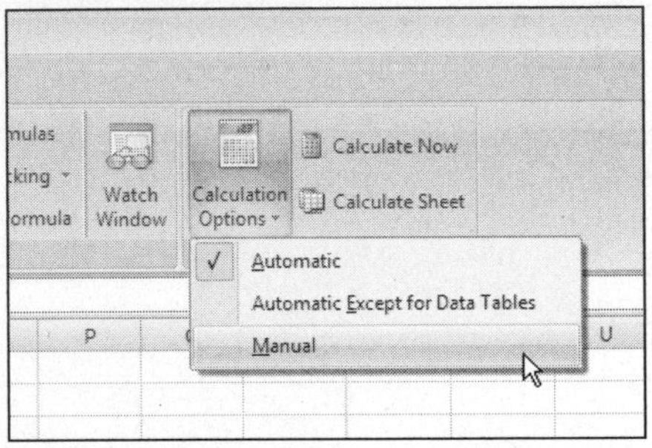

TIP If your worksheet uses any data tables (described in Chapter 36), you may want to select the option labeled `Automatically Except For Data Tables`. Large data tables calculate notoriously slowly. Note: A data table is not the same as a table created by choosing Insert ➪ Tables ➪ Table.

When you're working in Manual Calculation mode, Excel displays `Calculate` in the status bar when you have any uncalculated formulas. You can use the following shortcut keys to recalculate the formulas:

- **F9:** Calculates the formulas in all open workbooks.

- **Shift+F9:** Calculates only the formulas in the active worksheet. Other worksheets in the same workbook aren't calculated.

- **Ctrl+Alt+F9:** Forces a complete recalculation of all formulas.

- **Ctrl+Alt+Shift+F9:** Re-evaluates all formula dependencies and forces a complete recalculation.

NOTE Excel's Calculation mode isn't specific to a particular worksheet. When you change the Calculation mode, it affects all open workbooks, not just the active workbook.

Using Advanced Naming Techniques

Using range names can make your formulas easier to understand, easier to modify, and even help prevent errors. It's much easier to deal with a meaningful name such as AnnualSales than with a range reference such as AB12:AB68.

CROSS-REF   See Chapter 5 for basic information regarding working with names.

Excel offers a number of advanced techniques that make using names even more useful. I discuss these techniques in the sections that follow.

Using names for constants

Many Excel users don't realize that you can give a name to an item that doesn't appear in a cell. For example, if formulas in your worksheet use a sales-tax rate, you would probably insert the tax-rate value into a cell and use this cell reference in your formulas. To make things easier, you would probably also name this cell something similar to SalesTax.

Here's how to provide a name for a value that doesn't appear in a cell:

1. **Choose Formulas ➪ Defined Names ➪ Define Name.** Excel displays the New Name dialog box.
2. **Enter the name (in this case, SalesTax) into the field labeled Name.**
3. **Select a scope in which the name will be valid (either the entire workbook or a specific worksheet).**
4. **Click the Refers To box, delete its contents, and replace the old contents with a value (such as .075).**
5. **Use the Comment box to provide a comment about the name (optional).**
6. **Click OK to close the New Name dialog box and create the name.**

You just created a name that refers to a constant rather than a cell or range. Now if you type **=SalesTax** into a cell that's within the scope of the name, this simple formula returns 0.075 — the constant that you defined. You also can use this constant in a formula, such as =A1*SalesTax.

TIP   A constant also can be text. For example, you can define a constant for your company's name.

NOTE   Named constants don't appear in the Name box or in the Go To dialog box. This makes sense because these constants don't reside anywhere tangible. They do appear in the drop-down list that's displayed when you enter a formula — which is handy because you use these names in formulas.

Using names for formulas

Just as you can create a named constant, you can also create named formulas. As with named constants, named formulas don't appear in the worksheet.

You create named formulas the same way you create named constants — by using the New Name dialog box. For example, you might create a named formula that calculates the monthly interest rate from an annual rate; Figure 11.16 shows an example. In this case, the name MonthlyRate refers to the following formula:

```
=Sheet1!$B$1/12
```

FIGURE 11.16

Excel lets you give a name to a formula that doesn't exist in a worksheet cell.

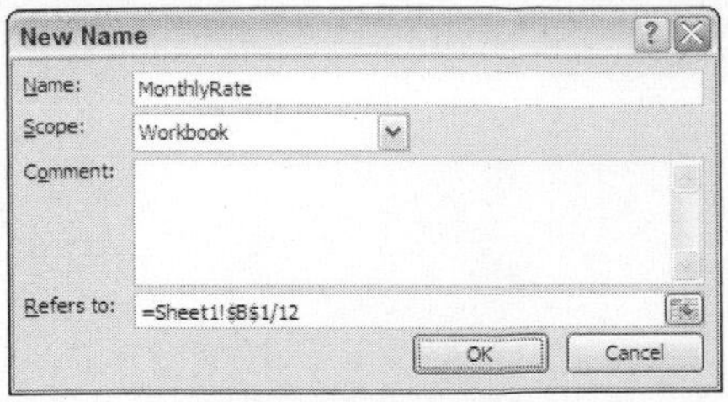

When you use the name `MonthlyRate` in a formula, it uses the value in B1 divided by 12. Notice that the cell reference is an absolute reference.

Naming formulas gets more interesting when you use relative references rather than absolute references. When you use the pointing technique to create a formula in the Refers To box of the New Name dialog box, Excel always uses absolute cell references — which is unlike its behavior when you create a formula in a cell.

For example, activate cell B1 on `Sheet1` and create the name **Cubed** for the following formula:

```
=Sheet1!A1^3
```

In this example, the relative reference points to the cell to the left of the cell in which the name is used. Therefore, make certain that cell B1 is the active cell *before* you open the New Name dialog box; this is very important. The formula contains a relative reference; when you use this named formula in a worksheet, the cell reference is always relative to the cell that contains the formula. For example, if you enter **=Cubed** into cell D12, then cell D12 displays the contents of cell C12 raised to the third power (C12 is the cell directly to the left of D12).

Using range intersections

This section describes a concept known as *range intersections* — individual cells that two ranges have in common. Excel uses an *intersection operator* — a space character — to determine the overlapping references in two ranges. Figure 11.17 shows a simple example.

You can use a range-intersection formula to determine values.

The formula in cell B9 is

    =B1:B6 A3:D3

This formula returns 10, the value in cell B3 — that is, the value at the intersection of the two ranges.

The intersection operator is one of three reference operators used with ranges. Table 11.4 lists these operators.

Reference Operators for Ranges

Operator	What It Does
: (colon)	Specifies a range.
, (comma)	Specifies the union of two ranges. This operator combines multiple range references into a single reference.
(space)	Specifies the intersection of two ranges. This operator produces cells that are common to two ranges.

The real value of knowing about range intersections is apparent when you use names. Examine Figure 11.18, which shows a table of values. I selected the entire table and then used Formulas ⇨ Defined Names ⇨ Create From Selection to create names automatically by using the top row and left column.

FIGURE 11.18

When you use names, using a range-intersection formula to determine values is even more useful.

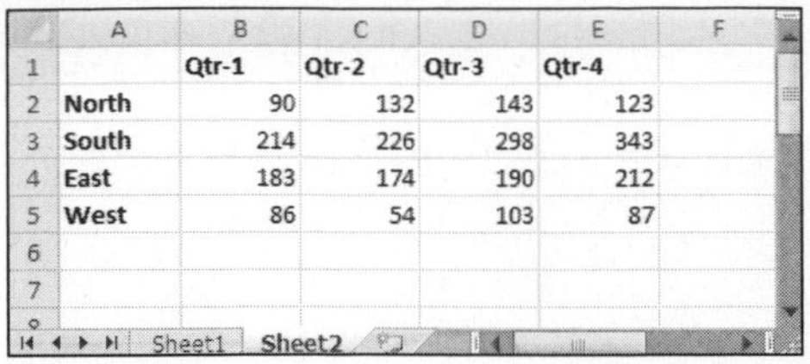

Excel created the following names:

North	=Sheet1!$B$2:$E$2	Qtr1	=Sheet1!$B$2:$B$5
South	=Sheet1!$B$3:$E$3	Qtr2	=Sheet1!$C$2:$C$5
West	=Sheet1!$B$4:$E$4	Qtr3	=Sheet1!$D$2:$D$5
East	=Sheet1!$B$5:$E$5	Qtr4	=Sheet1!$E$2:$E$5

With these names defined, you can create formulas that are easy to read and use. For example, to calculate the total for Quarter 4, just use this formula:

```
=SUM(Qtr4)
```

To refer to a single cell, use the intersection operator. Move to any blank cell and enter the following formula:

```
=Qtr1 West
```

This formula returns the value for the first quarter for the West region. In other words, it returns the value that exists where the Qtr1 range intersects with the West range. Naming ranges in this manner can help you create very readable formulas.

Applying names to existing references

When you create a name for a cell or a range, Excel doesn't automatically use the name in place of existing references in your formulas. For example, suppose you have the following formula in cell F10:

```
=A1-A2
```

If you define a name Income for A1 and Expenses for A2, Excel won't automatically change your formula to =Income-Expenses. Replacing cell or range references with their corresponding names is fairly easy, however.

To apply names to cell references in formulas after the fact, start by selecting the range that you want to modify. Then choose Formulas ➪ Defined Names ➪ Define Name ➪ Apply Names. Excel displays the Apply Names dialog box, as shown in Figure 11.19. Select the names that you want to apply by clicking them and then click OK. Excel replaces the range references with the names in the selected cells.

Use the Apply Names dialog box to replace cell or range references with defined names.

Tips for Working with Formulas

In this section, I offer a few additional tips and pointers relevant to formulas.

Don't hard-code values

When you create a formula, think twice before you use any specific value in the formula. For example, if your formula calculates sales tax (which is 6.5 percent), you may be tempted to enter a formula, such as the following:

```
+A1*.065
```

A better approach is to insert the sales tax rate in a cell — and use the cell reference. Or you can define the tax rate as a named constant, using the technique presented earlier in this chapter. Doing so makes modifying and maintaining your worksheet easier. For example, if the sales tax rate changed to 6.75 percent, you would have to modify every formula that used the old value. If you store the tax rate in a cell, however, you simply change that one cell — and Excel updates all the formulas.

Using the Formula bar as a calculator

If you simply need to perform a calculation, you can use the Formula bar as a calculator. For example, enter the following formula — but don't press Enter:

```
=(145*1.05)/12
```

If you press Enter, Excel enters the formula into the cell. But because this formula always returns the same result, you may prefer to store the formula's *result* rather than the formula itself. To do so, press F9 — and watch the result appear in the Formula bar. Press Enter to store the result in the active cell. (This technique also works if the formula uses cell references or worksheet functions.)

Making an exact copy of a formula

When you copy a formula, Excel adjusts its cell references when you paste the formula to a different location. Sometimes, you may want to make an exact copy of the formula. One way to do this is to convert the cell references to absolute values, but this isn't always desirable. A better approach is to select the formula in Edit mode and then copy it to the Clipboard as text. You can do this in several ways. Here's a step-by-step example of how to make an exact copy of the formula in A1 — and copy it to A2:

1. **Double-click A1 (or press F2) to get into Edit mode.**
2. **Drag the mouse to select the entire formula.** You can drag from left to right or from right to left. To select the entire formula with the keyboard, press Shift+Home.
3. **Choose Home ➪ Clipboard ➪ Copy(or press Ctrl+C).** This copies the selected text (which will become the copied formula) to the Clipboard.
4. **Press Esc to get out of Edit mode.**
5. **Select cell A2.**
6. **Home ➪ Clipboard ➪ Paste (or press Ctrl+V) to paste the text into cell A2.**

You also can use this technique to copy just *part* of a formula, if you want to use that part in another formula. Just select the part of the formula that you want to copy by dragging the mouse, and then use any of the available techniques to copy the selection to the Clipboard. You can then paste the text to another cell.

Formulas (or parts of formulas) copied in this manner won't have their cell references adjusted when they are pasted to a new cell. That's because the formulas are being copied as text, not as actual formulas.

TIP You can also convert a formula to text by adding an apostrophe (') in front of the equal sign. Then, copy the formula as usual and paste it to its new location. Remove the apostrophe from the pasted formula, and it will be identical to the original formula. And don't forget to remove the apostrophe from the original formula as well.

Converting formulas to values

If you have a range of formulas that will always produce the same result (that is, *dead formulas*), you may want to convert them to values. If, say, range A1:A20 contains formulas that have calculated results that will never change — or that you don't want to change. For example, if you use the RANDBETWEEN function to create a set of random numbers and you don't want Excel to recalculate those random numbers each time you press Enter, you can convert the formulas to values. Just follow these steps:

1. **Select A1:A20.**
2. **Choose Home ➪ Clipboard ➪ Copy (or press Ctrl+C).**
3. **Choose Home ➪ Clipboard ➪ Paste Values**
4. **Press Esc to cancel Copy mode.**

Chapter 12

Creating Formulas That Manipulate Text

Excel is, of course, best known for its ability to crunch numbers. It's also quite versatile, however, with handling text. As you know, you can enter text for such things as row and column headings, customer names and addresses, part numbers, and just about anything else. In addition (as you may expect), you can use formulas to manipulate the text contained in cells.

This chapter contains many examples of formulas that use a variety of functions to manipulate text. Some of these formulas perform feats that you may not have thought possible.

A Few Words About Text

When you enter data into a cell, Excel immediately goes to work and determines whether you're entering a formula, a number (including a date or time), or anything else. That "anything else" is considered text.

> **NOTE** You may hear the term *string* used instead of *text.* You can use these terms interchangeably. Sometimes they even appear together, as in *text string.*

How many characters in a cell?

A single cell can hold up to 32,000 characters. To put things into perspective, this chapter contains about 31,690 characters. How do I know that? I copied the entire chapter and pasted it into a single cell. Then I used the LEN function to count the characters. I certainly don't recommend putting that much text into a cell. Performance is extremely sluggish, and it's very likely that Excel will crash.

IN THIS CHAPTER

How Excel handles text entered into cells

Excel's worksheet functions that handle text

Examples of advanced text formulas

When a number isn't treated as a number

If you import data into Excel, you may be aware of a common problem: Sometimes the imported values are treated as text. Here's a quick way to convert these non-numbers to actual values. Activate any empty cell and choose Home ➪ Clipboard ➪ Copy (or press Ctrl+C). Then select the range that contains the values you need to fix. Choose Home ➪ Clipboard ➪ Paste Special. In the Paste Special dialog box, select the Add operation and then click OK. This procedure essentially adds zero to each cell — and, in the process, forces Excel to treat the non-numbers as actual values.

Excel may display a Smart Tag to identify numbers stored as text. If the cell contains a Smart Tag, you'll see a small rectangle in the upper left corner of the cells. Activate the cell, and you can respond to the Smart Tag. To force the number to be treated as an actual number, select Convert To Number on the Smart Tag's list of options.

Numbers as text

As I mentioned, Excel distinguishes between numbers and text. If you want to *force* a number to be considered as text, you can do one of the following:

- Apply the Text Number format to the cell. To do so, use the Number Format drop-down list on the Number group of the Home tab. If you haven't applied other horizontal alignment formatting, the value will appear left-aligned (like normal text) in the cell.
- Precede the number with an apostrophe. The apostrophe isn't displayed, but the cell entry will be treated as if it were text.

Even though a cell is formatted as Text (or it uses an apostrophe), you can still perform *some* mathematical operations on the cell if the entry *looks* like a number. For example, assume cell A1 contains a value preceded by an apostrophe. The formula that follows displays the value in A1, incremented by 1:

```
=A1+1
```

Functions, however, treat the contents of cell A1 as 0, which gives you an incorrect result. Here's an example:

```
=SUM(A1:A10)
```

Bottom line? Be aware of Excel's inconsistency in how it treats a number formatted as text; the accompanying sidebar is a good place to start.

Text Functions

Excel has an excellent assortment of worksheet functions that can handle text. You can access these functions just where you'd expect: from the Text control in the Function Library group of the Formula tab.

A few other functions that are relevant to text manipulation appear in other function categories.

CROSS-REF Refer to Appendix A for a listing of the functions in the Text category — or you can peruse these functions in the Insert Function dialog box. Activate an empty cell, and choose Formulas ⇨ Function Library ⇨ Insert Function. In the Insert Function dialog box, select the Text category and scroll through the list. To find out more about a particular function, click the <u>Help On This Function</u> link.

Most text functions are not limited to use with text; they can also operate with cells that contain values. You'll find that Excel is very accommodating when it comes to treating numbers as text and text as numbers.

The examples discussed in this section demonstrate some common (and useful) things you can do with text. You may need to adapt some of these examples for your own use.

Determining whether a cell contains text

In some situations, you may need a formula that determines the type of data contained in a particular cell. For example, you may use an IF function to return a result only if a cell contains text. The easiest way to make this determination is to use the ISTEXT function.

NOTE If you're browsing through the Text functions, you won't find the ISTEXT function. The ISTEXT function is in the Information category, which is accessed from the More control in the Function Library group.

The ISTEXT function takes a single argument and returns TRUE if the argument contains text and FALSE if it doesn't contain text. The formula that follows returns TRUE if A1 contains a string:

```
=ISTEXT(A1)
```

Working with character codes

Every character you see on your screen has an associated code number. For Windows systems, Excel uses the standard ANSI character set. The ANSI character set consists of 255 characters, numbered (not surprisingly) from 1 to 255.

Figure 12.1 shows a portion of an Excel worksheet that displays all of the 255 characters. This example uses the Wingdings 3 font. (Other fonts may have different characters.)

ON the CD-ROM The companion CD-ROM includes a copy of this workbook, which also includes some simple VBA macros that enable you to display the character set for any font installed on your system. The file is named **character set.xlsm**.

Two functions come into play when dealing with character codes: CODE and CHAR. These functions may not be very useful by themselves, but they can prove quite useful in conjunction with other functions. I discuss these functions in the following sections.

FIGURE 12.1

The ANSI character set (for the Wingdings 3 font).

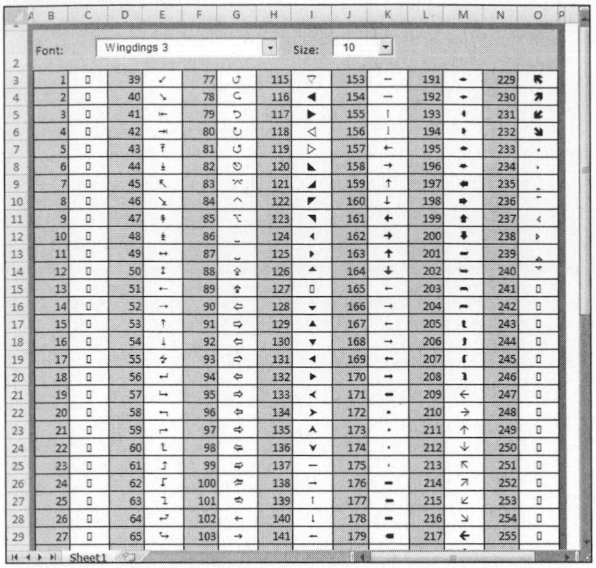

Font: Wingdings 3		Size: 10												
1	□	39	✓	77	↻	115	▽	153	↔	191	◆	229	➘
2	□	40	↘	78	↺	116	◀	154	↔	192	◆	230	➚
3	□	41	↤	79	↻	117	▶	155	↕	193	◆	231	➙
4	□	42	↦	80	↺	118	◁	156	↕	194	●	232	➘
5	□	43	↥	81	↻	119	▷	157	←	195	●	233	·
6	□	44	↨	82	↻	120	◤	158	→	196	●	234	·
7	□	45	↖	83	✳	121	◢	159	↑	197	◆	235	·
8	□	46	↘	84	∧	122	◥	160	↓	198	◆	236	ˉ
9	□	47	↕	85	∨	123	◣	161	←	199	↑	237	◀
10	□	48	↕	86	_	124	◀	162	→	200	↓	238	▶
11	□	49	↔	87	_	125	▶	163	↑	201	↔	239	▲
12	□	50	↕	88	⇑	126	▲	164	↓	202	↔	240	▼
13	□	51	←	89	⇑	127	□	165	↖	203	↔	241	□
14	□	52	→	90	⇐	128	▼	166	↗	204	↔	242	□
15	□	53	↑	91	⇒	129	▲	167	↘	205	↕	243	□
16	□	54	↓	92	⇐	130	▼	168	↙	206	↕	244	□
17	□	55	↔	93	⇔	131	◀	169	←	207	↕	245	□
18	□	56	↵	94	⇐	132	▶	170	→	208	↕	246	□
19	□	57	↴	95	⇒	133	◀	171	←	209	←	247	□
20	□	58	↱	96	⇔	134	▶	172	·	210	→	248	□
21	□	59	↰	97	⇔	135	▲	173	·	211	↑	249	□
22	□	60	↳	98	⇔	136	▼	174	·	212	↓	250	□
23	□	61	↲	99	⇔	137	↔	175	·	213	↖	251	□
24	□	62	↥	100	⇔	138	→	176	■	214	↗	252	□
25	□	63	↧	101	⇕	139	↕	177	■	215	↙	253	□
26	□	64	↩	102	←	140	↓	178	■	216	↘	254	□
27	□	65	↪	103	→	141	↔	179	■	217	←	255	□

The CODE function

Excel's CODE function returns the character code for its argument. The formula that follows returns 65, the character code for uppercase *A*:

```
=CODE("A")
```

If the argument for CODE consists of more than one character, the function uses only the first character. Therefore, this formula also returns 65:

```
=CODE("Abbey Road")
```

The CHAR function

The CHAR function is essentially the opposite of the CODE function. Its argument should be a value between 1 and 255, and the function should return the corresponding character. The following formula, for example, returns the letter *A*:

```
=CHAR(65)
```

To demonstrate the opposing nature of the CODE and CHAR functions, try entering this formula:

```
=CHAR(CODE("A"))
```

This formula, which is illustrative rather than useful, returns the letter *A*. First, it converts the character to its code value (65), and then it converts this code back to the corresponding character.

Inserting special characters

If you need to insert special characters not found on your keyboard, you can use the Symbol dialog box (which is accessed using Insert ⇨ Text ⇨ Symbol). This dialog box simplifies inserting special characters (including Unicode characters) into cells. For example, you may want to display the Greek letter *pi* (π) in your spreadsheet. Access Excel's Symbol dialog box and select the Symbol font (see the accompanying figure). Examine the characters, locate the pi character, and click Insert. You'll see (in the Character Code area of the Symbol dialog box) that this character has a numerical code of 112.

In addition, Excel has several built-in AutoCorrect symbols. For example, if you type **(c)**, Excel converts it to a copyright symbol. To see the other symbols that you can enter this way, display the AutoCorrect dialog box. To display this dialog box, choose Office ⇨ Excel Options and select the Proofing tab in the Excel Options dialog box. Then click the AutoCorrect Options button. You can then scroll through the list to see which autocorrections are enabled (and delete those that you don't want).

If you find that Excel makes an autocorrection that you don't want, press Ctrl+Z to undo the autocorrection.

Assume cell A1 contains the letter *A* (uppercase). The following formula returns the letter *a* (lowercase):

```
=CHAR(CODE(A1)+32)
```

This formula takes advantage of the fact that the alphabetic characters all appear in alphabetical order within the character set; lowercase letters follow uppercase letters (with a few other characters tossed in between). Each lowercase letter lies exactly 32 character positions higher than its corresponding uppercase letter.

Determining whether two strings are identical

You can set up a simple logical formula to determine whether two cells contain the same entry. For example, use this formula to determine whether cell A1 has the same contents as cell A2:

```
=A1=A2
```

This formula will return either TRUE of FALSE. However, Excel is a bit lax in its comparisons when text is involved. Consider the case in which A1 contains the word January (initial capitalization), and A2 contains JANUARY (all-uppercase). You'll find that the previous formula returns TRUE, even though the contents of the two cells are not really the same — the comparison is not case-sensitive.

Often, you don't need to worry about the case of the text. But if you need to make an exact, case-sensitive comparison, you can use the EXACT function. The formula that follows returns TRUE only if cells A1 and A2 contain *exactly* the same entry:

    =EXACT(A1,A2)

When you compare text, be careful with space characters — which are often difficult to spot. The following formula returns FALSE because the first string contains a trailing space:

    =EXACT("Canada ","Canada")

Joining two or more cells

Excel uses an ampersand (&) as its concatenation operator. *Concatenation* is simply a fancy term that describes what happens when you join the contents of two or more cells. For example, if cell A1 contains the text Tucson and cell A2 contains the text Arizona, the following formula will return TucsonArizona:

    =A1&A2

Notice that the two strings are joined together without an intervening space. To add a space between the two entries (to get Tucson Arizona), use a formula like this one:

    =A1&" "&A2

Or, even better, use a comma and a space to produce Tucson, Arizona:

    =A1&", "&A2

If you'd like to force the second string to be on a new line, concatenate the strings using CHAR(10), which inserts a line-break character. Also, make sure that you apply the Wrap Text format to the cell. The following example joins the text in cell A1 and the text in cell B1, with a line break in between:

    =A1&CHAR(10)&B1

TIP To apply Wrap Text formatting, select the cells and then use Home ➪ Alignment ➪ Wrap Text.

Here's another example of the CHAR function. The following formula returns the string Stop by concatenating four characters returned by the CHAR function:

    =CHAR(83)&CHAR(116)&CHAR(111)&CHAR(112)

Here's a final example of using the & operator. In this case, the formula combines text with the result of an expression that returns the maximum value in column C:

    ="The largest value in Column C is " &MAX(C:C)

NOTE Excel also has a CONCATENATE function, which takes up to 255 arguments. For example:

    =CONCATENATE(A1,B1,C1,D1)

This function simply combines the arguments into a single string. You can use this function if you like, but using the & operator results in shorter formulas.

Displaying formatted values as text

The TEXT function enables you to display a value in a specific number format. Figure 12.2 shows a simple worksheet. The formula in cell D3 is

```
="The net profit is " & B3
```

The formula in D3 doesn't display the formatted number.

	A	B	C	D	E	F
1	Gross	$354,234				
2	Expenses	$123,440				
3	Net	$230,794		The net profit is 230794		
4						
5						
6						

This formula essentially combines a text string with the contents of cell B3 and displays the result. Note, however, that the contents of B3 are not formatted in any way. You might want to display the contents of B3 using a Currency number format.

NOTE Contrary to what you might expect, applying a number format to the cell that contains the formula has no effect. This is because the formula returns a string, not a value.

Here's a revised formula that uses the TEXT function to apply formatting to the value in B3:

```
="The net profit is " & TEXT(B3," $#,##0")
```

This formula displays the text along with a nicely formatted value:

```
The net profit is $230,794
```

The second argument for the TEXT function consists of a standard Excel number format string. You can enter any valid number format code for this argument.

The preceding example uses a simple cell reference (B3). You can, of course, use an expression instead. Here's an example that combines text with a number resulting from a computation:

```
="Average Expenditure: "& TEXT(AVERAGE(A:A),"$#,##0.00")
```

This formula might return a string such as Average Expenditure: $7,794.57.

Here's another example that uses the NOW function (which returns the current date and time). The TEXT function displays the date and time, nicely formatted.

```
="Report printed on "&TEXT(NOW(),"mmmm d, yyyy at h:mm AM/PM")
```

The formula might display the following:

```
Report printed on March 22, 2007 at 3:23 PM
```

CROSS-REF Refer to Chapter 24 for details on Excel number formats.

Displaying formatted currency values as text

The Excel `DOLLAR` function converts a number to text using the currency format. It takes two arguments: the number to convert, and the number of decimal places to display. The `DOLLAR` function uses the regional currency symbol (for example, a $).

You can sometimes use the `DOLLAR` function in place of the `TEXT` function. The `TEXT` function, however, is much more flexible because it doesn't limit you to a specific number format.

The following formula returns `Total: $1,287.37` (the second argument for the `DOLLAR` function specifies the number of decimal places):

```
="Total: "&DOLLAR(1287.367, 2)
```

Repeating a character or string

The `REPT` function repeats a text string (first argument) any number of times you specify (second argument). For example, this formula returns `HoHoHo`:

```
=REPT("Ho",3)
```

You can also use this function to create crude vertical dividers between cells. This example displays a squiggly line, 20 characters in length:

```
=REPT("~",20)
```

Creating a text histogram

A clever use for the `REPT` function is to create a simple *histogram* (or frequency-distribution chart) directly in a worksheet. Figure 12.3 shows an example of such a histogram. You'll find this type of graphical display especially useful when you need a visual summary of many values, and a standard chart is unwieldy.

CROSS-REF **The new conditional formatting features in Excel 2007 provide a much better way to display a simple histogram directly in cells. See Chapter 21 for details.**

FIGURE 12.3

Using the `REPT` function to create a histogram in a worksheet range.

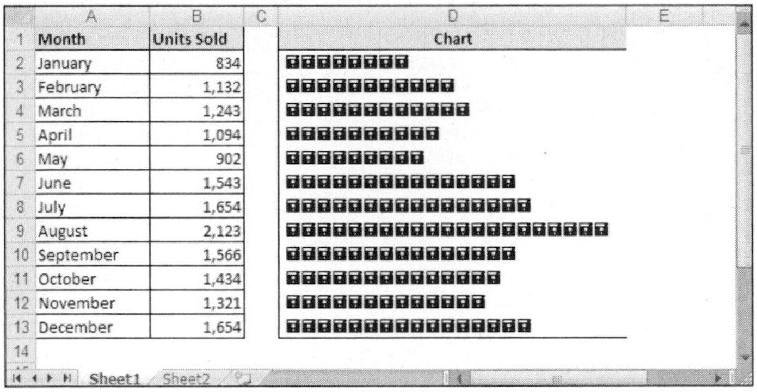

Month	Units Sold	Chart
January	834	
February	1,132	
March	1,243	
April	1,094	
May	902	
June	1,543	
July	1,654	
August	2,123	
September	1,566	
October	1,434	
November	1,321	
December	1,654	

The formulas in column D graphically depict the sales numbers in column B by displaying a series of characters in the Wingdings font. This example uses character code 61 (an equal sign), which appears on-screen as a small floppy disc the Wingdings font. A formula using the REPT function determines the number of characters displayed. The formula in cell D2 is:

```
=REPT("=",B2/100)
```

Assign the Wingdings font to cells D2, and then copy the formulas down the column to accommodate all the data. Depending on the numerical range of your data, you may need to change the scaling. Experiment by replacing the 100 value in the formulas. You can substitute any character you like for the equal sign character in the formula to produce a different character in the chart.

ON the CD-ROM The workbook shown in Figure 12.3 also appears on the companion CD-ROM. The file is named **text histogram.xlsx.**

Padding a number

You're probably familiar with a common security measure (frequently used on printed checks) in which numbers are padded with asterisks on the right. The following formula displays the value in cell A1, along with enough asterisks to make a total of 24 characters:

```
=(A1 & REPT("*",24-LEN(A1)))
```

If you'd prefer to pad the number with asterisks on the left instead, use this formula:

```
=REPT("*",24-LEN(A1))&A1
```

The formula below displays 12 asterisks on both sides of the number.

```
=REPT("*",12)&A1&REPT("*",12)
```

The preceding formulas are a bit deficient because they don't show any number formatting. This revised version displays the value in A1 (formatted), along with the asterisk padding on the right:

```
=(TEXT(A1,"$#,##0.00")&REPT("*",24-LEN(TEXT(A1,"$#,##0.00"))))
```

Figure 12.4 shows this formula in action.

FIGURE 12.4

Using a formula to pad a number with asterisks.

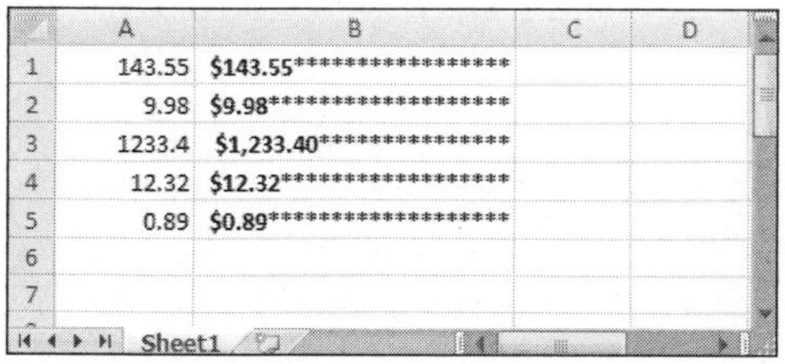

You can also pad a number by using a custom number format. To repeat the next character in that format until it fills the column width, include an asterisk (*) in the custom number format code. For example, use this number format to pad the number with dashes:

```
$#,##0.00*-
```

213

To pad the number with asterisks, use two asterisks in the number-format code, like this:

```
$#,##0.00**
```

CROSS-REF Refer to Chapter 24 for more information about custom number formats, including additional examples using the asterisk format code.

Removing excess spaces and nonprinting characters

Often data imported into an Excel worksheet contains excess spaces or strange (often unprintable) characters. Excel provides you with two functions to help whip your data into shape: TRIM and CLEAN:

- TRIM removes all leading and trailing spaces and replaces internal strings of multiple spaces by a single space.

- CLEAN removes all nonprinting characters from a string. These "garbage" characters often appear when you import certain types of data.

This example uses the TRIM function. The formula returns Fourth Quarter Earnings (with no excess spaces):

```
=TRIM("   Fourth    Quarter    Earnings    ")
```

Counting characters in a string

Excel's LEN function takes one argument and returns the number of characters in the argument. For example, assume the string September Sales is contained in cell A1. The following formula will return 15:

```
=LEN(A1)
```

Notice that space characters are included in the character count.

The following formula returns the total number of characters in the range A1:A3:

```
=LEN(A1)+LEN(A2)+LEN(A3)
```

CROSS-REF You see example formulas that demonstrate how to count the number of specific characters within a string later in this chapter. Chapter 14 covers counting techniques further.

Changing the case of text

Excel provides three handy functions to change the case of text:

- UPPER converts the text to ALL UPPERCASE.

- LOWER converts the text to all lowercase.

- PROPER converts the text to Proper Case (the first letter in each word is capitalized, as in a proper name).

These functions are quite straightforward. The formula that follows, for example, converts the text in cell A1 to proper case.

```
=PROPER(A1)
```

If cell A1 contained the text MR. JOHN Q. PUBLIC, the formula would return Mr. John Q. Public.

Transforming Data with Formulas

Many of the examples in this chapter describe how to use functions to transform data in some way. For example, you can use the UPPER function to transform text into uppercase. Often, you'll want to replace the original data with the transformed data. To do so, use the Paste Special dialog box. Specifically, follow these steps:

1. **Create your formulas to transform the original data.**
2. **Select the formula cells.**
3. **Choose Home ⇨ Clipboard ⇨ Copy (or press Ctrl+C).**
4. **Select the original data cells.**
5. **Choose Home ⇨ Clipboard ⇨ Paste Values.**

This procedure replaces the original data with the transformed data; then you can delete the formulas.

These functions operate only on alphabetic characters; they simply ignore all other characters and return them unchanged.

Extracting characters from a string

Excel users often need to extract characters from a string. For example, you may have a list of employee names (first and last names) and need to extract the last name from each cell. Excel provides several useful functions for extracting characters:

■ LEFT returns a specified number of characters from the beginning of a string.

■ RIGHT returns a specified number of characters from the end of a string.

■ MID returns a specified number of characters beginning at any position within a string.

The formula that follows returns the last 10 characters from cell A1 (if A1 contains fewer than 10 characters, the formula returns all text in the cell):

```
=RIGHT(A1,10)
```

This next formula uses the MID function to return five characters from cell A1, beginning at character position 2. In other words, it returns characters 2–6.

```
=MID(A1,2,5)
```

The following example returns the text in cell A1 with only the first letter in uppercase. It uses the LEFT function to extract the first character and convert it to uppercase. This then concatenates to another string that uses the RIGHT function to extract all but the first character (converted to lowercase). Here's what it looks like:

```
=UPPER(LEFT(A1))&RIGHT(LOWER(A1),LEN(A1)-1)
```

If cell A1 contained the text FIRST QUARTER, the formula would return First quarter.

> **NOTE**   This is different than the result obtained using the PROPER function. The PROPER function makes the first character in each word uppercase.

Replacing text with other text

In some situations, you may need to replace a part of a text string with some other text. For example, you may import data that contains asterisks, and you need to convert the asterisks to some other character. You could use Excel's Home ➪ Editing ➪ Find & Select ➪ Replace command to make the replacement. If you prefer a formula-based solution, you can take advantage of either of two functions:

- SUBSTITUTE replaces specific text in a string. Use this function when you know the character(s) to be replaced but not the position.

- REPLACE replaces text that occurs in a specific location within a string. Use this function when you know the position of the text to be replaced but not the actual text.

The following formula uses the SUBSTITUTE function to replace 2006 with 2007 in the string 2006 Budget. The formula returns 2007 Budget.

```
=SUBSTITUTE("2006 Budget","2006","2007")
```

The following formula uses the SUBSTITUTE function to remove all spaces from a string. In other words, it replaces all space characters with an empty string. The formula returns 2007OperatingBudget.

```
=SUBSTITUTE("2007 Operating Budget"," ","")
```

The following formula uses the REPLACE function to replace one character beginning at position 5 with nothing. In other words, it removes the fifth character (a hyphen) and returns Part544.

```
=REPLACE("Part-544",5,1,"")
```

Finding and searching within a string

Excel's FIND and SEARCH functions enable you to locate the starting position of a particular substring within a string:

- **FIND** finds a substring within another text string and returns the starting position of the substring. You can specify the character position at which to begin searching. Use this function for case-sensitive text comparisons. Wildcard comparisons are not supported.

- **SEARCH** finds a substring within another text string and returns the starting position of the substring. You can specify the character position at which to begin searching. Use this function for non-case-sensitive text or when you need to use wildcard characters.

The following formula uses the FIND function and returns 7, the position of the first *m* in the string. Notice that this formula is case-sensitive.

```
=FIND("m","Big Mama Thornton",1)
```

The formula that follows, which uses the SEARCH function, returns 5, the position of the first *m* (either uppercase or lowercase):

```
=SEARCH("m","Big Mama Thornton",1)
```

You can use the following wildcard characters within the first argument for the SEARCH function:

- Question mark (?) matches any single character.
- Asterisk (*) matches any sequence of characters.

TIP If you want to find an actual question mark or asterisk character, type a tilde (~) before the question mark or asterisk.

The next formula examines the text in cell A1 and returns the position of the first three-character sequence that has a hyphen in the middle of it. In other words, it looks for any character followed by a hyphen and any other character. If cell A1 contains the text Part-A90, the formula returns 4.

```
=SEARCH("?-?",A1,1)
```

Searching and replacing within a string

You can use the REPLACE function in conjunction with the SEARCH function to replace part of a text string with another string. In effect, you use the SEARCH function to find the starting location used by the REPLACE function.

For example, assume that cell A1 contains the text Annual Profit Figures. The following formula searches for the 6-letter word Profit and replaces it with the word Loss:

```
=REPLACE(A1,SEARCH("Profit",A1),6,"Loss")
```

This next formula uses the SUBSTITUTE function to accomplish the same effect in a more efficient manner:

```
=SUBSTITUTE(A1,"Profit","Loss")
```

Advanced Text Formulas

The examples in this section appear more complex than the examples in the preceding section. But as you can see, these examples can perform some very useful text manipulations. Space limitations prevent a detailed explanation of how these formulas work, but this section gives you a basic introduction.

ON the CD-ROM You can access all of the examples in this section on the companion CD-ROM. The file is named text formula examples.xlsx.

Counting specific characters in a cell

This formula counts the number of *B*s (uppercase only) in the string in cell A1:

```
=LEN(A1)-LEN(SUBSTITUTE(A1,"B",""))
```

This formula works by using the SUBSTITUTE function to create a new string (in memory) that has all the *B*s removed. Then the length of this string is subtracted from the length of the original string. The result reveals the number of *B*s in the original string.

The following formula is a bit more versatile; it counts the number of *B*s (both uppercase and lowercase) in the string in cell A1. Using the UPPER function to convert the string makes this formula work with both uppercase and lowercase characters:

```
=LEN(A1)-LEN(SUBSTITUTE(UPPER(A1),"B",""))
```

Counting the occurrences of a substring in a cell

The formulas in the preceding section count the number of occurrences of a particular character in a string. The following formula works with more than one character. It returns the number of occurrences of a particular substring (contained in cell B1) within a string (contained in cell A1). The substring can consist of any number of characters.

```
=(LEN(A1)-LEN(SUBSTITUTE(A1,B1,"")))/LEN(B1)
```

For example, if cell A1 contains the text Blonde On Blonde and B1 contains the text Blonde, the formula returns 2.

The comparison is case sensitive, so if B1 contains the text blonde, the formula returns 0. The following formula is a modified version that performs a case-insensitive comparison by converting the characters to uppercase:

```
=(LEN(A1)-LEN(SUBSTITUTE(UPPER(A1),UPPER(B1),"")))/LEN(B1)
```

Extracting a filename from a path specification

The following formula returns the filename from a full path specification. For example, if cell A1 contains c:\windows\important\myfile.xlsx, the formula returns myfile.xlsx.

```
=MID(A1,FIND("*",SUBSTITUTE(A1,"\","*",LEN(A1)-
LEN(SUBSTITUTE(A1,"\",""))))+1,LEN(A1))
```

This formula assumes that the system path separator is a backslash (\). It essentially returns all text that follows the last backslash character. If cell A1 doesn't contain a backslash character, the formula returns an error.

Extracting the first word of a string

To extract the first word of a string, a formula must locate the position of the first space character and then use this information as an argument for the LEFT function. The following formula does just that:

```
=LEFT(A1,FIND(" ",A1)-1)
```

This formula returns all of the text prior to the first space in cell A1. However, the formula has a slight problem: It returns an error if cell A1 consists of a single word. A slightly more complex formula that checks for the error using the IFERROR function solves that problem:

```
=IFERROR(LEFT(A1,FIND(" ",A1)-1),A1)
```

CAUTION The preceding formula uses the IFERROR function, which is new to Excel 2007. If your workbook will be used with previous versions of Excel, use this formula:

```
=IF(ISERR(FIND(" ",A1)),A1,LEFT(A1,FIND(" ",A1)-1))
```

Extracting the last word of a string

Extracting the last word of a string is more complicated because the FIND function only works from left to right. Therefore the problem is locating the *last* space character. The formula that follows, however, solves this problem by returning the last word of a string (all text following the last space character):

```
=RIGHT(A1,LEN(A1)-FIND("*",SUBSTITUTE(A1," ","*",LEN(A1)-
LEN(SUBSTITUTE(A1," ","")))))
```

This formula, however, has the same problem as the first formula in the preceding section: It fails if the string does not contain at least *one* space character. The following modified formula uses the new IFERROR function to test for an error (that is, no spaces). If the first argument returns an error, then the formula returns the complete contents of cell A1.

```
=IFERROR(RIGHT(A1,LEN(A1)-FIND("*",SUBSTITUTE(A1," ","*",LEN(A1)-
LEN(SUBSTITUTE(A1," ","")))))),A1)
```

Following is a modification that doesn't use the IFERROR function. This formula works for all versions of Excel.

```
=IF(ISERR(FIND(" ",A1)),A1,RIGHT(A1,LEN(A1)-FIND("*",SUBSTITUTE(A1,
" ","*",LEN(A1)-LEN(SUBSTITUTE(A1," ","")))))))
```

Extracting all but the first word of a string

The following formula returns the contents of cell A1, except for the first word:

```
=RIGHT(A1,LEN(A1)-FIND(" ",A1,1))
```

If cell A1 contains 2007 Operating Budget, the formula returns Operating Budget.

The formula below, which uses the new IFERROR function, returns the entire contents of cell A1 if the cell doesn't have a space character:

```
=IFERROR(RIGHT(A1,LEN(A1)-FIND(" ",A1,1)),A1)
```

A modification that works in all versions of Excel is

```
=IF(ISERR(FIND(" ",A1)),A1,RIGHT(A1,LEN(A1)-FIND(" ",A1,1)))
```

Extracting first names, middle names, and last names

Suppose you have a list consisting of people's names in a single column. You have to separate these names into three columns: one for the first name, one for the middle name or initial, and one for the last name. This task is more complicated than you may think because it must handle the situation for a missing middle initial. However, you can still do it.

NOTE The task becomes a *lot* more complicated if the list contains names with titles (such as *Mr.* or *Dr.*) or names followed by additional details (such as *Jr.* or *III*). In fact, the following formulas will *not* handle these complex cases. However, they still give you a significant head start if you're willing to do a bit of manual editing to handle special cases.

The formulas that follow all assume that the name appears in cell A1.

You can easily construct a formula to return the first name:

```
=LEFT(A1,FIND(" ",A1)-1)
```

This formula returns the last name:

```
=RIGHT(A1,LEN(A1)-FIND("*",SUBSTITUTE(A1," ","*",LEN(A1)-
LEN(SUBSTITUTE(A1," ","")))))
```

The next formula extracts the middle name and requires that you use the other formulas to extract the first name and the last name. It assumes that the first name is in B1 and the last name is in D1. Here's what it looks like:

```
=IF(LEN(B1&D1)+2>=LEN(A1),"",MID(A1,LEN(B1)+2,LEN(A1)-LEN(B1&D1)-2))
```

As you can see in Figure 12.5, the formulas work fairly well. There are a few problems, however, notably names that contain four "words." But, as I mentioned earlier, you can clean these cases up manually.

FIGURE 12.5

This worksheet uses formulas to extract the first name, last name, and middle name (or initial) from a list of names in column A.

	A	B	C	D	E	F
1	Full Name	First	Middle	Last		
2	John Q. Public	John	Q.	Public		
3	Lisa Smith	Lisa		Smith		
4	J. R. Robins	J.	R.	Robins		
5	Dr. Lester B. Jones	Dr.	Lester B.	Jones		
6	J. R. R. Tolkien	J.	R. R.	Tolkien		
7	Franklin H. Lee	Franklin	H.	Lee		
8	Melvina Pryce	Melvina		Pryce		
9	Suzette I. Thorson	Suzette	I.	Thorson		
10	J. Frank	J.		Frank		
11	Amanda M. Rowe	Amanda	M.	Rowe		
12	Melvin H. Hodges	Melvin	H.	Hodges		
13	Aaron E. Pacheco	Aaron	E.	Pacheco		
14	Dennis Michael Batie	Dennis	Michael	Batie		
15	Lloyd Benedict Arnold	Lloyd	Benedict	Arnold		
16	Agnes K. Saterfiel	Agnes	K.	Saterfiel		
17	Robert M. Simmons	Robert	M.	Simmons		
18	Joseph Q. Glenn	Joseph	Q.	Glenn		
19	Jeffrey George Bishop	Jeffrey	George	Bishop		
20	Henrietta D. Markowski	Henrietta	D.	Markowski		
21	William R. Gordon	William	R.	Gordon		

Sheet1

Removing titles from names

You can use the formula that follows to remove three common titles (*Mr.*, *Ms.*, and *Mrs.*) from a name. For example, if cell A1 contains Mr. Fred Munster, the formula would return Fred Munster.

```
=IF(OR(LEFT(A1,2)="Mr",LEFT(A1,3)="Mrs",LEFT(A1,2)="Ms"),
RIGHT(A1,LEN(A1) -FIND(" ",A1)),A1)
```

Creating an ordinal number

An *ordinal number* is an adjective form of a number. Examples include 1st, 2nd, 5th, 23rd, and so on.

The formula that follows displays the value in cell A1 as an ordinal number:

```
=A13&IF(OR(VALUE(RIGHT(A1,2))={11,12,13}),"th",
IF(OR(VALUE(RIGHT(A1))={1,2,3}),CHOOSE(RIGHT(A1),
"st","nd","rd"),"th"))
```

The formula is rather complex because it must determine whether the number will end in th, st, nd, or rd. This formula also uses literal arrays (enclosed in brackets), which are described in Chapter 17.

Counting the number of words in a cell

The following formula returns the number of words in cell A1:

```
=LEN(TRIM(A1))-LEN(SUBSTITUTE( (A1)," ",""))+1
```

Splitting text strings without using formulas

In many cases, you can eliminate the use of formulas and use Excel's Text To Columns command to parse strings into their component parts. This command is found in the Data Tools group of the Data tab. The Text To Columns command displays the Convert Text To Columns Wizard, which consists of a series of dialog boxes that walk you through the steps to convert a single column of data into multiple columns. Generally, you want to select the Delimited option (in Step 1) and use Space as the delimiter (in Step 2), as shown in the following figure.

The formula uses the TRIM function to remove excess spaces. It then uses the SUBSTITUTE function to create a new string (in memory) that has all the space characters removed. The length of this string is subtracted from the length of the original (trimmed) string to get the number of spaces. This value is then incremented by 1 to get the number of words.

Note that this formula will return 1 if the cell is empty. The following modification solves that problem:

```
=IF(LEN(A1)=0,0,LEN(TRIM(A1))-LEN(SUBSTITUTE(TRIM(A1)," ",""))+1)
```

Chapter 13

Working with Dates and Times

eginners often find that working with dates and times in Excel can be frustrating. To work with dates and times, you need a good understanding of how Excel handles time-based information. This chapter provides the information you need to create powerful formulas that manipulate dates and times.

NOTE   The dates in this chapter correspond to the United States English date format: month/day/year. For example, the date 3/1/1952 refers to March 1, 1952, not January 3, 1952. I realize that this setup may seem illogical, but that's the way Americans have been trained. I trust that the non-American readers of this book can make the adjustment.

IN THIS CHAPTER

An overview of using dates and times in Excel

Excel's date-related functions

Excel's time-related functions

How Excel Handles Dates and Times

This section presents a quick overview of how Excel deals with dates and times. It includes coverage of the Excel program's date and time serial number system, and it offers tips for entering and formatting dates and times.

Understanding date serial numbers

To Excel, a date is simply a number. More precisely, a date is a *serial number* that represents the number of days since the fictitious date of January 0, 1900. A serial number of 1 corresponds to January 1, 1900; a serial number of 2 corresponds to January 2, 1900, and so on. This system makes it possible to deal with dates in formulas. For example, you can create a formula to calculate the number of days between two dates (just subtract one from the other).

Excel support dates from January 1, 1900, through December 31, 9999 (serial number = 2,958,465).

Choose Your Date System: 1900 or 1904

Excel actually supports two date systems: the 1900 date system and the 1904 date system. Which system you use in a workbook determines what date serves as the basis for dates. The 1900 date system uses January 1, 1900, as the day assigned to date serial number 1. The 1904 date system uses January 1, 1904, as the base date. By default, Excel for Windows uses the 1900 date system, and Excel for Macintosh uses the 1904 date system. Excel for Windows supports the 1904 date system for compatibility with Macintosh files. You can choose the date system for the active workbook in the Advanced section of the Excel Options dialog box. (It's in the subsection titled When Calculating This Workbook.) You can't change the date system if you use Excel for Macintosh.

Generally, you should use the default 1900 date system. And you should exercise caution if you use two different date systems in workbooks that are linked together. For example, assume that Book1 uses the 1904 date system and contains the date 1/15/1999 in cell A1. Assume that Book2 uses the 1900 date system and contains a link to cell A1 in Book1. Book2 displays the date as 1/14/1995. Both workbooks use the same date serial number (34713), but they're interpreted differently.

One advantage to using the 1904 date system is that it enables you to display negative time values. With the 1900 date system, a calculation that results in a negative time (for example, 4:00 PM–5:30 PM) cannot be displayed. When using the 1904 date system, the negative time displays as –1:30 (that is, a difference of 1 hour and 30 minutes).

You may wonder about January 0, 1900. This *nondate* (which corresponds to date serial number 0) is actually used to represent times that aren't associated with a particular day. This nondate business becomes clear later in this chapter (see "Entering times").

To view a date serial number as a date, you must format the cell as a date. Choose Home ➪ Number ➪ Number Format. This drop-down control provides you with two date formats. To select from additional date formats, see "Formatting dates and times," later in this chapter.

Entering dates

You can enter a date directly as a serial number (if you know it), but more often, you enter a date using any of several recognized date formats. Excel automatically converts your entry into the corresponding date serial number (which it uses for calculations), and it also applies the default date format to the cell so that it displays as an actual date rather than as a cryptic serial number.

For example, if you need to enter June 18, 2007, you can simply enter the date by typing **June 18, 2007** (or any of several different date formats). Excel interprets your entry and stores the value 39251, the date serial number for that date. It also applies the default date format so that the cell contents may not appear exactly as you typed them.

NOTE Depending on your regional settings, entering a date in a format, such as June 18, 2007, may be interpreted as a text string. In such a case, you'd need to enter the date in a format that corresponds to your regional settings, such as 18 June, 2007.

When you activate a cell that contains a date, the Formula bar shows the cell contents formatted by using the default date format — which corresponds to your system's *short date format*. The Formula bar doesn't display the date's serial number. If you need to find out the serial number for a particular date, format the cell using a nondate number format.

 To change the default date format, you need to change a system-wide setting. Access the Windows Control Panel and select Regional and Language Options. Then click the Customize button to display the Customize Regional Options dialog box. Select the Date tab. The item selected in the Short Date Format drop-down list box determines the default date format used by Excel. These instructions apply to Windows XP and may vary with other versions of Windows.

Table 13.1 shows a sampling of the date formats that Excel recognizes (using the U.S. settings). Results will vary if you use a different regional setting.

TABLE 13.1

Date Entry Formats Recognized by Excel

Entry	Excel's Interpretation (U.S. Settings)
6-18-07	June 18, 2007
6-18-2007	June 18, 2007
6/18/07	June 18, 2007
6/18/2007	June 18, 2007
6-18/07	June 18, 2007
June 18, 2007	June 18, 2007
Jun 18	June 18 of the current year
June 18	June 18 of the current year
6/18	June 18 of the current year
6-18	June 18 of the current year
18-Jun-2007	June 18, 2007
2007/6/18	June 18, 2007

As you can see in Table 13.1, Excel is rather intelligent when it comes to recognizing dates entered into a cell. It's not perfect, however. For example, Excel does *not* recognize any of the following entries as dates:

- June 18 2007
- Jun-18 2007
- Jun-18/2007

Rather, it interprets these entries as text. If you plan to use dates in formulas, make sure that Excel can recognize the date you enter as a date; otherwise, the formulas that refer to these dates will produce incorrect results.

If you attempt to enter a date that lies outside of the supported date range, Excel interprets it as text. If you attempt to format a serial number that lies outside of the supported range as a date, the value displays as a series of hash marks (########).

Searching for Dates

If your worksheet uses many dates, you may need to search for a particular date by using the Find And Replace dialog box (which you can access by choosing Home ➪ Editing ➪ Find & Select ➪ Find or by pressing Ctrl+F). Excel is rather picky when it comes to finding dates. You must enter a full four-digit year into the Find What field in the Find dialog box. In addition, you must enter the date in the same format used to display dates in the Formula bar.

Understanding time serial numbers

When you need to work with time values, you simply extend the Excel date serial number system to include decimals. In other words, Excel works with times by using fractional days. For example, the date serial number for June 1, 2007, is 39234. Noon (halfway through the day) is represented internally as 39234.5.

The serial number equivalent of one minute is approximately 0.00069444. The formula that follows calculates this number by multiplying 24 hours by 60 minutes, and dividing the result into 1. The denominator consists of the number of minutes in a day (1,440).

```
=1/(24*60)
```

Similarly, the serial number equivalent of one second is approximately 0.00001157, obtained by the following formula: 1 divided by 24 hours times 60 minutes times 60 seconds. In this case, the denominator represents the number of seconds in a day (86,400).

```
=1/(24*60*60)
```

In Excel, the smallest unit of time is one one-thousandth of a second. The time serial number shown here represents 23:59:59.999 (or one one-thousandth of a second before midnight):

```
0.99999999
```

Table 13.2 shows various times of day along with each associated time serial numbers.

TABLE 13.2

Times of Day and Their Corresponding Serial Numbers

Time of Day	Time Serial Number
12:00:00 AM (midnight)	0.00000000
1:30:00 AM	0.06250000
3:00:00 AM	0.12500000
4:30:00 AM	0.18750000
6:00:00 AM	0.25000000
7:30:00 AM	0.31250000
9:00:00 AM	0.37500000

Time of Day	Time Serial Number
10:30:00 AM	0.43750000
12:00:00 PM (noon)	0.50000000
1:30:00 PM	0.56250000
3:00:00 PM	0.62500000
4:30:00 PM	0.68750000
6:00:00 PM	0.75000000
7:30:00 PM	0.81250000
9:00:00 PM	0.87500000
10:30:00 PM	0.93750000

Entering times

As with entering dates, you normally don't have to worry about the actual time serial numbers. Just enter the time into a cell using a recognized format. Table 13.3 shows some examples of time formats that Excel recognizes.

TABLE 13.3

Time Entry Formats Recognized by Excel

Entry	Excel's Interpretation
11:30:00 am	11:30 AM
11:30:00 AM	11:30 AM
11:30 pm	11:30 PM
11:30	11:30 AM
13:30	1:30 PM

Because the preceding samples don't have a specific day associated with them, Excel (by default) uses a date serial number of 0, which corresponds to the nonday January 0, 1900. Often, you'll want to combine a date and time. Do so by using a recognized date-entry format, followed by a space, and then a recognized time-entry format. For example, if you enter **6/18/2007 11:30** in a cell, Excel interprets it as 11:30 a.m. on June 18, 2007. Its date/time serial number is 39251.4791666667.

When you enter a time that exceeds 24 hours, the associated date for the time increments accordingly. For example, if you enter **25:00:00** into a cell, it's interpreted as 1:00 AM on January 1, 1900. The day part of the entry increments because the time exceeds 24 hours. Keep in mind that a time value without a date uses January 0, 1900 as the date.

Similarly, if you enter a date *and* a time (and the time exceeds 24 hours), the date that you entered is adjusted. If you enter **9/18/2007 25:00:00**, for example, it's interpreted as 9/19/2007 1:00:00 AM.

If you enter a time only (without an associated date), into an unformatted cell, the maximum time that you can enter into a cell is 9999:59:59 (just under 10,000 hours). Excel adds the appropriate number of days. In this case, 9999:59:59 is interpreted as 3:59:59 PM on 02/19/1901. If you enter a time that exceeds 10,000 hours, the entry is interpreted as a text string rather than a time.

Formatting dates and times

You have a great deal of flexibility in formatting cells that contain dates and times. For example, you can format the cell to display the date part only, the time part only, or both the date and time parts.

You format dates and times by selecting the cells and then using the Number tab of the Format Cells dialog box, as shown in Figure 13.1. To display this dialog box, click the dialog box launcher icon in the Number group of the Home tab. Or, you can click the Number Format control and select More Number Formats from the list that appears.

The Date category shows built-in date formats, and the Time category shows built-in time formats. Some formats include both date and time displays. Just select the desired format from the Type list and click OK.

FIGURE 13.1

Use the Number tab in the Format Cells dialog box to change the appearance of dates and times.

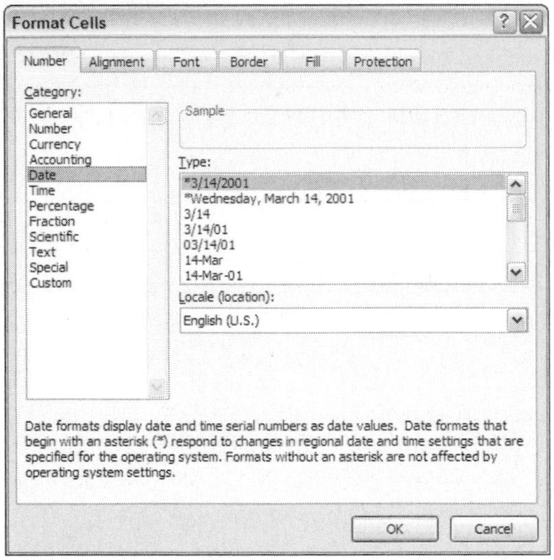

TIP When you create a formula that refers to a cell containing a date or a time, Excel automatically formats the formula cell as a date or a time. Sometimes, this automation is very helpful; other times, it's completely inappropriate and downright annoying. To return the number formatting to the default General format, choose Home ➪ Number ➪ Number Format, and select General from drop-down list Or, use this shortcut-key combination: Ctrl+Shift+~.

If none of the built-in formats meets your needs, you can create a custom number format. Select the Custom category and then type the custom format codes into the Type box. (See Chapter 24 for information on creating custom number formats.)

Problems with dates

Excel has some problems when it comes to dates. Many of these problems stem from the fact that Excel was designed many years ago, before the acronym *Y2K* was even thought of. And, as I describe, the Excel designers basically emulated the Lotus 1-2-3 program's limited date and time features, which contain a nasty bug duplicated intentionally in Excel.

If Excel were being designed from scratch today, I'm sure it would be much more versatile in dealing with dates. Unfortunately, users are currently stuck with a product that leaves much to be desired in the area of dates.

Excel's leap year bug

A leap year, which occurs every four years, contains an additional day (February 29). Although the year 1900 was not a leap year, Excel treats it as such. In other words, when you type **2/29/1900** into a cell, Excel interprets it as a valid date and assigns a serial number of 60.

If you type **2/29/1901**, however, Excel correctly interprets it as a mistake and doesn't convert it to a date. Rather, it simply makes the cell entry a text string.

How can a product used daily by millions of people contain such an obvious bug? The answer is historical. The original version of Lotus 1-2-3 contained a bug that caused it to consider 1900 as a leap year. When Excel was released some time later, the designers knew of this bug and chose to reproduce it in Excel to maintain compatibility with Lotus worksheet files.

Why does this bug still exist in later versions of Excel? Microsoft asserts that the disadvantages of correcting this bug outweigh the advantages. If the bug were eliminated, it would mess up millions of existing workbooks. In addition, correcting this problem would possibly affect compatibility between Excel and other programs that use dates. As it stands, this bug really causes very few problems because most users don't use dates before March 1, 1900.

Pre-1900 dates

The world, of course, didn't begin on January 1, 1900. People who use Excel to work with historical information often need to work with dates before January 1, 1900. Unfortunately, the only way to work with pre-1900 dates is to enter the date into a cell as text. For example, you can enter **July 4, 1776** into a cell, and Excel won't complain.

You can't, however, perform any manipulation on dates entered as text. For example, you can't change its numeric formatting, you can't determine which day of the week this date occurred on, and you can't calculate the date that occurs seven days later.

> **NOTE** My Power Utility Pak add-in includes eight new worksheet functions that enable you to work with any date in the years 0100 through 9999. Figure 13.2 shows a worksheet that uses these extended date functions in columns E though H to perform calculations that involve pre-1900 dates. You can download a trial version of Power Utility Pak from my Web site (http://j-walk.com/ss), or use the coupon in the back of the book to order a copy at a discounted price.

FIGURE 13.2

The author's Extended Date Functions add-in enables you to work with pre-1900 dates.

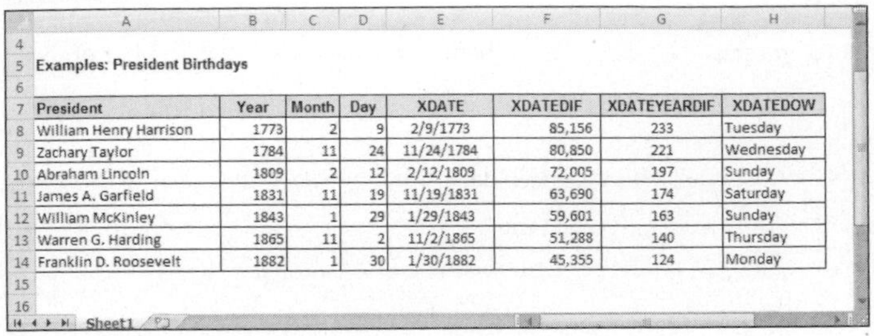

	A	B	C	D	E	F	G	H
4								
5	Examples: President Birthdays							
6								
7	President	Year	Month	Day	XDATE	XDATEDIF	XDATEYEARDIF	XDATEDOW
8	William Henry Harrison	1773	2	9	2/9/1773	85,156	233	Tuesday
9	Zachary Taylor	1784	11	24	11/24/1784	80,850	221	Wednesday
10	Abraham Lincoln	1809	2	12	2/12/1809	72,005	197	Sunday
11	James A. Garfield	1831	11	19	11/19/1831	63,690	174	Saturday
12	William McKinley	1843	1	29	1/29/1843	59,601	163	Sunday
13	Warren G. Harding	1865	11	2	11/2/1865	51,288	140	Thursday
14	Franklin D. Roosevelt	1882	1	30	1/30/1882	45,355	124	Monday
15								
16								

Sheet1

Inconsistent date entries

You need to exercise caution when entering dates by using two digits for the year. When you do so, Excel has some rules that kick in to determine which century to use. And those rules vary, depending on the version of Excel that you use.

Two-digit years between 00 and 29 are interpreted as 21st century dates, and two-digit years between 30 and 99 are interpreted as 20th-century dates. For example, if you enter 12/15/28, Excel interprets your entry as December 15, 2028. But if you enter 12/15/30, Excel sees it as December 15, 1930, because Windows uses a default boundary year of 2029. You can keep the default as is or change it by using the Windows Control Panel. In Windows XP, display the Regional And Language Options dialog box. Then click the Customize button to display the Customize Regional Options dialog box. Select the Date tab and then specify a different year. This procedure may vary with different versions of Windows.

> **TIP** The best way to avoid any surprises is to simply enter *all* years using all four digits for the year.

Date-Related Functions

Excel has quite a few functions that work with dates. These functions are accessible by choosing Formulas ⇨ Function Library ⇨ Date & Time.

Table 13.4 summarizes the date-related functions available in Excel.

TABLE 13.4

Date-Related Functions

Function	Description
DATE	Returns the serial number of a particular date
DATEVALUE	Converts a date in the form of text to a serial number
DAY	Converts a serial number to a day of the month
DAYS360	Calculates the number of days between two dates based on a 360-day year

Function	Description
EDATE*	Returns the serial number of the date that represents the indicated number of months before or after the start date
EOMONTH*	Returns the serial number of the last day of the month before or after a specified number of months
MONTH	Converts a serial number to a month
NETWORKDAYS*	Returns the number of whole work days between two dates
NOW	Returns the serial number of the current date and time
TODAY	Returns the serial number of today's date
WEEKDAY	Converts a serial number to a day of the week
WEEKNUM*	Returns the week number in the year
WORKDAY*	Returns the serial number of the date before or after a specified number of workdays
YEAR	Converts a serial number to a year
YEARFRAC*	Returns the year fraction representing the number of whole days between start_date and end_date

* In versions prior to Excel 2007, these functions are available only when the Analysis ToolPak add-in is installed.

Displaying the current date

The following function displays the current date in a cell:

```
=TODAY()
```

You can also display the date combined with text. The formula that follows, for example, displays text, such as *Today is Monday, April 9, 2007.*

```
="Today is "&TEXT(TODAY(),"dddd, mmmm d, yyyy")
```

It's important to understand that the TODAY function is updated whenever the worksheet is calculated. For example, if you enter either of the preceding formulas into a worksheet, the formulas display the current date. But when you open the workbook tomorrow, they will display the current date (not the date when you entered the formula).

> **TIP** To enter a date stamp into a cell, press Ctrl+; (semicolon). This action enters the date directly into the cell and does not use a formula. Therefore, the date will not change.

Displaying any date

You can easily enter a date into a cell by simply typing it while using any of the date formats that Excel recognizes. You can also create a date by using the DATE function, which takes three arguments: the year, the month, and the day. The following formula, for example, returns a date comprised of the year in cell A1, the month in cell B1, and the day in cell C1:

```
=DATE(A1,B1,C1)
```

TIP

The DATE function accepts invalid arguments and adjusts the result accordingly. For example, the following formula uses 13 as the month argument and returns January 1, 2008. The month argument is automatically translated as month 1 of the following year.

```
=DATE(2007,13,1)
```

Often, you'll use the DATE function with other functions as arguments. For example, the formula that follows uses the YEAR and TODAY functions to return the date for Independence Day (July 4th) of the current year:

```
=DATE(YEAR(TODAY()),7,4)
```

The DATEVALUE function converts a text string that looks like a date into a date serial number. The following formula returns 39316, the date serial number for August 22, 2007:

```
=DATEVALUE("8/22/2007")
```

To view the result of this formula as a date, you need to apply a date number format to the cell.

CAUTION

Be careful when using the DATEVALUE function. A text string that looks like a date in your country may not look like a date in another country. The preceding example works fine if your system is set for U.S. date formats, but it returns an error for other regional date formats because Excel is looking for the eighth day of the 22nd month!

Generating a series of dates

Often, you want to insert a series of dates into a worksheet. For example, in tracking weekly sales, you may want to enter a series of dates, each separated by seven days. These dates will serve to identify the sales figures.

The most efficient way to enter a series of dates doesn't require any formulas. Use the Excel AutoFill feature to insert a series of dates. Enter the first date and drag the cell's fill handle while pressing the right mouse button. Release the mouse button and select an option from the shortcut menu (see Figure 13.3) — either Fill Days, Fill Weekdays, Fill Months, or Fill Years.

FIGURE 13.3

Using Excel's AutoFill feature to create a series of dates.

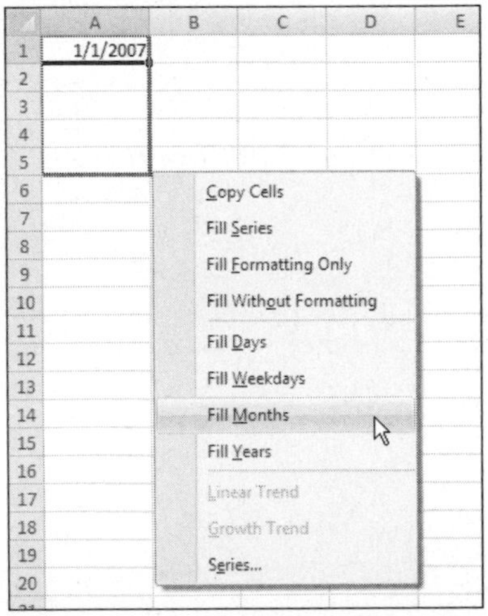

The advantage of using formulas (instead of the AutoFill feature) to create a series of dates is that you can change the first date, and the others update automatically. You need to enter the starting date into a cell and then use formulas (copied down the column) to generate the additional dates.

The following examples assume that you entered the first date of the series into cell A1 and the formula into cell A2. You can then copy this formula down the column as many times as needed.

To generate a series of dates separated by seven days, use this formula:

```
=A1+7
```

To generate a series of dates separated by one month, use this formula:

```
=DATE(YEAR(A1),MONTH(A1)+1,DAY(A1))
```

To generate a series of dates separated by one year, use this formula:

```
=DATE(YEAR(A1)+1,MONTH(A1),DAY(A1))
```

To generate a series of week days only (no Saturdays or Sundays), use the formula that follows. This formula assumes that the date in cell A1 is not a weekend day.

```
=IF(WEEKDAY(A1)=6,A1+3,A1+1)
```

Converting a nondate string to a date

You may import data that contains dates coded as text strings. For example, the following text represents August 21, 2007 (a four-digit year followed by a two-digit month, followed by a two-digit day):

```
20070821
```

To convert this string to an actual date, you can use a formula, such as this one. (It assumes that the coded data is in cell A1.)

```
=DATE(LEFT(A1,4),MID(A1,5,2),RIGHT(A1,2))
```

This formula uses text functions (LEFT, MID, and RIGHT) to extract the digits, and then it uses these extracted digits as arguments for the DATE function.

CROSS-REF Refer to Chapter 12 for more information about using formulas to manipulate text.

Calculating the number of days between two dates

A common type of date calculation determines the number of days between two dates. For example, you may have a financial worksheet that calculates interest earned on a deposit account. The interest earned depends on the number of days the account is open. If your sheet contains the open date and the close date for the account, you can calculate the number of days the account was open.

Because dates are stored as consecutive serial numbers, you can use simple subtraction to calculate the number of days between two dates. For example, if cells A1 and B1 both contain a date, the following formula returns the number of days between these dates:

```
=A1-B1
```

Excel automatically formats this formula cell as a date rather than as a numeric value. Therefore, you will need to change the number format so that the result is displayed as a nondate. If cell B1 contains a more recent date than the date in cell A1, the result will be negative.

> **NOTE**   If this formula does not display the correct value, make sure that A1 and B1 both contain actual dates — not text that *looks* like a date.

Sometimes, calculating the difference between two days is more difficult. To demonstrate, consider the common *fence-post analogy.* If somebody asks you how many units make up a fence, you can respond with either of two answers: the number of fence posts or the number of gaps between the fence posts. The number of fence posts is always one more than the number of gaps between the posts.

To bring this analogy into the realm of dates, suppose that you start a sales promotion on February 1 and end the promotion on February 9. How many days was the promotion in effect? Subtracting February 1 from February 9 produces an answer of eight days. Actually, the promotion lasted nine days. In this case, the correct answer involves counting the fence posts, not the gaps. The formula to calculate the length of the promotion (assuming that you have appropriately named cells) appears like this:

```
=EndDay-StartDay+1
```

Calculating the number of work days between two dates

When calculating the difference between two dates, you may want to exclude weekends and holidays. For example, you may need to know how many business days fall in the month of November. This calculation should exclude Saturdays, Sundays, and holidays. The NETWORKDAYS function can help out.

> **NEW FEATURE**   In versions prior to Excel 2007, the NETWORKDAYS function was available only when the Analysis ToolPak add-in was installed. The function is now part of Excel 2007.

The NETWORKDAYS function calculates the difference between two dates, excluding weekend days (Saturdays and Sundays). As an option, you can specify a range of cells that contain the dates of holidays, which are also excluded. Excel has absolutely no way of determining which days are holidays, so you must provide this information in a range.

Figure 13.4 shows a worksheet that calculates the work days between two dates. The range A2:A11 contains a list of holiday dates. The two formulas in column C calculate the work days between the dates in column A and column B. For example, the formula in cell C15 is

```
=NETWORKDAYS(A15,B15,A2:A11)
```

This formula returns 4, which means that the seven-day period beginning with January 1 contains four work days. In other words, the calculation excludes one holiday, one Saturday, and one Sunday. The formula in cell C16 calculates the total number of work days in the year.

> **ON the CD-ROM**   This workbook is available on the companion CD-ROM. The file is named **work days.xlsx.**

Offsetting a date using only work days

The WORKDAY function is the opposite of the NETWORKDAYS function. For example, if you start a project on January 4, and the project requires ten working days to complete, the WORKDAY function can calculate the date you will finish the project.

FIGURE 13.4

Using the NETWORKDAYS function to calculate the number of working days between two dates.

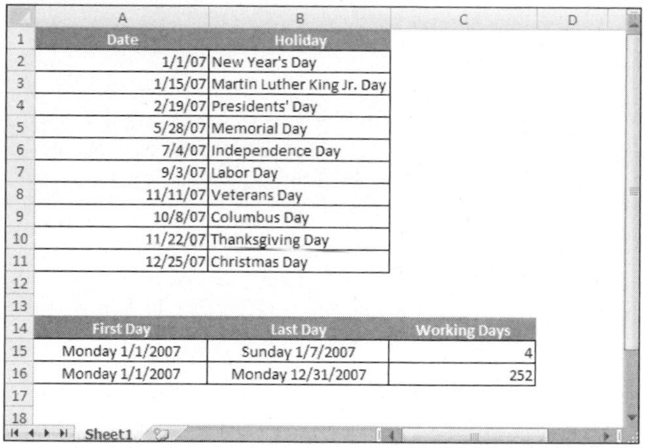

	A	B	C	D
1	**Date**	**Holiday**		
2	1/1/07	New Year's Day		
3	1/15/07	Martin Luther King Jr. Day		
4	2/19/07	Presidents' Day		
5	5/28/07	Memorial Day		
6	7/4/07	Independence Day		
7	9/3/07	Labor Day		
8	11/11/07	Veterans Day		
9	10/8/07	Columbus Day		
10	11/22/07	Thanksgiving Day		
11	12/25/07	Christmas Day		
12				
13				
14	**First Day**	**Last Day**	**Working Days**	
15	Monday 1/1/2007	Sunday 1/7/2007	4	
16	Monday 1/1/2007	Monday 12/31/2007	252	
17				
18				

NEW FEATURE In versions prior to Excel 2007, the WORKDAY function was available only when the Analysis ToolPak add-in was installed. The function is now part of Excel 2007.

The following formula uses the WORKDAY function to determine the date that is ten working days from January 4, 2008. A working day consists of a week day (Monday through Friday).

```
=WORKDAY("1/4/2008",10)
```

The formula returns a date serial number, which must be formatted as a date. The result is January 18, 2008 (four weekend dates fall between January 4 and January 18).

CAUTION The preceding formula may return a different result, depending on your regional date setting. (The hard-coded date may be interpreted as April 1, 2008.) A better formula is

```
=WORKDAY(DATE(2008,1,4),10)
```

The second argument for the WORKDAY function can be negative. And, as with the NETWORKDAYS function, the WORKDAY function accepts an optional third argument (a reference to a range that contains a list of holiday dates).

Calculating the number of years between two dates

The following formula calculates the number of years between two dates. This formula assumes that cells A1 and B1 both contain dates:

```
=YEAR(A1)-YEAR(B1)
```

This formula uses the YEAR function to extract the year from each date and then subtracts one year from the other. If cell B1 contains a more recent date than the date in cell A1, the result will be negative.

Note that this function doesn't calculate *full* years. For example, if cell A1 contains 12/31/2007 and cell B1 contains 01/01/2008, the formula returns a difference of one year, even though the dates differ by only one day. See the next section for another way to calculate the number of full years.

Calculating a person's age

A person's age indicates the number of full years that the person has been alive. The formula in the previous section (for calculating the number of years between two dates) won't calculate this value correctly. You can use two other formulas, however, to calculate a person's age.

The following formula returns the age of the person whose date of birth you enter into cell A1. This formula uses the YEARFRAC function.

```
=INT(YEARFRAC(TODAY(),A1,1))
```

NEW FEATURE In versions prior to Excel 2007, the YEARFRAC function was available only when the Analysis ToolPak add-in was installed. The function is now part of Excel 2007.

The following formula uses the DATEDIF function to calculate an age. (See the sidebar, "Where's the DATEDIF Function?")

```
=DATEDIF(A1,TODAY(),"Y")
```

Where's the DATEDIF Function?

One of Excel's mysteries is the DATEDIF function. You may notice that this function does not appear in the drop-down function list for the Date & Time category, nor does it appear in the Insert Function dialog box. Therefore, when you use this function, you must always enter it manually.

The DATEDIF function has its origins in Lotus 1-2-3, and apparently Excel provides it for compatibility purposes. For some reason, Microsoft wants to keep this function a secret. The function has been available since Excel 5, but Excel 2000 is the only version that ever documented it in its Help system.

DATEDIF is a handy function that calculates the number of days, months, or years between two dates. The function takes three arguments: start_date, end_date, and a code that represents the time unit of interest. The following table displays valid codes for the third argument. (You must enclose the codes in quotation marks.)

Unit Code	Returns
"y"	The number of complete years in the period.
"m"	The number of complete months in the period.
"d"	The number of days in the period.
"md"	The difference between the days in start_date and end_date. The months and years of the dates are ignored.
"ym"	The difference between the months in start_date and end_date. The days and years of the dates are ignored.
"yd"	The difference between the days of start_date and end_date. The years of the dates are ignored.

The start_date argument must be earlier than the end_date argument, or the function returns an error.

Determining the day of the year

January 1 is the first day of the year, and December 31 is the last day. But what about all those days in between? The following formula returns the day of the year for a date stored in cell A1:

```
=A1-DATE(YEAR(A1),1,0)
```

The following formula returns the number of days remaining in the year after a particular date (assumed to be in cell A1):

```
=DATE(YEAR(A1),12,31)-A1
```

When you enter either of these formulas, Excel applies date formatting to the cell. You need to apply a non-date number format to view the result as a number.

To convert a particular day of the year (for example, the 90th day of the year) to an actual date in a specified year, use the formula that follows. This formula assumes that the year is stored in cell A1 and the day of the year is stored in cell B1.

```
=DATE(A1,1,B1)
```

Determining the day of the week

The WEEKDAY function accepts a date argument and returns an integer between 1 and 7 that corresponds to the day of the week. The following formula, for example, returns 3 because the first day of the year 2008 falls on a Tuesday:

```
=WEEKDAY(DATE(2008,1,1))
```

The WEEKDAY function uses an optional second argument that specifies the day numbering system for the result. If you specify 2 as the second argument, the function returns 1 for Monday, 2 for Tuesday, and so on. If you specify 3 as the second argument, the function returns 0 for Monday, 1 for Tuesday, and so on.

> **TIP** You can also determine the day of the week for a cell that contains a date by applying a custom number format. A cell that uses the following custom number format displays the day of the week, spelled out:
>
> ```
> dddd
> ```

Determining the date of the most recent Sunday

You can use the following formula to return the date for the previous Sunday. If the current day is a Sunday, the formula returns the current date:

```
=TODAY()-MOD(TODAY()-1,7)
```

To modify this formula to find the date of a day other than Sunday, change the 1 to a different number between 2 (for Monday) and 7 (for Saturday).

Determining the first day of the week after a date

This next formula returns the specified day of the week that occurs after a particular date. For example, use this formula to determine the date of the first Monday after June 1, 2007. The formula assumes that cell A1 contains a date and cell A2 contains a number between 1 and 7 (1 for Sunday, 2 for Monday, and so on).

```
=A1+A2-WEEKDAY(A1)+(A2<WEEKDAY(A1))*7
```

If cell A1 contains June 1, 2007 (a Friday), and cell A2 contains 2 (for Monday), the formula returns June 4, 2007. This is the first Monday after June 1, 2004.

Determining the nth occurrence of a day of the week in a month

You may need a formula to determine the date for a particular occurrence of a week day. For example, suppose that your company payday falls on the second Friday of each month, and you need to determine the paydays for each month of the year. The following formula will make this type of calculation:

```
=DATE(A1,A2,1)+A3-WEEKDAY(DATE(A1,A2,1))+
(A4-(A3>=WEEKDAY(DATE(A1,A2,1))))*7
```

The formula in this section assumes that:

- Cell A1 contains a year.
- Cell A2 contains a month.
- Cell A3 contains a day number (1 for Sunday, 2 for Monday, and so on).
- Cell A4 contains the occurrence number (for example, 2 to select the second occurrence of the weekday specified in cell A3).

If you use this formula to determine the date of the second Friday in November 2007, it returns November 11, 2007.

NOTE If the value in cell A4 exceeds the number of the specified day in the month, the formula returns a date from a subsequent month. For example, if you attempt to determine the date of the fifth Friday in November 2007 (there is no such date), the formula returns the first Friday in December.

Calculating dates of holidays

Determining the date for a particular holiday can be tricky. Some, such as New Year's Day and U.S. Independence Day are no-brainers because they always occur on the same date. For these kinds of holidays, you can simply use the DATE function. To enter New Year's Day (which always falls on January 1) for a specific year in cell A1, you can enter this function:

```
=DATE(A1,1,1)
```

Other holidays are defined in terms of a particular occurrence of a particular week day in a particular month. For example, Labor Day falls on the first Monday in September.

Figure 13.5 shows a workbook with formulas that calculate the date for ten U.S. holidays. The formulas, which reference the year in cell A1, are listed in the sections that follow.

Using formulas to determine the date for various holidays.

	Holiday	Description	Date	Weekday
6	New Year's Day	1st Day in January	January 1, 2007	Monday
7	Martin Luther King Jr. Day	3rd Monday in January	January 15, 2007	Monday
8	Presidents' Day	3rd Monday in February	February 19, 2007	Monday
9	Memorial Day	Last Monday in May	May 28, 2007	Monday
10	Independence Day	4th Day of July	July 4, 2007	Wednesday
11	Labor Day	1st Monday in September	September 3, 2007	Monday
12	Veterans Day	11th Day of November	November 11, 2007	Sunday
13	Columbus Day	2nd Monday in October	October 8, 2007	Monday
14	Thanksgiving Day	4thThursday in November	November 22, 2007	Thursday
15	Christmas Day	25th Day of December	December 25, 2007	Tuesday

(Cell A1 contains 2007, with "<-- Enter the year" in B1; "Holiday Calculations" title spans the table.)

ON the CD-ROM The workbook shown in Figure 13.5 also appears on the companion CD-ROM. The file is named holidays.xlsx.

New Year's Day

This holiday always falls on January 1:

```
=DATE(A1,1,1)
```

Martin Luther King, Jr. Day

This holiday occurs on the third Monday in January. This formula calculates Martin Luther King, Jr. Day for the year in cell A1:

```
=DATE(A1,1,1)+IF(2<WEEKDAY(DATE(A1,1,1)),7-WEEKDAY
(DATE(A1,1,1))+2,2-WEEKDAY(DATE(A1,1,1)))+((3-1)*7)
```

Presidents' Day

Presidents' Day occurs on the third Monday in February. This formula calculates Presidents' Day for the year in cell A1:

```
=DATE(A1,2,1)+IF(2<WEEKDAY(DATE(A1,2,1)),7-WEEKDAY
(DATE(A1,2,1))+2,2-WEEKDAY(DATE(A1,2,1)))+((3-1)*7)
```

Memorial Day

The last Monday in May is Memorial Day. This formula calculates Memorial Day for the year in cell A1:

```
=DATE(A1,6,1)+IF(2<WEEKDAY(DATE(A1,6,1)),7-WEEKDAY
(DATE(A1,6,1))+2,2-WEEKDAY(DATE(A1,6,1)))+((1-1)*7)-7
```

Notice that this formula actually calculates the first Monday in June and then subtracts 7 from the result to return the last Monday in May.

Independence Day

This holiday always falls on July 4:

```
=DATE(A1,7,4)
```

Labor Day

Labor Day occurs on the first Monday in September. This formula calculates Labor Day for the year in cell A1:

```
=DATE(A1,9,1)+IF(2<WEEKDAY(DATE(A1,9,1)),7-WEEKDAY
(DATE(A1,9,1))+2,2-WEEKDAY(DATE(A1,9,1)))+((1-1)*7)
```

Veterans Day

This holiday always falls on November 11:

```
=DATE(A1,11,11)
```

Columbus Day

This holiday occurs on the second Monday in October. This formula calculates Columbus Day for the year in cell A1:

```
=DATE(A1,10,1)+IF(2<WEEKDAY(DATE(A1,10,1)),7-WEEKDAY
(DATE(A1,10,1))+2,2-WEEKDAY(DATE(A1,10,1)))+((2-1)*7)
```

Thanksgiving Day

Thanksgiving Day is celebrated on the fourth Thursday in November. This formula calculates Thanksgiving Day for the year in cell A1:

```
=DATE(A1,11,1)+IF(5<WEEKDAY(DATE(A1,11,1)),7-WEEKDAY
(DATE(A1,11,1))+5,5-WEEKDAY(DATE(A1,11,1)))+((4-1)*7)
```

Christmas Day

This holiday always falls on December 25:

```
=DATE(A1,12,25)
```

Determining the last day of a month

To determine the date that corresponds to the last day of a month, you can use the DATE function. However, you need to increment the month by 1 and use a day value of 0. In other words, the "0th" day of the next month is the last day of the current month.

The following formula assumes that a date is stored in cell A1. The formula returns the date that corresponds to the last day of the month.

```
=DATE(YEAR(A1),MONTH(A1)+1,0)
```

You can use a variation of this formula to determine how many days comprise a specified month. The formula that follows returns an integer that corresponds to the number of days in the month for the date in cell A1:

```
=DAY(DATE(YEAR(A1),MONTH(A1)+1,0))
```

Determining whether a year is a leap year

To determine whether a particular year is a leap year, you can write a formula that determines whether the 29th day of February occurs in February or March. You can take advantage of the fact that Excel's DATE function adjusts the result when you supply an invalid argument — for example, a day of 29 when February contains only 28 days.

The following formula returns TRUE if the year of the date in cell A1 is a leap year. Otherwise, it returns FALSE.

```
=IF(MONTH(DATE(YEAR(A1),2,29))=2,TRUE,FALSE)
```

CAUTION This function returns the wrong result (TRUE) if the year is 1900. See "Excel's leap year bug," earlier in this chapter.

Determining a date's quarter

For financial reports, you may find it useful to present information in terms of quarters. The following formula returns an integer between 1 and 4 that corresponds to the calendar quarter for the date in cell A1:

```
=ROUNDUP(MONTH(A1)/3,0)
```

This formula divides the month number by 3 and then rounds up the result.

Time-Related Functions

Excel also includes a number of functions that enable you to work with time values in your formulas. This section contains examples that demonstrate the use of these functions.

Table 13.5 summarizes the time-related functions available in Excel. When you use the Insert Function dialog box, these functions appear in the Date & Time function category.

TABLE 13.5

Time-Related Functions

Function	Description
HOUR	Converts a serial number to an hour
MINUTE	Converts a serial number to a minute
MONTH	Converts a serial number to a month
NOW	Returns the serial number of the current date and time
SECOND	Converts a serial number to a second
TIME	Returns the serial number of a particular time
TIMEVALUE	Converts a time in the form of text to a serial number

Displaying the current time

This formula displays the current time as a time serial number (or as a serial number without an associated date):

```
=NOW()-TODAY()
```

You need to format the cell with a time format to view the result as a recognizable time. The quickest way is to choose Home ➪ Number ➪ Format Number and select Time from the drop-down list.

 This formula is updated only when the worksheet is calculated.

 To enter a time stamp (that doesn't change) into a cell, press Ctrl+Shift+: (colon).

Displaying any time

One way to enter a time value into a cell is to just type it, making sure that you include at least one colon (:). You can also create a time by using the TIME function. For example, the following formula returns a time comprised of the hour in cell A1, the minute in cell B1, and the second in cell C1:

```
=TIME(A1,B1,C1)
```

Like the DATE function, the TIME function accepts invalid arguments and adjusts the result accordingly. For example, the following formula uses 80 as the minute argument and returns 10:20:15 AM. The 80 minutes are simply added to the hour, with 20 minutes remaining.

```
=TIME(9,80,15)
```

CAUTION If you enter a value greater than 24 as the first argument for the TIME function, the result may not be what you expect. Logically, a formula such as the one that follows should produce a date/time serial number of 1.041667 (that is, one day and one hour).

```
=TIME(25,0,0)
```

In fact, this formula is equivalent to the following:

```
=TIME(1,0,0)
```

You can also use the DATE function along with the TIME function in a single cell. The formula that follows generates a date and time with a serial number of 39420.7708333333 — which represents 6:30 PM on December 4, 2007:

```
=DATE(2007,12,4)+TIME(18,30,0)
```

The TIMEVALUE function converts a text string that looks like a time into a time serial number. This formula returns 0.2395833333, the time serial number for 5:45 AM:

```
=TIMEVALUE("5:45 am")
```

To view the result of this formula as a time, you need to apply number formatting to the cell. The TIMEVALUE function doesn't recognize all common time formats. For example, the following formula returns an error because Excel doesn't like the periods in "a.m."

```
=TIMEVALUE("5:45 a.m.")
```

Calculating the difference between two times

Because times are represented as serial numbers, you can subtract the earlier time from the later time to get the difference. For example, if cell A2 contains 5:30:00 and cell B2 contains 14:00:00, the following formula returns 08:30:00 (a difference of eight hours and 30 minutes):

    =B2-A2

If the subtraction results in a negative value, however, it becomes an invalid time; Excel displays a series of hash marks (#######) because a time without a date has a date serial number of 0. A negative time results in a negative serial number, which is not permitted.

If the direction of the time difference doesn't matter, you can use the ABS function to return the absolute value of the difference:

    =ABS(B2-A2)

This "negative time" problem often occurs when calculating an elapsed time — for example, calculating the number of hours worked given a start time and an end time. This presents no problem if the two times fall in the same day. But if the work shift spans midnight, the result is an invalid negative time. For example, you may start work at 10:00 PM and end work at 6:00 AM the next day. Figure 13.6 shows a worksheet that calculates the hours worked. As you can see, the shift that spans midnight presents a problem (cell C3).

FIGURE 13.6

Calculating the number of hours worked returns an error if the shift spans midnight.

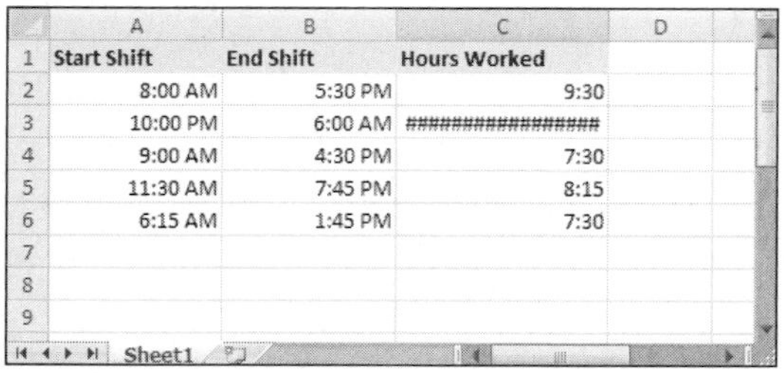

	A	B	C	D
1	Start Shift	End Shift	Hours Worked	
2	8:00 AM	5:30 PM	9:30	
3	10:00 PM	6:00 AM	################	
4	9:00 AM	4:30 PM	7:30	
5	11:30 AM	7:45 PM	8:15	
6	6:15 AM	1:45 PM	7:30	

Using the ABS function (to calculate the absolute value) isn't an option in this case because it returns the wrong result (16 hours). The following formula, however, *does* work:

    =IF(B2<A2,B2+1,B2)-A2

TIP Negative times *are* permitted if the workbook uses the 1904 date system. To switch to the 1904 date system, use the Advanced section of the Excel Options dialog box. Place a check mark next to the Use 1904 Date System option. But beware! When changing the workbook's date system, if the workbook uses dates, the dates will be off by four years. For more information about the 1904 date system, see the sidebar titled "Choose Your Date System: 1900 or 1904," earlier in this chapter.

Summing times that exceed 24 hours

Many people are surprised to discover that when you sum a series of times that exceed 24 hours, Excel doesn't display the correct total. Figure 13.7 shows an example. The range B2:B8 contains times that represent the hours and minutes worked each day. The formula in cell B9 is

```
=SUM(B2:B8)
```

As you can see, the formula returns a seemingly incorrect total (17 hours, 45 minutes). The total should read 41 hours, 45 minutes. The problem is that the formula is displaying the total as a date/time serial number of 1.7395833, but the cell formatting is not displaying the *date* part of the date/time. The answer is incorrect because cell B9 has the wrong number format.

FIGURE 13.7

Incorrect cell formatting makes the total appear incorrectly.

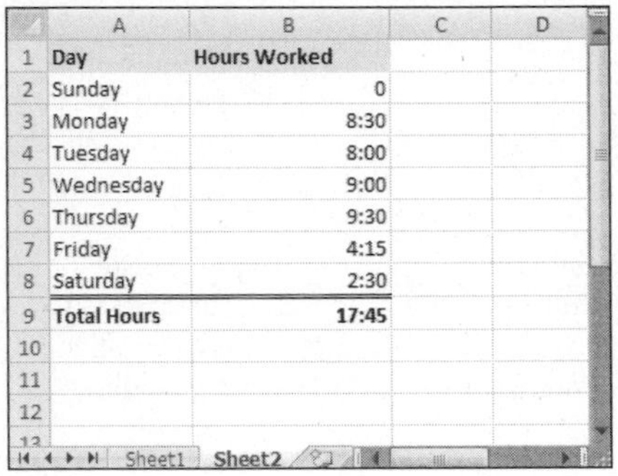

	A	B	C	D
1	Day	Hours Worked		
2	Sunday	0		
3	Monday	8:30		
4	Tuesday	8:00		
5	Wednesday	9:00		
6	Thursday	9:30		
7	Friday	4:15		
8	Saturday	2:30		
9	Total Hours	17:45		
10				
11				
12				

To view a time that exceeds 24 hours, you need to apply a custom number format for the cell so that square brackets surround the *hour* part of the format string. Applying the number format here to cell B9 displays the sum correctly:

```
[h]:mm
```

CROSS-REF For more information about custom number formats, see Chapter 24.

Figure 13.8 shows another example of a worksheet that manipulates times. This worksheet keeps track of hours worked during a week (regular hours and overtime hours).

ON the CD-ROM This workbook is available on the companion CD-ROM. The file name is time sheet.xlsm. The workbook contains a few macros to make it easier to use.

The week's starting date appears in cell D5, and the formulas in column B fill in the dates for the days of the week. Times appear in the range D8:G14, and formulas in column H calculate the number of hours worked each day. For example, the formula in cell H8 is

```
=IF(E8<D8,E8+1-D8,E8-D8)+IF(G8<F8,G8+1-G8,G8-F8)
```

FIGURE 13.8

An employee timesheet workbook.

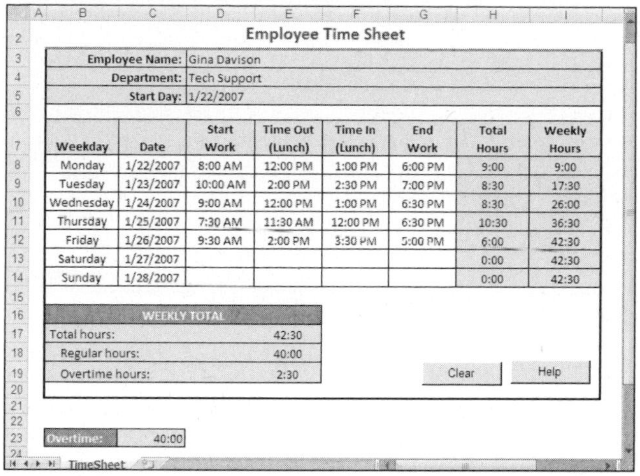

Employee Time Sheet

Employee Name: Gina Davison
Department: Tech Support
Start Day: 1/22/2007

Weekday	Date	Start Work	Time Out (Lunch)	Time In (Lunch)	End Work	Total Hours	Weekly Hours
Monday	1/22/2007	8:00 AM	12:00 PM	1:00 PM	6:00 PM	9:00	9:00
Tuesday	1/23/2007	10:00 AM	2:00 PM	2:30 PM	7:00 PM	8:30	17:30
Wednesday	1/24/2007	9:00 AM	12:00 PM	1:00 PM	6:30 PM	8:30	26:00
Thursday	1/25/2007	7:30 AM	11:30 AM	12:00 PM	6:30 PM	10:30	36:30
Friday	1/26/2007	9:30 AM	2:00 PM	3:30 PM	5:00 PM	6:00	42:30
Saturday	1/27/2007					0:00	42:30
Sunday	1/28/2007					0:00	42:30

WEEKLY TOTAL	
Total hours:	42:30
Regular hours:	40:00
Overtime hours:	2:30

The first part of this formula subtracts the time in column D from the time in column E to get the total hours worked before lunch. The second part subtracts the time in column F from the time in column G to get the total hours worked after lunch. I use `IF` functions to accommodate graveyard shift cases that span midnight — for example, an employee may start work at 10:00 PM and begin lunch at 2:00 AM. Without the `IF` function, the formula returns a negative result.

The following formula in cell H17 calculates the weekly total by summing the daily totals in column H:

```
=SUM(H8:H14)
```

This worksheet assumes that hours in excess of 40 hours in a week are considered overtime hours. The worksheet contains a cell named *Overtime*, in cell C23. This cell contains 40:00. If your standard workweek consists of something other than 40 hours, you can change this formula.

The following formula (in cell H18) calculates regular (nonovertime) hours. This formula returns the smaller of two values: the total hours or the overtime hours.

```
=MIN(E17,Overtime)
```

The final formula, in cell H19, simply subtracts the regular hours from the total hours to yield the overtime hours.

```
=E17-E18
```

The times in H17:H19 may display time values that exceed 24 hours, so these cells use a custom number format:

```
[h]:mm
```

Converting from military time

Military time is expressed as a four-digit number from 0000 to 2359. For example, 1:00 AM is expressed as 0100 hours, and 3:30 PM is expressed as 1530 hours. The following formula converts such a number (assumed to be in cell A1) to a standard time:

```
=TIMEVALUE(LEFT(A1,2)&":"&RIGHT(A1,2))
```

The formula returns an incorrect result if the contents of cell A1 do not contain four digits. The following formula corrects the problem, and it returns a valid time for any military time value from 0 to 2359:

```
=TIMEVALUE(LEFT(TEXT(A1,"0000"),2)&":"&RIGHT(A1,2))
```

Following is a simpler formula that uses the TEXT function to return a formatted string, and then it uses the TIMEVALUE function to express the result in terms of a time.

```
=TIMEVALUE(TEXT(A1,"00\:00"))
```

Converting decimal hours, minutes, or seconds to a time

To convert decimal hours to a time, divide the decimal hours by 24. For example, if cell A1 contains 9.25 (representing hours), this formula returns 09:15:00 (nine hours, 15 minutes):

```
=A1/24
```

To convert decimal minutes to a time, divide the decimal hours by 1,440 (the number of minutes in a day). For example, if cell A1 contains 500 (representing minutes), the following formula returns 08:20:00 (eight hours, 20 minutes):

```
=A1/1440
```

To convert decimal seconds to a time, divide the decimal hours by 86,400 (the number of seconds in a day). For example, if cell A1 contains 65,000 (representing seconds), the following formula returns 18:03:20 (18 hours, three minutes, and 20 seconds):

```
=A1/86400
```

Adding hours, minutes, or seconds to a time

You can use the TIME function to add any number of hours, minutes, or seconds to a time. For example, assume that cell A1 contains a time. The following formula adds 2 hours and 30 minutes to that time and displays the result:

```
=A1+TIME(2,30,0)
```

You can use the TIME function to fill a range of cells with incremental times. Figure 13.9 shows a worksheet with a series of times in 10-minute increments. Cell A1 contains a time that was entered directly. Cell A2 contains the following formula, which copied down the column:

```
=A1+TIME(0,10,0)
```

FIGURE 13.9

Using a formula to create a series of incremental times.

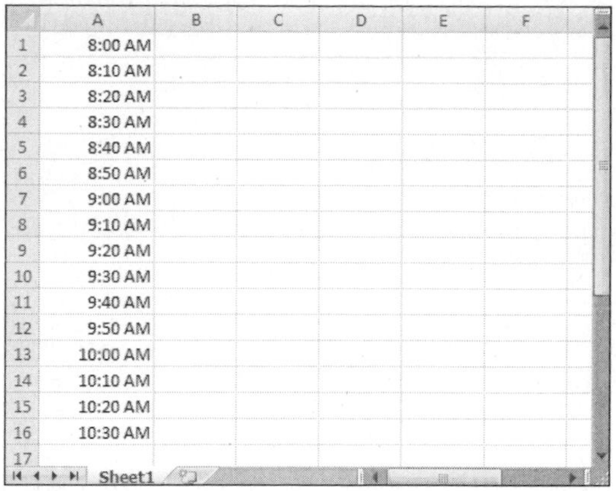

	A	B	C	D	E	F
1	8:00 AM					
2	8:10 AM					
3	8:20 AM					
4	8:30 AM					
5	8:40 AM					
6	8:50 AM					
7	9:00 AM					
8	9:10 AM					
9	9:20 AM					
10	9:30 AM					
11	9:40 AM					
12	9:50 AM					
13	10:00 AM					
14	10:10 AM					
15	10:20 AM					
16	10:30 AM					
17						

Sheet1

Rounding time values

You may need to create a formula that rounds a time to a particular value. For example, you may need to enter your company's time records rounded to the nearest 15 minutes. This section presents examples of various ways to round a time value.

The following formula rounds the time in cell A1 to the nearest minute:

```
=ROUND(A1*1440,0)/1440
```

The formula works by multiplying the time by 1440 (to get total minutes). This value is passed to the ROUND function, and the result is divided by 1440. For example, if cell A1 contains 11:52:34, the formula returns 11:53:00.

The following formula resembles this example, except that it rounds the time in cell A1 to the nearest hour:

```
=ROUND(A1*24,0)/24
```

If cell A1 contains 5:21:31, the formula returns 5:00:00.

The following formula rounds the time in cell A1 to the nearest 15 minutes (a quarter of an hour):

```
=ROUND(A1*24/0.25,0)*(0.25/24)
```

In this formula, 0.25 represents the fractional hour. To round a time to the nearest 30 minutes, change 0.25 to 0.5, as in the following formula:

```
=ROUND(A1*24/0.5,0)*(0.5/24)
```

Working with non-time-of-day values

Sometimes, you may want to work with time values that don't represent an actual time of day. For example, you may want to create a list of the finish times for a race or record the time you spend jogging each day. Such times don't represent a time of day. Rather, a value represents the time for an event (in hours, minutes, and seconds). The time to complete a test, for example, may be 35 minutes and 45 seconds. You can enter that value into a cell as:

    00:35:45

Excel interprets such an entry as 12:35:45 AM, which works fine. (Just make sure that you format the cell so that it appears as you like.) When you enter such times that do not have an hour component, you must include at least one zero for the hour. If you omit a leading zero for a missing hour, Excel interprets your entry as 35 hours and 45 minutes.

Figure 13.10 shows an example of a worksheet set up to keep track of a person's jogging activity. Column A contains simple dates. Column B contains the distance in miles. Column C contains the time it took to run the distance. Column D contains formulas to calculate the speed in miles per hour. For example, the formula in cell D2 is

    =B2/(C2*24)

FIGURE 13.10

This worksheet uses times not associated with a time of day.

	A	B	C	D	E	F	G	H
				Speed	Pace	YTD	Cumulative	
1	Date	Distance	Time	(mph)	(min/mile)	Distance	Time	
2	1/1/2007	1.50	00:18:45	4.80	12.50	1.50	00:18:45	
3	1/2/2007	1.50	00:17:40	5.09	11.78	3.00	00:36:25	
4	1/3/2007	2.00	00:21:30	5.58	10.75	5.00	00:57:55	
5	1/4/2007	1.50	00:15:20	5.87	10.22	6.50	01:13:15	
6	1/5/2007	2.40	00:25:05	5.74	10.45	8.90	01:38:20	
7	1/6/2007	3.00	00:31:06	5.79	10.37	11.90	02:09:26	
8	1/7/2007	3.80	00:41:06	5.55	10.82	15.70	02:50:32	
9	1/8/2007	5.00	01:09:00	4.35	13.80	20.70	03:59:32	
10	1/9/2007	4.00	00:45:10	5.31	11.29	24.70	04:44:42	
11	1/10/2007	3.00	00:29:06	6.19	9.70	27.70	05:13:48	
12	1/11/2007	5.50	01:08:30	4.82	12.45	33.20	06:22:18	
13								
14								

Sheet1

Column E contains formulas to calculate the pace, in minutes per mile. For example, the formula in cell E2 is

    =(C2*60*24)/B2

Columns F and G contain formulas that calculate the year-to-date distance (using column B) and the cumulative time (using column C). The cells in column G are formatted using the following number format (which permits time displays that exceed 24 hours):

    [hh]:mm:ss

ON the CD-ROM   You can also access the workbook shown in Figure 13.10 on the companion CD-ROM. The file is named **jogging log.xlsx.**

Chapter 14

Creating Formulas That Count and Sum

Many of the most common spreadsheet questions involve counting and summing values and other worksheet elements. It seems that people are always looking for formulas to count or to sum various items in a worksheet. If I've done my job, this chapter answers the vast majority of such questions. It contains many examples that you can easily adapt to your own situation.

Counting and Summing Worksheet Cells

Generally, a *counting formula* returns the number of cells in a specified range that meet certain criteria. A *summing formula* returns the sum of the values of the cells in a range that meet certain criteria. The range you want counted or summed may or may not consist of a worksheet database.

Table 14.1 lists the Excel worksheet functions that come into play when creating counting and summing formulas. Not all these functions are covered in this chapter. If none of the functions in Table 14.1 can solve your problem, it's likely that an array formula can come to the rescue.

CROSS-REF See Chapters 17 and 18 for detailed information and examples of array formulas used for counting and summing.

NOTE If your data is in the form of a table, you can use autofiltering to accomplish many counting and summing operations. Just set the autofilter criteria, and the table displays only the rows that match your criteria (the nonqualifying rows in the table are hidden). Then you can select formulas to display counts or sums in the table's total row. Refer to Chapter 6 for more information on using tables.

IN THIS CHAPTER

IN THIS CHAPTER

Information on counting and summing cells

Basic counting formulas

Advanced counting formulas

Formulas for performing common summing tasks

Conditional summing formulas using a single criterion

Conditional summing formulas using multiple criteria

TABLE 14.1

Excel's Counting and Summing Functions

Function	Description
COUNT	Returns the number of cells that contain a numeric value
COUNTA	Returns the number of nonblank cells
COUNTBLANK	Returns the number of blank cells
COUNTIF	Returns the number of cells that meet a specified criterion
COUNTIFS*	Returns the number of cells that meet multiple criteria
DCOUNT	Counts the number of records that meet specified criteria; used with a worksheet database.
DCOUNTA	Counts the number of nonblank records that meet specified criteria; used with a worksheet database.
DEVSQ	Returns the sum of squares of deviations of data points from the sample mean; used primarily in statistical formulas
DSUM	Returns the sum of a column of values that meet specified criteria; used with a worksheet database.
FREQUENCY	Calculates how often values occur within a range of values and returns a vertical array of numbers. Used only in a multicell array formula,
SUBTOTAL	When used with a first argument of 2, 3, 102, or 103, returns *a count* of cells that comprise a subtotal; when used with a first argument of 9 or 109, returns *the sum* of cells that comprise a subtotal
SUM	Returns the sum of its arguments
SUMIF	Returns the sum of cells that meet a specified criterion
SUMIFS*	Returns the sum of cells that meet multiple criteria
SUMPRODUCT	Multiplies corresponding cells in two or more ranges and returns the sum of those products
SUMSQ	Returns the sum of the squares of its arguments; used primarily in statistical formulas
SUMX2PY2	Returns the sum of the sum of squares of corresponding values in two ranges; used primarily in statistical formulas
SUMXMY2	Returns the sum of squares of the differences of corresponding values in two ranges; used primarily in statistical formulas
SUMX2MY2	Returns the sum of the differences of squares of corresponding values in two ranges; used primarily in statistical formulas

* These are new functions, available only in Excel 2007.

Getting a Quick Count or Sum

Excel's status bar can display useful information about the currently selected cells — no formulas required. Normally, the status bar displays the sum and count of the values in the selected range. You can, however, right-click to bring up a menu with other options. You can choose any or all of the following: Average, Count, Numerical Count, Minimum, Maximum, and Sum.

5	78	31	56	6	35	90	67	14	8
70	24	41	80	59	91	49	98	75	73
59	22	75	44	10	7	4	41	91	79
39	32	41	3	87	15	92	94	25	32
99	43	18	43	15	8	57	94	95	66
29	72	30	95	57	75	55	33	52	42
17	45	77	47	65	47	91	29	65	74
77	89	68	64	19	89	48	44	67	27
37	47	98	68	59	5	89	97	48	37

Average: 52.82857143   Count: 35   Min: 3   Max: 98   Sum: 1849   100%

Basic Counting Formulas

The basic counting formulas presented here are all straightforward and relatively simple. They demonstrate the capability of the Excel counting functions to count the number of cells in a range that meet specific criteria. Figure 14.1 shows a worksheet that uses formulas (in column E) to summarize the contents of range A1:B10 — a 20-cell range named *Data*. This range contains a variety of information, including values, text, logical values, errors, and empty cells.

FIGURE 14.1

Formulas in column E display various counts of the data in A1:B10.

	A	B	C	D	E	F
1	Jan	Feb		Total cells:	20	
2	525	718		Blank cells:	6	
3				Nonblank cells:	14	
4	3			Numeric values:	7	
5	552	911		Non-text cells:	17	
6	250	98		Text cells:	3	
7				Logical values:	2	
8	TRUE	FALSE		Error values:	2	
9		#DIV/0!		#N/A errors:	0	
10	Total	#NAME?		#NULL! errors:	0	
11				#DIV/0! errors:	1	
12				#VALUE! errors:	0	
13				#REF! errors:	0	
14				#NAME? errors:	1	
15				#NUM! errors:	0	
16						

Sheet1

ON the CD-ROM This workbook is available on the companion CD-ROM. The file is named basic counting.xlsx.

About This Chapter's Examples

Most of the examples in this chapter use named ranges for function arguments. When you adapt these formulas for your own use, you'll need to substitute either the actual range address or a range name defined in your workbook.

Also, some examples consist of array formulas. An *array formula* is a special type of formula that enables you to perform calculations that would not otherwise be possible. You can spot an array formula because it's enclosed in curly brackets when it's displayed in the Formula bar. In addition, I use this syntax for the array formula examples presented in this book. For example:

```
{=Data*2}
```

When you enter an array formula, press Ctrl+Shift+Enter (not just Enter) and *don't* type the brackets. (Excel inserts the brackets for you.) If you need to edit an array formula, don't forget to use Ctrl+Shift+Enter when you've finished editing (otherwise, the array formula will revert to a normal formula and it will return an incorrect result). Refer to Chapter 17 for an introduction to array formulas.

Counting the total number of cells

To get a count of the total number of cells in a range (empty and non-empty cells), use the following formula. This formula returns the number of cells in a range named *Data*. It simply multiplies the number of rows (returned by the ROWS function) by the number of columns (returned by the COLUMNS function).

```
=ROWS(Data)*COLUMNS(Data)
```

This formula will not work if the Data range consists of noncontiguous cells. In other words, Data must be a rectangular range of cells.

Counting blank cells

The following formula returns the number of blank (empty) cells in a range named *Data*:

```
=COUNTBLANK(Data)
```

The COUNTBLANK function also counts cells containing a formula that returns an empty string. For example, the formula that follows returns an empty string if the value in cell A1 is greater than 5. If the cell meets this condition, the COUNTBLANK function counts that cell.

```
=IF(A1>5,"",A1)
```

You can use the COUNTBLANK function with an argument that consists of entire rows or columns. For example, this next formula returns the number of blank cells in column A:

```
=COUNTBLANK(A:A)
```

The following formula returns the number of empty cells on the entire worksheet named Sheet1. You must enter this formula on a sheet other than Sheet1, or it will create a circular reference.

```
=COUNTBLANK(Sheet1!1:1048576)
```

Counting nonblank cells

To count nonblank cells, use the COUNTA function. The following formula uses the COUNTA function to return the number of nonblank cells in a range named *Data*:

```
=COUNTA(Data)
```

The COUNTA function counts cells that contain values, text, or logical values (TRUE or FALSE).

> **NOTE** If a cell contains a formula that returns an empty string, that cell is included in the count returned by COUNTA, even though the cell appears to be blank.

Counting numeric cells

To count only the numeric cells in a range, use the following formula (which assumes the range is named *Data*):

```
=COUNT(Data)
```

Cells that contain a date or a time are considered to be numeric cells. Cells that contain a logical value (TRUE or FALSE) aren't considered to be numeric cells.

Counting text cells

To count the number of text cells in a range, you need to use an array formula. The array formula that follows returns the number of text cells in a range named *Data*:

```
{=SUM(IF(ISTEXT(Data),1))}
```

Counting nontext cells

The following array formula uses Excel's ISNONTEXT function, which returns TRUE if its argument refers to any nontext cell (including a blank cell). This formula returns the count of the number of cells not containing text (including blank cells):

```
{=SUM(IF(ISNONTEXT(Data),1))}
```

Counting logical values

The following array formula returns the number of logical values (TRUE or FALSE) in a range named *Data*:

```
{=SUM(IF(ISLOGICAL(Data),1))}
```

Counting error values in a range

Excel has three functions that help you determine whether a cell contains an error value:

- ISERROR: Returns TRUE if the cell contains any error value (#N/A, #VALUE!, #REF!, #DIV/0!, #NUM!, #NAME?, or #NULL!)
- ISERR: Returns TRUE if the cell contains any error value except #N/A
- ISNA: Returns TRUE if the cell contains the #N/A error value

You can use these functions in an array formula to count the number of error values in a range. The following array formula, for example, returns the total number of error values in a range named *Data*:

```
{=SUM(IF(ISERROR(data),1))}
```

Depending on your needs, you can use the ISERR or ISNA function in place of ISERROR.

If you would like to count specific types of errors, you can use the COUNTIF function. The following formula, for example, returns the number of #DIV/0! error values in the range named *Data*:

```
=COUNTIF(Data,"#DIV/0!")
```

Advanced Counting Formulas

Most of the basic examples I presented earlier in this chapter use functions or formulas that perform conditional counting. The advanced counting formulas that I present here represent more complex examples for counting worksheet cells, based on various types of criteria.

CROSS-REF   Some of these examples are array formulas. Refer to Chapters 17 and 18 for more information about array formulas.

Counting cells by using the COUNTIF function

Excel's COUNTIF function is useful for single-criterion counting formulas. The COUNTIF function takes two arguments:

- *range*: The range that contains the values that determine whether to include a particular cell in the count
- *criteria*: The logical criteria that determine whether to include a particular cell in the count

Table 14.2 lists several examples of formulas that use the COUNTIF function . These formulas all work with a range named *Data*. As you can see, the *criteria* argument proves quite flexible. You can use constants, expressions, functions, cell references, and even wildcard characters (* and ?).

TABLE 14.2

Examples of Formulas Using the COUNTIF Function

=COUNTIF(Data,12)	Returns the number of cells containing the value 12
=COUNTIF(Data,"<0")	Returns the number of cells containing a negative value
=COUNTIF(Data,"<>0")	Returns the number of cells not equal to 0
=COUNTIF(Data,">5")	Returns the number of cells greater than 5
=COUNTIF(Data,A1)	Returns the number of cells equal to the contents of cell A1
=COUNTIF(Data,">"&A1)	Returns the number of cells greater than the value in cell A1
=COUNTIF(Data,"*")	Returns the number of cells containing text
=COUNTIF(Data,"???")	Returns the number of text cells containing exactly three characters
=COUNTIF(Data,"budget")	Returns the number of cells containing the single word *budget* (not case sensitive)

=COUNTIF(Data,"*budget*")	Returns the number of cells containing the text *budget* anywhere within the text
=COUNTIF(Data,"A*")	Returns the number of cells containing text that begins with the letter *A* (not case sensitive):
=COUNTIF(Data,TODAY())	Returns the number of cells containing the current date
=COUNTIF(Data,">"&AVERAGE(Data))	Returns the number of cells with a value greater than the average
=COUNTIF(Data,">"&AVERAGE(Data)+ STDEV(Data)*3)	Returns the number of values exceeding three standard deviations above the mean
=COUNTIF(Data,3)+COUNTIF(Data,-3)	Returns the number of cells containing the value 3 or –3
=COUNTIF(Data,TRUE)	Returns the number of cells containing logical TRUE
=COUNTIF(Data,TRUE)+ COUNTIF(Data,FALSE)	Returns the number of cells containing a logical value (TRUE or FALSE)
=COUNTIF(Data,"#N/A")	Returns the number of cells containing the #N/A error value

Counting cells by using multiple criteria

In many cases, your counting formula will need to count cells only if two or more criteria are met. These criteria can be based on the cells that are being counted or based on a range of corresponding cells.

Figure 14.2 shows a simple worksheet that I use for the examples in this section. This sheet shows sales data categorized by Month, SalesRep, and Type. The worksheet contains named ranges that correspond to the labels in row 1.

ON the CD-ROM **This workbook is available on the companion CD-ROM. The file is named multiple criteria counting.xlsx.**

NEW FEATURE **Several of the examples in this section use the COUNTIFS function, which is new to Excel 2007. I also present alternative versions of the formulas, which should be used if you plan to share your workbook with others who don't use Excel 2007.**

FIGURE 14.2

This worksheet demonstrates various counting techniques that use multiple criteria.

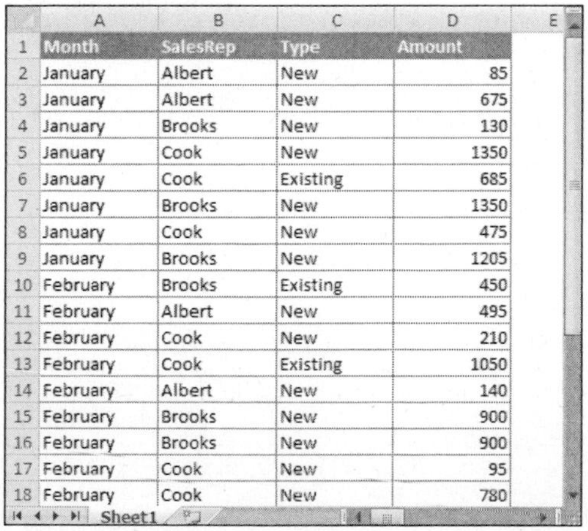

	A	B	C	D	E
1	Month	SalesRep	Type	Amount	
2	January	Albert	New	85	
3	January	Albert	New	675	
4	January	Brooks	New	130	
5	January	Cook	New	1350	
6	January	Cook	Existing	685	
7	January	Brooks	New	1350	
8	January	Cook	New	475	
9	January	Brooks	New	1205	
10	February	Brooks	Existing	450	
11	February	Albert	New	495	
12	February	Cook	New	210	
13	February	Cook	Existing	1050	
14	February	Albert	New	140	
15	February	Brooks	New	900	
16	February	Brooks	New	900	
17	February	Cook	New	95	
18	February	Cook	New	780	

Sheet1

Using And criteria

An And criterion counts cells if all specified conditions are met. A common example is a formula that counts the number of values that fall within a numerical range. For example, you may want to count cells that contain a value greater than 100 *and* less than or equal to 200. For this example, the new COUNTIFS function will do the job:

```
=COUNTIFS(Amount,">100",Amount,"<=200")
```

> **NOTE** If the data is contained in a table, you can use the new Excel 2007 method of referencing data within a table. For example, if the table is named Table1, you can rewrite the preceding formula as:
>
> ```
> =COUNTIFS(Table1[Amount],">100",Table1[Amount],"<=200")
> ```
>
> **This method of writing formulas does not require named ranges.**

The COUNTIFS function accepts any number of paired arguments. The first member of the pair is the range to be counted (in this case, the range named Amount); the second member of the pair is the criterion. The preceding example contains two sets of paired arguments and returns the number of cells in which Amount is greater than 100 and less than or equal to 200.

Prior to Excel 2007, you would need to use a formula like this:

```
=COUNTIF(Amount,">100")-COUNTIF(Amount,">200")
```

The formula counts the number of values that are great than 100 and then subtracts the number of values that are greater than or equal to 200. The result is the number of cells that contain a value greater than 100 and less than or equal to 200. This formula can be confusing because the formula refers to a condition ">200" even though the goal is to count values that are less than or equal to 200. Yet another alternate technique is to use an array formula, like the one that follows. You may find it easier to create this type of formula:

```
{=SUM((Amount>100)*(Amount<=200))}
```

> **NOTE** When you enter an array formula, remember to use Ctrl+Shift+Enter and don't type the brackets.

Sometimes, the counting criteria will be based on cells other than the cells being counted. You may, for example, want to count the number of sales that meet the following criteria:

- Month is January, *and*
- SalesRep is Brooks, *and*
- Amount is greater than 1000

The following formula (for Excel 2007 only) returns the number of items that meets all three criteria. Note that the COUNTIFS function uses three sets of pairs of arguments.

```
=COUNTIFS(Month,"January",SalesRep,"Brooks",Amount,">1000")
```

An alternative formula, which works with all versions of Excel, uses the SUMPRODUCT function. The following formula returns the same result as the previous formula.

```
=SUMPRODUCT((Month="January")*(SalesRep="Brooks")*(Amount>1000))
```

Yet another way to perform this count is to use an array formula:

```
{=SUM((Month="January")*(SalesRep="Brooks")*(Amount>1000))}
```

Using Or criteria

To count cells by using an Or criterion, you can sometimes use multiple COUNTIF functions. The following formula, for example, counts the number of sales made in January or February:

```
=COUNTIF(Month,"January")+COUNTIF(Month,"February")
```

You can also use the COUNTIF function in an array formula. The following array formula, for example, returns the same result as the previous formula:

```
{=SUM(COUNTIF(Month,{"January","February"}))}
```

But if you base your Or criteria on cells other than the cells being counted, the COUNTIF function won't work. (Refer to Figure 14.2.) Suppose that you want to count the number of sales that meet the following criteria:

- Month is January, *or*
- SalesRep is Brooks, *or*
- Amount is greater than 1000

If you attempt to create a formula that uses COUNTIF, some double counting will occur. The solution is to use an array formula like this:

```
{=SUM(IF((Month="January")+(SalesRep="Brooks")+(Amount>1000),1))}
```

Combining And and Or criteria

In some cases, you may need to combine And and Or criteria when counting. For example, perhaps you want to count sales that meet the following criteria:

- Month is January, *and*
- SalesRep is Brooks, *or* SalesRep is Cook

This array formula returns the number of sales that meet the criteria:

```
{=SUM((Month="January")*IF((SalesRep="Brooks")+
(SalesRep="Cook"),1))}
```

Counting the most frequently occurring entry

The MODE function returns the most frequently occurring value in a range. Figure 14.3 shows a worksheet with values in range A1:A10 (named *Data*). The formula that follows returns 10 because that value appears most frequently in the *Data* range:

```
=MODE(Data)
```

The MODE function returns the most frequently occurring value in a range.

	A	B	C	D	E
1	1		10	<-- Mode	
2	4		4	<-- Frequency of the mode	
3	4				
4	10				
5	10				
6	10				
7	10				
8	12				
9	14				
10	14				
11					

To count the number of times the most frequently occurring value appears in the range (in other words, the frequency of the mode), use the following formula:

```
=COUNTIF(Data,MODE(Data))
```

This formula returns 4, because the modal value (10) appears four times in the *Data* range.

The MODE function works only for numeric values. It simply ignores cells that contain text. To find the most frequently occurring text entry in a range, you need to use an array formula.

To count the number of times the most frequently occurring item (text or values) appears in a range named *Data*, use the following array formula:

```
{=MAX(COUNTIF(Data,Data))}
```

This next array formula operates like the MODE function, except that it works with both text and values:

```
{=INDEX(Data,MATCH(MAX(COUNTIF(Data,Data)),COUNTIF(Data,Data),0))}
```

Counting the occurrences of specific text

The examples in this section demonstrate various ways to count the occurrences of a character or text string in a range of cells. Figure 14.4 shows a worksheet used for these examples. Various text strings appear in the range A1:A10 (named *Data*); cell B1 is named *Text*.

ON the CD-ROM The companion CD-ROM contains a workbook that demonstrates the formulas in this section. The file is named **counting text in a range.xlsx**.

FIGURE 14.4

This worksheet demonstrates various ways to count characters in a range.

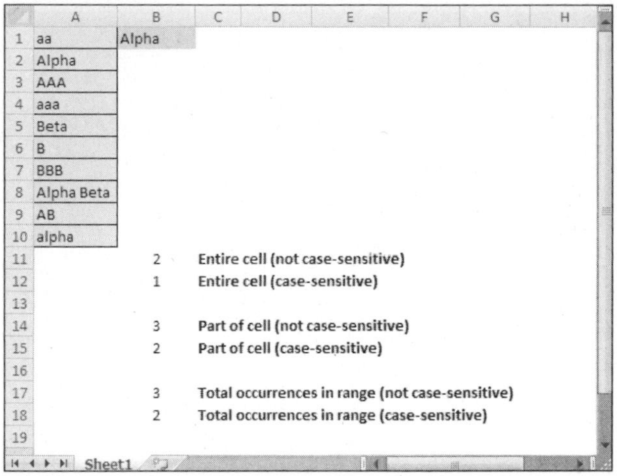

	A	B	C	D	E	F	G	H
1	aa	Alpha						
2	Alpha							
3	AAA							
4	aaa							
5	Beta							
6	B							
7	BBB							
8	Alpha Beta							
9	AB							
10	alpha							
11		2	Entire cell (not case-sensitive)					
12		1	Entire cell (case-sensitive)					
13								
14		3	Part of cell (not case-sensitive)					
15		2	Part of cell (case-sensitive)					
16								
17		3	Total occurrences in range (not case-sensitive)					
18		2	Total occurrences in range (case-sensitive)					
19								

Sheet1

Entire cell contents

To count the number of cells containing the contents of the *Text* cell (and nothing else), you can use the COUNTIF function as the following formula demonstrates.

```
=COUNTIF(Data,Text)
```

For example, if the *Text* cell contains the string "Alpha", the formula returns 2 because two cells in the *Data* range contain this text. This formula is not case sensitive, so it counts both "Alpha" (cell A2) and "alpha" (cell A10). Note, however, that it does not count the cell that contains "Alpha Beta" (cell A8).

The following array formula is similar to the preceding formula, but this one is case sensitive:

```
{=SUM(IF(EXACT(Data,Text),1))}
```

Partial cell contents

To count the number of cells that contain a string that includes the contents of the *Text* cell, use this formula:

```
=COUNTIF(Data,"*"&Text&"*")
```

For example, if the *Text* cell contains the text "Alpha", the formula returns 3 because three cells in the *Data* range contain the text "alpha" (cells A2, A8, and A10). Note that the comparison is not case sensitive.

If you need a case-sensitive count, you can use the following array formula:

```
{=SUM(IF(LEN(Data)-LEN(SUBSTITUTE(Data,Text,""))>0,1))}
```

If the *Text* cells contain the text "Alpha", the preceding formula returns 2 because the string appears in two cells (A2 and A8).

Total occurrences in a range

To count the total number of occurrences of a string within a range of cells, use the following array formula:

```
{=(SUM(LEN(Data))-SUM(LEN(SUBSTITUTE(Data,Text,""))))/
LEN(Text)}
```

If the *Text* cell contains the character "B", the formula returns 7 because the range contains seven instances of the string. This formula is case sensitive.

The following array formula is a modified version that is not case sensitive:

```
{=(SUM(LEN(Data))-SUM(LEN(SUBSTITUTE(UPPER(Data),
UPPER(Text),""))))/LEN(Text)}
```

Counting the number of unique values

The following array formula returns the number of unique values in a range named *Data*:

```
{=SUM(1/COUNTIF(Data,Data))}
```

NOTE The preceding formula is one of those "classic" Excel formulas that gets passed around the Internet. I don't think anyone knows who originated it.

Useful as it is, this formula does have a serious limitation: If the range contains any blank cells, it returns an error. The following array formula solves this problem:

```
{=SUM(IF(COUNTIF(Data,Data)=0,"",1/COUNTIF(Data,Data)))}
```

CROSS-REF To find out how to create an array formula that returns a list of unique items in a range, refer to Chapter 18.

ON the CD-ROM The companion CD-ROM contains a workbook that demonstrates this technique. The file is named **count unique.xlsx**.

Creating a frequency distribution

A *frequency distribution* basically comprises a summary table that shows the frequency of each value in a range. For example, an instructor may create a frequency distribution of test scores. The table would show the count of A's, B's, C's, and so on. Excel provides a number of ways to create frequency distributions. You can

- Use the FREQUENCY function
- Use the Analysis ToolPak add-in
- Create your own formulas
- Use a pivot table

ON the CD-ROM A workbook that demonstrates these four techniques appears on the companion CD-ROM. The file is named **frequency distribution.xlsx**.

The FREQUENCY function

Using the FREQUENCY function to create a frequency distribution can be a bit tricky. This function always returns an array, so you must use it in an array formula that's entered into a multicell range.

Figure 14.5 shows some data in range A1:E25 (named *Data*). These values range from 1 to 500. The range G2:G11 contains the bins used for the frequency distribution. Each cell in this bin range contains the upper limit for the bin. In this case, the bins consist of <=50, 51–100, 101–150, and so on.

FIGURE 14.5

Creating a frequency distribution for the data in A1:E25.

	A	B	C	D	E	F	G	H
1	55	316	223	185	124		Bins	
2	124	93	163	213	314		50	
3	211	41	231	241	212		100	
4	118	113	400	205	254		150	
5	262	1	201	12	101		200	
6	167	479	205	337	118		250	
7	489	15	89	362	148		300	
8	179	248	125	197	177		350	
9	456	153	269	49	127		400	
10	289	500	198	317	300		450	
11	126	114	303	314	270		500	
12	151	279	347	314	170			
13	250	175	93	209	61			
14	166	113	356	124	242			
15	152	384	157	233	99			
16	277	195	436	6	240			
17	147	80	173	211	244			
18	386	93	330	400	141			
19	332	173	129	323	188			
20	338	263	444	84	220			
21	221	402	498	98	2			
22	201	400	3	190	105			
23	35	225	12	265	329			
24	43	302	125	301	444			
25	56	9	135	500	398			
26								

To create the frequency distribution, select a range of cells that corresponds to the number of cells in the bin range (in this example, H2:H11). Then enter the following array formula (press Ctrl+Shift+Enter it):

```
{=FREQUENCY(Data,G2:G11)}
```

The array formula returns the count of values in the *Data* range that fall into each bin. To create a frequency distribution that consists of percentages, use the following array formula:

```
{=FREQUENCY(Data,G2:G11)/COUNT(Data)}
```

Figure 14.6 shows two frequency distributions — one in terms of counts and one in terms of percentages. The figure also shows a chart (histogram) created from the frequency distribution.

FIGURE 14.6

Frequency distributions created by using the FREQUENCY function

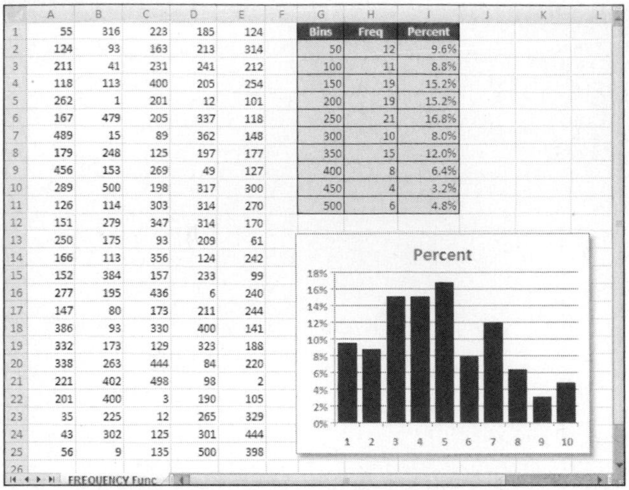

Using formulas to create a frequency distribution

Figure 14.7 shows a worksheet that contains test scores for 50 students in column B (the range is named *Grades*). Formulas in columns G and H calculate a frequency distribution for letter grades. The minimum and maximum values for each letter grade appear in columns D and E. For example, a test score between 80 and 89 (inclusive) earns a B. In addition, a chart displays the distribution of the test scores.

The formula in cell G2 that follows is an array formula that counts the number of scores that qualify for an A:

```
=COUNTIFS(Grades,">="&D2,Grades,"<="&E2)
```

You may recognize this formula from a previous section in this chapter (see "Counting cells by using multiple criteria"). This formula was copied to the four cells below G2.

> **NOTE** The preceding formula uses the COUNTIFS function, which is new to Excel 2007. For compatibility with previous Excel versions, use this array formula:

```
{=SUM((Grades>=D2)*(Grades<=E2))}
```

The formulas in column H calculate the percentage of scores for each letter grade. The formula in H2, which was copied to the four cells below H2, is

```
=G2/SUM($G$2:$G$6)
```

Creating a frequency distribution of test scores.

Using the Analysis ToolPak to create a frequency distribution

The Analysis ToolPak add-in, distributed with Excel, provides another way to calculate a frequency distribution. Start by entering your bin values in a range. Then choose Data ⇨ Analysis ⇨ Analysis to display the Data Analysis dialog box. If this command is not available, see the sidebar, "Is the Analysis Toolpak Installed?".

In the Data Analysis dialog box, select Histogram and click OK. You should see the Histogram dialog box shown in Figure 14.8.

Specify the ranges for your data (Input Range), bins (Bin Range), and results (Output Range), and then select any options. Figure 14.9 shows a frequency distribution (and chart) created with the Histogram option.

NOTE Note that the frequency distribution consists of values, not formulas. Therefore, if you make any changes to your input data, you need to rerun the Histogram procedure to update the results.

FIGURE 14.8

The Analysis ToolPak's Histogram dialog box.

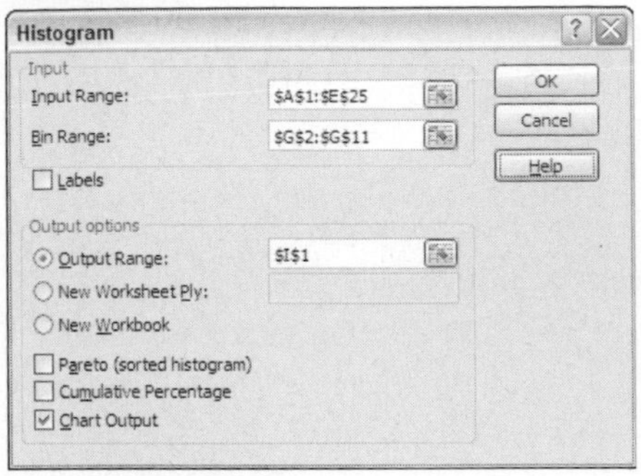

FIGURE 14.9

A frequency distribution and chart generated by the Analysis ToolPak's Histogram option.

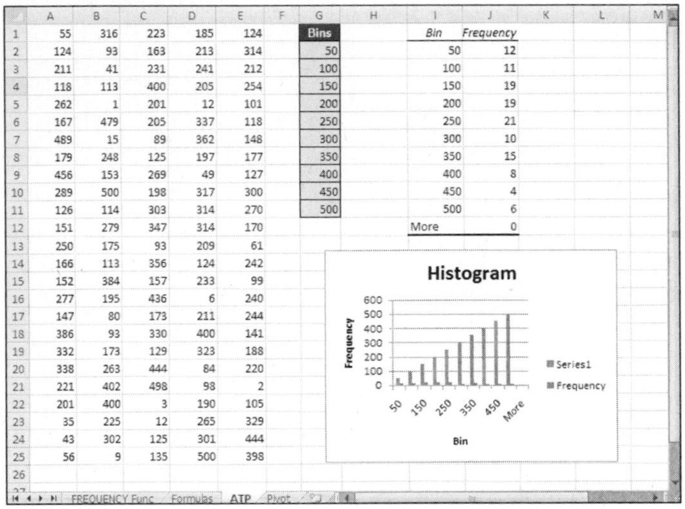

	A	B	C	D	E	F	G	H	I	J
1	55	316	223	185	124		Bins		*Bin*	*Frequency*
2	124	93	163	213	314		50		50	12
3	211	41	231	241	212		100		100	11
4	118	113	400	205	254		150		150	19
5	262	1	201	12	101		200		200	19
6	167	479	205	337	118		250		250	21
7	489	15	89	362	148		300		300	10
8	179	248	125	197	177		350		350	15
9	456	153	269	49	127		400		400	8
10	289	500	198	317	300		450		450	4
11	126	114	303	314	270		500		500	6
12	151	279	347	314	170				More	0
13	250	175	93	209	61					
14	166	113	356	124	242					
15	152	384	157	233	99					
16	277	195	436	6	240					
17	147	80	173	211	244					
18	386	93	330	400	141					
19	332	173	129	323	188					
20	338	263	444	84	220					
21	221	402	498	98	2					
22	201	400	3	190	105					
23	35	225	12	265	329					
24	43	302	125	301	444					
25	56	9	135	500	398					
26										

Using a pivot table to create a frequency distribution

If your data is in the form of a table, you may prefer to use a pivot table to create a histogram. Figure 14.10 shows the student grade data summarized in a pivot table. The data bars were added using the new conditional formatting features in Excel 2007.

CROSS-REF **I cover pivot tables in detail in Chapters 34 and 35, and you can learn more about the conditional formatting data bars in Chapter 21.**

Is the Analysis Toolpak Installed?

To make sure that the Analysis Toolpak add-in is installed, click the Data tab. If the Ribbon displays the Data Analysis command in the Analysis group, you're all set. If not, you'll need to install the add-in:

1. **Choose Office ⇨ Excel Options to display the Excel Options dialog box.**
2. **Click the Add-ins tab on the left.**
3. **Select Excel Add-Ins from the drop-down labeled Manage.**
4. **Click Go to display the Add-Ins dialog box.**
5. **Place a check mark next to Analysis ToolPak.**
6. **Click OK.**

Note: In the Add-Ins dialog box, you see an additional add-in, Analysis ToolPak - VBA. This add-in is for programmer, and you don't need to install it.

FIGURE 14.10

Using data bars within a pivot table to display a histogram.

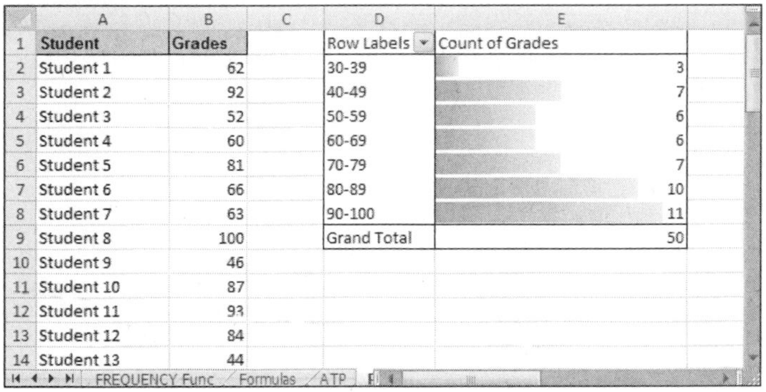

Summing Formulas

The examples in this section demonstrate how to perform common summing tasks by using formulas. The formulas range from very simple to relatively complex array formulas that compute sums by using multiple criteria.

Summing all cells in a range

It doesn't get much simpler than this. The following formula returns the sum of all values in a range named *Data*:

```
=SUM(Data)
```

The SUM function can take up to 255 arguments. The following formula, for example, returns the sum of the values in five noncontiguous ranges:

```
=SUM(A1:A9,C1:C9,E1:E9,G1:G9,I1:I9)
```

You can use complete rows or columns as an argument for the SUM function. The formula that follows, for example, returns the sum of all values in column A. If this formula appears in a cell in column A, it generates a circular reference error.

```
=SUM(A:A)
```

The following formula returns the sum of all values on Sheet1 by using a range reference that consists of all rows. To avoid a circular reference error, this formula must appear on a sheet other than Sheet1.

```
=SUM(Sheet1!1:1048576)
```

The SUM function is very versatile. The arguments can be numerical values, cells, ranges, text representations of numbers (which are interpreted as values), logical values, and even embedded functions. For example, consider the following formula:

```
=SUM(B1,5,"6",,SQRT(4),A1:A5,TRUE)
```

This odd formula, which is perfectly valid, contains all of the following types of arguments, listed here in the order of their presentation:

- A single cell reference
- A literal value
- A string that looks like a value
- A missing argument
- An expression that uses another function
- A range reference
- A logical TRUE value

CAUTION   The SUM function is versatile, but it's also inconsistent when you use logical values (TRUE or FALSE). Logical values stored in cells are always treated as 0. But logical TRUE, when used as an argument in the SUM function, is treated as 1.

Computing a cumulative sum

You may want to display a cumulative sum of values in a range — sometimes known as a "running total." Figure 14.11 illustrates a cumulative sum. Column B shows the monthly amounts, and column C displays the cumulative (year-to-date) totals.

The formula in cell C2 is

```
=SUM(B$2:B2)
```

Notice that this formula uses a *mixed reference* — that is, the first cell in the range reference always refers to the same row (in this case, row 2). When this formula is copied down the column, the range argument adjusts such that the sum always starts with row 2 and ends with the current row. For example, after copying this formula down column C, the formula in cell C8 is

```
=SUM(B$2:B8)
```

FIGURE 14.11

Simple formulas in column C display a cumulative sum of the values in column B.

	A	B	C	D
1	**Month**	**Amount**	**Year-to-Date**	
2	January	850	850	
3	February	900	1,750	
4	March	750	2,500	
5	April	1,100	3,600	
6	May	600	4,200	
7	June	500	4,700	
8	July	1,200	5,900	
9	August		5,900	
10	September		5,900	
11	October		5,900	
12	November		5,900	
13	December		5,900	
14	TOTAL	5,900		
15				

You can use an `IF` function to hide the cumulative sums for rows in which data hasn't been entered. The following formula, entered in cell C2 and copied down the column, is

```
=IF(B2<>"",SUM(B$2:B2),"")
```

Figure 14.12 shows this formula at work.

FIGURE 14.12

Using an `IF` function to hide cumulative sums for missing data.

	A	B	C	D
1	**Month**	**Amount**	**Year-to-Date**	
2	January	850	850	
3	February	900	1,750	
4	March	750	2,500	
5	April	1,100	3,600	
6	May	600	4,200	
7	June	500	4,700	
8	July	1,200	5,900	
9	August			
10	September			
11	October			
12	November			
13	December			
14	TOTAL	5,900		
15				

ON the CD-ROM This workbook is available on the companion CD-ROM. The file is named **cumulative sum.xlsx.**

Summing the "top n" values

In some situations, you may need to sum the *n* largest values in a range — for example, the top ten values. If your data resides in a table, you can use autofiltering to hide all but the top *n* rows and then display the sum of the visible data in the table's total row.

Another approach is to sort the range in descending order and then use the SUM function with an argument consisting of the first *n* values in the sorted range.

A better solution — which doesn't require a table or sorting — uses an array formula like this one:

```
{=SUM(LARGE(Data,{1,2,3,4,5,6,7,8,9,10}))}
```

This formula sums the ten largest values in a range named *Data*. To sum the ten smallest values, use the SMALL function instead of the LARGE function:

```
{=SUM(SMALL(Data,{1,2,3,4,5,6,7,8,9,10}))}
```

These formulas use an array constant comprised of the arguments for the LARGE or SMALL function. If the value of *n* for your top-*n* calculation is large, you may prefer to use the following variation. This formula returns the sum of the top 30 values in the *Data* range. You can, of course, substitute a different value for 30.

```
{=SUM(LARGE(Data,ROW(INDIRECT("1:30"))))}
```

CROSS-REF See Chapter 17 for more information about using array constants.

Conditional Sums Using a Single Criterion

Often, you need to calculate a *conditional sum*. With a conditional sum, values in a range that meet one or more conditions are included in the sum. This section presents examples of conditional summing by using a single criterion.

The SUMIF function is very useful for single-criterion sum formulas. The SUMIF function takes three arguments:

- *range*: The range containing the values that determine whether to include a particular cell in the sum.
- *criteria*: An expression that determines whether to include a particular cell in the sum.
- *sum_range*: Optional. The range that contains the cells you want to sum. If you omit this argument, the function uses the range specified in the first argument.

The examples that follow demonstrate the use of the SUMIF function. These formulas are based on the worksheet shown in Figure 14.13, set up to track invoices. Column F contains a formula that subtracts the date in column E from the date in column D. A negative number in column F indicates a past-due payment. The worksheet uses named ranges that correspond to the labels in row 1.

ON the CD-ROM All the examples in this section also appear on the companion CD-ROM. The file is named **conditional sum.xlsx**.

FIGURE 14.13

A negative value in column F indicates a past-due payment.

	A	B	C	D	E	F	G
1	InvoiceNum	Office	Amount	DateDue	Today	Difference	
2	AG-0145	Oregon	$5,000.00	4/1/2007	5/5/2007	-34	
3	AG-0189	California	$450.00	4/19/2007	5/5/2007	-16	
4	AG-0220	Washington	$3,211.56	4/28/2007	5/5/2007	-7	
5	AG-0310	Oregon	$250.00	4/30/2007	5/5/2007	-5	
6	AG-0355	Washington	$125.50	5/4/2007	5/5/2007	-1	
7	AG-0409	Washington	$3,000.00	5/10/2007	5/5/2007	5	
8	AG-0581	Oregon	$2,100.00	5/23/2007	5/5/2007	18	
9	AG-0600	Oregon	$335.39	5/23/2007	5/5/2007	18	
10	AG-0602	Washington	$65.00	5/28/2007	5/5/2007	23	
11	AG-0633	California	$250.00	5/30/2007	5/5/2007	25	
12	TOTAL		$14,787.45			26	
13							

Sheet1

Summing only negative values

The following formula returns the sum of the negative values in column F. In other words, it returns the total number of past-due days for all invoices. For this worksheet, the formula returns –63.

```
=SUMIF(Difference,"<0")
```

Because you omit the third argument, the second argument ("<0") applies to the values in the *Difference* range.

You don't need to hard-code the arguments for the SUMIF function into your formula. For example, you can create a formula, such as the following, which gets the criteria argument from the contents of cell G2:

```
=SUMIF(Difference,G2)
```

This formula returns a new result if you change the criteria in cell G2.

Summing values based on a different range

The following formula returns the sum of the past-due invoice amounts (in column C):

```
=SUMIF(Difference,"<0",Amount)
```

This formula uses the values in the *Difference* range to determine if the corresponding values in the *Amount* range contribute to the sum.

Summing values based on a text comparison

The following formula returns the total invoice amounts for the Oregon office:

```
=SUMIF(Office,"=Oregon",Amount)
```

Using the equal sign is optional. The following formula has the same result:

```
=SUMIF(Office,"Oregon",Amount)
```

To sum the invoice amounts for all offices *except* Oregon, use this formula:

```
=SUMIF(Office,"<>Oregon",Amount)
```

Let a Wizard Create Your Formula

Excel ships with an add-in called Conditional Sum Wizard. After you install this add-in, you can invoke the wizard by choosing Formulas ➪ Solutions ➪ Conditional Sum.

You can specify various conditions for your summing, and the add-in creates the formula for you (always an array formula). The Conditional Sum Wizard add-in, although a handy tool, is not all that versatile. For example, you can combine multiple criteria by using an And condition but not an Or condition.

Conditional Sum Wizard - Step 1 of 4

The Conditional Sum Wizard helps you write formulas that sum specific values in a column based on other values in the list.

Region	Code	Sales Amount	
North	Retail	$413	$413
East	Wholesale	$166	
North	Retail	$538	$538
North	Wholesale	$230	+
			$951

Where is the list that contains the values to sum, including the column labels?

Sheet1!$A$1:$A$34

Cancel   < Back   Next >   Finish

To install the Conditional Sum Wizard add-in:

1. **Choose Office ➪ Excel Options to display the Excel Options dialog box.**
2. **Click the Add-ins tab on the left.**
3. **Select Excel Add-Ins from the drop-down list labeled Manage.**
4. **Click Go to display the Add-Ins dialog box.**
5. **Place a check mark next to Conditional Sum Wizard.**
6. **Click OK.**

Summing values based on a date comparison

The following formula returns the total invoice amounts that have a due date after May 1, 2007:

```
=SUMIF(DateDue,">="&DATE(2007,5,1),Amount)
```

Notice that the second argument for the SUMIF function is an expression. The *expression* uses the DATE function, which returns a date. Also, the comparison operator, enclosed in quotes, is concatenated (using the & operator) with the result of the DATE function.

The formula that follows returns the total invoice amounts that have a future due date (including today):

```
=SUMIF(DateDue,">="&TODAY(),Amount)
```

Conditional Sums Using Multiple Criteria

The examples in the preceding section all used a single comparison criterion. The examples in this section involve summing cells based on multiple criteria.

Figure 14.14 shows the sample worksheet again, for your reference. The worksheet also shows the result of several formulas that demonstrate summing by using multiple criteria.

Using And criteria

Suppose that you want to get a sum of the invoice amounts that are past due *and* associated with the Oregon office. In other words, the value in the Amount range will be summed only if both of the following criteria are met:

- The corresponding value in the Difference range is negative.
- The corresponding text in the Office range is "Oregon."

FIGURE 14.14

This worksheet demonstrates summing based on multiple criteria.

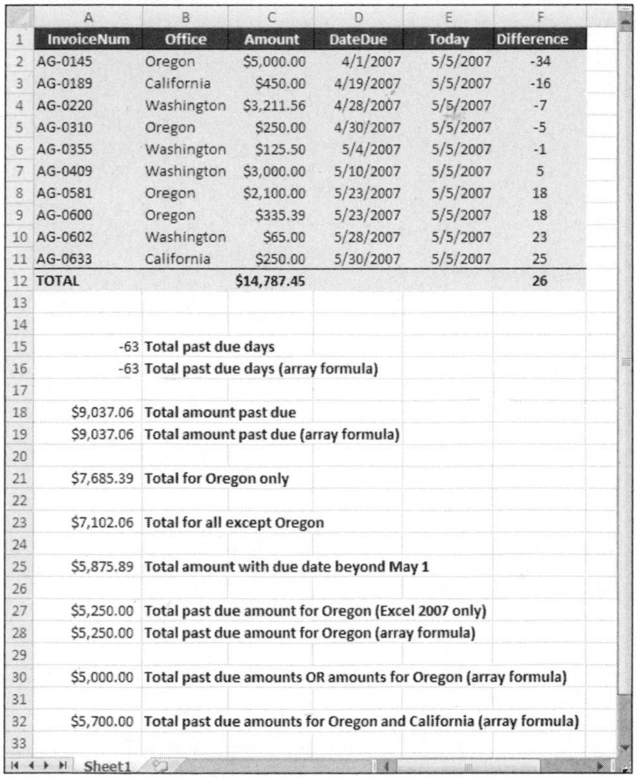

	A	B	C	D	E	F
1	InvoiceNum	Office	Amount	DateDue	Today	Difference
2	AG-0145	Oregon	$5,000.00	4/1/2007	5/5/2007	-34
3	AG-0189	California	$450.00	4/19/2007	5/5/2007	-16
4	AG-0220	Washington	$3,211.56	4/28/2007	5/5/2007	-7
5	AG-0310	Oregon	$250.00	4/30/2007	5/5/2007	-5
6	AG-0355	Washington	$125.50	5/4/2007	5/5/2007	-1
7	AG-0409	Washington	$3,000.00	5/10/2007	5/5/2007	5
8	AG-0581	Oregon	$2,100.00	5/23/2007	5/5/2007	18
9	AG-0600	Oregon	$335.39	5/23/2007	5/5/2007	18
10	AG-0602	Washington	$65.00	5/28/2007	5/5/2007	23
11	AG-0633	California	$250.00	5/30/2007	5/5/2007	25
12	TOTAL		$14,787.45			26
13						
14						
15		-63	Total past due days			
16		-63	Total past due days (array formula)			
17						
18		$9,037.06	Total amount past due			
19		$9,037.06	Total amount past due (array formula)			
20						
21		$7,685.39	Total for Oregon only			
22						
23		$7,102.06	Total for all except Oregon			
24						
25		$5,875.89	Total amount with due date beyond May 1			
26						
27		$5,250.00	Total past due amount for Oregon (Excel 2007 only)			
28		$5,250.00	Total past due amount for Oregon (array formula)			
29						
30		$5,000.00	Total past due amounts OR amounts for Oregon (array formula)			
31						
32		$5,700.00	Total past due amounts for Oregon and California (array formula)			
33						

Sheet1

If you're using Excel 2007, the following formula does the job:

```
=SUMIFS(Amount,Difference,"<0",Office,"Oregon")
```

The array formula that follows returns the same result and will work in all versions of Excel.

```
{=SUM((Difference<0)*(Office="Oregon")*Amount)}
```

Using Or criteria

Suppose that you want to get a sum of past-due invoice amounts *or* ones associated with the Oregon office. In other words, the value in the Amount range will be summed if either of the following criteria is met:

- The corresponding value in the Difference range is negative.
- The corresponding text in the Office range is "Oregon".

This example requires an array formula:

```
{=SUM(IF((Office="Oregon")+(Difference<0),1,0)*Amount)}
```

A plus sign (+) joins the conditions; you can include more than two conditions.

Using And and Or criteria

As you may expect, things get a bit tricky when your criteria consists of both And and Or operations. For example, you may want to sum the values in the Amount range when both of the following conditions are met:

- The corresponding value in the Difference range is negative.
- The corresponding text in the Office range is "Oregon" or "California".

Notice that the second condition actually consists of two conditions joined with Or. The following array formula does the trick:

```
{=SUM((Difference<0)*IF((Office="Oregon")+
(Office="California"),1)*Amount)}
```

Chapter 15

Creating Formulas That Look Up Values

This chapter discusses various techniques that you can use to look up a value in a range of data. Excel has three functions (LOOKUP, VLOOKUP, and HLOOKUP) designed for this task, but you may find that these functions don't quite cut it.

This chapter provides many lookup examples, including alternative techniques that go well beyond the Excel program's normal lookup capabilities.

Introducing Lookup Formulas

A *lookup formula* essentially returns a value from a table by looking up another related value. A common telephone directory provides a good analogy. If you want to find a person's telephone number, you first locate the name (look it up) and then retrieve the corresponding number.

> **NOTE** I use the term *table* to describe a rectangular range of data. The range does not necessarily need to be an "official" table, as created by Excel's Insert ⇨ Tables ⇨ Table command.

Figure 15.1 shows a simple worksheet that uses several lookup formulas. This worksheet contains a table of employee data, beginning in row 7. This range is named *EmpData*. When you enter a last name into cell C2, lookup formulas in D2:G2 retrieve the matching information from the table. The following lookup formulas use the VLOOKUP function:

D2	=VLOOKUP(C2,EmpData,2,FALSE)
E2	=VLOOKUP(C2,EmpData,3,FALSE)
F2	=VLOOKUP(C2,EmpData,4,FALSE)
G2	=VLOOKUP(C2,EmpData,5,FALSE)

About This Chapter's Examples

Most of the examples in this chapter use named ranges for function arguments. When you adapt these formulas for your own use, you need to substitute the actual range address or a range name defined in your workbook.

FIGURE 15.1

Lookup formulas in row 2 look up the information for the employee name in cell C2.

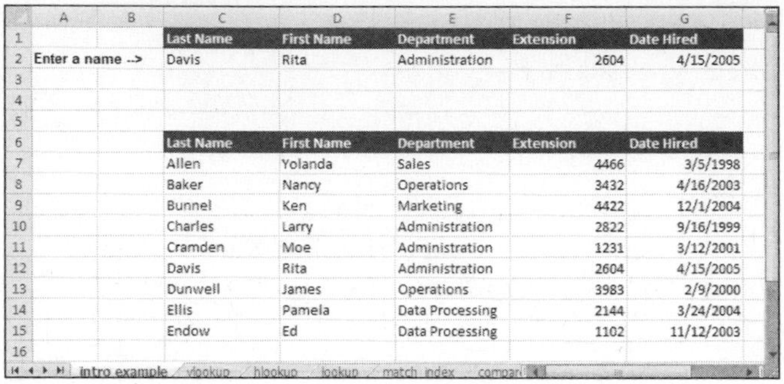

	A	B	C	D	E	F	G
1			Last Name	First Name	Department	Extension	Date Hired
2	Enter a name -->		Davis	Rita	Administration	2604	4/15/2005
3							
4							
5							
6			Last Name	First Name	Department	Extension	Date Hired
7			Allen	Yolanda	Sales	4466	3/5/1998
8			Baker	Nancy	Operations	3432	4/16/2003
9			Bunnel	Ken	Marketing	4422	12/1/2004
10			Charles	Larry	Administration	2822	9/16/1999
11			Cramden	Moe	Administration	1231	3/12/2001
12			Davis	Rita	Administration	2604	4/15/2005
13			Dunwell	James	Operations	3983	2/9/2000
14			Ellis	Pamela	Data Processing	2144	3/24/2004
15			Endow	Ed	Data Processing	1102	11/12/2003
16							

This particular example uses four formulas to return information from the *EmpData* range. In many cases, you want only a single value from the table, so use only one formula.

Functions Relevant to Lookups

Several Excel functions are useful when writing formulas to look up information in a table. Table 15.1 lists and describes these functions.

TABLE 15.1

Functions Used in Lookup Formulas

Function	Description
CHOOSE	Returns a specific value from a list of values (up to 29) supplied as arguments.
HLOOKUP	Horizontal lookup. Searches for a value in the top row of a table and returns a value in the same column from a row you specify in the table.
IF	Returns one value if a condition you specify is TRUE, and returns another value if the condition is FALSE.
IFERROR*	If the first argument returns an error, the second argument is evaluated and returned.
INDEX	Returns a value (or the reference to a value) from within a table or range.

Function	Description
LOOKUP	Returns a value either from a one-row or one-column range. Another form of the LOOKUP function works like VLOOKUP but is restricted to returning a value from the last column of a range.
MATCH	Returns the relative position of an item in a range that matches a specified value.
OFFSET	Returns a reference to a range that is a specified number of rows and columns from a cell or range of cells.
VLOOKUP	Vertical lookup. Searches for a value in the first column of a table and returns a value in the same row from a column you specify in the table.

* Available in Excel 2007 only.

The examples in this chapter use the functions listed in Table 15.1.

Basic Lookup Formulas

You can use the Excel basic lookup functions to search a column or row for a lookup value to return another value as a result. Excel provides three basic lookup functions: HLOOKUP, VLOOKUP, and LOOKUP. In addition, the MATCH and INDEX functions are often used together to return a cell or relative cell reference for a lookup value.

Using the IF Function for Simple Lookups

The IF function is very versatile and is often suitable for simple decision-making problems. The accompanying figure shows a worksheet with student grades in column B. Formulas in column C use the IF function to return text: either Pass (a score of 65 or higher) or Fail (a score below 65). For example, the formula in cell C2 is

```
=IF(B2>=65,"Pass","Fail")
```

	A	B	C
1	Student	Score	Grade
2	Andy	82	Pass
3	Barbara	57	Fail
4	Chris	73	Pass
5	Dennis	54	Fail
6	Elsie	82	Pass
7	Francine	72	Pass
8			
9			

Sheet1

You can "nest" IF functions to provide even more decision-making ability. This formula, for example, returns one of four strings: Excellent, Very Good, Fair, or Poor.

```
=IF(B2>=90,"Excellent",IF(B2>=70,"Very Good",IF(B2>=50,"Fair","Poor")))
```

This technique is fine for situations that involve only a few choices. But using nested IF functions can quickly become complicated and unwieldy. The lookup techniques described in this chapter provide a much better solution.

The VLOOKUP function

The VLOOKUP function looks up the value in the first column of the lookup table and returns the corresponding value in a specified table column. The lookup table is arranged vertically (which explains the V in the function's name). The syntax for the VLOOKUP function is

    VLOOKUP(lookup_value,table_array,col_index_num,range_lookup)

The VLOOKUP function's arguments are as follows:

- *lookup_value*: The value to be looked up in the first column of the lookup table.
- *table_array*: The range that contains the lookup table.
- *col_index_num*: The column number within the table from which the matching value is returned.
- *range_lookup*: Optional. If TRUE or omitted, an approximate match is returned. (If an exact match is not found, the next largest value that is less than *lookup_value* is returned.) If FALSE, VLOOKUP will search for an exact match. If VLOOKUP can't find an exact match, the function returns #N/A.

> **NOTE**
> If the *range_lookup* argument is TRUE or omitted, the first column of the lookup table must be in ascending order. If *lookup_value* is smaller than the smallest value in the first column of *table_array*, VLOOKUP returns #N/A. If the *range_lookup* argument is FALSE, the first column of the lookup table need not be in ascending order. If an exact match is not found, the function returns #N/A.

> **TIP**
> If the *lookup_value* argument is text, it can include wildcard characters * and ?.

A very common use for a lookup formula involves an income tax rate schedule (see Figure 15.2). The tax rate schedule shows the income tax rates for various income levels. The following formula (in cell B3) returns the tax rate for the income in cell B2:

    =VLOOKUP(B2,D2:F7,3)

> **ON the CD-ROM**
> The examples in this section are available on the companion CD-ROM. They're contained in a file named basic lookup examples.xlsx.

FIGURE 15.2

Using VLOOKUP to look up a tax rate.

	A	B	C	D	E	F	G
1				Income is Greater Than or Equal To...	But Less Than or Equal To...	Tax Rate	
2	Enter Income:	$45,500		$0	$2,650	15.00%	
3	The Tax Rate is:	31.00%		$2,651	$27,300	28.00%	
4				$27,301	$58,500	31.00%	
5				$58,501	$131,800	36.00%	
6				$131,801	$284,700	39.60%	
7				$284,701		45.25%	
8							

intro example **vlookup** hlookup lookup match indi

The lookup table resides in a range that consists of three columns (D2:F7). Because the last argument for the VLOOKUP function is 3, the formula returns the corresponding value in the third column of the lookup table.

Note that an exact match is not required. If an exact match is not found in the first column of the lookup table, the VLOOKUP function uses the next largest value that is less than the lookup value. In other words, the function uses the row in which the value you want to look up is greater than or equal to the row value but less than the value in the next row. In the case of a tax table, this is exactly what you want to happen.

The HLOOKUP function

The HLOOKUP function works just like the VLOOKUP function except that the lookup table is arranged horizontally instead of vertically. The HLOOKUP function looks up the value in the first row of the lookup table and returns the corresponding value in a specified table row.

The syntax for the HLOOKUP function is

    HLOOKUP(lookup_value,table_array,row_index_num,range_lookup)

The HLOOKUP function's arguments are as follows

- **lookup_value:** The value to be looked up in the first row of the lookup table.
- **table_array:** The range that contains the lookup table.
- **row_index_num:** The row number within the table from which the matching value is returned.
- **range_lookup:** Optional. If TRUE or omitted, an approximate match is returned. (If an exact match is not found, the next largest value less than *lookup_value* is returned.) If FALSE, VLOOKUP will search for an exact match. If VLOOKUP can't find an exact match, the function returns #N/A.

> **TIP**   If the *lookup_value* argument is text, it can include wildcard characters * and ?.

Figure 15.3 shows the tax rate example with a horizontal lookup table (in the range E1:J3). The formula in cell B3 is

    =HLOOKUP(B2,E1:J3,3)

FIGURE 15.3

Using HLOOKUP to look up a tax rate.

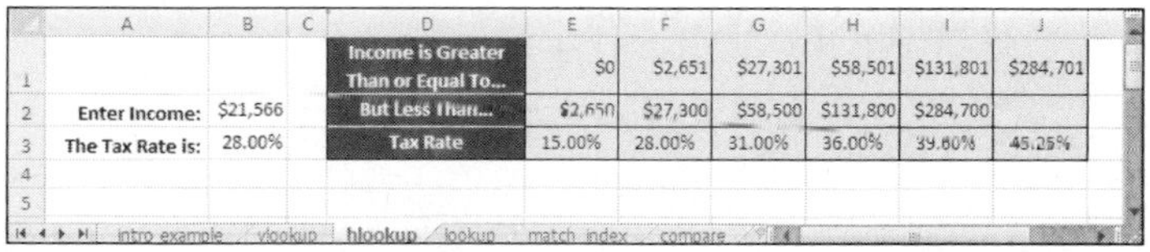

The LOOKUP function

The LOOKUP function has the following syntax:

    LOOKUP(lookup_value,lookup_vector,result_vector)

The function's arguments are as follows:

- **lookup_value:** The value to be looked up in the *lookup_vector*.
- **lookup_vector:** A single-column or single-row range that contains the values to be looked up. These values must be in ascending order.
- **result_vector:** The single-column or single-row range that contains the values to be returned. It must be the same size as the *lookup_vector*.

The LOOKUP function looks in a one-row or one-column range (*lookup_vector*) for a value (*lookup_value*) and returns a value from the same position in a second one-row or one-column range (*result_vector*).

CAUTION Values in the *lookup_vector* must be in ascending order. If *lookup_value* is smaller than the smallest value in *lookup_vector*, LOOKUP returns #N/A.

Figure 15.4 shows the tax table again. This time, the formula in cell B3 uses the LOOKUP function to return the corresponding tax rate. The formula in cell B3 is

    =LOOKUP(B2,D2:D7,F2:F7)

CAUTION If the values in the first column are not arranged in ascending order, the LOOKUP function may return an incorrect value.

Note that LOOKUP (as opposed to VLOOKUP) requires two range references (a range to be looked in, and a range that contains result values). VLOOKUP, on the other hand, uses a single range for the lookup table, and the third argument determines which column to use for the result. This argument, of course, can consist of a cell reference.

FIGURE 15.4

Using LOOKUP to look up a tax rate.

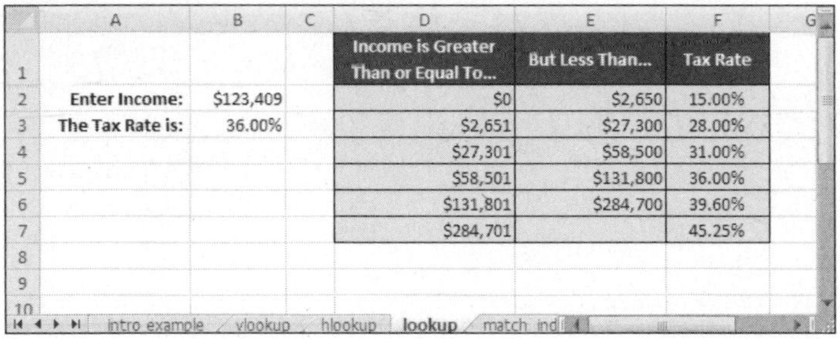

	A	B	C	D	E	F	G
1				Income is Greater Than or Equal To...	But Less Than...	Tax Rate	
2	Enter Income:	$123,409		$0	$2,650	15.00%	
3	The Tax Rate is:	36.00%		$2,651	$27,300	28.00%	
4				$27,301	$58,500	31.00%	
5				$58,501	$131,800	36.00%	
6				$131,801	$284,700	39.60%	
7				$284,701		45.25%	
8							
9							
10							

intro example / vlookup / hlookup / **lookup** / match ind

Combining the MATCH and INDEX functions

The MATCH and INDEX functions are often used together to perform lookups. The MATCH function returns the relative position of a cell in a range that matches a specified value. The syntax for MATCH is

    MATCH(lookup_value,lookup_array,match_type)

The MATCH function's arguments are as follows:

- *lookup_value*: The value you want to match in *lookup_array*. If *match_type* is 0 and the *lookup_value* is text, this argument can include wildcard characters "*" and "?"
- *lookup_array*: The range being searched.
- *match_type*: An integer (–1, 0, or 1) that specifies how the match is determined.

NOTE If *match_type* is 1, MATCH finds the largest value less than or equal to *lookup_value*. (*lookup_array* must be in ascending order.) If *match_type* is 0, MATCH finds the first value exactly equal to *lookup_value*. If *match_type* is –1, MATCH finds the smallest value greater than or equal to *lookup_value*. (*lookup_array* must be in descending order.) If you omit the *match_type* argument, this argument is assumed to be 1.

When a Blank Is Not a Zero

The Excel lookup functions treat empty cells in the result range as zeros. The worksheet in the accompanying figure contains a two-column lookup table, and this formula looks up the name in cell B1 and returns the corresponding amount:

```
=VLOOKUP(B1,D2:E8,2)
```

Note that the Amount cell for Charlie is blank, but the formula returns a 0.

	A	B	C	D	E	F
1	Name:	Charlie		Name	Amount	
2	Amount:	0		Bob	45	
3				Charlie		
4				David	0	
5				Frank	32	
6				George	9	
7				Harry	0	
8				Mike	1	
9						
10						

If you need to distinguish zeros from blank cells, you must modify the lookup formula by adding an IF function to check whether the length of the returned value is 0. When the looked up value is blank, the length of the return value is 0. In all other cases, the length of the returned value is non-zero. The following formula displays an empty string (a blank) whenever the length of the looked-up value is zero and the actual value whenever the length is anything but zero:

```
=IF(LEN(VLOOKUP(B1,D2:E8,2))=0,"",(VLOOKUP(B1,D2:E8,2)))
```

Alternatively, you can specifically check for an empty string, as in the following formula:

```
=IF(VLOOKUP(B1,D2:E8,2)="","",(VLOOKUP(B1,D2:E8,2)))
```

The INDEX function returns a cell from a range. The syntax for the INDEX function is

```
INDEX(array,row_num,column_num)
```

The INDEX function's arguments are as follows:

- *array*: A range
- *row_num*: A row number within *array*
- *col_num*: A column number within *array*

> **NOTE** If *array* contains only one row or column, the corresponding *row_num* or *column_num* argument is optional.

Figure 15.5 shows a worksheet with dates, day names, and amounts in columns D, E, and F. When you enter a date in cell B1, the following formula (in cell B2) searches the dates in column D and returns the corresponding amount from column F. The formula in cell B2 is

```
=INDEX(F2:F21,MATCH(B1,D2:D21,0))
```

To understand how this formula works, start with the MATCH function. This function searches the range D2:D21 for the date in cell B1. It returns the relative row number where the date is found. This value is then used as the second argument for the INDEX function. The result is the corresponding value in F2:F21.

FIGURE 15.5

Using the INDEX and MATCH functions to perform a lookup.

	A	B	C	D	E	F	G
1	Date:	1/12/2007		Date	Weekday	Amount	
2	Amount:	189		1/1/2007	Monday	23	
3				1/2/2007	Tuesday	179	
4				1/3/2007	Wednesday	149	
5				1/4/2007	Thursday	196	
6				1/5/2007	Friday	131	
7				1/6/2007	Saturday	179	
8				1/7/2007	Sunday	134	
9				1/8/2007	Monday	179	
10				1/9/2007	Tuesday	193	
11				1/10/2007	Wednesday	191	
12				1/11/2007	Thursday	176	
13				1/12/2007	Friday	189	
14				1/13/2007	Saturday	163	
15				1/14/2007	Sunday	121	
16				1/15/2007	Monday	100	
17				1/16/2007	Tuesday	109	
18				1/17/2007	Wednesday	151	
19				1/18/2007	Thursday	138	
20				1/19/2007	Friday	114	
21				1/20/2007	Saturday	156	
22							

vlookup / hlookup / lookup / **match** index

Specialized Lookup Formulas

You can use additional types of lookup formulas to perform more specialized lookups. For example, you can look up an exact value, search in another column besides the first in a lookup table, perform a case-sensitive lookup, return a value from among multiple lookup tables, and perform other specialized and complex lookups.

ON the CD-ROM The examples in this section are available on the companion CD-ROM. The file is named specialized lookup examples.xlsx.

Looking up an exact value

As demonstrated in the previous examples, VLOOKUP and HLOOKUP don't necessarily require an exact match between the value to be looked up and the values in the lookup table. An example is looking up a tax rate in a tax table. In some cases, you may require a perfect match. For example, when looking up an employee number, you would probably require a perfect match for the number.

To look up an exact value only, use the VLOOKUP (or HLOOKUP) function with the optional fourth argument set to FALSE.

Figure 15.6 shows a worksheet with a lookup table that contains employee numbers (column C) and employee names (column D). The lookup table is named ***EmpList***. The formula in cell B2, which follows, looks up the employee number entered in cell B1 and returns the corresponding employee name:

```
=VLOOKUP(B1,EmpList,2,FALSE)
```

Because the last argument for the `VLOOKUP` function is FALSE, the function returns a value only if an exact match is found. If the value is not found, the formula returns `#N/A`. This result, of course, is exactly what you want to happen because returning an approximate match for an employee number makes no sense. Also, notice that the employee numbers in column C are not in ascending order. If the last argument for `VLOOKUP` is FALSE, the values need not be in ascending order.

TIP **If you prefer to see something other than `#N/A` when the employee number is not found, you can use the `IFERROR` function to test for the error result and substitute a different string. The following formula displays the text `Not Found` rather than `#N/A`:**

```
=IFERROR(VLOOKUP(B1,EmpList,2,FALSE),"Not Found")
```

`IFERROR` is new to Excel 2007. For compatibility with previous versions, use the following formula:

```
=IF(ISNA(VLOOKUP(B1,EmpList,2,FALSE)),"Not Found",
VLOOKUP(B1,EmpList,2,FALSE))
```

FIGURE 15.6

This lookup table requires an exact match.

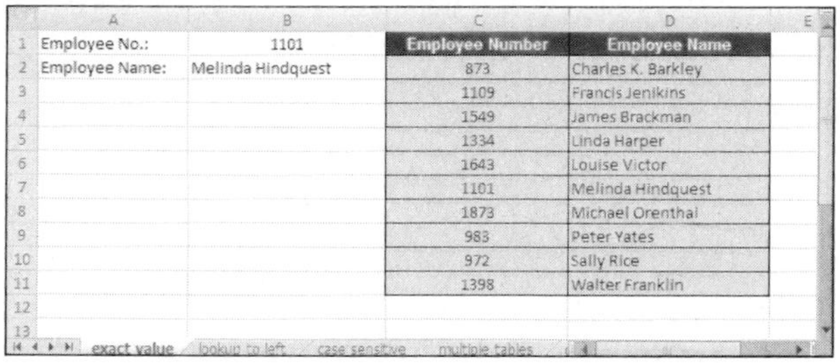

	A	B	C	D
1	Employee No.:	1101	Employee Number	Employee Name
2	Employee Name:	Melinda Hindquest	873	Charles K. Barkley
3			1109	Francis Jenikins
4			1549	James Brackman
5			1334	Linda Harper
6			1643	Louise Victor
7			1101	Melinda Hindquest
8			1873	Michael Orenthal
9			983	Peter Yates
10			972	Sally Rice
11			1398	Walter Franklin

Looking up a value to the left

The `VLOOKUP` function always looks up a value in the first column of the lookup range. But what if you want to look up a value in a column other than the first column? It would be helpful if you could supply a negative value for the third argument for `VLOOKUP` — but Excel doesn't allow it.

Figure 15.7 illustrates the problem. Suppose that you want to look up the batting average (column B, in a range named *Averages*) of a player in column C (in a range named *Players*). The player you want data for appears in a cell named *LookupValue*. The `VLOOKUP` function won't work because the data isn't arranged correctly. One option is to rearrange your data, but sometimes that's not possible.

One solution is to use the `LOOKUP` function, which requires two range arguments. The following formula (in cell F3) returns the batting average from column B of the player name contained in the cell named *LookupValue*:

```
=LOOKUP(LookupValue,Players,Averages)
```

Using the VLOOKUP function requires that the lookup range (in this case, the *Players* range) is in ascending order. In addition to this limitation, the formula suffers from a slight problem: If you enter a nonexistent player (in other words, the *LookupValue* cell contains a value not found in the *Players* range), the formula returns an erroneous result.

A better solution uses the INDEX and MATCH functions. The formula that follows works just like the previous one except that it returns #N/A if the player is not found. Another advantage is that the player names need not be sorted.

```
=INDEX(Averages,MATCH(LookupValue,Players,0))
```

FIGURE 15.7

The VLOOKUP function can't look up a value in column B, based on a value in column C.

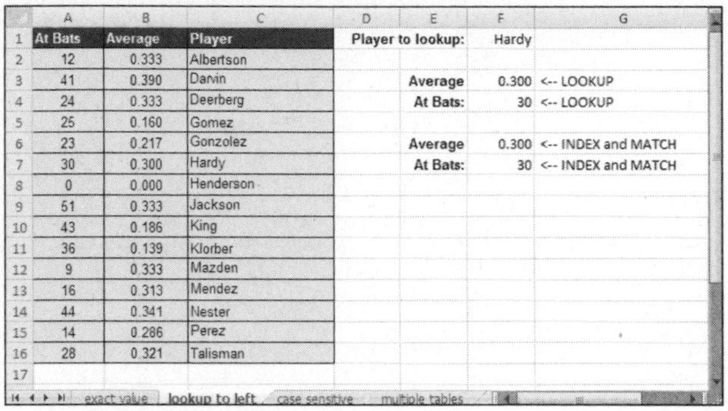

	A	B	C	D	E	F	G
1	At Bats	Average	Player		Player to lookup:	Hardy	
2	12	0.333	Albertson				
3	41	0.390	Darvin		Average	0.300	<-- LOOKUP
4	24	0.333	Deerberg		At Bats:	30	<-- LOOKUP
5	25	0.160	Gomez				
6	23	0.217	Gonzolez		Average	0.300	<-- INDEX and MATCH
7	30	0.300	Hardy		At Bats:	30	<-- INDEX and MATCH
8	0	0.000	Henderson				
9	51	0.333	Jackson				
10	43	0.186	King				
11	36	0.139	Klorber				
12	9	0.333	Mazden				
13	16	0.313	Mendez				
14	44	0.341	Nester				
15	14	0.286	Perez				
16	28	0.321	Talisman				
17							

exact value | **lookup to left** | case sensitive | multiple tables

Performing a case-sensitive lookup

The Excel lookup functions (LOOKUP, VLOOKUP, and HLOOKUP) are not case sensitive. For example, if you write a lookup formula to look up the text *budget*, the formula considers any of the following a match: *BUDGET*, *Budget*, or *BuDgEt*.

Figure 15.8 shows a simple example. Range D2:D7 is named *Range1*, and range E2:E7 is named *Range2*. The word to be looked up appears in cell B1 (named *Value*).

FIGURE 15.8

Using an array formula to perform a case-sensitive lookup.

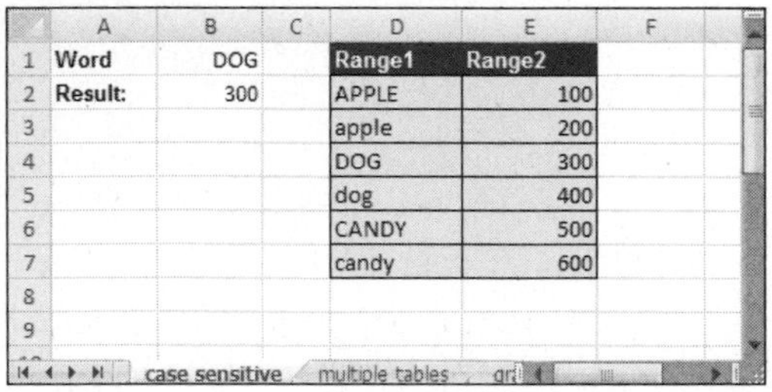

	A	B	C	D	E	F
1	Word	DOG		Range1	Range2	
2	Result:	300		APPLE	100	
3				apple	200	
4				DOG	300	
5				dog	400	
6				CANDY	500	
7				candy	600	
8						
9						

case sensitive | multiple tables | grid

The array formula that follows is in cell B2. This formula does a case-sensitive lookup in *Range1* and returns the corresponding value in *Range2*.

```
{=INDEX(Range2,MATCH(TRUE,EXACT(Value,Range1),0))}
```

The formula looks up the word *DOG* (uppercase) and returns 300. The following standard LOOKUP formula (which is not case sensitive) returns 400:

```
=LOOKUP(Value,Range1,Range2)
```

> **NOTE** When entering an array formula, remember to use Ctrl+Shift+Enter.

Choosing among multiple lookup tables

You can, of course, have any number of lookup tables in a worksheet. In some situations, your formula may need to decide which lookup table to use. Figure 15.9 shows an example.

This workbook calculates sales commission and contains two lookup tables: G3:H9 (named *CommTable1*) and J3:K8 (named *CommTable2*). The commission rate for a particular sales representative depends on two factors: the sales rep's years of service (column B) and the amount sold (column C). Column D contains formulas that look up the commission rate from the appropriate table. For example, the formula in cell D2 is

```
=VLOOKUP(C2,IF(B2<3,CommTable1,CommTable2),2)
```

FIGURE 15.9

This worksheet demonstrates the use of multiple lookup tables.

	A	B	C	D	E	F	G	H	I	J	K
1	Sales Rep	Years	Sales	Comm. Rate	Commission		<3 Years Tenure			3+ Years Tenure	
2	Benson	2	120,000	7.00%	8,400		Amt Sold	Rate		Amt Sold	Rate
3	Davidson	1	210,921	7.00%	14,764		0	1.50%		0	2.00%
4	Ellison	1	100,000	7.00%	7,000		5,000	3.25%		50,000	6.25%
5	Gomez	2	87,401	6.00%	5,244		10,000	3.50%		100,000	7.25%
6	Hernandez	6	310,983	9.25%	28,766		20,000	5.00%		200,000	8.25%
7	Kelly	3	43,902	2.00%	878		50,000	6.00%		300,000	9.25%
8	Martin	2	121,021	7.00%	8,471		100,000	7.00%		500,000	10.00%
9	Oswald	3	908	2.00%	18		250,000	8.00%			
10	Reginald	1	0	1.50%	0						
11	Veras	4	359,832	9.25%	33,284						
12	Wilmington	4	502,983	10.00%	50,298						

case sensitive   multiple tables   grade lookup 1   grade lookup 2   GP

The second argument for the VLOOKUP function consists of an IF formula that uses the value in column B to determine which lookup table to use.

The formula in column E simply multiplies the sales amount in column C by the commission rate in column D. The formula in cell E2, for example, is

```
=C2*D2
```

Determining letter grades for test scores

A common use of a lookup table is to assign letter grades for test scores. Figure 15.10 shows a worksheet with student test scores. The range E2:F6 (named *GradeList*) displays a lookup table used to assign a letter grade to a test score.

Column C contains formulas that use the VLOOKUP function and the lookup table to assign a grade based on the score in column B. The formula in cell C2, for example, is

```
=VLOOKUP(B2,GradeList,2)
```

When the lookup table is small (as in the example shown earlier in Figure 15.10), you can use a literal array in place of the lookup table. The formula that follows, for example, returns a letter grade without using a lookup table. Rather, the information in the lookup table is hard-coded into an array. See Chapter 17 for more information about arrays.

```
=VLOOKUP(B2,{0,"F";40,"D";70,"C";80,"B";90,"A"},2)
```

Another approach, which uses a more legible formula, is to use the LOOKUP function with two array arguments:

```
=LOOKUP(B2,{0,40,70,80,90},{"F","D","C","B","A"})
```

FIGURE 15.10

Looking up letter grades for test scores.

	A	B	C	D	E	F	G
1	Student	Score	Grade		Score	Grade	
2	Adams	36	F		0	F	
3	Baker	68	D		40	D	
4	Camden	50	D		70	C	
5	Dailey	77	C		80	B	
6	Gomez	92	A		90	A	
7	Hernandez	100	A				
8	Jackson	74	C				
9	Maplethorpe	45	D				
10	Paulson	60	D				
11	Ramirez	89	B				
12	Sosa	99	A				
13	Thompson	91	A				
14	Wilson	59	D				
15							

case sensitive / multiple tables / gra

Calculating a grade-point average

A student's *grade-point average* (GPA) is a numerical measure of the average grade received for classes taken. This discussion assumes a letter grade system, in which each letter grade is assigned a numeric value (A=4, B=3, C=2, D=1, and F=0). The GPA comprises an average of the numeric grade values weighted by the credit hours of the course. A one-hour course, for example, receives less weight than a three-hour course. The GPA ranges from 0 (all Fs) to 4.00 (all As).

Figure 15.11 shows a worksheet with information for a student. This student took five courses, for a total of 13 credit hours. Range B2:B6 is named *CreditHours*. The grades for each course appear in column C. (Range C2:C6 is named *Grades*.) Column D uses a lookup formula to calculate the grade value for each course. The lookup formula in cell D2, for example, follows. This formula uses the lookup table in G2:H6 (named *GradeTable*).

```
=VLOOKUP(C2,GradeTable,2,FALSE)
```

FIGURE 15.11

Using multiple formulas to calculate a GPA.

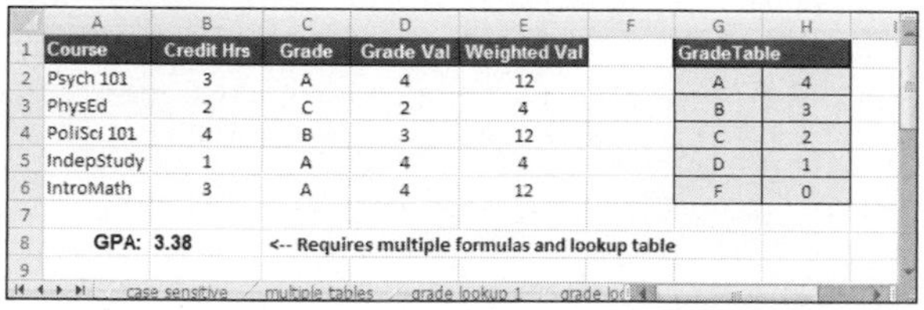

Course	Credit Hrs	Grade	Grade Val	Weighted Val		GradeTable	
Psych 101	3	A	4	12		A	4
PhysEd	2	C	2	4		B	3
PoliSci 101	4	B	3	12		C	2
IndepStudy	1	A	4	4		D	1
IntroMath	3	A	4	12		F	0
GPA:	3.38	<-- Requires multiple formulas and lookup table					

Formulas in column E calculate the weighted values. The formula in cell E2 is

```
=D2*B2
```

Cell B8 computes the GPA by using the following formula:

```
=SUM(E2:E6)/SUM(B2:B6)
```

The preceding formulas work fine, but you can streamline the GPA calculation quite a bit. In fact, you can use a single array formula to make this calculation and avoid using the lookup table and the formulas in columns D and E. This array formula does the job:

```
{=SUM((MATCH(Grades,{"F","D","C","B","A"},0)-1)*CreditHours)
/SUM(CreditHours)}
```

Performing a two-way lookup

Figure 15.12 shows a worksheet with a table that displays product sales by month. To retrieve sales for a particular month and product, the user enters a month in cell B1 and a product name in cell B2.

FIGURE 15.12

This table demonstrates a two-way lookup.

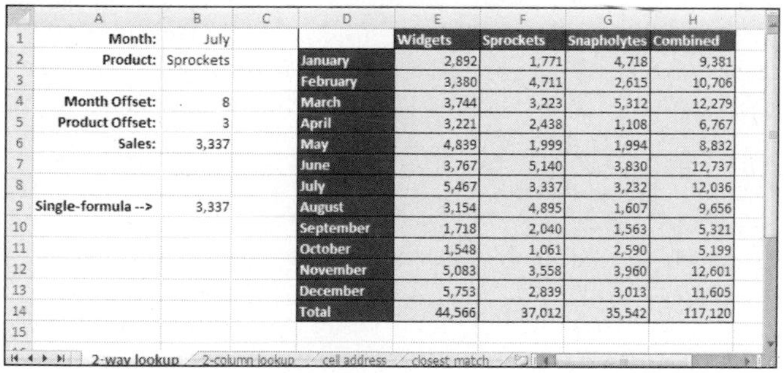

				Widgets	Sprockets	Snapholytes	Combined
Month:	July						
Product:	Sprockets		January	2,892	1,771	4,718	9,381
			February	3,380	4,711	2,615	10,706
Month Offset:	8		March	3,744	3,223	5,312	12,279
Product Offset:	3		April	3,221	2,438	1,108	6,767
Sales:	3,337		May	4,839	1,999	1,994	8,832
			June	3,767	5,140	3,830	12,737
			July	5,467	3,337	3,232	12,036
Single-formula -->	3,337		August	3,154	4,895	1,607	9,656
			September	1,718	2,040	1,563	5,321
			October	1,548	1,061	2,590	5,199
			November	5,083	3,558	3,960	12,601
			December	5,753	2,839	3,013	11,605
			Total	44,566	37,012	35,542	117,120

To simplify things, the worksheet uses the following named ranges:

Name	Refers To
Month	B1
Product	B2
Table	D1:H14
MonthList	D1:D14
ProductList	D1:H1

The following formula (in cell B4) uses the MATCH function to return the position of the *Month* within the *MonthList* range. For example, if the month is January, the formula returns 2 because January is the second item in the *MonthList* range (the first item is a blank cell, D1).

```
=MATCH(Month,MonthList,0)
```

The formula in cell B5 works similarly but uses the *ProductList* range.

```
=MATCH(Product,ProductList,0)
```

The final formula, in cell B6, returns the corresponding sales amount. It uses the INDEX function with the results from cells B4 and B5.

```
=INDEX(Table,B4,B5)
```

You can, of course, combine these formulas into a single formula, as shown here:

```
=INDEX(Table,MATCH(Month,MonthList,0),MATCH(Product,ProductList,0))
```

 You can use the Lookup wizard add-in to create this type of formula. The Lookup wizard add-in is distributed with Excel. When this add-in is installed, access it by choosing Formulas ➪ Solutions ➪ Lookup.

 Another way to accomplish a two-way lookup is to provide a name for each row and column of the table. A quick way to do so is to select the table and choose Formulas ➪ Defined Names ➪ Create From Selection. In the Create Names From Selection dialog box, select the Top Row and Left Column check boxes. After creating the names, you can use a simple formula, such as:

```
= Sprockets July
```

This formula, which uses the range intersection operator (a space), returns July sales for Sprockets. See Chapter 11 for details about the range intersection operator.

Performing a two-column lookup

Some situations may require a lookup based on the values in two columns. Figure 15.13 shows an example.

FIGURE 15.13

This workbook performs a lookup by using information in two columns (D and E).

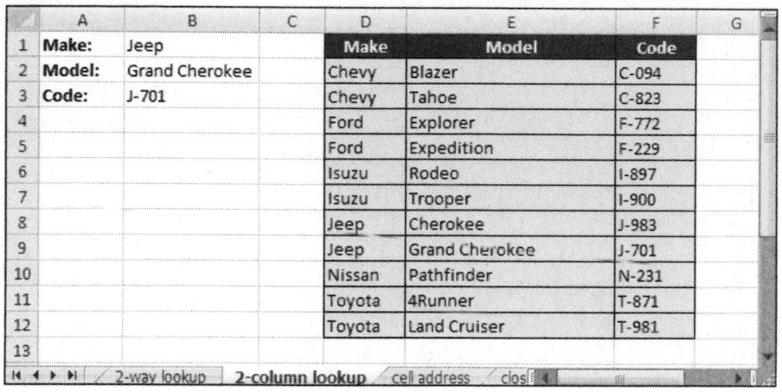

	A	B	C	D	E	F	G
1	**Make:**	Jeep		Make	Model	Code	
2	**Model:**	Grand Cherokee		Chevy	Blazer	C-094	
3	**Code:**	J-701		Chevy	Tahoe	C-823	
4				Ford	Explorer	F-772	
5				Ford	Expedition	F-229	
6				Isuzu	Rodeo	I-897	
7				Isuzu	Trooper	I-900	
8				Jeep	Cherokee	J-983	
9				Jeep	Grand Cherokee	J-701	
10				Nissan	Pathfinder	N-231	
11				Toyota	4Runner	T-871	
12				Toyota	Land Cruiser	T-981	
13							

The lookup table contains automobile makes and models and a corresponding code for each. The worksheet uses named ranges, as shown here:

F2:F12	*Code*
B1	*Make*
B2	*Model*
D2:D12	*Makes*
E2:E12	*Models*

The following array formula displays the corresponding code for an automobile make and model:

```
{=INDEX(Code,MATCH(Make&Model,Makes&Models,0))}
```

This formula works by concatenating the contents of *Make* and *Model* and then searching for this text in an array consisting of the concatenated corresponding text in *Makes* and *Models*.

Determining the cell address of a value within a range

Most of the time, you want your lookup formula to return a value. You may, however, need to determine the cell address of a particular value within a range. For example, Figure 15.14 shows a worksheet with a range of numbers that occupies a single column (named *Data*). Cell B1, which contains the value to look up, is named *Target*.

FIGURE 15.14

The formula in cell B2 returns the address in the *Data* range for the value in cell B1.

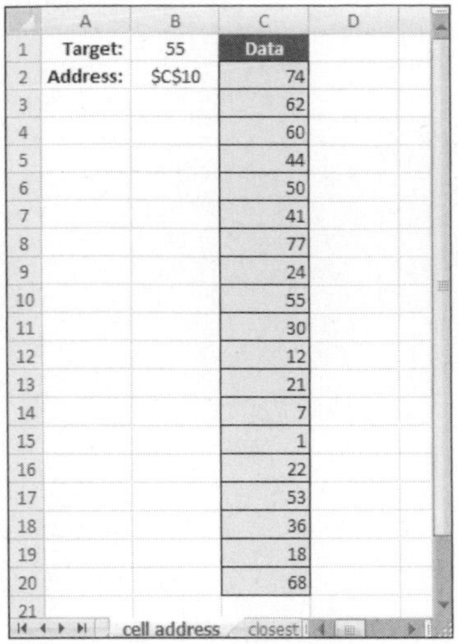

	A	B	C	D
1	Target:	55	Data	
2	Address:	$C$10	74	
3			62	
4			60	
5			44	
6			50	
7			41	
8			77	
9			24	
10			55	
11			30	
12			12	
13			21	
14			7	
15			1	
16			22	
17			53	
18			36	
19			18	
20			68	
21				

The formula in cell B2, which follows, returns the address of the cell in the *Data* range that contains the *Target* value:

```
=ADDRESS(ROW(Data)+MATCH(Target,Data,0)-1,COLUMN(Data))
```

If the *Data* range occupies a single row, use this formula to return the address of the *Target* value:

```
=ADDRESS(ROW(Data),COLUMN(Data)+MATCH(Target,Data,0)-1)
```

If the *Data* range contains more than one instance of the *Target* value, the address of the first occurrence is returned. If the *Target* value isn't found in the *Data* range, the formula returns #N/A.

Looking up a value by using the closest match

The VLOOKUP and HLOOKUP functions are useful in the following situations:

- You need to identify an exact match for a target value. Use FALSE as the function's fourth argument.
- You need to locate an approximate match. If the function's fourth argument is TRUE or omitted and an exact match is not found, the next largest value less than the lookup value is returned.

But what if you need to look up a value based on the *closest* match? Neither VLOOKUP nor HLOOKUP can do the job.

Figure 15.15 shows a worksheet with student names in column A and values in column B. Range B2:B20 is named *Data*. Cell E2, named *Target*, contains a value to search for in the *Data* range. Cell E3, named *ColOffset*, contains a value that represents the column offset from the *Data* range.

FIGURE 15.15

This workbook demonstrates how to perform a lookup by using the closest match.

	A	B	C	D	E	F
1	**Student**	**Data**				
2	Ann	9,101		Target Value -->	8025	
3	Betsy	8,873		Column Offset -->	-1	
4	Chuck	6,000				
5	David	9,820		Student:	Leslie	
6	George	10,500				
7	Hilda	3,500				
8	James	12,873				
9	John	5,867				
10	Keith	8,989				
11	Leslie	8,000				
12	Michelle	1,124				
13	Nora	9,099				
14	Paul	6,800				
15	Peter	5,509				
16	Rasmusen	5,460				
17	Sally	8,400				
18	Theresa	7,777				
19	Violet	3,600				
20	Wendy	5,400				
21						

closest match

The array formula that follows identifies the closest match to the *Target* value in the *Data* range and returns the names of the corresponding student in column A (that is, the column with an offset of −1). The formula returns Leslie (with a matching value of 8,000, which is the one closest to the *Target* value of 8,025).

```
{=INDIRECT(ADDRESS(ROW(Data)+MATCH(MIN(ABS(Target-Data)),
ABS(Target-Data),0)-1,COLUMN(Data)+ColOffset))}
```

If two values in the *Data* range are equidistant from the *Target* value, the formula uses the first one in the list.

The value in *ColOffset* can be negative (for a column to the left of *Data*), positive (for a column to the right of *Data*), or 0 (for the actual closest match value in the *Data* range).

To understand how this formula works, you need to understand the INDIRECT function. This function's first argument is a text string in the form of a cell reference (or a reference to a cell that contains a text string). In this example, the text string is created by the ADDRESS function, which accepts a row and column reference and returns a cell address.

Chapter 16

Creating Formulas for Financial Applications

I t's a safe bet that the most common use of Excel is to perform calculations involving money. Every day, people make hundreds of thousands of financial decisions based on the numbers that are calculated in a spreadsheet. These decisions range from simple (*Can I afford to buy a new car?*) to complex (*Will purchasing XYZ Corporation result in a positive cash flow in the next 18 months?*). This chapter discusses basic financial calculations that you can perform with the assistance of Excel.

The Time Value of Money

The face value of money may not always be what it seems. A key consideration is the time value of money. This concept involves calculating the value of money in the past, present, or future. It is based on the premise that money increases in value over time because of interest earned by the money. In other words, a dollar invested today will be worth more tomorrow.

For example, imagine that your rich uncle decided to give away some money and asked you to choose one of the following options:

- Receive $8,000 today
- Receive $9,500 in one year
- Receive $12,000 in five years
- Receive $150 per month for five years

If your goal is to maximize the amount received, you need to take into account not only the face value of the money but also the *time value* of the money when it arrives in your hands.

The time value of money depends on your perspective. In other words, you're either a lender or a borrower. When you take out a loan to purchase an automobile, you're a borrower, and the institution that provides the funds to you is the lender. When you invest money in a bank savings account, you're a lender; you're lending your money to the bank, and the bank is borrowing it from you.

Several concepts contribute to the time value of money:

- **Present Value (PV):** This is the *principal* amount. If you deposit $5,000 in a bank savings account, this amount represents the principal, or present value, of the money you invested. If you borrow $15,000 to purchase a car, this amount represents the principal or present value of the loan. Present Value may be positive or negative.

- **Future Value (FV):** This is the principal plus interest. If you invest $5,000 for five years and earn 6 percent annual interest, you receive $6,312.38 at the end of the five-year term. This amount is the future value of your $5,000 investment. If you take out a three-year auto loan for $15,000 and pay 7 percent annual interest, you pay a total of $16,673.16. This amount represents the principal plus the interest you paid. Future Value may be positive or negative, depending on the perspective (lender or borrower).

- **Payment (PMT):** This is either principal or principal plus interest. If you deposit $100 per month into a savings account, $100 is the payment. If you have a monthly mortgage payment of $825, then $825 is made up of principal and interest.

- **Interest Rate:** Interest is a percentage of the principal, usually expressed on an annual basis. For example, you may earn 5.5 percent annual interest on a bank CD (Certificate of Deposit). Or your mortgage loan may have a 7.75 percent interest rate.

- **Period:** This represents the point in time when interest is paid or earned (for example, a bank CD that pays interest quarterly or an auto loan that requires monthly payments).

- **Term:** This is the amount of time of interest. A 12-month bank CD has a term of one year. A 30-year mortgage loan has a term of 30 years.

Loan Calculations

This section describes how to calculate various components of a loan. Think of a loan as consisting of the following components:

- The loan amount
- The interest rate
- The number of payment periods
- The periodic payment amount

If you know any three of these components, you can create a formula to calculate the unknown component.

NOTE The loan calculations in this section all assume a fixed-rate loan with a fixed term.

Worksheet functions for calculating loan information

This section describes five functions: PMT, PPMT, IPMT, RATE, and PV. For information about the arguments used in these functions, see Table 16.1.

TABLE 16.1	

Financial Function Arguments

Function Argument	Description
rate	The interest rate per period. If the rate is expressed as an annual interest rate, you must divide it by the number of periods.
nper	The total number of payment periods.
per	A particular period. The period must be less than or equal to nper.
pmt	The payment made each period (a constant value that does not change).
fb	The future value after the last payment is made. If you omit fv, it is assumed to be 0. (The future value of a loan, for example, is 0.)
type	Indicates when payments are due — either 0 (due at the end of the period) or 1 (due at the beginning of the period). If you omit type, it is assumed to be 0.

The PMT function

The PMT function returns the loan payment (principal plus interest) per period, assuming constant payment amounts and a fixed interest rate. The syntax for the PMT function is

```
PMT(rate,nper,pv,fv,type)
```

The following formula returns the monthly payment amount for a $5,000 loan with a 6 percent annual percentage rate. The loan has a term of four years (48 months).

```
=PMT(.06/12,48,-5000)
```

This formula returns $117.43, the monthly payment for the loan. Notice that the third argument (*pv*, for present value) is negative and represents money owed.

The PPMT function

The PPMT function returns the *principal* part of a loan payment for a given period, assuming constant payment amounts and a fixed interest rate. The syntax for the PPMT function is

```
PPMT(rate,per,nper,pv,fv,type)
```

The following formula returns the amount paid to principal for the first month of a $5,000 loan with a 6 percent annual percentage rate. The loan has a term of four years (48 months).

```
=PPMT(.06/12,1,48,-5000)
```

The formula returns $92.43 for the principal, which is about 78.7 percent of the total loan payment. If I change the second argument to 48 (to calculate the principal amount for the last payment), the formula returns $116.84, or about 99.5 percent of the total loan payment.

NOTE   To calculate the cumulative principal paid between any two payment periods, use the CUMPRINC function. This function uses two additional arguments: *start_period* and *end_period*. In Excel versions prior to Excel 2007, the CUMPRINC is available only when you install the Analysis ToolPak add-in.

The IPMT Function

The IPMT function returns the *interest* part of a loan payment for a given period, assuming constant payment amounts and a fixed interest rate. The syntax for the IPMT function is

```
IPMT(rate,per,nper,pv,fv,type)
```

The following formula returns the amount paid to interest for the first month of a $5,000 loan with a 6 percent annual percentage rate. The loan has a term of four years (48 months).

```
=IPMT(.06/12,1,48,-5000)
```

This formula returns an interest amount of $25.00. By the last payment period for the loan, the interest payment is only $0.58.

NOTE To calculate the cumulative interest paid between any two payment periods use the CUMIPMT function. This function uses two additional arguments: *start_period* and *end_period.* In Excel versions prior to Excel 2007, the CUMIPMT is available only when you install the Analysis ToolPak add-in.

The RATE function

The RATE function returns the periodic interest rate of a loan, given the number of payment periods, the periodic payment amount, and the loan amount. The syntax for the RATE function is

```
RATE(nper,pmt,pv,fv,type,guess)
```

The following formula calculates the annual interest rate for a 48-month loan for $5,000 that has a monthly payment amount of $117.43.

```
=RATE(48,117.43,-5000)*12
```

This formula returns 6.00 percent. Notice that the result of the function multiplies by 12 to get the annual percentage rate.

The NPER function

The NPER function returns the number of payment periods for a loan, given the loan's amount, interest rate, and periodic payment amount. The syntax for the NPER function is

```
NPER(rate,pmt,pv,fv,type)
```

The following formula calculates the number of payment periods for a $5,000 loan that has a monthly payment amount of $117.43. The loan has a 6 percent annual interest rate.

```
=NPER(0.06/12,117.43,-5000)
```

This formula returns 47.997 (that is, 48 months). The monthly payment was rounded to the nearest penny, causing the minor discrepancy.

The PV Function

The PV function returns the present value (that is, the original loan amount) for a loan, given the interest rate, the number of periods, and the periodic payment amount. The syntax for the PV function is

```
PV(rate,nper,pmt,fv,type)
```

The following formula calculates the original loan amount for a 48-month loan that has a monthly payment amount of $117.43. The annual interest rate is 6 percent.

```
=PV(0.06/12,48,-117.43)
```

This formula returns $5,000.21. The monthly payment was rounded to the nearest penny, causing the $0.21 discrepancy.

A loan calculation example

Figure 16.1 shows a worksheet set up to calculate the periodic payment amount for a loan. The loan amount is in cell B1, and the annual interest rate is in cell B2. Cell B3 contains the payment period expressed in months. For example, if cell B3 is 1, the payment is due monthly. If cell B3 is 3, the payment is due every three months, or quarterly. Cell B4 contains the number of periods of the loan. The example shown in this figure calculates the payment for a $10,000 loan at 9.5 percent annual interest with monthly payments for 36 months. The formula in cell B6 is

```
=PMT(B2*(B3/12),B4,-B1)
```

FIGURE 16.1

Using the PMT function to calculate a periodic loan payment amount.

	A	B	C	D
1	Loan Amount:	10,000.00		
2	Annual Interest Rate:	9.5%		
3	Payment Period (months):	1		
4	Number of Periods:	36		
5				
6	Payment per Period:	$320.33		
7				
8				
9	Period	3		
10	Principal Amount	$245.00		
11	Interest Amount	$75.33		
12				

Sheet1 / Chart

Notice that the first argument is an expression that calculates the *periodic interest rate* by using the annual interest rate and the payment period. Therefore, if payments are made quarterly on a three-year loan, the payment period is 3, the number of periods is 12, and the periodic interest rate would be calculated as the annual interest rate multiplied by 3/12.

In the worksheet in Figure 16.1, range A9:B11 is set up to calculate the principal and interest amount for a particular payment period. Cell B9 contains the payment period used by the formulas in B10:B11. (The payment period must be less than or equal to the value in cell B4.)

The formula in cell B10, shown here, calculates the amount of the payment that goes toward principal for the payment period in cell B9:

```
=PPMT(B2*(B3/12),B9,B4,-B1)
```

The following formula, in cell B11, calculates the amount of the payment that goes toward interest for the payment period in cell B9:

```
=IPMT(B2*(B3/12),B9,B4,-B1)
```

You should note that the sum of B10 and B11 is equal to the total loan payment calculated in cell B6. However, the relative proportion of principal and interest amounts varies with the payment period. (An increasingly larger proportion of the payment is applied toward principal as the loan progresses.) Figure 16.2 shows this graphically.

FIGURE 16.2

This chart shows the relative interest and principal amounts for the payment periods of a loan.

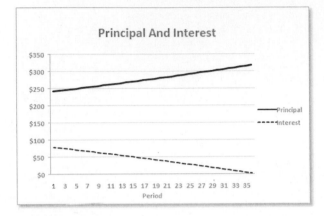

The workbook described in this section is available on the companion CD-ROM. The file is named **loan payment.xlsx.**

Credit-card payments

Do you ever wonder how long it would take to pay off a credit-card balance if you make the minimum payment amount each month? Figure 16.3 shows a worksheet set up to make this type of calculation.

The workbook shown in Figure 16.3 is available on the companion CD-ROM. The file is named **credit card payments.xlsx.**

Range B1:B5 stores input values. In this example, the credit card has a balance of $1,000, and the lender charges 18.25 percent annual percentage rate (APR). The minimum payment is 2.00 percent (typical of many credit-card lenders). Therefore, the minimum payment amount for this example is $20. You can enter a different payment amount in cell B5, but it must be greater than or equal to the value in cell B4. For example, you may choose to pay $50 per month.

Range B7:B9 holds formulas that perform various calculations. The formula in cell B7, which follows, calculates the number of months required to pay off the balance:

```
=NPER(B2/12,B5,-B1,0)
```

The formula in B8 calculates the total amount you will pay. This formula is

```
=B7*B5
```

The formula in cell B9 calculates the total interest paid:

```
=B8-B1
```

FIGURE 16.3

This worksheet calculates the number of payments required to pay off a credit-card balance by paying the minimum payment amount each month.

	A	B	C
1	Credit Card Balance	$1,000.00	
2	Annual Interest Rate:	18.25%	
3	Minimum Payment Pct:	2.00%	
4	Minimum Monthly Payment Amount:	$20.00	
5	Your Actual Monthly Payment:	$20.00	
6			
7	No. of Payments Required:	94.7	
8	Total Amount Paid:	$1,893.29	
9	Total Interest Paid:	$893.29	
10			

Sheet1

In this example, it would take about 95 months (more than seven years) to pay off the credit-card balance if the borrower made the minimum monthly payment. The total interest paid on the $1,000 loan would be $893.29. This calculation assumes, of course, that no additional charges are made on the account. This example may help explain why you receive so many credit-card solicitations in the mail.

Figure 16.4 shows some additional calculations for the credit-card example. For example, if you want to pay off the credit card in 12 months, you need to make monthly payments of $91.80. (This amount results in total payments of $1,101.59 and total interest of $101.59.) The formula in B13 is

```
=PMT($B$2/12,A13,-$B$1)
```

FIGURE 16.4

Column B shows the payment required to pay off the credit-card balance for various payoff periods.

	A	B	C	D
11				
12	Other Payoff Periods (months)	Pmt Required	Total Pmts	Total Interest
13	12	$91.80	$1,101.59	$101.59
14	24	$50.04	$1,201.08	$201.08
15	36	$36.28	$1,306.01	$306.01
16	48	$29.51	$1,416.28	$416.28
17	60	$25.53	$1,531.78	$531.78
18	72	$22.95	$1,652.35	$652.35
19	84	$21.16	$1,777.83	$777.83
20	96	$19.88	$1,908.00	$908.00
21	108	$18.91	$2,042.66	$1,042.66
22	120	$18.18	$2,181.57	$1,181.57
23				

Sheet1

Creating a loan amortization schedule

A *loan amortization schedule* is a table of values that shows various pieces of information for each payment period of a loan. Figure 16.5 shows a worksheet that uses formulas to calculate an amortization schedule.

A loan amortization schedule.

This workbook available on the companion CD-ROM. The file is named **loan amortization schedule.xlsx**.

The loan parameters are entered into B1:B4, and the formulas beginning in row 9 use these values for the calculations. Table 16.2 shows the formulas in row 9 of the schedule. These formulas were copied down to row 488. Therefore, the worksheet can calculate amortization schedules for a loan with as many as 480 payment periods (40 years of monthly payments).

NOTE Formulas in the rows that extend beyond the number of payments return an error value. The worksheet uses conditional formatting to hide the data in these rows. See Chapter 21 for more information about conditional formatting.

TABLE 16.2

Formulas Used to Calculate an Amortization Schedule

Cell	Formula	Description
A9	=A8+1	Returns the payment number
B9	=PMT($B$2*($B$3/12),$B$4,-$B$1)	Calculates the periodic payment amount
C9	=C8+B9	Calculates the cumulative payment amounts
D9	=IPMT($B$2*($B$3/12),A9,$B$4,-$B$1)	Calculates the interest portion of the periodic payment
E9	=E8+D9	Calculates the cumulative interest paid

Cell	Formula	Description
F9	=PPMT($B$2*($B$3/12),A9,$B$4,-$B$1)	Calculates the principal portion of the periodic payment
G9	=G8+F9	Calculates the cumulative amount applied toward principal
H9	=H8-F9	Returns the principal balance at the end of the period

Summarizing loan options by using a data table

Excel's Data Table feature is probably one of the most underutilized tools in Excel. It's a handy way to summarize calculations that depend on one or two "changing" cells. In this example, I use a data table to summarize various loan options. This section describes how to create one-way and two-way data tables.

CROSS-REF Refer to Chapter 36 for more information about setting up data tables.

ON the CD-ROM A workbook that demonstrates one- and two-way data tables is available on the companion CD-ROM. The file is named loan data tables.xlsx.

Creating a one-way data table

A *one-way data table* shows the results of any number of calculations for different values of a single input cell.

Figure 16.6 shows a one-way data table (in B10:I13) that displays three calculations (payment amount, total payments, and total interest) for a loan, using seven interest rates ranging from 7.00 percent to 8.50 percent. In this example, the input cell is cell B2.

To create this one-way data table, follow these steps:

1. **Enter the formulas that return the results for use in the data table.** In this example, the formulas are in B6:B8.
2. **Enter various values for a single input cell in successive columns.** In this example, the input value is interest rate, and the values for various interest rates appear in C10:I10.
3. **Create a reference to the formula cells in the column to the left of the input values.** In this example, the range B11:B13 contains simple formulas that reference other cells. For example, cell B11 contains the following formula:

   =B6
4. **Select the rectangular range that contains the entries from the previous steps.** In this example, select B10:I13.
5. **Choose Data ➪ Data Tools ➪ What-If Analysis ➪ Data Table.** Excel displays the Data Table dialog box, shown in Figure 16.7.

FIGURE 16.6

Using a one-way data table to display three loan calculations for various interest rates.

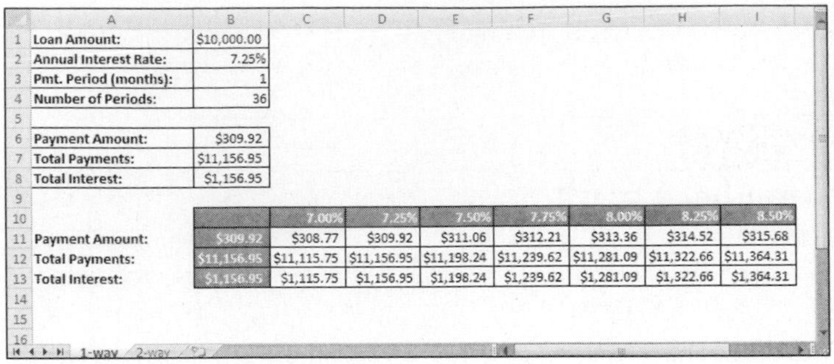

	A	B	C	D	E	F	G	H	I
1	Loan Amount:	$10,000.00							
2	Annual Interest Rate:	7.25%							
3	Pmt. Period (months):	1							
4	Number of Periods:	36							
5									
6	Payment Amount:	$309.92							
7	Total Payments:	$11,156.95							
8	Total Interest:	$1,156.95							
9									
10			7.00%	7.25%	7.50%	7.75%	8.00%	8.25%	8.50%
11	Payment Amount:	$309.92	$308.77	$309.92	$311.06	$312.21	$313.36	$314.52	$315.68
12	Total Payments:	$11,156.95	$11,115.75	$11,156.95	$11,198.24	$11,239.62	$11,281.09	$11,322.66	$11,364.31
13	Total Interest:	$1,156.95	$1,115.75	$1,156.95	$1,198.24	$1,239.62	$1,281.09	$1,322.66	$1,364.31

6. **For the Row input cell field, specify the cell reference that corresponds to the variable in your Data Table column header row.** In this example, the Row input cell is B2.
7. **Leave the Column input cell field empty.** The Column input field is used for two-way data tables, described in the next section.
8. **Click OK.** Excel inserts an array formula that uses the `TABLE` function with a single argument.
9. **If you like, you can format the data table.** For example, you may want to apply shading to the row and column headers.

FIGURE 16.7

The Data Table dialog box.

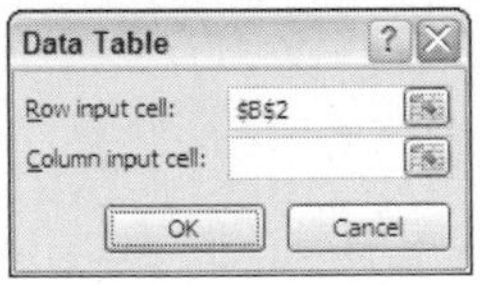

Note that the array formula is not entered into the entire range that you selected in Step 4. The first column and first row of your selection are not changed.

TIP **When you create a data table, the leftmost column of the data table (the column that contains the references entered in Step 3) contains the calculated values for the input cell. In this example, those values are repeated in column D. You may want to hide the values in column B by making the font color the same color as the background.**

Creating a two-way data table

A *two-way data table* shows the results of a single calculation for different values of two input cells. Figure 16.8 shows a two-way data table (in B10:I16) that displays a calculation (payment amount) for a loan, using seven interest rates and six loan amounts.

To create this two-way data table, follow these steps:

1. **Enter a formula that returns the results that will be used in the data table.** In this example, the formula is in cell B6. The formulas in B7:B8 are not used.
2. **Enter various values for the first input in successive columns.** In this example, the first input value is interest rate, and the values for various interest rates appear in C10:I10.

FIGURE 16.8

Using a two-way data table to display payment amounts for various loan amounts and interest rates.

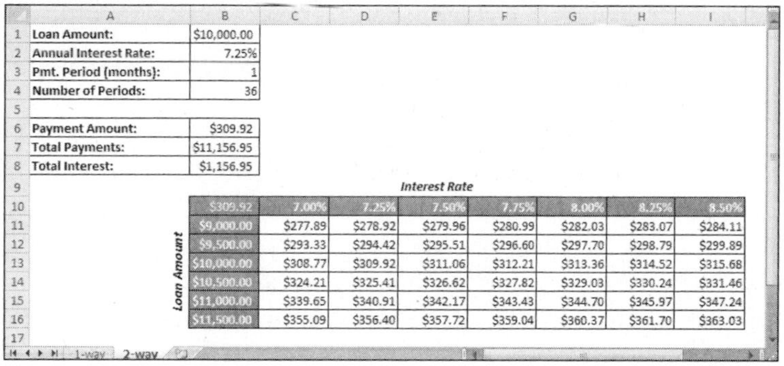

	A	B	C	D	E	F	G	H	I
1	Loan Amount:	$10,000.00							
2	Annual Interest Rate:	7.25%							
3	Pmt. Period (months):	1							
4	Number of Periods:	36							
5									
6	Payment Amount:	$309.92							
7	Total Payments:	$11,156.95							
8	Total Interest:	$1,156.95							
9					Interest Rate				
10		$309.92	7.00%	7.25%	7.50%	7.75%	8.00%	8.25%	8.50%
11		$9,000.00	$277.89	$278.92	$279.96	$280.99	$282.03	$283.07	$284.11
12		$9,500.00	$293.33	$294.42	$295.51	$296.60	$297.70	$298.79	$299.89
13	Loan Amount	$10,000.00	$308.77	$309.92	$311.06	$312.21	$313.36	$314.52	$315.68
14		$10,500.00	$324.21	$325.41	$326.62	$327.82	$329.03	$330.24	$331.46
15		$11,000.00	$339.65	$340.91	$342.17	$343.43	$344.70	$345.97	$347.24
16		$11,500.00	$355.09	$356.40	$357.72	$359.04	$360.37	$361.70	$363.03
17									

3. **Enter various values for the second input cell in successive rows, to the left and below the input values for the first input.** In this example, the second input value is loan amount, and the values for various loan amounts are in B11:B16.
4. **Create a reference to the formula that will be calculated in the table.** This reference goes in the upper-left corner of the data table range. In this example, cell B10 contains the following formula:

   ```
   =B6
   ```
5. **Select the rectangular range that contains the entries from the previous steps.** In this example, select B10:I16.
6. **Choose Data ➪ Data Tools ➪ What-If Analysis ➪ Data Table.** Excel displays the Data Table dialog box.
7. **For the Row input cell field, specify the cell reference that corresponds to the first input cell.** In this example, the Row input cell is B2.
8. **For the Column input cell field, specify the cell reference that corresponds to the second input cell.** In this example, the Row input cell is B1.
9. **Click OK.** Excel inserts an array formula that uses the `TABLE` function with two arguments.

After you create the two-way data table, you can change the calculated cell by changing the cell reference in the upper-left cell of the data table. In this example, you can change the formula in cell B10 to =B8 so that the data table displays total interest rather than payment amounts.

TIP If you create very large data tables, the calculation speed of your workbook may be slowed down. Excel has a special calculation mode for calculation-intensive data tables. To change the calculation mode, choose Formulas ➪ Calculation ➪ Calculation Options ➪ Automatic Except For Data Tables.

Calculating a loan with irregular payments

So far, the loan calculation examples in this chapter have involved loans with regular periodic payments. In some cases, loan payback is irregular. For example, you may loan some money to a friend without a formal agreements as to how he will pay the money back. You still collect interest on the loan, so you need a way to perform the calculations based on the actual payment dates.

Figure 16.9 shows a worksheet set up to keep track of such a loan. The annual interest rate for the loan is stored in cell B1 (named *APR*). The original loan amount and loan date are stored in row 5. Formulas, beginning in row 6, track the irregular loan payments and perform calculations.

FIGURE 16.9

This worksheet tracks loan payments that are made on an irregular basis.

	Payment Number	Payment Amount	Payment Date	Amount to Interest	Amount to Principal	Cumulative Payments	Cumulative Interest	Loan Balance
5	Original Loan	($10,000.00)	09/12/05					$10,000.00
6	1	$200.00	10/29/05	$83.70	$116.30	$200.00	$83.70	$9,883.70
7	2	$200.00	11/13/05	$26.40	$173.60	$400.00	$110.10	$9,710.10
8	3	$200.00	12/29/05	$79.54	$120.46	$600.00	$189.64	$9,589.64
9	4	$100.00	03/15/06	$129.79	($29.79)	$700.00	$319.43	$9,619.43
10	5	$250.00	04/25/06	$70.24	$179.76	$950.00	$389.67	$9,439.67
11	Addition to Principal	($500.00)	05/08/06	$21.05	($521.85)	$450.00	$411.52	$9,961.52
12	6	$200.00	05/18/06	$17.74	$182.26	$650.00	$429.26	$9,779.26
13	7	$100.00	06/03/06	$27.86	$72.14	$750.00	$457.12	$9,707.12
14	8	$1,000.00	06/12/06	$15.56	$984.44	$1,750.00	$472.68	$8,722.68
15	9	$250.00	06/27/06	$23.30	$226.70	$2,000.00	$495.98	$8,495.98
16	10	$200.00	07/14/06	$25.72	$174.28	$2,200.00	$521.70	$8,321.70
17	11	$200.00	07/31/06	$25.19	$174.81	$2,400.00	$546.90	$8,146.90
18	12	$1,000.00	08/15/06	$21.76	$978.24	$3,400.00	$568.66	$7,168.66
19	13	$100.00	08/27/06	$15.32	$84.68	$3,500.00	$583.98	$7,083.98
20	14	$200.00	09/13/06	$21.45	$178.55	$3,700.00	$605.42	$6,905.42
21	15	$200.00	09/30/06	$20.91	$179.09	$3,900.00	$626.33	$6,726.33
22	16	$100.00	10/16/06	$19.17	$80.83	$4,000.00	$645.49	$6,645.49
23	17	$100.00	10/26/06	$11.83	$88.17	$4,100.00	$657.33	$6,557.33
24	Addition to Principal	($500.00)	12/13/06	$56.05	($556.05)	$3,600.00	$713.38	$7,113.38
25	18	$100.00	02/13/07	$78.54	$21.46	$3,700.00	$791.92	$7,091.92
26	19	$100.00	02/26/07	$16.42	$83.58	$3,800.00	$808.34	$7,008.34
27	20	$200.00	03/28/07	$37.44	$162.56	$4,000.00	$845.78	$6,845.78
28	21	$250.00	04/18/07	$25.60	$224.40	$4,250.00	$871.38	$6,621.38
29	22							

Interest Rate (APR): 6.50%

Sheet1

Column B stores the payment amount made on the date in column C. Notice that the payments are not made on a regular basis. Also, notice that in two cases (row 11 and row 24), the payment amount is negative. These entries represent additional borrowed money added to the loan balance. Formulas in columns D and E calculate the amount of the payment credited toward interest and principal. Columns F and G keep a running tally of the cumulative payments and interest amounts. Formulas in column H compute the new loan balance after each payment. Table 16.3 lists and describes the formulas in row 6. Note that each formula uses an IF function to determine whether the payment date in column C is missing. If so, the formula returns an empty string, so no data appears in the cell.

TABLE 16.3

Formulas to Calculate a Loan with Irregular Payments

Cell	Formula	Description
D6	`=IF(C6<>"",(C6-C5)/365*H5*APR,"")`	The formula calculates the interest, based on the payment date.
E6	`=IF(C6<>"",B6-D6,"")`	The formula subtracts the interest amount from the payment to calculate the amount credited to principal.
F6	`=IF(C6<>"",F5+B6,"")`	The formula adds the payment amount to the running total.
G6	`=IF(C6<>"",G5+D6,"")`	The formula adds the interest to the running total.
H6	`=IF(C6<>"",H5-E6,"")`	The formula calculates the new loan balance by subtracting the principal amount from the previous loan balance.

ON the CD-ROM This workbook is available on the companion CD-ROM. The file name is **irregular payments.xlsx**.

Investment Calculations

Investment calculations involve calculating interest on fixed-rate investments, such as bank savings accounts, Certificates of Deposit (CDs), and annuities. You can make these interest calculations for investments that consist of a single deposit or multiple deposits.

ON the CD-ROM The companion CD-ROM contains a workbook with all of the interest calculation examples in this section. The file is named **investment calculations.xlsx**.

Future value of a single deposit

Many investments consist of a single deposit that earns interest over the term of the investment. This section describes calculations for simple interest and compound interest.

Calculating simple interest

Simple interest refers to the fact that interest payments are not compounded. The basic formula for computing interest is

```
Interest = Principal * Rate * Term
```

For example, suppose that you deposit $1,000 into a bank CD that pays a 5 percent simple annual interest rate. After one year, the CD matures, and you withdraw your money. The bank adds $50, and you walk away with $1,050. In this case, the interest earned is calculated by multiplying the principal ($1,000) by the interest rate (.05) by the term (one year).

If the investment term is less than one year, the simple interest rate is adjusted accordingly, based on the term. For example, $1,000 invested in a six-month CD that pays 5 percent simple annual interest earns $25 when the CD matures. In this case, the annual interest rate multiplies by 6/12.

Figure 16.10 shows a worksheet set up to make simple interest calculations. The formula in cell B7, shown here, calculates the interest due at the end of the term:

```
=B3*B4*B5
```

The formula in B8 simply adds the interest to the original investment amount.

FIGURE 16.10

This worksheet calculates simple interest payments.

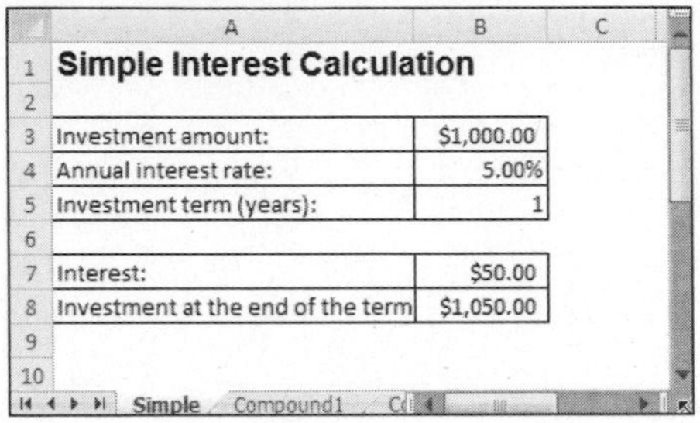

	A	B	C
1	**Simple Interest Calculation**		
2			
3	Investment amount:	$1,000.00	
4	Annual interest rate:	5.00%	
5	Investment term (years):	1	
6			
7	Interest:	$50.00	
8	Investment at the end of the term	$1,050.00	
9			
10			

H ◀ ▶ H   Simple Compound1 C

Calculating compound interest

Most fixed-term investments pay interest by using some type of compound interest calculation. *Compound interest* refers to the fact that interest is credited to the investment balance, and the investment then earns interest on the interest.

For example, suppose that you deposit $1,000 into a bank CD that pays 5 percent annual interest rate, compounded monthly. Each month, the interest is calculated on the balance, and that amount is credited to your account. The next month's interest calculation will be based on a higher amount because it also includes the previous month's interest payment. One way to calculate the final investment amount involves a series of formulas (see Figure 16.11).

Column B contains formulas to calculate the interest for one month. For example, the formula in B10 is

```
=C9*($B$5*(1/12))
```

The formulas in column C simply add the monthly interest amount to the balance. For example, the formula in C10 is

```
=C9+B10
```

At the end of the 12-month term, the CD balance is $1,051.16. In other words, monthly compounding results in an additional $1.16 (compared to simple interest).

FIGURE 16.11

Using a series of formulas to calculate compound interest.

	A	B	C
1	**Compound Interest Calculation**		
2	*Monthly compounding*		
3			
4	Investment amount:	$1,000.00	
5	Annual interest rate:	5.00%	
6	Investment term (months)	12	
7			
8	Month	Interest Earned	Balance
9	Beginning Balance		$1,000.00
10	1	$4.17	$1,004.17
11	2	$4.18	$1,008.35
12	3	$4.20	$1,012.55
13	4	$4.22	$1,016.77
14	5	$4.24	$1,021.01
15	6	$4.25	$1,025.26
16	7	$4.27	$1,029.53
17	8	$4.29	$1,033.82
18	9	$4.31	$1,038.13
19	10	$4.33	$1,042.46
20	11	$4.34	$1,046.80
21	12	$4.36	$1,051.16
22			

H ◀ ▶ H   Simple   Compound1   Compou

You can use the FV (Future Value) function to calculate the final investment amount without using a series of formulas. Figure 16.12 shows a worksheet set up to calculate compound interest. Cell B6 is an input cell that holds the number of compounding periods per year. For monthly compounding, the value in B6 would be 12. For quarterly compounding, the value would be 4. For daily compounding, the value would be 365. Cell B7 holds the term of the investment expressed in years.

FIGURE 16.12

Using a single formula to calculate compound interest.

	A	B
1	**Compound Interest Calculation**	
2	*Single formula general solution*	
3		
4	Investment amount:	$5,000.00
5	Annual interest rate:	5.75%
6	Compounding periods/year	4
7	Term (years)	3
8		
9	Periodic interest rate:	1.44%
10	Investment value at end of term	$5,934.07
11	Total interest earned:	$934.07
12		
13	Annual yield:	6.23%
14		

H ◀ ▶ H   Compound2   compou

Cell B9 contains the following formula that calculates the periodic interest rate. This value is the interest rate used for each compounding period.

```
=B5*(1/B6)
```

The formula in cell B10 uses the FV function to calculate the value of the investment at the end of the term. The formula is

```
=FV(B9,B6*B7,,-B4)
```

The first argument for the FV function is the periodic interest rate, which is calculated in cell B9. The second argument represents the total number of compounding periods. The third argument (pmt) is omitted, and the fourth argument is the original investment amount (expressed as a negative value).

The total interest is calculated with a simple formula in cell B11:

```
=B10-B4
```

Another formula, in cell B13, calculates the annual yield on the investment:

```
=(B11/B4)/B7
```

For example, suppose that you deposit $5,000 into a three-year CD with a 5.75 percent annual interest rate compounded quarterly. In this case, the investment has four compounding periods per year, so you enter 4 into cell B6. The term is three years, so you enter 3 into cell B7. The formula in B10 returns $5,934.07.

Perhaps you want to see how this rate stacks up against a competitor's account that offers daily compounding. Figure 16.13 shows a calculation with daily compounding, using a $5,000 investment (compare this to Figure 16.12). As you can see, the difference is very small ($934.07 versus. $941.28). Over a period of three years, the account with daily compounding earns a total of $7.21 more interest. In terms of annual yield, quarterly compounding earns 6.23%, and daily compounding earns 6.28%.

FIGURE 16.13

Calculating interest by using daily compounding.

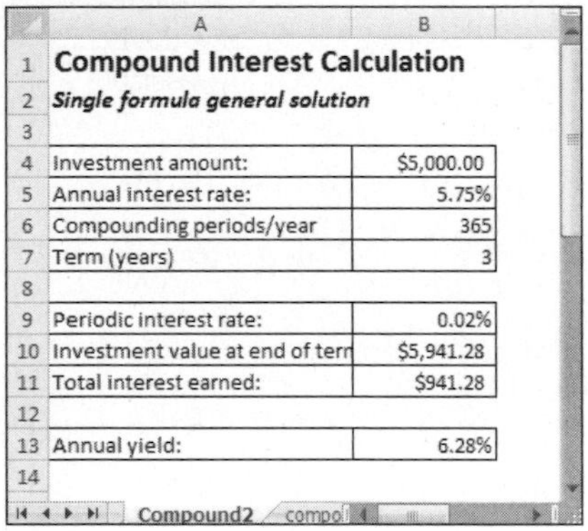

	A	B
1	**Compound Interest Calculation**	
2	*Single formula general solution*	
3		
4	Investment amount:	$5,000.00
5	Annual interest rate:	5.75%
6	Compounding periods/year	365
7	Term (years)	3
8		
9	Periodic interest rate:	0.02%
10	Investment value at end of term	$5,941.28
11	Total interest earned:	$941.28
12		
13	Annual yield:	6.28%
14		

Compound2 / compo

Calculating interest with continuous compounding

The term *continuous compounding* refers to interest that is accumulated continuously. In other words, the investment has an infinite number of compounding periods per year. The following formula calculates the future value of a $5,000 investment at 5.75 percent compounded continuously for three years:

```
=5000*EXP(0.0575*3)
```

The formula returns $5,941.36, which is an additional $0.08 compared to daily compounding.

> **NOTE** You can calculate compound interest without using the FV function. The general formula to calculate compound interest is
>
> ```
> Principal * (1 + periodic rate) ^ number of periods
> ```
>
> For example, consider a five-year, $5,000 investment that earns an annual interest rate of 5 percent, compounded monthly. The formula to calculate the future value of this investment is
>
> ```
> =5000*(1+.05/12)^(12*5)
> ```

Future value of a series of deposits

Now, consider another type of investment, one in which you make a regular series of deposits. This type of investment is known as an *annuity*.

The worksheet functions discussed in the "Loan Calculations" section earlier in this chapter also apply to annuities, but you need to use the perspective of a lender, not a borrower. A simple example of this type of investment is a holiday club savings program offered by some banking institutions. A fixed amount is deducted from each of your paychecks and deposited into an interest-earning account. At the end of the year, you withdraw the money (with accumulated interest) to use for holiday expenses.

Suppose that you deposit $200 at the beginning of each month (for 12 months) into an account that pays 4.25 percent annual interest compounded monthly. The following formula calculates the future value of your series of deposits:

```
=FV(0.0425/12,12,-200,,1)
```

This formula returns $2,455.97, which represents the total of your deposits ($2,400) plus the interest ($55.97). The last argument for the FV function is 1, which means that you make payments at the beginning of the month. Figure 16.14 shows a worksheet set up to calculate annuities. Table 16.4 describes the contents of this sheet.

> **ON the CD-ROM** The workbook shown in Figure 16.14 is available on the companion CD-ROM. The file is named annuity calculator.xlsx.

The Rule of 72

Need to make an investment decision, but don't have a computer handy? You can use the *Rule of 72* to determine the number of years required to double your money at a particular interest rate, using annual compounding. Just divide 72 by the interest rate. For example, consider a $10,000 investment at 6 percent interest. How many years will it take to turn that 10 grand into 20 grand? Take 72, divide it by 6, and you get 12 years. What if you can get a 7 percent interest rate? If so, you can double your money in a little over 10 years.

How accurate is the Rule of 72? The table that follows shows Rule of 72 estimated values versus the actual values for various interest rates. As you can see, this simple rule is remarkably accurate. However, for interest rates that exceed 30 percent, the accuracy drops off considerably.

Interest Rate	Rule of 72	Actual
1%	72.00	69.66
2%	36.00	35.00
3%	24.00	23.45
4%	18.00	17.67
5%	14.40	14.21
6%	12.00	11.90
7%	10.29	10.24
8%	9.00	9.01
9%	8.00	8.04
10%	7.20	7.27
15%	4.80	4.96
20%	3.60	3.80
25%	2.88	3.11
30%	2.40	2.64

The Rule of 72 also works in reverse. For example, if you want to double your money in six years, divide 6 into 72; you'll discover that you need to find an investment that pays an annual interest rate of about 12 percent.

This worksheet contains formulas to calculate annuities.

	A	B	C
1	**Annuity Calculator**		
2			
3	Deposits...		
4	Initial investment:	$0.00	
5	Periodic deposit amount:	$200.00	
6	No. periodic deposits per year :	12	
7	Deposits made at beginning of period?	TRUE	
8			
9	Investment Period...		
10	Length of investment (years):	1	
11			
12	Interest Rate...		
13	Annual interest rate:	4.25%	
14			
15	Calculations		
16	Initial investment	$0.00	
17	Additional deposits:	$2,400.00	
18	Total amount invested:	$2,400.00	
19	Periodic interest rate:	0.35%	
20	Value of investment at end of term:	$2,455.97	
21	Interest earned on investment:	$55.97	
22			
23			

H ◄ ► H Sheet1

The Annuity Calculator Worksheet

Cell	Formula	Description
B4	None (input cell)	Initial investment (can be 0)
B5	None (input cell)	The amount deposited on a regular basis
B6	None (input cell)	The number of deposits made in 12 months
B7	None (input cell)	TRUE if you make deposits at the beginning of period; FALSE otherwise
B10	None (input cell)	The length of the investment, in years (can be fractional)
B13	None (input cell)	The annual interest rate
B16	=B4	Displays the initial investment amount
B17	=B5*B6*B10	Calculates the total of all regular deposits
B18	=B16+B17	Adds the initial investment to the sum of the deposits
B19	=B13*(1/B6)	Calculates the periodic interest rate
B20	=FV(B19,B6*B10,-B5,-B4,IF(B7,1,0))	Calculates the future value of the investment
B21	=B20-B18	Calculates the interest earned from the investment

Depreciation Calculations

Excel offers five functions to calculate depreciation of an asset over time. Depreciating an asset places a value on the asset at a point in time, based on the original value and its useful life. The function that you choose depends on the type of *depreciation method* that you use.

Table 16.5 summarizes the Excel depreciation functions and the arguments used by each. For complete details, consult the Excel online Help system.

TABLE 16.5

Excel's Depreciation Functions

Function	Depreciation Method	Arguments*
SLN	Straight-line. The asset depreciates by the same amount each year of its life.	Cost, Salvage, Life
DB	Declining balance. Computes depreciation at a fixed rate.	Cost, Salvage, Life, Period, [Month]
DDB	Double-declining balance. Computes depreciation at an accelerated rate. Depreciation is highest in the first period and decreases in successive periods.	Cost, Salvage, Life, Period, Month, [Factor]
SYD	Sum of the year's digits. Allocates a large depreciation in the earlier years of an asset's life.	Cost, Salvage, Life, Period
VDB	Variable-declining balance. Computes the depreciation of an asset for any period (including partial periods) using the double-declining balance method or some other method you specify.	Cost, Salvage, Life, Start Period, End Period, [Factor], [No Switch]

* Arguments in brackets are optional.

Here are the arguments for the depreciation functions:

- *Cost*: Original cost of the asset.
- *Salvage*: Salvage cost of the asset after it has fully depreciated.
- *Life*: Number of periods over which the asset will depreciate.
- *Period*: Period in the life for which the calculation is being made.
- *Month*: Number of months in the first year; if omitted, Excel uses 12.
- *Factor*: Rate at which the balance declines; if omitted, it is assumed to be 2 (that is, double-declining).
- *Rate*: Interest rate per period. If you make payments monthly, for example, you must divide the annual interest rate by 12.
- *No Switch*: True or False. Specifies whether to switch to straight-line depreciation when depreciation is greater than the declining balance calculation.

Figure 16.15 shows depreciation calculations using the SLN, DB, DDB, and SYD functions. The asset's original cost, $10,000, is assumed to have a useful life of 10 years, with a salvage value of $1,000. The range labeled Depreciation Amount shows the annual depreciation of the asset. The range labeled Value of Asset shows the asset's depreciated value over its life.

ON the CD-ROM This workbook is available on the companion CD-ROM. The file is named **depreciation calculations.xlsx.**

Figure 16.16 shows a chart that graphs the asset's value. As you can see, the SLN function produces a straight line; the other functions produce a curved line because the depreciation is greater in the earlier years of the asset's life.

FIGURE 16.15

A comparison of four depreciation functions.

	A	B	C	D	E
1	Asset:	Office Furniture			
2	Original Cost:	$10,000			
3	Life (years):	10			
4	Salvage Value:	$1,000			
5					
6	*Depreciation Amount*				
7	Year	SLN	DB	DDB	SYD
8	1	$900.00	$2,060.00	$2,000.00	$1,636.36
9	2	$900.00	$1,635.64	$1,600.00	$1,472.73
10	3	$900.00	$1,298.70	$1,280.00	$1,309.09
11	4	$900.00	$1,031.17	$1,024.00	$1,145.45
12	5	$900.00	$818.75	$819.20	$981.82
13	6	$900.00	$650.08	$655.36	$818.18
14	7	$900.00	$516.17	$524.29	$654.55
15	8	$900.00	$409.84	$419.43	$490.91
16	9	$900.00	$325.41	$335.54	$327.27
17	10	$900.00	$258.38	$268.44	$163.64
18					
19					
20	*Value of Asset*				
21	Year	SLN	DB	DDB	SYD
22	0	$10,000.00	$10,000.00	$10,000.00	$10,000.00
23	1	$9,100.00	$7,940.00	$8,000.00	$8,363.64
24	2	$8,200.00	$6,304.36	$6,400.00	$6,890.91
25	3	$7,300.00	$5,005.66	$5,120.00	$5,581.82
26	4	$6,400.00	$3,974.50	$4,096.00	$4,436.36
27	5	$5,500.00	$3,155.75	$3,276.80	$3,454.55
28	6	$4,600.00	$2,505.67	$2,621.44	$2,636.36
29	7	$3,700.00	$1,989.50	$2,097.15	$1,981.82
30	8	$2,800.00	$1,579.66	$1,677.72	$1,490.91
31	9	$1,900.00	$1,254.25	$1,342.18	$1,163.64
32	10	$1,000.00	$995.88	$1,073.74	$1,000.00
33					

Depreciation / VBD

FIGURE 16.16

This chart shows an asset's value over time, using four depreciation functions.

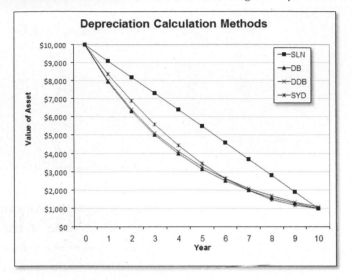

The VBD function is useful if you need to calculate depreciation for multiple periods (for example, years 2 and 3). Figure 16.17 shows a worksheet set up to calculate depreciation using the VBD function. The formula in cell B11 is

    =VDB(B2,B4,B3,B6,B7,B8,B9)

FIGURE 16.17

Using the VBD function to calculate depreciation for multiple periods.

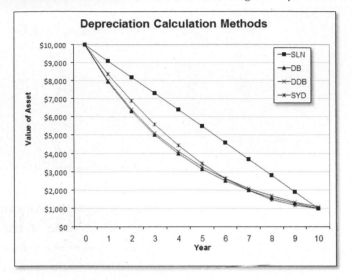

The formula displays the depreciation for the first three years of an asset (starting period of 0 and ending period of 3).

Chapter 17

Introducing Array Formulas

IN THIS CHAPTER

The definition of an array and an array formula

One-dimensional versus two-dimensional arrays

How to work with array constants

Techniques for working with array formulas

Examples of multicell array formulas

Examples of array formulas that occupy a single cell

O ne of Excel's most interesting (and most powerful) features is its ability to work with arrays in formulas. When you understand this concept, you'll be able to create elegant formulas that appear to perform spreadsheet magic.

This chapter introduces the concept of arrays and is required reading for anyone who wants to become a master of Excel formulas. Chapter 18 continues with lots of useful examples.

Understanding Array Formulas

If you do any computer programming, you've probably been exposed to the concept of an array. An *array* is simply a collection of items operated on collectively or individually. In Excel, an array can be one dimensional or two dimensional. These dimensions correspond to rows and columns. For example, a *one-dimensional array* can be stored in a range that consists of one row (a horizontal array) or one column (a vertical array). A *two-dimensional array* can be stored in a rectangular range of cells. Excel doesn't support three-dimensional arrays (but its VBA programming language does).

As you'll see, arrays need not be stored in cells. You can also work with arrays that exist only in Excel's memory. You can then use an *array formula* to manipulate this information and return a result. An array formula can occupy multiple cells or reside in a single cell.

This section presents two array formula examples: an array formula that occupies multiple cells and another array formula that occupies only one cell.

A multicell array formula

Figure 17.1 shows a simple worksheet set up to calculate product sales. Normally, you'd calculate the value in column D (total sales per product) with a formula such as the one that follows, and then you'd copy this formula down the column.

```
=B2*C2
```

After copying the formula, the worksheet contains six formulas in column D.

FIGURE 17.1

Column D contains formulas to calculate the total for each product.

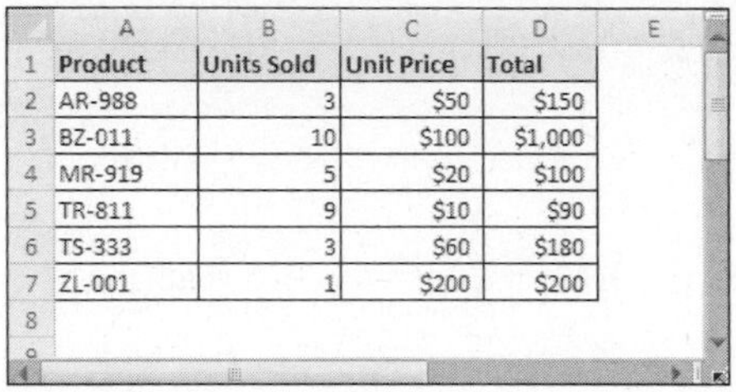

	A	B	C	D	E
1	Product	Units Sold	Unit Price	Total	
2	AR-988	3	$50	$150	
3	BZ-011	10	$100	$1,000	
4	MR-919	5	$20	$100	
5	TR-811	9	$10	$90	
6	TS-333	3	$60	$180	
7	ZL-001	1	$200	$200	
8					

An alternative method uses a *single* formula (an array formula) to calculate all six values in D2:D7. This single formula occupies six cells and returns an array of six values.

To create a single array formula to perform the calculations, follow these steps:

1. **Select a range to hold the results.** In this case, the range is D2:D7.
2. **Enter the following formula:**
   ```
   =B2:B7*C2:C7
   ```
3. **Press Ctrl+Shift+Enter to enter the formula.** Normally, you press Enter to enter a formula. Because this is an array formula, however, press Ctrl+Shift+Enter.

CAUTION You can't insert a multicell array formula into a range that has been designated a table. You designate a table using the Excel 2007 Insert ➪ Tables ➪ Table command). In addition, you can't convert a range that contains a multicell array formula to a table.

The formula is entered into all six of the selected cells. If you examine the Formula bar, you see the following:

```
{=B2:B7*C2:C7}
```

Excel places curly brackets around the formula to indicate that it's an array formula.

This formula performs its calculations and returns a six-item array. The array formula actually works with two other arrays, both of which happen to be stored in ranges. The values for the first array are stored in B2:B7, and the values for the second array are stored in C2:C7.

Because you can't display more than one value in a single cell, six cells are required to display the resulting array — which explains why you selected six cells before you entered the array formula.

This array formula, of course, returns exactly the same values as these six normal formulas entered into individual cells in D2:D7:

```
=B2*C2
=B3*C3
=B4*C4
=B5*C5
=B6*C6
=B7*C7
```

Using a single array formula rather than individual formulas does offer a few advantages:

- It's a good way of ensuring that all formulas in a range are identical.
- Using a multicell array formula makes it less likely that you'll overwrite a formula accidentally. You can't change one cell in a multicell array formula. Excel displays an error message if you attempt to do so.
- Using a multicell array formula will almost certainly prevent novices from tampering with your formulas.

Using a multicell array formula as described in the preceding list also has some potential disadvantages:

- It's impossible to insert a new row into the range. But in some cases, the inability to insert a row is a positive feature.
- If you add new data to the bottom of the range, you need to modify the array formula to accommodate the new data.

A single-cell array formula

Now it's time to take a look at a single-cell array formula. Check out Figure 17.2, which is similar to Figure 17.1. Notice, however, that the formulas in column D have been deleted. The goal is to calculate the sum of the total product sales without using the individual calculations that were in column D.

FIGURE 17.2

The array formula in cell C10 calculates the total sales without using intermediate formulas.

	A	B	C	D
1	Product	Units Sold	Unit Price	
2	AR-988	3	$50	
3	BZ-011	10	$100	
4	MR-919	5	$20	
5	TR-811	9	$10	
6	TS-333	3	$60	
7	ZL-001	1	$200	
8				
9				
10		Total Sales:	$1,720	
11				

The following array formula is in cell C10:

```
{=SUM(B2:B7*C2:C7)}
```

315

When you enter this formula, make sure that you use Ctrl+Shift+Enter (and don't type the curly brackets).

This formula works with two arrays, both of which are stored in cells. The first array is stored in B2:B7, and the second array is stored in C2:C7. The formula multiplies the corresponding values in these two arrays and creates a new array (which exists only in memory). The SUM function then operates on this new array and returns the sum of its values.

> **NOTE** In this case, you can use Excel's SUMPRODUCT function to obtain the same result without using an array formula:
>
> =SUMPRODUCT(B2:B7,C2:C7)

As you see, however, array formulas allow many other types of calculations that are otherwise not possible.

Creating an array constant

The examples in the preceding section used arrays stored in worksheet ranges. The examples in this section demonstrate an important concept: An array need not be stored in a range of cells. This type of array, which is stored in memory, is referred to as an *array constant*.

To create an array constant, list its items and surround them with brackets. Here's an example of a five-item vertical array constant:

    {1,0,1,0,1}

The following formula uses the SUM function, with the preceding array constant as its argument. The formula returns the sum of the values in the array (which is 3).

    =SUM({1,0,1,0,1})

Notice that this formula uses an array, but the formula itself isn't an array formula. Therefore, you don't use Ctrl+Shift+Enter to enter the formula — although entering it as an array formula will still produce the same result.

> **NOTE** When you specify an array directly (as shown previously), you must provide the brackets around the array elements. When you enter an array formula, on the other hand, you do not supply the brackets.

At this point, you probably don't see any advantage to using an array constant. The formula that follows, for example, returns the same result as the previous formula:

    =SUM(1,0,1,0,1)

The advantages, however, will become apparent.

Following is a formula that uses two array constants:

    =SUM({1,2,3,4}*{5,6,7,8})

This formula creates a new array (in memory) that consists of the product of the corresponding elements in the two arrays. The new array is

    {5,12,21,32}

This new array is then used as an argument for the SUM function, which returns the result (70). The formula is equivalent to the following formula, which doesn't use arrays:

    =SUM(1*5,2*6,3*7,4*8)

Alternatively, you can use the SUMPRODUCT function. The formula that follows is not an array formula, but it uses two array constants.

```
=SUMPRODUCT({1,2,3,4},{5,6,7,8})
```

A formula can work with both an array constant and an array stored in a range. The following formula, for example, returns the sum of the values in A1:D1, each multiplied by the corresponding element in the array constant:

```
=SUM((A1:D1*{1,2,3,4}))
```

This formula is equivalent to:

```
=SUM(A1*1,B1*2,C1*3,D1*4)
```

Array constant elements

An array constant can contain numbers, text, logical values (TRUE or FALSE), and even error values, such as #N/A. Numbers can be in integer, decimal, or scientific format. You must enclose text in double quotation marks. You can use different types of values in the same array constant, as in this example:

```
{1,2,3,TRUE,FALSE,TRUE,"Moe","Larry","Curly"}
```

An array constant can't contain formulas, functions, or other arrays. Numeric values can't contain dollar signs, commas, parentheses, or percent signs. For example, the following is an invalid array constant:

```
{SQRT(32),$56.32,12.5%}
```

Understanding the Dimensions of an Array

As stated previously, an array can be either one dimensional or two dimensional. A one-dimensional array's orientation can be either vertical or horizontal.

One-dimensional horizontal arrays

The elements in a one-dimensional horizontal array are separated by commas. The following example is a one-dimensional horizontal array constant:

```
{1,2,3,4,5}
```

To display this array in a range requires five consecutive cells in a row. To enter this array into a range, select a range of cells that consists of one row and five columns. Then enter **={1,2,3,4,5}** and press Ctrl+Shift+Enter.

> **NOTE** If you enter this array into a horizontal range that consists of more than five cells, the extra cells will contain #N/A (which denotes unavailable values). If you enter this array into a *vertical* range of cells, only the first item (1) will appear in each cell.

The following example is another horizontal array; it has seven elements and is made up of text strings:

```
{"Sun","Mon","Tue","Wed","Thu","Fri","Sat"}
```

To enter this array, select seven cells in a row and type the following (followed by Ctrl+Shift+Enter):

```
={"Sun","Mon","Tue","Wed","Thu","Fri","Sat"}
```

One-dimensional vertical arrays

The elements in a one-dimensional vertical array are separated by semicolons. The following is a six-element vertical array constant:

```
{10;20;30;40;50;60}
```

Displaying this array in a range requires six cells in a column. To enter this array into a range, select a range of cells that consists of six rows and one column. Then enter the following formula, followed by Ctrl+Shift+Enter:

```
={10;20;30;40;50;60}
```

The following is another example of a vertical array; this one has four elements:

```
{"Widgets";"Sprockets";"Doodads";"Thingamajigs"}
```

Two-dimensional arrays

A two-dimensional array uses commas to separate its horizontal elements and semicolons to separate its vertical elements. The following example shows a 3 × 4 array constant:

```
{1,2,3,4;5,6,7,8;9,10,11,12}
```

Displaying this array in a range requires 12 cells. To enter this array into a range, select a range of cells that consists of three rows and four columns. Then type the following formula, followed by Ctrl+Shift+Enter:

```
={1,2,3,4;5,6,7,8;9,10,11,12}
```

Figure 17.3 shows how this array appears when entered into a range (in this case, B2:E4).

If you enter an array into a range that has more cells than array elements, Excel displays #N/A in the extra cells. Figure 17.4 shows a 3 × 4 array entered into a 10 × 5 cell range.

Each row of a two-dimensional array must contain the same number of items. The array that follows, for example, isn't valid, because the third row contains only three items:

```
{1,2,3,4;5,6,7,8;9,10,11}
```

Excel doesn't allow you to enter a formula that contains an invalid array.

FIGURE 17.3

A 3 × 4 array entered into a range of cells.

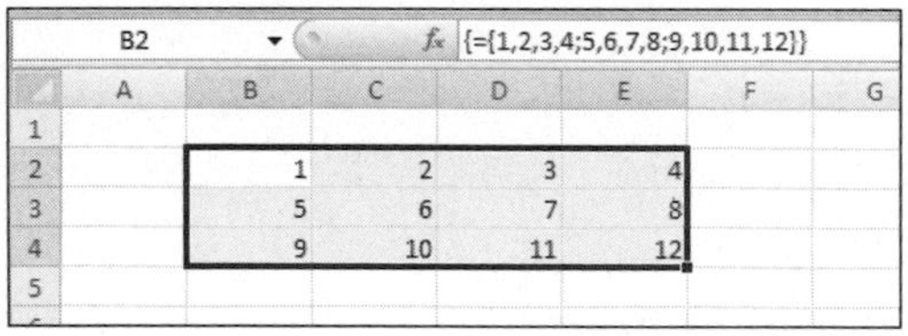

FIGURE 17.4

A 3 × 4 array entered into a 10 × 5 cell range.

	A	B	C	D	E	F	G	H
1								
2		1	2	3	4	#N/A		
3		5	6	7	8	#N/A		
4		9	10	11	12	#N/A		
5		#N/A	#N/A	#N/A	#N/A	#N/A		
6		#N/A	#N/A	#N/A	#N/A	#N/A		
7		#N/A	#N/A	#N/A	#N/A	#N/A		
8		#N/A	#N/A	#N/A	#N/A	#N/A		
9		#N/A	#N/A	#N/A	#N/A	#N/A		
10		#N/A	#N/A	#N/A	#N/A	#N/A		
11		#N/A	#N/A	#N/A	#N/A	#N/A		
12								
13								

Naming Array Constants

You can create an array constant, give it a name, and then use this named array in a formula. Technically, a named array is a named formula.

CROSS-REF Chapter 5 covers the topic of names and named formulas.

Figure 17.5 shows a named array being created with the help of the New Name dialog box. (Access this dialog box by choosing Formulas ➪ Defined Names ➪ Define Name.) The name of the array is *DayNames*, and it refers to the following array constant:

    {"Sun","Mon","Tue","Wed","Thu","Fri","Sat"}

Notice that, in the New Name dialog box, the array is defined (in the Refers To box) using a leading equal sign (=). Without this equal sign, the array is interpreted as a text string rather than an array. Also, you must type the curly brackets when defining a named array constant; Excel does not enter them for you.

After creating this named array, you can use it in a formula. Figure 17.6 shows a worksheet that contains a single array formula entered into the range A1:G1. The formula is

    {=DayNames}

FIGURE 17.5

Creating a named array constant.

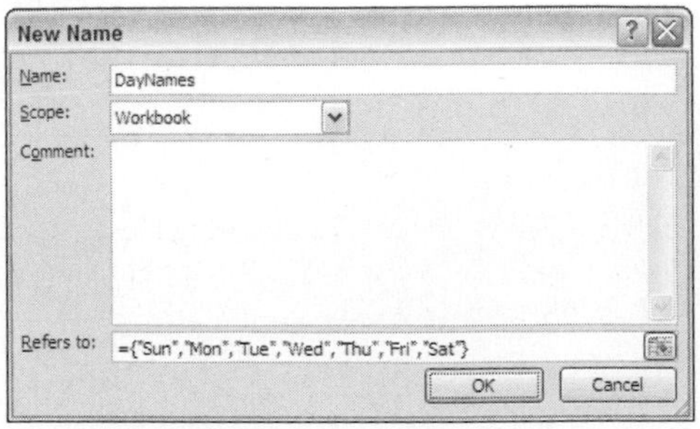

FIGURE 17.6

Using a named array in an array formula.

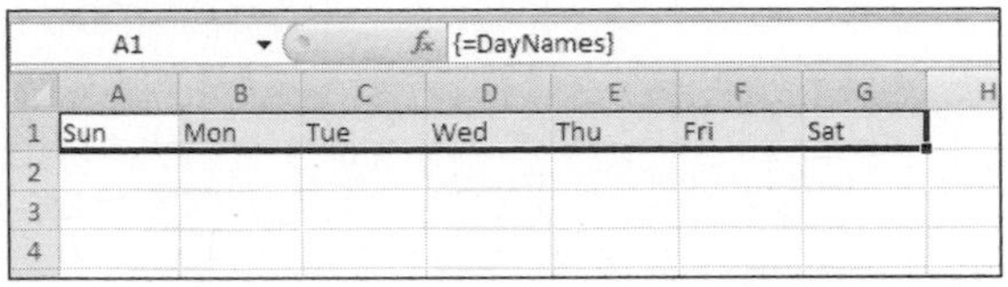

Because commas separate the array elements, the array has a horizontal orientation. Use semicolons to create a vertical array. Or you can use the Excel TRANSPOSE function to insert a horizontal array into a vertical range of cells (see "Transposing an array," later in this chapter). The following array formula, which is entered into a seven-cell vertical range, uses the TRANSPOSE function:

```
{=TRANSPOSE(DayNames)}
```

You also can access individual elements from the array by using the Excel INDEX function. The following formula, for example, returns *Wed*, the fourth item in the *DayNames* array:

```
=INDEX(DayNames,4)
```

Working with Array Formulas

This section deals with the mechanics of selecting cells that contain arrays and entering and editing array formulas. These procedures differ a bit from working with ordinary ranges and formulas.

Entering an array formula

When you enter an array formula into a cell or range, you must follow a special procedure so that Excel knows that you want an array formula rather than normal formula. You enter a normal formula into a cell by pressing Enter. You enter an array formula into one or more cells by pressing Ctrl+Shift+Enter.

Don't enter the curly brackets when you create an array formula; Excel inserts them for you. If the result of an array formula consists of more than one value, you must select all the cells in the results range *before* you enter the formula. If you fail to do so, only the first element of the result is returned.

Selecting an array formula range

You can select the cells that contain a multicell array formula manually by using the normal cell selection procedures. Or you can use either of the following methods:

- Activate any cell in the array formula range. Display the Go To dialog box by choosing Home ⇨ Editing ⇨ Find & Select ⇨ Go To (or just press F5). In the Go To dialog box, click the Special button and then choose the Current Array option. Click OK to close the dialog box.

- Activate any cell in the array formula range and press Ctrl+/ to select the entire array.

Editing an array formula

If an array formula occupies multiple cells, you must edit the entire range as though it were a single cell. The key point to remember is that you can't change just one element of an array formula. If you attempt to do so, Excel displays the message shown in Figure 17.7.

FIGURE 17.7

Excel's warning message reminds you that you can't edit just one cell of a multicell array formula.

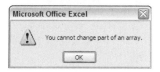

The following rules apply to multicell array formulas. If you try to do any of these things, Excel lets you know about it:

- You can't change the contents of any individual cell that makes up an array formula.

- You can't move cells that make up part of an array formula (but you can move an entire array formula).

- You can't delete cells that form part of an array formula (but you can delete an entire array).

- You can't insert new cells into an array range. This rule includes inserting rows or columns that would add new cells to an array range.

- You can't use multicell array formulas inside of a table that was created by choosing Insert ⇨ Tables ⇨ Table. Similarly, you can't convert a range to a table if the range contains a multicell array formula.

To edit an array formula, select all the cells in the array range and activate the Formula bar as usual (click it or press F2). Excel removes the brackets from the formula while you edit it. Edit the formula and then press Ctrl+Shift+Enter to enter the changes. All the cells in the array now reflect your editing changes.

CAUTION   If you accidentally press Ctrl+Enter (instead of Ctrl+Shift+Enter) after editing an array formula, the formula will be entered into each selected cell, but it will no longer be an array formula. And it will probably return an incorrect result. Just reselect the cells, press F2, and then press Ctrl+Shift+Enter.

Although you can't change any individual cell that makes up a multicell array formula, you can apply formatting to the entire array or to only parts of it.

Expanding or contracting a multicell array formula

Often, you may need to expand a multicell array formula (to include more cells) or contract it (to include fewer cells). Doing so requires a few steps:

1. **Select the entire range that contains the array formula.**
2. **Press F2 to enter Edit mode.**
3. **Press Ctrl+Enter.** This step enters an identical (non-array) formula into each selected cell.
4. **Change your range selection to include additional or fewer cells.**
5. **Press F2 to re-enter Edit mode.**
6. **Press Ctrl+Shift+Enter.**

Array Formulas: The Downside

If you've followed along in this chapter, you probably understand some of the advantages of using array formulas. The main advantage, of course, is that an array formula enables you to perform otherwise impossible calculations. As you gain more experience with arrays, however, you undoubtedly will also discover some disadvantages.

Array formulas are one of the least understood features of Excel. Consequently, if you plan to share a workbook with someone who may need to make modifications, you should probably avoid using array formulas. Encountering an array formula when you don't know what it is can be very confusing.

You might also discover that you can easily forget to enter an array formula by pressing Ctrl+Shift+Enter. (And don't forget: If you edit an existing array, you must remember to use this key combination to complete the edits.) Except for logical errors, this is probably the most common problem that users have with array formulas. If you press Enter by mistake after editing an array formula, just press F2 to get back into Edit mode and then press Ctrl+Shift+Enter.

Another potential problem with array formulas is that they can slow your worksheet's recalculations, especially if you use very large arrays. On a faster system, this delay in speed may not be a problem. But, conversely, using an array formula is almost always faster than using a custom VBA function. See Chapter 40 for more information about creating custom VBA functions.

Using Multicell Array Formulas

This section contains examples that demonstrate additional features of *multicell array formulas* (array formulas that are entered into a range of cells). These features include creating arrays from values, performing operations, using functions, transposing arrays, and generating consecutive integers.

Creating an array from values in a range

The following array formula creates an array from a range of cells. Figure 17.8 shows a workbook with some data entered into A1:C4. The range D8:F11 contains a single array formula:

```
{=A1:C4}
```

The array in D8:F11 is linked to the range A1:C4. Change any value in A1:C4, and the corresponding cell in D8:F11 reflects that change. It's a one-way link, of course. You can change a value in D8:F11.

FIGURE 17.8

Creating an array from a range.

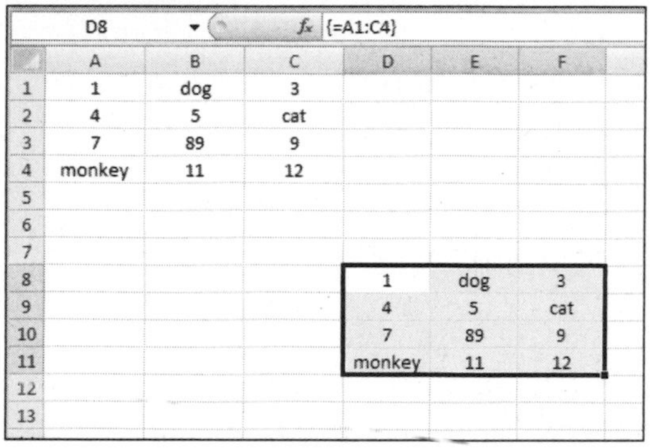

Creating an array constant from values in a range

In the preceding example, the array formula in D8:F11 essentially created a link to the cells in A1:C4. It's possible to sever this link and create an array constant made up of the values in A1:C4:

1. **To do so, select the cells that contain the array formula (the range D8:F11, in this example).**
2. **Press F2 to edit the array formula.**
3. **Press F9 to convert the cell references to values.**
4. **Press Ctrl+Shift+Enter to re-enter the array formula (which now uses an array constant).**

The array constant is

```
{1,"dog",3;4,5,"cat";7,8,9;"monkey",11,12}
```

Figure 17.9 shows how this looks in the Formula bar.

FIGURE 17.9

After you've pressed F9, the Formula bar displays the array constant.

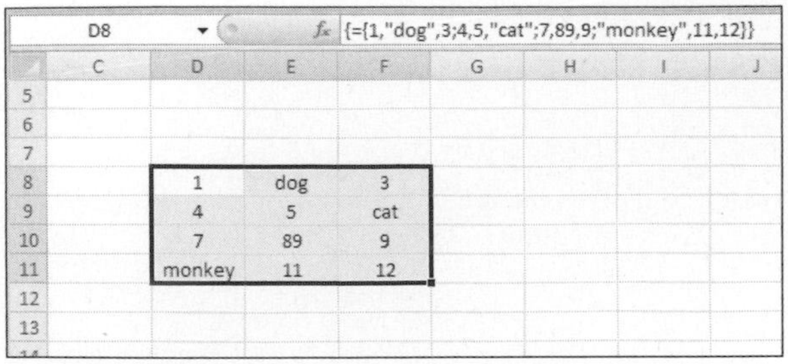

	C	D	E	F	G	H	I	J
5								
6								
7								
8		1	dog	3				
9		4	5	cat				
10		7	89	9				
11		monkey	11	12				
12								
13								

D8 f_x {={1,"dog",3;4,5,"cat";7,89,9;"monkey",11,12}}

Performing operations on an array

So far, most of the examples in this chapter simply entered arrays into ranges. The following array formula creates a rectangular array and multiplies each array element by 2:

```
{={1,2,3,4;5,6,7,8;9,10,11,12}*2}
```

Figure 17.10 shows the result when you enter this formula into a range:

FIGURE 17.10

Performing a mathematical operation on an array.

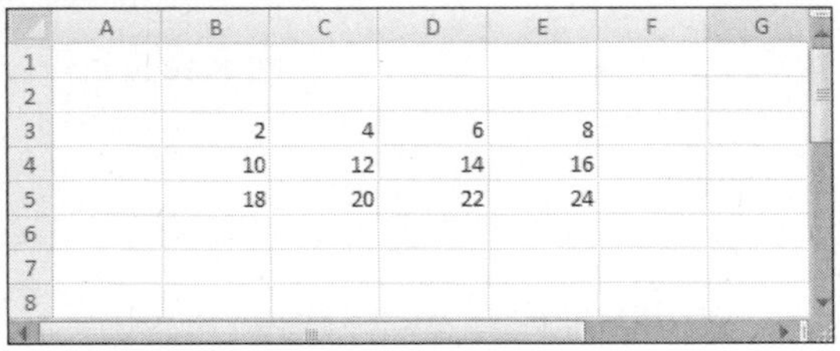

	A	B	C	D	E	F	G
1							
2							
3		2	4	6	8		
4		10	12	14	16		
5		18	20	22	24		
6							
7							
8							

The following array formula multiplies each array element by itself. Figure 17.11 shows the result when you enter this formula into a range:

```
{={1,2,3,4;5,6,7,8;9,10,11,12}*{1,2,3,4;5,6,7,8;9,10,11,12}}
```

The following array formula is a simpler way of obtaining the same result:

```
{={1,2,3,4;5,6,7,8;9,10,11,12}^2}
```

If the array is stored in a range (such as A1:C4), the array formula returns the square of each value in the range, as follows:

```
{=A1:C4^2}
```

FIGURE 17.11

Multiplying each array element by itself.

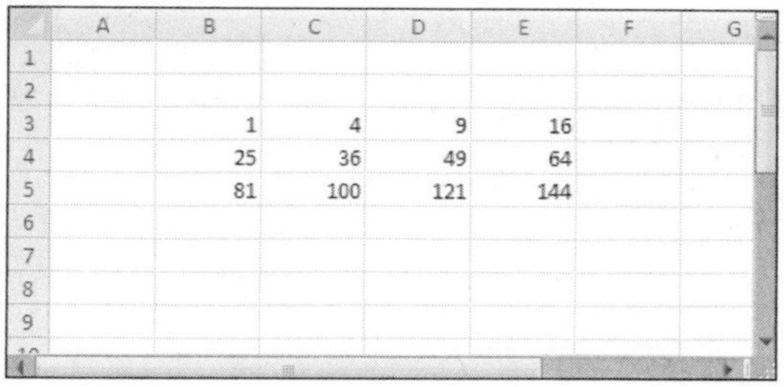

	A	B	C	D	E	F	G
1							
2							
3		1	4	9	16		
4		25	36	49	64		
5		81	100	121	144		
6							
7							
8							
9							

Using functions with an array

As you may expect, you also can use functions with an array. The following array formula, which you can enter into a 10-cell vertical range, calculates the square root of each array element in the array constant:

```
{=SQRT({1;2;3;4;5;6;7;8;9;10})}
```

If the array is stored in a range, an array formula such as the one that follows returns the square root of each value in the range:

```
{=SQRT(A1:A10)}
```

Transposing an array

When you transpose an array, you essentially convert rows to columns and columns to rows. In other words, you can convert a horizontal array to a vertical array (and vice versa). Use the TRANSPOSE function to transpose an array.

Consider the following one-dimensional horizontal array constant:

```
{1,2,3,4,5}
```

You can enter this array into a vertical range of cells by using the TRANSPOSE function. To do so, select a range of five cells that occupy five rows and one column. Then enter the following formula and press Ctrl+Shift+Enter:

```
=TRANSPOSE({1,2,3,4,5})
```

The horizontal array is transposed, and the array elements appear in the vertical range.

Transposing a two-dimensional array works in a similar manner. Figure 17.12 shows a two-dimensional array entered into a range normally and entered into a range by using the TRANSPOSE function. The formula in A1:D3 is

```
{={1,2,3,4;5,6,7,8;9,10,11,12}}
```

The formula in A6:C9 is

```
{=TRANSPOSE({1,2,3,4;5,6,7,8;9,10,11,12})}
```

You can, of course, use the TRANSPOSE function to transpose an array stored in a range. The following formula, for example, uses an array stored in A1:C4 (four rows, three columns). You can enter this array formula into a range that consists of three rows and four columns.

```
{=TRANSPOSE(A1:C4)}
```

FIGURE 17.12

Using the TRANSPOSE function to transpose a rectangular array.

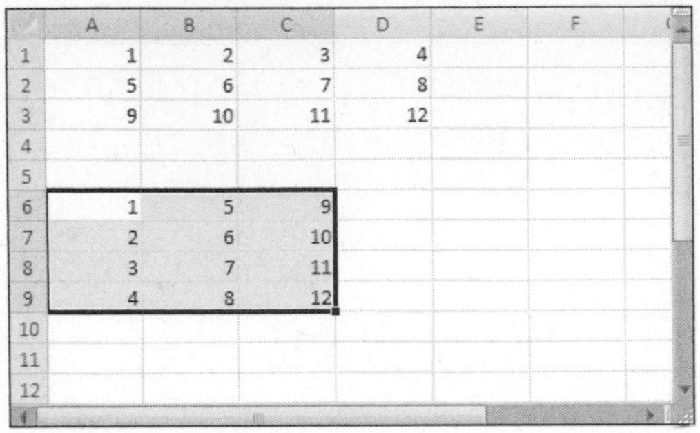

Generating an array of consecutive integers

As you can see in Chapter 18, generating an array of consecutive integers for use in an array formula is often useful. The ROW function, which returns a row number, is ideal for this. Consider the array formula shown here, entered into a vertical range of 12 cells:

```
{=ROW(1:12)}
```

This formula generates a 12-element array that contains integers from 1 to 12. To demonstrate, select a range that consists of 12 rows and one column and enter the array formula into the range. You'll find that the range is filled with 12 consecutive integers (as shown in Figure 17.13).

If you want to generate an array of consecutive integers, a formula like the one shown previously is good — but not perfect. To see the problem, insert a new row above the range that contains the array formula. Excel adjusts the row references so that the array formula now reads

```
{=ROW(2:13)}
```

The formula that originally generated integers from 1 to 12 now generates integers from 2 to 13.

For a better solution, use this formula:

```
{=ROW(INDIRECT("1:12"))}
```

This formula uses the INDIRECT function, which takes a text string as its argument. Excel does not adjust the references contained in the argument for the INDIRECT function. Therefore, this array formula *always* returns integers from 1 to 12.

CROSS-REF Chapter 18 contains several examples that use the technique for generating consecutive integers.

Worksheet Functions That Return an Array

Several of the Excel worksheet functions use arrays; you must enter a formula that uses one of these functions into multiple cells as an array formula. These functions are FORECAST, FREQUENCY, GROWTH, LINEST, LOGEST, MINVERSE, MMULT, and TREND. Consult Excel's Help system for more information.

FIGURE 17.13

Using an array formula to generate consecutive integers.

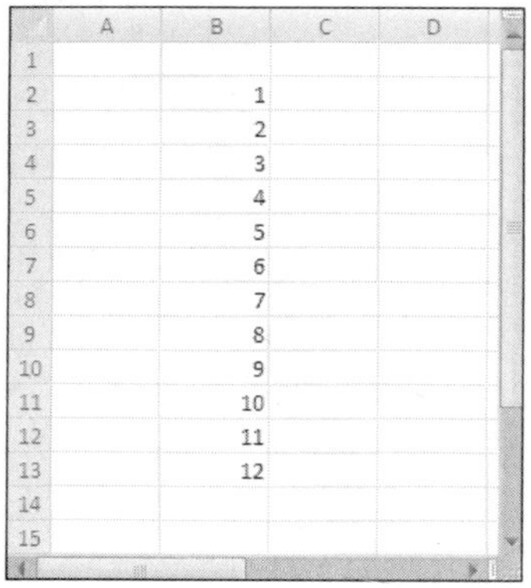

	A	B	C	D
1				
2		1		
3		2		
4		3		
5		4		
6		5		
7		6		
8		7		
9		8		
10		9		
11		10		
12		11		
13		12		
14				
15				

Using Single-Cell Array Formulas

The examples in the preceding section all used a multicell array formula — a single array formula that's entered into a range of cells. The real power of using arrays becomes apparent when you use single-cell array formulas. This section contains examples of array formulas that occupy a single cell.

Counting characters in a range

Suppose that you have a range of cells that contains text entries (see Figure 17.14). If you need to get a count of the total number of characters in that range, the "traditional" method involves creating a formula like the one that follows and copying it down the column:

```
=LEN(A1)
```

Then you use a SUM formula to calculate the sum of the values returned by these intermediate formulas.

The following array formula does the job without using any intermediate formulas:

```
{=SUM(LEN(A1:A14))}
```

FIGURE 17.14

The goal is to count the number of characters in a range of text.

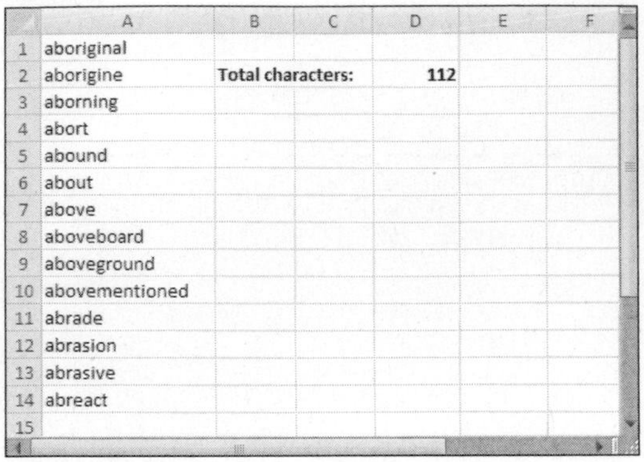

	A	B	C	D	E	F
1	aboriginal					
2	aborigine	Total characters:		112		
3	aborning					
4	abort					
5	abound					
6	about					
7	above					
8	aboveboard					
9	aboveground					
10	abovementioned					
11	abrade					
12	abrasion					
13	abrasive					
14	abreact					
15						

The array formula uses the LEN function to create a new array (in memory) that consists of the number of characters in each cell of the range. In this case, the new array is

    {10,9,8,5,6,5,5,10,11,14,6,8,8,7}

The array formula is then reduced to:

    =SUM({10,9,8,5,6,5,5,10,11,14,6,8,8,7})

The formula returns the sum of the array elements, 112.

Summing the three smallest values in a range

If you have values in a range named *Data*, you can determine the smallest value by using the SMALL function:

    =SMALL(Data,1)

You can determine the second smallest and third smallest values by using these formulas:

    =SMALL(Data,2)
    =SMALL(Data,3)

To add the three smallest values, you could use a formula like this:

    =SUM(SMALL(Data,1), SMALL(Data,2), SMALL(Data,3)

This formula works fine, but using an array formula is more efficient. The following array formula returns the sum of the three smallest values in a range named *Data*:

    {=SUM(SMALL(Data,{1,2,3}))}

The formula uses an array constant as the second argument for the SMALL function. This generates a new array, which consists of the three smallest values in the range. This array is then passed to the SUM function, which returns the sum of the values in the new array.

Figure 17.15 shows an example in which the range A1:A10 is named *Data*. The SMALL function is evaluated three times, each time with a different second argument. The first time, the SMALL function has a second argument of 1, and it returns –5. The second time, the second argument for the SMALL function is 2, and it returns 0 (the second smallest value in the range). The third time, the SMALL function has a second argument of 3 and returns the third smallest value of 2.

FIGURE 17.15

An array formula returns the sum of the three smallest values in A1:A10.

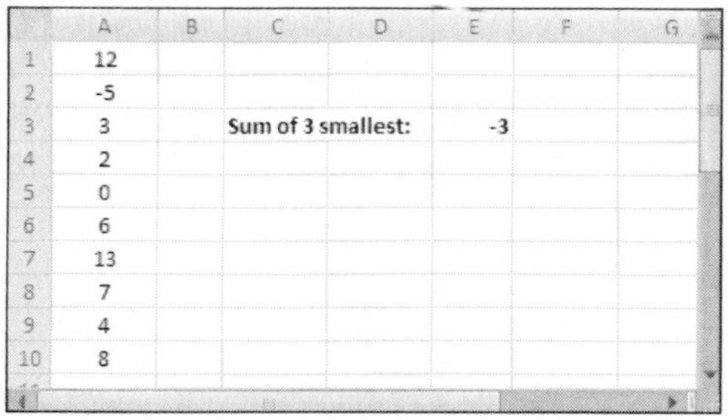

Therefore, the array that's passed to the SUM function is

    {-5,0,2}

The formula returns the sum of the array (–3).

Counting text cells in a range

Suppose that you need to count the number of text cells in a range. The COUNTIF function seems like it might be useful for this task — but it's not. COUNTIF is useful only if you need to count values in a range that meet some criterion (for example, values greater than 12).

To count the number of text cells in a range, you need an array formula. The following array formula uses the IF function to examine each cell in a range. It then creates a new array (of the same size and dimensions as the original range) that consists of 1s and 0s, depending on whether the cell contains text. This new array is then passed to the SUM function, which returns the sum of the items in the array. The result is a count of the number of text cells in the range.

    {=SUM(IF(ISTEXT(A1:D5),1,0))}

CROSS-REF This general array formula type (that is, an IF function nested in a SUM function) is very useful for counting. Refer to Chapter 14 for additional examples.

Figure 17.16 shows an example of the preceding formula in cell C8. The array created by the IF function is

    {0,1,1,1;1,0,0,0;1,0,0,0;1,0,0,0;1,0,0,0}

Notice that this array contains four rows of three elements (the same dimensions as the range).

A slightly more efficient variation on this formula follows:

    {=SUM(ISTEXT(A1:D5)*1)}

This formula eliminates the need for the IF function and takes advantage of the fact that:

```
TRUE * 1 = 1
```

and

```
FALSE * 1 = 0
```

FIGURE 17.16

An array formula returns the number of text cells in the range.

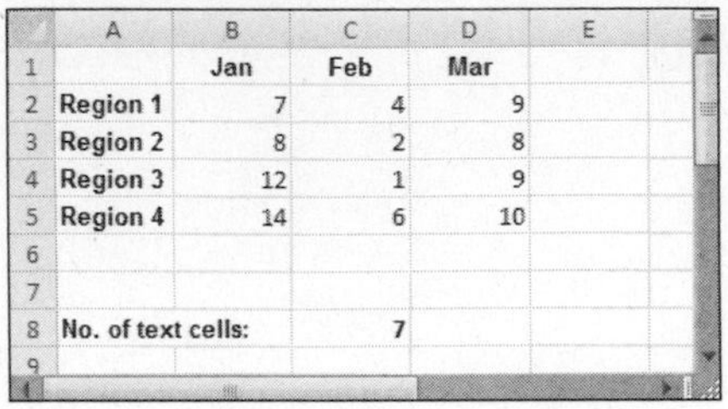

	A	B	C	D	E
1		Jan	Feb	Mar	
2	Region 1	7	4	9	
3	Region 2	8	2	8	
4	Region 3	12	1	9	
5	Region 4	14	6	10	
6					
7					
8	No. of text cells:		7		
9					

Eliminating intermediate formulas

One key benefit of using an array formula is that you can often eliminate intermediate formulas in your worksheet, which makes your worksheet more compact and eliminates the need to display irrelevant calculations. Figure 17.17 shows a worksheet that contains pre-test and post-test scores for students. Column D contains formulas that calculate the changes between the pre-test and the post-test scores. Cell D17 contains a formula, shown here, that calculates the average of the values in column D:

```
=AVERAGE(D2:D15)
```

With an array formula, you can eliminate column D. The following array formula calculates the average of the changes but does not require the formulas in column D:

```
{=AVERAGE(C2:C15-B2:B15)}
```

How does it work? The formula uses two arrays, the values of which are stored in two ranges (B2:B15 and C2:C15). The formula creates a *new* array that consists of the differences between each corresponding element in the other arrays. This new array is stored in Excel's memory, not in a range. The AVERAGE function then uses this new array as its argument and returns the result.

The new array consists of the following elements:

```
{11,15,-6,1,19,2,0,7,15,1,8,23,21,-11}
```

The formula, therefore, is reduced to

```
=AVERAGE({11,15,-6,1,19,2,0,7,15,1,8,23,21,-11})
```

Excel evaluates the function and displays the results, 7.57.

You can use additional array formulas to calculate other measures for the data in this example. For example, the following array formula returns the largest change (that is, the greatest improvement). This formula returns 23, which represents Linda's test scores.

```
{=MAX(C2:C15-B2:B15)}
```

Without an array formula, calculating the average change requires intermediate formulas in column D.

	A	B	C	D
1	Student	Pre-Test	Post-Test	Change
2	Andy	56	67	11
3	Beth	59	74	15
4	Cindy	98	92	-6
5	Duane	78	79	1
6	Eddy	81	100	19
7	Francis	92	94	2
8	Georgia	100	100	0
9	Hilda	92	99	7
10	Isabel	54	69	15
11	Jack	91	92	1
12	Kent	80	88	8
13	Linda	45	68	23
14	Michelle	71	92	21
15	Nancy	94	83	-11
16				
17		Average Change:		7.57
18				

The following array formula returns the smallest change (that is, the least improvement). This formula returns –11, which represents Nancy's test scores.

```
{=MIN(C2:C15-B2:B15)}
```

Using an array in lieu of a range reference

If your formula uses a function that requires a range reference, you may be able to replace that range reference with an array constant. This is useful in situations in which the values in the referenced range do not change.

NOTE A notable exception to using an array constant in place of a range reference in a function is with the database functions that use a reference to a criteria range (for example, DSUM). Unfortunately, using an array constant instead of a reference to a criteria range does not work.

CROSS-REF For information about lookup formulas, refer to Chapter 15.

Figure 17.18 shows a worksheet that uses a lookup table to display a word that corresponds to an integer. For example, looking up a value of 9 returns *Nine* from the lookup table in D1:E10. The formula in cell C1 is

```
=VLOOKUP(B1,D1:E10,2,FALSE)
```

FIGURE 17.18

You can replace the lookup table in D1:E10 with an array constant.

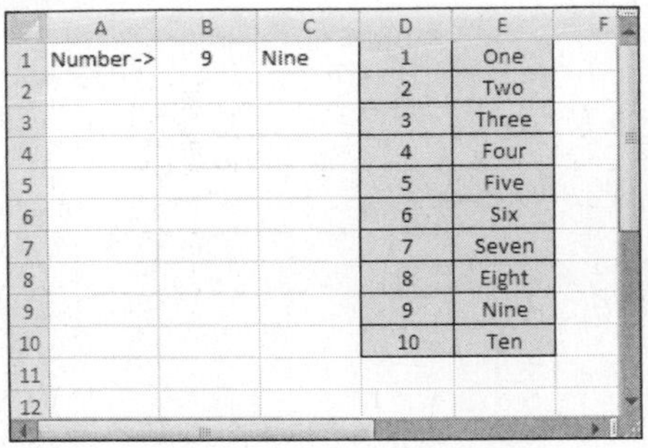

	A	B	C	D	E	F
1	Number ->	9	Nine	1	One	
2				2	Two	
3				3	Three	
4				4	Four	
5				5	Five	
6				6	Six	
7				7	Seven	
8				8	Eight	
9				9	Nine	
10				10	Ten	
11						
12						

You can use a two-dimensional array in place of the lookup range. The following formula returns the same result as the previous formula, but it does not require the lookup range in D1:E1:

```
=VLOOKUP(B1,{1,"One";2,"Two";3,"Three";4,"Four";5,"Five";
6,"Six";7,"Seven";8,"Eight";9,"Nine";10,"Ten"},2,FALSE)
```

This chapter introduced arrays. Chapter 18 explores the topic further and provides some additional examples.

Chapter 18

Performing Magic with Array Formulas

The preceding chapter provides an introduction to arrays and array formulas and presented some basic examples to whet your appetite. This chapter continues the saga and provides many useful examples that further demonstrate the power of this feature.

I selected the examples in this chapter to provide a good assortment of the various uses for array formulas. You can use most of them as-is. You will, of course, need to adjust the range names or references used. Also, you can modify many of the examples easily to work in a slightly different manner.

IN THIS CHAPTER

More examples of single-cell array formulas

More examples of multicell array formulas

Returning an array from a custom VBA function

Working with Single-Cell Array Formulas

As I describe in the preceding chapter, you enter single-cell array formulas into a single cell (not into a range of cells). These array formulas work with arrays contained in a range or that exist in memory. This section provides some additional examples of such array formulas.

ON the CD-ROM The examples in this section are available on the companion CD-ROM. The file is named single-cell array formulas.xlsx.

Summing a range that contains errors

You may have discovered that the SUM function doesn't work if you attempt to sum a range that contains one or more error values (such as #DIV/0! or #N/A). Figure 18.1 shows an example. The formula in cell C11 returns an error value because the range that it sums (C4:C10) contains errors.

The following array formula, in cell C13, overcomes this problem and returns the sum of the values, even if the range contains error values:

```
{=SUM(IF(ISERROR(C4:C10),"",C4:C10))}
```

This formula works by creating a new array that contains the original values but without the errors. The IF function effectively filters out error values by replacing them with an empty string. The SUM function then works on this "filtered" array. This technique also works with other functions, such as AVERAGE, MIN, and MAX.

NEW FEATURE If only Excel 2007 users will use your worksheet, you can use this more efficient version, which uses the new IFERROR function:

```
{=SUM(IFERROR(G1:G7,""))}
```

FIGURE 18.1

An array formula can sum a range of values, even if the range contains errors.

	A	B	C	D	E	F
1	Summing a range that contains error values					
2						
3	Total	Number	Per Unit			
4	80	10	8.00			
5	120	6	20.00			
6	144	12	12.00			
7			#DIV/0!			
8			#DIV/0!			
9	100	20	5.00			
10	50	5	10.00			
11	TOTAL:		#DIV/0!			
12						
13			55.000 <-- SUM, excluding errors			
14						

Counting the number of error values in a range

The following array formula is similar to the previous example, but it returns a count of the number of error values in a range named *Data*:

```
{=SUM(IF(ISERROR(Data),1,0))}
```

This formula creates an array that consists of 1s (if the corresponding cell contains an error) and 0s (if the corresponding cell does not contain an error value).

You can simplify the formula a bit by removing the third argument for the IF function. If this argument isn't specified, the IF function returns FALSE if the condition is not satisfied (that is, the cell does not contain an error value). In this context, Excel treats FALSE as a 0 value. The array formula shown here performs exactly like the previous formula, but it doesn't use the third argument for the IF function:

```
{=SUM(IF(ISERROR(Data),1))}
```

Actually, you can simplify the formula even more:

```
{=SUM(ISERROR(Data)*1)}
```

This version of the formula relies on the fact that:

```
TRUE * 1 = 1
```

and

```
FALSE * 1 = 0
```

Summing the n largest values in a range

The following array formula returns the sum of the 10 largest values in a range named *Data*:

```
{=SUM(LARGE(Data,ROW(INDIRECT("1:10"))))}
```

The LARGE function is evaluated 10 times, each time with a different second argument (1, 2, 3, and so on up to 10). The results of these calculations are stored in a new array, and that array is used as the argument for the SUM function.

To sum a different number of values, replace the 10 in the argument for the INDIRECT function with another value.

If the number of cells to sum is contained in cell C17, use the following array formula, which uses the concatenation operator (&) to create the range address for the INDIRECT function:

```
{=SUM(LARGE(Data,ROW(INDIRECT("1:"&C17))))}
```

To sum the *n smallest* values in a range, use the SMALL function instead of the LARGE function.

Computing an average that excludes zeros

Figure 18.2 shows a simple worksheet that calculates average sales. The formula in cell B14 is

```
=AVERAGE(B5:B12)
```

FIGURE 18.2

The calculated average includes cells that contain a 0.

	A	B	C	D	E	F
1	Exclude zero from average					
2						
3						
4	Sales Person	Sales				
5	Abner	23,991				
6	Baker	15,092				
7	Charleston	0				
8	Davis	11,893				
9	Ellerman	32,116				
10	Flugelhart	29,089				
11	Gallaway	0				
12	Harrison	33,211				
13						
14		18,174	<-- Average with zeros			
15		24,232	<-- Average without zeros (array formula)			
16						

Sheet4 **Sheet5** Sheet6 She

Two of the sales staff had the week off, however, so including their 0 sales in the calculated average doesn't accurately describe the average sales per representative.

NOTE   The AVERAGE function ignores blank cells, but it does not ignore cells that contain 0.

The following array formula returns the average of the range but excludes the cells containing 0:

```
{=AVERAGE(IF(B5:B12<>0,B5:B12))}
```

This formula creates a new array that consists only of the nonzero values in the range. The AVERAGE function then uses this new array as its argument.

You also can get the same result with a regular (non-array) formula:

```
=SUM(B5:B12)/COUNTIF(B5:B12,"<>0")
```

This formula uses the COUNTIF function to count the number of nonzero values in the range. This value is divided into the sum of the values.

Determining whether a particular value appears in a range

To determine whether a particular value appears in a range of cells, you can choose Edit ➪ Find and do a search of the worksheet. But you also can make this determination by using an array formula.

Figure 18.3 shows a worksheet with a list of names in A5:E24 (named *NameList*). An array formula in cell D3 checks the name entered into cell C3 (named *TheName*). If the name exists in the list of names, the formula displays the text *Found*. Otherwise, it displays *Not Found*.

FIGURE 18.3

Using an array formula to determine whether a range contains a particular value.

	A	B	C	D	E
1	Is a value contained in a range?				
2					
3	Enter a Name -->		Wendy	**Found**	
4					
5	Al	Daniel	Harold	Lyle	Richard
6	Allen	Dave	Ian	Maggie	Rick
7	Andrew	David	Jack	Margaret	Robert
8	Anthony	Dennis	James	Marilyn	Rod
9	Arthur	Don	Jan	Mark	Roger
10	Barbara	Donald	Jeff	Marvin	Ronald
11	Bernard	Doug	Jeffrey	Mary	Russ
12	Beth	Douglas	Jerry	Matt	Sandra
13	Bill	Ed	Jim	Mel	Scott
14	Bob	Edward	Joe	Merle	Simon
15	Brian	Eric	John	Michael	Stacy
16	Bruce	Fran	Joseph	Michelle	Stephen
17	Cark	Frank	Kathy	Mike	Steven
18	Carl	Fred	Kathy	Norman	Stuart
19	Charles	Gary	Keith	Patrick	Susan
20	Chris	George	Kenneth	Paul	Terry
21	Chuck	Glenn	Kevin	Peter	Thomas
22	Clark	Gordon	Larry	Phillip	Timothy
23	Curt	Greg	Leonard	Ray	Vincent
24	Dan	Gregory	Louise	Rebecca	Wendy
25					

Sheet4 / Sheet5 / **Sheet6**

The array formula in cell D3 is

```
{=IF(OR(TheName=NameList),"Found","Not Found")}
```

This formula compares *TheName* to each cell in the *NameList* range. It builds a new array that consists of logical TRUE or FALSE values. The OR function returns TRUE if any one of the values in the new array is TRUE. The IF function uses this result to determine which message to display.

A simpler form of this formula follows. This formula displays TRUE if the name is found and returns FALSE otherwise.

```
{=OR(TheName=NameList)}
```

Yet another approach uses the COUNTIF function in a non-array formula:

```
=IF(COUNTIF(NameList,TheName)>0,"Found","Not Found")
```

Counting the number of differences in two ranges

The following array formula compares the corresponding values in two ranges (named *MyData* and *YourData*) and returns the number of differences in the two ranges. If the contents of the two ranges are identical, the formula returns 0.

```
{=SUM(IF(MyData=YourData,0,1))}
```

NOTE The two ranges must be the same size and of the same dimensions.

This formula works by creating a new array of the same size as the ranges being compared. The IF function fills this new array with 0s and 1s. (0 if a difference is found, and 1 if the corresponding cells are the same.) The SUM function then returns the sum of the values in the array.

The following formula, which is simpler, is another way of calculating the same result:

```
{=SUM(1*(MyData<>YourData))}
```

This version of the formula relies on the fact that:

```
TRUE * 1 = 1
```

and

```
FALSE * 1 = 0
```

Returning the location of the maximum value in a range

The following array formula returns the row number of the maximum value in a single-column range named *Data*:

```
{=MIN(IF(Data=MAX(Data),ROW(Data), ""))}
```

The IF function creates a new array that corresponds to the *Data* range. If the corresponding cell contains the maximum value in *Data*, the array contains the row number; otherwise, it contains an empty string. The MIN function uses this new array as its second argument, and it returns the smallest value, which corresponds to the row number of the maximum value in *Data*.

If the *Data* range contains more than one cell that has the maximum value, the row of the first maximum cell is returned.

The following array formula is similar to the previous one, but it returns the actual cell address of the maximum value in the *Data* range. It uses the ADDRESS function, which takes two arguments: a row number and a column number.

```
{=ADDRESS(MIN(IF(Data=MAX(Data),ROW(Data), "")),COLUMN(Data))}
```

The previous formulas work only with a single-column range. The following variation works with any sized range and returns the address of the smallest value in the range named *Data*:

```
{=ADDRESS(MIN(IF(Data=MAX(data),ROW(Data), "")),
MIN(IF(Data=MAX(data),COLUMN(Data), "")))}
```

Finding the row of a value's nth occurrence in a range

The following array formula returns the row number within a single-column range named *Data* that contains the *n*th occurrence of the value in a cell named *Value*:

```
{=SMALL(IF(Data=Value,ROW(Data), ""),n)}
```

The IF function creates a new array that consists of the row number of values from the *Data* range that are equal to *Value*. Values from the *Data* range that aren't equal to *Value* are replaced with an empty string. The SMALL function works on this new array and returns the *n*th smallest row number.

The formula returns #NUM! if the *Value* is not found or if *n* exceeds the number of the values in the range.

Returning the longest text in a range

The following array formula displays the text string in a range (named *Data*) that has the most characters. If multiple cells contain the longest text string, the first cell is returned.

```
{=INDEX(Data,MATCH(MAX(LEN(Data)),LEN(Data),FALSE),1)}
```

This formula works with two arrays, both of which contain the length of each item in the *Data* range. The MAX function determines the largest value, which corresponds to the longest text item. The MATCH function calculates the offset of the cell that contains the maximum length. The INDEX function returns the contents of the cell containing the most characters. This function works only if the *Data* range consists of a single column.

Determining whether a range contains valid values

You may have a list of items that you need to check against another list. For example, you may import a list of part numbers into a range named *MyList*, and you want to ensure that all the part numbers are valid. You can do so by comparing the items in the imported list to the items in a master list of part numbers (named *Master*).

The following array formula returns TRUE if every item in the range named *MyList* is found in the range named *Master*. Both ranges must consist of a single column, but they don't need to contain the same number of rows.

```
{=ISNA(MATCH(TRUE,ISNA(MATCH(MyList,Master,0)),0))}
```

The array formula that follows returns the number of invalid items. In other words, it returns the number of items in *MyList* that do not appear in *Master*.

```
{=SUM(1*ISNA(MATCH(MyList,Master,0)))}
```

To return the first invalid item in *MyList*, use the following array formula:

```
{=INDEX(MyList,MATCH(TRUE,ISNA(MATCH(MyList,Master,0)),0))}
```

Summing the digits of an integer

I can't think of any practical application for the example in this section, but it's a good demonstration of the power of an array formula. The following array formula calculates the sum of the digits in a positive integer, which is stored in cell A1. For example, if cell A1 contains the value 409, the formula returns 13 (the sum of 4, 0, and 9).

```
{=SUM(MID(A1,ROW(INDIRECT("1:"&LEN(A1))),1)*1)}
```

To understand how this formula works, start with the ROW function, as shown here:

```
{=ROW(INDIRECT("1:"&LEN(A1)))}
```

This function returns an array of consecutive integers beginning with 1 and ending with the number of digits in the value in cell A1. For example, if cell A1 contains the value 409, the LEN function returns 3, and the array generated by the ROW functions is

```
{1,2,3}
```

 CROSS-REF For more information about using the INDIRECT function to return this array, see Chapter 17.

This array is then used as the second argument for the MID function. The MID part of the formula, simplified a bit and expressed as values, is the following:

```
{=MID(409,{1,2,3},1)*1}
```

This function generates an array with three elements:

```
{4,0,9}
```

By simplifying again and adding the SUM function, the formula looks like this:

```
{=SUM({4,0,9})}
```

This formula produces the result of 13.

NOTE The values in the array created by the MID function are multiplied by 1 because the MID function returns a string. Multiplying by 1 forces a numeric value result. Alternatively, you can use the VALUE function to force a numeric string to become a numeric value.

Notice that the formula doesn't work with a negative value because the negative sign is not a numeric value. The following formula solves this problem by using the ABS function to return the absolute value of the number. Figure 18.4 shows a worksheet that uses this formula in cell B4.

```
{=SUM(VALUE(MID(ABS(A4),ROW(INDIRECT("1:"&LEN(ABS(A4)))),1)))}
```

The formula was copied down to calculate the sum of the digits for other values in column A.

An array formula calculates the sum of the digits in an integer.

	A	B	C	D
1	Sum of the digits of a value			
2				
3	**Number**	**Sum of Digits**		
4	132	6		
5	9	9		
6	111111	6		
7	980991	36		
8	-980991	36		
9	409	13		
10		0		
11	12	3		
12	123	6		
13				
14				

Sheet12 She

Summing rounded values

Figure 18.5 shows a simple worksheet that demonstrates a common spreadsheet problem: rounding errors. As you can see, the grand total in cell E7 appears to display an incorrect amount. (That is, it's off by a penny.) The values in column E use a number format that displays two decimal places. The actual values, however, consist of additional decimal places that do not display due to rounding (as a result of the number format). The net effect of these rounding errors is a seemingly incorrect total. The total, which is actually $168.320997, displays as $168.32.

Using an array formula to correct rounding errors.

	A	B	C	D	E	F
1	Summing rounded values					
2						
3	**Description**	**Quantity**	**Unit Price**	**Discount**	**Total**	
4	Widgets	6	$11.69	5.23%	$66.47	
5	Sprockets	8	$9.74	5.23%	$73.84	
6	Snapholytes	3	$9.85	5.23%	$28.00	
7	GRAND TOTAL				$168.32	
8						
9				Sum of rounded values:	$168.31	
10						
11						

Sheet13 Sheet14 Sheet15

The following array formula creates a new array that consists of values in column E, rounded to two decimal places:

```
{=SUM(ROUND(E4:E6,2))}
```

This formula returns $168.31.

You also can eliminate these types of rounding errors by using the ROUND function in the formula that cal-culates each row total in column E (which does not require an array formula).

Summing every nth value in a range

Suppose that you have a range of values and you want to compute the sum of every third value in the list — the first, the fourth, the seventh, and so on. One solution is to hard-code the cell addresses in a formula. But a better solution is to use an array formula.

In Figure 18.6, the values are stored in a range named *Data*, and the value of *n* is in cell D2 (named *n*).

FIGURE 18.6

An array formula returns the sum of every *n*th value in the range.

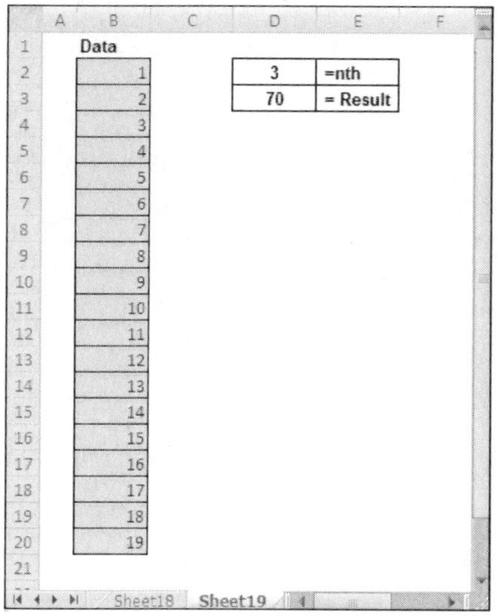

The following array formula returns the sum of every *n*th value in the range:

```
{SUM(IF(MOD(ROW(INDIRECT("1:"&COUNT(Data)))-1,n)=0,Data,""))}
```

This formula returns 70, which is the sum of every third value in the range.

This formula generates an array of consecutive integers, and the MOD function uses this array as its first argument. The second argument for the MOD function is the value of *n*. The MOD function creates another array that consists of the remainders when each row number is divided by *n*. When the array item is 0 (that is, the row is evenly divisible by *n*), the corresponding item in the *Data* range will be included in the sum.

You find that this formula fails when *n* is 0 (that is, when it sums no items). The modified array formula that follows uses an IF function to handle this case:

```
{=IF(n=0,0,SUM(IF(MOD(ROW(INDIRECT("1:"&COUNT(data)))-
1,n)=0,data,"")))}
```

Using Excel's Formula Evaluator

If you would like to better understand how some of these complex array formulas work, consider using a handy tool: The Formula Evaluator. Select the cell that contains the formula and then choose Formulas ⇨ Formula Auditing ⇨ Evaluate Formula. You'll see the Evaluate Formula dialog box shown in the figure.

Click the Evaluate button repeatedly to see the intermediate results as the formula is being calculated. It's like watching a formula calculate in slow motion.

This formula works only when the *Data* range consists of a single column of values. It does not work for a multicolumn range or for a single row of values.

To make the formula work with a horizontal range, you need to transpose the array of integers generated by the ROW function. Excel's TRANPOSE function is just the ticket. The modified array formula that follows works only with a horizontal *Data* range:

```
{=IF(n=0,0,SUM(IF(MOD(TRANSPOSE(ROW(INDIRECT("1:"&COUNT(Data))))-
1,n)=0,Data,"")))}
```

Removing non-numeric characters from a string

The following array formula extracts a number from a string that contains text. For example, consider the string *ABC145Z*. The formula returns the numeric part, 145.

```
{=MID(A1,MATCH(0,(ISERROR(MID(A1,ROW(INDIRECT
("1:"&LEN(A1))),1)*1)*1),0),LEN(A1)-SUM((ISERROR
(MID(A1,ROW(INDIRECT("1:"&LEN(A1))),1)*1)*1)))}
```

This formula works only with a single embedded number. For example, it fails with a string like *X45Z99* because the string contains two embedded numbers.

Determining the closest value in a range

The array formula that follows returns the value in a range named *Data* that is closest to another value (named *Target*):

```
{=INDEX(Data,MATCH(SMALL(ABS(Target-Data),1),ABS(Target-Data),0))}
```

If two values in the *Data* range are equidistant from the *Target* value, the formula returns the first one in the list. Figure 18.7 shows an example of this formula. In this case, the *Target* value is 45. The array formula in cell D5 returns 48 — the value closest to 45.

FIGURE 18.7

An array formula returns the closest match.

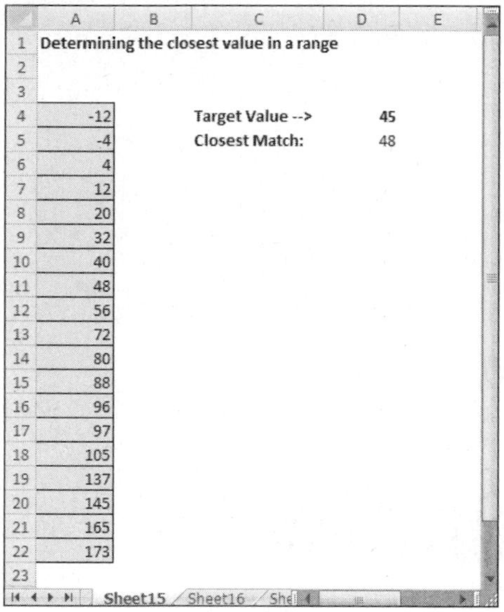

Returning the last value in a column

Suppose that you have a worksheet that you update frequently by adding new data to columns. You may need a way to reference the last value in column A (the value most recently entered). If column A contains no empty cells, the solution is relatively simple and doesn't require an array formula:

```
=OFFSET(A1,COUNTA(A:A)-1,0)
```

This formula uses the COUNTA function to count the number of nonempty cells in column A. This value (minus 1) is used as the second argument for the OFFSET function. For example, if the last value is in row 100, COUNTA returns 100. The OFFSET function returns the value in the cell 99 rows down from cell A1 in the same column.

If column A has one or more empty cells interspersed, which is frequently the case, the preceding formula won't work because the COUNTA function doesn't count the empty cells.

The following array formula returns the contents of the last nonempty cell in the first 500 rows of column A:

```
{=INDEX(A1:A500,MAX(ROW(A1:A500)*(A1:A500<>"")))}
```

You can, of course, modify the formula to work with a column other than column A. To use a different column, change the four column references from A to whatever column you need. If the last nonempty cell occurs in a row beyond row 500, you need to change the two instances of 500 to a larger number. The fewer rows referenced in the formula, the faster the calculation speed.

> **CAUTION** You can['t use this formula, as written, in the same column with which it's working. Attempting to do so generates a circular reference. You can, however, modify it. For example, to use the function in cell A1, change the references so that they begin with row 2 instead of row 1.

Returning the last value in a row

The following array formula is similar to the previous formula, but it returns the last nonempty cell in a row (in this case, row 1):

```
{=INDEX(1:1,MAX(COLUMN(1:1)*(1:1<>"")))}
```

To use this formula for a different row, change the 1:1 reference to correspond to the row.

Ranking data with an array formula

Often, computing the rank orders for the values in a range of data is helpful. If you have a worksheet containing the annual sales figures for 20 salespeople, for example, you may want to know how each person ranks, from highest to lowest.

If you've used the Excel program's RANK function, you may have noticed that the ranks produced by this function don't handle ties the way that you may like. For example, if two values are tied for third place, the RANK function gives both of them a rank of 3. You may prefer a commonly-used approach that assigns each an average (or midpoint) of the ranks—in other words, a rank of 3.5 for both values tied for third place.

Figure 18.8 shows a worksheet that uses two methods to rank a column of values (named *Sales*). The first method (column C) uses the Excel RANK function. Column D uses array formulas to compute the ranks.

The following is the array formula in cell D5:

```
{=SUM(1*(B5<=Sales))-(SUM(1*(B5=Sales))-1)/2}
```

This formula is copied to the cells below it.

> **NOTE** Each ranking is computed with a separate array formula, not with an array formula entered into multiple cells.

Each array function works by computing the number of higher values and subtracting one half of the number of equal values minus 1.

FIGURE 18.8

Ranking data with the Excel program's `RANK` function and with array formulas.

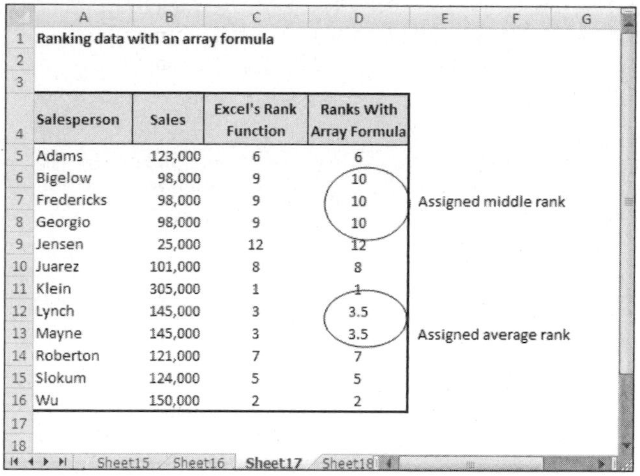

Ranking data with an array formula

Salesperson	Sales	Excel's Rank Function	Ranks With Array Formula
Adams	123,000	6	6
Bigelow	98,000	9	10
Fredericks	98,000	9	10
Georgio	98,000	9	10
Jensen	25,000	12	12
Juarez	101,000	8	8
Klein	305,000	1	1
Lynch	145,000	3	3.5
Mayne	145,000	3	3.5
Roberton	121,000	7	7
Slokum	124,000	5	5
Wu	150,000	2	2

Working with Multicell Array Formulas

The preceding chapter introduced array formulas entered into multicell ranges. In this section, I present a few more array multicell formulas. Most of these formulas return some or all of the values in a range, but rearranged in some way.

ON the CD-ROM **The examples in this section are available on the companion CD-ROM. The file is named multi-cell array formulas.xlsx.**

Returning only positive values from a range

The following array formula works with a single-column vertical range (named *Data*). The array formula is entered into a range that's the same size as *Data* and returns only the positive values in the *Data* range. (Zeroes and negative numbers are ignored.)

```
{=INDEX(Data,SMALL(IF(Data>0,ROW(INDIRECT("1:"&ROWS(Data)))),
ROW(INDIRECT("1:"&ROWS(Data)))))}
```

As you can see in Figure 18.9, this formula works, but not perfectly. The *Data* range is A5:A24, and the array formula is entered into C5:C24. However, the array formula displays `#NUM!` error values for cells that don't contain a value.

This modified array formula, entered into range E5:E24, use the `IFERROR` function to avoid the error value display:

```
{=IFERROR(INDEX(Data,SMALL(IF(Data>0,ROW(INDIRECT("1:"&ROWS(Data)))),RO
W(INDIRECT("1:"&ROWS(Data))))),"")}
```

The IFERROR function is new to Excel 2007. For compatibility with older versions, use this formula:

```
{=IF(ISERR(SMALL(IF(Data>0,ROW(INDIRECT("1:"&ROWS(Data))))),
ROW(INDIRECT("1:"&ROWS(Data))))),"",INDEX(Data,SMALL(IF
(Data>0,ROW(INDIRECT("1:"&ROWS(Data)))),ROW(INDIRECT
("1:"&ROWS(Data)))))))}
```

FIGURE 18.9

Using an array formula to return only the positive values in a range.

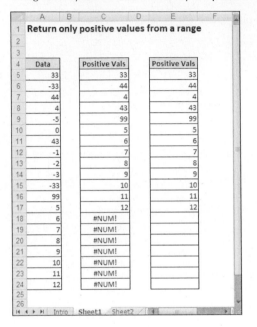

Returning nonblank cells from a range

The following formula is a variation on the formula in the preceding section. This array formula works with a single-column vertical range named *Data*. The array formula is entered into a range of the same size as *Data* and returns only the nonblank cell in the *Data* range.

```
{=IFERROR(INDEX(Data,SMALL(IF(Data<>"",ROW(INDIRECT("1:"&ROWS(Data)))),
ROW(INDIRECT("1:"&ROWS(Data))))),"")}
```

For compatibility with versions prior to Excel 2007, use this formula:

```
{=IF(ISERR(SMALL(IF(Data<>"",ROW(INDIRECT("1:"&ROWS(Data))))),
ROW(INDIRECT("1:"&ROWS(Data))))),"",INDEX(Data,SMALL(IF(Data
<>"",ROW(INDIRECT("1:"&ROWS(Data)))),ROW(INDIRECT("1:"&ROWS
(Data)))))))}
```

Returning a list of unique items in a range

If you have a single-column range named *Data*, the following array formula returns a list of the unique items in the range (the list with no duplicated items):

```
{=INDEX(Data,SMALL(IF(MATCH(Data,Data,0)=ROW(INDIRECT
("1:"&ROWS(Data))),MATCH(Data,Data,0),""),ROW(INDIRECT
("1:"&ROWS(Data))))))}
```

This formula doesn't work if the *Data* range contains any blank cells. The unfilled cells of the array formula display #NUM!.

The following modified version eliminates the #NUM!. display by using the Excel 2007 IFERROR function.

```
{=IFERROR(INDEX(Data,SMALL(IF(MATCH(Data,Data,0)=ROW(INDIRECT
("1:"&ROWS(data))),MATCH(Data,Data,0),""),ROW(INDIRECT
("1:"&ROWS(Data)))))),"")}
```

Figure 18.10 shows an example. Range A5:A23 is named *Data*, and the array formula is entered into range C5:C23. Range E5:E23 contains the array formula that uses the IFERROR function.

FIGURE 18.10

Using an array formula to return unique items from a list.

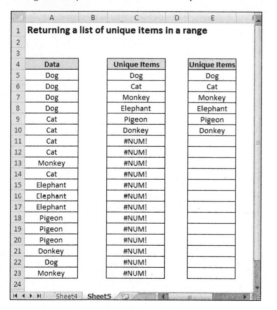

Displaying a calendar in a range

Figure 18.11 shows the results of one of my favorite multicell array formulas, a "live" calendar displayed in a range of cells. If you change the date at the top, the calendar recalculates to display the dates for the month and year.

ON the CD-ROM This workbook is available on the companion CD-ROM. The file is named array formula calendar.xlsx.

To create this calendar in the range B2:H9, follow these steps:

1. **Select B2:H2 and merge the cells by choosing Home ➪ Alignment ➪ Merge & Center.**
2. **Enter a date into the merged range.** The day of the month isn't important.
3. **Enter the abbreviated day names in the range B3:H3.**
4. **Select B4:H9 and enter this array formula.** Remember, to enter an array formula, use Ctrl+Shift+Enter (not just Enter).

```
{=IF(MONTH(DATE(YEAR(B2),MONTH(B2),1))<>MONTH(DATE(YEAR(B2),
MONTH(B2),1)-(WEEKDAY(DATE(YEAR(B2),MONTH(B2),1))-1)+
{0;1;2;3;4;5}*7+{1,2,3,4,5,6,7}-1),"",
DATE(YEAR(B2),MONTH(B2),1)-(WEEKDAY(DATE(YEAR(B2),MONTH(B2),1))-1)+
{0;1;2;3;4;5}*7+{1,2,3,4,5,6,7}-1)}
```

5. **Format the range B4:H9 to use this custom number format: d.** This step formats the dates to show only the day. Use the Custom category in the Number tab of the Format Cells dialog box to specify this custom number format.
6. **Adjust the column widths and format the cells as you like.**

Change the month and year in cell B2, and the calendar will update automatically. After creating this calendar, you can copy the range to any other worksheet or workbook.

FIGURE 18.11

Displaying a calendar by using a single array formula.

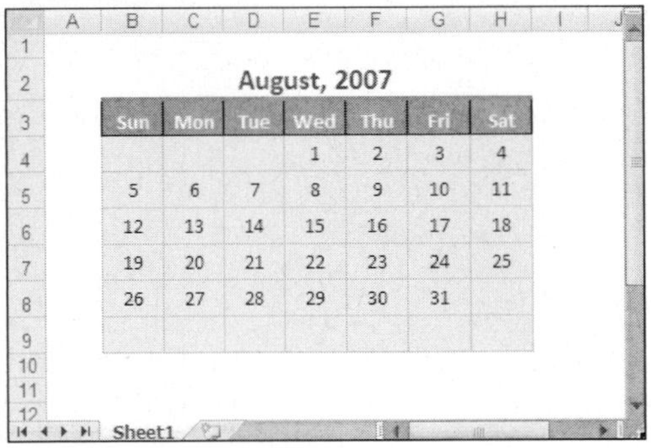

The array formula actually returns date values, but the cells are formatted to display only the day portion of the date. Also, notice that the array formula uses array constants.

CROSS-REF See Chapter 17 for more information about array constants.

Part III

Creating Charts and Graphics

The four chapters in this section deal with charts and graphics. You'll discover how to use Excel's graphics capabilities to display your data in a chart. In addition, you'll learn to use Excel's other drawing tools to enhance your worksheets.

Chapter 19

Getting Started Making Charts

W hen most people think of Excel, they think of crunching rows and columns of numbers. But as you probably know already, Excel is no slouch when it comes to presenting data visually in the form of a chart. In fact, it's a safe bet that Excel is the most commonly used software for creating charts.

This chapter presents an introductory overview of the Excel program's charting ability.

What Is a Chart?

A *chart* is a visual representation of numeric values. Charts (also known as *graphs*) have been an integral part of spreadsheets since the early days of Lotus 1-2-3. Charts generated by early spreadsheet products were quite crude but have improved significantly over the years. Excel provides you with the tools to create a wide variety of highly customizable charts.

NEW FEATURE Excel 2007 charting is a good news/bad news situation. The good news is that Excel 2007 charts have a great new look. The bad news is that Microsoft did not provide any new chart types or any significant new features.

Displaying data in a well-conceived chart can make your numbers more understandable. Because a chart presents a picture, charts are particularly useful for summarizing a series of numbers and their interrelationships. Making a chart can often help you spot trends and patterns that may otherwise go unnoticed.

Figure 19.1 shows a worksheet that contains a simple column chart that depicts a company's sales volume by month. Viewing the chart makes it very apparent that sales were down in the summer months (June through August), but they increased steadily during the final four months of the year. You could, of course,

IN THIS CHAPTER

Charting overview

How Excel handles charts

Embedded charts versus chart sheets

The parts of a chart

Examples of each chart type

arrive at this same conclusion simply by studying the numbers. But viewing the chart makes the point much more quickly.

FIGURE 19.1

A simple column chart depicts the monthly sales volume.

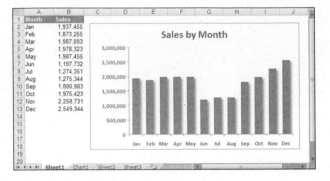

A column chart is just one of many different types of charts that you can create with Excel.

Understanding How Excel Handles Charts

Before you can create a chart, you must have some numbers — sometimes known as *data.* The data, of course, is stored in the cells in a worksheet. Normally, the data that a chart uses resides in a single worksheet, but that's not a strict requirement. A chart can use data that's stored in any number of worksheets, and the worksheets can even be in different workbooks.

A chart is essentially an *object* that Excel creates upon request. This object consists of one or more *data series,* displayed graphically. The appearance of the data series depends on the selected *chart type.* For example, if you create a line chart that uses two data series, the chart contains two lines, each representing one data series. The data for each series is stored in a separate row or column. Each point on the line is determined by the value in a single cell and is represented by a marker. You can distinguish each of the lines by its thickness, line style, color, or data markers (squares, circles, and so on).

Figure 19.2 shows a line chart that plots two data series across a 12-month period. I used different data markers (squares versus circles) to identify the two series, as shown in the *legend* at the bottom of the chart. The chart clearly shows the sales in the Eastern Region are declining steadily, while Western Region sales are increasing at a slower rate.

A key point to keep in mind is that charts are *dynamic.* In other words, a chart series is linked to the data in your worksheet. If the data changes, the chart is updated automatically to reflect those changes.

After you've created a chart, you can always change its type, change the formatting, add new data series to it, or change an existing data series so that it uses data in a different range.

Before you create a chart, you need to determine whether you want it to be an embedded chart or one that resides on a chart sheet. However, you can change your mind later on because it's very easy to move an embedded chart to a chart sheet (and vice versa).

FIGURE 19.2

This line chart displays two data series.

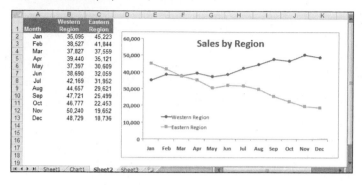

Embedded charts

An *embedded chart* basically floats on top of a worksheet, on the worksheet's draw layer. The charts shown previously in this chapter are both embedded charts.

As with other drawing objects (such as Shapes or SmartArt), you can move an embedded chart, resize it, change its proportions, adjust its borders, and perform other operations. Using embedded charts enables you to print the chart next to the data that it uses.

To make any changes to the actual chart in an embedded chart object, you must click it to *activate* the chart. When a chart is activated, Excel displays the Chart Tools context tab. The Ribbon provides many tools for working with charts.

Chart sheets

When you create a chart on a chart sheet, the chart occupies the entire sheet. If you plan to print a chart on a page by itself, using a chart sheet is often your better choice. If you have many charts to create, you may want to create each one on a separate chart sheet to avoid cluttering your worksheet. This technique also makes locating a particular chart easier because you can change the names of the chart sheets' tabs to provide a description of the chart that it contains.

The Excel Ribbon changes when a chart sheet is active, similar to the way it changes when you select an embedded chart.

Excel displays a chart in a chart sheet in WYSIWYG (What You See Is What You Get) mode: The printed chart looks just like the image on the chart sheet. If the chart doesn't fit in the window, you can use the scroll bars to scroll it or adjust the zoom factor. You also can change its orientation (tall or wide) by using Page Layout ➪ Page Setup ➪ Orientation.

If you create a chart on a chart sheet, you can easily convert it to an embedded chart. Choose Chart Tools ➪ Design ➪ Location ➪ Move Chart to display the Move Chart dialog box. Select the worksheet that will hold the embedded chart from the As Object In drop-down box. Excel deletes the chart sheet and moves the chart to the sheet that you specify. This operation also works in the opposite direction: You can select an embedded chart and relocate it to a new chart sheet.

Parts of a Chart

Refer to the accompanying chart as you read the following description of the chart's elements.

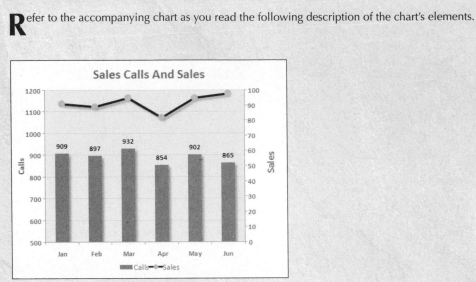

This particular chart is a *combination chart* that displays two *data series:* Calls and Sales. Calls are plotted as vertical columns, and the Sales are plotted as a line with round markers. Each column (or marker on the line) represents a single *data point* (the value in a cell).

The chart has a horizontal axis, known as the *category axis.* This axis represents the category for each data point (January, February, and so on).

Notice that this chart has two vertical axes, known as *value axes,* and each one has a different scale. The axis on the left is for the columns (Calls), and the axis on the right is for the line (Sales).

The value axes also display scale values. The axis on the left displays scale values from 500 to 1,200, in *major unit* increments of 100. The value axis on the right uses a different scale: 0 to 100, in increments of 10.

A chart with two value axes is appropriate because the two data series vary dramatically in scale. If the Sales data were plotted using the left axis, the line wouldn't even be visible.

Most charts provide some method of identifying the data series or data points. A *legend,* for example, is often used to identify the various series in a chart. In this example, the legend appears on the bottom of the chart. Some charts also display *data labels* to identify specific data points. The example chart displays data labels for the Calls series, but not for the Sales series. In addition, most charts (including the example chart) contain a *chart title* and additional labels to identify the axes or categories.

The example chart also contains horizontal *grid lines* (which correspond to the left value axis). Grid lines are basically extensions of the value axis scale, which makes it easier for the viewer to determine the magnitude of the data points.

In addition, all charts have a *chart area* (the entire background area of the chart) and a *plot area*. The plot area shows the actual chart, and in this example, the plot area has a different background color.

Charts can have additional parts or fewer parts, depending on the chart type. For example, a pie chart has *slices* and no axes. A 3-D chart may have *walls* and a *floor*. You can also add many other types of items to a chart. For example, you can add a *trend line* or display *error bars. In other words, after you create a chart, you have a great deal of flexibility in customizing the chart.*

Creating a Chart

Creating a chart is fairly simple:

1. **Make sure that your data is appropriate for a chart.**
2. **Select the range that contains your data.**
3. **Select a chart type by clicking a chart icon in the Insert ⇨ Charts.** These icons display drop-down lists that display subtypes.
4. **(Optional) Use the commands in the Chart Tools context menu to change the look or layout of the chart or add or delete chart elements.**

 **TIP** You can create a chart with a single keystroke. Select the range to be used in the chart and press F11. Excel inserts a new chart sheet and displays the chart of the selected data using the default chart type.

Hands On: Creating and Customizing a Chart

This section contains a step-by-step example of creating a chart and applying some customizations. If you've never created a chart, this is a good opportunity to get a feel for how it works.

Figure 19.3 shows a worksheet with a range of data. This data is customer survey results by month, broken down by customers in three age groups. In this case, the data resides in a table (created by choosing Insert ⇨ Tables ⇨ Table), but that's not a requirement to create a chart.

ON the CD-ROM This workbook, named **hands-on example.xlsx**, is available on the companion CD-ROM.

FIGURE 19.3

The source data for the hands-on chart example.

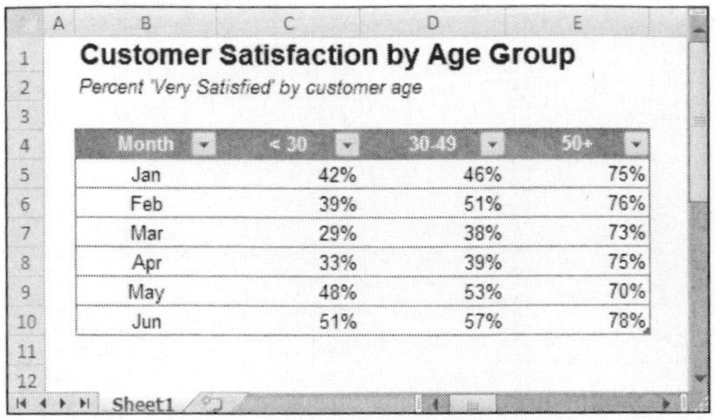

	A	B	C	D	E
1		**Customer Satisfaction by Age Group**			
2		*Percent 'Very Satisfied' by customer age*			
3					
4		Month	< 30	30-49	50+
5		Jan	42%	46%	75%
6		Feb	39%	51%	76%
7		Mar	29%	38%	73%
8		Apr	33%	39%	75%
9		May	48%	53%	70%
10		Jun	51%	57%	78%
11					
12					

Sheet1

Selecting the data

The first step is to select the data for the chart. Your selection should include such items as labels and series identifiers (row and column headings).

For this example, select the range B4:E10. This range includes the category labels but not the title (which is in B1).

NOTE The data that you use in a chart need not be in contiguous cells. You can press Ctrl and make a multiple selection. The initial data, however, must be on a single worksheet. If you need to plot data that exists on more than one worksheet, you can add more series after the chart is created. In all cases, however, data for a single chart series must reside on one sheet.

Choosing a chart type

After you've selected the data, select a chart type from the Insert ➪ Charts. Each control in this group is a drop-down list, which lets you further refine your choice by selecting a subtype.

For this example, choose Insert ➪ Charts ➪ Column ➪ Clustered Column. In other words, you're creating a column chart, using the clustered column subtype. Excel displays the chart shown in Figure 19.4.

FIGURE 19.4

A clustered columns chart.

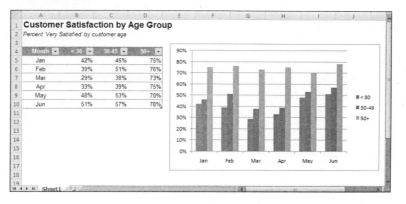

Experimenting with different layouts

The chart shown in Figure 19.4 looks pretty good, but it's just one of several predefined layouts for a clustered column chart.

To see some other configurations for the chart, select the chart and apply a few other layouts in the Chart Tools ➪ Design ➪ Chart Layoutsgroup.

NOTE Every chart type has a set of layouts that you can choose from. A layout contains additional chart elements, such as a title, data labels, axes, and so on. You can add your own elements to your chart, but often using a predefined layout saves time. Even if the layout isn't exactly what you want, it may be close enough that you need to make only a few adjustments.

Figure 19.5 shows the chart after selecting a layout that adds a chart title and moves the legend to the bottom.

FIGURE 19.5

The chart, after selecting a different layout.

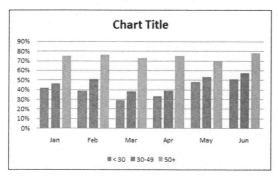

The chart title is a text element that you can select and edit. Alternatively, you can link the chart title to a cell so the title always displays the contents of a particular cell. To create a link to a cell, click the chart title, type an equal sign (=), and click the cell. Excel displays the link in the Formula bar. In the example, the contents of cell A1 is perfect for the chart title.

Experiment with the Chart Tools ➪ Layout tab to make other changes to the chart. For example, you can remove the grid lines, add axis titles, relocate the legend, and so on. Making these changes is easy and intuitive.

Trying another view of the data

The chart, at this point, shows six clusters (months) of three data points in each (age groups). Would the data be easier to understand if we plotted the information in the opposite way?

Try it. Select the chart and then choose Chart Tools ➪ Design ➪ Data ➪ Switch Row/Column. Figure 19.6 shows the result of this change. I also selected a different layout, which provides more separation between the three clusters.

> **NOTE** The orientation of the data has a drastic effect on the look of your chart. Excel has its own rules that it uses to determine the initial data orientation when you create a chart. If Excel's orientation doesn't match your expectation, it's easy enough to change.

The chart, with this new orientation, reveals information that wasn't so apparent in the original version. The <30 and 30-49 age groups both show a decline in satisfaction for March and April. The 50+ age group didn't have this problem, however.

FIGURE 19.6

The chart, after changing the row and column orientation.

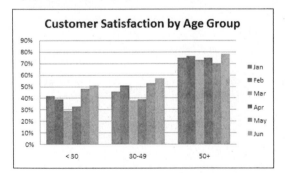

Trying other chart types

Although a clustered column chart seems to work well for this data, there's no harm in checking out some other chart types. Choose Design ➪ Type ➪ Change Chart Type to experiment with other chart types. This command displays the Change Chart Type dialog box, shown in Figure 19.7. The main categories are listed on the left, and the subtypes are shown as icons. Select an icon, click OK, and Excel displays the chart using the new chart type. If you don't like the result, select Undo.

Figure 19.8 shows a few different chart type options.

FIGURE 19.7

Use this dialog box to change the chart type.

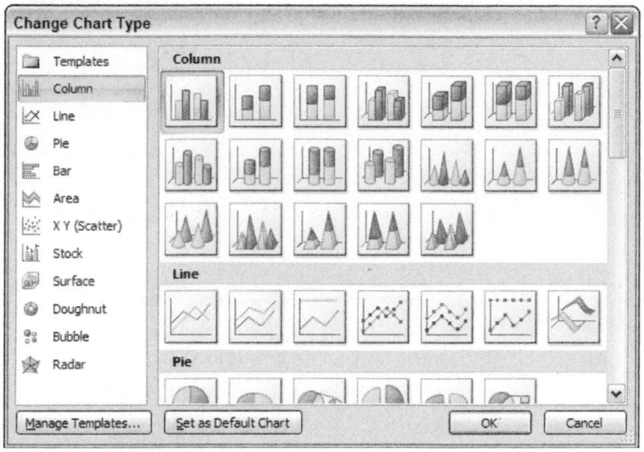

FIGURE 19.8

The customer satisfaction chart, using four different chart types.

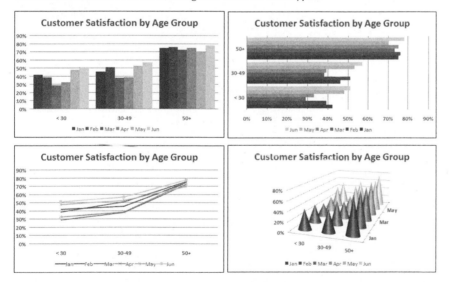

Trying other chart styles

If you'd like to try some of the prebuilt chart styles, select the chart and choose Chart Tools ➪ Design ➪ Chart Styles gallery. You'll find an amazing selection of different colors and effects, all available with a single mouse click.

> **TIP**   The styles displayed in the gallery depend on the workbook's theme. When you choose Page Layout ➪ Themes to apply a different theme, you'll have a new selection of chart styles designed for the selected theme.

Figure 19.9 shows the chart after drastically changing its appearance by applying a new chart style, which adds a three-dimensional look to the columns.

FIGURE 19.9

A single click applies a new style and dramatically changes the chart's look.

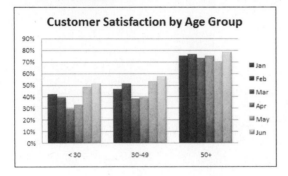

Working with Charts

This section covers some common chart modifications:

- Moving and resizing charts
- Copying a chart
- Deleting a chart
- Adding chart elements
- Moving and deleting chart elements
- Formatting chart elements
- Printing charts

> **NOTE**   Before you can modify a chart, the chart must be activated. To activate an embedded chart, click it. Doing so activates the chart and also selects the element that you click. To activate a chart on a chart sheet, just click its sheet tab.

Moving and resizing a chart

If your chart is an embedded chart, you can freely move and resize it with you mouse. Click the chart's border and then drag the border to move the chart. Drag any of the eight "handles" to resize the chart. The handles are the black dots that appear on the chart's corners and edges when you click the chart's border. When the mouse pointer turns into a double arrow, click and drag to resize the chart.

When a chart is selected, you can use the Format ⇨ Size controls to adjust the height and width of the chart. Use the spinners, or type the dimensions directly into the Height and Width controls.

You also can use standard cut and paste techniques to move an embedded chart. In fact, this is the only way move a chart from one worksheet to another. Select the chart and choose Home ⇨ Clipboard ⇨ Cut (or press Ctrl+X). Then activate a cell near the desired location and choose Home ⇨ Clipboard ⇨ Paste (or press Ctrl+V). The new location can be in a different worksheet or even in a different workbook. If you paste the chart to a different workbook, it will be linked to the data in the original workbook.

To move an embedded chart to a chart sheet (or vice versa), select the chart and choose Chart Tools ⇨ Location ⇨ Move Chart to display the Move Chart dialog box.

Copying a chart

To make an exact copy of an embedded chart, press and hold down the Ctrl key. Click the chart and then drag the mouse pointer to a new location. To make a copy of a chart sheet, use the same procedure, but drag the chart sheet's tab.

You also can use standard copy and paste techniques to copy a chart. Select the chart (an embedded chart or a chart sheet) and choose Home ⇨ Clipboard ⇨ Copy (or press Ctrl+C). Then activate a cell near the desired location and choose Home ⇨ Clipboard ⇨ Paste (or press Ctrl+V). The new location can be in a different worksheet or even in a different workbook. If you paste the chart to a different workbook, it will be linked to the data in the original workbook.

Deleting a chart

To delete an embedded chart, press Ctrl and click the chart (this selects the chart as an object). Then press Delete. When the Ctrl key is pressed, you can select multiple charts, and then delete them all with a single press of the Del key.

To delete a chart sheet, right-click its sheet tab and choose Delete from the shortcut menu. To delete multiple chart sheets, select them by pressing Ctrl while you click the sheet tabs.

Adding chart elements

To add new elements to a chart (such as a title, legend, data labels, or gridlines), use the controls in the Chart Tools ⇨ Layout group. These controls are arranged into logical groups, and they all display a drop-down list of options.

Moving and deleting chart elements

Some of the elements within a chart can be moved. The movable chart elements include the titles, the legend, and data labels. To move a chart element, simply click it to select it. Then drag its border. The easiest way to delete a chart element is to select it and then press Delete. You can also use the controls in the Chart Tools ⇨ Layout group to turn of the display of a particular chart element. For example, to delete data labels, choose Chart Tools ⇨ Layout ⇨ Labels ⇨ Data Labels ⇨ None.

A few chart elements consist of multiple objects. For example, the data labels element consists of one label for each data point. To more or delete one data label, click once to select the entire element and then click a second time to select the specific data label. You can then move or delete the single data label.

Formatting chart elements

Many users are content to stick with the predefined chart layouts and chart styles. For more precise customizations, Excel allows you to work with individual chart elements and apply additional formatting. You can use the Ribbon commands for some modifications, but the easiest way to format chart elements is to right-click the element and choose Format from the shortcut menu. The exact command depends on the element you select. For example, if you right-click the chart's title, the shortcut menu command is Format Chart Title.

The Format command displays a stay-on-top tabbed dialog box with options for the selected element.

Figure 19.10 shows the Format Axis dialog box, which I displayed by right-clicking the vertical axis and selecting Format Axis from the shortcut menu.

TIP If you've applied formatting to a chart element and decide that it wasn't such a good idea, you can revert to the original formatting for the particular chart style. Right-click the chart element and choose Reset To Match Style from the shortcut menu. To reset the entire chart, select the chart area when you issue the command.

FIGURE 19.10

Each chart element has a formatting dialog box. This one is used to format a chart axis.

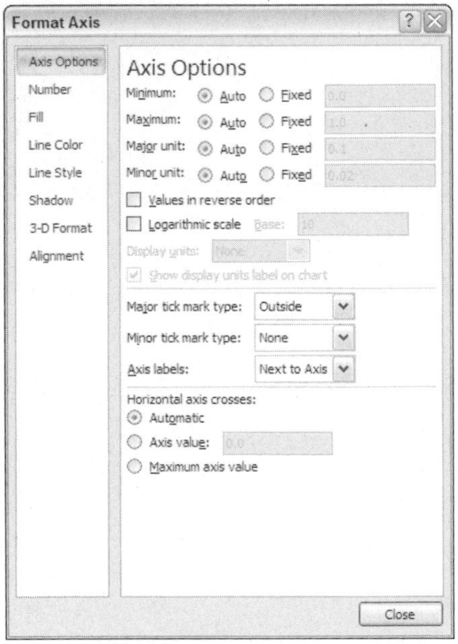

 In previous versions of Excel, double-clicking a chart element displayed its Format dialog box. That mouse action no longer works in Excel 2007.

CROSS-REF   Refer to Chapter 20 for more information about customizing and formatting charts.

Printing Charts

Printing embedded charts is nothing special; you print them the same way that you print a worksheet. As long as you include the embedded chart in the range that you want to print, Excel prints the chart as it appears on-screen. When printing a sheet that contains embedded charts, it's a good idea to preview first (or use Page Layout View) to ensure that your charts do not span multiple pages. If you created the chart on a chart sheet, Excel always prints the chart on a page by itself.

TIP   If you select an embedded chart and use Office ⇨ Print, Excel prints the chart on a page by itself and does *not* print the worksheet.

If you don't want a particular embedded chart to appear on your printout, select the chart and display the Size And Properties dialog box. Choose Chart Tools ⇨ Format, and then click the dialog box launcher in the Size group. In the Size And Properties dialog box, click the Properties tab and remove the check mark from the Print Object check box.

Understanding Chart Types

People who create charts usually do so to make a point or to communicate a specific message. Often, the message is explicitly stated in the chart's title or in a text box within the chart. The chart itself provides visual support.

Choosing the correct chart type is often a key factor in the effectiveness of the message. Therefore, it's often well worth your time to experiment with various chart types to determine which one conveys your message best.

In almost every case, the underlying message in a chart is some type of *comparison*. Examples of some general types of comparisons include

- **Compare item to other items**: For example, a chart may compare sales in each of a company's sales regions.
- **Compare data over time:** For example, a chart may display sales by month and indicate trends over time.
- **Make relative comparisons:** An example is a common pie chart that depicts relative values in terms of pie "slices."
- **Compare data relationships:** An XY chart is ideal for this comparison. For example, you might show the relationship between marketing expenditures and sales.
- **Frequency comparison:** You can use a common histogram, for example, to display the number (or percentage) of students who scored within a particular grade range.
- **Identify "outliers" or unusual situations:** If you have thousands of data points, creating a chart may help identify data that is not representative.

Choosing a chart type

A common question among Excel users is "How do I know which chart type to use for my data?" Unfortunately, this question has no cut-and-dried answer to. Perhaps the best answer is a vague one: Use the chart type that gets your message across in the simplest way.

Figure 19.11 shows the same set of data plotted by using six different chart types. Although all six charts represent the same information (monthly Web site visitors), they look quite different from one another.

The column chart (upper left) is probably the best choice for this particular set of data because it clearly shows the information for each month in discrete units. The bar chart (upper right) is similar to a column chart, but the axes are swapped. Most people are more accustomed to seeing time-based information extend from left to right rather than from top to bottom.

The line chart (middle left) may not be the best choice because it seems to imply that the data is continuous — that points exist in between the 12 actual data points. This same argument may be made against using an area chart (middle right).

The pie chart (lower left) is simply too confusing and does nothing to convey the time-based nature of the data. Pie charts are most appropriate for a data series in which you want to emphasize proportions among a relatively small number of data points. If you have too many data points, a pie chart can be impossible to interpret.

FIGURE 19.11

The same data, plotted by using six chart types.

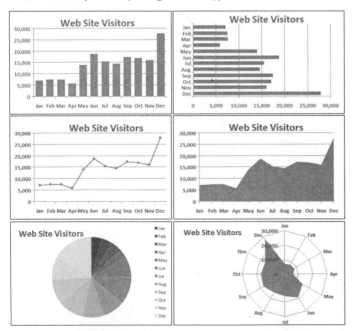

The radar chart (lower right) is clearly inappropriate for this data. People aren't accustomed to viewing time-based information in a circular direction!

Fortunately, changing a chart's type is an easy procedure, so you can experiment with various chart types until you find the one that represents your data accurately, clearly, and as simply as possible.

The remainder of this chapter contains lots of information about Excel's various chart types. The examples and discussion may give you a better handle on determining the most appropriate chart type for your data.

Chart type examples

After you select the data to use in a chart, the next step is to select the type of chart. The commands in the Insert ⇨ Charts group are all drop-down controls. Click a control, and you see icons that represent the subtypes for the chart type. For example, a Line chart has seven subtypes.

The remainder of this section discusses each of Excel's standard chart types and shows examples of each.

Column charts

Probably the most common chart type is column charts. A *column chart* displays each data point as a vertical column, the height of which corresponds to the value. The value scale is displayed on the vertical axis, which is usually on the left side of the chart. You can specify any number of data series, and the corresponding data points from each series can be stacked on top of each other. Typically, each data series is depicted in a different color or pattern.

Column charts are often used to compare discrete items, and they can depict the differences between items in a series or items across multiple series. Excel offers seven column-chart subtypes.

ON the CD-ROM A workbook that contains the charts in this section is available on the companion CD-ROM. The file is named **column charts.xlsx**.

Figure 19.12 shows an example of a clustered column chart that depicts monthly sales for two products. From this chart, it is clear that Sprocket sales have always exceeded Widget sales. In addition, Widget sales have been declining over the five-month period, whereas Sprocket sales are increasing.

FIGURE 19.12

This clustered column chart compares monthly sales for two products.

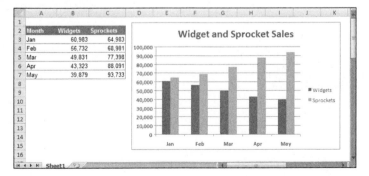

The same data, in the form of a stacked column chart, is shown in Figure 19.13. This chart has the added advantage of depicting the combined sales over time. It shows that total sales have remained fairly steady each month, but the relative proportions of the two products have changed.

Figure 19.14 shows the same sales data plotted as a 100% stacked column chart. This chart type shows the relative contribution of each product by month. Notice that the vertical axis displays percentage values, not sales amounts. This chart provides no information about the actual sales volumes. This type of chart is often a good alternative to using several pie charts. Instead of using a pie to show the relative sales volume in each year, the chart uses a column for each year.

The data is plotted with a 3-D clustered column chart in Figure 19.15. The name is a bit deceptive, because the chart uses only two dimensions, not three. Many people use this type of chart because it has more visual pizzazz. Compare this chart with a "true" 3-D column chart, shown in Figure 19.16. This type of chart may be appealing visually, but precise comparisons are difficult because of the distorted perspective view.

You can also choose from column variations known as cylinder, cone, and pyramid charts. The only difference among these chart types and a standard column chart is the shape of the columns.

FIGURE 19.13

This stacked column chart displays sales by product and depicts the total sales.

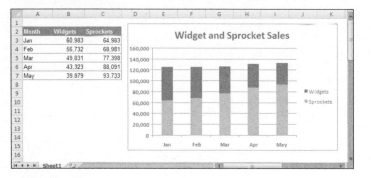

FIGURE 19.14

This 100% stacked column chart display monthly sales as a percentage.

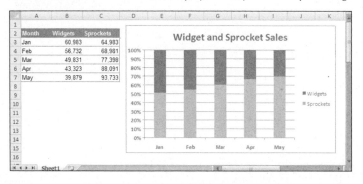

FIGURE 19.15

A 3-D column chart.

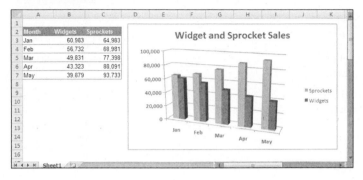

FIGURE 19.16

A true 3-D column chart.

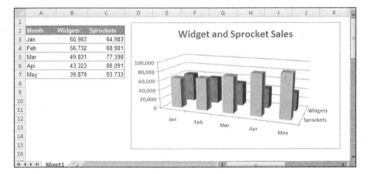

Bar charts

A *bar chart* is essentially a column chart that has been rotated 90 degrees clockwise. One distinct advantage to using a bar chart is that the category labels may be easier to read. Figure 19.17 shows a bar chart that displays a value for each of ten survey items. The category labels are lengthy, and displaying them legibly with a column chart would be difficult. Excel offers six bar chart subtypes.

ON the CD-ROM A workbook that contains the chart in this section is available on the companion CD-ROM. The file is named **bar charts.xlsx.**

FIGURE 19.17

If you have lengthy category labels, a bar chart may be a good choice.

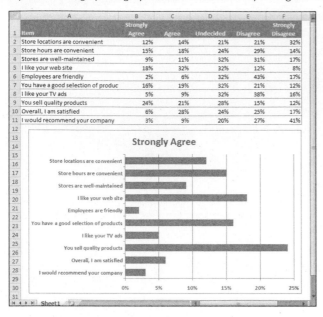

Unlike a column chart, no subtype displays multiple series along a third axis. (That is, Excel does not provide a 3-D Bar Chart subtype.)

As with a column chart, you can include any number of data series in a bar chart. In addition, the bars can be "stacked" from left to right.

Line charts

Line charts are often used to plot continuous data and are useful for identifying trends. For example, plotting daily sales as a line chart may enable you to identify sales fluctuations over time. Normally, the category axis for a line chart displays equal intervals. Excel supports seven line chart subtypes.

See Figure 19.18 for an example of a line chart that depicts daily sales (200 data points). Although the data varies quite a bit on a daily basis, the chart clearly depicts an upward trend.

A workbook that contains the charts in this section is available on the companion CD-ROM. The file is named **line charts.xlsx**.

FIGURE 19.18

A line chart often can help you spot trends in your data.

A line chart can use any number of data series, and you distinguish the lines by using different colors, line styles, or markers. Figure 19.19 shows a line chart that has three series. The series are distinguished by both markers and different line colors.

FIGURE 19.19

This line chart displays three series.

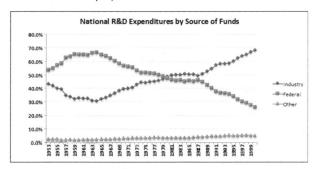

The final line chart example, shown in Figure 19.20, is a *3-D line chart*. Although it has a nice visual appeal (especially with the shadow effect), it's certainly not the clearest way to present the data.

FIGURE 19.20

This 3-D line chart does not present the data very well.

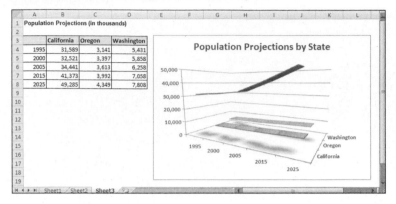

Pie charts

A *pie chart* is useful when you want to show relative proportions or contributions to a whole. A pie chart uses only one data series. Pie charts are most effective with a small number of data points. Generally, a pie chart should use no more than five or six data points (or slices). A pie chart with too many data points can be very difficult to interpret.

NOTE The values used in a pie chart must all be positive numbers. If you create a pie chart that uses one or more negative values, the negative values will be converted to positive values — which is probably not what you intended!

You can "explode" one or more slices of a pie chart for emphasis (see Figure 19.21). Activate the chart and click any pie slice to select the entire pie. Then click the slice that you want to explode and drag it away from the center.

ON the CD-ROM A workbook that contains the charts in this section is available on the companion CD-ROM. The file is named pie charts.xlsx.

The pie of pie and bar of pie chart types enables you to display a secondary chart that provides more detail for one of the pie slices. Figure 19.22 shows an example of a bar of pie chart. The pie chart shows the breakdown of four expense categories Rent, Supplies, Miscellaneous, and Salary. The secondary bar chart provides an additional regional breakdown of the Salary category.

The data used in the chart resides in A2:B8. When the chart was created, Excel made a guess at which categories belong to the secondary chart. In this case, the guess was to use the last three data points for the secondary chart — and the guess was incorrect.

To correct the chart, right-click any of the pie slices and choose Format Data Series. In the dialog box, select the Series Options tab and make the changes. In this example, I chose Split Series By Position and specified that the Second Plot Contains The Last 4 Values In The Series. I also replaced the default category name (Other) with Salary.

FIGURE 19.21

A pie chart with one slice exploded.

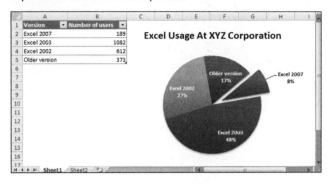

FIGURE 19.22

A bar of pie chart that shows detail for one of the pie slices.

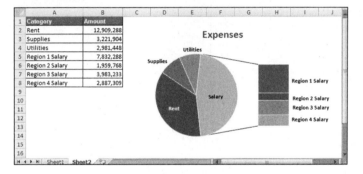

XY (scatter) charts

Another common chart type is an *XY chart* (also known as scattergrams or scatter plots). An XY chart differs from most other chart types in that both axes display values. (An XY chart has no category axis.)

This type of chart often is used to show the relationship between two variables. Figure 19.23 shows an example of an XY chart that plots the relationship between sales calls made (horizontal axis) and actual sales (vertical axis). Each point in the chart represents one month. The chart shows that these two variables are positively related: Months in which more calls were made typically had higher sales volumes.

 A workbook that contains the charts in this section is available on the companion CD-ROM. The file is named xy charts.xlsx.

NOTE   Although these data points correspond to time, the chart doesn't convey any time-related information. In other words, the data points are plotted based only on their two values.

Figure 19.24 shows another XY chart, this one with lines that connect the XY points. This chart plots a hypocycloid curve with 200 data points. It's set up with three parameters. Change any of the parameters, and you'll get a completely different curve. This is a very minimalist chart. I deleted all the chart elements except the data series itself.

If this type of design looks familiar, it's because a hypocycloid curve is the basis for a popular children's drawing toy.

FIGURE 19.23

An XY chart shows the relationship between two variables.

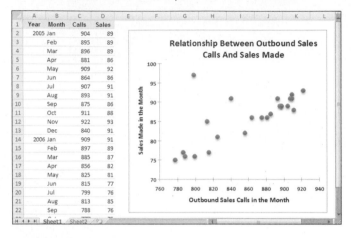

FIGURE 19.24

A hypocycloid curve, plotted as an XY chart.

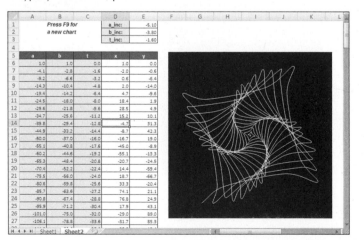

Area charts

Think of an *area chart* as a line chart in which the area below the line has been colored in. Figure 19.25 shows an example of a stacked area chart. Stacking the data series enables you to see clearly the total, plus the contribution by each series.

ON the CD-ROM A workbook that contains the charts in this section is available on the companion CD-ROM. The file is named **area charts.xlsx**.

FIGURE 19.25

A stacked area chart.

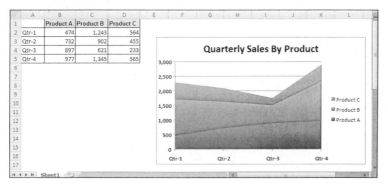

Figure 19.26 shows the same data, plotted as a 3-D area chart. As you can see, it's not an example of an effective chart. The data for products B and C are obscured. In some cases, the problem can be resolved by rotating the chart or using transparency. But I think the best way to salvage this particular chart is to select a new chart type.

FIGURE 19.26

This 3-D area chart is not a good choice.

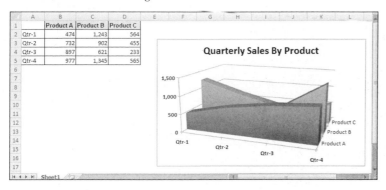

Doughnut charts

A *doughnut chart* is similar to a pie chart, with two exceptions: It has a hole in the middle, and it can display more than one series of data. Doughnut charts are listed in the Other Charts category.

Figure 19.27 shows an example of a doughnut chart with two series (1st Half Sales and 2nd Half Sales). The legend identifies the data points. Because a doughnut chart doesn't provide a direct way to identify the series, I added arrows and series descriptions manually.

ON the CD-ROM A workbook that contains the charts in this section is available on the companion CD-ROM. The file is named **doughnut charts.xlsx**.

FIGURE 19.27

A doughnut chart with two data series.

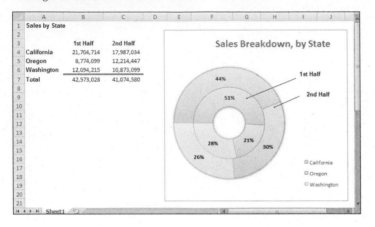

Notice that Excel displays the data series as concentric rings. As you can see, a doughnut chart with more than one series can be very difficult to interpret. For example, the relatively larger sizes of the slices toward the outer part of the doughnut can be deceiving. Consequently, you should use doughnut charts sparingly. Perhaps the best use for a doughnut chart is to plot a single series as a visual alternative to a pie chart.

In many cases, a stacked column chart for such comparisons expresses your meaning better than does a doughnut chart (see Figure 19.28).

Radar charts

Radar charts are listed in the Other Charts category. You may not be familiar with this type of chart. A *radar chart* is a specialized chart that has a separate axis for each category, and the axes extend outward from the center of the chart. The value of each data point is plotted on the corresponding axis.

Figure 19.29 shows an example of a radar chart. This chart plots two data series across 12 categories (months) and shows the seasonal demand for snow skis versus water skis. Note that the water-ski series partially obscures the snow-ski series.

ON the CD-ROM A workbook that contains the charts in this section is available on the companion CD-ROM. The file is named **radar charts.xlsx**.

FIGURE 19.28

Using a stacked column chart is a better choice.

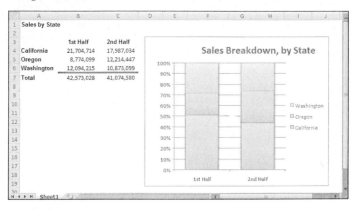

FIGURE 19.29

Plotting ski sales using a radar chart with 12 categories and 2 series.

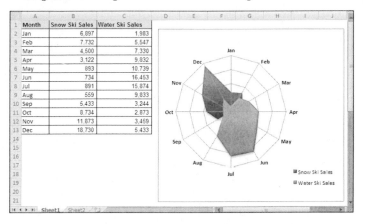

Using a radar chart to show seasonal sales may be an interesting approach, but it's not the best. As you can see in Figure 19.30, a stacked bar chart shows the information much more clearly.

A more appropriate use for radar charts is shown in Figure 19.31. These four charts each plot a color. More precisely, each chart shows the RGB components (the contributions of red, green, and blue) that make up a color. Each chart has one series, and three categories. The categories extend from 0 to 255.

NOTE If you view the charts in color, you'll see that they actually depict the color that they describe. The data series colors were applied manually.

FIGURE 19.30

A stacked bar chart is a better choice for the ski sales data.

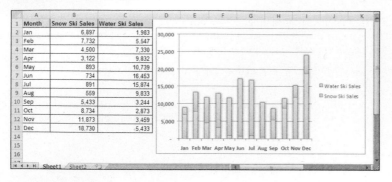

FIGURE 19.31

These radar charts depict the red, green, and blue contributions for each of four colors.

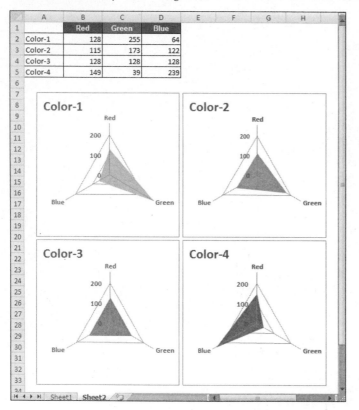

Surface charts

Surface charts display two or more data series on a surface. Surface charts are listed in the Other Charts category.

As Figure 19.32 shows, these charts can be quite interesting. Unlike other charts, Excel uses color to distinguish values, not to distinguish the data series. The number of colors used is determined by the major unit scale setting for the value axis. Each color corresponds to one major unit.

 A workbook that contains the charts in this section is available on the companion CD-ROM. The file is named **surface charts.xlsx**.

NOTE It's important to understand that a surface chart does not plot 3-D data points. The series axis for a surface chart, as with all other 3-D charts, is a category axis — not a value axis. In other words, if you have data that is represented by x, y, and z coordinates, it can't be plotted accurately on a surface chart unless the x and y values are equally spaced.

FIGURE 19.32

A surface chart.

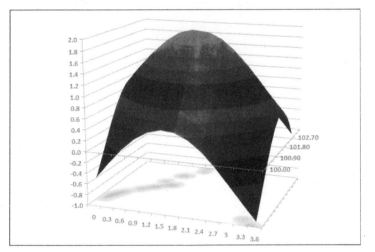

Bubble charts

Think of a *bubble chart* as an XY chart that can display an additional data series, which is represented by the size of the bubbles. As with an XY chart, both axes are value axes (there is no category axis). Bubble charts are listed in the Other Charts category.

Figure 19.33 shows an example of a bubble chart that depicts the results of a weight-loss program. The horizontal value axis represents the original weight, the vertical value axis shows the number of weeks in the program, and the size of the bubbles represents the amount of weight lost.

 A workbook that contains the charts in this section is available on the companion CD-ROM. The file is named **bubble charts.xlsx**.

Figure 19.34 shows another bubble chart, made up of nine series that represent mouse face parts. The size and position of each bubble required some experimentation.

A bubble chart.

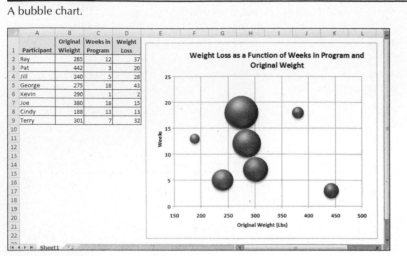

This bubble chart depicts a mouse.

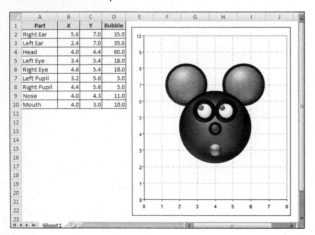

Stock charts

Stock charts are most useful for displaying stock-market information. These charts require three to five data series, depending on the subtype. This chart type is listed in the Other Charts category.

Figure 19.35 shows an example of each of the four stock chart types. The two charts on the bottom display the trade volume and use two value axes. The daily volume, represented by columns, uses the axis on the left. The *up-bars,* sometimes referred to as *candlesticks,* are the vertical lines that depict the difference between the opening and closing price. A black up-bar indicates that the closing price was lower than the opening price.

ON the CD-ROM A workbook that contains the charts in this section is available on the companion CD-ROM. The file is named **stock charts.xlsx.**

Stock charts aren't just for stock price data. Figure 19.36 shows a chart that depicts the high, low, and average temperatures for each day in May. This is a high-low-close chart.

FIGURE 19.35

The four stock chart subtypes.

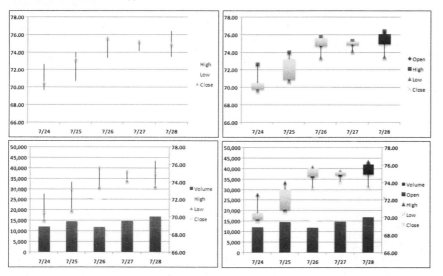

FIGURE 19.36

Plotting temperature data with a stock chart.

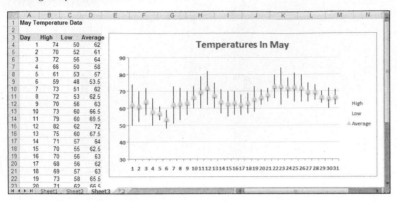

Learning More

This chapter introduced Excel charts, including examples of the types of charts that you can create. For many uses, the information in this chapter is sufficient to create a wide variety of charts.

Those who require control over every aspect of their charts can find the information they need in the next chapter. It picks up where this one left off and covers the details involved in creating the perfect chart.

Chapter 20

Learning Advanced Charting

The preceding chapter introduced charting in Excel and described how to create basic charts. This chapter takes the topic to the next level. You learn how to customize your charts to the maximum so that they look exactly as you want. You also pick up some slick charting tricks that will make your charts even more impressive.

Understanding Chart Customization

Excel 2007 makes creating a basic chart easier than ever. Select your data, choose a chart type, and you're finished. You may take a few extra seconds and select one of the prebuilt Chart Layouts, and maybe even select one of the Chart Styles. But if your goal is to create the most effective chart possible, you probably want to take advantage of the additional customization techniques available in Excel.

Customizing a chart involves changing its appearance, as well as possibly adding new elements to it. These changes can be purely cosmetic (such as changing colors modifying line widths, or adding a shadow) or quite substantial (such as changing the axis scales or adding a second Value Axis). Chart elements that you might add include such features as a data table, a trend line, or error bars.

Selecting Chart Elements

Modifying a chart is similar to everything else you do in Excel: First you make a selection (in this case, select a chart element), and then you issue a command to do something with the selection.

You can select only one chart element (or one group of chart elements) at a time. For example, if you want to change the font for two axis labels, you must work on each set of axis labels separately.

Excel provides three ways, described in the following sections, to select a particular chart element:

- Use the mouse
- Use the keyboard
- Use the Chart Elements control

Selecting with the mouse

To select a chart element with your mouse, just click it. The chart element appears with small circles at the corners.

TIP   To ensure that you've selected the chart element that you intended to select, view the Chart Element control, located in the Chart Tools ⇨ Format ⇨ Current Selection group of the Ribbon (see Figure 20.1).

FIGURE 20.1

The Chart Element control displays the name of the selected chart element. In this example, the Vertical (Value) Axis is selected.

When you move the mouse over a chart, a small *chart tip* displays the name of the chart element under the mouse pointer. When the mouse pointer is over a data point, the chart tip also displays the value of the data point.

> **TIP** If you find these chart tips annoying, you can turn them off. Choose Office ➪ Excel Options and click the Advanced tab in the Excel Options dialog box. Locate the Display section and remove the check mark from either or both items labeled Show Chart Element Names On Hover or Show Data Point Values On Hover.

Some chart elements (such as a series, a legend, and data labels) consist of multiple items. For example, a chart series element is made up of individual data points. To select a particular data point, click twice: First click the series to select it and then click the specific element within the series (for example, a column or a line chart marker). Selecting the element enables you to apply formatting only to a particular data point in a series.

You may find that some chart elements are difficult to select with the mouse. If you rely on the mouse for selecting a chart element, you may have to click it several times before the desired element is actually selected. Fortunately, Excel provides other ways to select a chart element, and it's worth your while to be familiar with them.

Selecting with the keyboard

When a chart is active, you can use the up-arrow and down-arrow keys on your keyboard to cycle among the chart's elements. Again, keep your eye on the Chart Elements control to ensure that the chart element that's selected is what you think it is.

When a chart series is selected, use the left-arrow and right-arrow keys to select an individual item within the series. Similarly, when a set of data labels is selected, you can select a specific data label by using the left-arrow or right-arrow key. And when a legend is selected, you can select individual elements within the legend by using the left-arrow or right-arrow keys.

Selecting with the Chart Element control

The Chart Element control is located in the Chart Tools ➪ Format ➪ Current Selection group. This control displays the name of the currently selected chart element. But it's a drop-down control, and you can also use it to select a particular element in the active chart (see Figure 20.2).

This control lists only the top-level elements in the chart. To select an individual data point within a series, for example, you need to select the series and then use the left and right arrow keys (or your mouse) to select the desired data point.

FIGURE 20.2

Using the Chart Element drop-down control to select a chart element.

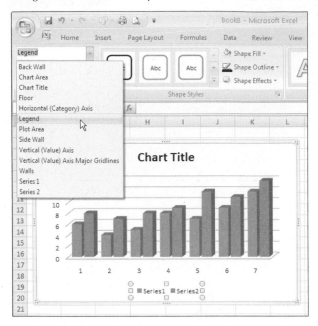

> **NOTE** When a single data point is selected, the Chart Element control *will* display the name of the selected element, even though it's not actually available for selection in the drop-down list.

> **TIP** If you do a lot of work with charts, you may want to add the Chart Element control to your Quick Access Toolbar. That way, it will always be visible regardless of which Ribbon tab is selected. To add the control to your QAT, right-click it and choose Add To Quick Access Toolbar.

User Interface Choices for Modifying Chart Elements

You have two main ways of working with chart elements. You can use the Format dialog box or use the Ribbon and Mini toolbar.

Using the Format dialog box

When a chart element is selected, you can access the element's Format dialog box to format or set options for the element. Each chart element has a unique Format dialog box that contains controls specific to the element (although many Format dialog boxes have controls in common). To access the Format dialog box, use either of these methods:

- Right-click the chart element and choose Format xxxx from the shortcut menu (where xxxx is the name of the element).

- Select a chart element and then choose Chart Tools ➪ Format ➪ Current Selection ➪ Format Selection.

- Select a chart element and press Ctrl+1.

Any of these methods displays a tabbed Format dialog box that enables you to make many changes to the selected chart element. For example, Figure 20.3 shows the dialog box that appears when a chart's legend is selected.

TIP The Format dialog box is a modeless dialog box, so you can leave it open while you're working on a chart. If you select a different chart element, the Format dialog box changes to display the options appropriate for the new element.

FIGURE 20.3

Use the Format dialog box to set the properties of a selected chart element — in this case, the chart's legend.

Using the Ribbon and Mini Toolbar

When a chart element is selected, you can also use the commands on the Ribbon to change some aspects of its formatting. For example, to change the color of the bars in a column chart, use the commands in the Chart Tools ➪ Format ➪ Shape Styles group. For some types of chart element formatting, you need to leave the Chart Tools tab. For example, to adjust font-related properties, use the commands in the Home ➪ Font Group.

TIP   If you need to adjust a text element in a chart, it may be more efficient to right-click the element and use the Mini Toolbar that pop up.

The Ribbon controls do *not* comprise a comprehensive set of tools for chart elements. The Format dialog box presents many additional options. But then again, the Format dialog box is missing some formatting options. For example, if you want to apply Glow or Soft Edges formatting, you need to use the Ribbon commands.

Modifying the Chart Area

The *Chart Area* is an object that contains all other elements in the chart. You can think of it as a chart's master background or container.

The only modifications that you can make to the Chart Area are cosmetic. You can change its fill color, outline, or effects.

Note that if you set the Chart Area to use No Fill, the underlying cells are visible. Figure 20.4 shows a chart that uses No Fill and No Outline in its Chart Area. The Plot Area, Legend, and Chart Title *do* use a fill color. Adding a shadow to these other elements make them appear to be floating on the worksheet.

The Chart Area element also controls all the fonts used in the chart. For example, if you want to change every font in the chart, you don't need to format each text element separately. Just select the Chart Area and then make the change using the control on the Home ⇨ Font group or by using the Mini toolbar.

FIGURE 20.4

The Chart Area element uses No Fill, so the underlying cells are visible.

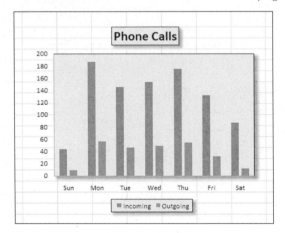

Resetting Chart Element Formatting

If you go overboard formatting a chart element, you can always reset it to its original state. Just select the element and choose Chart Tools ➪ Format ➪ Current Selection ➪ Reset to Match Style. Or, right-click the chart element and choose Reset To Match Style from the shortcut menu.

To reset all formatting changes in the entire chart, select the Chart Area before you issue the Reset to Match Style command.

Modifying the Plot Area

The *Plot Area* is the part of the chart that contains the actual chart.

> **TIP** If you set the Shape Fill property to No Fill, the Plot Area will be transparent. Therefore, the fill color applied to the Chart Area will show through.

You can move and resize the Plot Area if you like. Select the Plot Area and then drag a border to move it. To change the size of the Plot Area, drag on one of the corner handles.

Different chart types vary in how they respond to changes in the Plot Area dimensions. For example, you can't change the relative dimensions of the Plot Area of a pie chart or a radar chart. The Plot Area of these charts is always square. But with other chart types, you can change the aspect ratio of the Plot Area by changing either the height or the width.

Figure 20.5 shows a chart in which the Plot Area was resized in order to make room for a Shape that contains text.

FIGURE 20.5

Reducing the size of the Plot Area makes room for the Shape.

In some cases, the size of the Plot Area changes automatically when you adjust other elements of your chart. For example, if you add a legend to a chart, the size of the Plot Area may be reduced to accommodate the legend.

> **TIP** Changing the size and position of the Plot Area can have a dramatic effect on the overall look of your chart. When you're fine-tuning a chart, you'll probably want to experiment with various sizes and positions for the Plot Area.

Working with Chart Titles

A chart can have several different types of titles:

- Chart title
- Category (X) axis title
- Value (Y) axis title
- Second category (X) axis title
- Second value (Y) axis title
- Depth axis title (for true 3-D charts)

The number of titles that you can use depends on the chart type. For example, a pie chart supports only a chart title because it has no axes.

To add a chart title, activate the chart and choose Chart Tools ➪ Layout ➪ Labels ➪ Chart Title. To add a title to one or more of the axes, choose Chart Tools ➪ Layout ➪ Labels ➪ Axis Titles. These controls are drop-down lists, and each has several options.

After you add a title, you can replace the default text and drag the titles to a different position. However, you can't change the size of a title by dragging. The only way to change the size of a title is to change the font size.

The chart title or any of the axis titles can also use a cell reference. For example, you can create a link so the chart always displays the text contained in cell A1 as its title. To create a link, select the title, type an equal sign (=), and then point to the cell and press Enter. After you create the link, the Formula bar displays the cell reference when you select the title.

Adding Free-Floating Text to a Chart

Text in a chart is not limited to titles. In fact, you can add free-floating text anywhere you want. To do so, activate the chart and choose Chart Tools ➪ Layout ➪ Insert ➪ Text Box. Excel adds a text box to the chart. You can resize the text box, move it, change its formatting, and so on. You can also add a Shape to the chart and then add text to the Shape.

Many people prefer to use a text box in place of a chart's "official" title elements. Resizing a title is not possible (except by changing its font size). But if you use a text box, you can resize it by dragging its corners, change the text alignment, and even rotate it.

Working with the Legend

A chart's *legend* consists of text and keys that make it easier to identify the data series. A *key* is a small graphic that corresponds to the chart's series (one key for each series).

To add a legend to your chart, choose Chart Tools ➪ Layout ➪ Labels ➪ Legend. This drop-down control contains several options for the legend placement. After you've added a legend, you can drag it to move it anywhere you like.

> **TIP** If you move a legend from its default position, you may want to change the size of the Plot Area to fill in the gap left by the legend. Just select the Plot Area and drag a border to make it the desired size.

The quickest way to remove a legend is to select the legend and then press Delete.

You can select individual items within a legend and format them separately. For example, you may want to make the text bold to draw attention to a particular data series. To select an element in the legend, first select the legend and then click the desired element.

If you didn't include legend text when you originally selected the cells to create the chart, Excel displays Series 1, Series 2, and so on in the legend. To add series names, choose Chart Tools ➪ Design ➪ Select Data to display the Select Data Source dialog box (see Figure 20.6). Select the series name and click the Edit button. In the Edit Series dialog box, type the series name or enter a cell reference that contains the series name. Repeat for each series that needs naming.

In some cases, you may prefer to omit the legend and use callouts to identify the data series. Figure 20.7 shows a chart with no legend. Instead, it uses Shapes to identify each series. These Shapes are from the Callouts section of the Chart Tools ➪ Layout ➪ Insert ➪ Shapes gallery.

FIGURE 20.6

Use the Select Data Source dialog box to change the name of a data series.

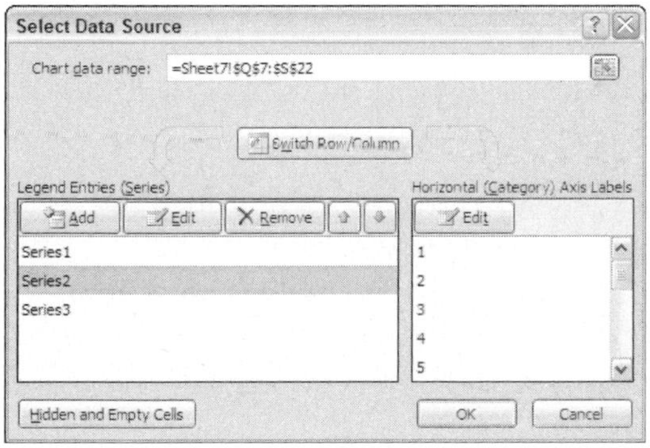

FIGURE 20.7

Using Shapes in lieu of a legend.

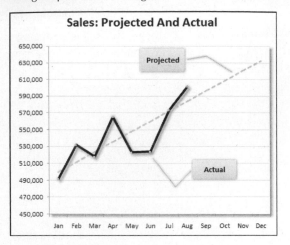

CROSS-REF For more information about using chart templates, see "Creating Chart Templates," later in this chapter.

Copying Chart Formatting

You created a killer chart and spent hours customizing it. Now you need to create another one just like it, but with a different set of data. What are your options? You have several choices:

- **Copy the formatting.** Create your new chart with the default formatting. Then select your original chart and choose Home ⇨ Clipboard ⇨ Copy (or press Ctrl+C). Click your new chart and choose Home ⇨ Clipboard ⇨ Paste ⇨ Paste Special. In the Paste Special dialog box, select the Formats option.

- **Copy the chart; change the data sources.** Press Ctrl while you click the original chart and drag. This creates an exact copy of your chart. Then choose Chart Tools ⇨ Design ⇨ Data ⇨ Select Data. In the Select Data Source dialog box, specify the data for the new chart.

- **Create a chart template.** Select your chart and then choose Chart Tools ⇨ Design ⇨ Type ⇨ Save As Template. Excel prompts you for a name. When you create your next chart, use this template as the chart type.

Working with Gridlines

Gridlines can help the viewer determine what the chart series represents numerically. Gridlines simply extend the tick marks on an axis. Some charts look better with gridlines; others appear more cluttered. Sometimes, horizontal gridlines alone are enough, although XY charts often benefit from both horizontal and vertical gridlines.

To add or remove gridlines, choose Chart Tools ⇨ Layout ⇨ Axes ⇨ Gridlines. This drop-down control contains options for all possible gridlines in the active chart.

NOTE Each axis has two sets of gridlines: major and minor. Major units display a label. Minor units are located between the labels.

To modify the color or thickness of a set of gridlines, click one of the gridlines and use the commands in the Chart Tools ⇨ Format ⇨ Shape Styles group.

If gridlines seem too overpowering, consider changing them to a lighter color or one of the dashed options.

Modifying the Axes

Charts vary in the number of axes that they use. Pie and doughnut charts have no axes. All 2-D charts have two axes (three, if you use a secondary-value axis; four, if you use a secondary-category axis in an XY chart). True 3-D charts have three axes.

Excel gives you a great deal of control over these axes, via the Format Axis dialog box. The content of this dialog box varies depending on the type of axis selected.

Value axis options

Figure 20.8 shows the Axis Options tab of the Format Axis dialog box when a Value Axis is selected. The other tabs in the dialog box deal with cosmetic formatting.

In the Axis Options tab, the four sets of option buttons at the top determine the scale of the axis (it's minimum, maximum, and intervals). By default, Excel determines these values based on the numerical range of the data, and the settings are set to Auto. You can override Excel's choice and set any or all of them to Fixed and then enter your own values.

Adjusting the scale of a Value Axis can dramatically affect the chart's appearance. Manipulating the scale, in some cases, can present a false picture of the data. Figure 20.9 shows two line charts,, which depict the same data. The top chart uses Excel's default axis scale values, which extend from 8,000 to 9,200. In the bottom chart, the Minimum scale value was set to 0, and the Maximum scale value was set to 10,000. The top chart makes the differences in the data seem more prominent. The lower chart gives the impression that there is not much change over time.

FIGURE 20.8

These options are available for a Value Axis.

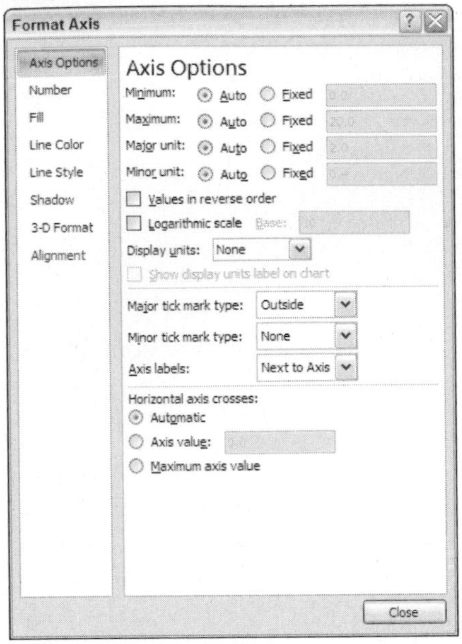

The actual scale that you use depends on the situation. There are no hard-and-fast rules regarding setting scale values, except that you shouldn't misrepresent data by manipulating the chart to prove a point that doesn't exist.

TIP If you're preparing several charts that use similarly scaled data, keeping the scales the same is a good idea so that the charts can be compared more easily.

Another option in the Format Axis dialog box is Values In Reverse Order. The top chart in Figure 20.10 uses default axis settings. The bottom chart uses the Values In Reverse Order option, which reverses the scale's direction. Notice that the Category Axis is at the top. If you would prefer that it remain at the bottom of the chart, select the Maximum Axis Value option for the Horizontal Axis Crosses setting.

If the values to be plotted cover a very large range, you may want to use a logarithmic scale for the Value Axis. A log scale is most often used for scientific applications. Figure 20.11 shows two charts. The top chart uses a standard scale, and the bottom chart uses a logarithmic scale.

NOTE The Base setting is 10, so each scale value in the chart is 10 times greater than the one below it. Increasing the major unit to 100 results in a scale in which each tick mark value is 100 times greater than the one below. You can specify a Base value between 2 and 1,000.

FIGURE 20.9

These two charts show the same data, but use a different Value Axis scales.

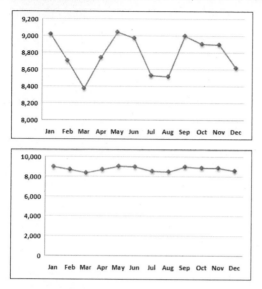

FIGURE 20.10

The bottom chart uses the Values In Reverse Order option.

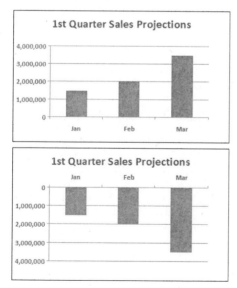

FIGURE 20.11

These charts display the same data, but the lower chart uses a logarithmic scale.

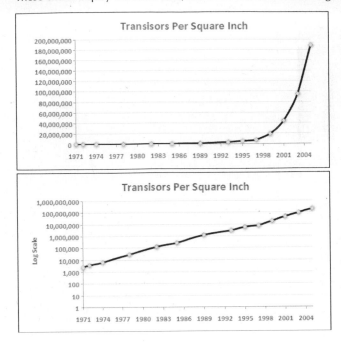

ON the CD-ROM   This workbook, log scale.xlsx, is available on the companion CD-ROM.

If your chart uses very large numbers, you may want to change the Display Units settings. Figure 20.12 shows a chart that uses very large numbers. The chart below uses the Display Units as Millions settings, with the option to Show Display Units Labels On Chart.

The Major and Minor Tick Mark options control how the tick marks are displayed. Major tick marks are the axis tick marks that normally have labels next to them. Minor tick marks are between the major tick marks.

Excel lets you position the axis labels at three different locations: Next To Axis, High, and Low. Each axis extends from -10 to +10. When you combine these settings with the Axis Crosses At option, you have a great deal of flexibility, as shown in Figure 20.13.

FIGURE 20.12

The lower chart uses display units of millions.

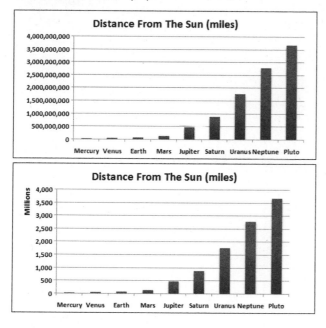

FIGURE 20.13

Various ways to display axis labels and crossing points.

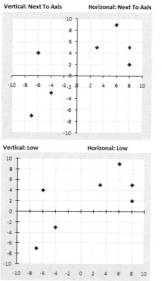
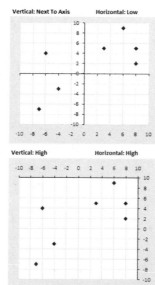

Category axis options

Figure 20.14 shows the Axis Options tab of the Format Axis dialog box when a Category Axis is selected. Some options are the same as those for a Value Axis.

FIGURE 20.14

These options are available for a Category Axis.

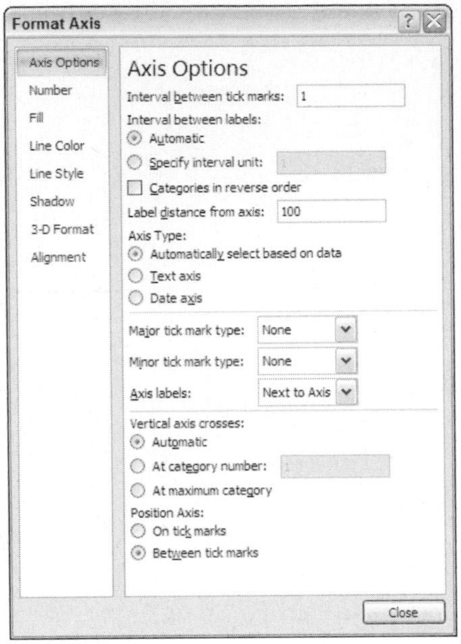

Excel chooses how to display category labels, but you can override its choice. Figure 20.15 shows a column chart with month labels. Excel displays the labels at an angle. If you make the chart wider, the labels will then appear horizontally.

You can adjust the Interval Between Labels settings to skip some labels and cause the text to display horizontally. Figure 20.16 shows the chart with an Interval Between Labels setting of 3.

When you create a chart, Excel recognizes whether your category axis contains date or time values. If so, it uses a time-based category axis. Figure 20.17 shows a simple example. Column A contains dates, and column B contains the values plotted in the column chart. The data consists of values for only 10 dates, yet Excel created the chart with 30 intervals on the category axis. It recognized that the category axis values were dates and created an equal-interval scale.

You can override Excel's decision to use a time-based category axis by choosing the Text Axis option for Axis Type. Using a time-based category axis presents a truer picture of the data.

FIGURE 20.15

Excel determines how to display Category Axis labels.

FIGURE 20.16

Changing the Interval Between Labels makes the labels display horizontally.

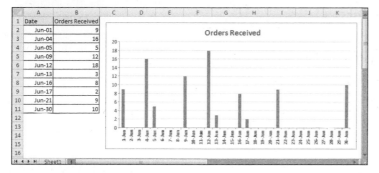

FIGURE 20.17

Excel recognizes dates and creates a time-based category axis.

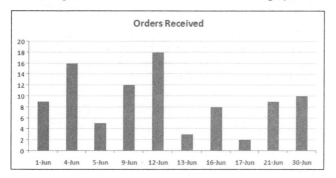

Don't Be Afraid to Experiment (but on a Copy)

I'll let you in on a secret: The key to mastering charts in Excel is experimentation, otherwise known as trial and error. Excel's charting options can be overwhelming, even to experienced users. This book doesn't even pretend to cover all the charting features. Your job, as a potential charting guru, is to dig deep and try out the various options in your charts. With a bit of creativity, you can create really original-looking charts.

After you've created a basic chart, you may want to make a copy of the chart for your experimentation. That way, if you mess it up, you can always revert to the original and start again. To make a copy of an embedded chart, press the Ctrl key while you click the chart and drag the mouse pointer to a new location. To make a copy of a chart sheet, press Ctrl while you click the sheet tab and drag it to a new location among the other tabs.

Working with Data Series

Every chart consists of one or more data series. This data translates into chart columns, bars, lines, pie slices, and so on. This section discusses some common operations that involve a chart's data series.

When you select a data series in a chart, Excel:

- Displays the series name in the Chart Elements control (located in the Chart Tools ⇨ Layout ⇨ Current Selection group).
- Displays the `Series` formula in the Formula bar.
- Highlights the cells used for the selected series by outlining them in color.

You can make changes to a data series by using the Ribbon or by using the Format Data Series dialog box. This dialog box varies, depending on the type of data series you're working on (column, line, pie, and so on).

Deleting a data series

To delete a data series in a chart, select the data series and press the Delete key. The data series disappears from the chart. The data in the worksheet, of course, remains intact.

NOTE You can delete all data series from a chart. If you do so, the chart appears empty. It retains its settings, however. Therefore, you can add a data series to an empty chart, and it again looks like a chart.

Adding a new data series to a chart

In some situations, you may need to add another data series to an existing chart. You can re-create the chart and include the new data series, but adding the data to the existing chart is usually easier, and your chart retains any customization that you've made.

Figure 20.19 shows a column chart that has two data series (Jan and Feb). The March figures just became available, and now the chart needs to be updated to include the new data.

FIGURE 20.18

This chart needs a new data series.

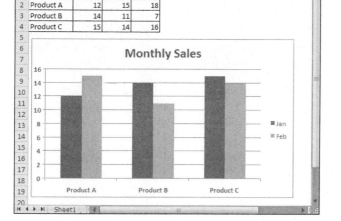

Excel provides two ways to add a new data series to a chart:

■ Activate the chart and choose Chart Tools ➪ Design ➪ Data ➪ Select Data. In the Select Data Source dialog box, click the Add button, and Excel displays the Edit Series dialog box. Specify the Series Name (as a cell reference or text) and the range that contains the Series Values.

■ Select the range to add and copy it to the Clipboard. Then activate the chart and press Ctrl+V to paste the data into the chart.

 **NOTE** In previous versions of Excel, you could add a new data series by selecting a range of data and "dragging" it into an embedded chart. Excel 2007 doesn't support that action.

Changing data used by a series

You may find that you need to modify the range that defines a data series. For example, you may need to add new data points or remove old ones from the data set. The following sections describe several ways to change the range used by a data series.

TIP An easy way to handle data ranges that change over time is to use a table as the data source. When you add rows to a table, the chart updates automatically.

Changing the data range by dragging the range outline

The easiest way to change the data range for a data series is to drag the range outline (this technique works only for embedded charts). When you select a series in a chart, Excel outlines the data range used by that series (see Figure 20.19 You can drag the small dot in the lower-right corner of the range outline to extend or contract the data series. Most of the time, you'll also need to adjust the range that contains the category labels as well.

FIGURE 20.19

Changing a chart's data series by dragging the range outline.

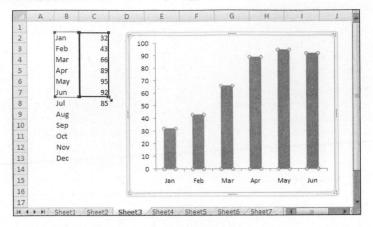

Using the Edit Series dialog box

Another way to update the chart to reflect a different data range is to use the Edit Series dialog box. A quick way to display this dialog box is to right-click the series in the chart and choose Select Data from the short-cut menu. Excel displays the Select Source Data dialog box. Select the data series in the list, and click Edit to display the Edit Series dialog box, shown in Figure 20.20

You can change the entire data range used by the chart by adjusting the range references in the Chart Data Range field. Or, select a Series from the list and click Edit to modify the selected series.

FIGURE 20.20

The Edit Series dialog box.

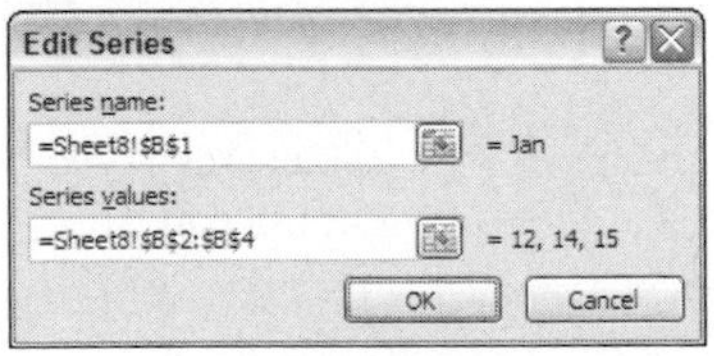

Editing the Series formula

Every data series in a chart has an associated `Series` formula, which appears in the Formula bar when you select a data series in a chart. If you understand how a `Series` formula is constructed, you can edit the range references in the `Series` formula directly to change the data used by the chart.

NOTE The `Series` formula is not a real formula: In other words, you can't use it in a cell, and you can't use worksheet functions within the Series formula. You can, however, edit the arguments in the `Series` formula.

A Series formula has the following syntax:

```
=SERIES(series_name, category_labels, values, order, sizes)
```

The arguments that you can use in the Series formula include

- **series_name:** (Optional) A reference to the cell that contains the series name used in the legend. If the chart has only one series, the name argument is used as the title. This argument can also consist of text in quotation marks. If omitted, Excel creates a default series name (for example, Series 1).

- **category_labels:** (Optional) A reference to the range that contains the labels for the category axis. If omitted, Excel uses consecutive integers beginning with 1. For XY charts, this argument specifies the X values. A noncontiguous range reference is also valid. The ranges' addresses are separated by commas and enclosed in parentheses. The argument could also consist of an array of comma-separated values (or text in quotation marks) enclosed in curly brackets.

- **values:** (Required) A reference to the range that contains the values for the series. For XY charts, this argument specifies the Y values. A noncontiguous range reference is also valid. The ranges addresses are separated by a comma and enclosed in parentheses. The argument could also consist of an array of comma-separated values enclosed in curly brackets.

- **order:** (Required) An integer that specifies the plotting order of the series. This argument is relevant only if the chart has more than one series. Using a reference to a cell is not allowed.

- **sizes:** (Only for bubble charts) A reference to the range that contains the values for the size of the bubbles in a bubble chart. A noncontiguous range reference is also valid. The ranges addresses are separated by commas and enclosed in parentheses. The argument can also consist of an array of values enclosed in curly brackets.

Range references in a Series formula are always absolute, and they always include the sheet name. For example:

```
=SERIES(Sheet1!$B$1,,Sheet1!$B$2:$B$7,1)
```

> **TIP** You can substitute range names for the range references. If you do so, Excel changes the reference in the Series formula to include the workbook. For example:

```
=SERIES(Sheet1!$B$1,,budget.xlsx!MyData,1)
```

Displaying data labels in a chart

Sometimes, you may want your chart to display the actual numerical values for each data point. You specify data labels by choosing Chart Tools ➪ Layout ➪ Labels ➪ Data Labels. This drop-down control contains several data label options.

Figure 20.21 shows a chart with data labels.

FIGURE 20.21

This chart uses data labels.

Use the Format Data Labels dialog box to customize the data labels. For example, you can include the series name and the category name along with the value.

The data labels are linked to the worksheet, so if your data changes, the labels also change. If you want to override the data label with other text, select the label and enter the new text.

> **TIP**
>
> Often, the data labels aren't positioned properly — for example, a label may be obscured by another data point. If you select an individual data label, you can drag the label to a better location.

As you work with data labels, you discover that the Excel data labels feature leaves a bit to be desired. For example, it would be nice to be able to specify an arbitrary range of text to be used for the data labels. This capability would be particularly useful in XY charts in which you want to identify each data point with a particular text item. Despite what must amount to thousands of requests, Microsoft still hasn't added this feature to Excel. You need to add data labels and then manually edit each label.

Handling missing data

Sometimes, data that you're charting may be missing one or more data points. As shown in Figure 20.22, Excel offers three ways to handle the missing data:

- **Gaps:** Missing data is simply ignored, and the data series will have a gap. This is the default.
- **Zero:** Missing data is treated as zero.
- **Connect With Line:** Missing data is interpolated — calculated by using data on either side of the missing point(s). This option is available only for line charts, area charts, and XY charts.

FIGURE 20.22

Three options for dealing with missing data.

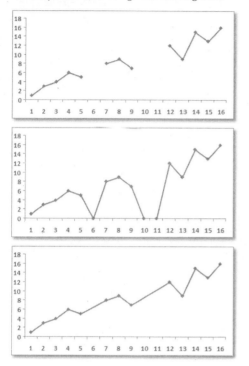

To specify how to deal with missing data for a chart, choose Chart Tools ➪ Design ➪ Data ➪ Select Data. In the Select Data Source, click the Hidden and Empty Cells button. Excel displays its Hidden and Empty Cell Settings dialog box. Make your choice in the dialog box. The option that you choose applies to the entire chart, and you can't set a different option for different series in the same chart.

 **TIP** Normally, a chart doesn't display data that's in a hidden row or columns. You can use the Hidden and Empty Cell Settings dialog box to force a chart to use hidden data.

Adding error bars

Some chart types support error bars. *Error bars* often are used to indicate "plus or minus" information that reflects uncertainty in the data. Error bars are appropriate only for area, bar, column, line, and XY charts.

To add error bars, select a data series and then choose Chart Tools ➪ Layout ➪ Analysis >>Error Bars. This drop-down control has several options. You can fine-tune the error bar settings using the Format Error Bars dialog box. The types of error bars are

- **Fixed value:** The error bars are fixed by an amount that you specify.
- **Percentage:** The error bars are a percentage of each value.

- **Standard Deviation(s):** The error bars are in the number of standard-deviation units that you specify. (Excel calculates the standard deviation of the data series.)
- **Standard Error:** The error bars are one standard error unit. (Excel calculates the standard error of the data series.)
- **Custom:** You set the error bar units for the upper or lower error bars. You can enter either a value or a range reference that holds the error values that you want to plot as error bars.

The chart shown in Figure 20.23 displays error bars based on percentage.

FIGURE 20.23

This line chart series displays error bars based on percentage.

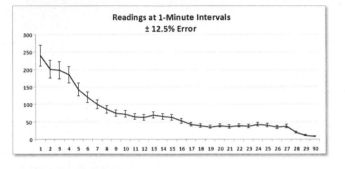

> **TIP** A data series in an XY chart can have error bars for both the X values and Y values.

Adding a trendline

When you're plotting data over time, you may want to plot a trendline that describes the data. A *trendline* points out general trends in your data. In some cases, you can forecast future data with trendlines. A single series can have more than one trendline.

To add a trendline, select the data series and choose Chart Tools ➪ Layout ➪ Analysis ➪ >Trendline. This drop-down control contains options for the type of trendline. The type of trendline that you choose depends on your data. Linear trends are most common, but some data can be described more effectively with another type.

Figure 20.24 shows an XY chart with a linear trendline and the (optional) equation for the trendline. The trendline describes the "best fit" of the height and weight data.

For more control over trendlines, use the Format Trendline dialog box. One option, Moving Average, is useful for smoothing out data that has a lot of variation (that is, "noisy" data).

The Moving Average option enables you to specify the number of data points to include in each average. For example, if you select 5, Excel averages every five data points. Figure 20.25 shows a chart that uses a moving average trendline.

FIGURE 20.24

This linear trendline forecasts sales for three additional time periods.

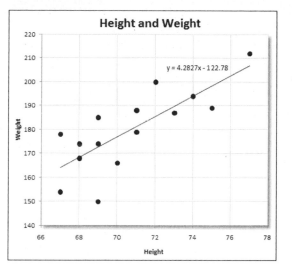

FIGURE 20.25

The dashed line displays a 10-interval moving average.

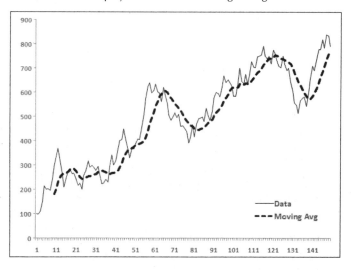

Modifying 3-D charts

3-D charts have a few additional elements that you can customize. For example, most 3-D charts have a floor and walls, and the true 3-D charts also have an additional axis. You can select these chart elements and format them to your liking using the Format dialog box.

One area in which 3-D charts differ from Excel's 2-D charts is in the perspective — or *viewpoint* — from which you see the chart. In some cases, the data may be viewed better if you change the order of the series.

Figure 20.26 shows two versions of 3-D column chart with two data series. The top chart is the original, and the bottom chart shows the effect of changing the series order. To change the series order, choose Chart Tools ➪ Design ➪ Data ➪ Select Data. In the Select Data Source dialog box, select a series and use the arrow buttons to change its order.

FIGURE 20.26

A 3-D column chart, before and after changing the series order.

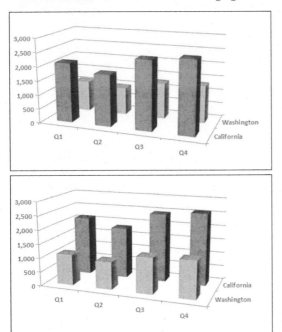

Fortunately, Excel allows you to change the viewing angle of 3-D charts. Doing so may reveal portions of the chart that are otherwise hidden. To rotate a 3-D chart, choose Chart Tools ➪ Layout ➪ Background ➪ 3-D Rotation, which displays the 3-D Rotation tab of the Format Chart Area dialog box. You can make your rotations and perspective changes by clicking the appropriate controls.

Figure 20.27 shows four different views of the same chart. As you can see, you can accidentally distort the chart to make it virtually worthless in terms of visualizing information.

FIGURE 20.27

Four different views of the same 3-D column chart.

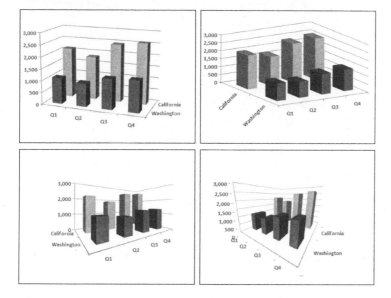

Creating combination charts

A *combination chart* is a single chart that consists of series that use different chart types. A combination chart may also include a second value axis. For example, you may have a chart that shows both columns and lines, with two value axes. The value axis for the columns is on the left, and the value axis for the line is on the right. A combination chart requires at least two data series.

Creating a combination chart simply involves changing one or more of the data series to a different chart type. Select the data series to change and then choose Chart Tools ➪ Design ➪ Type ➪ Change Chart Type. In the Change Chart Type dialog box, select the chart type that you want to apply to the selected series. Using a second Value Axis is optional.

NOTE If anything other than a series is selected when you issue the Chart Tools ➪ Design ➪ Type ➪ Change Chart Type, all the series in the chart change.

Figure 20.28 shows a column chart with two data series. The values for the Precipitation series are very low — so low that they're barely visible on the Value Axis scale. This is a good candidate for a combination chart.

The following steps describe how to convert this chart into a combination chart (column and line) that uses a second Value Axis.

1. **Select the Precipitation data series**
2. **Right-click and choose Format Data Series for the shortcut menu.**
3. **In the Format Data Series dialog box, click the Series Options tab and select the Secondary Axis option.**

4. With the Precipitation data series still selected, choose Chart Tools ➪ Design ➪ Type ➪ Change Chart Type.

5. In the Change Chart Type dialog box, select the Line type and click OK.

Figure 20.29 shows the modified chart. The Precipitation data appears as a line, and it uses the Value Axis on the right.

FIGURE 20.28

The Precipitation series is barely visible.

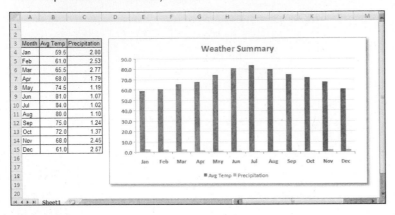

FIGURE 20.29

The Precipitation series is now visible.

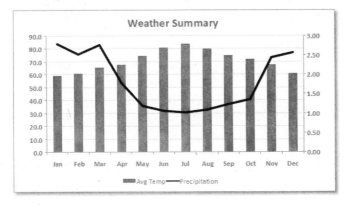

ON the CD-ROM This workbook is available on the companion CD-ROM. The filename is **weather combination chart.xlsx.**

In some cases, you can't combine chart types. For example, you can't create a combination chart that involves a bubble chart or a 3-D chart. If you choose an incompatible chart type for the series, Excel lets you know.

Figure 20.30 demonstrates just how far you can go with a combination chart. This chart combines five different chart types: Pie, Area, Column, Line, and XY. I can't think of any situation that would warrant such a chart, but it's an interesting demo.

FIGURE 20.30

A five-way combination chart.

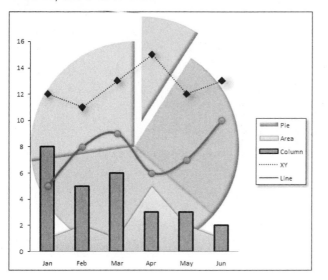

Displaying a data table

In some cases, you may want to display a *data table,* which displays the chart's data in tabular form, directly in the chart.

To add a data table to a chart, choose Chart Tools ➪ Layout ➪ Labels ➪ Data Table. This control is a drop-down list with a few options to choose from. For more options, use the Format Data Table dialog box. Figure 20.31 shows a chart with a data table.

Using a data table is probably best suited for charts on chart sheets. If you need to show the data used in an embedded chart, you can do so using data in cells, which provide you with a lot more flexibility in terms of formatting.

This combination chart includes a data table that displays the values of the data points.

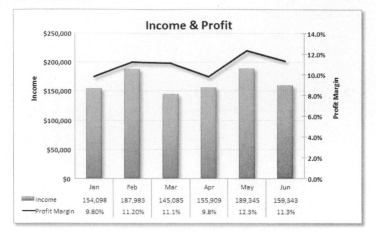

Creating Chart Templates

This section describes how to create your own custom chart templates. A template includes customized chart formatting and settings. When you create a new chart, you can choose to use your template rather than a built-in chart type.

If you find that you are continually customizing your charts in the same way, you can probably save some time by creating a template. Or, if you create lots of combination charts, you can create a combination chart template and avoid making the manual adjustments required for a combination chart.

To create a chart template:

1. **Create a chart to serve as the basis for your template.** The data you use for this chart is not critical; but for best results, it should be typical of the data that you'll eventually be plotting with your custom chart type.

2. **Apply any formatting and customizations that you like.** This step determines how the appearance of the charts created from the template.

3. **Activate the chart and choose Chart Tools ➪ Design ➪ Type ➪ Save As Template.** Excel displays its Save Chart Template dialog box.

4. **Provide a name for the template and click Save.**

> **NOTE** Chart templates, by default, are stored in the following directory:
>
>   C:\Documents And Settings\<user name>Application Data\
>   Microsoft\Templates\Charts

To create a chart based on a template:

1. **Select the data to be used in the chart.**

2. **Choose Insert ➪ Charts ➪ Other Charts ➪ All Chart Types.** Excel displays its Insert Chart dialog box.

3. **In the left side of the Insert Chart dialog box, select Templates.** Excel displays an icon for each custom template that has been created.

4. **Click the icon that represents the template you want to use and click OK.** Excel creates the chart based on the template you selected.

NOTE   You can also apply a template to an existing chart. Select the chart and use Chart Tools ⇨ Design ⇨ Change Chart Type.

Learning Some Chart-Making Tricks

This section describes some interesting (and perhaps useful) chart-making tricks. Some of these tricks use little-known features, and several tricks enable you to make charts that you may have considered impossible to create.

Creating picture charts

Excel makes it easy to incorporate a pattern, texture, or graphic file for elements in your chart. Figure 20.32 shows a chart that uses a photo as the background for a chart's Chart Area element.

FIGURE 20.32

The Chart Area contains a photo.

To display an image in a chart element, use the Fill tab in the element's Format dialog box. Select the Picture Or Texture Fill option and then click the button that corresponds to the image source (File, Clipboard, or ClipArt). If you use the Clipboard button, make sure that you've copied your image first. The other two options prompt you for the image.

Figure 20.33 shows two more examples: a pie chart that uses Office clipart as its fill, and a column chart that uses a Shape, which was inserted on a worksheet and then copied to the Clipboard.

ON the CD-ROM   The examples in this section are available on the companion CD-ROM. The filename is **picture charts.xlsx.**

Using images in a chart offers unlimited potential for creativity. The key, of course, is to resist the temptation to go overboard. A chart's primary goal is to convey information, not to impress the viewer with your artistic skills.

CAUTION Using images, especially photos, in charts can dramatically increase the size of your workbooks.

Creating a thermometer chart

You're probably familiar with a "thermometer" type display that shows the percentage of a task that's completed. Creating such a display in Excel is very easy. The trick involves creating a chart that uses a single cell (which holds a percentage value) as a data series.

Figure 20.34 shows a worksheet set up to track daily progress toward a goal: 1,000 new customers in a 15-day period. Cell B18 contains the goal value, and cell B19 contains a simple formula that calculates the sum. Cell B21 contains a formula that calculates the percent of goal:

```
=B19/B18
```

FIGURE 20.33

The top chart uses clipart, while the bottom chart uses a Shape that was copied to the Clipboard.

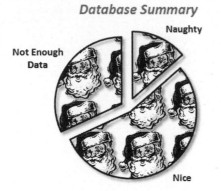

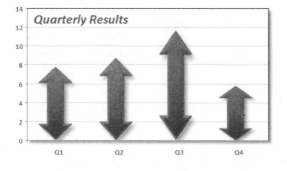

As you enter new data in column B, the formulas display the current results.

A workbook with this example is available on the companion CD-ROM. The filename is ther- mometer chart.xlsx.

To make the thermometer chart, select cell B21 and create a column chart from that single cell. Notice the blank cell above cell B21. Without this blank cell, Excel uses the entire data block for the chart, not just the single cell. Because B21 is isolated from the other data, only the single cell is used.

Other changes required:

- Select the horizontal category axis and press Delete to remove the category axis from the chart.
- Remove the legend.
- Add a text box, linked to cell B21 to display the percent accomplished.
- In the Format Data Series dialog box (Series Options tab), set the Gap width to 0, which makes the column occupy the entire width of the plot area.
- Select the Value Axis and display the Format Value Axis dialog box. In the Axis Options tab, set the Minimum to 0 and the Maximum to 1.

Make any other cosmetic adjustments to get the look you desire.

FIGURE 20.34

This chart displays progress toward a goal.

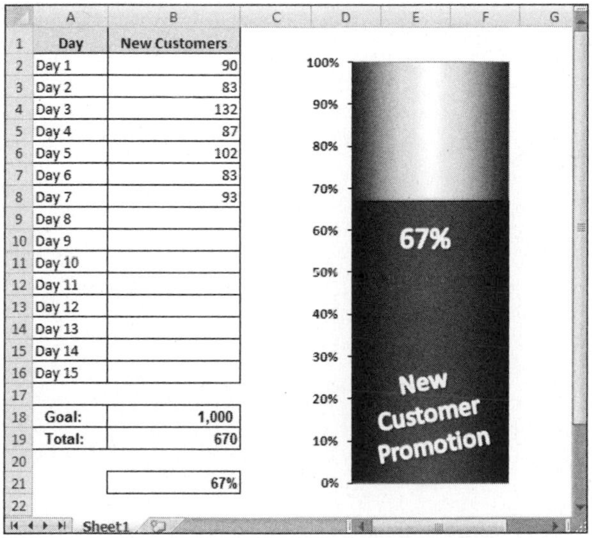

Creating a gauge chart

Figure 20.35 shows another chart based on a single cell. It's a pie chart set up to resemble a gauge. Although this chart displays only one value (entered in cell B1), it actually uses three data points (in A4:A6).

One slice of the pie — the slice at the bottom — always consists of 50 percent, and that slice is hidden. (The slice uses No Fill and No Outline.) The other two slices are apportioned based on the value in cell B1. The formula in cell 44 is

```
=MIN(B1,100%)/2
```

This formula uses the MIN function to display the smaller of two values: either the value in cell B1 or 100 percent. It then divides this value by 2 because only the top half of the pie is relevant. Using the MIN function prevents the chart from displaying more than 100 percent.

The formula in cell A5 simply calculates the remaining part of the pie — the part to the right of the gauge's needle:

FIGURE 20.35

This chart resembles a speedometer gauge and displays a value between 0 and 100 percent.

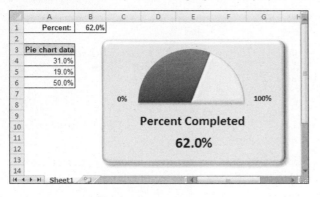

```
=50%-A4
```

The chart's title was moved below the half-pie. The chart also contains a text box, linked cell B1, that displays the percent completed.

Displaying conditional colors in a column chart

You may have noticed that the Fill tab of the Format Data Series dialog box has an option labeled Vary Colors By Point. This option simply uses more colors for the data series. Unfortunately, the colors aren't related to the values of the data series.

This section describes how to create a column chart in which the color of each column depends on the value that it's displaying. Figure 20.36 shows such a chart (it's more impressive when you see it in color). The data used to create the chart is in range A1:F14.

FIGURE 20.36

The color of the column depends varies with the value.

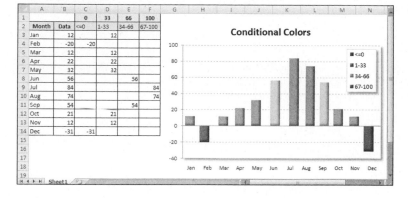

A workbook with this example is available on the companion CD-ROM. The filename is **conditional colors.xlsx.**

This chart displays four data series, but some data is missing for each series. The data for the chart is entered in column B. Formulas in columns C:F determine which series the number belongs to by referencing the bins in Row 1. For example, the formula in cell C3 is

```
=IF(B3<=$C$1,B3,"")
```

If the value in column B is less than the value in cell C1, then the value goes in this column. The formulas are set up such that a value in column B goes into only one column in the row.

The formula in cell D3 is a bit more complex because it must determine whether cell C3 is greater than the value in cell C1 and less than or equal to the value in cell D1:

```
=IF(AND($B3>C$1,$B3<=D$1),$B3,"")
```

The four data series are overlaid on top of each other in the chart. The trick involves setting the Series Overlap value to a large number. This setting determines the spacing between the series. Use the Series Options tab of the Format Data Series dialog box to adjust this setting.

NOTE Series Overlap is a single setting for the chart. If you change the setting for one series, the other series change to the same value.

Creating a comparative histogram

With a bit of creativity, you can create charts that you may have considered impossible. For example, Figure 20.37 shows a chart sometimes referred to as a *comparative histogram chart.* Such charts often display population data.

A workbook with this example is available on the companion CD-ROM. The filename is **comparative histogram.xlsx.**

FIGURE 20.37

A comparative histogram.

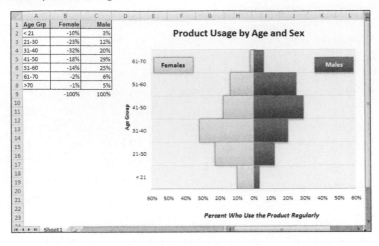

Here's how to create the chart:

1. **Enter the data in A1:C8, as shown in Figure 20.38.** Notice that the values for females are entered as negative values, which is very important.

2. **Select A1:C8 and create a bar chart.** Use the subtype labeled Clustered Bar.

3. **Select the horizontal axis and display the Format Axis dialog box.**

4. **Click the Number tab and specify the following custom number format:**

   0%;0%;0%

   This custom format eliminates the negative signs in the percentages.

5. **Select the vertical axis and display the Format Axis dialog box.**

6. **In the Axis Options tab, set all tick marks to None and set the Axis Labels option to Low.** This setting keeps the vertical axis in the center of the chart but displays the axis labels at the left side.

7. **Select either of the data series and display the Format Data Series dialog box.**

8. **In the Series Options tab, set the Series Overlap to 100% and the Gap Width to 0%.**

9. **Delete the legend and add two text boxes to the chart (Females and Males) to substitute for the legend.**

10. **Apply other formatting and labels as desired.**

Creating a Gantt chart

A *Gantt chart* is a horizontal bar chart often used in project management applications. Although Excel doesn't support Gantt charts per se, creating a simple Gantt chart is fairly easy. The key is getting your data set up properly.

Figure 20.38 shows a Gantt chart that depicts the schedule for a project, which is in the range A2:C13. The horizontal axis represents the total time span of the project, and each bar represents a project task. The viewer can quickly see the duration for each task and identify overlapping tasks.

ON the CD-ROM   A workbook with this example is available on the companion CD-ROM. The filename is gantt chart.xlsx.

Column A contains the task name, column B contains the corresponding start date, and column C contains the duration of the task, in days.

Follow these steps to create this chart:

1. **Select the range A2:C13, and create a Stacked Bar Chart.**
2. **Delete the legend.**
3. **Select the category (vertical) axis and display the Format Axis dialog box.**
4. **In the Format Axis dialog box, specify Categories In Reverse Order to display the tasks in order, starting at the top.** Choose Horizontal Axis Crosses At Maximum Category to display the dates at the bottom.
5. **Select the Start Date data series and display the Format Data Series dialog box.**
6. **In the Format Data Series dialog box, click the Series Options tab and set the Series Overlap to 100%. Click the Fill tab, and specify No Fill.** Click the Border Color tab and specify No Line. These steps effectively hide the data series.
7. **Select the value (horizontal) axis and display the Format Axis dialog box.**
8. **In the Format Axis dialog box, adjust the Minimum and Maximum settings to accommodate the dates that you want to display on the axis.** Unfortunately, you must enter these values as date serial numbers, not actual dates. In this example, the Minimum is 39181 (April 9, 2007) and the Maximum is 39261 (June 28, 2007). Specify 7 for the Major Unit, to display one-week intervals. Use the number tab to specify a date format for the axis labels.
9. **Apply other formatting as desired.**

FIGURE 20.38

You can create a simple Gantt chart from a bar chart.

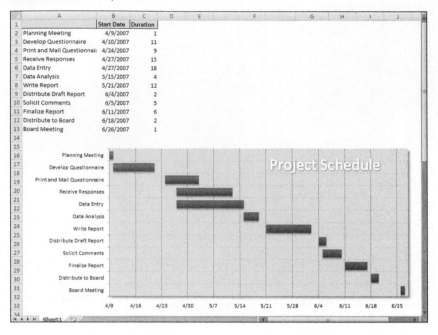

Plotting mathematical functions with one variable

An XY chart is useful for plotting various mathematical and trigonometric functions. For example, Figure 20.39 shows a plot of the SIN function. The charts plots y for values of x (expressed in radians) from –5 to +5 in increments of 0.5. Each pair of x and y values appears as a data point in the chart, and the points connect with a line.

The function is expressed as:

```
y = SIN(x)
```

The corresponding formula in cell B2 (which is copied to the cells below) is

```
=SIN(A2)
```

ON the CD-ROM   The companion CD-ROM contains a general-purpose single-variable plotting application. The file is named **function plot 2D.xlsx.**

FIGURE 20.39

This chart plots the SIN(x).

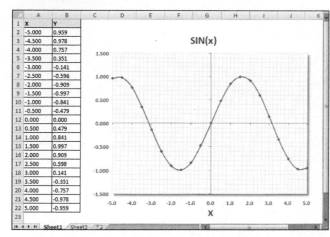

Plotting mathematical functions with two variables

The preceding section describes how to plot functions that use a single variable (x). You also can plot functions that use two variables. For example, the following function calculates a value of z for various values of two variables (x and y):

```
z = SIN(x)*COS(y)
```

Figure 20.40 shows a surface chart that plots the value of z for 21 x values ranging from 1 to 4, and for 21 y values ranging from 1 to 4. Both x and y use an increment of 0.15.

The formula in cell B2, copied across and down, is

```
=SIN($A2*COS(B$1))
```

 The companion CD-ROM contains a general–purpose, two-variable plotting application. The file is named **function plot 3D.xlsm.** This workbook contains a few simple VBA macros to allow you to change the chart's rotation and elevation.

FIGURE 20.40

Using a surface chart to plot a function with two variables.

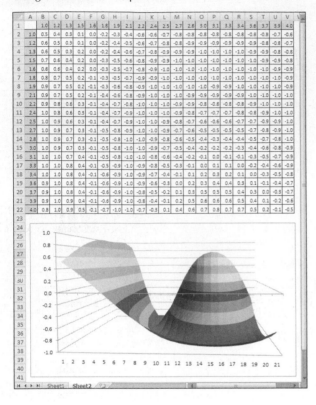

Visualizing Data Using Conditional Formatting

This chapter explores conditional formatting, one of Excel's most versatile features. You can apply conditional formatting to a cell so that the cells look different, depending on its content.

Conditional formatting has improved significantly in Excel 2007, and it's now a useful tool for visualizing numeric data. In some cases, you may be able to use conditional formatting in lieu of a chart.

About Conditional Formatting

Conditional formatting enables you to apply cell formatting selectively and automatically, based on the contents of the cells. For example, you can set things up so that all negative values in a range have a light-yellow background color. When you enter or change a value in the range, Excel examines the value and checks the conditional formatting rules for the cell. If the value is negative, the background is shaded. If not, no formatting is applied.

Conditional formatting is a useful way to quickly identify erroneous cell entries or cells of a particular type. You can use a format (such as bright-red cell shading) to make particular cells easy to identify.

Figure 21.1 shows a worksheet with nine ranges, each with a different type of conditional formatting rule applied. Here's a brief explanation of each:

- **Greater than 10:** Values greater than 10 are highlighted with a different background color. This rule is just one of many numeric value related rules that you can apply.

- **Above average:** Values that are higher than the average value are highlighted.

- **Duplicate values:** Values that appear more than one time are highlighted.

IN THIS CHAPTER

An overview of Excel's conditional formatting feature

How to use the graphical conditional formats

Examples of using conditional formatting formulas

Tips for using conditional formatting

- **Words that contain X:** If the cell contains X (upper or lower case), the cell is highlighted.

- **Data bars:** Each cell displays a horizontal bar, proportional to its value.

- **Color Scale:** The background color varies, depending on the value of the cells. You can choose from several different color scales or create your own.

- **Icon Set:** One of many icon sets. It displays a small graphic in the cell. The graphic varies, depending on the cell value.

- **Icon Set:** Another icon set.

- **Custom rule:** The rule for this checkerboard pattern is based on a formula:

  `=MOD(ROW(),2)=MOD(COLUMN(),2)`

FIGURE 21.1

This worksheet demonstrates a few conditional formatting rules.

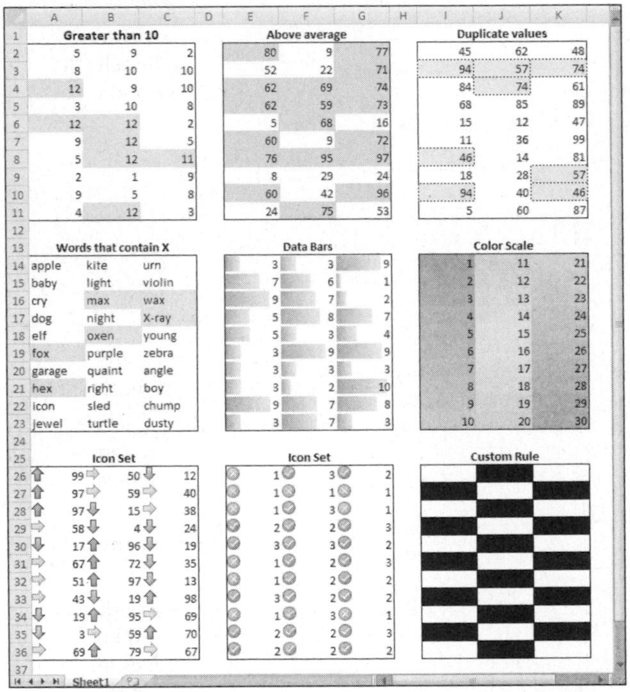

Specifying Conditional Formatting

To apply a conditional formatting rule to a cell or range, select the cells and then use one of the commands on the Home ➪ Styles ➪ Conditional Formatting drop-down to specify a rule. The choices are

- **Highlight Cell Rules:** Examples rules include highlighting cells that are greater than a particular value, between two values, contain specific text string, or are duplicated.

- **Top Bottom Rules:** Examples include highlighting the top 10 items, the items in the bottom 20 percent, and items that are above average.
- **Data Bars:** Applies graphic bars directly in the cells, proportional to the cell's value.
- **Color Scales:** Applies background color, proportional to the cell's value.
- **Icon Sets:** Displays icons directly in the cells. The icons depend on the cell's value.
- **New Rule:** Enables you to specify other conditional formatting rules, including rules based on a logical formula.
- **Clear Rules:** Deletes all the conditional formatting rules from the selected cells.
- **Manage Rules:** Displays the Conditional Formatting Rules Manager dialog box, in which you create new conditional formatting rules, edit rules, or delete rules.

Formatting types you can apply

When you select a conditional formatting rule, Excel displays a dialog box that's specific to that rule. These dialog boxes have one thing in a common: a drop-down list with common formatting suggestions. Figure 21.2 shows the dialog box that appears when you choose Home ➪ Styles ➪ Conditional Formatting ➪ Highlight Cells Rules ➪ Between. This particular rule applies the formatting if the value in the cell falls between two specified values. In this case, you enter the two values (or enter cell references), and then use the drop-down control to choose the type of formatting to display if the condition is met.

Excel 2007 Improvements

If you've used conditional formatting in a previous version of Excel, you'll find lots of improvements in Excel 2007, and the feature is now much easier to use:

- In the past, it was far too easy to accidentally wipe out conditional formatting by copying and pasting a range of cells to cells that contain conditional formatting. This problem has been corrected in Excel 2007.
- Excel 2007 includes conditional formatting visualizations based on a range of data. These formatting rules that previously required a formula are now built in. Improvements include visualizations include data bars, color scales, and icon sets.
- You're no longer limited to three conditional formatting rules per cell. In fact, you can specify any number of rules.
- In the past, if more than one conditional formatting rule evaluated to true, only the first conditional format was applied. In Excel 2007, all the format rules are applied. For example, assume that you have a cell with two rules: One rule makes the cell italic, and another rules makes the background color green. If both conditions are true, both formats are applied. When conflicts arise, (for example, red background versus green background), the first rule is used.
- Excel 2007 allows number formatting to result from conditional formatting
- In previous versions, a conditional formatting formula could not reference cells in a different worksheet. Excel 2007 removes that restriction.

FIGURE 21.2

One of several different conditional formatting dialog boxes.

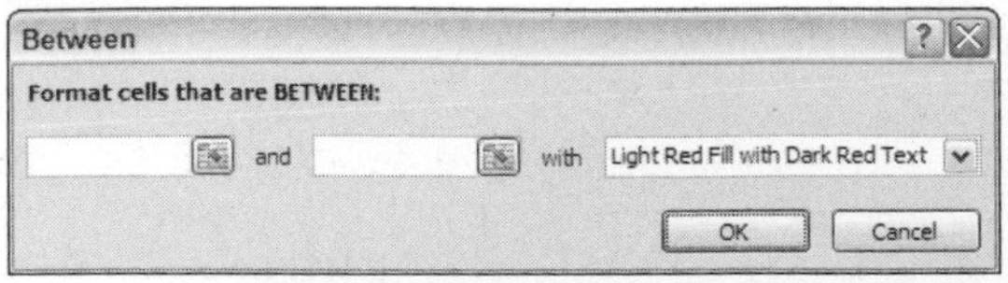

The formatting suggestions in the drop-down control are just a few of thousands of different formatting combinations. In most cases, none of Excel's suggestions is what you want, so you choose the Custom Format option to display the Format Cells dialog box. You can specify the format in any or all of the four tabs: Number, Font, Border, and Fill.

NOTE The Format Cells dialog box used for conditional formatting is a modified version of the standard Format Cells dialog box. It doesn't have the Number, Alignment, and Protection tabs; and some of the Font formatting options are disabled. The dialog box also includes a Clear button that clears any formatting already selected.

Making your own rules

For do-it-yourself types, Excel provides the New Formatting Rule dialog box, shown in Figure 21.3. Access this dialog box by choosing Home ➪ Styles ➪ Conditional Formatting ➪ New Rules.

The New Formatting Rule dialog box lets you recreate all the conditional format rules available via the Ribbon, as well as new rules.

FIGURE 21.3

Use the New Formatting Rule dialog box to create your own conditional formatting rules.

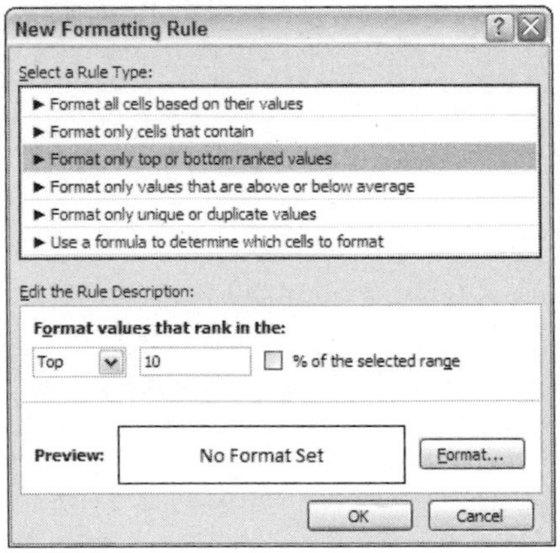

First, select a general rule type from the list at the top of the dialog box. The bottom part of the dialog box varies, depending on your selection at the top. After you specify the rule, click the Format button to specify the type of formatting to apply if the condition is met. An exception is the first rule type, which doesn't have a Format button (it uses graphics rather than cell formatting).

Following is a summary of the rule types:

- **Format all cells based on their values:** Use this rule type to create rules that display data bars, color scales, or icon sets.

- **Format only cells that contain:** Use this rule type to create rules that format cells based on mathematical comparisons (greater than, less than, greater than or equal to, less than or equal to, equal to, not equal to, between, not between). You can also create rules based on text, dates, blanks, nonblanks, and errors. This rule type is very similar to how conditional formatting was set up in previous versions of Excel.

- **Format only top or bottom ranked values:** Use this rule type to create rules that involve identifying cells in the top n, top n percent, bottom n, and bottom n percent.

- **Format only values that are above or below average:** Use this rule type to create rules that identify cells that are above average, below average, or within a specified standard deviation from the average.

- **Format only unique or duplicate values:** Use this rule type to create rules that format unique or duplicate values in a range.

- **Use a formula to determine which cells to format:** Use this rule type to create rules based on a logical formula. See "Formula-Based Conditions," later in this chapter.

Conditional Formats That Use Graphics

This section describes the three conditional formatting options that are new to Excel 2007: data bars, color scales, and icons sets. These types of conditional formatting can be useful for visualizing the values in a range.

Using data bars

The *data bars conditional format* displays horizontal bars directly in the cell. Length of the bar is based on the value of the cell, relative to the other values in the range.

A data bar example

Figure 21.4 shows a simple example of data bars. It's a list of customers and sales amounts. I applied data bar conditional formatting to the values in column B. You can tell at a glance where the higher values are.

ON the CD-ROM The examples in the section are available on the companion CD-ROM. The workbook is named **data bars examples.xlsx.**

FIGURE 21.4

The length of the data bars is proportional to the value in the cell.

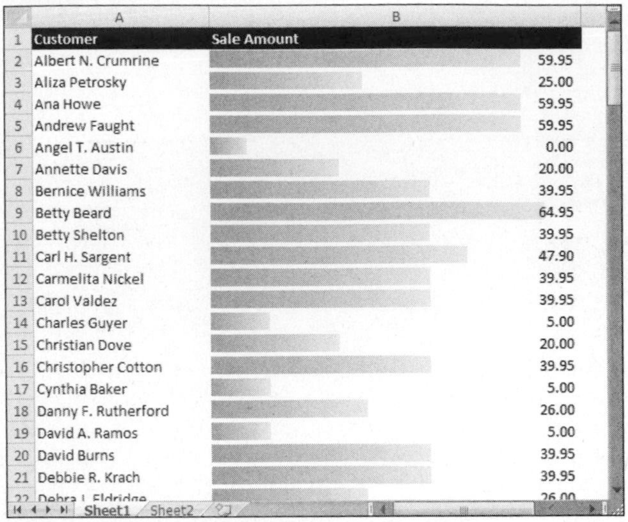

	A	B
1	Customer	Sale Amount
2	Albert N. Crumrine	59.95
3	Aliza Petrosky	25.00
4	Ana Howe	59.95
5	Andrew Faught	59.95
6	Angel T. Austin	0.00
7	Annette Davis	20.00
8	Bernice Williams	39.95
9	Betty Beard	64.95
10	Betty Shelton	39.95
11	Carl H. Sargent	47.90
12	Carmelita Nickel	39.95
13	Carol Valdez	39.95
14	Charles Guyer	5.00
15	Christian Dove	20.00
16	Christopher Cotton	39.95
17	Cynthia Baker	5.00
18	Danny F. Rutherford	26.00
19	David A. Ramos	5.00
20	David Burns	39.95
21	Debbie R. Krach	39.95
22	Debra L Eldridge	26.00

Sheet1 / Sheet2

TIP The differences among the bar lengths become more prominent when you increase the column width.

Excel provides quick access to six data bar colors via the Home ➪ Styles ➪ Conditional Formatting ➪ Data Bars command. For additional choices, click the More Rules option, which displays the New Formatting Rule dialog box. Use this dialog box to:

- Show the bar only (hide the numbers)
- Adjust how the bars relate to the values (use the Type and Value controls)
- Change the color of the bars

NOTE Data bars are always displayed as a color gradient (from dark to light), and you can't change the display style. Also, the colors used are not theme colors. If you apply a new document theme, the data bar colors do not change.

If you make adjustments in this dialog box, you can use the Preview button to see the formats before you commit to them with the OK button.

NOTE You may notice something odd about the data bars in Figure 21.4. Contrary to what you may expect, a cell with a zero value displays a data bar. Data bar conditional formatting always displays a bar for every cell, even for zero values. The smallest value in the range always has a bar length equal to 10 percent of the cell's width. Unfortunately, Excel provides no direct way to modify the minimum percent setting. But, if you're familiar with VBA, you can use a statement like the following to set the minimum display width for a range that uses conditional formatting data bars:

```
Range("B2:B123").FormatConditions(1).PercentMin = 1
```

After this statement is executed, the minimum value in the range will display a bar length equal to 1 percent of the cell's width — and zero value cells will not display a data bar.

Using data bars in lieu of a chart

Using the data bars conditional formatting can sometimes serve as a quick alternative to creating a chart. Figure 21.5 shows a three-column table of data, with data bars applied in the third column. The third column of the table contains references to the values in the second column. The conditional formatting in the third column uses the Show Bars Only option.

FIGURE 21.5

This table uses data bars conditional formatting.

Month	Incoming Calls	Chart
January	2,984	
February	3,683	
March	4,123	
April	4,092	
May	4,532	
June	3,194	
July	2,765	
August	2,893	
September	4,256	
October	3,983	
November	4,234	
December	6,233	
Total Calls	46,972	

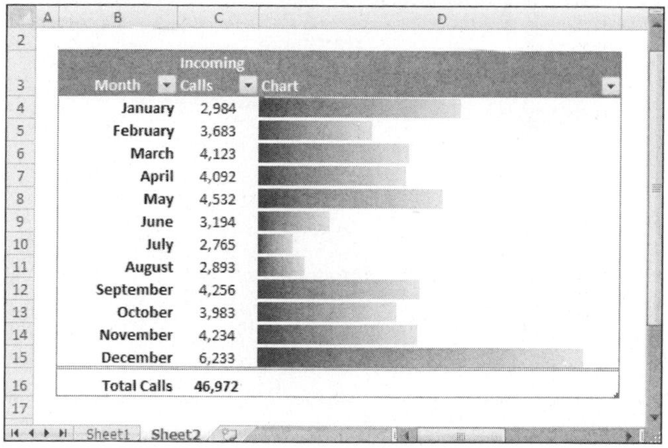

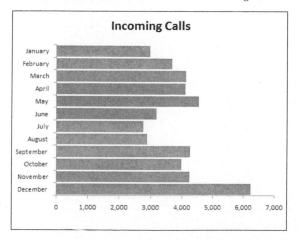

Figure 21.6 shows an actual bar chart created from the same data. The bar chart takes about the same amount of time to create and is a lot more flexible. But for a quick and dirty chart, data bars are a good option — especially when you need to create several such charts.

FIGURE 21.6

A real Excel bar chart (not conditional formatting data bars).

Using color scales

The *color scale conditional formatting option* varies the background color of a cell based on the cell's value, relative to other cells in the range.

A color scale example

Figure 21.7 shows a range of cells that use color scale conditional formatting. It depicts the number of employees on each day of the year. This is a 3-color scale that uses red for the lowest value, yellow for the midpoint, and green for the highest value. Values in between are displayed using a color within the gradient.

ON the CD-ROM **This workbook, named daily staffing level.xlsx, is available on the companion CD-ROM.**

Excel provides four 2-color scale presets and four 3-color scales presets, which you can apply to the selected range by choosing Home ➪ Styles ➪ Conditional Formatting ➪ Color Scales.

To customize the colors and other options, choose Home ➪ Styles ➪ Conditional Formatting ➪ Color Scales ➪ More Rules. This command displays the New Formatting Rule dialog box, shown in Figure 21.8.

FIGURE 21.7

A range that uses color scale conditional formatting.

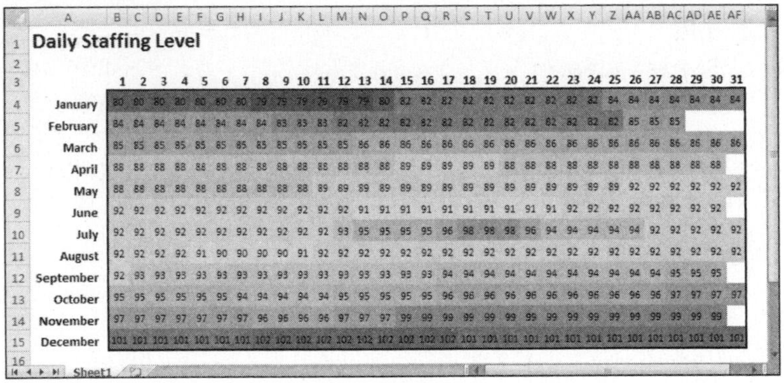

	1	2	3	4	5	6	7	8	9	10	11	12	13	14	15	16	17	18	19	20	21	22	23	24	25	26	27	28	29	30	31
January	80	80	80	80	80	80	80	79	79	79	79	79	79	80	82	82	82	82	82	82	82	82	82	82	84	84	84	84	84	84	84
February	84	84	84	84	84	84	84	84	83	83	83	82	82	82	82	82	82	82	82	82	82	82	82	82	82	85	85	85			
March	85	85	85	85	85	85	85	85	85	85	85	85	86	86	86	86	86	86	86	86	86	86	86	86	86	86	86	86	86	86	86
April	88	88	88	88	88	88	88	88	88	88	88	88	88	88	89	89	89	89	89	88	88	88	88	88	88	88	88	88	88	88	
May	88	88	88	88	88	88	88	88	88	88	89	89	89	89	89	89	89	89	89	89	89	89	89	89	89	92	92	92	92	92	92
June	92	92	92	92	92	92	92	92	92	92	92	92	91	91	91	91	91	91	91	91	91	91	92	92	92	92	92	92	92	92	
July	92	92	92	92	92	92	92	92	92	92	92	93	95	95	95	95	96	98	98	98	96	94	94	94	94	94	92	92	92	92	92
August	92	92	92	92	91	90	90	90	90	91	92	92	92	92	92	92	92	92	92	92	92	92	92	92	92	92	92	92	92	92	92
September	92	93	93	93	93	93	93	93	93	93	93	93	93	93	93	93	94	94	94	94	94	94	94	94	94	94	94	95	95	95	
October	95	95	95	95	95	95	94	94	94	94	94	95	95	95	95	95	96	96	96	96	96	96	96	96	96	96	96	97	97	97	97
November	97	97	97	97	97	97	97	96	96	96	96	97	97	97	99	99	99	99	99	99	99	99	99	99	99	99	99	99	99	99	
December	101	101	101	101	101	101	101	102	102	102	102	102	102	102	102	102	102	101	101	101	101	101	101	101	101	101	101	101	101	101	101

FIGURE 21.8

Use the New Formatting Rule dialog box to customize a color scale.

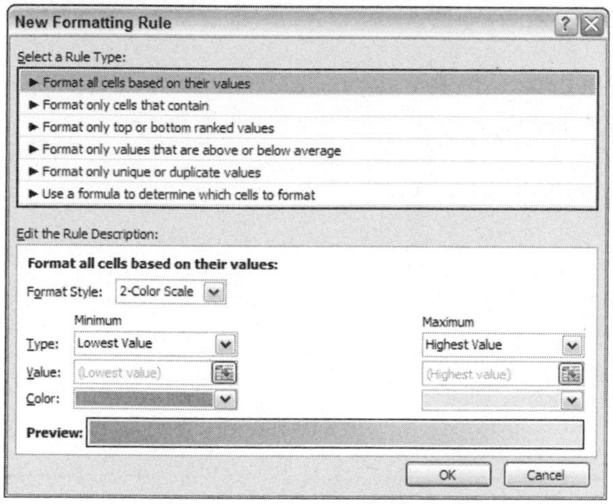

New Formatting Rule	? X

Select a Rule Type:

▶ Format all cells based on their values
▶ Format only cells that contain
▶ Format only top or bottom ranked values
▶ Format only values that are above or below average
▶ Format only unique or duplicate values
▶ Use a formula to determine which cells to format

Edit the Rule Description:

Format all cells based on their values:

Format Style: 2-Color Scale

	Minimum		Maximum	
Type:	Lowest Value		Highest Value	
Value:	(Lowest value)		(Highest value)	
Color:				

Preview:

OK Cancel

An extreme color scale example

It's important to understand that color scale conditional formatting uses a gradient. For example, if you format a range using a 2-color scale, you will get a lot more than two colors. You'll get colors with the gradient between the two specified colors.

Figure 21.9 shows an extreme example that uses color scale conditional formatting on a range of 10,000 cells (100 rows X 100 columns). The worksheet is zoomed down to 20% to display a very smooth 3-color gradient. The range contains formulas like this one, in cell C5:

=SIN($A2)+COS(B$1)Values in column A and row 1 range from 0 to 4.0, in increments of 0.04.

When viewed on your screen, the result is stunning (it loses a lot when converted to greyscale).

 This workbook, named **extreme color scale.xlsx,** is available on the companion CD-ROM.

NOTE You can't hide the cell contents when using a color scale rule, so I formatted the cells using this custom number format:

;;;

FIGURE 21.9

This worksheet, which uses color scale conditional formatting, is zoomed to 20%.

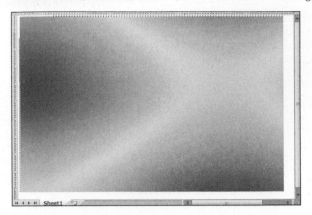

Using Icon Sets

Yet another conditional formatting option is to display an icon in the cell. The icon displayed depends on the value of the cells.

To assign an icon set to a range, select the cells and choose Home ➪ Styles ➪ Conditional Formatting ➪ Icon Sets. Excel provides 17 icon sets to choose from (and you can't create your set of icons). The number of icons in the sets ranges from 3 to 5.

An icon set example

Figure 21.10 shows a simple example that uses the icon set named Three Symbols (Uncircled). The symbols graphically depict the status of each project, based on the value in column C.

ON the CD-ROM All the icon set examples in this section are available on the companion CD-ROM. The work-book is named **icon set examples.xlsx.**

FIGURE 21.10

Using an icon set to indicate the status of projects.

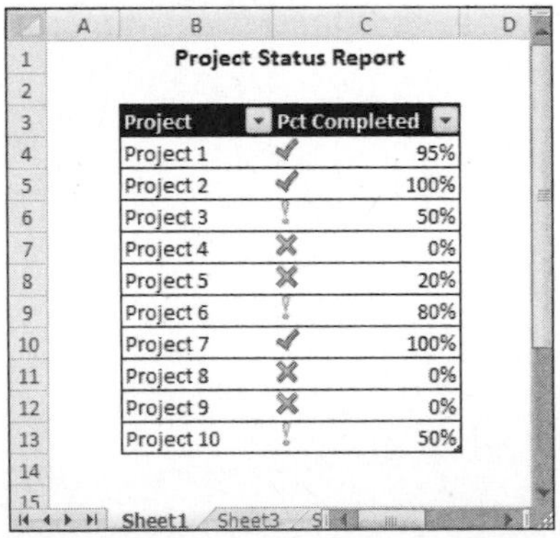

	Project	Pct Completed
1	Project Status Report	
3	Project	Pct Completed
4	Project 1	95%
5	Project 2	100%
6	Project 3	50%
7	Project 4	0%
8	Project 5	20%
9	Project 6	80%
10	Project 7	100%
11	Project 8	0%
12	Project 9	0%
13	Project 10	50%

By default, the symbols are assigned using percentiles. For a 3-symbol set, the items are grouped into three percentiles. For a 4-symbol set, they're grouped into 4 percentiles. And for a 5-symbol set, the items are grouped into five percentiles.

If you would like more control over how the icons are assigned, choose Home ➪ Styles ➪ Conditional Formatting ➪ Icon Sets ➪ More Rules to display the New Formatting Rule dialog box. Figure 21.11 shows how to modify the icon set rules such that only projects that are 100% completed get the check mark icons. Projects which are 0% completed get the X icon. All other projects get the exclamation point icon.

Figure 21.12 shows the task list after making this change.

FIGURE 21.11

Changing the icon assignment rule.

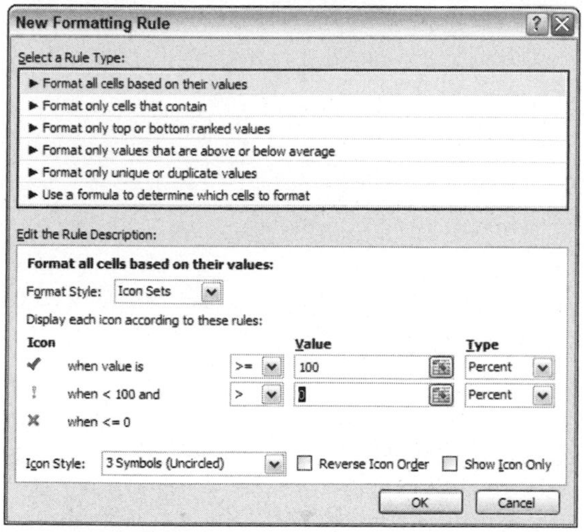

FIGURE 21.12

Using a customized icon set to indicate the status of projects.

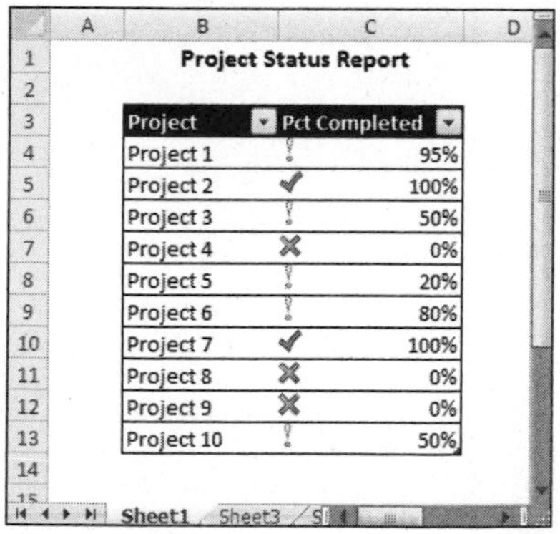

Another icon set example

Figure 21.13 shows a table that contains two test scores for each student. The Change column contains a formula that calculates the difference between the two tests. The Trend column uses an icon set to display the trend graphically.

This example uses the icon set named 3 Arrows, and I customized the rule:

- **Up Arrow:** When value is >=5
- **Level Arrow:** When value <5 and >= -5
- **Down Arrow:** When value is >=5

In other words, difference of five points or less in either direction is considered an even trend. An improvement of more than five points is considered a positive trend, and a decline of more than five points is considered a negative trend.

FIGURE 21.13

The arrows depict the trend from Test 1 to Test 2.

	A	B	C	D	E	F
1						
2	Student	Test 1	Test 2	Change	Trend	
3	Amy	59	65	6	⬆	
4	Bob	82	78	-4	⇨	
5	Calvind	98	92	-6	⬇	
6	Doug	56	69	13	⬆	
7	Ephraim	98	89	-9	⬇	
8	Frank	67	75	8	⬆	
9	Gretta	78	87	9	⬆	
10	Harold	87	95	8	⬆	
11	Inez	56	85	29	⬆	
12	June	87	72	-15	⬇	
13	Kenny	87	88	1	⇨	
14	Lance	92	92	0	⇨	
15	Marvin	82	73	-9	⬇	
16	Noel	98	100	2	⇨	
17	Opie	84	73	-11	⬇	
18	Paul	94	93	-1	⇨	
19	Quinton	68	92	24	⬆	
20	Rasmus	91	90	-1	⇨	
21	Sam	85	86	1	⇨	
22	Ted	72	92	20	⬆	
23	Ursie	80	71	-9	⬇	
24	Valerie	77	65	-12	⬇	
25	Wally	64	45	-19	⬇	
26	Xerxes	59	63	4	⇨	
27	Yolanda	89	99	10	⬆	
28	Zippy	85	82	-3	⇨	
29						

Sheet1   **Sheet3**   Sheet2   SH

The Trend column contains a formula that references the Change column. I used the Show Icon Only option in the Trend column, which also centers the icon in the column.

Displaying only one icon

In some cases, you may want to display only one icon from an icon set. Excel doesn't provide this option directly, but displaying a single icon is possible if you use two rules. Figure 21.14 shows a range of values. Only the values greater than or equal to 80 display an icon.

FIGURE 21.14

It's possible to display only one icon.

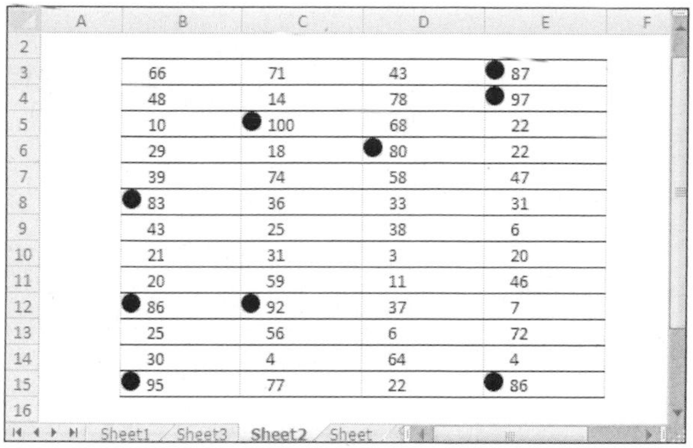

Here's how to set up an icon set such that only values greater than or equal to 80 display an icon:

1. **Select the cells, choose Home ⇨ Styles ⇨ Conditional Formatting ⇨ Icon Sets, and select any icon set.** Keep in mind that only the last icon of the set will be used.

2. **With the range selected, choose Home ⇨ Styles ⇨ Conditional Formatting ⇨ Manage Rules.** Excel displays its Conditional Formatting Rules Manager dialog box.

3. **Click Edit Rule to display the Edit Formatting Rule dialog box.**

4. **Change the first icon setting to When Value Is >= 80 and specify Number as the Type; leave the other icon settings as they are, and click OK to return to the Conditional Formatting Rules Manager.**

5. **Click New Rule and then choose this rule type: Format Only Cells That Contain.**

6. **In the bottom section of the dialog box, specify Cell Value Less Than 80 and click OK to return to the Conditional Formatting Rules Manager.** The range now has two rules.

7. **Place a check mark next to Stop If True for the first rule.** Figure 21.15 shows the completed dialog box.

8. **Click OK.**

The first rule checks to see whether the value is less than 80. If so, rule checking stops, and no conditional formatting is applied. If the value is greater than or equal to 80, the second rule kicks in. This rule indicates that values greater than or equal to 80 are displayed with an icon.

FIGURE 21.15

The Conditional Formatting Rules Manager dialog box.

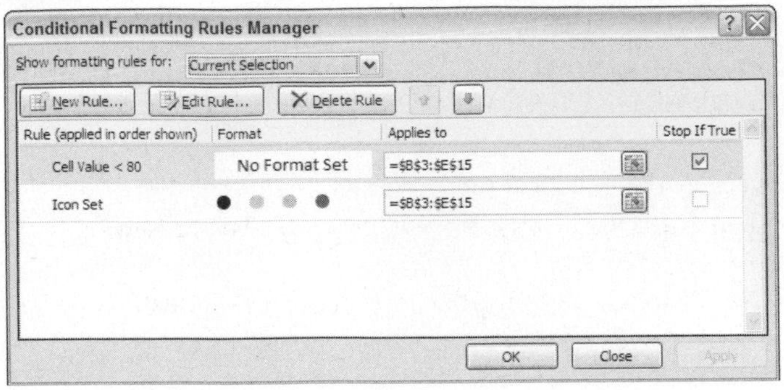

Creating Formula-Based Rules

Excel's conditional formatting feature is versatile, but sometimes it's just not quite versatile enough. Fortunately, you can extend its versatility by writing conditional formatting formulas.

The examples later in this section describe how to create conditional formatting formulas for the following:

- To identify text entries
- To identify dates that fall on a weekend
- To format cells that are in odd-numbered rows or columns (for dynamic alternate row or columns shading)
- To format groups of rows (for example, shade every two groups of rows).
- To display a sum only when all precedent cells contain values

Some of these formulas may be useful to you. If not, they may inspire you to create other conditional formatting formulas.

To specify conditional formatting based on a formula, select the cells and then choose Home ➪ Styles ➪ Conditional Formatting ➪ New Rule. This command displays the New Formatting Rule dialog box. Click the rule type labeled Use A Formula To Determine Which Cells To Format, and you'll be able to specify the formula.

You can type the formula directly into the box, or you can enter a reference to an existing formula. As with normal Excel formulas, the formula you enter here must begin with an equal sign (=).

NOTE The formula must be a logical formula that returns either TRUE or FALSE. If the formula evaluates to TRUE, the condition is satisfied, and the conditional formatting is applied. If the formula evaluates to FALSE, the conditional formatting is not applied.

Understanding relative and absolute references

If the formula that you enter into the Conditional Formatting dialog box contains a cell reference, that reference is considered a *relative reference,* based on the upper-left cell in the selected range.

For example, suppose that you want to set up a conditional formatting condition that applies shading to cells in range A1:B10 only if the cell contains text. None of Excel's conditional formatting options can do this task, so you need to create a formula that will return TRUE if the cell contains text and FALSE otherwise. Follow these steps:

1. **Select the range A1:B10 and ensure that cell A1 is the active cell.**
2. **Choose Home ➪ Styles ➪ Conditional Formatting ➪ New Rule to display the New Formatting Rule dialog box.**
3. **Click the rule type labeled Use A Formula To Determine Which Cells To Format.**
4. **Enter the following formula in the Formula box:**
    ```
    =ISTEXT(A1)
    ```
5. **Click the Format button to display the Format Cells dialog box.**
6. **In the Format Cells dialog box, click the Fill tab and specify the cell shading that will be applied if the formula returns TRUE.**
7. **Click OK to return to the New Formatting Rule dialog box (refer to Figure 21.16).**
8. **In the New Formatting Rule dialog box, click the Preview button to make sure that the formula is working correctly and to see a preview of your selected formatting.**
9. **If the preview looks correct, click OK to close the New Formatting Rule dialog box.**

Notice that the formula entered in Step 4 contains a relative reference to the upper-left cell in the selected range.

Generally, when entering a conditional formatting formula for a range of cells, you'll use a reference to the active cell, which is normally the upper-left cell in the selected range. One exception is when you need to refer to a specific cell. For example, suppose that you select range A1:B10, and you want to apply formatting to all cells in the range that exceed the value in cell C1. Enter this conditional formatting formula:

```
=A1>$C$1
```

In this case, the reference to cell C1 is an *absolute reference;* it will not be adjusted for the cells in the selected range. In other words, the conditional formatting formula for cell A2 looks like this:

```
=A2>$C$1
```

The relative cell reference is adjusted, but the absolute cell reference is not.

FIGURE 21.16

Creating a conditional formatting rule based on a formula.

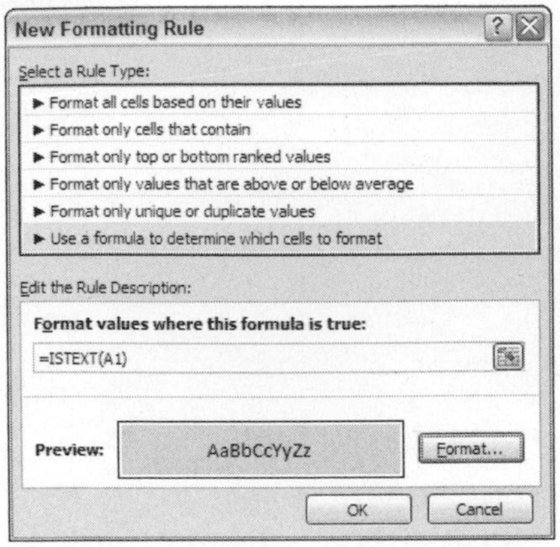

Conditional formatting formula examples

Each of these examples uses a formula entered directly into the New Formatting Rule dialog box, after selecting the rule type labeled Use A Formula To Determine Which Cells To Format. You decide the type of formatting that you apply conditionally.

ON the CD-ROM The companion CD-ROM contains all the examples in this section. The file is named conditional formatting formulas.xlsx.

Identifying weekend days

Excel provides a number of conditional formatting rules that deal with dates, but it doesn't let you identify dates that fall on a weekend. Use this formula to identify weekend dates:

```
=OR(WEEKDAY(A1)=7,WEEKDAY(A1)=1)
```

This formula assumes that a range is selected and that cell A1 is the active cell.

Displaying alternate-row shading

The conditional formatting formula that follows was applied to the range A1:D18, as shown in Figure 21.17, to apply shading to alternate rows.

```
=MOD(ROW(),2)=0
```

Alternate row shading can make your spreadsheets easier to read. If you add or delete rows within the conditional formatting area, the shading is updated automatically.

This formula uses the ROW function (which returns the row number) and the MOD function (which returns the remainder of its first argument divided by its second argument). For cells in even-numbered rows, the MOD function returns 0, and cells in that row are formatted.

For alternate shading of columns, use the COLUMN function instead of the ROW function.

FIGURE 21.17

Using conditional formatting to apply formatting to alternate rows.

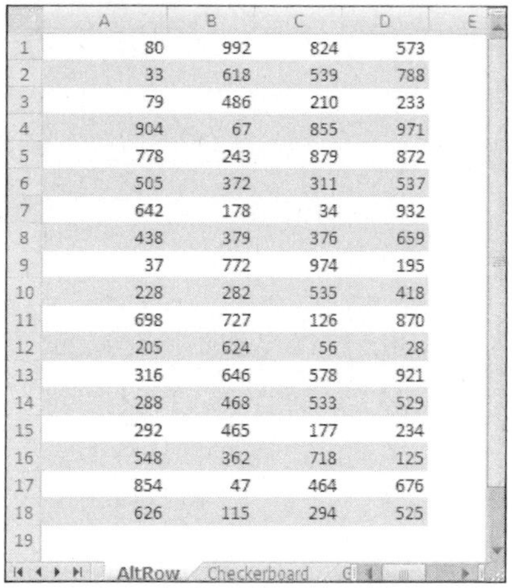

	A	B	C	D	E
1	80	992	824	573	
2	33	618	539	788	
3	79	486	210	233	
4	904	67	855	971	
5	778	243	879	872	
6	505	372	311	537	
7	642	178	34	932	
8	438	379	376	659	
9	37	772	974	195	
10	228	282	535	418	
11	698	727	126	870	
12	205	624	56	28	
13	316	646	578	921	
14	288	468	533	529	
15	292	465	177	234	
16	548	362	718	125	
17	854	47	464	676	
18	626	115	294	525	
19					

AltRow / Checkerboard / C

Creating checkerboard shading

The following formula is a variation on the example in the preceding section. It applies formatting to alternate rows and columns, creating a checkerboard effect.

```
=MOD(ROW(),2)=MOD(COLUMN(),2)
```

Shading groups of rows

Here's another rows shading variation. The following formula shades alternate groups of rows. It produces four rows of shaded rows, followed by four rows of unshaded rows, followed by four more shaded rows, and so on.

```
=MOD(INT((ROW()-1)/4)+1,2)
```

Figure 21.18 shows an example.

For different sized groups, change the 4 to some other value. For example, use this formula to shade alternate groups of two rows:

```
=MOD(INT((ROW()-1)/2)+1,2)
```

Displaying a total only when all values are entered

Figure 21.19 shows a range with a formula that uses the SUM function in cell C6. Conditional formatting is used to hide the sum if any of the four cells above is blank. The conditional formatting formula for cell C6 (and cell C5, which contains a label) is

```
=COUNT($C$2:$C$5)=4
```

This formula returns TRUE only if C2:C5 contains no empty cells.

Figure 21.20 shows the worksheet when one of the values is missing.

FIGURE 21.18

Conditional formatting produces these groups of alternate shaded rows.

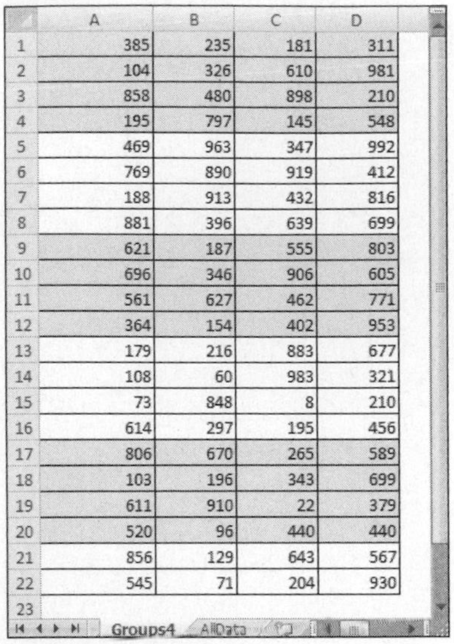

	A	B	C	D
1	385	235	181	311
2	104	326	610	981
3	858	480	898	210
4	195	797	145	548
5	469	963	347	992
6	769	890	919	412
7	188	913	432	816
8	881	396	639	699
9	621	187	555	803
10	696	346	906	605
11	561	627	462	771
12	364	154	402	953
13	179	216	883	677
14	108	60	983	321
15	73	848	8	210
16	614	297	195	456
17	806	670	265	589
18	103	196	343	699
19	611	910	22	379
20	520	96	440	440
21	856	129	643	567
22	545	71	204	930
23				

Groups4   AllData

FIGURE 21.19

The sum is displayed only when all four values have been entered.

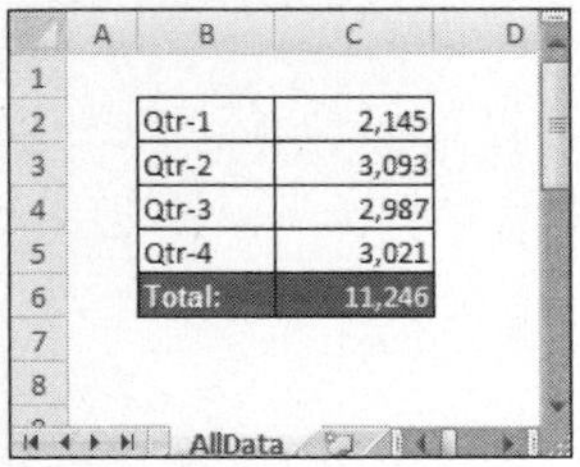

	A	B	C	D
1				
2		Qtr-1	2,145	
3		Qtr-2	3,093	
4		Qtr-3	2,987	
5		Qtr-4	3,021	
6		Total:	11,246	
7				
8				

AllData

FIGURE 21.20

A missing value causes the sum to be hidden.

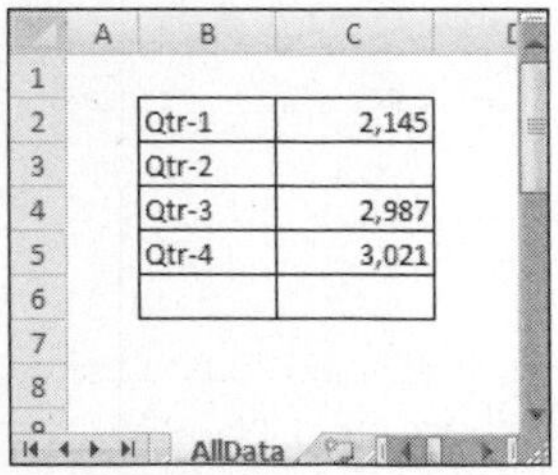

	A	B	C	D
1				
2		Qtr-1	2,145	
3		Qtr-2		
4		Qtr-3	2,987	
5		Qtr-4	3,021	
6				
7				
8				

AllData

Working with Conditional Formats

This section describes some additional information about conditional formatting that you may find useful.

Managing rules

The Conditional Formatting Rules Manager dialog box is useful for checking, editing, deleting, and adding conditional formats. Access this dialog box by choosing Home ➪ Styles ➪ Conditional Formatting ➪ Manage Rules.

You can specify as many rules as you like by clicking the New Rule button. As you can see in Figure 21.21, cells can even use data bars, color scales, and icon sets all at the same time — although I can't think of a good reason to do so.

FIGURE 21.21

This range uses data bars, color scales, and icon sets.

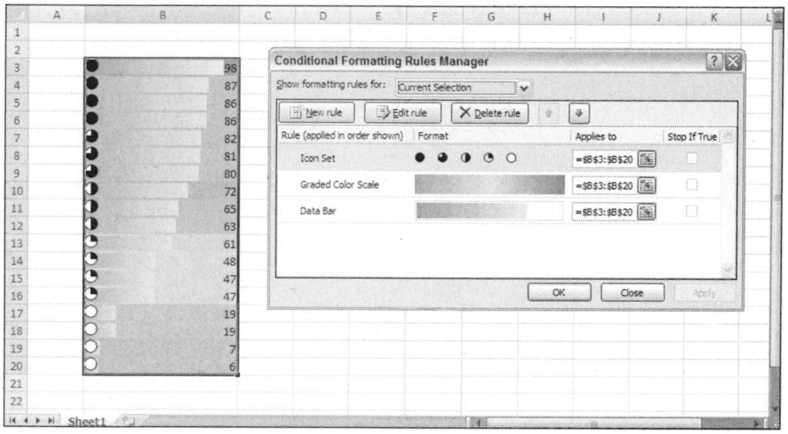

Copying cells that contain conditional formatting

Conditional formatting information is stored with a cell much like standard formatting information is stored with a cell. As a result, when you copy a cell that contains conditional formatting, you also copy the conditional formatting.

> **TIP**   To copy only the formatting (including conditional formatting), use the Paste Special dialog box and select the Formats option.

If you insert rows or columns within a range that contains conditional formatting, the new cells have the same conditional formatting.

Deleting conditional formatting

When you press Delete to delete the contents of a cell, you do not delete the conditional formatting for the cell (if any). To remove all conditional formats (as well as all other cell formatting), select the cell. Then choose Home ➪ Editing ➪ Clear ➪ Clear Formats. Or, choose Home ➪ Editing ➪ Clear ➪ Clear All to delete the cell contents and the conditional formatting.

To remove only conditional formatting (and leave the other formatting intact), use Home ➪ Styles ➪ Conditional Formatting ➪ Clear Rules.

Find and Replace limitations

Excel's Find And Replace dialog box includes a feature that allows you to search your worksheet to locate cells that contain specific formatting. This feature does *not* locate cells that contain formatting resulting from conditional formatting.

Locating cells that contain conditional formatting

You can't tell, just by looking at a cell, whether it contains conditional formatting. You can, however, use Excel's Go To dialog box to select such cells.

1. **Choose Home ➪ Editing ➪ Find & Select ➪ Go To Special.**
2. **In the Go To Special dialog box, select the Conditional Formats option.**
3. **To select all cells on the worksheet containing conditional formatting, select the All option; to select only the cells that contain the same conditional formatting as the active cell, select the Same option.**
4. **Click OK.** Excel selects the cells for you.

Chapter 22

Enhancing Your Work with Pictures and Drawings

When it comes to visual presentation, Excel has a lot more up its sleeve than charts. As you may know, you can insert a wide variety of graphics into your worksheet to add pizzazz to an otherwise boring report.

This chapter describes the non-chart-related graphic tools available in Excel. These tools consist of Shapes, SmartArt, WordArt, and imported or pasted images. In addition to enhancing your worksheets, you'll find that working with these objects can be a nice diversion. When you need a break from crunching numbers, you might enjoy creating an artistic masterpiece using Excel's graphic tools.

Using Shapes

Microsoft Office, including Excel, provides access to a variety of customizable graphic images known as *Shapes*. You can add a Shape to a worksheet's draw layer by selecting a Shape using the Insert ➪ Illustrations ➪ Shapes gallery, shown in Figure 22.1. The Shapes are organized into categories, and the category at the top displays the Shapes that you've used recently.

Inserting a Shape

To insert a Shape on a worksheet, just click the Shape in the Shapes gallery and then click in the worksheet. A default-sized shape is added to your worksheet. Alternatively, you can click the Shape and then drag it in the worksheet to create a larger or smaller Shape. When you release the mouse button, the object is selected, and its name appears in the Name box (as shown in Figure 22.2).

> **TIP** You can also insert a Shape into a chart. Just select the chart before you choose the Shape from the gallery and then click inside of the chart to insert the Shape. When a chart is selected, the Chart Tools context tab also displays an icon to access the Shape gallery: Chart Tools ➪ Layout ➪ Insert ➪ Shapes.

FIGURE 22.1

The Shapes gallery.

A few of the Shapes require a slightly different approach. For example, when adding a FreeForm Shape (from the Lines category), you can click repeatedly to create lines. Or click and drag to create a nonlinear shape. Double-click to finish drawing and create the Shape. The Curve and Scribble Shapes (in the Lines category) also require several clicks while drawing.

Following are a few tips to keep in mind when creating Shapes:

- Every Shape has a name. Some have generic names like *Shape 1* and *Shape 2*, but others are given more descriptive names (for example, *Rectangle 1*). To change the name of a Shape, select it, type a new name in the Name box, and press Enter.

- To select a specific shape, type its name in the Name box and press Enter.

- When you create a Shape by dragging, hold down the Shift key to maintain the object's default proportions.

■ You can control how objects appear on-screen in the Advanced tab of the Excel Options dialog box (choose Office ⇨ Excel Options). This setting appears in the section labeled Display Options for This Workbook. Normally, the All option is selected under For Objects Show. You can hide all objects by choosing Nothing (Hide Objects). Hiding objects may speed things up if your worksheet contains complex objects that take a long time to redraw.

FIGURE 22.2

This Shape was drawn on the worksheet. Its name (Quad Arrow 1) appears in the Name box.

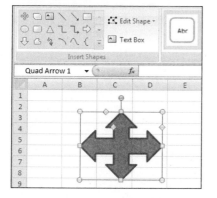

About the Drawing Layer

Every worksheet and chart sheet has what's known as a *drawing layer*. This invisible surface can hold Shapes, SmartArt, WordArt, graphic images, embedded charts, inserted objects, and so on.

You can move, resize, copy, and delete objects placed on the drawing layer, with no effect on any other elements in the worksheet. Objects on the drawing layer have properties that relate to how they're moved and sized when underlying cells are moved and sized. When you right-click a graphic object and choose Size And Properties from the shortcut menu, you get a tabbed dialog box. Click the Properties tab to adjust how the object moves or resizes with its underlying cells. Your choices are as follows:

■ **Move and Size with Cells:** If this option is selected, the object appears to be attached to the cells beneath it. For example, if you insert rows above the object, the object moves down. If you increase the column width, the object gets wider.

■ **Move But Don't Size with Cells:** If this option is checked, the object moves whenever rows or columns are inserted, but it never changes its size when you change row heights or column widths.

■ **Don't Move or Size with Cells:** This option makes the object completely independent of the underlying cells.

The preceding options control how an object is moved or sized with respect to the underlying cells. Excel also lets you *attach* an object to a cell. To do so, Display the Excel Options dialog box, click the Advanced tab, and place a check mark next to the check box labeled Cut, Copy, and Sort Inserted Objects With Their Parent Cells. After you do so, graphic objects on the drawing layer are attached to the underlying cells.

Adding text to a Shape

Many of the Shape objects can display text. To add text to such a Shape, select the Shape and start typing the text.

To change the formatting for all of the text in a Shape, Ctrl+Click the Shape object. You can then use the formatting commands on the Home tab of the Ribbon. To change the formatting of specific characters within the text, select only those characters, and use the Ribbon buttons or the Mini toolbar.

In addition, you can dramatically change the look of the text by using the tools in the Drawing Tools ➪ Format ➪ WordArt Styles group.

Selecting and Hiding Objects

An easy way to select an object is to use the Selection and Visibility task pane. To display this task pane, select any Shape and choose Drawing Tools ➪ Format ➪ Arrange ➪ Selection Pane. As with all task panes, you can undock it from the side of the window and make it free-floating. The accompanying figure shows the Selection and Visibility task pane as a floating window.

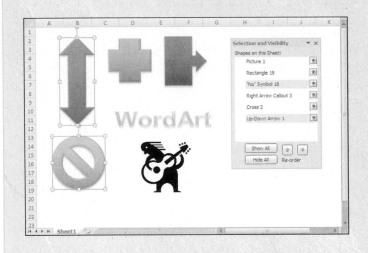

Each object on the active worksheet is listed in the task pane. Just click the object's name to select it. To select multiple objects, press Ctrl while you click the names.

To hide an object, click the "eye" icon to the right of its name. Use the buttons at the bottom of the task pane to quickly hide (or show) all items.

Formatting Shapes

When you select a Shape, Excel displays its Drawing Tools ➪ Format context tab, with the following groups of commands:

- **Insert Shapes:** Insert new Shapes; change a Shape to a different Shape.
- **Shape Styles:** Change the overall style of a Shape; modify the Shape's fill, outline, or effects.
- **WordArt Styles:** Modify the appearance of the text within a Shape.
- **Arrange:** Adjust the "stack order" of Shapes, align Shapes, group multiple Shapes, and rotate Shapes.
- **Size:** Change the size of a Shape.

Many of the commands that are available in the Ribbon are also available in the Shape's shortcut menu, which you access by right-clicking the Shape. In addition, you can use your mouse to perform some operations directly (for example, resize or rotate a Shape).

Figure 22.3 shows a worksheet with some Shapes that use various types of formatting.

FIGURE 22.3

A variety of Shapes.

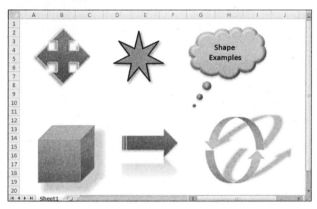

As an alternative to the Ribbon, you can use the Format Shape dialog box. Right-click the Shape and select Format Shape from the shortcut menu. You'll get a stay-on-top tabbed dialog box that contains some additional formatting options that aren't on the Ribbon.

I could probably write 20 pages about formatting Shapes, but it would be a waste of paper and certainly not a very efficient way of learning about Shape formatting. The best way, by far, to learn about formatting Shapes is to experiment. Create some shapes, click some commands, and see what happens. The commands are fairly intuitive, and you can always use Undo if something unexpected happens.

Grouping objects

Excel lets you combine two or more Shape objects into a single object. This feature is known as *grouping*. For example, if you create a design that uses four separate Shapes, you can combine them into a group. Then you can manipulate this group as a single object (move it, resize it, and so on).

To group two or more objects, press Ctrl while you click the objects to be included in the group. Then right-click and choose Group ➪ Group from the shortcut menu.

When objects are grouped, you can still work with an individual object in the group. Click once to select the group; then click again to select the object.

To ungroup a group, right-click the group object and choose Group ➪ Ungroup from the shortcut menu. This command breaks the object into its original components.

Aligning and spacing objects

When you have several objects on a worksheet, you may want to align and evenly space these objects. You can, of course, drag the objects with your mouse (which isn't very precise). Or, you can use the keyboard arrow keys to move a selected object one pixel at a time. The fastest way to align and space objects is to let Excel do it for you.

To align multiple objects, start by selecting them (press Ctrl and click the objects). Then use the tools in the Drawing Tools ➪ Format ➪ Arrange ➪ Align drop-down control.

NOTE   Unfortunately, you can't specify which object is used as the basis for the alignment. When you're aligning objects to the left (or right), they're always aligned with the leftmost (or rightmost) object that's selected. When you're aligning objects to the top (or bottom), they're always aligned with the topmost (or bottommost) object. Aligning the centers (or middles) of objects will align them along an axis halfway between the left and right (or top and bottom) extremes of the selected shapes.

You can instruct Excel to distribute three or more objects so that they're equally spaced horizontally or vertically. Use the Drawing Tools ➪ Format ➪ Arrange ➪ Align drop-down control and select Distribute Horizontally or Distribute Vertically.

Reshaping Shapes

Excel has many Shapes to choose from, but sometimes the Shape you need isn't in the gallery. In such a case, you may be able to modify one of the existing shapes using one of these techniques:

- **Rotate the Shape:** When you select a Shape, it displays a small green dot. Click and drag this dot to rotate the Shape.

- **Group multiple Shapes:** You may be able to create the Shape you need by combining two or more Shapes and then grouping them (see "Grouping objects," earlier in this chapter).

- **Reconfigure the Shape:** Many of the Shapes display one or more small yellow diamonds when the Shape is selected. You can click and drag this diamond to change the Shape's outline. The exact behavior varies with the AutoShape, so you should experiment and see what happens. Figure 22.4 shows an up-down arrow, before and after changing its shape (this particular shape has two yellow diamonds).

- **Create a Freeform Shape:** Select the Freeform Shape (in the Lines category of the Shapes gallery) to create custom Shape. Figure 22.5 shows a Freeform Shape, with eyes and a mouth added. I applied the Perspective effect to create the shadow.

- **Convert an existing Shape to a Freeform Shape**: If an existing Shape is close to what you want, convert it to a Freeform Shape and then edit its points. Select the Shape and choose Drawing Tools ➪ Format ➪ Insert Shapes ➪ Edit Shape ➪ Convert To Freeform. Then, with the Shape still selected, choose Drawing Tools ➪ Format ➪ Insert Shapes ➪ Edit Shape ➪ Edit Points. You can then drag the points to reconfigure the Shape.

FIGURE 22.4

A Shape, before and after being modified.

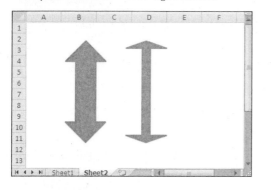

FIGURE 22.5

When none of the existing Shapes will do, create your own Freeform Shape.

Printing objects

By default, objects are printed along with the worksheet. To avoid printing a Shape, right-click the Shape and choose Size And Properties. In the Size And Properties dialog box, select the Properties tab and remove the check mark from the Print Object check box.

Exporting a Graphic

If you create a graphic in Excel using Shapes, SmartArt, or WordArt, you may want to save the graphic as a separate file for use in another program. Unfortunately, Excel doesn't provide a direct way to export a graphic, but here's a trick you can use. Make sure that your graphic appears the way you want it and then follow these steps:

1. **Save your workbook.**
2. **Choose Office ➪ Save As to save your workbook as a Web Page.** In the Save As dialog box, select Web Page (*.htm; *.html) from the Save As Type drop-down list.
3. **Close the workbook.**
4. **Use Windows Explorer to locate the HTML file you saved in Step 2.** You'll notice that Excel also created a companion directory for the HTML file. If you save the file as myart.htm, the directory will be named myart_files.
5. **Open the directory, and you'll find *.png graphic files — one for each graphic object in your workbook.** The *.png files have a transparent background.

Using SmartArt

Excel's Shapes are certainly impressive, but the SmartArt feature is downright amazing. Using SmartArt, you can insert a wide variety of highly customizable diagrams into a worksheet, and you can change the overall look of the diagram with a few mouse clicks. This Office 2007 feature is probably more useful for PowerPoint users, but I think many Excel users will find a need for SmartArt.

 SmartArt is new to Excel 2007.

Inserting SmartArt

To insert SmartArt into a worksheet, choose Insert ➪ SmartArt. Excel displays the dialog box shown in Figure 22.6. The diagrams are arranged in categories along the left. When you find one that looks appropriate, click it for a larger view in the panel on the right, which also provides some usage tips. Click OK to insert the graphic.

NOTE Don't be concerned about the number of elements in the SmartArt graphics. You can customize the SmartArt to display the number of elements you need.

FIGURE 22.6

Inserting a SmartArt graphic.

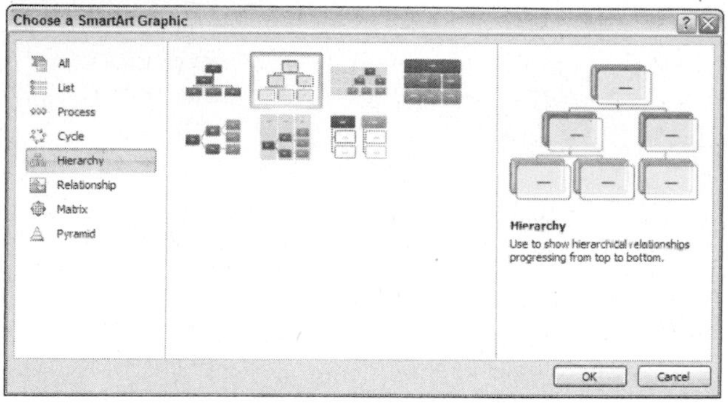

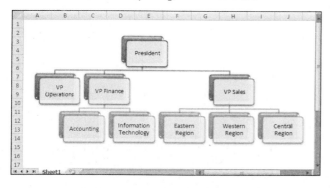

Figure 22.7 shows a SmartArt diagram, after I customized it and added text. When you insert or select a SmartArt diagram, Excel displays its SmartArt Tools context tab, which provides many customization options.

FIGURE 22.7

This SmartArt shows a simple organizational chart.

Customizing SmartArt

Figure 22.8 shows a SmartArt graphic (from the Process category) immediately after I inserted it into a worksheet. The Type Your Text Here window makes it very easy to enter text into the elements of the image. If you prefer, you can click one of the [Text] areas in the image and type the text directly.

FIGURE 22.8

This SmartArt needs to be customized.

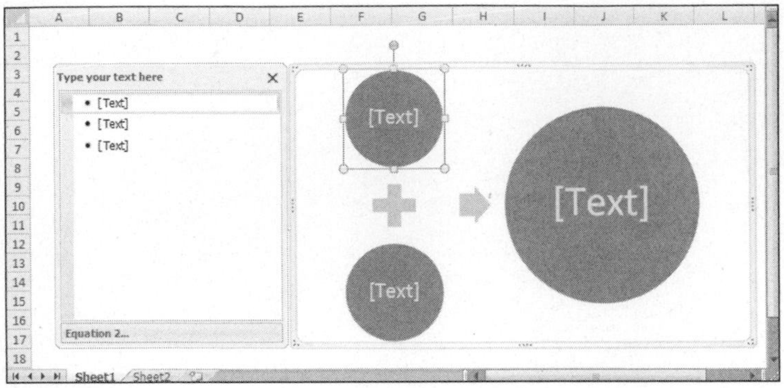

Figure 22.9 shows the SmartArt after I added some text.

FIGURE 22.9

The SmartArt now has text.

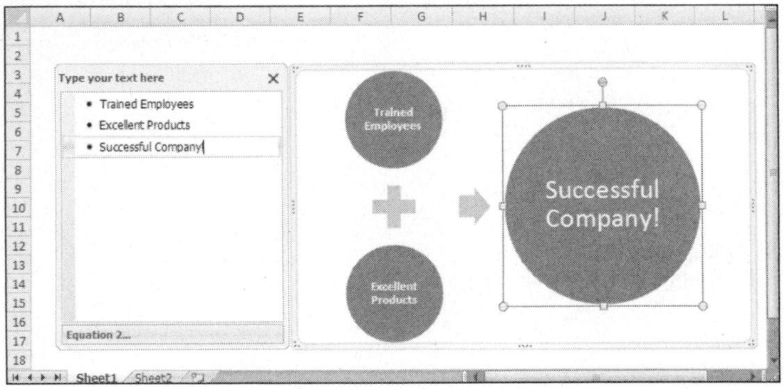

This particular diagram depicts two items combining into a third item. Suppose that your boss sees this graphic and tells you that you need a third item: Advanced Technology. To add an element to the SmartArt graphic, just select an item and choose SmartArt Tools ➪ Design ➪ Create Graphic ➪ Add Shape. Or you can just select an item and press Enter. Figure 22.10 shows the modified SmartArt.

When working with SmartArt, keep in mind that you can move, resize, or format individually any element within the graphic. Select the element and then use the tools in the SmartArt Tools ➪ Format tab.

Changing the layout

You can easily change the layout of a SmartArt diagram. Select the object and then choose SmartArt Tools ➪ Design ➪ Layouts. Any text that you've entered remains intact. Figure 22.11 shows a few alternate layouts for the previous example.

FIGURE 22.10

The SmartArt, after adding a new element.

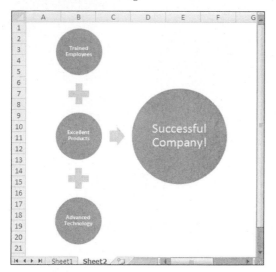

FIGURE 22.11

A few different layouts for the SmartArt.

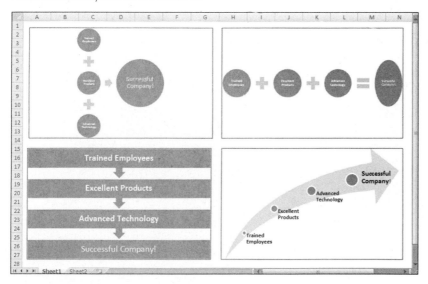

Changing the Style

Once you decide on a layout, you may want to consider other styles or colors available in the SmartArt Tools ⇨ Design ⇨ SmartArt Styles group. Figure 22.12 shows the diagram after you choose a different style and changing the color.

TIP The SmartArt styles available vary, depending on the document theme assigned to the workbook. To change a workbook's theme, choose Page Layout ⇨ Themes. Switching to a different theme can have a dramatic impact on the appearance of SmartArt diagrams.

FIGURE 22.12

A few mouse clicks changed the style of this diagram.

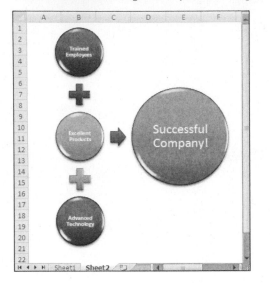

Learning more about SmartArt

This section provided a basic introduction to SmartArt. The topic is complex enough to deserve an entire book, but I think most users can master SmartArt simply by experimenting with the commands.

Using WordArt

WordArt has been available in previous versions of Excel, but this feature has gotten a well-needed facelift in Excel 2007. You can use WordArt to create graphical effects in text. Figure 22.13 shows a few examples of WordArt.

To insert a WordArt graphic on a worksheet, choose Insert ⇨ WordArt and then select a style from the gallery. Excel inserts an object with the text "Your text here." Replace that text with your own, resize it, and apply other formatting if you like.

When you select a WordArt image, Excel displays its Drawing Tools context menu. Use the controls to vary the look of your WordArt.

NOTE The controls in the Drawing Tools ⇨ Format ⇨ Shape Styles group operate on the shape that contains the text, not the text. If you want to apply text formatting, use the control in the Drawing Tools ⇨ Format ⇨ WordArt Styles group. You can also use some of the standard formatting controls on the Home tab or the Mini toolbar. In addition, right-click the WordArt and select Format Text Effects for more formatting options.

FIGURE 22.13

WordArt examples.

Working with Other Graphic Types

Excel can import a wide variety of graphics into a worksheet. You have several choices:

- Use the Clip Art task pane to locate and insert an image.
- Import a graphic file directly.
- Copy and paste an image using the Windows Clipboard.

About graphics files

Graphics files come in two main categories: *bitmap* and *vector* (picture). Bitmap images are made up of discrete dots. They usually look pretty good at their original size, but often lose clarity if you increase the size. Vector-based images, on the other hand, are comprised of points and paths that are represented by mathematical equations, so they retain their crispness regardless of their size. Examples of common bitmap file formats include BMP, PNG, JPG, and GIF. Examples of common vector file formats include CGM, WMF, and EPS.

Want a Great Graphics File Viewer?

Many users are content to use the graphics file-viewing capabilities built into Windows. But if you do a lot of work with graphics files, you owe it to yourself to get a *real* file-viewing program.

Many graphics viewers are available, but one of the best products in its class is IrfanView. It enables you to view just about any graphics file you can find, and it has features and options that will satisfy even hard-core graphics mavens. Best of all, it's free. To download a copy, visit `www.irfanview.com`.

You can find thousands of graphics files free for the taking on the Internet. Be aware, however, that some graphic files have copyright restrictions.

CAUTION   Using bitmap graphics in a worksheet can dramatically increase the size of your workbook, resulting in more memory usage and longer load and save times.

Using the Clip Art task pane

The Clip Art task pane is a shared program that is also accessible from other Microsoft Office applications. Besides providing an easy way to locate and insert images, the task pane lets you insert sound and video files. This tool also gives you direct access to Microsoft's Design Gallery Live on the Web.

Display the Clip Art task pane by choosing Insert ➪ Clip Art. You can search for clip art by using the controls at the top of the task pane. Figure 22.14 shows the task pane, along with the thumbnail images resulting from a search for "banjo". To insert an image into the active worksheet, just double-click the thumbnail. For additional options, right-click the thumbnail image.

FIGURE 22.14

Use the Excel task pane to search for clip art and other multimedia files.

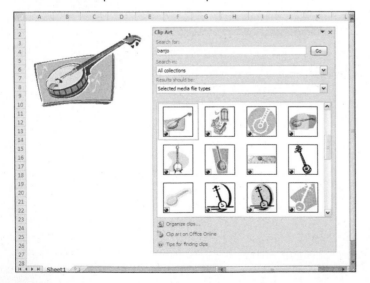

You may prefer to use the Microsoft Clip Organizer to access image files. Clip Organizer is essentially a stand-alone version of the Clip Art task pane. To display the Clip Organizer, click the Organize Clips hyperlink at the bottom of the task pane. Figure 22.15 shows the Microsoft Clip Organizer.

You can also add new files to the Clip Organizer. You may want to do so if you tend to insert a particular graphic file (such as your company logo) into your worksheets quite often.

If you can't find a suitable image, you can go online and browse through the extensive clip art at Microsoft's Clip Gallery Live Web site. Click the Clip Art On Office Online hyperlink (at the bottom of the task pane), and your Web browser will be activated, at which point you can view the images (or listen to the sounds) and add those you want to your Clip Organizer.

FIGURE 22.15

Microsoft Clip Organizer.

Inserting graphics files

If the graphic image that you want to insert is available in a file, you can easily import the file into your worksheet. Choose Insert ➪ Picture. Excel displays its Insert Picture dialog box, which enables you to browse for the file.

When you insert a picture on a worksheet, you can modify the picture in a number of ways by choosing Picture Tools ➪ Format context tab. This tab appears automatically when you select a picture object. For example, you can adjust the color, contrast, and brightness. In addition, you can add borders, shadows, reflections, and so on — similar to the operations available for Shapes.

Don't overlook the Picture Tools ➪ Format ➪ Picture Styles group. These commands can transform your image in some very interesting ways. Figure 22.16 shows various styles for a picture.

FIGURE 22.16

Displaying a picture in a number of different styles.

Copying graphics by using the Clipboard

In some cases, you may want to use a graphic image that's not stored in a separate file or is in a file that Excel can't import. For example, you may have an obscure drawing program that uses a file format that Excel doesn't support. You may be able to export the file to a supported format, but it may be easier to load the file into the drawing program and copy the image to the Clipboard (using that program's Edit ➪ Copy command). Then you can activate Excel and paste the image to the drawing layer by choosing Home ➪ Clipboard ➪ Paste.

Suppose that you see a graphic displayed on-screen, but you can't select it — it may be part of a program's logo, for example. In this case, you can copy the entire screen to the Clipboard and then paste it into Excel. To copy all or part of the screen, use the following keyboard commands:

■ **PrintScreen:** Copies the entire screen to the Clipboard.

■ **Alt+PrintScreen:** Copies the active window to the Clipboard.

Taking Pictures of Ranges

One of Excel's best-kept secrets is its ability to copy and paste "live" pictures of cells and charts. You can copy a cell or range and then paste a picture (as an object) of the cell or range on any worksheet or chart. If you change the contents of a cell that's in a picture, the picture changes.

To "take a picture" of a range:

1. **Select the range.**
2. **Press Ctrl+C to copy the range.**
3. **Choose Home ⇨ Clipboard ⇨ Paste ⇨ As Picture ⇨ Paste Picture Link**

The result is a live picture of the range you selected in Step 1.

If you use this feature frequently, you can save some time by adding Excel's Camera tool to your Quick Access Toolbar (QAT):

1. **Right-click your QAT and choose Customize Quick Access Toolbar.**
2. **In the Customization tab of the Excel Options dialog box, select Command Not In The Ribbon from the drop-down list on the left.**
3. **Select Camera from the list and click Add.**
4. **Click OK to close the Excel Options dialog box.**

After you've added the Camera tool to your QAT, you can select a range of cells and click the Camera tool to take a "picture" of the range. Then click in the worksheet, and Excel places a live picture of the selected range on the worksheet's draw layer. If you make changes to the original ranges, the changes are shown in the picture of the range.

Most of the time, you don't want the entire screen — just a portion of it. The solution is to crop the image by choosing Picture Tools ⇨ Format ⇨ Size ⇨ Crop. This command adds cropping marks to the corners of the image. Just drag the cropping marks to crop the image.

Displaying a worksheet background image

If you want to use a graphic image for a worksheet's background (similar to wallpaper on the Windows desktop), choose Page Layout ⇨ Page Setup ⇨ Background and select a graphics file. The selected graphics file is tiled on the worksheet. Unfortunately, worksheet background images are for on-screen display only. These images do not appear when the worksheet is printed.

Part IV

Using Advanced Excel Features

A number of Excel's features can probably be fairly called advanced features if for no better reason than the ways in which they expand the definitions of what a spreadsheet program can do. The chapters in this part cover some useful features that you may not have used in the past but may find very valuable.

Chapter 23

Customizing the Quick Access Toolbar

I n previous versions of Excel, it was relatively easy for end users to make changes to the user interface. They could create custom toolbars that contained frequently used commands, and they could even remove menu items that they never used. Users could display any number of toolbars and move them wherever they liked. Those days are over.

With the introduction of the new Ribbon-based user interface in Office 2007, end-user customization is severely curtailed. Although you can modify the Ribbon, it's a rather complicated process, and it's not something a casual user would do. In Office 2007, user-interface customization is limited to the Quick Access Toolbar, or QAT, which is the topic of this chapter.

IN THIS CHAPTER
About the Quick Access Toolbar
Adding frequently used commands to the QAT
Adding commands that are otherwise not available

About the QAT

The QAT is always visible, regardless of which Ribbon tab is selected. After you customize the QAT, your frequently used commands will always be one click away.

> **NOTE** The only situation in which the QAT is not visible is in Full Screen mode, which is enabled by choosing View ➪ Workbook Views ➪ Full Screen. To cancel Full Screen mode, right-click any cell and select Close Full Screen or press Escape.

By default, the QAT is located on the left side of Excel's title bar (see Figure 23.1). It includes three tools:

- **Save:** Saves the active workbook.
- **Undo:** Reverses the effect of the last action.
- **Redo:** Reverses the effect of the last undo.

If you prefer, you can move the QAT below the Ribbon. To do so, right-click the QAT and select Show Quick Access Toolbar Below The Ribbon. Moving the QAT below the Ribbon uses additional vertical space on your screen. In other words, you'll be able to see one less row of your worksheet if you move the QAT from its default location.

FIGURE 23.1

The default location for the QAT is on the left side of Excel's title bar.

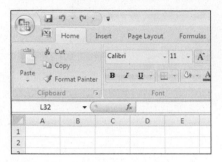

Commands on the QAT always appear as a small icon, with no text. When you hover your mouse pointer over an icon, you see the name of the command and a brief description.

Customizing the QAT consists of adding new commands to it. If you find that you use some Excel commands frequently, you can make these commands easily accessible by adding them to your QAT.

As far as I can tell, there is no limit to the number of commands that you can add. But regardless of the number of icons, the QAT always displays a single line of icons. If the number of icons exceeds Excel's window width, it displays an additional icon at the end: More Controls. Click the More Controls icon, and the hidden QAT icons appear in a pop-up window.

Adding New Commands to the QAT

You can add a new command to the QAT in three ways:

- Click the QAT drop-down control, which is located on the right side of the QAT (see Figure 23.2). The list contains a few commonly used commands. Select a command from the list, and Excel adds it to your QAT.

- Right-click any control on the Ribbon and choose Add To Quick Access Toolbar. The control is added to your QAT, after the last control.

- Use the Customization tab in the Excel Options dialog box. A quick way to access this dialog box is to right-click any Ribbon control and select Customize Quick Access Toolbar.

The remainder of this section discusses the Customization tab in the Excel Options dialog box, shown in Figure 23.3.

The left side of the dialog box displays a list of Excel commands, and the right side shows the commands that are currently in your QAT. Above the command list on the left is a drop-down control that lets you filter the list. Select an item for the drop-down, and the list displays only the commands for that item.

FIGURE 23.2

The QAT drop-down list is one way to add a new command to the QAT.

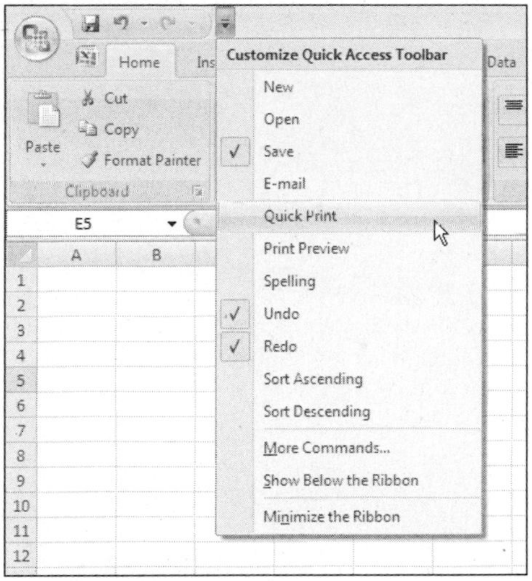

FIGURE 23.3

Use the Customization tab in the Excel Options dialog box to customize the QAT.

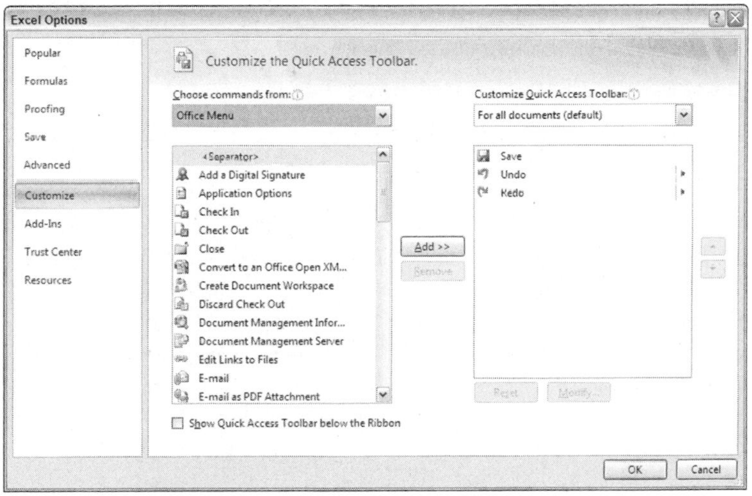

Some of the items in the drop-down are

■ Popular Commands: Displays commands that Excel users commonly use.

■ Commands Not In The Ribbon: Displays a list of commands that you cannot access from the Ribbon.

- All Commands: Displays a complete list of Excel commands.
- Macros: Displays a list of all available macros.
- Office Menu: Displays the commands available in the Office menu.
- Home Tab: Displays all commands that are available when the Home tab is active.

In addition, the drop-down contains an item for every other tab.

To add an item to your QAT, select it from the list on the right, and click Add. Notice some of the commands in the list on the left display an icon. The icon tells you what form the command will take: A drop-down, a split button, and edit control, or a Ribbon group. If the command doesn't display an icon, it's a button control.

If you add a macro to your QAT, you can click the Modify button to change the text and choose a different icon for the macro.

TIP   The only times you ever *need* to use the Customize tab in the Excel Options dialog box is when you want to add a command that's not in the Ribbon, or add a command that executes a macro. In all other situations, it's much easier to locate the command in the Ribbon, right-click the command, and choose Add To Quick Access Toolbar.

Other QAT Actions

Other QAT actions include the following:

- **Rearranging the QAT icons:** If you want to change the order of your QAT icons, you can do so in the Customization tab in the Excel Options dialog box. Select the command and then use the Up and Down arrow buttons on the right to move the icon.

- **Removing QAT icons:** The easiest way to remove an icon from your QAT is to right-click the icon and select Remove From Quick Access Toolbar. You can also use the Customization tab in the Excel Options dialog box. Just select the command in the list on the right and click Remove.

- **Resetting the QAT:** If you want to return the QAT to its default state, display the Customization tab in the Excel Options dialog box and click the Reset button. All your customizations disappear, and the QAT then displays its three default commands.

CAUTION   You can't undo resetting the QAT.

Behind the Scenes

You may be curious about how Excel keeps track of your customized QAT. The information is stored in an XML file named `excel.qat`. The file is located here:

```
C:\Documents and Settings\<username>\Local Settings\Application
Data\Microsoft\Office
```

You can view this file with a text editor or an XML viewer. If you make a copy of the file and rename it with an XML extension, you can even open it with Excel (when prompted for how to open the file, specify as an XML table). However, you cannot modify the `excel.qat` file using Excel.

If you create the ultimate QAT, you can share your `excel.qat` file with your colleagues.

Chapter 24

Using Custom Number Formats

When you enter a number into a cell, you can display that number in a variety of different formats. Excel has quite a few built-in number formats, but you may find that none of them suit your needs.

This chapter describes how to create custom number formats and provides many examples that you can use as-is or adapt to your needs.

About Number Formatting

By default, all cells use the General number format. This format is basically "what you type is what you get." But if the cell isn't wide enough to show the entire number, the General format rounds numbers with decimals and uses scientific notation for large numbers. In many cases, the General number format works just fine. But most people prefer to specify a different number format for consistency.

The key thing to remember about number formatting is that it affects only how a value is *displayed*. The actual number remains intact, and any formulas that use a formatted number use the actual number.

NOTE An exception to this rule occurs if you specify the Set Precision As Displayed option in the Advanced tab in the Excel Options dialog box. If that option is in effect, formulas use the values that are actually displayed in the cells. In general, using this option is not a good idea because it changes the underlying values in your worksheet.

One more thing to keep in mind: If you use Excel's Find And Replace dialog box (displayed by choosing Home ➪ Editing ➪ Find & Select ➪ Find, characters that are displayed as a result of number formatting (for example, a currency symbol) are not searchable.

Automatic number formatting

Excel is smart enough to perform some formatting for you automatically. For example, if you enter **12.3%** into a cell, Excel knows that you want to use a percentage format and applies it automatically. If you use commas to separate thousands (such as 123,456), Excel applies comma formatting for you. And if you precede your value with a currency symbol, Excel formats the cell for currency.

> **NOTE**   You have an option when it comes to entering values into cells formatted as percentages. Access the Excel Options and click the Advanced tab. If the check box labeled Enable Automatic Percent Entry is checked (the default setting), you can simply enter a normal value into a cell formatted to display as a percent (for example, enter 12.5 for 12.5%). If this check box isn't checked, you must enter the value as a decimal (for example, .125 for 12.5%).

Excel automatically applies a built-in number format to a cell based on the following criteria:

- If a number contains a slash (/), it may be converted to a date format or a fraction format.
- If a number contains a hyphen (-), it may be converted to a date format.
- If a number contains a colon (:) or is followed by a space and the letter A or P, it may be converted to a time format.
- If a number contains the letter E (in either uppercase or lowercase), it may be converted to scientific notation or exponential format.

> **TIP**   To avoid automatic number formatting when you enter a value, preformat the cell with the desired number format or precede your entry with an apostrophe. (The apostrophe makes the entry text, so number formatting is not applied to the cell.)

Formatting numbers by using the Ribbon

The Number group on the Home tab of the Ribbon contains several controls that enable you to apply common number formats quickly. The Number Format drop-down control gives you quick access to 11 common number formats. In addition, the Number group contains some buttons. When you click one of these buttons, the selected cells take on the specified number format. Table 24.1 summarizes the formats that these buttons perform in the U.S. English version of Excel.

> **NOTE**   Some of these buttons actually apply predefined styles to the selected cells. Access Excel's styles by using the style gallery, in the Styles group on the Home tab.

TABLE 24.1

Number-Formatting Buttons on the Ribbon

Button Name	Formatting Applied
Accounting Number Format	Adds a dollar sign to the left, separates thousands with a comma, and displays the value with two digits to the right of the decimal point. This is a drop-down control, so you can select other common currency symbols.
Percent Style	Displays the value as a percentage, with no decimal places.
Comma Style	Separates thousands with a comma and displays the value with two digits to the right of the decimal place.
Increase Decimal	Increases the number of digits to the right of the decimal point by one.
Decrease Decimal	Decreases the number of digits to the right of the decimal point by one.

Using shortcut keys to format numbers

Another way to apply number formatting is to use shortcut keys. Table 24.2 summarizes the shortcut key combinations that you can use to apply common number formatting to the selected cells or range.

TABLE 24.2

Number-Formatting Keyboard Shortcuts

Key Combination	Formatting Applied
Ctrl+Shift+~	General number format (that is, unformatted values).
Ctrl+Shift+$	Currency format with two decimal places. (Negative numbers appear in parentheses.)
Ctrl+Shift+%	Percentage format with no decimal places.
Ctrl+Shift+^	Scientific notation number format with two decimal places.
Ctrl+Shift+#	Date format with the day, month, and year.
Ctrl+Shift+@	Time format with the hour, minute, and AM or PM.
Ctrl+Shift+!	Two decimal places, thousands separator, and a hyphen for negative values.

Using the Format Cells dialog box to format numbers

For maximum control of number formatting, use the Number tab in the Format Cells dialog box. You can access this dialog box in any of several ways:

- Click the dialog box selector in the Home ⇨ Number group
- Choose Home ⇨ Number ⇨ Number Format ⇨ More Number Formats
- Press Ctrl+1

The Number tab in the Format Cells dialog box contains 12 categories of number formats from which to choose. When you select a category from the list box, the right side of the dialog box changes to display appropriate options.

Following is a list of the number-format categories along with some general comments:

- **General:** The default format; it displays numbers as integers, decimals, or in scientific notation if the value is too wide to fit into the cell.
- **Number:** Enables you to specify the number of decimal places, whether to use your system thousands separator (for example, a comma) to separate thousands, and how to display negative numbers.
- **Currency:** Enables you to specify the number of decimal places, to choose a currency symbol, and to display negative numbers. This format always uses the system thousands separator symbol (for example, a comma) to separate thousands.
- **Accounting:** Differs from the Currency format in that the currency symbols always line up vertically, regardless of the number of digits displayed in the value.
- **Date:** Enables you to choose from a variety of date formats and select the locale for your date formats.

- **Time:** Enables you to choose from a number of time formats and select the locale for your time formats.

- **Percentage:** Enables you to choose the number of decimal places; always displays a percent sign.

- **Fraction:** Enables you to choose from among nine fraction formats.

- **Scientific:** Displays numbers in exponential notation (with an E): 2.00E+05 = 200,000. 2.05E+05 = 205,000. You can choose the number of decimal places to display to the left of E.

- **Text:** When applied to a value, causes Excel to treat the value as text (even if it looks like a value). This feature is useful for such items as numerical part numbers and credit-card numbers.

- **Special:** Contains additional number formats. The list varies, depending on the Locale you choose. For the English (United States) locale, the formatting options are Zip Code, Zip Code +4, Phone Number, and Social Security Number.

- **Custom:** Enables you to define custom number formats not included in any of the other categories.

NOTE If the cell displays a series of hash marks after you apply a number format (such as ##########), it usually means that the column isn't wide enough to display the value by using the number format that you selected. Either make the column wider (by dragging the right border of the column header) or change the number format. A series of hash marks also can mean that the cell contains an invalid date or time.

Creating a Custom Number Format

The Custom category on the Number tab in the Format Cells dialog box (see Figure 24.1) enables you to create number formats not included in any of the other categories. Excel gives you a great deal of flexibility in creating custom number formats.

FIGURE 24.1

The Number tab in the Format Cells dialog box.

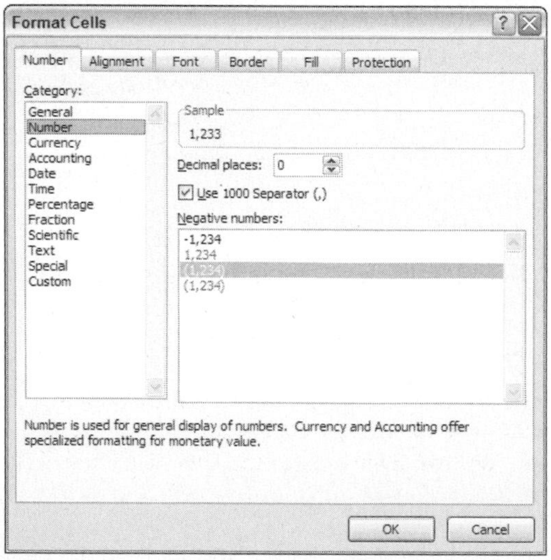

TIP   Custom number formats are stored with the workbook in which they are defined. To make the custom format available in a different workbook, you can just copy a cell that uses the custom format to the other workbook.

You construct a number format by specifying a series of codes as a *number format string*. You enter this code sequence in the Type field after you select the Custom category on the Number tab in the Format Cells dialog box. Here's an example of a simple number format code:

```
0.000
```

This code consists of placeholders and a decimal point; it tells Excel to display the value with three digits to the right of the decimal place. Here's another example:

```
00000
```

This custom number format has five placeholders and displays the value with five digits (no decimal point). This format is good to use when the cell holds a five-digit Zip Code. (In fact, this is the code actually used by the Zip Code format in the Special category.) When you format the cell with this number format and then enter a Zip Code, such as 06604 (Bridgeport, CT), the value is displayed with the leading zero. If you enter this number into a cell with the General number format, it displays 6604 (no leading zero).

Scroll through the list of number formats in the Custom category in the Format Cells dialog box to see many more examples. In many cases, you can use one of these codes as a starting point, and you'll only need to customize it slightly.

ON the CD-ROM   The companion CD-ROM contains a workbook with many custom number format examples. The file is named `number formats.xlsx`.

Parts of a number format string

A custom format string can have up to four sections, which enables you to specify different format codes for positive numbers, negative numbers, zero values, and text. You do so by separating the codes with a semicolon. The codes are arranged in the following order:

```
Positive format; Negative format; Zero format; Text format
```

If you don't use all four sections of a format string, Excel interprets the format string as follows:

- If you use only one section, the format string applies to all types of entries.
- If you use two sections, the first section applies to positive values and zeros, and the second section applies to negative values.
- If you use three sections, the first section applies to positive values, the second section applies to negative values, and the third section applies to zeros.
- If you use all four sections, the last section applies to text stored in the cell.

The following is an example of a custom number format that specifies a different format for each of these types:

```
[Green]General;[Red]General;[Black]General;[Blue]General
```

This custom number format example takes advantage of the fact that colors have special codes. A cell formatted with this custom number format displays its contents in a different color, depending on the value. When a cell is formatted with this custom number format, a positive number is green, a negative number is red, a zero is black, and text is blue.

Preformatting Cells

Usually, you'll apply number formats to cells that already contain values. You also can format cells with a specific number format *before* you make an entry. Then, when you enter information, it takes on the format that you specified. You can preformat specific cells, entire rows or columns, or even the entire worksheet.

Rather than preformat an entire worksheet, however, you can change the number format for the Normal style. (Unless you specify otherwise, all cells use the Normal style.) Change the Normal style by displaying the Style gallery. Choose Home ➪ Styles. Right-click the Normal style icon and choose Modify to display the Style dialog box. In the Style dialog box, click the Format button and then choose the new number format that you want to use for the Normal style.

CROSS-REF If you want to apply cell formatting automatically (such as text or background color) based on the cell's contents, a much better solution is to use Excel's Conditional Formatting feature. Chapter 21 covers conditional formatting.

Custom number format codes

Table 24.3 lists the formatting codes available for custom formats, along with brief descriptions. I use most of these codes in examples later in this chapter.

TABLE 24.3

Codes Used to Create Custom Number Formats

Code	Comments
General	Displays the number in General format.
#	Digit placeholder. Displays only significant digits, and does not display insignificant zeros.
0 (zero) in the format.	Digit placeholder. Displays insignificant zeros if a number has fewer digits than there are zeros
?	Digit placeholder. Adds spaces for insignificant zeros on either side of the decimal point so that decimal points align when formatted with a fixed-width font. You can also use ? for fractions that have varying numbers of digits.
.	Decimal point.
%	Percentage.
,	Thousands separator.
E- E+ e- e+	Scientific notation
$ - + / ( ) : space	Displays this character.
\	Displays the next character in the format.
*	Repeats the next character, to fill the column width.

Code	Comments
_ (underscore)	Leaves a space equal to the width of the next character.
"text"	Displays the text inside the double quotation marks.
@	Text placeholder.
[color]	Displays the characters in the color specified. Can be any of the following text strings (not case sensitive): Black, Blue, Cyan, Green, Magenta, Red, White, or Yellow.
[Color n]	Displays the corresponding color in the color palette, where *n* is a number from 0 to 56.
[condition value]	Enables you to set your own criterion for each section of a number format.

Table 24.4 lists the codes used to create custom formats for dates and times.

TABLE 24.4

Codes Used in Creating Custom Formats for Dates and Times

Code	Comments
m	Displays the month as a number without leading zeros (1–12).
mm	Displays the month as a number with leading zeros (01–12).
mmm	Displays the month as an abbreviation (Jan–Dec).
mmmm	Displays the month as a full name (January–December).
mmmmm	Displays the first letter of the month (J–D).
d	Displays the day as a number without leading zeros (1–31).
dd	Displays the day as a number with leading zeros (01–31).
ddd	Displays the day as an abbreviation (Sun–Sat).
dddd	Displays the day as a full name (Sunday–Saturday).
yy or yyyy	Displays the year as a two-digit number (00–99) or as a four-digit number (1900–9999).
h or hh	Displays the hour as a number without leading zeros (0–23) or as a number with leading zeros (00–23).
m or mm	Displays the minute as a number without leading zeros (0–59) or as a number with leading zeros (00–59).
s or ss	Displays the second as a number without leading zeros (0–59) or as a number with leading zeros (00–59).
[ ]	Displays hours greater than 24 or minutes or seconds greater than 60.
AM/PM	Displays the hour using a 12-hour clock; if no AM/PM indicator is used, the hour uses a 24.hour clock.

Where Did Those Number Formats Come From?

Excel may create custom number formats without you realizing it. When you use the Increase Decimal or Decrease Decimal button on the Home ⇨ Number group of the Ribbon (or in the Mini toolbar), Excel creates new custom number formats, which appear on the Number tab in the Format Cells dialog box. For example, if you click the Increase Decimal button five times, the following custom number formats are created:

```
0.0
0.000
0.0000
0.000000
```

A format string for two decimal places is not created because that format string is built-in.

Custom Number Format Examples

The remainder of this chapter consists of useful examples of custom number formats. You can use most of these format codes as-is. Others may require slight modification to meet your needs.

Scaling values

You can use a custom number format to scale a number. For example, if you work with very large numbers, you may want to display the numbers in thousands (that is, display 1,200,000 as 1,200). The actual number, of course, will be used in calculations that involve that cell. The formatting affects only how it is displayed.

Displaying values in thousands

The following format string displays values without the last three digits to the left of the decimal place and no decimal places. In other words, the value appears as if it's divided by 1,000 and rounded to no decimal places.

```
#,###,
```

A variation of this format string follows. A value with this number format appears as if it's divided by 1,000 and rounded to two decimal places.

```
#,###.00,
```

Table 24.5 shows examples of these number formats:

TABLE 24.5

Examples of Displaying Values in Thousands

Value	Number Format	Display
123456	#,###,	123
1234565	#,###,	1,235
−323434	#,###,	−323

Value	Number Format	Display
123123.123	#,###,	123
499	#,###,	(blank)
500	#,###,	1
123456	#,###.00,	123.46
1234565	#,###.00,	1,234.57
–323434	#,###.00,	–323.43
123123.123	#,###.00,	123.12
499	#,###.00,	.50
500	#,###.00,	.50

Displaying values in hundreds

The following format string displays values in hundreds, with two decimal places. A value with this number format appears as if it's divided by 100 and rounded to two decimal places.

```
0"."00
```

Table 24.6 shows examples of these number formats:

TABLE 24.6

Examples of Displaying Values in Hundreds

Value	Number Format	Display
546	0"."00	5.46
100	0"."00	1.00
9890	0"."00	98.90
500	0"."00	5.00≥
–500	0"."00	–5.00
0	0"."00	0.00

Displaying values in millions

The following format string displays values in millions with no decimal places. A value with this number appears as if it's divided by 1,000,000 and rounded to no decimal places.

```
#,###,,
```

A variation of this format string follows. A value with this number appears as if it's divided by 1,000,000 and rounded to two decimal places.

```
#,###.00,,
```

Another variation follows. This adds the letter M to the end of the value.

```
#,###,,M
```

The following format string is a bit more complex. It adds the letter M to the end of the value — and also displays negative values in parentheses as well as displaying zeros.

```
#,###.0,,"M"_);(#,###.0,,"M)";0.0"M"_)
```

Table 24.7 shows examples of these format strings.

TABLE 24.7

Examples of Displaying Values in Millions

Value	Number Format	Display
123456789	#,###,,	123
1.23457E+11	#,###,,	123,457
1000000	#,###,,	1
5000000	#,###,,	5
–5000000	#,###,,	–5
0	#,###,,	(blank)
123456789	#,###.00,,	123.46
1.23457E+11	#,###.00,,	123,457.00
1000000	#,###.00,,	1.00
5000000	#,###.00,,	5.00
–5000000	#,###.00,,	–5.00
0	#,###.00,,	.00
123456789	#,###,,"M"	123M
1.23457E+11	#,###,,"M"	123,457M
1000000	#,###,,"M"	1M
5000000	#,###,,"M"	5M
–5000000	#,###,,"M"	–5M
0	#,###,,"M"	M
123456789	#,###.0,,"M"_);(#,###.0,,"M)";0.0"M"_)	123.5M
1.23457E+11	#,###.0,,"M"_);(#,###.0,,"M)";0.0"M"_)	123,456.8M
1000000	#,###.0,,"M"_);(#,###.0,,"M)";0.0"M"_)	1.0M
5000000	#,###.0,,"M"_);(#,###.0,,"M)";0.0"M"_)	5.0M
–5000000	#,###.0,,"M"_);(#,###.0,,"M)";0.0"M"_)	(5.0M)
0	#,###.0,,"M"_);(#,###.0,,"M)";0.0"M"_)	0.0M

Adding zeros to a value

The following format string displays a value with three additional zeros and no decimal places. A value with this number format appears as if it's rounded to no decimal places and then multiplied by 1,000.

```
#",000"
```

Examples of this format string, plus a variation that adds six zeros, are shown in Table 24.8.

TABLE 24.8

Examples of Displaying a Value with Extra Zeros

Value	Number Format	Display
1	#",000"	1,000
1.5	#",000"	2,000
43	#",000"	43,000
−54	#",000"	−54,000
5.5	#",000"	6,000
0.5	#",000,000"	1,000,000
0	#",000,000"	,000,000
1	#",000,000"	1,000,000
1.5	#",000,000"	2,000,000
43	#",000,000"	43,000,000
−54	#",000,000"	−54,000,000
5.5	#",000,000"	6,000,000
0.5	#",000,000"	1,000,000

Displaying leading zeros

To display leading zeros, create a custom number format that uses the 0 character. For example, if you want all numbers to display with ten digits, use the number format string that follows. Values with fewer than ten digits will display with leading zeros.

```
0000000000
```

You also can force all numbers to display with a fixed number of leading zeros. The format string that follows, for example, appends three zeros to the beginning of each number:

```
"000"#
```

In the following example, the format string uses the repeat character code (an asterisk) to apply enough leading zeros to fill the entire width of the cell:

```
*00
```

Displaying fractions

Excel supports quite a few built-in fraction number formats (select the Fraction category on the Number tab in the Format Cells dialog box). For example, to display the value .125 as a fraction with 8 as the denominator, select As Eighths (4/8) from the Type list (see Figure 24.2).

Selecting a number format to display a value as a fraction.

You can use a custom format string to create other fractional formats. For example, the following format string displays a value in 50ths:

```
# ??/50
```

The following format string displays a value in terms of fractional dollars. For example, the value 154.87 is displayed as *154 and 87/100 Dollars*.

```
0 "and "??/100 "Dollars"
```

The following example displays the value in sixteenths, with a quotation mark appended to the right. This format string is useful when you deal with inches (for example, 2/16").

```
# ??/16\"
```

Displaying a negative sign on the right

The following format string displays negative values with the negative sign to the right of the number. Positive values have an additional space on the right, so both positive and negative numbers align properly on the right.

```
0.00_-;0.00-
```

Testing Custom Number Formats

When you create a custom number format, don't overlook the Sample box on the Number tab in the Format Cells dialog box. This box displays the value in the active cell using the format string in the Type box.

It's a good idea to test your custom number formats by using the following data: a positive value, a negative value, a zero value, and text. Often, creating a custom number format takes several attempts. Each time you edit a format string, it is added to the list. When you finally get the correct format string, access the Format Cells dialog box one more time and delete your previous attempts.

To make the negative numbers more prominent, you can add a color code to the negative part of the number format string:

```
0.00_-;[Red]0.00-
```

Formatting dates and times

When you enter a date into a cell, Excel formats the date using the system short date format. You can change this format by using the Windows Control Panel (Regional and Language Options).

Excel provides many useful, built-in date and time formats. Table 24.9 shows some other date and time formats that you may find useful. The first column of the table shows the date/time serial number.

TABLE 24.9

Useful Built-In Date and Time Formats

Value	Number Format	Display
39264	mmmm d, yyyy (dddd)	July 1, 2007 (Sunday)
39264	"It's" dddd!	It's Sunday!
39264	dddd, mm/dd/yyyy	Sunday, 07/01/2007
39264	"Month: "mmm	Month: July
39264	General (m/d/yyyy)	39264 (7/1/2007)
0.345	h "Hours"	8 Hours
0.345	h:mm o'clock	8:16 o'clock
0.345	h:mm a/p"m"	8:16 am
0.78	h:mm a/p".m."	6:43 p.m.

CROSS-REF See Chapter 13 for more information about Excel's date and time serial number system.

Displaying text with numbers

The ability to display text with a value is one of the most useful benefits of using a custom number format. To add text, just create the number format string as usual (or use a built-in number format as a starting point) and put the text within quotation marks. The following number format string, for example, displays a value with the text *(US Dollars)* added to the end:

```
#,##0.00 "(US Dollars)"
```

Here's another example that displays text before the number:

```
"Average: "0.00
```

If you use the preceding number format, you'll find that the negative sign appears before the text for negative values. To display number signs properly, use this variation:

```
"Average: "0.00;"Average: "-0.00
```

The following format string displays a value with the words *Dollars and Cents*. For example, the number 123.45 displays as *123 Dollars and .45 Cents*.

```
0 "Dollars and" .00 "Cents"
```

Suppressing certain types of entries

You can use number formatting to hide certain types of entries. For example, the following format string displays text but not values:

```
;;
```

This format string displays values but not text or zeros:

```
0.0;-0.0;;
```

This format string displays everything except zeros:

```
0.0;-0.0;;@
```

Formatting Numbers by Using the TEXT Function

Excel's TEXT function accepts a number format string as its second argument. For example, the following formula displays the contents of cell A1 using a custom number format that displays a fraction:

```
=TEXT(A1,"# ??/50")
```

However, not all formatting codes work when used in this manner. For example, colors and repeating characters are ignored. The following formula does not display the contents of cell A1 in red:

```
=TEXT(A1,"[Red]General")
```

You can use the following format string to completely hide the contents of a cell:

```
;;;
```

Note that when the cell is activated, however, the cell's contents are visible on the Formula bar.

Filling a cell with a repeating character

The asterisk (*) symbol specifies a repeating character in a number format string. The repeating character completely fills the cell and adjusts if the column width changes. The following format string, for example, displays the contents of a cell padded on the right with dashes:

```
General*-;-General*-;General*-;General*-
```

Using Data Validation

his chapter explores a very useful Excel feature known as data validation. Data validation enables you to add useful dynamic elements to your worksheet without using any macro programming.

About Data Validation

Excel's *data validation* feature enables you to set up certain rules that dictate what can be entered into a cell. For example, you may want to limit data entry in a particular cell to whole numbers between 1 and 12. If the user makes an invalid entry, you can display a custom message, such as the one shown in Figure 25.1.

Excel makes it easy to specify the validation criteria, and you can also use a formula for more complex criteria.

CAUTION The data validation suffers from a potentially serious problem: If the user copies a cell that does not use data validation and pastes it to a cell that *does* use data validation, the data validation rules are deleted. In other words, the cell then accepts any type of data.

FIGURE 25.1

Displaying a message when the user makes an invalid entry.

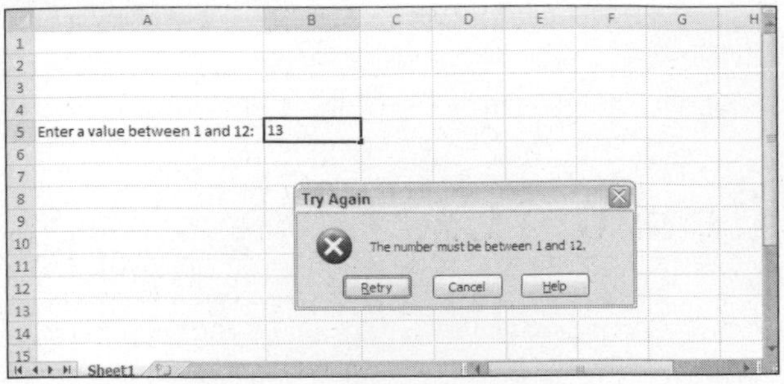

Specifying Validation Criteria

To specify the type of data allowable in a cell or range, follow these steps:

1. **Select the cell or range.**
2. **Choose Data ⇨ Data Tools ⇨ Data Validation. Excel displays its Data Validation dialog box.**
3. **Click the Settings tab (see Figure 25.2).**

FIGURE 25.2

The Settings tab of the Data Validation dialog box.

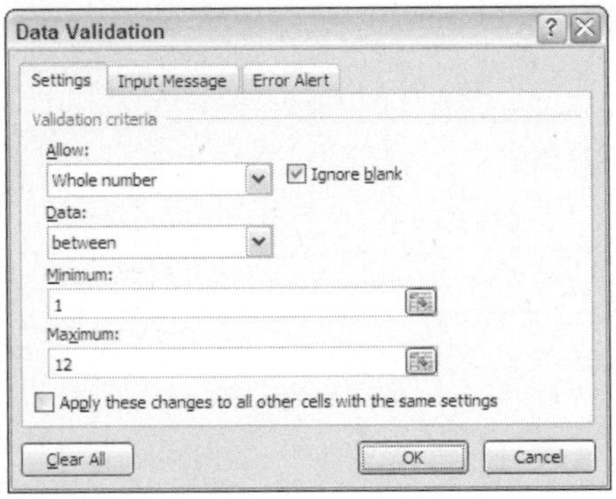

4. **Choose an option from the drop-down box labeled Allow.** The contents of the Data Validation dialog box will change, displaying controls based on your choice. To specify a formula, select Custom.
5. **Specify the conditions by using the displayed controls.** Your selection in Step 4 determines what other controls you can access.
6. **(Optional) Click the Input Message tab and specify which message to display when a user selects the cell.** You can use this optional step to tell the user what type of data is expected. If this step is omitted, no message will appear when the user selects the cell.

7. **(Optional.) Click the Error Alert tab and specify which error message to display when a user makes an invalid entry.** The selection for Style determines what choices users have when they make invalid entries. To prevent an invalid entry, choose Stop. If this step is omitted, a standard message will appear if the user makes an invalid entry.

8. **Click OK.**

After you've performed these steps, the cell or range contains the validation criteria you specified.

Types of Validation Criteria You Can Apply

The Settings tab of the Data Validation dialog box enables you to specify a wide variety of data validation criteria. The following options are available in the Allow drop-down box. Keep in mind that the other controls in the Settings tab vary, depending on your choice in the Allow drop-down box.

- **Any Value:** Selecting this option removes any existing data validation. Note, however, that the input message, if any, still displays if the check box is checked in the Input Message tab.

- **Whole Number:** The user must enter a whole number. You specify a valid range of whole numbers by using the Data drop-down list. For example, you can specify that the entry must be a whole number greater than or equal to 100.

- **Decimal:** The user must enter a number. You specify a valid range of numbers by using the Data drop-down list. For example, you can specify that the entry must be greater than or equal to 0 and less than or equal to 1.

- **List:** The user must choose from a list of entries you provide. This option is very useful, and I discuss it in detail later in this chapter (see "Creating a drop-down list").

- **Date:** The user must enter a date. You specify a valid date range by using the Data drop-down list. For example, you can specify that the entered data must be greater than or equal to January 1, 2007, and less than or equal to December 31, 2007.

- **Time:** The user must enter a time. You specify a valid time range by using the Data drop-down list. For example, you can specify that the entered data must be greater than 12:00 p.m.

- **Text Length:** The length of the data (number of characters) is limited. You specify a valid length by using the Data drop-down list. For example, you can specify that the length of the entered data be 1 (a single alphanumeric character).

- **Custom:** To use this option, you must supply a logical formula that determines the validity of the user's entry (a logical formula returns either `True` or `False`). You can enter the formula directly into the Formula control (which appears when you select the Custom option), or you can specify a cell reference that contains a formula. This chapter contains examples of useful formulas.

The Settings tab of the Data Validation dialog box contains two other check boxes:

- **Ignore Blank:** If checked, blank entries are allowed.

- **Apply These Changes to All Other Cells with the Same Setting:** If checked, the changes you make apply to all other cells that contain the original data validation criteria.

It's important to understand that, even with data validation in effect, the user can enter invalid data. If the Style setting in the Error Alert tab of the Data Validation dialog box is set to anything except Stop, invalid data *can* be entered. Also, remember that data validation does not apply to the calculated results of formulas. In other words, if the cell contains a formula, applying conditional formatting to that cell will have no effect.

> **TIP** The Data ➪ Data Tools ➪ Data Validation drop-down control contains an item named Circle Invalid Data. When you click this item, circles appear around cells that contain incorrect entries. If you correct an invalid entry, the circle disappears. To get rid of the circles, choose Data ➪ Data Tools ➪ Data Validation ➪ Clear Validation Circles. In Figure 25.3, invalid entries are defined as values that are greater than 100.

FIGURE 25.3

Excel can draw circles around invalid entries (in this case, cells that contains values greater than 100).

	A	B	C	D	E	F	G
1	17	45	17	60	51		
2	65	35	31	59	95		
3	35	70	75	10	108		
4	58	12	88	95	84		
5	4	101	95	7	27		
6	54	74	45	81	30		
7	50	44	66	51	46		
8	89	42	86	91	45		
9	89	20	15	22	99		
10	84	13	21	108	78		
11	105	38	100	1	44		
12	7	97	15	85	43		
13	18	4	66	96	29		
14	37	7	21	7	23		
15	42	10	107	106	16		
16	35	18	2	50	97		
17	18	97	57	86	11		
18	98	87	25	58	74		
19	42	48	24	105	26		
20	99	85	24	86	57		
21							

Sheet1

Creating a Drop-Down List

Perhaps one of the most common uses of data validation is to create a drop-down list in a cell. Figure 25.4 shows an example that uses the month names in A1:A12 as the list source.

To create a drop-down list in a cell:

1. **Enter the list items into a single-row or single-column range.** These items are the ones that appear in the drop-down list.
2. **Select the cell that will contain the drop-down list and access the Data Validation dialog box.**
3. **In the Settings tab, select the List option and specify the range that contains the list using the Source control.**
4. **Make sure that the In-Cell Dropdown check box is checked.**
5. **Set any other Data Validation options as desired.**

After performing these steps, the cell displays a drop-down arrow when it's activated. Click the arrow and choose an item from the list that appears.

> **TIP** If you have a short list, you can enter the items directly into the Source control in the Settings tab of the Data Validation dialog box. (This control appears when you choose the List option in the Allow drop-down list.) Just separate each item with list separators specified in your regional settings (a comma if you use the U.S. regional settings).

FIGURE 25.4

This drop-down list was created using data validation.

	A	B	C	D	E	F	G
1	January						
2	February						
3	March						
4	April		Select a month:				
5	May			January			
6	June			February			
7	July			March			
8	August			April			
9	September			May			
10	October			June			
11	November			July			
12	December			August			
13							
14							
15							
16							

Sheet1

TIP If you specify a range for a list, the range must be on the same sheet. If your list is in a range on a different worksheet, you can provide a name for the range and then use the name as your list source (preceded by an equal sign). For example, if the list is on a different sheet in a range named *MyList*, enter the following:

```
=MyList
```

Using Formulas for Data Validation Rules

For simple data validation, the data validation feature is quite straightforward and easy to use. But the real power of this feature becomes apparent when you use data validation formulas.

NOTE The formula that you specify must be a logical formula that returns either `True` or `False`. If the formula evaluates to `True`, the data is considered valid and remains in the cell. If the formula evaluates to `False`, a message box appears that displays the message specified in the Error Alert tab of the Data Validation dialog box.

You can specify a formula in the Data Validation dialog box by selecting the Custom option in the Allow drop-down list of the Settings tab. You can enter the formula directly into the Formula control, or you can enter a reference to a cell that contains a formula. The Formula control appears in the Setting tab of the Data Validation dialog box when the Custom option is selected.

Understanding Cell References

If the formula that you enter into the Data Validation dialog box contains a cell reference, that reference is considered a *relative reference*, based on the upper-left cell in the selected range.

The following example clarifies this concept. Suppose that you want to allow only an odd number to be entered into the range B2:B10. None of Excel's Data Validation rules can limit entry to odd numbers, so a formula is required.

Follow these steps:

1. **Select the range B2:B10 and ensure that cell B2 is the active cell.**
2. **Choose Data ➪ Data Tools ➪ Data Validation.** The Data Validation dialog box appears.
3. **Click the Settings tab and select Custom from the Allow drop-down list.**
4. **Enter the following formula in the Formula box, as shown in Figure 25.5:**

   `=ISODD(B2)`

   This formula uses Excel's ISODD function, which returns True if its numeric argument is an odd number. Notice that the formula refers to the active cell, which is cell B2.
5. **Click the Error Alert tab and choose Stop for the Style and type** An odd number is required here **as the Error Message.**
6. **Click OK to close the Data Validation dialog box.**

Notice that the formula entered contains a reference to the upper-left cell in the selected range. This Data Validation formula was applied to a range of cells, so you might expect that each cell would contain the same Data Validation formula. Because you entered a relative cell reference as the argument for the ISODD function, Excel adjusts the Data Validation formula for the other cells in the B2:B10 range. To demonstrate that the reference is relative, select cell B5 and examine its Data Validation formula. You'll see that the formula for this cell is

   `=ISODD(B5)`

Entering a Data Validation formula.

Generally, when entering a Data Validation formula for a range of cells, you use a reference to the active cell, which is normally the upper-left cell in the selected range. An exception is when you need to refer to a specific cell. For example, suppose that you select range A1:B10, and you want your Data Validation to allow only values that are greater than C1. You would use this Data Validation formula:

   `=A1>$C$1`

In this case, the reference to cell C1 is an *absolute reference;* it will not be adjusted for the cells in the selected range — which is just what you want. The Data Validation formula for cell A2 looks like this:

```
=A2>$C$1
```

The relative cell reference is adjusted, but the absolute cell reference is not.

Data Validation Examples

The following sections contain a few data validation examples that use a formula entered directly into the Formula control on the Settings tab of the Data Validation dialog box. These examples help you understand how to create your own Data Validation formulas.

ON the CD-ROM   All the examples in this section are available on the companion CD-ROM. The file is named **data validation examples.xlsx.**

Accepting text only

Excel has a Data Validation option to limit the length of text entered into a cell, but it doesn't have an option to force text (rather than a number) into a cell. To force a cell or range to accept only text (no values), use the following data validation formula:

```
=ISTEXT(A1)
```

This formula assumes that the active cell in the selected range is cell A1.

Accepting a larger value than the previous cell

The following data validation formula enables the user to enter a value only if it's greater than the value in the cell directly above it:

```
=A2>A1
```

This formula assumes that A2 is the active cell in the selected range. Note that you can't use this formula for a cell in row 1.

Accepting nonduplicate entries only

The following data validation formula does not permit the user to make a duplicate entry in the range A1:C20:

```
=COUNTIF($A$1:$C$20,A1)=1
```

This formula assumes that A1 is the active cell in the selected range. Note that the first argument for COUNTIF is an absolute reference. The second argument is a relative reference, and it adjusts for each cell in the validation range. Figure 25.6 shows this validation criterion in effect, using a custom error alert message. The user is attempting to enter 17 into cell B6.

Using data validation to prevent duplicate entries in a range.

Accepting text that begins with A

The following Data Validation formula demonstrates how to check for a specific character. In this case, the formula ensures that the user's entry is a text string that begins with the letter *A* (either uppercase or lowercase).

```
=LEFT(A1)="a"
```

This formula assumes that the active cell in the selected range is cell A1.

The following formula is a variation of this validation formula. In this case, the formula ensures that the entry begins with the letter *A* and contains exactly five characters.

```
=COUNTIF(A1,"A????")=1
```

Accepting only a date that's a Monday

The following Data Validation formula ensures that the cell entry is a date, and the date is a Monday.

```
=WEEKDAY(A1)=2
```

This formula assumes that the active cell in the selected range is cell A1. It uses the WEEKDAY function, which returns 1 for Sunday, 2 for Monday, and so on.

Accepting only values that don't exceed a total

Figure 25.7 shows a simple budget worksheet, with the budget item amounts in the range B1:B6. The total budget is in cell E5, and the user is attempting to enter a value in cell B4 that would cause the total to exceed the budget. The following Data Validation formula ensures that the sum of the budget items does not exceed the budget:

```
=SUM($B$1:$B$6)<=$E$5
```

FIGURE 25.7

Using data validation to ensure that the sum of a range does not exceed a certain value.

Creating and Using Worksheet Outlines

IN THIS CHAPTER

Introducing worksheet outlines

Creating an outline

Using outlines

I f you use a word processor, you may be familiar with the concept of an outline. Most word processors (including Microsoft Word) have an outline mode that lets you view only the headings and subheadings in your document. You can easily expand a heading to show the text below it. Using an outline makes visualizing the structure of your document easy.

Excel also is capable of using outlines, and understanding this feature can make working with certain types of worksheets much easier for you.

Introducing Worksheet Outlines

You can use outlines to create summary reports in which you don't want to show all the details. You'll find that some worksheets are more suitable for outlines than others. If your worksheet uses hierarchical data with subtotals, it's probably a good candidate for an outline.

The best way to understand how worksheet outlining works is to look at an example. Figure 26.1 shows a simple sales summary sheet without an outline. Formulas are used to calculate subtotals by region and by quarter.

Figure 26.2 shows the same worksheet after the outline was created. Notice that Excel adds a new section to the left of the screen. This section contains outline controls that enable you to determine which level to view. This particular outline has three levels: States, Regions (each region consists of states grouped into categories such as West, East, and Central), and Grand Total (the sum of each region's subtotal).

Figure 26.3 depicts the outline after clicking the 2 button, which displays the second level of details. Now, the outline shows only the totals for the regions (the detail rows are hidden). You can partially expand the outline to show the detail for a particular region by clicking one of the + buttons. Collapsing the outline to level 1 shows only the headers and the Grand Total row.

Excel can create outlines in both directions. In the preceding examples, the outline was a row (vertical) outline. Figure 26.4 shows the same model after a column (horizontal) outline was added. Now, Excel also displays outline controls at the top.

FIGURE 26.1

A simple sales summary with subtotals.

FIGURE 26.2

The worksheet after creating an outline.

FIGURE 26.3

The worksheet after collapsing the outline to the second level.

FIGURE 26.4

The worksheet after adding a column outline.

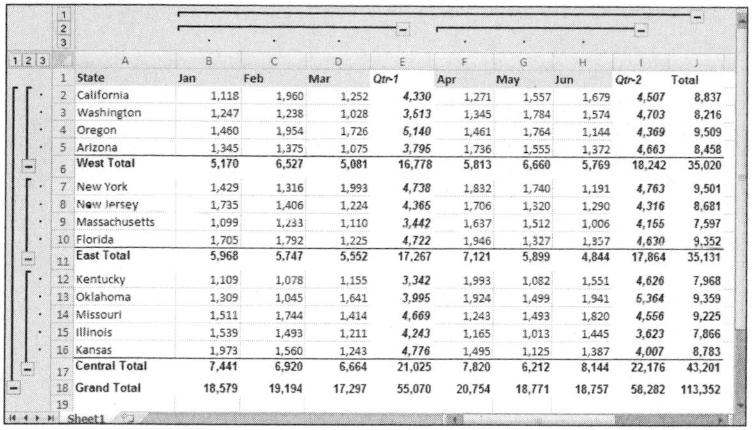

	A	B	C	D	E	F	G	H	I	J
1	State	Jan	Feb	Mar	Qtr-1	Apr	May	Jun	Qtr-2	Total
2	California	1,118	1,960	1,252	4,330	1,271	1,557	1,679	4,507	8,837
3	Washington	1,247	1,238	1,028	3,513	1,345	1,784	1,574	4,703	8,216
4	Oregon	1,460	1,954	1,726	5,140	1,461	1,764	1,144	4,369	9,509
5	Arizona	1,345	1,375	1,075	3,795	1,736	1,555	1,372	4,663	8,458
6	West Total	5,170	6,527	5,081	16,778	5,813	6,660	5,769	18,242	35,020
7	New York	1,429	1,316	1,993	4,738	1,832	1,740	1,191	4,763	9,501
8	New Jersey	1,735	1,406	1,224	4,365	1,706	1,320	1,290	4,316	8,681
9	Massachusetts	1,099	1,233	1,110	3,442	1,637	1,512	1,006	4,155	7,597
10	Florida	1,705	1,792	1,225	4,722	1,946	1,327	1,357	4,630	9,352
11	East Total	5,968	5,747	5,552	17,267	7,121	5,899	4,844	17,864	35,131
12	Kentucky	1,109	1,078	1,155	3,342	1,993	1,082	1,551	4,626	7,968
13	Oklahoma	1,309	1,045	1,641	3,995	1,924	1,499	1,941	5,364	9,359
14	Missouri	1,511	1,744	1,414	4,669	1,243	1,493	1,820	4,556	9,225
15	Illinois	1,539	1,493	1,211	4,243	1,165	1,013	1,445	3,623	7,866
16	Kansas	1,973	1,560	1,243	4,776	1,495	1,125	1,387	4,007	8,783
17	Central Total	7,441	6,920	6,664	21,025	7,820	6,212	8,144	22,176	43,201
18	Grand Total	18,579	19,194	17,297	55,070	20,754	18,771	18,757	58,282	113,352
19										

If you create both a row and a column outline in a worksheet, you can work with each outline independent of the other. For example, you can show the row outline at the second level and the column outline at the first level. Figure 26.5 shows the model with both outlines collapsed at the second level. The result is a nice summary table that gives regional totals by quarter.

FIGURE 26.5

The worksheet with both outlines collapsed at the second level.

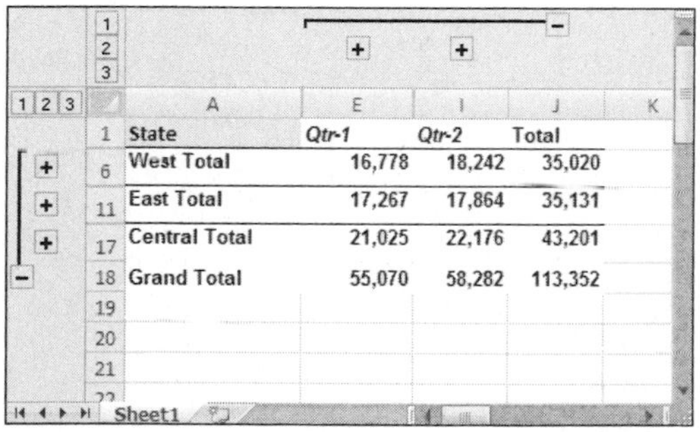

	A	E	I	J	K
1	State	Qtr-1	Qtr-2	Total	
6	West Total	16,778	18,242	35,020	
11	East Total	17,267	17,864	35,131	
17	Central Total	21,025	22,176	43,201	
18	Grand Total	55,070	58,282	113,352	
19					
20					
21					

ON the CD-ROM You can find the workbook used in the preceding examples on this book's CD-ROM. The file is named outline example.xlsx.

The following are points to keep in mind about worksheet outlines:

- A worksheet can have only one outline. If you need to create more than one outline, move the data to a new worksheet.

- You can either create an outline manually or have Excel do it for you automatically. If you choose the latter option, you may need to do some preparation to get the worksheet in the proper format.

- You can create an outline for either all data on a worksheet or just a selected data range.

- You can remove an outline with a single command (but the data remains).
- You can hide the outline symbols (to free screen space) but retain the outline.
- An outline can have up to eight nested levels.

Worksheet outlines can be quite useful. But if your main objective is to summarize a large amount of data, you may be better off using a pivot table. A pivot table is much more flexible and doesn't require that you create the subtotal formulas; it does the summarizing for you automatically.

CROSS-REF   I discuss pivot tables in Chapters 34 and 35.

Creating an Outline

This section describes the two ways to create an outline: automatically and manually. Before you create an outline, you need to ensure that data is appropriate for an outline and that the formulas are set up properly.

Preparing the data

What type of data is appropriate for an outline? Generally, the data should be arranged in a hierarchy, such as a budget that consists of an arrangement similar to the following:

Company

      Division

           Department

               Budget Category

               Budget Item

In this case, each budget item (for example, airfare and hotel expenses) is part of a budget category (for example, travel expenses). Each department has its own budget, and the departments are rolled up into divisions. The divisions make up the company. This type of arrangement is well suited for a row outline.

After you create such an outline, you can view the information at any level of detail that you want by clicking the outline controls. When you need to create reports for different levels of management, consider using an outline. Upper management may want to see only the division totals. Division managers may want to see totals by department, and each department manager needs to see the full details for his or her department.

You can include time-based information that is rolled up into larger units (such as months and quarters) in a column outline. Column outlines work just like row outlines, however, and the levels need not be time-based.

Before you create an outline, you need to make sure that all the summary formulas are entered correctly and consistently. *Consistently* means that the formulas are in the same relative location. Generally, formulas that compute summary formulas (such as subtotals) are entered below the data to which they refer. In some cases, however, the summary formulas are entered above the referenced cells. Excel can handle either method, but you must be consistent throughout the range that you outline. If the summary formulas aren't consistent, automatic outlining won't produce the results that you want.

 If your summary formulas aren't consistent (that is, some are above and some are below the data), you still can create an outline, but you must do it manually.

Creating an outline automatically

Excel can create an outline for you automatically in a few seconds, whereas it may take you 10 minutes or more to do the same thing manually.

 If you have created a table for your data (by using Insert ➪ Tables ➪ Table), Excel can't create an outline automatically. You can create an outline from a table, but you must do so manually.

To have Excel create an outline, move the cell pointer anywhere within the range of data that you're outlining. Then, choose Data ➪ Outline ➪ Group ➪ Auto Outline. Excel analyzes the formulas in the range and creates the outline. Depending on the formulas that you have, Excel creates a row outline, a column outline, or both.

If the worksheet already has an outline, Excel asks whether you want to modify the existing outline. Click Yes to force Excel to remove the old outline and create a new one.

 Excel automatically creates an outline when you choose Data ➪ Outline ➪ Subtotal, which inserts subtotal formulas automatically. See the sidebar, "Let Excel Insert the Subtotal Formulas."

Creating an outline manually

Usually, letting Excel create the outline is the best approach. It's much faster and less error-prone. If the outline that Excel creates isn't what you have in mind, however, you can create an outline manually.

When Excel creates a row outline, the summary rows must all be below the data or all above the data (they can't be mixed). Similarly, for a column outline, the summary columns must all be to the right of the data or to the left of the data. If your worksheet doesn't meet these requirements, you have two choices:

- Rearrange the worksheet so that it does meet the requirements.
- Create the outline manually.

You also need to create an outline manually if the range doesn't contain any formulas. You may have imported a file and want to use an outline to display it better. Because Excel uses the positioning of the formulas to determine how to create the outline, it isn't able to make an outline without formulas.

Creating an outline manually consists of creating groups of rows (for row outlines) or groups of columns (for column outlines). To create a group of rows, click the row numbers for all the rows that you want to include in the group—but do not select the row that has the summary formulas. Then, choose Data ➪ Outline ➪ Group ➪ Group. Excel displays outline symbols for the group. Repeat this process for each group that you want to create. When you collapse the outline, Excel hides rows in the group, but the summary row, which isn't in the group, remains in view.

 If you select a range of cells (rather than entire rows or columns) before you create a group, Excel displays a dialog box asking what you want to group. It then groups entire rows or columns based on the range that you select.

You can also select groups of groups to create multilevel outlines. When you create multilevel outlines, always start with the innermost groupings and then work your way out. If you realize that you grouped the wrong rows, you can ungroup the group by choosing Data ➪ Outline ➪ Ungroup ➪ Ungroup.

Excel has keyboard shortcuts that speed up the process of grouping and ungrouping:

- **Alt+Shift+right arrow:** Groups selected rows or columns.
- **Alt+Shift+left arrow:** Ungroups selected rows or columns.

Creating outlines manually can be confusing at first, but if you stick with it, you'll become a pro in no time.

Working with Outlines

This section discusses the basic operations that you can perform with a worksheet outline.

Displaying levels

To display various outline levels, click the appropriate outline symbol. These symbols consist of buttons with numbers on them (1, 2, and so on) and buttons with either a plus sign (+) or a minus sign (–). Refer to Figure 26.5, which shows these symbols for a row and column outline.

Clicking the 1 button collapses the outline so that it displays no detail (just the highest summary level of information), clicking the 2 button expands the outline to show one level, and so on. The number of numbered buttons depends on the number of outline levels. Choosing a level number displays the detail for that level, plus any lower levels. To display all levels (the most detail), click the highest-level number.

You can expand a particular section by clicking its + button, or you can collapse a particular section by clicking its – button. In short, you have complete control over the details that Excel exposes or hides in an outline.

If you prefer, you can use the Hide Detail and Show Detail commands on the Data ➪ Outline group to hide and show details, respectively.

TIP   If you constantly adjust the outline to show different reports, consider using the Custom Views feature to save a particular view and give it a name. Then you can quickly switch among the named views. Choose View ➪ Workbook Views ➪ Custom Views.

Adding data to an outline

You may need to add additional rows or columns to an outline. In some cases, you may be able to insert new rows or columns without disturbing the outline, and the new rows or columns become part of the outline. In other cases, you'll find that the new row or column is not part of the outline. If you create the outline automatically, choose Data ➪ Outline ➪ Group ➪ Auto Outline. Excel makes you verify that you want to modify the existing outline. If you create the outline manually, you need to make the adjustments manually, as well.

Removing an outline

After you no longer need an outline, you can remove it by choosing Data ➪ Outline ➪ Ungroup ➪ Clear Outline. Excel fully expands the outline by displaying all hidden rows and columns, and the outline symbols disappear. Be careful before you remove an outline, however. You can't make it reappear using the Undo button. You must re-create the outline from scratch.

Hiding the outline symbols

The outline symbols Excel displays when an outline is present take up quite a bit of space. (The exact amount depends on the number levels.) If you want to see as much as possible on-screen, you can temporarily hide these symbols without removing the outline. Use Ctrl+8 to toggle the outline symbols on and off.

NOTE When you hide the outline symbols, the outline still is in effect, and the worksheet displays the data at the current outline level. That is, some rows or columns may be hidden.

The Custom Views feature, which saves named views of your outline, also saves the status of the outline symbols as part of the view, enabling you to name some views with the outline symbols and other views without them.

Chapter 27

Linking and Consolidating Worksheets

I n this chapter, I discuss two procedures that are common in the world of spreadsheets: linking and consolidation. *Linking* is the process of using references to cells in external workbooks to get data into your worksheet. *Consolidation* combines or summarizes information from two or more worksheets (which can be in multiple workbooks).

IN THIS CHAPTER

Linking workbooks

Consolidating worksheets

Linking Workbooks

When you link worksheets, you connect them together in such a way that one depends on the other. The workbook that contains the link formulas (also known as external reference formulas) is called the *dependent* workbook. The workbook that contains the information used in the external reference formula is called the *source* workbook.

When you consider linking workbooks, you may ask yourself the following question: If Workbook A needs to access data in another workbook (Workbook B), why not just enter the data into Workbook A in the first place? In some cases, you can. But the real value of linking becomes apparent when the source workbook is being continually updated by another person or group. Creating a link in Workbook A to Workbook B means that, in Workbook A, you always have access to the most recent information in Workbook B because Workbook A is updated whenever Workbook B changes.

Linking workbooks also can be helpful if you need to consolidate different files. For example, each regional sales manager may store data in a separate workbook. You can create a summary workbook that first uses link formulas to retrieve specific data from each manager's workbook and then calculates totals across all regions.

Linking also is useful as a way to break up a large workbook into smaller files. You can create smaller workbooks that are linked together with a few key external references.

Linking has its downside, however. External reference formulas are somewhat fragile, and accidentally severing the links that you create is relatively easy. You can prevent this mistake if you understand how linking works. Later in the chapter, I discuss some problems that may arise, as well as how to avoid them (see "Avoiding Potential Problems with External Reference Formulas").

Creating External Reference Formulas

You can create an external reference formula by using several different techniques:

- **Type the cell references manually.** These references may be lengthy because they include workbook and sheet names (and, possibly, even drive and path information). The advantage of manually typing the cell references is that the source workbook doesn't have to be open. The disadvantage is that it's very error-prone.

- **Point to the cell references.** If the source workbook is open, you can use the standard pointing techniques to create formulas that use external references.

- **Paste the links.** Copy your data to the Clipboard. Then, with the source workbook open, choose Home ➪ Clipboard ➪ Paste ➪ Paste Link. Excel pastes the copied data as external reference formulas.

- **Choose Data ➪ Data Tools ➪ Consolidate.** For more on this method, see the section "Consolidating worksheets by using the Consolidate command," later in this chapter.

Understanding the link formula syntax

The general syntax for an external reference formula is as follows:

```
=[WorkbookName]SheetName!CellAddress
```

Precede the cell address with the workbook name (in brackets), the worksheet name, and an exclamation point. Here's an example of a formula that uses cell A1 in the Sheet1 worksheet of a workbook named Budget:

```
=[Budget.xlsx]Sheet1!A1
```

If the workbook name or the sheet name in the reference includes one or more spaces, you must enclose the text in single quotation marks. For example, here's a formula that refers to cell A1 on Sheet1 in a workbook named **Annual Budget.xlsx**:

```
='[Annual Budget.xlsx]Sheet1'!A1
```

When a formula refers to cells in a different workbook, you don't need to open the other workbook. If the workbook is closed and not in the current folder, you must add the complete path to the reference; for example:

```
='C:\Data\Excel\Budget\[Annual Budget.xlsx]Sheet1'!A1
```

Creating a link formula by pointing

Entering external reference formulas manually is usually not the best approach because you can easily make an error. Instead, have Excel build the formula for you, as follows:

1. **Open the source workbook.**
2. **Select the cell in the dependent workbook that will hold the formula.**

3. **Enter the formula.** When you get to the part that requires the external reference, activate the source workbook and select the cell or range and press Enter. If you're simply creating a link and not using the external reference as part of a formula, just enter an equal sign (=) and then select the cell and press Enter.

4. **After you press Enter, you return to the dependent workbook, where you can finish the formula.**

When you point to the cell or range, Excel automatically takes care of the details and creates a syntactically correct external reference. When using this method, the cell reference is always an absolute reference (such as $A$1). If you plan to copy the formula to create additional link formulas, you need to change the absolute reference to a relative reference by removing the dollar signs for the cell address.

As long as the source workbook remains open, the external reference doesn't include the path to the workbook. If you close the source workbook, however, the external reference formulas change to include the full path.

CAUTION If you choose the Office ⇨ Save As command to save the source workbook with a different name, Excel changes the external references to use the new filename. In some cases — but not always — this change is exactly what you want.

Pasting links

Pasting links provides another way to create external reference formulas. This method is applicable when you want to create formulas that simply reference other cells. Follow these steps:

1. **Open the source workbook.**

2. **Select the cell or range that you want to link and then copy it to the Clipboard.**

3. **Activate the dependent workbook and select the cell in which you want the link formula to appear.** If you're pasting a copied range, just select the upper-left cell.

4. **Choose Home ⇨ Clipboard ⇨ Paste ⇨ Paste Link.**

Working with External Reference Formulas

This section discusses what you need to know about working with links.

Creating links to unsaved workbooks

Excel enables you to create link formulas to unsaved workbooks (and even to nonexistent workbooks). Assume that you have two workbooks open (Book1 and Book2), and you haven't saved either of them. If you create a link formula to Book1 in Book2 and then save Book2, Excel displays the dialog box shown in Figure 27.1.

FIGURE 27.1

This message indicates that the workbook you're saving contains references to a workbook that you haven't yet saved.

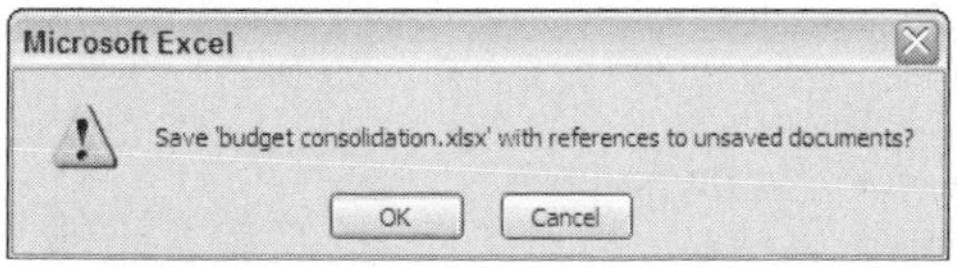

Microsoft Excel

⚠ Save 'budget consolidation.xlsx' with references to unsaved documents?

[OK] [Cancel]

Normally, you don't want to save a workbook that has links to an unsaved document. To avoid this prompt, simply save the source workbook first.

You also can create links to documents that don't exist. You may want to do so if you'll be using a source workbook from a colleague but the file hasn't yet arrived. When you enter an external reference formula that refers to a nonexistent workbook, Excel displays its Update Values dialog box, which resembles the Open dialog box. If you click Cancel, the formula retains the workbook name that you entered, but it returns a #REF! error. When the source workbook becomes available, you can choose Office ➪ Prepare ➪ Edit Links To Files to update the link (see "Updating links," later in this chapter). After doing so, the error goes away, and the formula displays its proper value.

Opening a workbook with external reference formulas

If you open a workbook that contains links, the links are updated to display the current values in the source workbook.

But what if the source workbook is no longer available? If Excel can't locate a source workbook that's referred to in a link formula, it displays a dialog box, shown in Figure 27.2, that asks you what to do. If you click Continue, the file opens, even though the links aren't valid (it displays the previous values for the links). If you click Edit Links, Excel displays its Edit Links dialog box, shown in Figure 27.3. You can use the Change Source button to specify a different workbook or click Break Link to destroy the link.

You can also access the Edit Links dialog box by choosing Office ➪ Prepare ➪ Edit Links To Files. The dialog box that appears lists all source workbooks, plus other types of links to other documents.

FIGURE 27.2

Excel displays this dialog box if it can't locate a linked file.

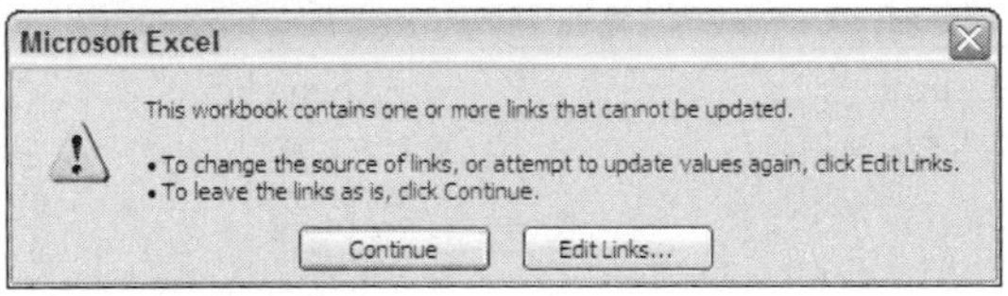

FIGURE 27.3

The Edit Links dialog box.

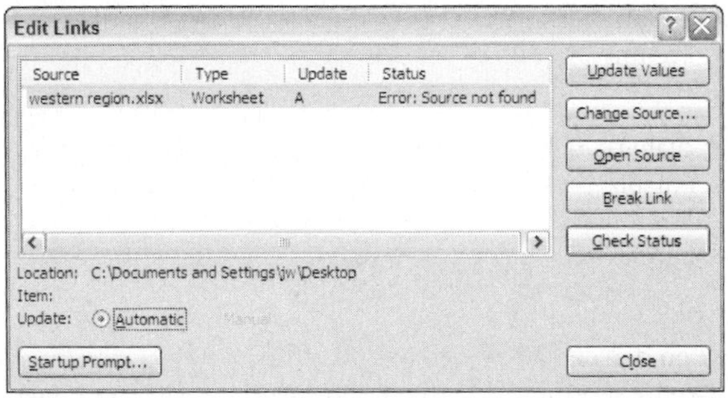

Changing the startup prompt

When you open a workbook that contains one or more external reference formulas, Excel, by default, retrieves the current values from the source workbooks and calculates the formulas. However, you can change this behavior by using the Startup Prompt dialog box (see Figure 27.4).

To display the Startup Prompt dialog box, choose Office ➪ Prepare ➪ Edit Links To Files, which displays the Edit Links dialog box. Then, in the Edit Links dialog box, click the Startup Prompt button. Select the option that describes how you want to handle the links.

FIGURE 27.4

Use the Startup Prompt dialog box to specify how Excel handles links when the workbook is opened.

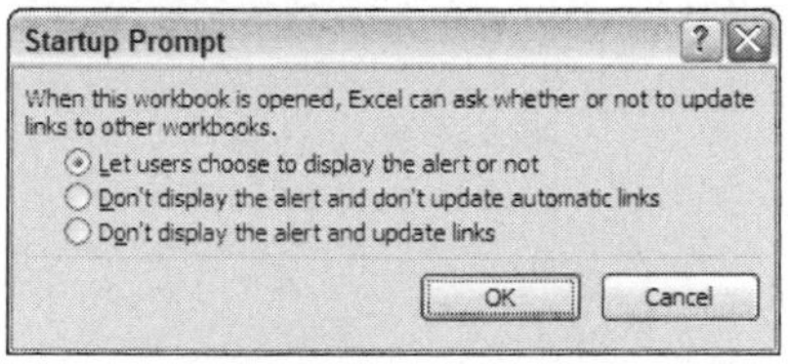

Updating links

If you want to ensure that your link formulas have the latest values from their source workbooks, you can force an update. For example, say that you just discovered that someone made changes to the source workbook and saved the latest version to your network server. In such a case, you may want to update the links to display the current data.

To update linked formulas with their current value, open the Edit Links dialog box (choose Office ➪ Prepare ➪ Edit Links To Files), choose the appropriate source workbook in the list, and then click the Update Values button. Excel updates the link formulas with the latest version of the source workbook.

> **NOTE** Excel always sets worksheet links to the Automatic Update option in the Edit Links dialog box, and you can't change them to Manual, which means that Excel updates the links only when you open the workbook. Excel doesn't automatically update links when the source file changes (unless the source workbook is open).

Changing the link source

In some cases, you may need to change the source workbook for your external references. For example, you may have a worksheet that has links to a file named Preliminary Budget, but you later receive a finalized version named Final Budget.

You can change the link source using the Edit Links dialog box. Select the source workbook that you want to change and click the Change Source button. Excel displays its Change Source dialog box, which enables you to select a new source file. After you select the file, all external reference formulas are updated.

Severing links

If you have external references in a workbook and then decide that you no longer need the links, you can convert the external reference formulas to values, thereby severing the links. To do so, access the Edit Links dialog box, select the linked file in the list, and click Break Link. Be sure to verify your intentions because you can't undo this operation.

Avoiding Potential Problems with External Reference Formulas

Using external reference formulas can be quite useful, but the links may be unintentionally severed. As long as the source file hasn't been deleted, you can almost always re-establish lost links. If you open the workbook and Excel can't locate the file, you see a dialog box that enables you to specify the workbook and re-create the links. You also can change the source file by using the Change Source button in the Edit Links dialog box. The following sections discuss some pointers that you must remember when you use external reference formulas.

Renaming or moving a source workbook

If you rename the source document or move it to a different folder, Excel won't be able to update the links. You need to use the Edit Links dialog box and specify the new source document.

> **NOTE**   If the source and destination folder reside in the same folder, you can move both of the files to a different folder. In such a case, the links remain intact.

Using the Save As command

If both the source workbook and the destination workbook are open, Excel doesn't display the full path in the external reference formulas. If you use the Office ➪ Save As command to give the source workbook a new name, Excel modifies the external references to use the new workbook name. In some cases, this change may be what you want. But in other cases, it may not. Bottom line? Be careful when you choose Office ➪ Save As with a workbook that is the source of a link in another open workbook.

Modifying a source workbook

If you open a workbook that is a source workbook for another workbook, be extremely careful if the destination workbook isn't opened. For example, if you add a new row to the source workbook, the cells all move down one row. When you open the destination workbook, it continues to use the old cell references — which is probably not what you want.

You can avoid this problem in the following ways:

- **Always open the destination workbook(s) when you modify the source workbook.** If you do so, Excel adjusts the external references in the destination workbook when you make changes to the source workbook.

- **Use names rather than cell references in your link formula.** This approach is the safest.

The following link formula refers to cell C21 on Sheet1 in the **budget.xlsx** workbook:

```
=[budget.xlsx]Sheet1!$C$21
```

If cell C21 is named *Total*, you can write the formula using that name:

```
=budget.xlsx!total
```

Using a name ensures that the link retrieves the correct value, even if you add or delete rows or columns from the source workbook.

> **CROSS-REF**   See Chapter 5 for more information about creating names for cells and ranges.

Intermediary links

Excel doesn't place many limitations on the complexity of your network of external references. For example, Workbook A can contain external references that refer to Workbook B, which can contain an external reference that refers to Workbook C. In this case, a value in Workbook A can ultimately depend on a value in Workbook C. Workbook B is an *intermediary link*.

I don't recommend these types of links, but if you must use them, be aware that Excel doesn't update external reference formulas if the workbook isn't open. In the preceding example, assume that Workbooks A and C are open. If you change a value in Workbook C, Workbook A won't reflect the change because you didn't open Workbook B (the intermediary link).

Consolidating Worksheets

The term *consolidation,* in the context of worksheets, refers to several operations that involve multiple worksheets or multiple workbook files. In some cases, consolidation involves creating link formulas. Here are two common examples of consolidation:

- The budget for each department in your company is stored in a single workbook, with a separate worksheet for each department. You need to consolidate the data and create a company-wide budget on a single sheet.
- Each department head submits a budget to you in a separate workbook file. Your job is to consolidate these files into a company-wide budget.

These types of tasks can be very difficult or quite easy. The task is easy if the information is laid out *exactly* the same in each worksheet. If the worksheets aren't laid out identically, they may be similar enough. In the second example, some budget files submitted to you may be missing categories that aren't used by a particular department. In this case, you can use a handy feature in Excel that matches data by using row and column titles. I discuss this feature in "Consolidating worksheets by using the Consolidate command," later in this chapter.

If the worksheets bear little or no resemblance to each other, your best bet may be to edit the sheets so that they correspond to one another. Better yet, return the files to the department heads and insist that they submit them using a standard format.

You can use any of the following techniques to consolidate information from multiple workbooks:

- Use external reference formulas.
- Copy the data and use Home ➪ Clipboard ➪ Paste ➪ Paste Link.
- Use the Consolidate dialog box, displayed by choosing Data ➪ Data Tools ➪ Consolidate.

Consolidating worksheets by using formulas

Consolidating with formulas simply involves creating formulas that use references to other worksheets or other workbooks. The primary advantages to using this method of consolidation are

- Dynamic updating — if the values in the source worksheets change, the formulas are updated automatically.
- The source workbooks don't need to be open when you create the consolidation formulas.

If you're consolidating the worksheets in the same workbook and all the worksheets are laid out identically, the consolidation task is simple. You can just use standard formulas to create the consolidations. For example, to compute the total for cell A1 in worksheets named Sheet2 through Sheet10, enter the following formula:

```
=SUM(Sheet2:Sheet10!A1)
```

You can enter this formula manually or use the multisheet selection technique discussed in Chapter 5. You can then copy this formula to create summary formulas for other cells.

If the consolidation involves other workbooks, you can use external reference formulas to perform your consolidation. For example, if you want to add the values in cell A1 from Sheet1 in two workbooks (named Region1 and Region2), you can use the following formula:

```
=[Region1.xlsx]Sheet1!B2+[Region2.xlsx]Sheet1!B2
```

You can include any number of external references in this formula, up to the 8,000-character limit for a formula. However, if you use many external references, such a formula can be quite lengthy and confusing if you need to edit it.

If the worksheets that you're consolidating aren't laid out the same, you can still use formulas, but you need to ensure that each formula refers to the correct cell.

Consolidating worksheets by using Paste Special

Another method of consolidating information is to use the Paste Special dialog box. This technique takes advantage of the fact that the Paste Special dialog box can perform a mathematical operation when it pastes data from the Clipboard. For example, you can use the Add option to add the copied data to the selected range. Figure 27.5 shows the Paste Special dialog box.

This method is applicable only when all the worksheets that you're consolidating are open. The disadvantage is that the consolidation isn't dynamic. In other words, it doesn't generate formulas. So, if any data that was consolidated changes, the consolidation is no longer accurate.

FIGURE 27.5

The Paste Special dialog box.

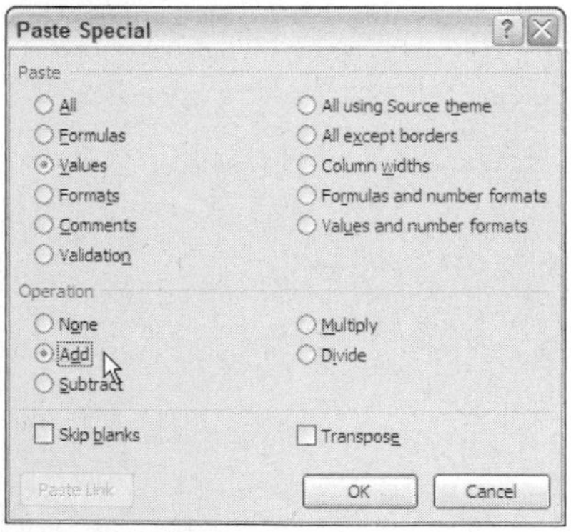

Here's how to use this method:

1. **Copy the data from the first source range.**
2. **Activate the destination workbook and select a location for the consolidated data.**
3. **Display the Paste Special dialog box (choose Home ⇨ Clipboard ⇨ Paste ⇨ Paste Special). Choose the Values option and the Add operation, and then click OK.**

Repeat these steps for each source range that you want to consolidate.

This method is probably the worst way of consolidating data. It can be rather error-prone, and the lack of formulas means that you have no way to verify the accuracy of the data.

Consolidating worksheets by using the Consolidate command

For the ultimate in data consolidation, use Excel's Consolidate dialog box. This method is very flexible, and in some cases, it even works if the source worksheets aren't laid out identically. This technique can create consolidations that are *static* (no link formulas) or *dynamic* (with link formulas). The Data Consolidate feature supports the following methods of consolidation:

- **By position:** This method is accurate only if the worksheets are laid out identically.
- **By category:** Excel uses row and column labels to match data in the source worksheets. Use this option if the data is laid out differently in the source worksheets or if some source worksheets are missing rows or columns.

Figure 27.6 shows the Consolidate dialog box, which appears when you choose Data ⇨ Data Tools ⇨ Consolidate. Following is a description of the controls in this dialog box:

FIGURE 27.6

The Consolidate dialog box enables you to specify ranges to consolidate.

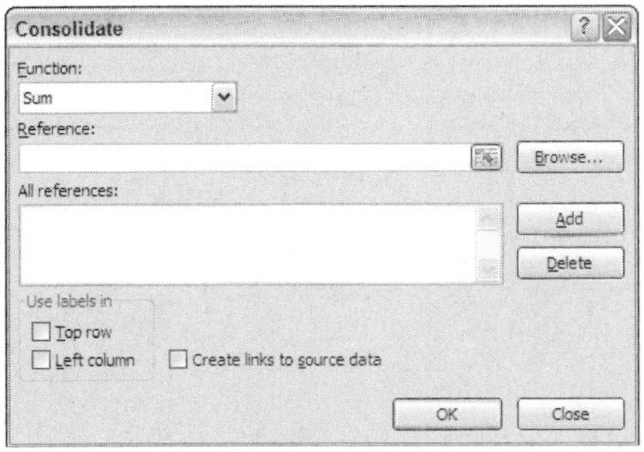

- **Function list box:** Specify the type of consolidation. Sum is the most commonly used consolidation function, but you also can select from ten other options.
- **Reference text box:** Specify a range from a source file that you want to consolidate. You can enter the range reference manually or use any standard pointing technique (if the workbook is open). After you enter the range in this box, click the Add button to add it to the All References list. If you consolidate by position, don't include labels in the range. If you consolidate by category, *do* include labels in the range.

- **All References list box:** Contains the list of references that you have added with the Add button.

- **Use Labels In check boxes:** Use to instruct Excel to perform the consolidation by examining the labels in the top row, the left column, or both positions. Use these options when you consolidate by category.

- **Create Links to Source Data check box:** When you select this option, Excel adds summary formulas for each label and creates an outline. If you don't select this option, the consolidation doesn't use formulas, and an outline isn't created.

- **Browse button:** Displays a dialog box that enables you to select a workbook to open. It inserts the filename in the Reference box, but you have to supply the range reference. You'll find that your job is much easier if all the workbooks to be consolidated are open.

- **Add button:** Adds the reference in the Reference box to the All References list. Make sure that you click this button after you specify each range.

- **Delete button:** Deletes the selected reference from the All References list.

An example

The simple example in this section demonstrates the power of Excel's Data Consolidate feature. Figure 27.7 shows three single-sheet workbooks that will be consolidated. These worksheets report product sales for three months. Notice, however, that they don't all report on the same products. In addition, the products aren't even listed in the same order. In other words, these worksheets aren't laid out identically. Creating consolidation formulas manually would be a very tedious task.

ON the CD-ROM These workbooks are available on the companion CD-ROM. The files are named region1.xlsx, region2.xlsx, and region3.xlsx.

To consolidate this information, start with a new workbook. You don't need to open the source workbooks, but consolidation is easier if they are open. Follow these steps to consolidate the workbooks:

1. **Choose Data ⇨ Data Tools ⇨ Consolidate. Excel displays its Consolidate dialog box.**

2. **Use the Function drop-down list to select the type of consolidation summary that you want to use.** Use Sum for this example.

3. **Enter the reference for the first worksheet to consolidate.** If the workbook is open, you can point to the reference. If it's not open, click the Browse button to locate the file on disk. The reference must include a range. You can use a range that includes complete columns, such as A:K. This range is larger than the actual range to consolidate, but using this range ensures that the consolidation will still work if new rows and columns are added to the source file. When the reference in the Reference box is correct, click Add to add it to the All References list.

4. **Enter the reference for the second worksheet.** You can point to the range in the Region2 workbook, or you can simply edit the existing reference by changing Region1 to Region2 and then clicking Add. This reference is added to the All References list.

5. **Enter the reference for the third worksheet.** Again, you can edit the existing reference by changing Region2 to Region3 and then clicking Add. This final reference is added to the All References list.

6. **Because the worksheets aren't laid out the same, select the Left column and Top row check boxes to force Excel to match the data by using the labels.**

7. **Select the Create Links to Source Data check box to make Excel create an outline with external references.**

8. **Click OK to begin the consolidation.**

FIGURE 27.7

Three worksheets to be consolidated.

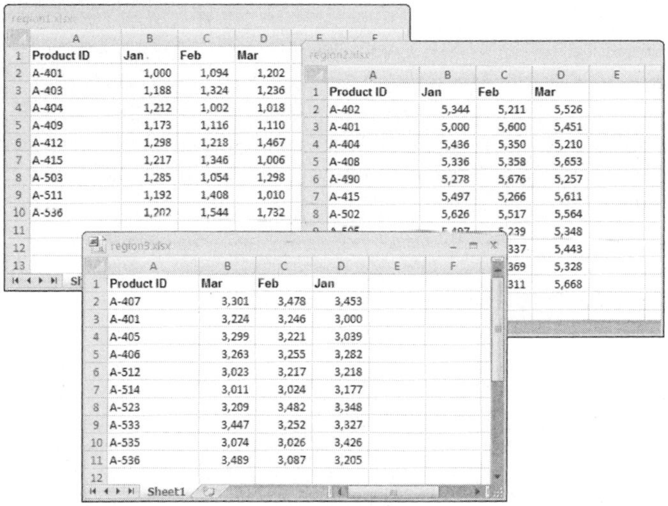

Excel creates the consolidation, beginning at the active cell. Notice that Excel created an outline, which is collapsed to show only the subtotals for each product. If you expand the outline (by clicking the number 2 or the + symbols in the outline), you can see the details. Examine it further, and you discover that each detail cell is an external reference formula that uses the appropriate cell in the source file. Therefore, the destination range is updated automatically if any data is changed.

Figure 27.8 shows the result of the consolidation, and Figure 27.9 shows the summary information (with the outline collapsed to hide the details).

CROSS-REF For more information about Excel outlines, see Chapter 26.

Refreshing a consolidation

When you choose the option to create formulas, the external references in the consolidation workbook are created only for data that exists at the time of the consolidation. Therefore, if new rows are added to any of the original workbooks, the consolidation must be re-done. Fortunately, the consolidation parameters are stored with the workbook, so it's a simple matter to re-run the consolidation if necessary. That's why specifying complete columns and including extra columns (in Step 3 in the preceding section) is a good idea.

Excel remembers the references that you entered in the Consolidate dialog box and saves them with the workbook. Therefore, if you want to refresh a consolidation later, you don't have to re-enter the references. Just display the Consolidate dialog box, verify that the ranges are correct, and click OK.

FIGURE 27.8

The result of consolidating the information in three workbooks.

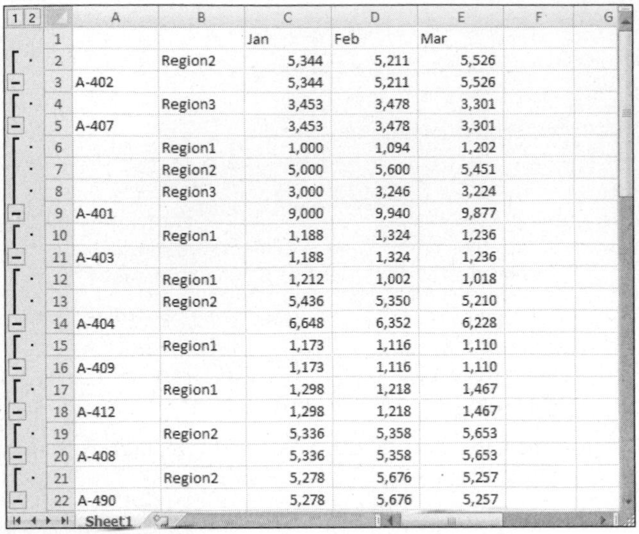

1 2		A	B	C	D	E	F	G
	1			Jan	Feb	Mar		
	2		Region2	5,344	5,211	5,526		
	3	A-402		5,344	5,211	5,526		
	4		Region3	3,453	3,478	3,301		
	5	A-407		3,453	3,478	3,301		
	6		Region1	1,000	1,094	1,202		
	7		Region2	5,000	5,600	5,451		
	8		Region3	3,000	3,246	3,224		
	9	A-401		9,000	9,940	9,877		
	10		Region1	1,188	1,324	1,236		
	11	A-403		1,188	1,324	1,236		
	12		Region1	1,212	1,002	1,018		
	13		Region2	5,436	5,350	5,210		
	14	A-404		6,648	6,352	6,228		
	15		Region1	1,173	1,116	1,110		
	16	A-409		1,173	1,116	1,110		
	17		Region1	1,298	1,218	1,467		
	18	A-412		1,298	1,218	1,467		
	19		Region2	5,336	5,358	5,653		
	20	A-408		5,336	5,358	5,653		
	21		Region2	5,278	5,676	5,257		
	22	A-490		5,278	5,676	5,257		

Sheet1

FIGURE 27.9

After collapsing the outline to show only the totals.

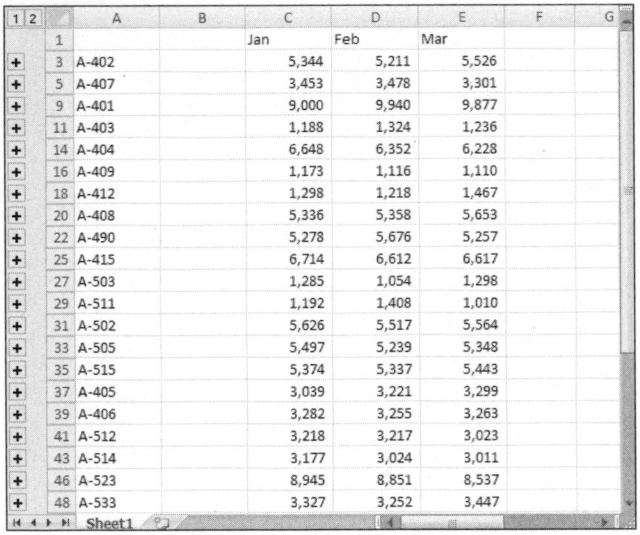

1 2		A	B	C	D	E	F	G
	1			Jan	Feb	Mar		
+	3	A-402		5,344	5,211	5,526		
+	5	A-407		3,453	3,478	3,301		
+	9	A-401		9,000	9,940	9,877		
+	11	A-403		1,188	1,324	1,236		
+	14	A-404		6,648	6,352	6,228		
+	16	A-409		1,173	1,116	1,110		
+	18	A-412		1,298	1,218	1,467		
+	20	A-408		5,336	5,358	5,653		
+	22	A-490		5,278	5,676	5,257		
+	25	A-415		6,714	6,612	6,617		
+	27	A-503		1,285	1,054	1,298		
+	29	A-511		1,192	1,408	1,010		
+	31	A-502		5,626	5,517	5,564		
+	33	A-505		5,497	5,239	5,348		
+	35	A-515		5,374	5,337	5,443		
+	37	A-405		3,039	3,221	3,299		
+	39	A-406		3,282	3,255	3,263		
+	41	A-512		3,218	3,217	3,023		
+	43	A-514		3,177	3,024	3,011		
+	46	A-523		8,945	8,851	8,537		
+	48	A-533		3,327	3,252	3,447		

Sheet1

More about consolidation

Excel is very flexible regarding the sources that you can consolidate. You can consolidate data from the following:

- Open workbooks.
- Closed workbooks. (You need to enter the reference manually, but you can use the Browse button to get the filename part of the reference.)
- The same workbook in which you're creating the consolidation.

And, of course, you can mix and match any of the preceding choices in a single consolidation.

If you perform the consolidation by matching labels, be aware that the matches must be exact. For example, *Jan* doesn't match *January*. The matching is not case-sensitive, however, so *April* does match *APRIL*. In addition, the labels can be in any order, and they don't need to be in the same order in all the source ranges.

If you don't choose the Create Links to Source Data check box, Excel generates a static consolidation. (It doesn't create formulas.) Therefore, if the data on any of the source worksheets changes, the consolidation doesn't update automatically. To update the summary information, you need to select the destination range and repeat the Data ⇨ Data Tools ⇨ Consolidate command.

If you choose the Create Links to Source Data check box, Excel creates a standard worksheet outline that you can manipulate by using the techniques described in Chapter 26.

Chapter 28

Excel and the Internet

Most people who use a computer are connected to the Internet. The Web has become an important way to share and gather information from myriad sources. To help you with these tasks, Excel has the capability to create files that you can use on the Internet and also to gather and process data from the Web. This chapter covers topics related to Excel and the Internet.

Understanding How Excel Uses HTML

HTML, an acronym for HyperText Markup Language, is the language of the World Wide Web. When you browse the Web, the documents that your browser retrieves and displays are usually in HTML format. An HTML file consists of text information plus special tags that describe how the text is to be formatted. The browser interprets the tags, applies the formatting, and displays the information.

> **CAUTION** In previous Excel versions, you could use HTML as a native file format. In other words, you could save a workbook in HTML format and then re-open the HTML file in Excel with no loss of functionality. You can no longer do so in Excel 2007. For example, all your formulas are converted to values. Therefore, if you save a file in HTML format using Excel 2007, make sure that you also save the file in a standard Excel format.

IN THIS CHAPTER

Saving Excel files in HTML format

Creating hyperlinks

Importing data from a Web page

Understanding the Different Web Formats

When you save an Excel workbook for viewing on the Web, you have two options:

- **An HTML file:** Produces a static Web page, plus a folder that contains support files. You can create the HTML file from the entire workbook or from a specific sheet.
- **A single file Web page:** Produces a file in the Web archive format (*.mht; *.mhtml). You can view these files only with Microsoft's Internet Explorer browser.

NOTE Previous versions of Excel included an additional option to create an interactive Web page, using the Microsoft ActiveX Spreadsheet Component. Users could perform standard Excel operations directly in the browser. This feature was removed from Excel 2007.

These options are described in the following sections. Both examples use a simple two-sheet workbook file. Each sheet has a table and a chart. Figure 28.1 shows one of these worksheets.

FIGURE 28. 1

This workbook will be saved in Excel's Web formats.

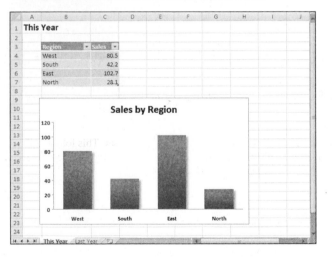

ON the CD-ROM This workbook, named webpage.xlsx, is available on the companion CD-ROM.

Creating an HTML file

To save a workbook as an HTML file, choose Office ➪ Save As. In the Save As dialog box, select Web Page (*.htm; *.html) from the Save As Type drop-down list and specify the Entire Workbook option. Name this file **webpage1.htm**. Click Save to create the HTML file.

Figure 28.2 shows how Sheet1 of the file looks in a browser. Notice that the workbook's sheet tabs appear along the bottom, and you can switch sheets just as you do in Excel.

FIGURE 28.2

Viewing the HTML file in a browser.

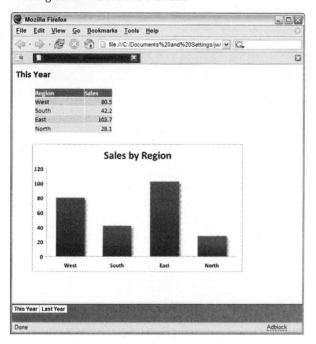

In addition to the **webpage1.htm** file, Excel also created a folder named **webpage1_files**. This folder contains additional files that must be kept with the main HTML file. Therefore, if you post such a file on a Web server, don't forget to also post the accompanying directory.

Creating a single file Web page

In the previous section, you saw that creating an HTML file with Excel also created a folder of additional files. To create a Web page that uses a single file, choose File ➪ Save As. In the Save As dialog box, select Single File Web Page (*.mht; *.mhtml) from the Save As Type drop-down list and specify the Entire Workbook option. Name this file **Webpage2.mht**. Click Save to create the file.

Figure 28.3 shows the file displayed in Microsoft Internet Explorer.

Web Options

If you save your work in HTML format, you should be aware of some additional options. In the Save As dialog box, click Tools and choose Web Options. You'll see the Web Options dialog box, which lets you control some aspects of the HTML file. Most of the time, the default settings work just fine. However, if you plan to save Excel files in HTML format, familiarizing yourself with the options available is worthwhile. These options are described in the Help system.

 You can view single file Web pages created from Excel only by using Microsoft's Internet Explorer browser.

FIGURE 28.3

Viewing the single file Web page.

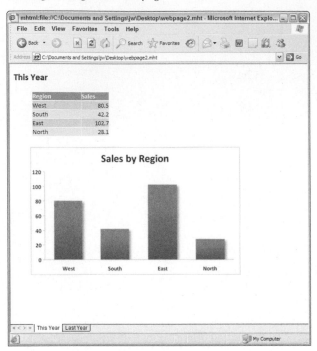

Opening an HTML File

Excel can open most HTML files, which can be stored on your local drive or on a Web server. Choose Office ➪ Open and locate the HTML file. If the file is on a server, you'll need to copy the URL and paste it into the File Name field in the Open dialog box.

How the HTML code renders in Excel varies considerably. Sometimes, the HTML file may look exactly as it does in a browser. Other times, it may bear little resemblance (especially if the HTML file uses CSS for layout).

Working with Hyperlinks

Hyperlinks are shortcuts that provide a quick way to jump to other workbooks and files. You can set up hyperlinks to jump to files on your own computer, your network, and the Web. For example, you can create a series of hyperlinks to serve as a table of contents for a workbook.

Inserting a hyperlink

You can create hyperlinks from cell text or graphic objects, such as shapes and pictures. To create a text hyperlink, choose Insert ➪ Links ➪ Hyperlink (or press Ctrl+K). Excel responds with the Insert Hyperlink dialog box, as shown in Figure 28.4.

FIGURE 28.4

Use the Insert Hyperlink dialog box to add hyperlinks to your Excel worksheets.

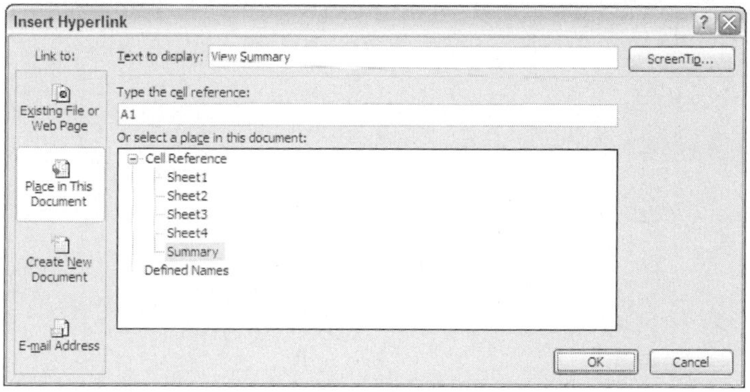

Select an icon in the Link To column that represents the type of hyperlink you want to create. Then, specify the location for the file that you want to link to. The dialog box changes, depending on the icon selected. If you like, click the Screen Tip button to provide some additional text that appears as a tool tip. Click OK, and Excel creates the hyperlink in the active cell.

You can create hyperlinks to a file on your hard drive, a Web page on the Internet, a new document, or a location in your current workbook. In addition, you can create a hyperlink that consists of an e-mail address.

Figure 28.5 shows a worksheet that contains hyperlinks.

FIGURE 28.5

Some hyperlinks.

Here's another way to create a link to a cell or range (which can be in any workbook):

1. **Select the cell or range.**
2. **Choose Home ➪ Clipboard ➪ Copy (or press Ctrl+C).**
3. **Activate the cell that will display the hyperlink.**
4. **Choose Home ➪ Clipboard ➪ Paste As Hyperlink.**

Excel creates a hyperlink to the cell or range that you copied in Step 3. This cell or range can be in any workbook or worksheet.

To add a hyperlink to a Shape, select the Shape and then choose Insert ➪ Links ➪ Hyperlink (or press Ctrl+K). Specify the required information in the Insert Hyperlink dialog box, as outlined earlier in this section.

Using hyperlinks

When you hover your mouse pointer over a cell that contains a hyperlink, the mouse pointer turns into a hand. Click the hyperlink and you're taken to the hyperlinked document.

> **TIP**   To select a cell that has a hyperlink with your mouse (without following the hyperlink), position your mouse over the cell, click, and hold for a second or two. Or just activate a nearby cell and use the arrow keys to select the cell that contains the hyperlink.

When you hover your pointer over a Shape that contains a hyperlink, the mouse pointer turns into a hand. To follow a hyperlink from a Shape, just point to the Shape and click.

If the hyperlink contains an e-mail address, your default e-mail program will be launched so that you can send an e-mail.

Using Web Queries

Excel enables you to pull in data contained in an HTML file by performing a Web query. The data is transferred to a worksheet, where you can manipulate it any way you like. Web queries are especially useful for data that is frequently updated — such as stock market quotes.

> **NOTE**   Performing a Web query doesn't actually open the HTML file in Excel — rather, it copies the information from the HTML file.

The best part about a Web query is that Excel remembers where the data came from. Therefore, after you create a Web query, you can *refresh* the query to pull in the most recent data.

To create a Web query, choose Data ➪ Get External Data ➪ From Web. Excel displays the New Web Query dialog box, shown in Figure 28.6. This dialog box is actually a resizable Web browser. You can click links to navigate or just type the URL of the HTML file in the Address box. The HTML file can be on the Internet, on a corporate intranet, or on a local or network drive. Each table is indicated by an arrow in a yellow box. Click an arrow to select the table or tables you want to import.

FIGURE 28. 6

Use the New Web Query dialog box to specify the source of the data.

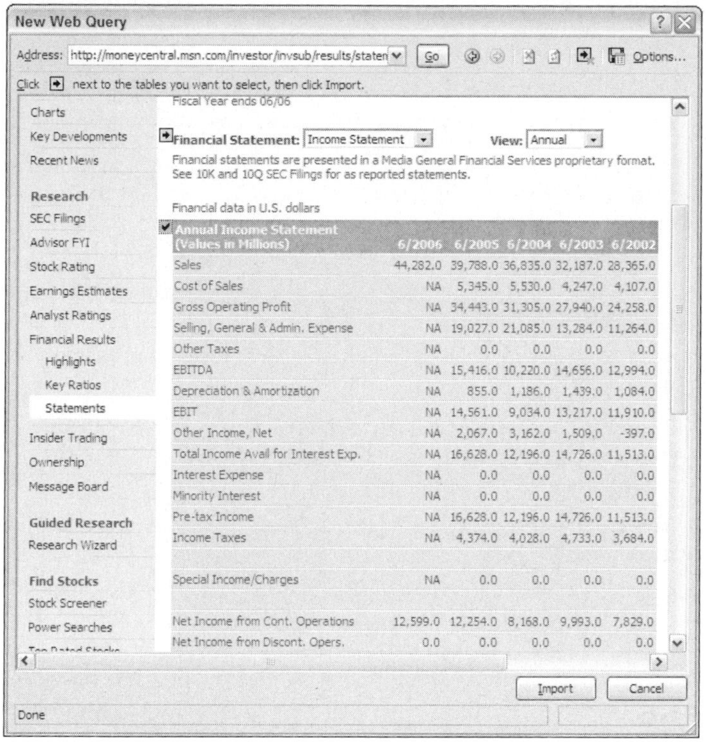

You can also control how the imported data is formatted. In the New Web Query dialog box, click Options to display the Web Query Options dialog box. Select the desired formatting and click OK to return to the New Web Query dialog box.

When you're ready to retrieve the information, click Import, and you get the Import Data dialog box, asking where you want to place the data.

The information on the Web page is retrieved and placed on your worksheet.

After you create your Web query, you have some options. Right-click any cell in the data range and select Data Range Properties from the shortcut menu. Excel displays the External Data Range Properties dialog box, shown in Figure 28.7. These settings control when the data is refreshed, how it is formatted, and what happens if the amount of data changes when the query is refreshed.

FIGURE 28.7

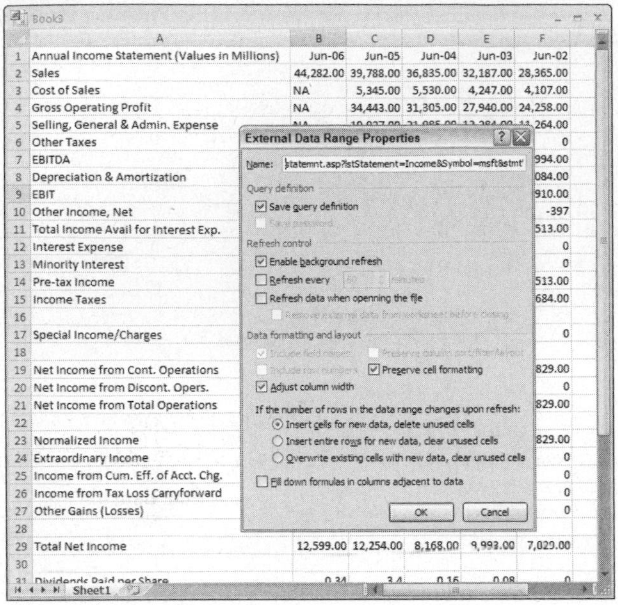

Chapter 29

Sharing Data with Other Applications

The applications in Microsoft Office are designed to work together. These programs have a common look and feel, and sharing data among these applications is usually quite easy. This chapter explores some ways in which you can make use of other applications while working with Excel, as well as some ways in which you can use Excel while working with other applications.

Understanding Data Sharing

Excel can import and export a variety of different file types. Besides sharing data using files, you can also transfer data to and from other open Windows applications in several other ways:

- Copy and paste, using either the Windows Clipboard or the Office Clipboard. Copying and pasting information creates a static copy of the data.
- Create a link so that changes in the source data are reflected in the destination document.
- Embed an entire object from one application into another application's document.

This chapter discusses these techniques and shows you how to use them.

Copying and Pasting

Copying information from one Windows application to another is quite easy. The application that contains the information that you're copying is called the *source* application, and the application to which you're copying the information is called the *destination* application.

521

Two Clipboards

I f you copy or cut information while working in a Microsoft Office application, the application places the copied information on both the Windows Clipboard and the Office Clipboard. After you copy information to the Windows Clipboard, it remains on the Windows Clipboard even after you paste it so that you can use it multiple times.

Because the Windows Clipboard can hold only one item at a time, when you copy or cut something else, the information previously stored on the Windows Clipboard is replaced. The Office Clipboard, unlike the Windows Clipboard, can hold up to 24 separate selections. The Office Clipboard operates in all Office applications; for example, you can copy two selections from Word and three from Excel and paste any or all of them in PowerPoint.

Following are the general steps that are required to copy from one application to another.

1. **Activate the source document window that contains the information that you want to copy.**

2. **Select the information by using the mouse or the keyboard.**

3. **If the source application is a Microsoft Office 2007 application, choose Home ⇨ Clipboard ⇨ Copy.** Most other applications have an Edit ⇨ Copy menu command. In most cases, pressing Ctrl+C copies the selection to the Clipboard.

4. **Activate the destination application.** If the program isn't running, you can start it without affecting the contents of the clipboard.

5. **Move to the appropriate position in the destination application (where you want to paste the copied material).**

6. **If the destination application is a Microsoft Office 2007 application, choose Home ⇨ Clipboard ⇨ Paste.** Most other applications have an Edit ⇨ Paste command, and you can usually use Ctrl+V to paste. If the Clipboard contents aren't appropriate for pasting, the Paste command is grayed (not available). You can sometimes select other paste options by choosing Home ⇨ Clipboard ⇨ Paste (or Edit ⇨ Paste Special).

In Step 3 in the preceding steps, you also can choose Home ⇨ Clipboard ⇨ Cut (or Edit ⇨ Cut) from the source application menu. This step deletes your selection from the source application after placing the selection on the Clipboard.

NOTE If you repeat Step 3 in any Office application, the Office Clipboard task pane appears automatically. If it doesn't appear, click the dialog launcher in the Home ⇨ Clipboard group.

Copying from Excel to Word

One of the most frequently used software combinations is a spreadsheet and a word processor. This section describes some of the ways to copy information from an Excel worksheet to a Word document.

Generally speaking, you can copy something from Excel and paste it into Word in one of two ways:

■ **As static information:** If the Excel data changes, the changes aren't reflected in the Word document.

■ **As a link:** If the Excel data changes, the changes are shown in the Word document.

You can find all the various paste options for Word in the Paste Special dialog box, which appears when you choose Home ➪ Clipboard ➪ Paste ➪ Paste Special.

> **NOTE** If you use Word's standard paste command (Home ➪ Clipboard ➪ Paste, or Ctrl+V), you'll find that the paste method varies, depending on what is pasted. An Excel range copied and pasted to Word is pasted as a static table. An Excel chart, on the other hand, is pasted as a link.

Pasting static information

Often, you don't need a link when you copy data from Excel to Word. For example, if you're preparing a report in your word processor and you simply want to include a range of data from an Excel worksheet, you probably don't need to create a link (unless the data in the Excel worksheet may be changed). After you've copied an Excel range, activate Word and choose Home ➪ Clipboard ➪ Paste or press Ctrl+V. The range appears as a Word table, and is not linked to the Excel workbook.

For more control over pasting, use the Paste Special dialog box. Figure 29.1 shows Word's Paste Special dialog box when you've copied an Excel range and chosen the Paste option. If you select one of the choices in the Paste Special dialog box with the Paste option selected, the data is pasted without creating a link.

FIGURE 29.1

Word's paste options when an Excel range is on the Clipboard.

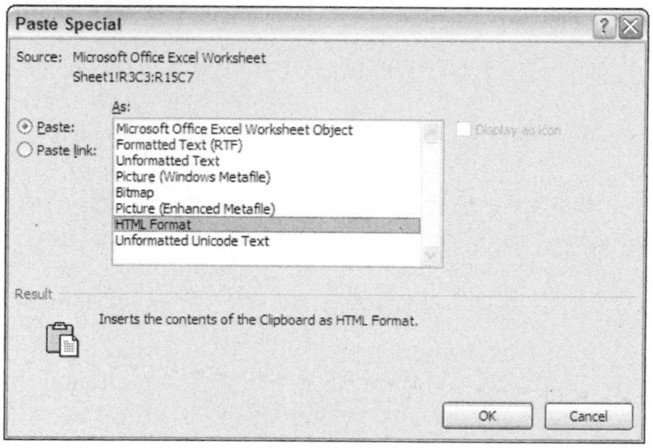

The paste options in Word's Paste Special dialog box when a range is copied include

- **Microsoft Office Excel Worksheet Object:** You can edit this object with Excel. Double-click, and Word's Ribbon is replaced with Excel's Ribbon. See "Embedding an Excel range in a Word document," later in this chapter.

- **Formatted Text (RTF):** The range is pasted as a table, with some formatting retained.

- **Unformatted Text:** Only the raw information is pasted, with no formatting. Cells are separated with a Tab character.

- **Picture (Windows Metafile):** The range is pasted as a picture.

- **Bitmap:** The range is pasted as a picture.

- **Picture (Enhanced Metafile):** The range is pasted as a picture.

- **HTML Format:** The range is pasted as a table, with all formatting retained. This format is pasted when you choose Home ⇨ Clipboard ⇨ Paste.

- **Unformatted Unicode Text:** Only the raw information is pasted, with no formatting. Cells are separated with a Tab character.

If you've copied an Excel chart to the Clipboard, Word's Paste Special dialog box displays different options. Figure 29.2 shows Word's Paste Special dialog box when an Excel chart is copied. The options are

FIGURE 29.2

Word's paste options when an Excel chart is on the Clipboard.

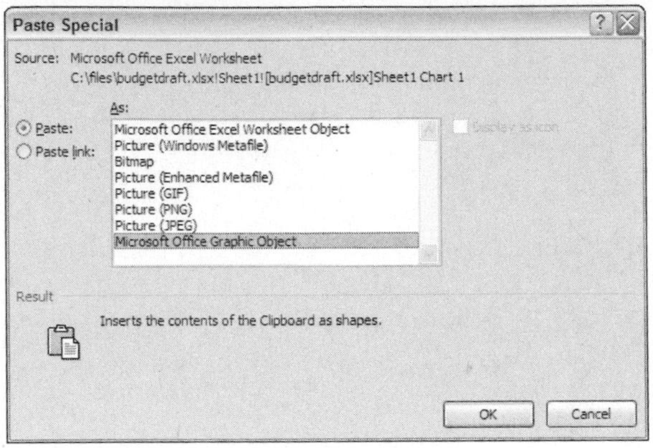

- **Microsoft Office Excel Worksheet Object:** You can edit this object with Excel. Double-click, and Word's Ribbon is replaced with Excel's Ribbon.

- **Picture (Windows Metafile):** The chart is pasted as a picture.

- **Bitmap:** The chart is pasted as bitmap image.

- **Picture (Enhanced Metafile):** The chart is pasted as a picture.

- **Picture (GIF):** The chart is pasted as a GIF image.

- **Picture (PNG):** The chart is pasted as a PNG (Portable Network Graphics) image.

- **Picture (JPEG):** The chart is pasted as a JPEG image, which usually results in a fuzzy image.

- **Microsoft Office Graphic Object:** The image is linked to the Excel range, and you can also edit it in Word. This format is pasted when you choose Home ⇨ Clipboard ⇨ Paste.

Pasting a link

If the data that you're copying will change, you may want to paste a link. When would you want to use this technique? If you generate proposals using Word, for example, you may need to refer to pricing information that you store in an Excel worksheet. If you set up a link between your Word document and the Excel worksheet, you can be sure that your proposals always quote the latest prices.

If you paste the data by using the Paste Link option in the Paste Special dialog box, you can make changes to the source document, and those changes appear in the destination application. You can test these changes by displaying both applications on-screen, making changes to the source document, and watching for them to appear in the destination document.

CAUTION
You can break links rather easily. If you move the source document to another directory or save it under a different name, for example, the destination document's application isn't able to update the link. In such a case, you need to re-establish the link manually.

Figure 29.3 shows Word's Paste Special dialog box when an Excel range has been copied and the Paste Link option is specified. Note that, with one exception, these options are the same ones available when you select the Paste option. The only format that isn't available for pasting a link is Picture (Enhanced Metafile).

FIGURE 29.3

Word's paste link options for an Excel range.

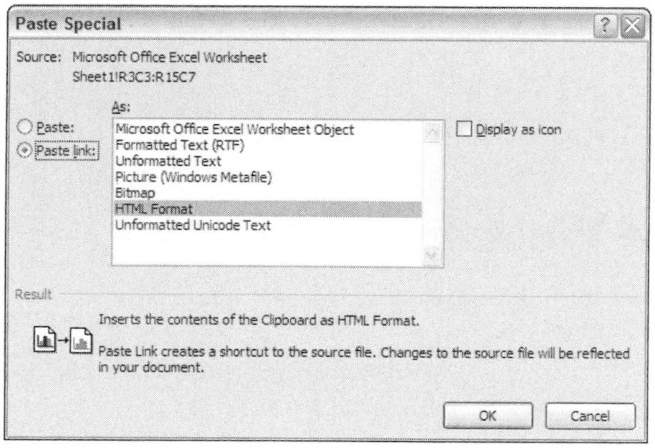

When an Excel chart is on the Clipboard, you can also choose the Paste Link option in Word's Paste Special dialog box.

NOTE
When you paste an Excel chart to Word using the Microsoft Office Graphic Object option, only the chart's data is linked. All other modifications (such as formatting or changing the chart type) aren't reflected in the copy pasted in the Word document. When you activate the chart in Word, you can use the Chart Tools context menu to make changes to the chart.

To edit (or break) a link, choose Office ⇨ Prepare ⇨ Edit Links To Files in Word, which displays the Links dialog box shown in Figure 29.4. Select the Source File from the list, and click the Break Link button. After breaking a link, the data remains in the destination document, but it's no longer linked to the source document.

FIGURE 29.4

Use Word's Links dialog box to modify or break links.

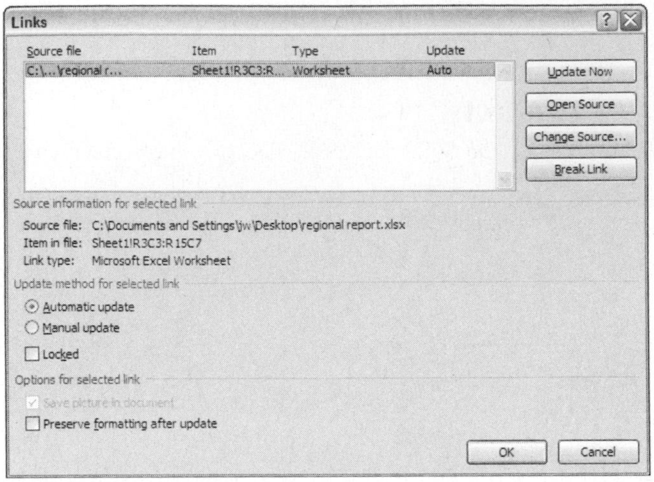

Embedding Objects in a Worksheet

Using *Object Linking and Embedding* (OLE), you can also embed an object to share information between Windows applications. This technique enables you to insert an object from another program and use that program's editing tools to manipulate it. The OLE objects can be such items as

- Text documents from other products, such as word processors
- Drawings or pictures from other products
- Information from special OLE server applications, such as Microsoft Equation
- Sound files
- Video or animation files

Many (but certainly not all) Windows applications support OLE. Embedding is often used for a document that you will distribute to others. It can eliminate the need to send multiple document files and help avoid broken link problems.

To embed an object into an Excel workbook, choose Insert ➪ Text ➪ Object, which displays the Object dialog box. This dialog box has two tabs, one for creating a new object and one for creating an object from an existing file.

Embedding Word documents

To embed an empty Word document into an Excel worksheet, choose Insert ➪ Text ➪ Object in Excel. In the Object dialog box, click the Create New tab and select Microsoft Office Word Document from the Object type list.

The result is a blank Word document, activated and ready for you to enter text. Notice that Word's Ribbon replaces Excel's Ribbon, giving you access to all Word's features.

To embed a copy of an existing Word file, use the Create From File tab in the Object dialog box and then locate the file on your hard drive. The Word document is inserted into your Excel worksheet. Double-click the document to display Word's Ribbon.

Embedding other types of documents

You can embed many other types of objects, including audio clips, video clips, MIDI sequences, and even an entire Microsoft PowerPoint presentation.

Figure 29.5 shows an MP3 audio file embedded in a worksheet. Clicking the object plays the song on the default MP3 players.

FIGURE 29.5

An MP3 file embedded in a worksheet.

	A	B	C	D	E	F
1						
2		Click below to play music while you work.				
3						
4						
5						
6		Madeleine Peyroux - No More.mp3				
7						
8						
9						

Sheet1

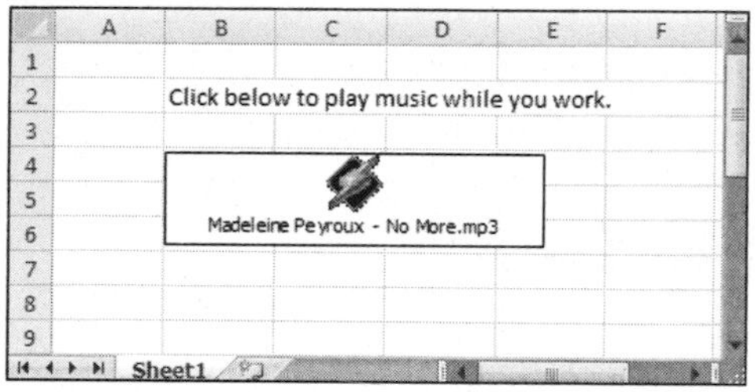

Microsoft Office includes several additional applications that you may find useful. For example, you can embed a Microsoft Equation object in an Excel document to graphically illustrate a formula that you use in a worksheet.

 Some of the object types listed in the Object dialog box can result in quite useful and interesting items when inserted into an Excel worksheet. If you're not sure what an object type is, try adding the object to a blank Excel workbook to see what is available. Keep in mind that not all the objects listed in this dialog box actually work with Excel. Attempting to use some of them may even crash Excel.

Embedding an Excel Workbook in a Word Document

You can embed an Excel workbook in a Word document in three ways:

- Copy a range and use Word's Paste Special dialog box.
- Open an existing Excel file using Word's Object dialog box.
- Create a new Excel workbook using Word's Object dialog box.

The following sections cover these methods.

Embedding a workbook in Word by copying

The example in this section describes how to embed an Excel workbook (shown in Figure 29.6) in a Word document.

FIGURE 29.6

This workbook will be embedded in a Word document.

	A	B	C
1	Region	Manager	ID
2	Region 1	Logan Tipton	L12172
3	Region 2	David D. Hill	D13168
4	Region 3	Rene Martin	R1139
5	Region 4	Janet Crane	J1169
6	Region 5	Albert Thomas	A13124
7	Region 6	Angel K. Bluhm	A1424
8	Region 7	Carol P. Barger	C15118
9	Region 8	Cassie Jones	C1287
10	Region 9	Lori V. Moore	L1315
11	Region 10	Jeffrey P. Moore	J1688
12	Region 11	Beverly Glenn	B1360
13	Region 12	Henry Baker	H1117
14			

Sheet1

To start, select A1:C13 and copy the range to the Clipboard. Then activate (or start) Word, open the document in which you want to embed the range, and move the insertion point to the location in the document where you want the table to appear. Choose Word's Home ➪ Clipboard ➪ Paste ➪ Paste Special command. Select the Paste option (not the Paste Link option) and choose the Microsoft Excel Worksheet Object format. Click OK, and the range appears in the Word document. Although it appears that only the range is embedded, the entire Excel workbook is actually embedded.

If you double-click the embedded object, you notice something unusual: Word's Ribbon is replaced by the Excel Ribbon. In addition, the embedded object appears with Excel's familiar row and column borders. In other words, you can edit this object *in place* by using Excel's commands. Figure 29.7 shows the Word document after double-clicking the embedded Excel workbook. To return to Word, just click anywhere in the Word document.

> **CAUTION**   Remember that no link is involved here. If you make changes to the embedded object in Word, these changes don't appear in the original Excel worksheet. The embedded object is a copy of the original workbook, and is completely independent from the original source.

You may have noticed that Microsoft Excel Worksheet Object also appears in the Paste Special dialog box when you choose the Paste Link option. If you paste the range using this option, the workbook isn't embedded in the Word document. When you double-click the object, Excel is activated so that you can edit the workbook.

Double-clicking the embedded Excel object enables you to edit it in place. Note that Word now displays Excel's Ribbon.

Embedding a saved workbook in Word

Another way to embed an Excel workbook in a Word document is to choose Insert ➪ Text ➪ Object in Word, which displays the Object dialog box. Select the Create From File tab, click Browse, and locate the Excel document. When you click OK, a copy of the workbook is embedded in the document. No link is created.

NOTE If you select the Link to File check box in the Object dialog box, you create a link to the workbook. In such a case, double-clicking the object in Word activates Excel so that you can edit the workbook.

Creating a new Excel object in Word

The preceding examples embed an existing workbook into a Word document. This section demonstrates how to create a new (empty) Excel object in Word, which is useful if you're creating a report and need to insert a table of values. If those values aren't available in an existing Excel workbook, you can embed a new Excel object and type them.

> **TIP** You could insert a normal Word table, but you can take advantage of Excel's formulas and functions in an embedded Excel worksheet.

To create a new Excel object in a Word document, choose Insert ➪ Text ➪ Object in Word. Word responds with the Object dialog box. Click the Create New tab, and you see a list of the types of objects that you can create. Select Microsoft Office Excel Worksheet from the list and click OK.

Word inserts an empty Excel worksheet object into the document and activates it for you. Again, you have full access to the Excel Ribbon, so you can enter whatever you want into the worksheet object. After you finish, click anywhere in the Word document. You can double-click this object at any time to make changes or additions.

You can change the size of the object while it's activated by dragging any of the sizing handles (the little black squares and rectangles) that appear on the borders of the object.

Chapter 30

Using Excel in a Workgroup

M ost people who use a computer in an office connect to others via a network. In fact, networks have also become common in homes. By enabling users to easily share data (and peripheral devices), networks make it much easier for people to work together on projects. Excel has a number of features that facilitate this type of cooperation, and those features are the subject of this chapter.

NOTE If you're working on a corporate network, you may need to consult with your network administrator before using any of the features described in this chapter.

Using Excel on a Network

A computer *network* consists of a group of PCs that are linked electronically. Users on a network can perform these tasks:

- Access files on other systems
- Share files with other users
- Share resources, such as printers, scanners, and fax modems
- Communicate with each other electronically

Excel has tools that enable you to work cooperatively with other Excel users on a project.

Understanding File Reservations

Networks provide users with the ability to share information stored on other computer systems. Sharing files on a network has two major advantages:

- It eliminates the need to have multiple copies of the files stored locally on user PCs.

- It ensures that the file is always up-to-date. For example, a group of users can work on a single document, as opposed to everyone working on his or her own document and then merging them all together.

> **NOTE** Some networks — generally known as *client-server networks* — designate specific computers as file servers. On these types of networks, the shared data files are normally stored on the file server. Excel doesn't care whether you're working on a client-server or a *peer-to-peer network* (where all the PCs have essentially equal functions).

Some software applications are *multiuser applications*. Most database software applications, for example, enable multiple users to work simultaneously on the same database files. One user may be updating customer records in the database, while another is extracting information for a report. But what if two users attempt to change a particular customer record at the same time? Multiuser database software contains record-locking safeguards that ensure that only one user at a time can modify a particular record.

Excel is *not* a multiuser application. When you open an Excel file, the entire file is loaded into memory. If the file is accessible to other users, you wouldn't want someone else to change the stored copy of a file that you've opened. If Excel allowed you to open and change a file that someone else on a network had already opened, the following scenario could happen.

Assume that your company keeps its sales information in an Excel file that is stored on a network server. Esther wants to add this week's data to the file, so she loads it from the server and begins adding new information. A few minutes later, Jim loads the file to correct some errors that he noticed last week. Esther finishes her work and saves the file. A while later, Jim finishes his corrections and saves the file. Jim's file overwrites the copy that Esther saved, and her additions are gone.

This scenario *can't happen* because Excel uses a concept known as *file reservation*. When Esther opens the sales workbook, she has the reservation for the file. When Jim tries to open the file, Excel informs him that Esther is using the file. If he insists on opening it, Excel opens the file as *read-only*. In other words, Jim can open the file, but he can't save it under the same name. Figure 30.1 shows the message that Jim receives if he tries to open a file that is in use by someone else.

FIGURE 30.1

The File In Use dialog box appears if you try to open a file that someone else is using.

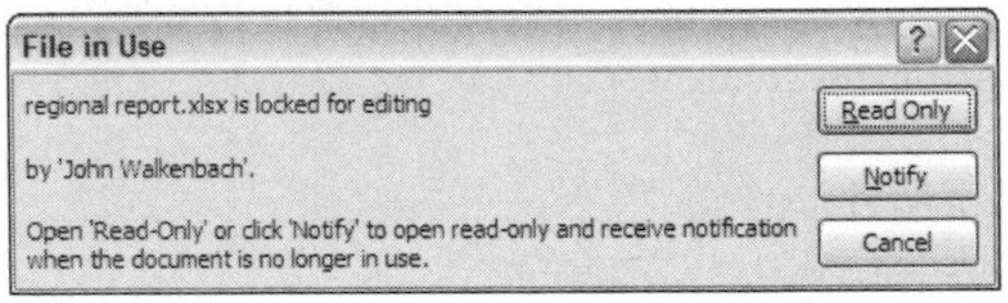

Jim has three choices:

- **Select Cancel, wait a while, and try again.** He may call the person who has the file reservation and ask when the file will be available.
- **Select Read Only.** This option lets him open the file to read it, but it doesn't let him save changes to the same filename.
- **Select Notify, which opens the file as read-only.** Excel pops up a message that notifies Jim when the person who has the file reservation is finished using the file.

Figure 30.2 shows the message that Jim receives when the file is available. If Jim opens the file as Read-Write, he receives another message if he makes any changes to his read-only version. He will have an opportunity to discard his changes or to save his file with a new name.

FIGURE 30.2

The File Now Available dialog box pops up with a new message when the file is available for editing.

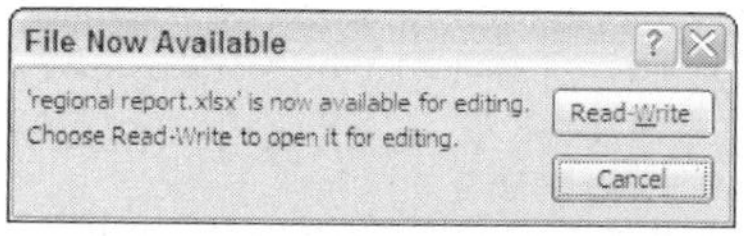

Sharing Workbooks

Although Excel isn't a true multiuser application, it does support a feature known as *shared workbooks*, which enables multiple users to work on the same workbook simultaneously. Excel keeps track of the changes and provides appropriate prompts to handle conflicts.

CAUTION Although the ability to share workbooks sounds great in theory, it can be confusing if more than a few users are sharing a single workbook. Also, be warned that this feature has been known to cause problems, and it's certainly not 100 percent reliable. Therefore, use caution and make frequent backup copies of your workbooks.

Understanding shared workbooks

You can share any Excel workbook with any number of users. Following are a few examples of workbooks that work well as shared workbooks:

- **Project tracking:** You may have a workbook that contains status information for projects. If multiple people are involved in the project, they can make changes and updates to the parts that are relevant to them.
- **Customer lists:** With a customer list, records are often added, deleted, and modified by multiple users.
- **Consolidations:** You may create a budget workbook in which each department manager is responsible for his or her department's budget. Usually, each department's budget appears on a separate sheet, with one sheet serving as the consolidation sheet.

If you plan to designate a workbook as shared, be aware that Excel imposes quite a few restrictions on the workbook. For example, a shared workbook may not contain any tables.

In addition, you can't perform any of the following actions while sharing the workbook (the relevant commands are grayed out in the Ribbon):

- Delete worksheets or chart sheets.
- Insert or delete a blocks of cells. However, you can insert or delete entire rows and columns.
- Merge cells.
- Define or apply conditional formats.
- Change or delete array formulas.
- Set up or change data-validation restrictions and messages.
- Insert or change charts, pictures, drawings, objects, or hyperlinks.
- Assign or modify a password to protect individual worksheets or the entire workbook.
- Create or modify pivot tables, scenarios, outlines, or data tables.
- Insert automatic subtotals.
- Write, change, view, record, or assign macros. However, you can record a macro while a shared workbook is active as long as you store the macro in another unshared workbook (such as your Personal Macro Workbook).

TIP

You may want to choose Review ⇨ Protect Sheet to further control what users can do while working in a shared workbook.

CAUTION

If you save an Excel 2007 shared workbook to an earlier version file format (such as *.xls), sharing is turned off, and the revision history (if any) is lost.

Designating a workbook as a shared workbook

To designate a workbook as a shared workbook, choose Review Changes ⇨ Share Workbook. Excel displays the Share Workbook dialog box, shown in Figure 30.3. This dialog box has two tabs: Editing and Advanced. In the Editing tab, select the check box to allow changes by multiple users and then click OK. Excel then prompts you to save the workbook.

FIGURE 30.3

Use the Share Workbook dialog box to control the sharing of your workbooks.

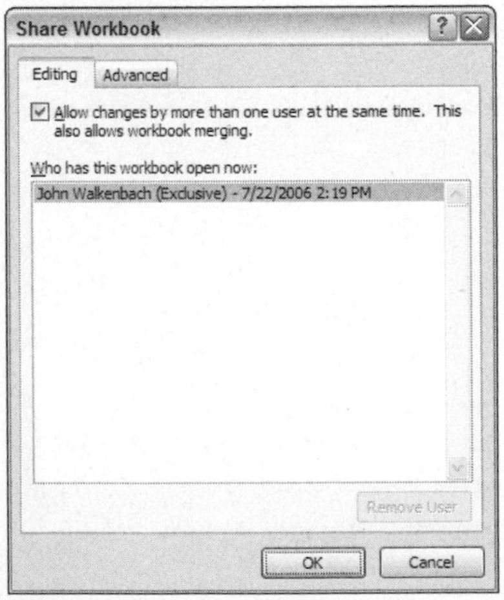

When you open a shared workbook, the workbook window's title bar displays [Shared]. If you no longer want other users to be able to use the workbook, remove the check mark from the Editing tab of the Share Workbook dialog box and save the workbook.

> **TIP** Whenever you're working with a shared workbook, you can find out whether any other users are working on the workbook. Choose Tools ➪ Share Workbook, and the Editing tab of the Share Workbook dialog box lists the names of the other users who have the file open, as well as the time that each user opened the workbook.

Controlling the advanced sharing settings

Excel enables you to set options for shared workbooks. Choose Tools ➪ Share Workbook and click the Advanced tab in the Share Workbook dialog box to access these options (see Figure 30.4).

FIGURE 30.4

Use the Advanced tab of the Share Workbook dialog box to set the advanced sharing options for your workbook.

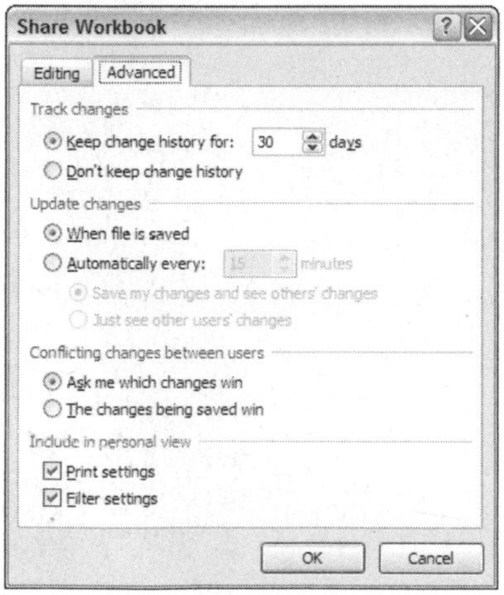

Tracking changes

Excel can keep track of the workbook's changes — which is known as *change history*. When you designate a workbook as a shared workbook, Excel automatically turns on the Change History option, enabling you to view information about previous (and perhaps conflicting) changes to the workbook. You can turn off change history by selecting the option labeled Don't Keep Change History. You can also specify the number of days for which Excel tracks change history.

Updating changes

While you're working on a shared workbook, you can choose Office ➪ Save to update the workbook with your changes. The Update Changes settings determine what happens when you save a shared workbook:

- **When File Is Saved:** You receive updates from other users when you save your copy of the shared workbook.

- **Automatically Every:** Lets you specify a time period for receiving updates from other users of the workbook. You can also specify whether Excel should save your changes automatically, too, or just show you the changes made by other users.

Sharing a Workbook with Yourself

If you plan to use shared workbooks, spend time experimenting with the various settings to ensure that you understand how sharing works. You don't need to enlist a colleague to help you—you can share a workbook with yourself. Just launch a second instance of Excel and then open a shared workbook in both instances. Make changes, save the file, adjust the settings, and so on. Before long, you'll have a good understanding of Excel's shared workbooks.

Resolving conflicting changes between users

As you may expect, multiple users working on the same file can result in some conflicts. For example, assume that you're working on a shared customer information workbook, and another user also has the workbook open. If you and the other user both make a change to the same cell, a conflict occurs. You can specify the manner in which Excel resolves the conflicts by selecting one of two options in the Advanced tab of the Share Workbook dialog box:

- **Ask Me Which Changes Win:** If you select this option, Excel displays a dialog box to let you determine how to settle the conflict.

- **The Changes Being Saved Win:** If you select this option, the most recently saved version always takes precedence.

CAUTION   Notice that the second option, The Changes Being Saved Win, has slightly deceptive wording. Even if the other user saves his changes, any changes you make will automatically override his changes when you save the workbook. This option may result in a loss of data because you won't have any warning that you've overwritten another user's changes.

Controlling the Include in Personal View settings

The final section of the Advanced tab of the Share Workbook dialog box enables you to specify settings that are specific to your view of the shared workbook. You can choose to use your own print settings and your own data-filtering settings. If you don't place check marks in these check boxes, you can't save your own print and filter settings.

Tracking Workbook Changes

Excel has a feature that enables you to track changes made to a workbook. You may want to use this feature if you send a workbook to someone for reviewing. When the file is returned, you can then see what changes were made and then accept or reject them accordingly.

Turning Track Changes on and off

To enable change tracking, choose Review ➪ Changes ➪ Track Changes ➪ Highlight Changes, which displays the Highlight Changes dialog box, shown in Figure 30.5. Then place a check mark in the Track Changes While Editing check box.

FIGURE 30.5

Use the Highlight Changes dialog box to track changes made to a workbook.

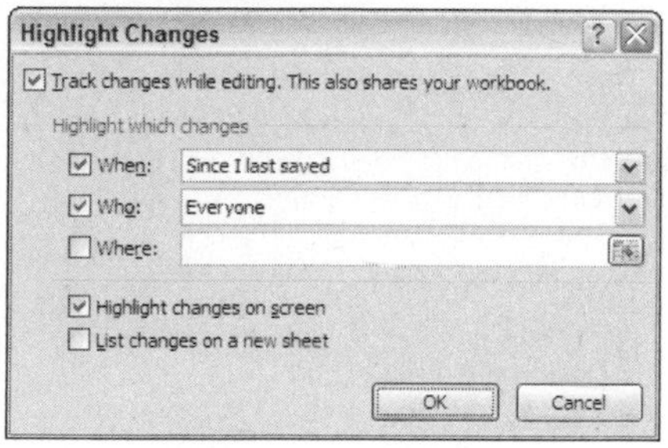

You can also specify the period to track (When), which users to track (Who), and specify a range of cells to track (Where). If you enable the Highlight Changes on Screen option, each changed cell displays a small triangle in its upper-left corner. And when a changed cell is selected, you see a cell comment that describes what change was made (see Figure 30.6).

After you select the option(s) that you want, click OK to close the Highlight Changes dialog box and enable tracking. To stop tracking changes, choose Review ⇨ Changes ⇨ Track Changes ⇨ Highlight Changes again, and then remove the check mark in the Track Changes While Editing check box.

CAUTION When tracking changes is enabled, the workbook always becomes a shared workbook — which severely limits the types of changes you can make. Shared workbooks are discussed earlier in this chapter (see "Sharing Workbooks").

FIGURE 30.6

Excel displays a descriptive note when you select a cell that has changed.

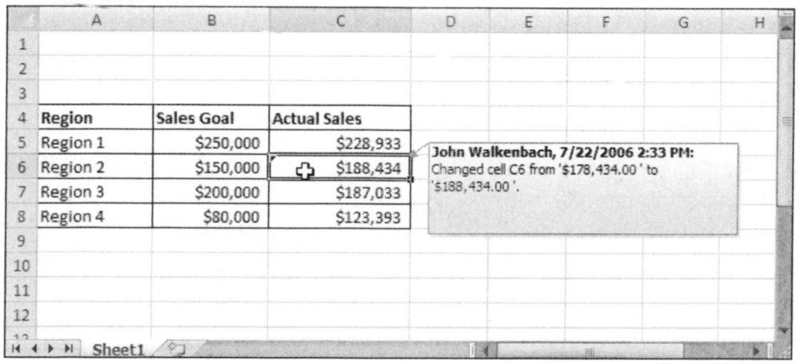

Following are some points to keep in mind when using the Track Changes feature:

- Changes made to cell contents are tracked, but other changes (such as formatting changes) aren't tracked.

- The change history is kept only for a set interval. When you turn on Track Changes, the changes are kept for 30 days. You can increase or decrease the number of days of history to keep in the Highlight Changes dialog box (use the When setting).

- If you would like to generate a list of the changes made, choose Review ➪ Changes ➪ Track Changes ➪ Highlight Changes and then enable the List Changes On A New Sheet check box. Click OK, and Excel inserts a new worksheet named History. This sheet shows detailed information about each change made.

- Only one level of changes is maintained. Thus, if you change the value of a cell several times, only the most recent change is remembered.

Reviewing the changes

To review the changes made while using the Track Changes features, choose Review ➪ Changes ➪ Track Changes ➪ Accept/Reject Changes. The Select Changes to Accept or Reject dialog box appears, enabling you to select the types of changes that you want to review. This dialog box is similar to the Highlight Changes dialog box. You can specify When, Who, and Where.

Click OK, and Excel displays each change in a new dialog box, as shown in Figure 30.7. Click Accept to accept the change or click Reject to reject the change. You can also click Accept All (to accept all changes) or Reject All (to reject all changes).

FIGURE 30.7

Chapter 31

Protecting
Your Work

The concept of "protection" gets a lot of attention in the Excel newsgroups and forums. It seems that many users want to learn how to protect their workbooks from being copied or modified. Excel has several protection-related features, and those features are covered in this chapter.

Types of Protection

Excel's protection-related features fall into three categories:

- **Worksheet protection:** Protecting a worksheet from being modified, or restricting the modifications to certain users.
- **Workbook protection:** Protecting a workbook from having sheets inserted or deleted, and also requiring the use of password in order to open the workbook.
- **VB protection:** Using a password to prevent others from viewing or modifying your VBA code.

CAUTION Before I discuss these features, you should understand the notion of security. Using a password to protect some aspect of your work doesn't guarantee that it's secure. Password-cracking utilities (and some simple tricks) have been around for a long time. Using passwords work in the vast majority of cases, but if someone is truly intent on getting to your data, he or she can usually find a way. If absolute security is critical, perhaps Excel isn't the proper tool.

About Information Rights Management

Excel supports a feature known as Information Rights Management (IRM), which allows you to specify access permissions for workbooks. Using IRM may help prevent sensitive information from being printed, e-mailed, or copied by unauthorized people. When IRM is applied to a workbook, the permission information is stored in the document file itself.

To use IRM, you must install Microsoft's Windows Rights Management Services (RMS) — an extra-cost product that isn't included with Microsoft Office. You can access the IRM settings by choosing Office ➪ Prepare ➪ Restrict Permission.

IRM is not covered in this book. If your company uses RMS, consult your system administrator for more information about how this feature is used within your organization.

Worksheet Protection

Excel users protect a worksheet for a variety of reasons. One reason is to prevent yourself or others from accidentally deleting formulas or other critical data. A common scenario is to protect a worksheet so that the data can be changed, but the formulas can't be changed.

To protect a worksheet, activate the worksheet and choose Review ➪ Changes ➪ Protect Sheet. Excel displays the Protect Sheet dialog box shown in Figure 31.1. Note that providing a password is optional. If you enter a password, that password will be required to unprotect the worksheet. If you accept the default options in the Protect Sheet dialog box, none of the cells on the worksheet can be modified.

FIGURE 31.1

Use the Protect Sheet dialog box to protect a worksheet.

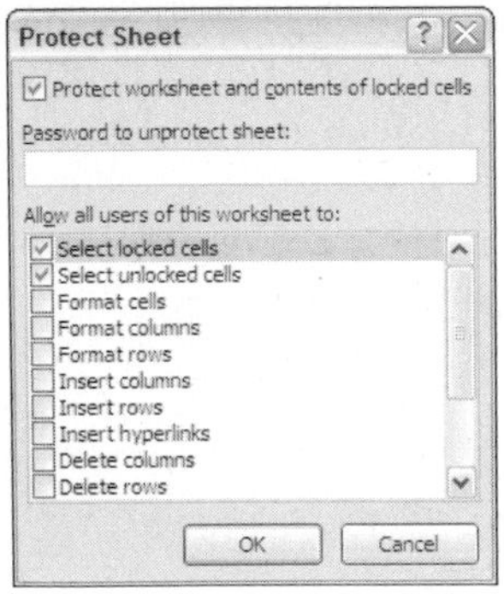

Unlocking cells

In many cases, you will want to allow *some* cells to be changed when the worksheet is protected. For example, your worksheet may have some input cells that are used by formula cells. In such a case, you would want the user to be able to change the input cells, but not the formula cells. Every cell has a Locked attribute, and that attribute determines whether the cell can be changed when the sheet is protected.

By default, all cells are locked. To change the locked attribute, select the cell or range and then use the Protection tab of the Format Cells dialog box (see Figure 31.2). To display this dialog box, right-click the cell or range and choose Format Cells from the shortcut menu (or press Ctrl+1). Remove the check mark from Locked and click OK.

FIGURE 31.2

Use the Protection tab in the Format Cells dialog box to change the Locked attribute of a cell or range.

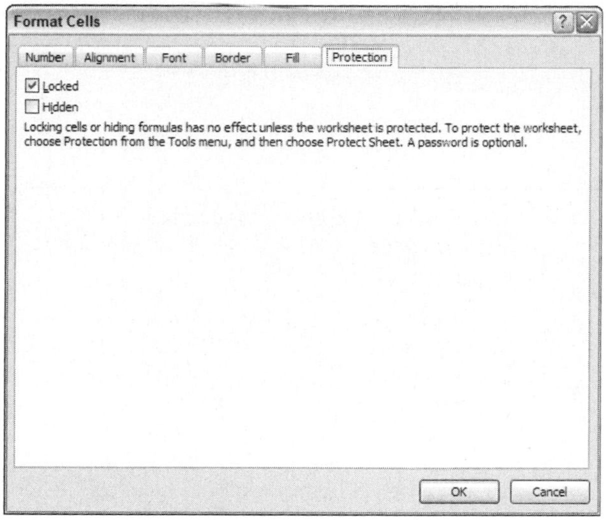

NOTE The Protection tab of the Format Cells dialog box has another attribute: Hidden. If checked, the contents of the cell don't appear in the Formula bar when the sheet is protected. The cell isn't hidden in the worksheet. You may want to set the Hidden attribute for formula cells to prevent users from seeing the formula when the cell is selected.

After you unlock the desired cells, choose Review ➪ Changes ➪ Protect Sheet to protect the sheet. After doing so, you can change the unlocked cells, but if you attempt to change a locked cell, Excel displays the dialog box shown in Figure 31.3.

FIGURE 31.3

Excel warns you if you attempt to change a locked cell.

To unprotect a protected sheet, choose Review ➪ Changes ➪ Unprotect Sheet. If the sheet is protected with a password, you're prompted to enter the password.

Sheet protection options

The Protect Sheet dialog box has several options, which determine what the user can do when the worksheet is protected.

- **Select locked cells:** If checked, the user can select locked cells using the mouse or the keyboard. This setting is checked, by default.
- **Select unlocked cells:** If checked, the user can select unlocked cells using the mouse or the keyboard. This setting is checked, by default.
- **Format cells:** If checked, the user can apply formatting to locked cells.
- **Format columns:** If checked, the user can hide or change the width of columns.
- **Format rows:** If checked, the user can hide or change the height of rows.
- **Insert columns:** If checked, the user can insert new columns.
- **Insert rows:** If checked, the user can insert new rows.
- **Insert hyperlinks:** If checked, the user can insert hyperlinks (even in locked cells).
- **Delete columns:** If checked, the user can delete columns.
- **Delete rows:** If checked, the user can delete rows.
- **Sort:** If checked, the user can sort data in a range (as long as the range doesn't contain any locked cells).
- **Use AutoFilter:** If checked, the user can use existing autofiltering.
- **Use PivotTable reports:** If checked, the user can change the layout of pivot tables or create new pivot tables.
- **Edit objects:** If checked, the user can make changes to objects (such as Shapes) and charts, as well as insert or delete comments.
- **Edit scenarios:** If checked, the user can use scenarios (see Chapter 36).

TIP   When the worksheet is protected and the Select Unlocked Cells option is set, pressing Tab moves to the next unlocked cell, making data entry much easier.

Assigning User Permissions

Excel also offers the ability to assign user-level permissions to different areas on a protected worksheet. You can specify which users can edit a particular range while the worksheet is protected. As an option, you can require a password to make changes.

This feature is rarely used, and the setup procedure is rather complicated. But if you need this level of protection, setting it up is worth the effort to get it.

Start by unprotecting the worksheet if it's protected. Then choose Review ➪ Changes ➪ Allow Users To Edit Ranges, which displays the dialog box shown in Figure 31.4. Then follow the prompts in the series of dialog boxes that follow. Make sure that you protect the sheet as the final step.

FIGURE 31.4

The Allow Users To Edit Ranges dialog box.

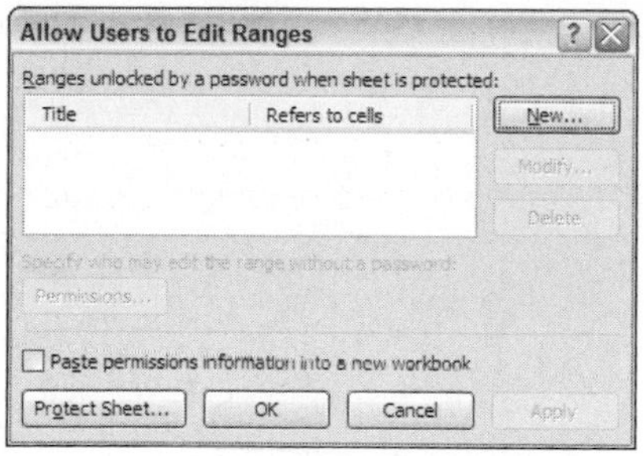

Workbook Protection

Excel provides three ways to protect a workbook:

- Require a password to open the workbook
- Prevent users from adding sheets, deleting sheets, hiding sheets, and unhiding sheets
- Prevent users from changing the size or position of windows

I discuss each of these methods in the sections that follow.

Requiring a password to open a workbook

Excel lets you save a workbook with a password. After doing so, whoever tries to open the workbook must enter the password.

To add a password to a workbook:

1. **Choose Office ⇨ Prepare ⇨ Encrypt Document.** Excel displays the Encrypt Document dialog box shown in Figure 31.5.
2. **Type a password and click OK.**
3. **Type the password again and click OK.**
4. **Save the workbook.**

NOTE You need to perform these steps only one time. You don't need to specify the password every time you resave the workbook.

To remove a password from a workbook, repeat the same procedure. In Step 2, however, delete the existing password symbols from the Encrypt Document dialog box, click OK, and save your workbook.

Figure 31.6 shows the Password dialog box that appears when you try to open a file saved with a password.

FIGURE 31.5

Specify a workbook password in the Encrypt Document dialog box.

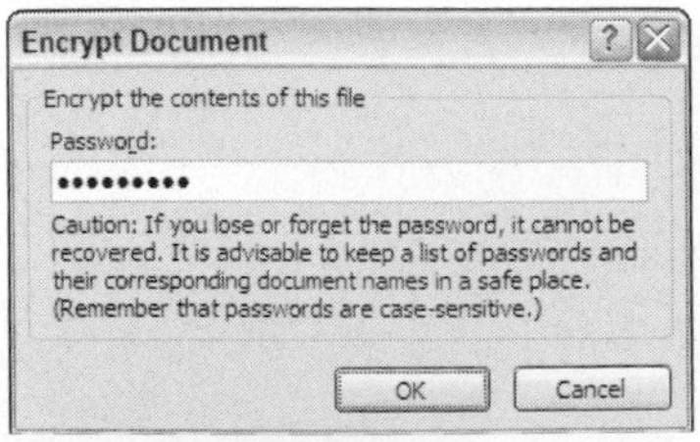

FIGURE 31.6

This workbook requires a password.

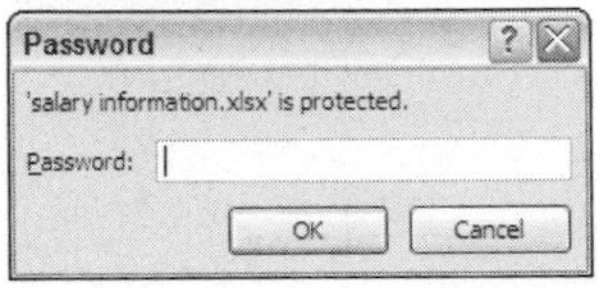

Excel provides another way to add a password to a document:

1. **Choose Office ⇨ Save As.**
2. **In the Save As dialog box, click the Tools button and choose General Options.** Excel displays the General Options dialog box.
3. **In the General Options dialog box, enter a password in the Password to Open field.**
4. **Click OK.** You're asked to re-enter the password before you return to the Save As dialog box.
5. **In the Save As dialog box, make sure that the filename, location, and type are correct and then click Save.**

NOTE The General Options dialog box has another password field: Password to Modify. If you specify a password for this field, the file opens in read-only mode (it can't be saved under the same name) unless the user knows the password. If you use the Read-Only Recommended check box without a password, Excel *suggests* that the file be opened in read-only mode, but the user can override this suggestion.

Protecting a workbook's structure

To prevent others (or yourself) from performing certain actions in a workbook, you can protect the workbook's structure. When a workbook's structure is protected, the user may not

- Add a sheet
- Delete a sheet
- Hide a sheet
- Unhide a sheet
- Rename a sheet
- Move a sheet

To protect a worksheet's structure:

1. **Choose Review ⇨ Changes ⇨ Protect Workbook to display the Protect Workbook dialog box (see Figure 31.7).**
2. **In the Protect Workbook dialog box, place a check mark next to Structure.**
3. **Enter a password, if desired.**
4. **Click OK.**

To unprotect the workbook's structure, choose Review ⇨ Changes ⇨ Unprotect Workbook. If the workbook's structure was protected with a password, you are prompted to enter the password.

FIGURE 31.7

The Protect Workbook dialog box.

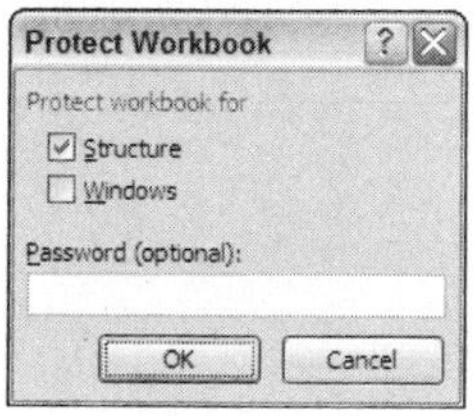

Protecting a workbook's windows

To prevent others (or yourself) from changing the size or position of a workbook's windows, you can protect the workbook's windows:

1. **Choose Review ⇨ Changes ⇨ Protect Workbook.**
2. **In the Protect Workbook dialog box, place a check mark next to Windows.**
3. **Enter a password, if desired.**
4. **Click OK.**

When a workbook's windows are protected, the user can't change anything related to the window size or position. For example, if the workbook window is maximized when the windows are protected, the user cannot unmaximize the window. The windows can, however, be zoomed.

To unprotect the workbook's windows, choose Review ⇨ Changes ⇨ Unprotect Workbook. If the workbook's windows were protected with a password, you are prompted to enter the password.

VB Project Protection

If your workbook contains any VBA macros, you may want to protect the VB Project to prevent others from viewing or modifying your macros. Another reason to protect a VB Project is to prevent its components from being expanded in the VB Editor Project window (which can avoid clutter while you're working on other VB project). To protect a VB Project:

1. **Activate the VB Editor.**

2. **Select your project in the Projects window.**

3. **Choose Tools -** *xxxx* **Properties (where** *xxxx* **corresponds to your Project name).** Excel displays the Project Properties dialog box.

4. **In the Project Properties dialog box, click the Protection tab (see Figure 31.8).**

5. **Place a check mark next to Lock project for viewing.**

6. **Enter a password (twice).**

7. **Click OK and then save your file.** When the file is closed and then re-opened, a password will be required to view or modify the VBA code.

FIGURE 31.8

Protecting a VB Project with a password.

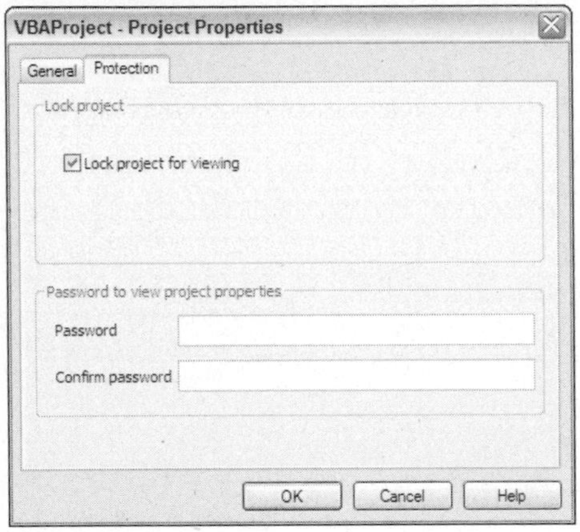

CROSS-REF Part VI discusses VBA macros.

Related Topics

This section covers additional topics related to protecting and distributing your work.

Saving a workbook as a PDF file

You can download a free Office 2007 add-in that enables you to save a workbook as a PDF file. Because of a legal dispute with Adobe Systems, Microsoft is not able to ship this add-in with Office 2007. You can download the add-in from:

```
http://office.microsoft.com/downloads
```

The PDF (Portable Document Format) file format is widely used as a way to present information in a read-only manner, with precise control over the layout. Software to display PDF files is available from a number of sources. Excel (with the assistance of the add-in) can create PDF files, but it cannot open them.

After installing the add-in, you can save your workbook in PDF or XPS format by choosing Office ➪ Save As ➪ PDF Or XPS. Excel displays its Publish As PDF Or XPS dialog box, in which you can specify a filename and location and set some other options.

NOTE XPS is another "electronic paper" format, developed by Microsoft as an alternative to the PDF format. At this time, there is very little third-party support for the XPS format.

Marking a workbook final

Excel lets you mark a document as "final." This action makes two changes to the workbook:

- It makes the workbook read-only so that the file can't be saved using the same name.
- It makes the workbook view-only so that nothing may be changed. When you open a finalized document, the status bar displays an additional icon. You'll find that most of the Ribbon commands are grayed out.

To finalize a workbook, choose Office ➪ Prepare ➪ Mark As Final. Excel displays a dialog box so that you can confirm your choice.

NEW FEATURE Finalizing a workbook is a new feature in Excel 2007.

CAUTION Marking a document as final is *not* a security measure. Anyone who opens the workbook can choose Office ➪ Prepare ➪ Mark As Final to cancel the mark as final designation. After the user selects that command, the workbook is no longer read-only or view-only. Therefore, this method doesn't guarantee that others will not change the workbook.

Inspecting a workbook

If you plan to distribute a workbook to others, you may want to have Excel check the file for hidden data and personal information. This tool can locate hidden information about you, your organization, or about the workbook that you may not want to share with others.

To do so, choose Office ➪ Prepare ➪ Inspect Document. You see the dialog box shown in Figure 31.9. Click Inspect, and Excel displays the results of the inspection and gives you the opportunity to remove the items it finds.

NEW FEATURE The Document Inspector is a new feature in Excel 2007.

CAUTION If Excel identifies items in the Document Inspector, it doesn't necessarily mean that they should be removed. In other words, you should not blindly use the Remove All buttons to remove the items that Excel locates. For example, you may have a hidden sheet that serves a critical purpose. Excel will identify that hidden sheet and make it very easy for you to delete it. To be on the safe side, always make a backup copy of your workbook before running the Document Inspector.

FIGURE 31.9

The Document Inspector dialog box identifies hidden and personal information in a workbook.

Using a digital signature

Excel lets you add a *digital signature* to a workbook. Using a digital signature is somewhat analogous to signing a paper document. A digital signature helps to assure the authenticity of the workbook and also ensures that the content hasn't been modified since it was signed.

After you sign a workbook, the signature is valid until you make changes and resave the file.

Getting a digital ID

In order to digitally sign a workbook, you must obtain a certificate from a certified authority who is able to verify the authenticity of your signature. Prices vary, depending on the certificate granting company.

Another option is to create your own digital ID, but others will not be able to verify the authenticity. Creating your own digital ID is useful if you want to ensure that no one has tampered with one of your signed workbooks.

Signing a workbook

Excel 2007 supports two types of digital signatures: a visible signature and an invisible signature.

To add a visible digital signature, choose Insert ➪ Text ➪ Signature Line ➪ Microsoft Office Signature Line. Excel displays its Signature Setup dialog box, and you're prompted for the information for the signature. After you add the signature box, double-click it to display the Sign dialog box, where you actually sign the document either by typing your name or uploading a scanned image of your signature.

Figure 31.10 shows a document with a visible digital signature.

FIGURE 31.10

This document has a digital signature.

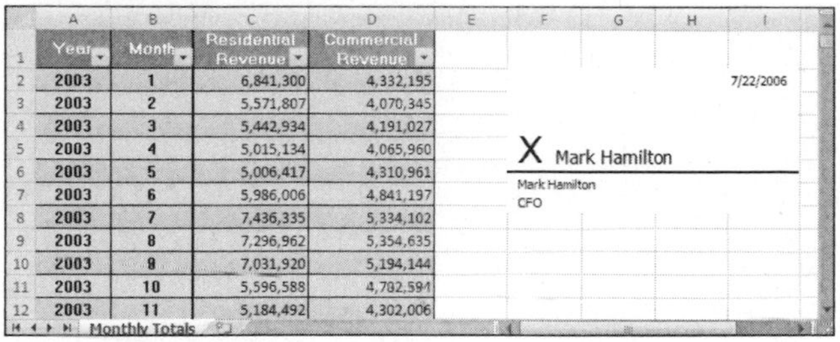

To add an invisible digital signature, choose Office ➪ Prepare ➪ Add a Digital Signature.

Chapter 32

Making Your Worksheets Error-Free

It goes without saying that you want your Excel worksheets to produce accurate results. Unfortunately, it's not always easy to be certain that the results are correct — especially if you deal with large, complex worksheets. This chapter introduces the tools and techniques available to help identify, correct, and prevent errors.

Finding and Correcting Formula Errors

Making a change in a worksheet — even a relatively minor change — may produce a ripple effect that introduces errors in other cells. For example, accidentally entering a value into a cell that previously held a formula is all too easy to do. This simple error can have a major impact on other formulas, and you may not discover the problem until long after you make the change — or you may never discover the problem.

Formula errors tend to fall into one of the following general categories:

- **Syntax errors:** You have a problem with the syntax of a formula. For example, a formula may have mismatched parentheses, or a function may not have the correct number of arguments.

- **Logical errors:** A formula doesn't return an error, but it contains a logical flaw that causes it to return an incorrect result.

- **Incorrect reference errors:** The logic of the formula is correct, but the formula uses an incorrect cell reference. As a simple example, the range reference in a Sum formula may not include all the data that you want to sum.

- **Semantic errors:** An example is a function name that is spelled incorrectly. Excel will attempt to interpret it as a name and will display the #NAME? error.

- **Circular references:** A circular reference occurs when a formula refers to its own cell, either directly or indirectly. Circular references are useful in a few cases, but most of the time a circular reference indicates a problem.

- **Array formula entry error:** When entering (or editing) an `Array` formula, you must use Ctrl+Shift+Enter to enter the formula. If you fail to do so, Excel doesn't recognize the formula as an `Array` formula, and you may get an error or incorrect results.

- **Incomplete calculation errors:** The formulas simply aren't calculated fully. Microsoft has acknowledged some problems with Excel's calculation engine in some versions of Excel. To ensure that your formulas are fully calculated, use Ctrl+Alt+F9.

Syntax errors are usually the easiest to identify and correct. In most cases, you'll know when your formula contains a syntax error. For example, Excel won't permit you to enter a formula with mismatched parentheses. Other syntax errors also usually result in an error display in the cell.

The following sections describe common formula problems and offers advice on identifying and correcting them.

Mismatched parentheses

In a formula, every left parenthesis must have a corresponding right parenthesis. If your formula has mismatched parentheses, Excel usually won't permit you to enter it. An exception to this rule involves a simple formula that uses a function. For example, if you enter the following formula (which is missing a closing parenthesis), Excel accepts the formula and provides the missing parenthesis.

```
=SUM(A1:A500
```

A formula may have an equal number of left and right parentheses, but the parentheses may not match properly. For example, consider the following formula, which converts a text string such that the first character is uppercase and the remaining characters are lowercase. This formula has five pairs of parentheses, and they match properly.

```
=UPPER(LEFT(A1))&RIGHT(LOWER(A1),LEN(A1)-1)
```

The following formula also has five pairs of parentheses, but they are mismatched. The result displays a syntactically correct formula that simply returns the wrong result.

```
=UPPER(LEFT(A1)&RIGHT(LOWER(A1),LEN(A1)-1))
```

Often, parentheses that are in the wrong location will result in a *syntax error* — which is usually a message that tells you that you entered too many or too few arguments for a function.

> **TIP**   Excel can help you out with mismatched parentheses. When you're editing a formula and you move the cursor over a parenthesis, Excel displays it (and its matching parenthesis) in bold for about one-half second. In addition, Excel color codes nested parentheses while you are editing a formula.

Cells are filled with hash marks

A cell is filled with a series of hash marks (#) for one of two reasons:

- The column is not wide enough to accommodate the formatted numeric value. To correct it, you can make the column wider or use a different number format.

- The cell contains a formula that returns an invalid date or time. For example, Excel doesn't support dates prior to 1900 or the use of negative time values. Attempting to display either of these values results in a cell filled with hash marks. Widening the column won't fix it.

Using Formula AutoCorrect

When you enter a formula that has a syntax error, Excel attempts to determine the problem and offers a suggested correction. The accompanying figure shows an example of a proposed correction.

Be careful when accepting corrections for your formulas from Excel because it doesn't always guess correctly. For example, I entered the following formula (which has mismatched parentheses):

`=AVERAGE(SUM(A1:A12,SUM(B1:B12))`

Excel then proposed the following correction to the formula:

`=AVERAGE(SUM(A1:A12,SUM(B1:B12)))`

You may be tempted to accept the suggestion without even thinking. In this case, the proposed formula is syntactically correct — but not what I intended. The correct formula is

`=AVERAGE(SUM(A1:A12),SUM(B1:B12))`

Blank cells are not blank

Some Excel users have discovered that by pressing the spacebar, the contents of a cell seem to erase. Actually, pressing the spacebar inserts an invisible space character, which isn't the same as erasing the cell.

For example, the following formula returns the number of nonempty cells in range A1:A10. If you "erase" any of these cells by using the spacebar, these cells are included in the count, and the formula returns an incorrect result.

`=COUNTA(A1:A10)`

If your formula doesn't ignore blank cells the way that it should, check to make sure that the blank cells are really blank cells. One way is to choose Home ➪ Editing ➪ Find & Select ➪ Go To (or press F5 or Ctrl+G), which displays the Go To dialog box. Click the Special button and then choose the Blanks option in the Go To Special dialog box. Excel will select all blank cells so that you can spot cells that appear to be empty but are not.

Extra space characters

If you have formulas or use procedures that rely on comparing text, be careful that your text doesn't contain additional space characters. Adding an extra space character is particularly common when data has been imported from another source.

Excel automatically removes trailing spaces from values that you enter, but trailing spaces in text entries are not deleted. It's impossible to tell, just by looking at a cell, if text contains one or more trailing space characters.

Formulas returning an error

A formula may return any of the following error values:

- #DIV/0!
- #N/A
- #NAME?
- #NULL!
- #NUM!
- #REF!
- #VALUE!

The following sections summarize possible problems that may cause these errors.

> **TIP**   Excel allows you to choose how error values are printed. To access this feature, display the Page Setup dialog box and click the Sheet tab. You can choose to print error values as displayed (the default), or as blank cells, dashes, or #N/A. To display the Page Setup dialog box, click the dialog box launcher on the Page Layout ⇨ Page Setup group.

#DIV/0! errors

Division by zero is not a valid operation. If you create a formula that attempts to divide by zero, Excel displays its familiar #DIV/0! error value.

Because Excel considers a blank cell to be zero, you also get this error if your formula divides by a missing value. This problem is common when you create formulas for data that you haven't entered yet, as shown in Figure 32.1. The formula in cell D2, which was copied to the cells below it, is

    =(C2-B2)/C2

This formula calculates the percent change between the values in columns B and C. Data isn't available for months beyond May, so the formula returns a #DIV/0! error.

To avoid the error display, you can use an IF function to check for a blank cell in column C:

    = IF(C2=0,"",(C2-B2)/C2)

This formula displays an empty string if cell C2 is blank or contains 0; otherwise, it displays the calculated value.

Another approach is to use an IFERROR function to check for *any* error condition. The following formula, for example, displays an empty string if the formula results in any type of error.

    =IFERROR((C2-B2)/C2,"")

Tracing Error Values

Often, an error in one cell is the result of an error in a precedent cell. For help in identifying the cell that is causing an error value to appear, activate the cell that contains the error and then use Formulas ⇨ Formula Auditing ⇨ Error Checking ⇨ Trace Error. Excel draws arrows to indicate which cell is the source of the error. When you've identified the error, use Formulas ⇨ Formula Auditing ⇨ Error Checking ⇨ Remove Errors to get rid of the arrow display.

NEW FEATURE The IFERROR function is new to Excel 2007. For compatibility with previous versions, use this formula:

```
=IF(ISERROR((C2-B2)/C2),"",(C2-B2)/C2)
```

#N/A errors

The #N/A error occurs if any cell referenced by a formula displays #N/A.

FIGURE 32.1

#DIV/0! errors occur when the data in column C is missing.

	A	B	C	D	E	F
1	Month	Last Year	This Year	Change		
2	January	175	188	6.9%		
3	February	156	166	6.0%		
4	March	198	175	-13.1%		
5	April	144	187	23.0%		
6	May	132	149	11.4%		
7	June	198		#DIV/0!		
8	July	202		#DIV/0!		
9	August	184		#DIV/0!		
10	September	140		#DIV/0!		
11	October	198		#DIV/0!		
12	November	232		#DIV/0!		
13	December	255		#DIV/0!		
14						

Sheet1

NOTE Some users like to enter =NA() or #N/A explicitly for missing data. This method makes it perfectly clear that the data is not available and hasn't been deleted accidentally.

The #N/A error also occurs when a LOOKUP function (HLOOKUP, LOOKUP, MATCH, or VLOOKUP) can't find a match.

#NAME? errors

The #NAME? error occurs under these conditions:

- The formula contains an undefined range or cell name.
- The formula contains text that Excel *interprets* as an undefined name. A misspelled function name, for example, generates a #NAME? error.
- The formula uses a worksheet function that's defined in an add-in, and the add-in is not installed.

NOTE Excel has a bit of a problem with range names. If you delete a name for a cell or range and the name is used in a formula, the formula continues to use the name, even though it's no longer defined. As a result, the formula displays #NAME?. You may expect Excel to automatically convert the names to their corresponding cell references, but this doesn't happen.

#NULL! errors

The #NULL! error occurs when a formula attempts to use an intersection of two ranges that don't actually intersect. Excel's intersection operator is a space. The following formula, for example, returns #NULL! because the two ranges don't intersect.

```
=SUM(B5:B14 A16:F16)
```

The following formula doesn't return #NULL! but displays the contents of cell B9 — which represents the intersection of the two ranges.

```
=SUM(B5:B14 A9:F9)
```

#NUM! errors

A formula returns a #NUM! error if any of the following occurs:

- You pass a non-numeric argument to a function when a numeric argument is expected.
- You pass an invalid argument to a function. For example, this formula returns #NUM!:

```
=SQRT(-12)
```

- A function that uses iteration can't calculate a result. Examples of functions that use iteration are IRR and RATE.
- A formula returns a value that is too large or too small. Excel supports values between –1E-307 and 1E+307.

#REF! errors

The #REF! error occurs when a formula uses an invalid cell reference. This error can occur in the following situations:

- You delete a cell that is referenced by the formula. For example, the following formula displays a #REF! error if row 1, column A, or column B is deleted.

```
=A1/B1
```

- You copy a formula to a location that invalidates the relative cell references. For example, if you copy the following formula from cell A2 to cell A1, the formula returns #REF! because it attempts to refer to a nonexistent cell.

```
=A1-1
```

- You cut a cell (by choosing Home ➪ Clipboard ➪ Cut) and then paste it to a cell that's referenced by a formula. The formula will display #REF!.

#VALUE! errors

The #VALUE! error is very common and can occur under the following conditions:

- An argument for a function is of an incorrect data type, or the formula attempts to perform an operation using incorrect data. For example, a formula that adds a value to a text string returns the #VALUE! error.
- A function's argument is a range when it should be a single value.
- A custom worksheet function is not calculated. You can use Ctrl+Alt+F9 to force a recalculation.
- A custom worksheet function attempts to perform an operation that is not valid. For example, custom functions can't modify the Excel environment or make changes to other cells.
- You forget to press Ctrl+Shift+Enter when entering an Array formula.

Absolute/relative reference problems

As described in Chapter 11, a cell reference can be relative (for example, A1), absolute (for example, $A$1), or mixed (for example, $A1 or A$1). The type of cell reference that you use in a formula is relevant only if the formula will be copied to other cells.

Pay Attention to the Colors

When you edit a cell that contains a formula, Excel color-codes the cell and range references in the formula. Excel also outlines the cells and ranges used in the formula by using corresponding colors. Therefore, you can see at a glance the cells that are used in the formula.

You also can manipulate the colored outline to change the cell or range reference. To change the references that are used in a formula, drag the outline's border or fill handle (at the lower-right corner of the outline). This technique is often easier than editing the formula.

A common problem is using a relative reference when you should use an absolute reference. As shown in Figure 32.2, cell C1 contains a tax rate, which is used in the formulas in column C. The formula in cell C4 is

```
=B4+(B4*$C$1)
```

FIGURE 32.2

Formulas in the range C4:C7 use an absolute reference to cell C1.

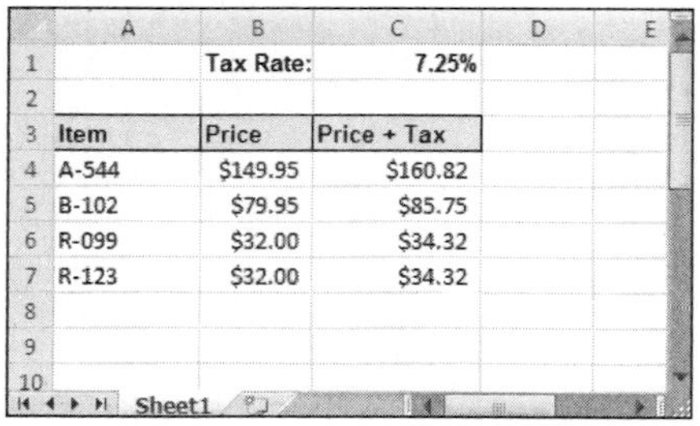

	A	B	C	D	E
1		Tax Rate:	7.25%		
2					
3	Item	Price	Price + Tax		
4	A-544	$149.95	$160.82		
5	B-102	$79.95	$85.75		
6	R-099	$32.00	$34.32		
7	R-123	$32.00	$34.32		
8					
9					
10					

Sheet1

Notice that the reference to cell C1 is an absolute reference. When the formula is copied to other cells in column C, the formula continues to refer to cell C1. If the reference to cell C1 were a relative reference, the copied formulas would return an incorrect result.

Operator precedence problems

Excel has some straightforward rules about the order in which mathematical operations are performed (see Chapter 11). When in doubt (or when you simply need to clarify your intentions), you should use parentheses to ensure that operations are performed in the correct order. For example, the following formula multiplies A1 by A2 and then adds 1 to the result. The multiplication is performed first because it has a higher order of precedence.

```
= 1+A1*A2
```

The following is a clearer version of this formula. The parentheses aren't necessary, but in this case, the order of operations is perfectly obvious.

```
=1+(A1*A2)
```

Notice that the negation operator symbol is exactly the same as the subtraction operator symbol. This, as you may expect, can cause some confusion. Consider these two formulas:

```
=-3^2
=0-3^2
```

The first formula, as expected, returns 9. The second formula, however, returns –9. Squaring a number always produces a positive result, so how is it that Excel can return the –9 result?

In the first formula, the minus sign is a *negation* operator and has the highest precedence. However, in the second formula, the minus sign is a *subtraction* operator, which has a lower precedence than the exponentiation operator. Therefore, the value 3 is squared, and the result is subtracted from zero, which produces a negative result.

Using parentheses, as shown in the following formula, causes Excel to interpret the operator as a minus sign rather than a negation operator. This formula returns –9.

```
=-(3^2)
```

Formulas are not calculated

If you use custom worksheet functions written in VBA, you may find that formulas that use these functions fail to get recalculated and may display incorrect results. To force a single formula to be recalculated, select the cell, press F2, and then press Enter. To force a recalculation of all formulas, press Ctrl+Alt+F9.

Actual versus displayed values

You may encounter a situation in which values in a range don't appear to add up properly. For example, Figure 32.3 shows a worksheet with the following formula entered into each cell in the range B3:B5:

```
=1/3
```

FIGURE 32.3

A simple demonstration of numbers that appear to add up incorrectly.

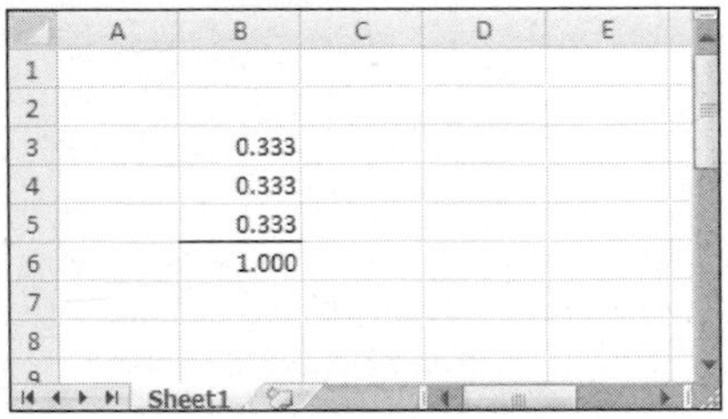

Cell B6 contains the following formula:

```
=SUM(B3:B5)
```

All the cells are formatted to display with three decimal places. As you can see, the formula in cell B6 appears to display an incorrect result. (You may expect it to display 0.999.) The formula, of course, *does* return the correct result. The formula uses the *actual* values in the range B3:B5, not the *displayed* values.

You can instruct Excel to use the displayed values by checking the Set Precision As Displayed check box on the Advanced section of the Excel Options dialog box. (Choose Office ➪ Excel Options to display this dialog box.)

> **CAUTION** Be very careful with the Set Precision As Displayed option. This option also affects normal values (nonformulas) that have been entered into cells. For example, if a cell contains the value 4.68 and is displayed with no decimal places (that is, 5), checking the Precision As Displayed check box converts 4.68 to 5.00. This change is permanent, and you can't restore the original value if you later uncheck the Set Precision As Displayed check box. A better approach is to use Excel's ROUND function to round off the values to the desired number of decimal places.

Floating point number errors

Computers, by their very nature, don't have infinite precision. Excel stores numbers in binary format by using eight bytes, which can handle numbers with 15-digit accuracy. Some numbers can't be expressed precisely by using eight bytes, so the number stores as an approximation.

To demonstrate how this lack of precision may cause problems, enter the following formula into cell A1:

```
=(5.1-5.2)+1
```

The result should be 0.9. However, if you format the cell to display 15 decimal places, you discover that Excel calculates the formula with a result of 0.899999999999999. This result occurs because the operation in parentheses is performed first, and this intermediate result stores in binary format by using an approximation. The formula then adds 1 to this value, and the approximation error is propagated to the final result.

In many cases, this type of error doesn't present a problem. However, if you need to test the result of that formula by using a logical operator, it *may* present a problem. For example, the following formula (which assumes that the previous formula is in cell A1) returns `False`:

```
=A1=.9
```

One solution to this type of error is to use Excel's ROUND function. The following formula, for example, returns `True` because the comparison is made by using the value in A1 rounded to one decimal place.

```
=ROUND(A1,1)=0.9
```

Here's another example of a "precision" problem. Try entering the following formula:

```
=(1.333-1.233)-(1.334-1.234)
```

This formula should return 0, but it actually returns −2.220446E-16 (a number very close to zero).

If that formula is in cell A1, the following formula returns `Not Zero`.

```
=IF(A1=0,"Zero","Not Zero")
```

One way to handle these "very close to zero" rounding errors is to use a formula like this:

```
=IF(ABS(A1)<1E-6,"Zero","Not Zero")
```

This formula uses the less-than (<) operator to compare the absolute value of the number with a very small number. This formula returns `Zero`.

"Phantom link" errors

You may open a workbook and see a message like the one shown in Figure 32.4. This message sometimes appears even when a workbook contains no linked formulas. Often, these phantom links are created when you copy a worksheet that contains names.

Excel's way of asking you if you want to update links in a workbook.

Microsoft Office Excel

This workbook contains one or more links that cannot be updated.

- To change the source of links, or attempt to update values again, click Edit Links.
- To leave the links as is, click Continue.

[Continue]   [Edit Links...]

First, try choosing Office ➪ Prepare ➪ Edit Links To Files to display the Edit Links dialog box. Then select each link and click Break Link. If that doesn't solve the problem, this phantom link may be caused by an erroneous name. Choose Formulas ➪ Defined Names ➪ Name Manager and scroll through the list of names. If you see a name that refers to #REF!, delete the name. The Name Manager dialog box has a Filter button that lets you filter the names. For example, you can filter the lists to display only the names with errors.

Using Excel's Auditing Tools

Excel includes a number of tools that can help you track down formula errors. This section describes the auditing tools built into Excel.

Identifying cells of a particular type

The Go To Special dialog box is a handy tool that enables you to locate cells of a particular type. To display this dialog box, choose Home ➪ Editing ➪ Find & Select ➪ Go To Special, which displays the Go To Special dialog box, as shown in Figure 32.5.

NOTE   If you select a multicell range before displaying the Go To Special dialog box, the command operates only within the selected cells. If a single cell is selected, the command operates on the entire worksheet.

You can use the Go To Special dialog box to select cells of a certain type, which can often help you identify errors. For example, if you choose the Formulas option, Excel selects all the cells that contain a formula. If you zoom the worksheet out to a small size, you can get a good idea of the worksheet's organization (see Figure 32.6).

FIGURE 32.5

The Go To Special dialog box.

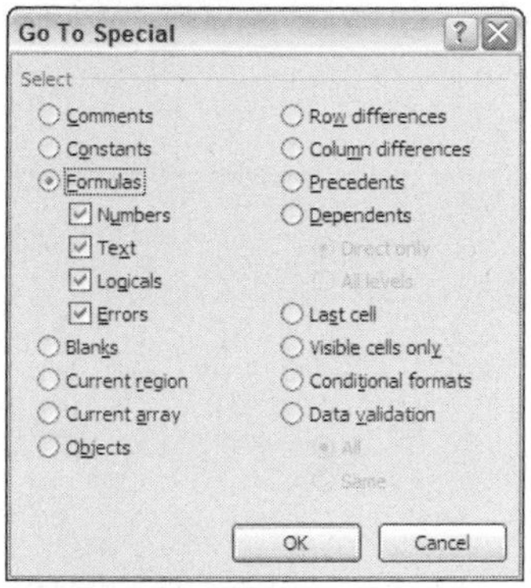

Go To Special

Select
- ○ Comments
- ○ Constants
- ⦿ Formulas
  - ☑ Numbers
  - ☑ Text
  - ☑ Logicals
  - ☑ Errors
- ○ Blanks
- ○ Current region
- ○ Current array
- ○ Objects

- ○ Row differences
- ○ Column differences
- ○ Precedents
- ○ Dependents
  - ○ Direct only
  - ○ All levels
- ○ Last cell
- ○ Visible cells only
- ○ Conditional formats
- ○ Data validation
  - ○ All
  - ○ Same

[OK] [Cancel]

FIGURE 32.6

Zooming out and selecting all formula cells can give you a good overview of how the worksheet is designed.

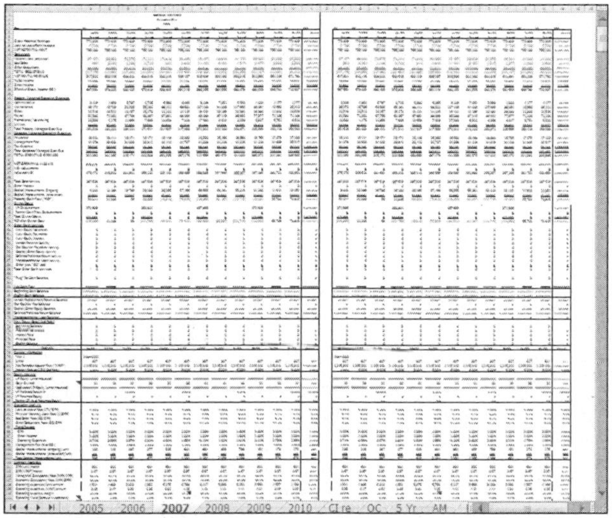

TIP Selecting the formula cells may also help you to spot a common error — a formula that has been replaced accidentally with a value. If you find a cell that's not selected amid a group of selected formula cells, chances are good that the cell previously contained a formula that has been replaced by a value.

Viewing formulas

You can become familiar with an unfamiliar workbook by displaying the formulas rather than the results of the formulas. To toggle the display of formulas, choose Formulas ➪ Formula Auditing ➪ Show Formulas. You may want to create a second window for the workbook before issuing this command. This way, you can see the formulas in one window and the results of the formula in the other window. Choose View ➪ Window ➪ New Window to open a new window.

> **TIP**
>
> You can also use Ctrl+` (that key is usually above the Tab key) to toggle between Formula view and Normal view.

Figure 32.7 shows an example of a worksheet displayed in two windows. The window on the top shows Normal view (formula results), and the window on the bottom displays the formulas. The View ➪ Window ➪ View Side By Side command, which allows synchronized scrolling, is also useful for viewing two windows (see Chapter 4 for more information about this command).

FIGURE 32.7

Displaying formulas (bottom window) and their results (top window).

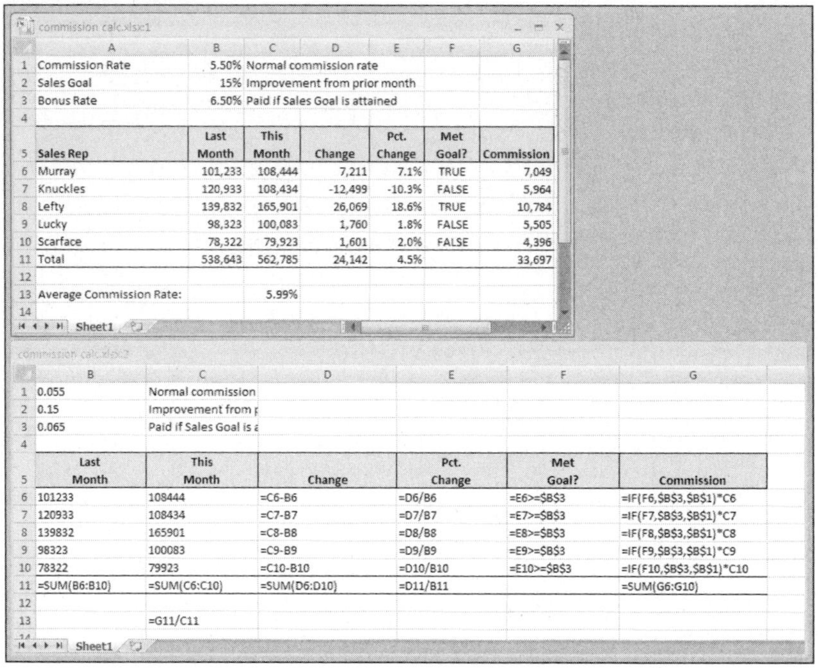

Tracing cell relationships

To understand how to trace cell relationships, you need to familiarize yourself with the following two concepts:

- **Cell precedents:** Applicable only to cells that contain a formula, a formula cell's precedents are all the cells that contribute to the formula's result. A *direct precedent* is a cell that you use directly in the formula. An *indirect precedent* is a cell that isn't used directly in the formula but is used by a cell that you refer to in the formula.

■ **Cell dependents:** These formula cells depend on a particular cell. A cell's dependents consist of all formula cells that use the cell. Again, the formula cell can be a *direct dependent* or an *indirect dependent.*

For example, consider this simple formula entered into cell A4:

```
=SUM(A1:A3)
```

Cell A4 has three precedent cells (A1, A2, and A3), which are all direct precedents. Cells A1, A2, and A3 each have a dependent cell (cell A4), and they're all direct dependents.

Identifying cell precedents for a formula cell often sheds light on why the formula isn't working correctly. Conversely, knowing which formula cells depend on a particular cell is also helpful. For example, if you're about to delete a formula, you may want to check to see whether it has any dependents.

Identifying precedents

You can identify cells used by a formula in the active cell in a number of ways:

■ **Press F2.** The cells that are used directly by the formula are outlined in color, and the color corresponds to the cell reference in the formula. This technique is limited to identifying cells on the same sheet as the formula.

■ **Display the Go To Special dialog box** (choose Home ⇨ Editing ⇨ Find & Select ⇨ Go To Special). Select the Precedents option and then select either Direct Only (for direct precedents only) or All Levels (for direct and indirect precedents). Click OK, and Excel selects the precedent cells for the formula. This technique is limited to identifying cells on the same sheet as the formula.

■ **Press Ctrl+[** to select all direct precedent cells on the active sheet.

■ **Press Ctrl+Shift+{** to select all precedent cells (direct and indirect) on the active sheet.

■ **Choose Formulas ⇨ Formula Auditing ⇨ Trace Precedents,** and Excel will draw arrows to indicate the cell's precedents. Click this button multiple times to see additional levels of precedents. Choose Formulas ⇨ Formula Auditing ⇨ Remove Arrows to hide the arrows. Figure 32.8 shows a worksheet with precedent arrows drawn to indicate the precedents for the formula in cell C13.

FIGURE 32.8

This worksheet displays arrows that indicate cell precedents for the formula in cell C13.

	A	B	C	D	E	F	G	H
1	Commission Rate	5.50%	Normal commission rate					
2	Sales Goal	15%	Improvement from prior month					
3	Bonus Rate	6.50%	Paid if Sales Goal is attained					
4								
5	Sales Rep	Last Month	This Month	Change	Pct. Change	Met Goal?	Commission	
6	Murray	101,233	108,444	7,211	7.1%	TRUE	7,049	
7	Knuckles	120,933	108,434	-12,499	-10.3%	FALSE	5,964	
8	Lefty	139,832	165,901	26,069	18.6%	TRUE	10,784	
9	Lucky	98,323	100,083	1,760	1.8%	FALSE	5,505	
10	Scarface	78,322	79,923	1,601	2.0%	FALSE	4,396	
11	Total	538,643	562,785	24,142	4.5%		33,697	
12								
13	Average Commission Rate:		5.99%					
14								
15								

Sheet1

Identifying dependents

You can identify formula cells that use a particular cell in a number of ways:

- **Display the Go To Special dialog box.** Select the Dependents option and then select either Direct Only (for direct dependents only) or All Levels (for direct and indirect dependents). Click OK. Excel selects the cells that depend on the active cell. This technique is limited to identifying cells on the active sheet only.

- **Press Ctrl+]** to select all direct dependent cells on the active sheet.

- **Press Ctrl+Shift+}** to select all dependent cells (direct and indirect) on the active sheet.

- **Choose Formulas ⇨ Formula Auditing ⇨ Trace Dependents,** and Excel will draw arrows to indicate the cell's dependents. Click this button multiple times to see additional levels of dependents. Choose Formulas ⇨ Formula Auditing ⇨ Remove Arrows to hide the arrows.

Tracing error values

If a formula displays an error value, Excel can help you identify the cell that is causing that error value. An error in one cell is often the result of an error in a precedent cell. Activate a cell that contains an error value and choose Formulas ⇨ Formula Auditing ⇨ Error Checking ⇨ Trace Error. Excel draws arrows to indicate the error source.

Fixing circular reference errors

If you accidentally create a circular reference formula, Excel displays a warning message, `Circular Reference` (with the cell address) in the status bar, and draws arrows on the worksheet to help you identify the problem. If you can't figure out the source of the problem, use Formulas ⇨ Formula Auditing ⇨ Error Checking ⇨ Circular References. This command displays a list of all cells that are involved in the circular references. Start by selecting the first cell listed and then work your way down the list until you figure out the problem.

Using background error-checking feature

Some people may find it helpful to take advantage of Excel's automatic error-checking feature. This feature is enabled or disabled by using the check box labeled Enable Background Error Checking, on the Formulas tab in the Excel Options dialog box shown in Figure 32.9. In addition, you can specify which types of errors to check for by using the check boxes in the Error Checking Rules section.

When error checking is turned on, Excel continually evaluates your worksheet, including its formulas. If a potential error is identified, Excel places a small triangle in the upper-left corner of the cell. When the cell is activated, a Smart Tag appears. Clicking this Smart Tag provides you with options. Figure 32.10 shows the options that appear when you click the Smart Tag in a cell that contains a #DIV/0 error. The options vary, depending on the type of error.

In many cases, you will choose to ignore an error by selecting the Ignore Error option. Selecting this option eliminates the cell from subsequent error checks. However, all previously ignored errors can be reset so that they appear again. (Use the Reset Ignored Errors button in the Formulas tab of the Excel Options dialog box.)

You can choose Formulas ⇨ Formula Auditing ⇨ Error Checking to display a dialog box that describes each potential error cell in sequence, much like using a spell-checking command. This command is available even if you disable background error checking. Figure 32.11 shows the Error Checking dialog box. Note that this dialog box is *modeless*, so that you can still access your worksheet when the Error Checking dialog box is displayed.

FIGURE 32.9

Excel can check your formulas for potential errors.

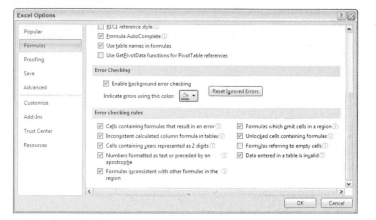

FIGURE 32.10

After you click an error, Smart Tag gives you a list of options.

	A	B	C	D	E	F	G
1	Month	Last Year	This Year	Change			
2	January	175	188	6.9%			
3	February	156	166	6.0%			
4	March	198	175	-13.1%			
5	April	144	187	23.0%			
6	May	132	149	11.4%			
7	June	198		#DIV/0!			
8	July	202		#DIV/0!			
9	August	184					
10	September	140					
11	October	198					
12	November	232					
13	December	255					

Smart Tag menu options:
- **Divide by Zero Error**
- **Help on this error**
- **Show Calculation Steps...**
- **Ignore Error**
- **Edit in Formula Bar**
- **Error Checking Options...**

CAUTION It's important to understand that the error-checking feature isn't perfect. In fact, it's not even close to perfect. In other words, you can't assume that you have an error-free worksheet simply because Excel doesn't identify any potential errors! Also, be aware that this error-checking feature won't catch a very common type of error — that of overwriting a formula cell with a value.

FIGURE 32.11

Using the Error Checking dialog box to cycle through potential errors identified by Excel.

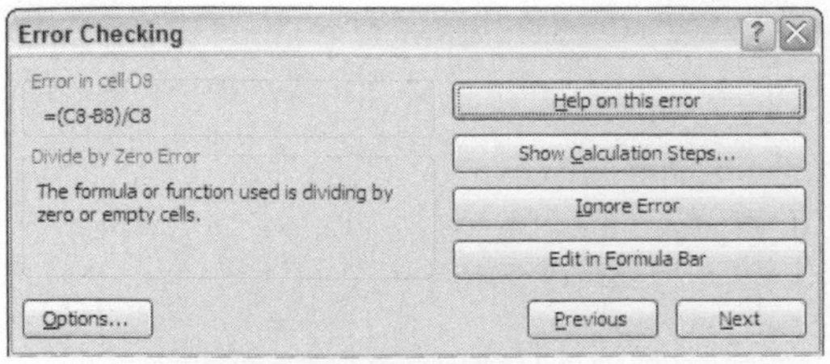

Error Checking

Error in cell D8
=(C8-B8)/C8

Divide by Zero Error

The formula or function used is dividing by zero or empty cells.

Help on this error
Show Calculation Steps...
Ignore Error
Edit in Formula Bar

Options...   Previous   Next

Using Excel Formula Evaluator

Excel's Formula Evaluator lets you see the various parts of a nested formula evaluated in the order that the formula is calculated. To use the Formula Evaluator, select the cell that contains the formula and choose Formula ➪ Formula Auditing ➪ Evaluate Formula to display the Evaluate Formula dialog box (see Figure 32.12).

FIGURE 32.12

Excel's Formula Evaluator shows a formula being calculated one step at a time.

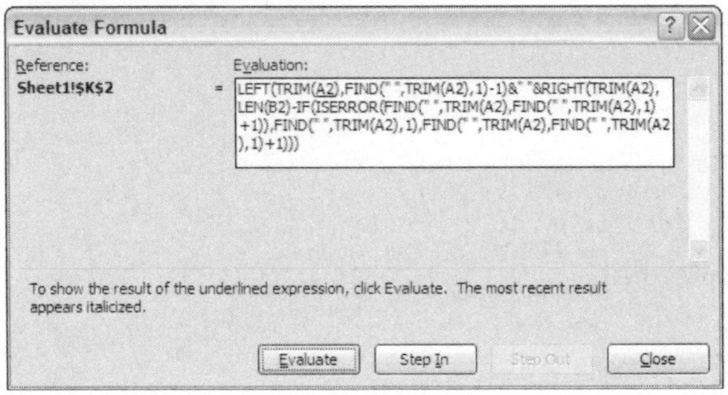

Evaluate Formula

Reference:
Sheet1!$K$2

Evaluation:
= LEFT(TRIM(A2),FIND(" ",TRIM(A2),1)-1)&" "&RIGHT(TRIM(A2),
LEN(B2)-IF(ISERROR(FIND(" ",TRIM(A2),FIND(" ",TRIM(A2),1)
+1)),FIND(" ",TRIM(A2),1),FIND(" ",TRIM(A2),FIND(" ",TRIM(A2
),1)+1)))

To show the result of the underlined expression, click Evaluate. The most recent result appears italicized.

Evaluate   Step In   Step Out   Close

Click the Evaluate button to show the result of calculating the expressions within the formula. Each click of the button performs another calculation. This feature may seem a bit complicated at first, but if you spend some time working with it, you'll understand how it works and see the value.

Excel provides another way to evaluate a part of a formula:

1. **Select the cell that contains the formula.**
2. **Press F2 to get into cell edit mode.**
3. **Use your mouse to highlight the portion of the formula you want to evaluate.** Or, press Shift and use the arrow keys.
4. **Press F9.**

The highlighted portion of the formula displays the calculated result. You can evaluate other parts of the formula or press Esc to cancel and return your formula to its previous state.

 Be careful when using this technique, because if you press Enter (rather than Escape), the formula will be modified to use the calculated values.

Searching and Replacing

Excel has a powerful search and replace feature that makes it easy to locate information in a worksheet or across multiple worksheets in a workbook. As an option, you can also search for text and replace it with other text.

To access the Find And Replace dialog box, start by selecting the range that you want to search. If you select any single cell, Excel searches the entire sheet. Choose Home ➪ Editing ➪ Find & Select ➪ Find (or click Ctrl+F). You'll see the dialog box shown in Figure 32.13. If you're simply looking for information in the worksheet, click the Find tab. If you want to replace existing text with new text, use the Replace tab. Also note that you can use the Options button to display (or hide) additional options. The dialog box shown in the figure displays these additional options.

FIGURE 32.13

Use the Find And Replace dialog box to locate information in a worksheet or workbook.

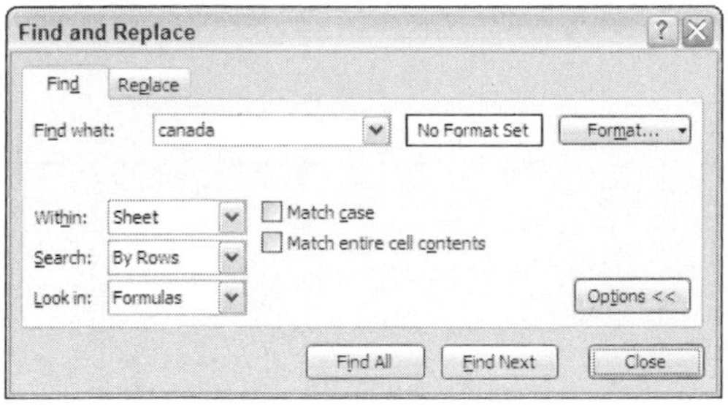

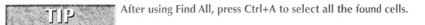

Searching for information

Enter the information to search for in the Find What text box and then specify any of the following options.

- Use the Within drop-down list to specify where to search (the current sheet or the entire workbook).
- Use the Search drop-down list to specify the direction (by rows or by columns).
- Use the Look In drop-down list to specify what cell parts to search (formulas, values, or comments).
- Use the Match Case check boxes to specify whether the search should be case sensitive.
- Use the Match Entire Cell Contents check box to specify whether the entire cell contents must be matched.
- Click the Format button to search for cells that have a particular formatting (see the upcoming "Searching for formatting" section).

Click Find Next to locate the matching cells one at a time or click Find All to locate all matches. If you use the Find All button, the Find And Replace dialog box expands to display the addresses of all matching cells in a list (see Figure 32.14). When you select an entry in this list, Excel scrolls the worksheet so that you can view it in context.

TIP After using Find All, press Ctrl+A to select all the found cells.

FIGURE 32.14

Displaying the result of a search in the Find And Replace dialog box.

| Find and Replace | ? ✕ |

| Find | Replace |

Find what: canada ▾ No Format Set   Format... ▾

Within: Sheet ▾   ☐ Match case
Search: By Rows ▾   ☐ Match entire cell contents
Look in: Formulas ▾   Options <<

   Find All   Find Next   Close

Book	Sheet	Name	Cell	Value	Formula
data...	Customers		$F$58	Canada	
data...	Customers		$F$61	Canada	
data...	Customers		$F$76	Canada	
data...	Customers		$F$147	Canada	
data...	Customers		$F$159	Canada	
data...	Customers		$F$183	Canada	
data...	Customers		$F$328	Canada	
data...	Customers		$F$378	Canada	
data...	Customers		$F$392	Canada	
data...	Customers		$F$421	Canada	
data...	Customers		$F$425	Canada	
data...	Customers		$F$429	Canada	

1135 cell(s) found

> **NOTE** The Find And Replace dialog box is *modeless*. Therefore, you can access the worksheet and make changes without the need to dismiss the dialog box.

Replacing information

To replace text with other text, use the Replace tab in the Find And Replace dialog box. Enter the text to be replaced in the Find What field and then enter the new text in the Replace With field. Specify other options as described in the previous section.

Click Find Next to locate the first matching item and then click Replace to do the replacement. When you click the Replace button, Excel then locates the next matching item. To override the replacement, click Find Next. To replace all items without verification, click Replace All.

> **TIP** To delete information, enter the text to be deleted in the Find What field, and leave the Replace With field empty.

Searching for formatting

The Find And Replace dialog box also enables you to locate cells that contain a particular type of formatting. As an option, you can replace that formatting with another type of formatting. For example, assume that you want to locate all cells that are formatted as bold and then change that formatting to bold and italic. Follow these steps:

1. **Choose Home ➪ Editing ➪ Find & Select ➪ Replace to display the Find And Replace dialog box (or press Ctrl+H).**
2. **Make sure that the Replace tab is displayed.**

3. **If the Find What and Replace With fields are not empty, delete their contents.**

4. **Click the top Format button to display the Find Format dialog box.** This dialog box resembles the standard Format Cells dialog box.

5. **In the Find Format dialog box, select the Font tab.**

6. **Select Bold in the Font Style list and then click OK.**

7. **Click the bottom Format button to display the Replace Format dialog box.**

8. **In the Replace Format dialog box, select the Font tab.**

9. **Select Bold Italic in the Font Style list and then click OK.** At this point, the Find And Replace dialog box resembles Figure 32.15. Notice that it displays previews of the formatting that will be found and replaced.

10. **In the Find And Replace dialog box, click Replace All.** Excel locates all cells that have bold formatting and changes the formatting to bold italic.

You can also find formatting based on a particular cell. In the Find Format dialog box, click the Choose Format From Cell button and then click the cell that contains the formatting you're looking for.

FIGURE 32.15

Using the Find And Replace dialog box to change formatting.

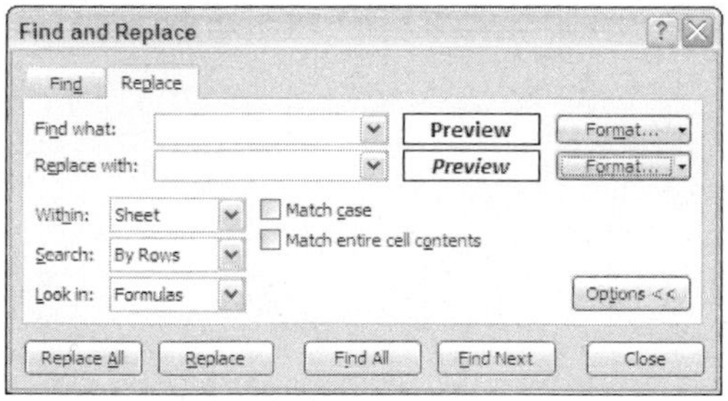

 **CAUTION** The Find And Replace dialog box cannot find background color formatting in tables that was applied using table styles, or formatting that is applied based on Conditional Formatting.

Spell Checking Your Worksheets

If you use a word-processing program, you probably run its spell checker before printing an important document. Spelling mistakes can be just as embarrassing when they appear in a spreadsheet. Fortunately, Microsoft includes a spell checker with Excel.

To access the spell checker, choose Review ➪ Proofing ➪ Spelling, or press F7. To check the spelling in just a particular range, select the range before you activate the spell checker.

If the spell checker finds any words it does not recognize as correct, it displays the Spelling dialog box, shown in Figure 32.16.

FIGURE 32.16

Use the Spelling dialog box to locate and correct spelling errors in your worksheets.

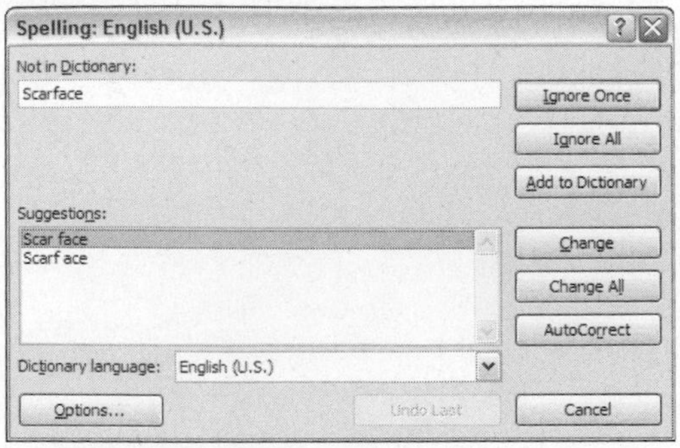

 The spell checker checks cell contents, text in graphic objects and charts, and page headers and footers. Even the contents of hidden rows and columns are checked.

The Spelling dialog box works similarly to other spell checkers with which you may be familiar. If Excel encounters a word that isn't in the current dictionary or that is misspelled, it offers a list of suggestions. You can respond by clicking one of these buttons:

- **Ignore Once:** Ignores the word and continues the spell check.
- **Ignore All:** Ignores the word and all subsequent occurrences of it.
- **Add To Dictionary:** Adds the word to the dictionary.
- **Change:** Changes the word to the selected word in the Suggestions list.
- **Change All:** Changes the word to the selected word in the Suggestions list and changes all subsequent occurrences of it without asking.
- **AutoCorrect:** Adds the misspelled word and its correct spelling (which you select from the list) to the AutoCorrect list.

Using AutoCorrect

AutoCorrect is a handy feature that automatically corrects common typing mistakes. You can also add to the list some words that Excel corrects automatically. The AutoCorrect dialog box appears in Figure 32.17. To access this feature, choose Office ➪ Excel Options. In the Excel Options dialog box, click the Proofing tab and then click the AutoCorrect Options button.

This dialog box has several options:

- **Correct TWo INitial CApitals:** Automatically corrects words with two initial uppercase letters. For example, BUdget is converted to Budget. This mistake is common among fast typists. You can click the Exceptions button to specify a list of exceptions to this rule.
- **Capitalize First Letter Of Sentences:** Capitalizes the first letter in a sentence (all other letters are unchanged).

- **Capitalize Names Of Days:** Capitalizes the days of the week. If you enter *monday*, Excel converts it to *Monday*.

- **Correct Accidental Use Of cAPS LOCK key:** Corrects errors caused if you accidentally hit the CapsLock key while typing.

- **Replace Text As You Type:** AutoCorrect automatically changes incorrect words as you type them.

FIGURE 32.17

Use the AutoCorrect dialog box to control the spelling corrections Excel makes automatically.

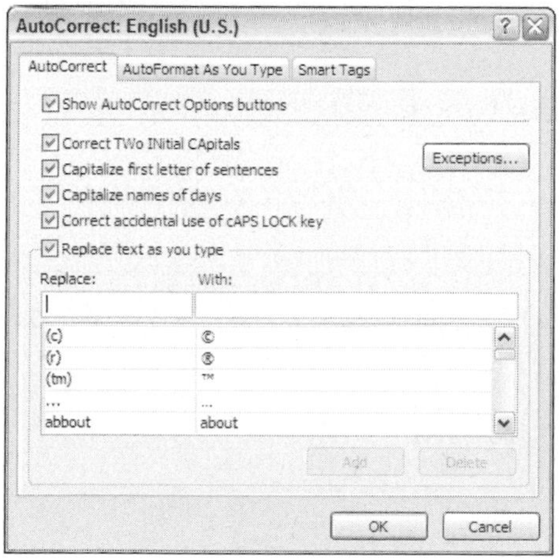

Excel includes a long list of AutoCorrect entries for commonly misspelled words. In addition, it has AutoCorrect entries for some symbols. For example, *(c)* is replaced with © and *(r)* is replaced with ®. You can also add your own AutoCorrect entries. For example, if you find that you frequently misspell the word *January* as *Janruary*, you can create an AutoCorrect entry so that it's changed automatically. To create a new AutoCorrect entry, enter the misspelled word in the Replace box and the correctly spelled word in the With box. You can also delete entries that you no longer need.

TIP You also can use the AutoCorrect feature to create shortcuts for commonly used words or phrases. For example, if you work for a company named Consolidated Data Processing Corporation, you can create an AutoCorrect entry for an abbreviation, such as cdp. Then, whenever you type cdp, Excel automatically changes it to Consolidated Data Processing Corporation. Just make sure that you don't use a combination of characters that might normally appear in your text.

NOTE In some cases, you may want to override the AutoCorrect feature. For example, you may need to enter (c) rather than the copyright symbol. You can do so by clicking the Undo button on the Quick Access Toolbar (or by pressing Ctrl+Z).

You can use the AutoFormat As You Type tab of the AutoCorrect dialog box to control a few other automatic settings in Excel.

Use the Smart Tags tab to make Excel show Smart Tags — similar to hyperlinks — for certain types of data in your worksheets. The types of Smart Tags Excel recognizes vary depending on the types of software that are installed on your system.

Part V

Analyzing Data with Excel

Excel is a superb data analysis tool if you know how to extract the information you really need. In this part, you'll learn how to obtain and analyze data in Excel. As you'll see, many of the data analysis capabilities in Excel are both surprisingly powerful and easy to use.

Chapter 33

Using Microsoft Query with External Database Files

Excel has some great analysis and presentation tools, but these tools require data. In many cases, the data that you need is available in an external database. For example, your company may have a database that contains customer information, sales data, and so on. This chapter is an introduction to retrieving data from external database files for use in Excel.

Understanding External Database Files

When you work with an Excel workbook, the entire workbook must be loaded into memory before you can begin working. Although loading all the data provides you with immediate access to the entire file and all the data it contains, it also means that you can't work with extremely large amounts of data. Although Excel 2007 supports more than a million rows, actually using that many rows can slow your system to a crawl — even if your system has plenty of memory.

When you access an external database file using Excel, you can perform a query to load just a subset of the data into your workbook.

Accessing external database files from Excel is useful in the following situations:

- You need to work with a subset of a very large database.
- You share the database with others; that is, other users have access to the database and may need to work with the data at the same time.
- The database is in a format that Excel can't import, or the database may be too large to import.
- The database contains multiple tables with relationships between those tables.

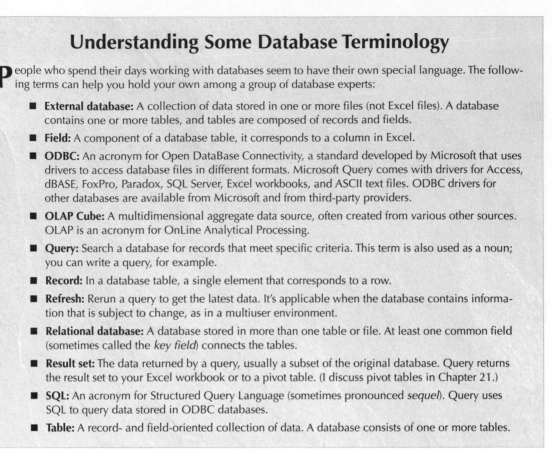

Understanding Some Database Terminology

People who spend their days working with databases seem to have their own special language. The following terms can help you hold your own among a group of database experts:

- **External database:** A collection of data stored in one or more files (not Excel files). A database contains one or more tables, and tables are composed of records and fields.

- **Field:** A component of a database table, it corresponds to a column in Excel.

- **ODBC:** An acronym for Open DataBase Connectivity, a standard developed by Microsoft that uses drivers to access database files in different formats. Microsoft Query comes with drivers for Access, dBASE, FoxPro, Paradox, SQL Server, Excel workbooks, and ASCII text files. ODBC drivers for other databases are available from Microsoft and from third-party providers.

- **OLAP Cube:** A multidimensional aggregate data source, often created from various other sources. OLAP is an acronym for OnLine Analytical Processing.

- **Query:** Search a database for records that meet specific criteria. This term is also used as a noun; you can write a query, for example.

- **Record:** In a database table, a single element that corresponds to a row.

- **Refresh:** Rerun a query to get the latest data. It's applicable when the database contains information that is subject to change, as in a multiuser environment.

- **Relational database:** A database stored in more than one table or file. At least one common field (sometimes called the *key field*) connects the tables.

- **Result set:** The data returned by a query, usually a subset of the original database. Query returns the result set to your Excel workbook or to a pivot table. (I discuss pivot tables in Chapter 21.)

- **SQL:** An acronym for Structured Query Language (sometimes pronounced *sequel*). Query uses SQL to query data stored in ODBC databases.

- **Table:** A record- and field-oriented collection of data. A database consists of one or more tables.

If you need to work with external databases, you may prefer Excel to other database programs. The advantage? After you bring the data into Excel, you can manipulate and format it by using familiar tools such as formulas and pivot tables. Of course, real database programs, such as Access, have advantages, too. For example, creating a complex database report in Access may be easier than creating it in Excel.

Importing Access Tables

Microsoft Access is included with some versions of Office 2007. An Access database contains one or more tables of data, and you can import an Access table directly into a worksheet by choosing Data ➪ Get External Data ➪ From Access. When you choose this command, Excel displays the Select Data Source dialog box, which you use to locate the Access file.

When you've located the Access database file, Excel displays the Select Table dialog box, in which you select the table (or view) to import. Figure 33.1 shows the tables and views available for Microsoft's Northwind Traders database, a sample database that's installed with Access. Select the table, click OK, and Excel displays its Import Data dialog box, shown in Figure 33.2. Use this dialog box to specify the location and whether you want a normal table or a pivot table.

FIGURE 33.1

Selecting an Access table to import.

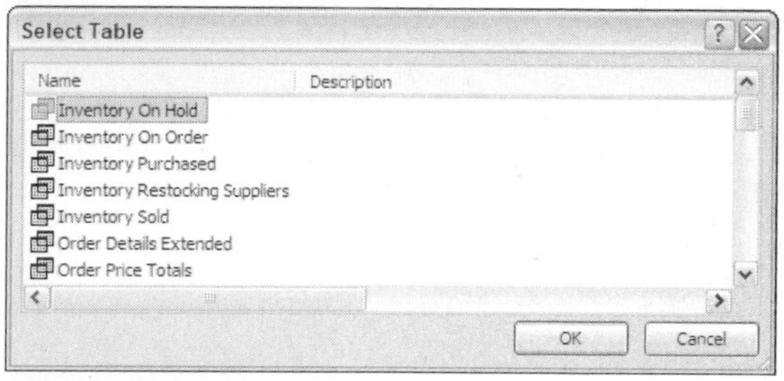

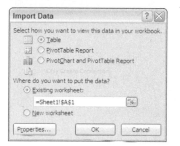

FIGURE 33.2

Use this dialog box to specify the location of the imported table.

Importing an Access table in this manner is all or none. You're not given an opportunity to query the database for specific records.

Figure 33.3 shows part of the Customers table from the Northwind Traders database. Excel converts the data to a table.

FIGURE 33.3

An Access table, imported into Excel.

ID	Company	First Name	Last Name	E-mail Address	Job Title	Busi
1	Company A	Anna	Bedecs		Owner	(123)
2	Company B	Antonio	Gratacos Solsona		Owner	(123)
3	Company C	Thomas	Axen		Purchasing Representative	(123)
4	Company D	Christina	Lee		Purchasing Manager	(123)
5	Company E	Martin	O'Donnell		Owner	(123)
6	Company F	Francisco	Pérez-Olaeta		Purchasing Manager	(123)
7	Company G	Ming-Yang	Xie		Owner	(123)
8	Company H	Elizabeth	Andersen		Purchasing Representative	(123)
9	Company I	Sven	Mortensen		Purchasing Manager	(123)
10	Company J	Roland	Wacker		Purchasing Manager	(123)
11	Company K	Peter	Krschne		Purchasing Manager	(123)
12	Company L	John	Edwards		Purchasing Manager	(123)
13	Company M	Andre	Ludick		Purchasing Representative	(123)
14	Company N	Carlos	Grilo		Purchasing Representative	(123)
15	Company O	Helena	Kupkova		Purchasing Manager	(123)
16	Company P	Daniel	Goldschmidt		Purchasing Representative	(123)
17	Company Q	Jean Philippe	Bagel		Owner	(123)
18	Company R	Catherine	Autier Miconi		Purchasing Representative	(123)
19	Company S	Alexander	Eggerer		Accounting Assistant	(123)
20	Company T	George	Li		Purchasing Manager	(123)
21	Company U	Bernard	Tham		Accounting Manager	(123)

Sheet1

Retrieving Data with Query: An Example

This section discusses Microsoft Query, an application that ships with Excel. Use Query to import a subset of a database.

NOTE To perform queries using external databases, Microsoft Query must be installed on your system. (This program is included with Excel.) If Query isn't installed, you're prompted to install it when you first choose Data ⇨ Get External Data ⇨ From Other Sources ⇨ From Microsoft Query.

The best way to become familiar with Microsoft Query is to walk through an example. In the following sections, you learn how to use Query to open a database file and import a specified set of records.

ON the CD-ROM The database file used in this example is available on the companion CD-ROM. It's an Access 2007 file named budget data.accdb.

The database file

The database file used in this example is a single-table Access file that consists of 31,680 records. This table contains the following fields:

- **Sort:** A numeric field that holds record sequence numbers.
- **Division:** A text field that specifies the company division (either Asia, Europe, N. America, Pacific Rim, or S. America).
- **Department:** A text field that specifies the department within the division. Each division is organized into the following departments: Accounting, Advertising, Data Processing, Human Resources, Operations, Public Relations, R&D, Sales, Security, Shipping, and Training.
- **Category:** A text field that specifies the budget category. The four categories are Compensation, Equipment, Facility, and Supplies & Services.

- **Item:** A text field that specifies the budget item. Each budget category has different budget items. For example, the Compensation category includes the following items: Benefits, Bonuses, Commissions, Conferences, Entertainment, Payroll Taxes, Salaries, and Training.
- **Month:** A text field that specifies the month (abbreviated as Jan, Feb, and so on).
- **Year:** A numeric field that stores the year (either 2005 or 2006).
- **Budget:** A numeric field that stores the budgeted amount.
- **Actual:** A numeric field that stores the actual amount spent.
- **Variance:** A numeric field that stores the difference between the Budget and Actual.

The task

The objective of this exercise is to create a report that shows the first quarter 2006 (January through March) Compensation expenditures of the Training Department in the North American Division. In other words, the query will extract records that meet all of the following criteria:

- The Division is **N. America**.
- The Department is **Training**.
- The Category is **Compensation**.
- The Month is **Jan**, **Feb**, or **Mar**.
- The Year is **2006**.

Using Query to get the data

One approach to this task is to import the entire Access file into a worksheet using the method described earlier in this chapter (see "Importing Access Tables"). When the table is imported, you can filter it to display only the rows that meet the specified criteria. This approach works because this particular table isn't very large. However, in some cases, the number of records in the table may exceed the number of rows in a worksheet. The advantage of using Query is that it imports only the data that's required. And, once you've imported the data, you can refresh the query at any time to bring in updated data.

Selecting a data source

Begin with an empty worksheet. Choose Data ➪ Get External Data ➪ From Other Sources ➪ From Microsoft Query, which displays the Choose Data Source dialog box, shown in Figure 33.4. This dialog box contains three tabs:

- **Databases:** Lists the data sources that are known to Query — this tab may be empty, depending on which data sources are defined on your system.
- **Queries:** Contains a list of stored queries. Again, this tab may or may not be empty.
- **OLAP Cubes:** Lists OLAP databases available for query.

Your system may have some data sources already defined. If so, they appear in the list on the Databases tab. To set up a new data source, use the <New Data Source> option. For this example, choose <New Data Source> and click OK. The Create New Data Source dialog box, which has four parts, appears (see Figure 33.5):

FIGURE 33.4

The Choose Data Source dialog box.

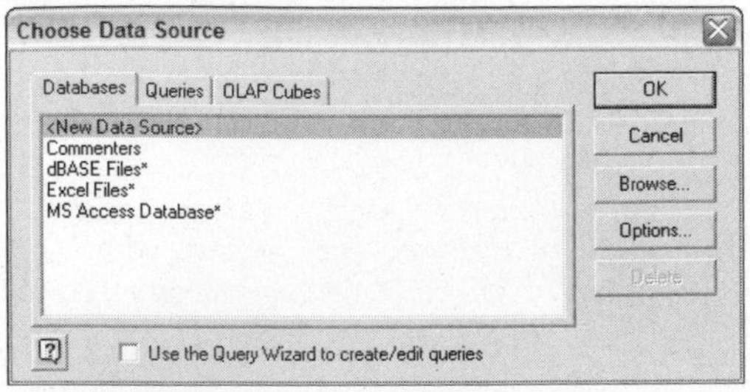

FIGURE 33.5

The Create New Data Source dialog box.

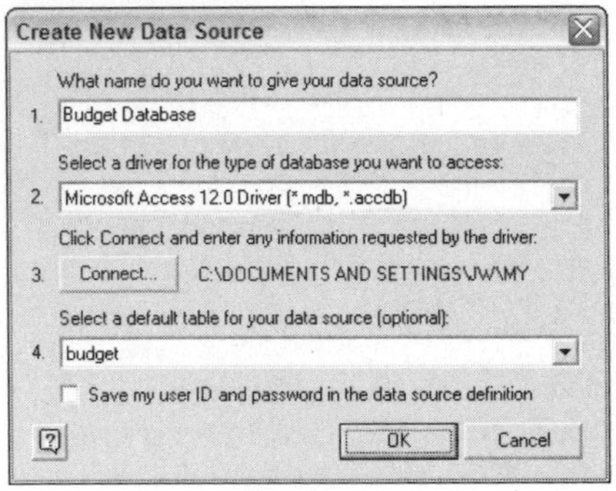

1. **Enter a descriptive name for the data source.** For this example, use the name Budget Database.

2. **Select a driver for the data source by selecting from the list of installed drivers.** For this example, choose Microsoft Access 12 Driver (*.mdb, *.accdb).

3. **Click the Connect button to display another dialog box that asks for information specific to the driver that you selected in Step 2.** In this example, you need to click the Select button and then locate the **budget data.accdb** file. Click OK to return to the previous dialog box and click OK again to return to the Create New Data Source dialog box.

4. **Select the default data table that you want to use.** For this example, the database file contains a single table named budget. If the database requires a password, you can also specify that the password be saved with the data source definition.

5. **When you've supplied all the information in the Create New Data Source dialog box, click OK.** You're returned to the Choose Data Source dialog box, which now displays the data source that you created.

NOTE You only have to go through these steps once for each data source. The next time that you need to access this data source, the Budget Database (and any other database sources that you've defined) appears in the Choose Data Source dialog box.

NOTE | The preceding steps are general steps that work with all supported database types. In some situations, you may prefer to open the database file directly and not create a named data source that will appear in the Choose Data Source dialog box. For example, if you won't be using the database again, you can open the file directly and not have to bother creating a new named data source. If you're using an Access file, you can select MS Access Database from the Databases tab in the Choose Data Source dialog box. Then, you can specify the file, and you're taken directly to Microsoft Query.

Using the Query Wizard

The Choose Data Source dialog box has a check box at the bottom that lets you specify whether to use the Query Wizard to create your query. The Query Wizard walks you through the steps used to create your query, and if you use the Query Wizard, you don't have to deal directly with Query. I highly recommend using the Query Wizard, and the examples in this chapter use this tool.

In the Choose Data Source dialog box:

1. **Select your data source (Budget Database, for this example).**
2. **Make sure that the Query Wizard check box is checked.**
3. **Click OK to start the Query Wizard.**

Query Wizard: Choosing the columns

In the first step of the Query Wizard, select the database columns that you want to appear in your query. Select one or more columns and click the > button to add them (see Figure 33.6). To select all fields, click the table name (`budget`) and click the > button.

FIGURE 33.6

In the first step of Query Wizard, you select the columns to use in your query.

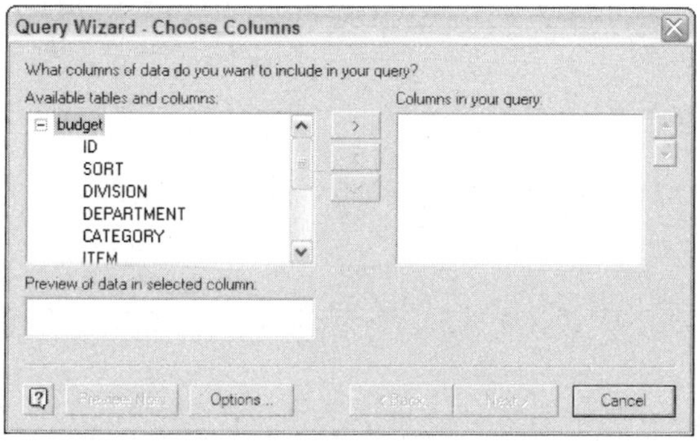

If you want to see the data for a particular column, select the column and click the Preview Now button. If you accidentally add a column that you don't need, select it in the right panel and click the < button to remove it.

For this example, add all the fields and then click the Next button.

Query Wizard: Filtering data

In the second Query Wizard dialog box, you specify your record selection criteria — how you want to filter the data. This step is optional. If you want to retrieve all the data, just click the Next button to proceed.

Figure 33.7 shows the Filter Data dialog box of the Query Wizard.

In the second step of the Query Wizard, you specify how you want to filter the data.

For the example, not all records are needed. Recall that you're interested only in the records in which one of the following applies:

- The Division is N. America.
- The Department is Training.
- The Category is Compensation.
- The Year is 2006.
- The Month is Jan, Feb, or Mar.

The criteria are entered by column. In this case, you have five criteria (one for each of five columns):

- In the Column To Filter list, select Division. In the right panel, select equals from the first drop-down list and select N. America from the second drop-down list.
- In the Column To Filter list, select Department. In the right panel, select equals from the first drop-down list and select Training from the second drop-down list.
- In the Column To Filter list, select Category. In the right panel, select equals from the first drop-down list and select Compensation from the second drop-down list.
- In the Column To Filter list, select Year. In the right panel, select equals from the first drop-down list and select 2006 from the second drop-down list.
- In the Column To Filter list, select Month. In the right panel, select equals from the first drop-down list and select Jan from the second drop-down list. Because this column is filtered by multiple values, click on the Or option and then select equals and Feb from the drop-down lists in the second row. Finally, select equals and Mar from the drop-down lists in the second row.

To review the criteria that you've entered, just select the column from the Column To Filter list. The Query Wizard displays the criteria that you entered for the selected column.

When you've entered all the criteria, click Next.

Query Wizard: Sort order

The third step of the query lets you specify how you want the records to be sorted (see Figure 33.8). This step is optional, and you can click Next to move to the next step if you don't want the data sorted or if you prefer to sort it after it's returned to your worksheet.

For this example, sort by Category in ascending order. You can specify as many sort fields as you like. Click Next to move on to the next step.

Query Wizard: Finish

The final step of the Query Wizard, shown in Figure 33.9, lets you save the query so that you can reuse it. To save the query, click Save Query and then enter a filename.

Select an option that corresponds to what you want to do with the returned data. Normally, you want to return the data to Excel. If you know how to use the Microsoft Query application, you can return the data to Query and examine it or even modify the selection criteria.

For this example, select Return Data to Microsoft Excel and click Finish.

FIGURE 33.8

In the third step of the Query Wizard, you specify the sort order.

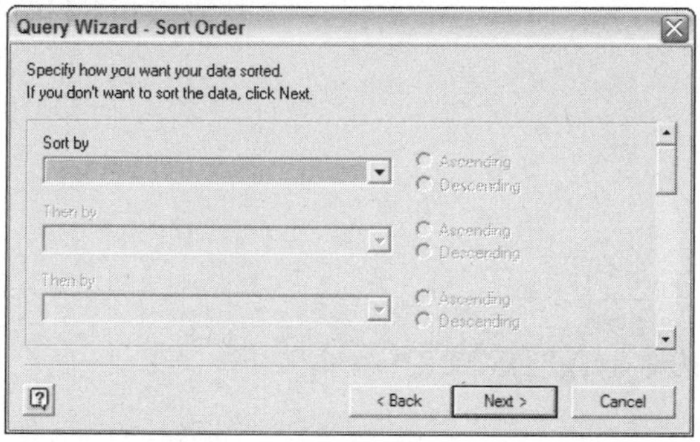

FIGURE 33.9

The final step of the Query Wizard.

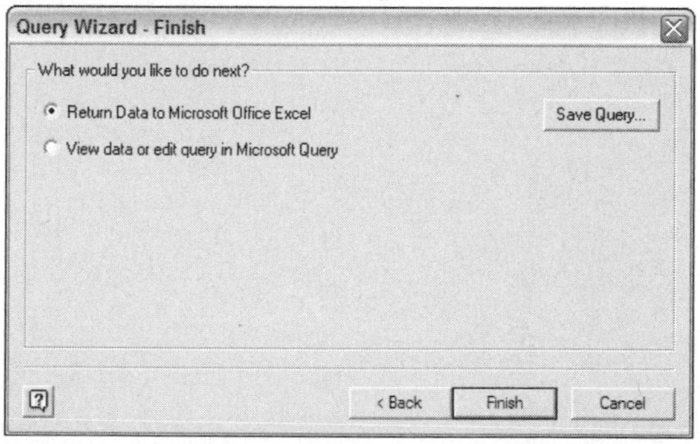

Specifying a location for the data

Figure 33.10 shows the Import Data dialog box, which appears when you click the Finish button in the Query Wizard dialog box.

FIGURE 33.10

Specifying what to do with the data.

For this example, select the Table option and place the data beginning in cell A1 of the existing worksheet.

> **NOTE**   If you choose PivotTable Report or PivotChart and PivotTable Report, you can specify the layout for a pivot table (see Chapters 34 and 35). In such a case, the database is used as the source for the pivot table, and the original data is not stored in your workbook.

Figure 33.11 shows the data that is returned to a worksheet.

FIGURE 33.11

The results of the query.

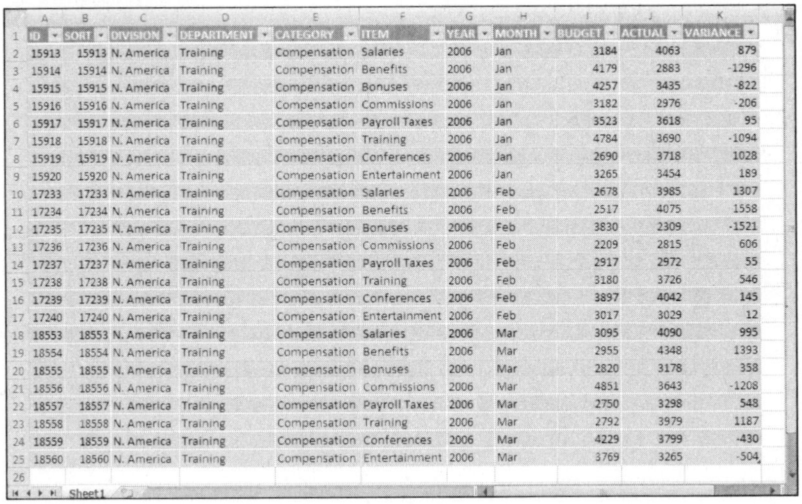

ID	SORT	DIVISION	DEPARTMENT	CATEGORY	ITEM	YEAR	MONTH	BUDGET	ACTUAL	VARIANCE
15913	15913	N. America	Training	Compensation	Salaries	2006	Jan	3184	4063	879
15914	15914	N. America	Training	Compensation	Benefits	2006	Jan	4179	2883	-1296
15915	15915	N. America	Training	Compensation	Bonuses	2006	Jan	4257	3435	-822
15916	15916	N. America	Training	Compensation	Commissions	2006	Jan	3182	2976	-206
15917	15917	N. America	Training	Compensation	Payroll Taxes	2006	Jan	3523	3618	95
15918	15918	N. America	Training	Compensation	Training	2006	Jan	4784	3690	-1094
15919	15919	N. America	Training	Compensation	Conferences	2006	Jan	2690	3718	1028
15920	15920	N. America	Training	Compensation	Entertainment	2006	Jan	3265	3454	189
17233	17233	N. America	Training	Compensation	Salaries	2006	Feb	2678	3985	1307
17234	17234	N. America	Training	Compensation	Benefits	2006	Feb	2517	4075	1558
17235	17235	N. America	Training	Compensation	Bonuses	2006	Feb	3830	2309	-1521
17236	17236	N. America	Training	Compensation	Commissions	2006	Feb	2209	2815	606
17237	17237	N. America	Training	Compensation	Payroll Taxes	2006	Feb	2917	2972	55
17238	17238	N. America	Training	Compensation	Training	2006	Feb	3180	3726	546
17239	17239	N. America	Training	Compensation	Conferences	2006	Feb	3897	4042	145
17240	17240	N. America	Training	Compensation	Entertainment	2006	Feb	3017	3029	12
18553	18553	N. America	Training	Compensation	Salaries	2006	Mar	3095	4090	995
18554	18554	N. America	Training	Compensation	Benefits	2006	Mar	2955	4348	1393
18555	18555	N. America	Training	Compensation	Bonuses	2006	Mar	2820	3178	358
18556	18556	N. America	Training	Compensation	Commissions	2006	Mar	4851	3643	-1208
18557	18557	N. America	Training	Compensation	Payroll Taxes	2006	Mar	2750	3298	548
18558	18558	N. America	Training	Compensation	Training	2006	Mar	2792	3979	1187
18559	18559	N. America	Training	Compensation	Conferences	2006	Mar	4229	3799	-430
18560	18560	N. America	Training	Compensation	Entertainment	2006	Mar	3769	3265	-504

Working with Data Returned by Query

Excel stores the data that Query returns in either a worksheet or a pivot table. When Excel stores data in a worksheet, it stores the data in a table that's a specially named range known as an *external data range;* Excel creates the name for this range automatically. In this example, the external data range is named `Table_Query_from_Budget_Database`.

You can manipulate data returned from a query just like any other worksheet range. For example, you can sort the data, format it, or create formulas that use the data.

The following sections describe what you can do with the data that Excel receives from Query and stores in a worksheet.

Adjusting the external data range properties

You can adjust various properties of the external data range by using the External Data Properties dialog box (see Figure 33.12).

To display this dialog box, the cell pointer must be within the external data range. You can open this dialog box by using either of three methods:

- Right-click and choose Table ⇨ External Data Properties from the shortcut menu.
- Choose Data ⇨ Manage Connections ⇨ Properties.

For more settings (applicable for advanced users), click the Properties icon, which is directly to the right of the Name box in the External Data Properties dialog box. Excel displays the Connection Properties dialog box.

FIGURE 33.12

The External Data Properties dialog box enables you to specify various options for an external data range.

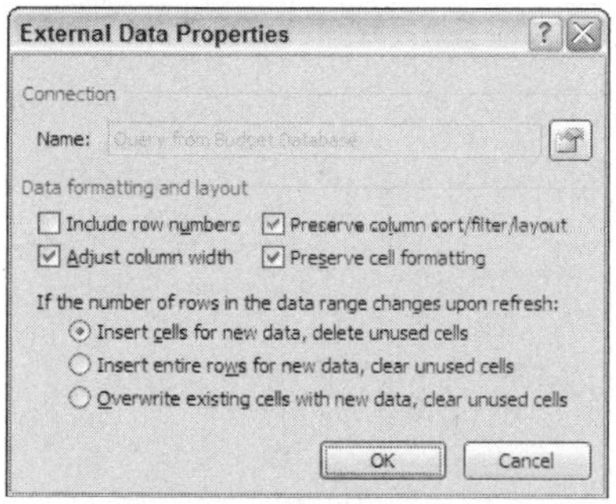

Refreshing a query

After performing a query, you can save the workbook file and then retrieve it later. The file contains the data that you originally retrieved from the external database. The external database may have changed, however, in the interim.

Fortunately, Excel saves the query definition with the workbook. Simply move the cell pointer anywhere within the external data table in the worksheet and then use one of the following methods to refresh the query:

- Right-click and choose Refresh from the shortcut menu.
- Choose Data ⇨ Manage Connections ⇨ Refresh All.
- Click Refresh in the Workbook Connections dialog box (displayed by choosing Data ⇨ Manage Connections ⇨ Connections).

Excel uses your original query to bring in the current data from the external database.

TIP   If you find that refreshing the query causes undesirable results, use Excel's Undo feature to "unrefresh" the data.

NOTE   A single workbook can hold as many external data ranges as you need. Excel gives each query a unique name, and you can work with each query independently. Excel automatically keeps track of the query that produces each external data range.

CAUTION   After performing a query, you may want to copy or move the external data range, which you can do by using the normal copy, cut, and paste techniques. However, make sure that you copy or cut the entire external data range — otherwise, the underlying query is not copied, and the copied data can't be refreshed.

Deleting a query

If you decide that you no longer need the data returned by a query, you can delete it by selecting the entire external data range and pressing Delete. Excel displays a warning and asks you to verify your intentions.

Changing your query

If you bring the query results into your worksheet and discover that you don't have what you want, you can modify the query. Move the cell pointer anywhere within the external data table in the worksheet. Right-click and choose Table ⇨ Edit Query from the shortcut menu. You need to edit the query using Microsoft Query. See the next section to learn how to work with Query directly.

Using Query Without the Wizard

When you choose Data ⇨ Get External Data ⇨ From Other Sources ⇨ From Microsoft Query, the Choose Data Source dialog box gives you the option of whether to use Query Wizard to create your query. If you choose not to use Query Wizard, Microsoft Query is launched in a new window. You also work directly with Query if you choose to edit a query that was created with Query Wizard.

NOTE   Microsoft Query is a relatively old application, and its user interface hasn't been updated to match the other Office 2007 programs. It works fine. It just looks old-fashioned.

Creating a query manually

Before you can create a query, you must display the Criteria pane. In Query, open the View menu and place a check next to the Criteria command. The Criteria pane appears in the middle of the window. Figure 33.13 shows Microsoft Query, after selecting the Budget Database from Excel's Choose Data Source dialog box. The Criteria pane also appears.

FIGURE 33.13

Display the Criteria pane as shown here so that you'll be able to create your query.

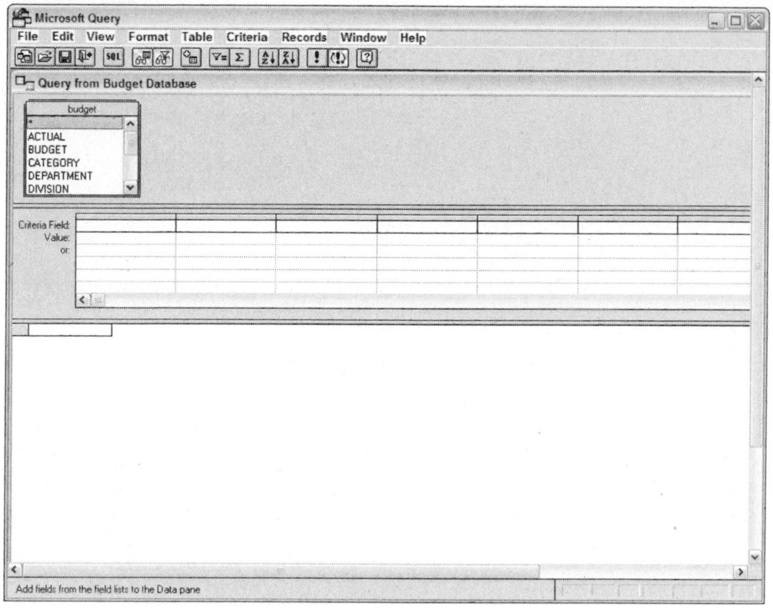

The Query window has three panes, which are split horizontally:

- **Tables pane:** The top pane, which holds the selected data tables for the database. Each data table window has a list of the fields in the table.
- **Criteria pane:** The middle pane, which holds the criteria that determine the rows that the query returns.
- **Data pane:** The bottom pane, which holds the data that passes the criteria.

Creating a query consists of the following steps:

1. **Drag fields from the Tables pane to the Data pane.** You can drag as many fields as you want. These fields are the columns that the query will return. You can also double-click a field instead of dragging it.

2. **Enter criteria in the Criteria pane.** When you activate this pane, the first row (labeled Criteria Field) displays a drop-down list that contains all the field names. Select a field and enter the criteria below it. Query updates the Data pane automatically, treating each row like an OR operator.

3. **Choose File ⇨ Return Data to Microsoft Excel to execute the query and place the data in a worksheet or pivot table.**

Figure 33.14 shows how the query for the example presented earlier in this chapter appears in Query.

TIP   Double-click a criteria box to display the Edit Criteria dialog box, which enables you to select an operator and value.

FIGURE 33.14

Add the fields and criteria to complete your query.

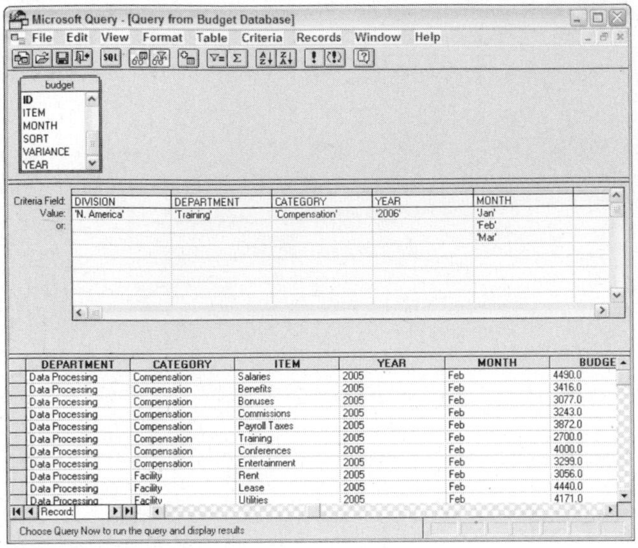

Using multiple database tables

The example in this chapter uses only one database table. Some databases, however, use multiple tables. These databases are known as *relational databases* because a common field links the tables. Query lets you use any number of tables in your queries.

> **NOTE** When you add tables to a query, the Tables pane in Query connects the linked fields with a line between the tables. If no links exist, you can create a link yourself by dragging a field from one table to the corresponding field in the other table.

Adding and editing records in external database tables

To add, delete, and edit data when you're using Query, make sure that a check mark appears next to the Records ⇨ Allow Editing command. Of course, you can't edit a database file that's set up as read-only.

> **CAUTION** Be careful with this feature because your changes are saved to disk as soon as you move the cell pointer out of the record that you're editing. (You do not need to choose File ⇨ Save.)

Formatting data

If you don't like the data's appearance in the Data pane, you can change the font used by choosing Format ⇨ Font. Be aware that selective formatting isn't allowed (unlike in Excel); changing the font affects all the data in the Data pane.

> **TIP** If you need to view the data in the Data pane in a different order, choose Records ⇨ Sort (or click the Sort Ascending or Sort Descending toolbar icon).

Learning More about Query

This chapter isn't intended to cover every aspect of Microsoft Query; rather, it discusses the basic features that are used most often. In fact, if you use the Query Wizard, you may never need to interact with Query itself. But if you do need to use Query, you can experiment and consult the online Help to learn more. As with anything related to Excel, the best way to master Query is to use it — preferably with data that's meaningful to you.

Chapter 34

Introducing Pivot Tables

The Pivot Table feature is perhaps the most technologically sophisticated component in Excel. With only a few mouse clicks, you can slice and dice a data table in dozens of different ways and get just about any type of summary you can think of.

If you haven't yet discovered the power of pivot tables, this chapter provides an introduction, and Chapter 35 continues with many examples that demonstrate how easy it is to create powerful data summaries using pivot tables.

About Pivot Tables

A *pivot table* is essentially a dynamic summary report generated from a database. The database can reside in a worksheet (in the form of a table) or in an external data file. A pivot table can help transform endless rows and columns of numbers into a meaningful presentation of the data.

For example, a pivot table can create frequency distributions and cross-tabulations of several different data dimensions. In addition, you can display subtotals and any level of detail that you want. Perhaps the most innovative aspect of a pivot table is its interactivity. After you create a pivot table, you can rearrange the information in almost any way imaginable and even insert special formulas that perform new calculations. You even can create post hoc groupings of summary items (for example, combine Northern Region totals with Western Region totals). And the icing on the cake: With a few mouse clicks, you can apply formatting to a pivot table to convert it into an attractive report.

One minor drawback to using a pivot table is that, unlike a formula-based summary report, a pivot table does not update automatically when you change information in the source data. This drawback doesn't pose a serious problem, however, because a single click of the Refresh button forces a pivot table to update itself with the latest data.

Pivot tables have been around since Excel 97. Unfortunately, many users overlook this feature because they think it's too complicated. The pivot table feature in Excel 2007 is vastly improved, and creating and working with pivot tables is easier than ever.

NOTE If you've used pivot tables in a previous version of Excel, be aware that the rarely used option to create a pivot table from "multiple consolidation ranges" is no longer available.

A pivot table example

The best way to understand the concept of a pivot table is to see one. Start with Figure 34.1, which shows a portion of the data used in creating the pivot table in this chapter.

FIGURE 34.1

This table is used to create a pivot table.

	A	B	C	D	E	F	G
1	Date	Amount	AcctType	OpenedBy	Branch	Customer	
2	Sep-01	5,000	IRA	New Accts	Central	Existing	
3	Sep-01	14,571	CD	Teller	Central	New	
4	Sep-01	500	Checking	New Accts	Central	Existing	
5	Sep-01	15,000	CD	New Accts	Central	Existing	
6	Sep-01	4,623	Savings	New Accts	North County	Existing	
7	Sep-01	8,721	Savings	New Accts	Westside	New	
8	Sep-01	15,276	Savings	New Accts	North County	Existing	
9	Sep-01	5,000	Savings	New Accts	Westside	Existing	
10	Sep-01	15,759	CD	Teller	Westside	Existing	
11	Sep-01	12,000	CD	New Accts	Westside	Existing	
12	Sep-01	7,177	Savings	Teller	North County	Existing	
13	Sep-01	6,837	Savings	New Accts	Westside	Existing	
14	Sep-01	3,171	Checking	New Accts	Westside	Existing	
15	Sep-01	50,000	Savings	New Accts	Central	Existing	
16	Sep-01	4,690	Checking	New Accts	North County	New	
17	Sep-01	12,438	Checking	New Accts	Central	Existing	
18	Sep-01	5,000	Checking	New Accts	North County	Existing	
19	Sep-01	7,000	Savings	New Accts	North County	New	
20	Sep-01	11,957	Checking	New Accts	Central	Existing	
21	Sep-01	13,636	CD	New Accts	North County	Existing	
22	Sep-01	16,000	CD	New Accts	Central	New	

| ◄ ◄ ► ► | **data** pt1 / pt2 / q1 / q2 / q3 / q4 / q5 / q6 | | |

This table consists of a month's worth of new account information for a three-branch bank. The table contains 712 rows, and each row represents a new account. The table has the following columns:

- The date the account was opened
- The opening amount
- The account type (CD, checking, savings, or IRA)
- Who opened the account (a teller or a new-account representative)
- The branch at which it was opened (Central, Westside, or North County)
- The type of customer (an existing customer or a new customer)

ON the CD-ROM This workbook, named **bank accounts.xlsx**, is available on the companion CD-ROM.

The bank accounts database contains quite a bit of information. But in its current form, the data doesn't reveal much. To make the data more useful, you need to summarize it. Summarizing a database is essentially the process of answering questions about the data. Following are a few questions that may be of interest to the bank's management:

- What is the daily total new deposit amount for each branch?
- How many accounts were opened at each branch, broken down by account type?
- What's the dollar distribution of the different account types?
- What types of accounts do tellers open most often?
- How does the Central branch compare to the other two branches?
- In which branch do tellers open the most checking accounts for new customers?

You can, of course, spend time sorting the data and creating formulas to answer these questions. Often, however, a pivot table is a much better choice. Creating a pivot table takes only a few seconds, doesn't require a single formula, and produces a nice-looking report. In addition, pivot tables are much less prone to error than creating formulas. (Later in this chapter, you'll see several pivot tables that answer the preceding questions.)

Figure 34.2 shows a pivot table created from the bank data. This pivot table shows the amount of new deposits, broken down by branch and account type. This particular summary represents one of dozens of summaries that you can produce from this data.

FIGURE 34.2

A simple pivot table.

Sum of Amount	AcctType					
Branch	CD	Checking	IRA	Savings	Grand Total	
Central	1,359,385	802,403	68,380	885,757	3,115,925	
North County	1,137,911	392,516	134,374	467,414	2,132,215	
Westside	648,549	292,995	10,000	336,088	1,287,632	
Grand Total	3,145,845	1,487,914	212,754	1,689,259	6,535,772	

Figure 34.3 shows another pivot table generated from the bank data. This pivot table uses a drop-down Report Filter for the Customer item (in row 1). In the figure, the pivot table displays the data only for Existing customers. (The user can also select New or All from the drop-down control.) Notice the change in the orientation of the table? For this pivot table, branches appear as column labels, and account types appear as row labels. This change, which took about five seconds to make, is another example of the flexibility of a pivot table.

> # Why "Pivot?"
>
> **A**re you curious about the term "pivot?" *Pivot*, as a verb, means to rotate or revolve. If you think of your data as a physical object, a pivot table lets you rotate the data summary and look at it from different angles or perspectives. A pivot table allows you to move fields around easily, nest fields within each other, and even create ad hoc groups of items.
>
> If you were handed a strange object and asked to identify it, you'd probably look at it from several different angles in an attempt to figure it out. Working with a pivot table is similar to investigating a strange object. In this case, the object happens to be your data. A pivot table invites experimentation, so feel free to rotate and manipulate the pivot table until you're satisfied. You may be surprised at what you discover.

FIGURE 34.3

A pivot table that uses a report filter.

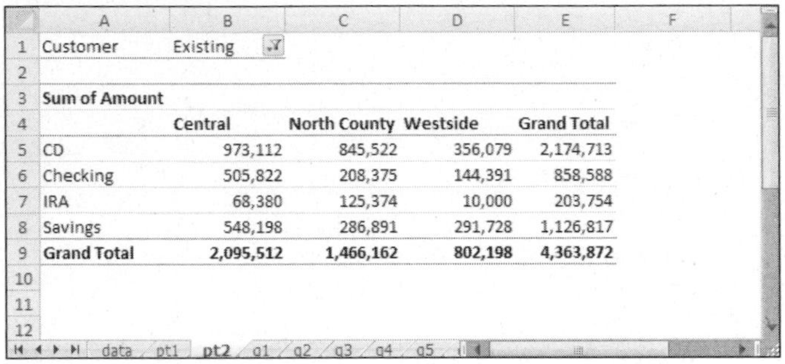

	A	B	C	D	E	F
1	Customer	Existing ⊽				
2						
3	Sum of Amount					
4		Central	North County	Westside	Grand Total	
5	CD	973,112	845,522	356,079	2,174,713	
6	Checking	505,822	208,375	144,391	858,588	
7	IRA	68,380	125,374	10,000	203,754	
8	Savings	548,198	286,891	291,728	1,126,817	
9	Grand Total	2,095,512	1,466,162	802,198	4,363,872	
10						
11						
12						

H ◀ ▶ H   data / pt1   pt2 / q1 / q2 / q3 / q4 / q5 ◀

Data appropriate for a pivot table

A pivot table requires that your data is in the form of a rectangular database. You can store the database in either a worksheet range (which can be a table or just a normal range) or an external database file. Although Excel can generate a pivot table from any database, not all databases benefit.

Generally speaking, fields in a database table consist of two types:

- **Data:** Contains a value or data to be summarized. For the bank account example, the Amount field is a data field.
- **Category:** Describes the data. For the bank account data, the Date, AcctType, OpenedBy, Branch, and Customer fields are category fields because they describe the data in the Amount field.

A single database table can have any number of data fields and category fields. When you create a pivot table, you usually want to summarize one or more of the data fields. Conversely, the values in the category fields appear in the pivot table as rows, columns, or filters.

Exceptions exist, however, and you may find Excel's pivot table feature useful even for databases that don't contain actual numerical data fields. Chapter 35 has an example of a pivot table created from non-numeric data.

Figure 34.4 shows an example of an Excel range that is *not* appropriate for a pivot table. This range contains descriptive information about each value, but it's not set up as a table. In fact, this range resembles a pivot table summary.

FIGURE 34.4

This range is not appropriate for a pivot table.

	North	South	East	West
Jan	132	233	314	441
Feb	143	251	314	447
Mar	172	252	345	450
Apr	184	290	365	452
May	212	299	401	453
Jun	239	317	413	457
Jul	249	350	427	460
Aug	263	354	448	468
Sep	291	373	367	472
Oct	294	401	392	479
Nov	302	437	495	484
Dec	305	466	504	490

Sheet1

Creating a Pivot Table

In this section, I describe the basic steps required to create a pivot table, using the bank account data. Creating a pivot table is an interactive process. It's not at all uncommon to experiment with various layouts until you find one that you're satisfied with.

Specifying the data

If your data is in a worksheet range, select any cell in that range and then choose Insert ➪ Tables ➪ PivotTable, which displays the dialog box shown in Figure 34.5.

Excel attempts to guess the range, based on the location of the active cell. If you're creating a pivot table from an external data source, you need to select that option and then click Choose Connection to specify the data source.

TIP **If you're creating a pivot table from data in a worksheet, it's a good idea to first create a table for the range (by choosing Insert ➪ Tables ➪ Table). Then, if you expand the table by adding new rows of data, Excel will refresh the pivot table without the need to manually indicate the new data range.**

FIGURE 34.5

In the Create PivotTable dialog box, you tell Excel where the data is and where you want the pivot table.

Specifying the location for the pivot table

Use the bottom section of the Create PivotTable dialog box to indicate the location for your pivot table. The default location is on a new worksheet, but you can specify any range on any worksheet, including the worksheet that contains the data.

Click OK, and Excel creates an empty pivot table and displays its PivotTable Field List, as shown in Figure 34.6.

> **TIP** The PivotTable Field List is normally docked on the right side of Excel's window. By dragging its title bar, you can move it anywhere you like. Also, if you click a cell outside the pivot table, the PivotTable Field List is hidden.

FIGURE 34.6

Use the PivotTable Field List to build the pivot table.

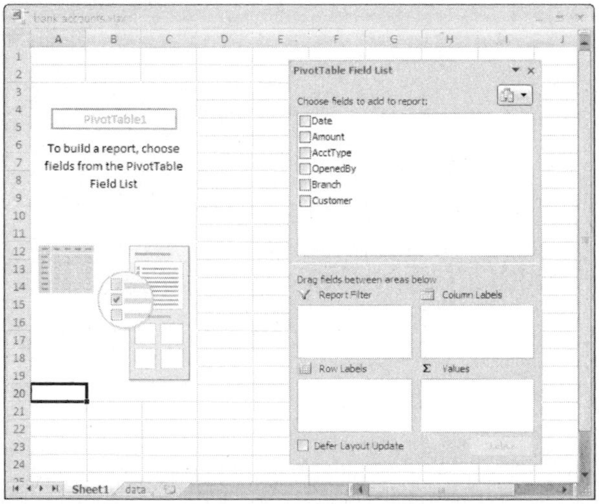

Laying out the pivot table

Next, set up the actual layout of the pivot table. You can do so by using either of these techniques:

- Drag the field names to one of the four boxes in the PivotTable Field List.
- Right-click a field name and choose its location from the shortcut menu.

NOTE In previous versions of Excel, you could drag items from the field list directly into the appropriate area of the pivot table. This feature is still available, but it's turned off by default. To enable this feature, choose PivotTable Tools ⇨ Options ⇨ PivotTable Options ⇨ Options to display the PivotTable Options dialog box. Click the Display tab and add a check mark next to Classic PivotTable Layout.

The following steps create the pivot table presented earlier in this chapter (see "A pivot table example"). For this example, I drag the items from the top of the PivotTable Field List to the areas in the bottom of the PivotTable Field List.

1. **Drag the Amount field into the Values area.** At this point, the pivot table displays the total of all the values in the Amount column.
2. **Drag the AcctType field into the Row Labels area.** Now the pivot table shows the total amount for each of the account types.
3. **Drag the Branch field into the Column Labels area.** The pivot table shows the amount for each account type, cross-tabulated by branch (see Figure 34.7).

FIGURE 34.7

After a few simple steps, the pivot table shows a summary of the data.

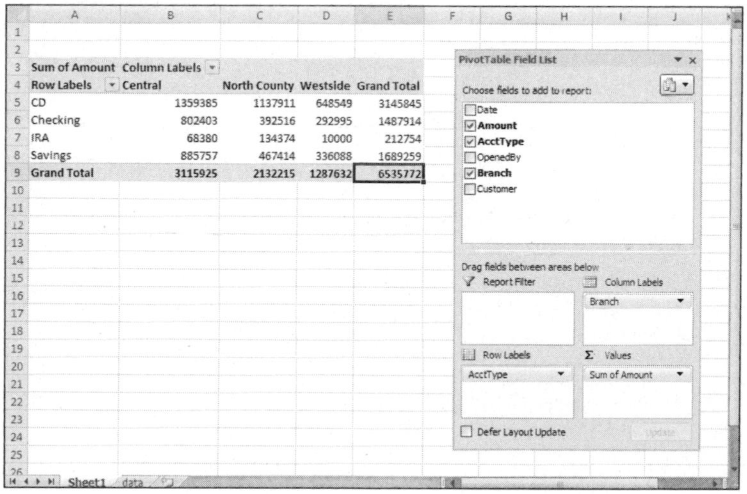

Pivot Table Terminology

Understanding the terminology associated with pivot tables is the first step in mastering this feature. Refer to the accompanying figure to get your bearings.

- **Column labels:** A field that has a column orientation in the pivot table. Each item in the field occupies a column. In the figure, Customer represents a column field that contains two items (Existing and New). You can have nested column fields.

- **Grand totals:** A row or column that displays totals for all cells in a row or column in a pivot table. You can specify that grand totals be calculated for rows, columns, or both (or neither). The pivot table in the figure shows grand totals for both rows and columns.

- **Group:** A collection of items treated as a single item. You can group items manually or automatically (group dates into months, for example). The pivot table in the figure does not have any defined groups.

- **Item:** An element in a field that appears as a row or column header in a pivot table. In the figure, Existing and New are items for the Customer field. The Branch field has three items: Central, North County, and Westside. AcctType has four items: CD, Checking, IRA (Investment Retirement Account), and Savings.

- **Refresh:** Recalculates the pivot table after making changes to the source data.

- **Row labels:** A field that has a row orientation in the pivot table. Each item in the field occupies a row. You can have nested row fields. In the figure, Branch and AcctType both represent row fields.

- **Source data:** The data used to create a pivot table. It can reside in a worksheet or an external database.

- **Subtotals:** A row or column that displays subtotals for detail cells in a row or column in a pivot table. The pivot table in the figure displays subtotals for each branch.

- **Table Filter:** A field that has a page orientation in the pivot table — similar to a slice of a three-dimensional cube. You can display only one item (or all items) in a page field at one time. In the figure, OpenedBy represents a page field that displays the New Accts item. In previous version of Excel, a table filter was known as a Page field.

- **Values area:** The cells in a pivot table that contain the summary data. Excel offers several ways to summarize the data (sum, average, count, and so on).

Formatting the pivot table

Notice that the pivot table uses General number formatting. To change the number format used, select any value and choose PivotTable Tools ➪ Options ➪ Active Field ➪ Field Settings to display the Data Field Settings dialog box. Click the Number Format button and change the number format.

You can apply any of several built-in styles to a pivot table. Select any cell in the pivot table and choose PivotTable Tools ➪ Design ➪ PivotTable Styles to select a style.

You also can use the controls in the PivotTable ➪ Design ➪ Layout group to control various elements in the pivot table. For example, you can choose to hide the grand totals if you prefer.

The PivotTable Tools ➪ Options Show/Hide group contains additional options that affect the appearance of your pivot table. For example, you use the Show Field Headers button to toggle the display of the field headings.

Still more pivot table options are available in the PivotTable Options dialog box, shown in Figure 34.8. To display this dialog box, choose PivotTable Tools ➪ Options ➪ PivotTable Options ➪ Options. Or, right-click any cell in the pivot table and choose Table Options from the shortcut menu.

FIGURE 34.8

The PivotTable Options dialog box.

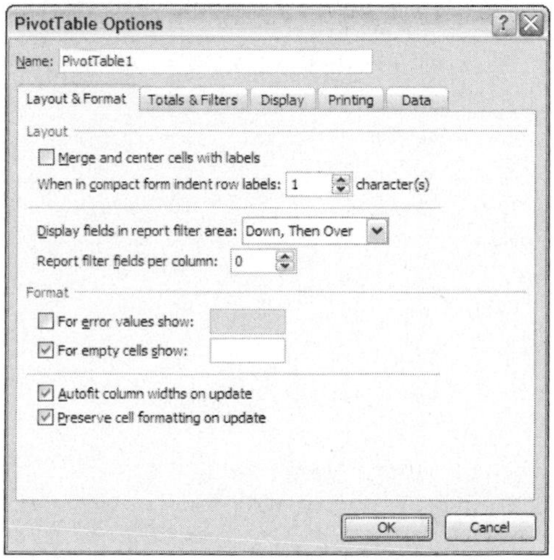

Pivot Table Calculations

Pivot table data is most frequently summarized using a sum. However, you can display your data using a number of different summary techniques. Select any cell in the Values area of your pivot table and then choose PivotTable Tools ⇨ Options ⇨ Active Field ⇨ Field Settings to display the Data Field Settings dialog box. This dialog box has two tabs: Summarize By and Show Values As.

Use the Summarize By tab to select a different summary function. Your choices are Sum, Count, Average, Max, Min, Product, Count Numbers, StdDev, StdDevp, Var, and Varp.

To display your values in a different form, use the drop-down control in the Show Values As tab. Your choices are described in the following table.

Function	Result
Difference From	Displays data as the difference from the value of the Base item in the Base field.
% Of	Displays data as a percentage of the value of the Base item in the Base field.
% Difference From	Displays data as the percentage difference from the value of the Base item in the Base field.
Running Total	Displays the data for successive items in the Base field as a running total.
% Of Row	Displays the data in each row or category as a percentage of the total for the row or category.
% Of Column	Displays all the data in each column or series as a percentage of the total for the column or series.
% Of Total	Displays data as a percentage of the grand total of all the data or data points in the report.
Index	Calculates data as follows: ((value in cell) x (Grand Total of Grand Totals)) / ((Grand Row Total) x (Grand Column Total))

Modifying the pivot table

Once you've created a pivot table, it's easy to change it. For example, you can add further summary information by using the PivotTable Field List. Figure 34.9 shows the pivot table after I dragged a second field (OpenedBy) to the Row Labels section in the PivotTable Field List.

FIGURE 34.9

Two fields are used for row labels.

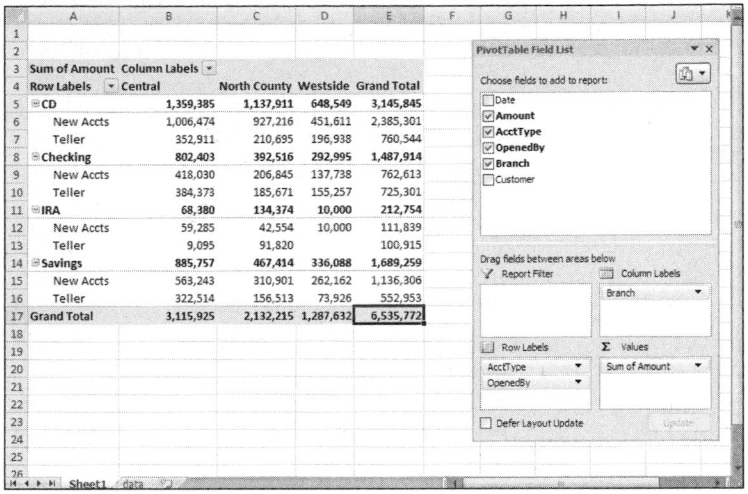

The following are some tips on other pivot table modifications you can make:

- To remove a field from the pivot table, select it in the bottom part of the PivotTable Field List and "drag it away."

- If an area has more than one field, you can change the order in which the fields are listed by dragging the field names. Doing so affects the appearance of the pivot table.

- To temporarily remove a field from the pivot table, remove the check mark from the field name in the top part of the PivotTable Field List. The pivot table is redisplayed without that field. Place the check mark back on the field name, and it appears in its previous section.

- If you add a field to the Report Filter section, the field items appear in a drop-down list, which allows you to filter the displayed data by one or more items. Figure 34.10 shows an example. I dragged the Date field to the Report Filter area. The report is now showing the data only for a single day (which I selected from the drop-down list).

Copying a Pivot Table

A pivot table is very flexible, but it does have some limitations. For example, you can't add new rows or columns, change any of the calculated values, or enter formulas within the pivot table. If you want to manipulate a pivot table in ways not normally permitted, make a copy of it.

To copy a pivot table, select the entire table and choose Home ➪ Clipboard ➪ Copy (or press Ctrl+C). Then select a new worksheet and choose Home Clipboard ➪ Paste ➪ Paste Values. The contents of the pivot table are copied to the new location so that you can do whatever you like to them. You also may want to copy the formats from the pivot table. Select the entire pivot table and then choose Home ➪ Clipboard ➪ Format Painter. Then click the upper-left corner of the copied range.

Note that the copied information is not a pivot table, and it is no longer linked to the source data. If the source data changes, your copied pivot table does not reflect these changes.

FIGURE 34.10

The pivot table is filtered by date.

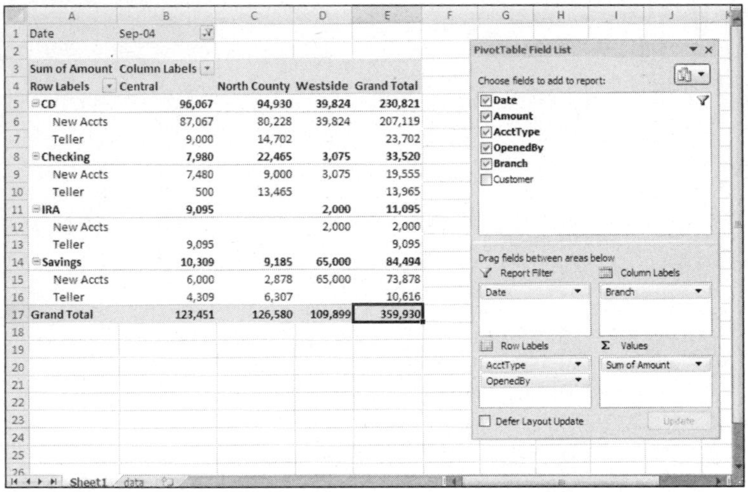

More Pivot Table Examples

To demonstrate the flexibility of this feature, I've created some additional pivot tables. The examples use the bank account data and answer the questions posed earlier in this chapter (see "A pivot table example").

Question 1

What is the daily total new deposit amount for each branch?

Figure 34.11 shows the pivot table that answers this question.

- The Branch field is in the Column Labels section.
- The Date field is in the Row Labels section.
- The Amount field is in the Value section and is summarized by Sum.

Note that the pivot table can also be sorted by any column. For example, you can sort the Grand Total column in descending order to find out which day of the month had the largest amount of new funds. To sort, just right-click any cell in the column to sort and choose Sort on the shortcut menu.

FIGURE 34.11

This pivot table shows daily totals for each branch.

Sum of Amount	Branch			
Date	Central	North County	Westside	Grand Total
Sep-01	135,345	57,402	51,488	244,235
Sep-02	79,642	81,794		161,436
Sep-03	59,119	65,530	20,117	144,766
Sep-04	123,451	126,580	109,899	359,930
Sep-05	101,480	50,294	97,415	249,189
Sep-06	188,018	91,724	52,738	332,480
Sep-07	271,227	196,188	53,525	520,940
Sep-08	67,999	24,123	47,329	139,451
Sep-09	14,475	41,248	36,172	91,895
Sep-10	91,367	24,238	8,512	124,117
Sep-11	104,166	32,018	89,258	225,442
Sep-12	70,300	43,621	39,797	153,718
Sep-13	143,921	176,698	29,075	349,694
Sep-14	117,800	114,418	36,064	268,282
Sep-15	88,566	41,635	78,481	208,682
Sep-16	79,579	21,152	6,534	107,265
Sep-17	56,187	29,380	7,037	92,604
Sep-18	46,673	42,882	41,300	130,855
Sep-19	208,916	213,728	53,721	476,365
Sep-20	125,276	140,739	56,444	322,459
Sep-21	79,355	35,753	3,419	118,527
Sep-22	132,403	149,447	97,210	379,060
Sep-23	56,106	15,823		71,929
Sep-24	75,606	23,285	28,457	127,348
Sep-25	143,283	113,740	57,371	314,394
Sep-26	150,139	29,040	94,310	273,489
Sep-27	56,379	72,948	43,472	172,799
Sep-28	62,192	43,217	12,128	117,537
Sep-29	186,955	33,570	36,359	256,884
Grand Total	3,115,925	2,132,215	1,287,632	6,535,772

data / pt1 / pt2 / q1 / q2 / q3 / q4

Question 2

How many accounts were opened at each branch, broken down by account type?

Figure 34.12 shows a pivot table that answers this question.

- The AcctType field is in the Column Labels section.
- The Branch field is in the Row Labels section.
- The Amount field is in the Value section and is summarized by Count.

The most common summary function used in pivot tables is Sum. In this case, I changed the summary function to Count. To change the summary function to Count, right-click any cell in the Value area and choose Summarize Data By ⇨ Count from the shortcut menu.

FIGURE 34.12

This pivot table uses the Count function to summarize the data.

	A	B	C	D	E	F
2						
3	Count of Amount	AcctType				
4	Branch	CD	Checking	IRA	Savings	Grand Total
5	Central	97	158	8	99	362
6	North County	60	61	15	61	197
7	Westside	54	59	5	35	153
8	Grand Total	211	278	28	195	712
9						
10						

`data  pt1  pt2  q1  q2  q3  q4  q5`

Question 3

What's the dollar distribution of the different account types?

Figure 34.13 shows a pivot table that answer this question. For example, 253 of the new accounts were for an amount of $5,000 or less.

This pivot table is unusual because it uses only one field: Amount.

- The Amount field is in the Row Labels section (grouped).
- The Amount field is also in the Values section and is summarized by Count.
- A third instance of the Amount field is the Values section, summarized by Percent of Total.

When I initially added the Amount field to the Row Labels section, the pivot table showed a row for each unique dollar amount. I right-clicked one of the Row Labels and selected Group. Then I used Excel's Grouping dialog box to set up bins of $5,000 increments.

The second instance of the Amount field (in the Values section) is summarized by Count. I right-clicked a value and chose Summarize Data By ⇨ Count.

I added another instance of Amount to the Values section, and I set it up to display the percentage. I used the Show Values As tab of the Data Field Settings dialog box and specified % Of Total. To display the Data Field Settings dialog box, right-click any cell and choose Summarize Data As ⇨ More Options.

FIGURE 34.13

This pivot table counts the number of accounts that fall into each value range.

	A	B	C	D
2				
3		Data		
4	Amount	No. Accounts	Pct.	
5	1-5000	253	35.53%	
6	5001-10000	193	27.11%	
7	10001-15000	222	31.18%	
8	15001-20000	19	2.67%	
9	20001-25000	3	0.42%	
10	25001-30000	1	0.14%	
11	30001-35000	3	0.42%	
12	40001-45000	3	0.42%	
13	45001-50000	5	0.70%	
14	60001-65000	2	0.28%	
15	70001-75000	5	0.70%	
16	85001-90000	3	0.42%	
17	Grand Total	712	100.00%	
18				

data pt1 pt2

Question 4

What types of accounts do tellers open most often?

Figure 34.14 shows that the most common account opened by tellers is a Checking account.

- The AcctType field is in the Row Labels section.
- The OpenedBy field is in the Report Filters section.
- The Amount field is in the Values section (summarized by Count).
- A second instance of the Amount field is in the Values section (summarized by % Of Total).

This pivot table uses the OpenedBy field as a Report Filter and is showing the data only for Tellers. I sorted the data so that the largest value is at the top, and I also used conditional formatting to display data bars for the percentages.

CROSS-REF Refer to Chapter 21 for more information about conditional formatting.

FIGURE 34.14

This pivot table uses a Report Filter to show only the Teller data.

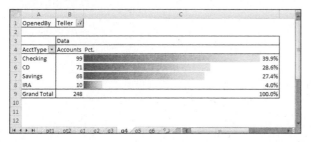

	A	B	C
1	OpenedBy	Teller	
2			
3		Data	
4	AcctType	Accounts	Pct.
5	Checking	99	39.9%
6	CD	71	28.6%
7	Savings	68	27.4%
8	IRA	10	4.0%
9	Grand Total	248	100.0%
10			
11			
12			

pt1 pt2 q1 q2 q3 q4 q5 q6

Question 5

How does the Central branch compare to the other two branches?

Figure 34.15 shows a pivot table that sheds some light on this rather vague question. It simply shows how the Central branch compares to the other two branches combined.

- The AcctType field is in the Row Labels section.
- The Branch field is in the Column Labels section.
- The Amount field is in the Values section.

I grouped the North County and Westside branches together and named the group Other. The pivot table shows the amount, by account type. I also created a pivot chart for good measure.

FIGURE 34.15

This pivot table (and pivot chart) compares the Central branch with the other two branches combined.

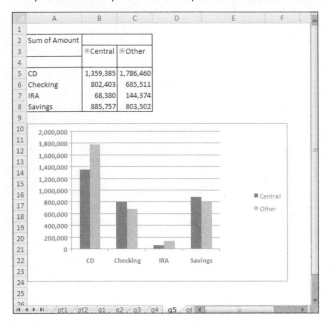

Question 6

In which branch do tellers open the most checking accounts for new customers?

Figure 34.16 shows a pivot table that answers this question. At the Central branch, tellers opened 23 checking accounts for new customers.

- The Customer field is in the Report Filters section.
- The OpenedBy field is in the Report Filters section.
- The AcctType field is in the Report Filters section.

- The Branch field is in the Row Labels section.
- The Amount field is in the Values section, summarized by Count.

This pivot table uses three Report Filters. The Customer field is filtered to show only New, the OpenedBy field is filtered to show only Teller, and the AcctType field is filtered to show only Checking.

FIGURE 34.16

This pivot table uses three Report Filters.

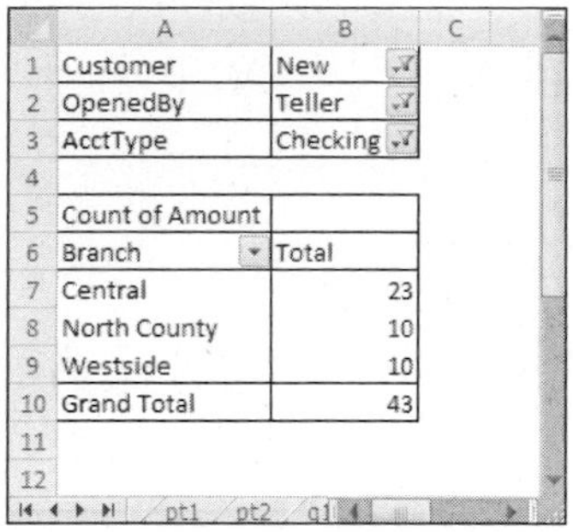

Learning More

If you've looked at the examples in this chapter, you should have an appreciation for the power and flexibility of Excel pivot tables. The next chapter digs a bit deeper and covers some advanced features — with lots of examples.

Chapter 35

Analyzing Data with Pivot Tables

T he previous chapter was an introduction to pivot tables. I presented several examples to demonstrate the types of pivot table summaries that you can generate from a set of data.

This chapter continues the discussion and explores the details of creating effective pivot tables. Creating a basic pivot table is very easy, and the examples in this chapter demonstrate additional pivot table features that you may find helpful. I urge you to try these techniques with your own data. If you don't have suitable data, use the files on the companion CD-ROM.

Working with Non-Numeric Data

Most pivot tables are created from numeric data, but pivot tables are also useful with some types of non-numeric data. Because you can't sum non-numbers, this technique involves counting.

Figure 35.1 shows a table and a pivot table generated from the table. The table is a list of 400 employees, along with their location and gender. As you can see, the table has no numeric values, but you can create a useful pivot table that counts the items rather than sums them. The pivot table cross-tabulates the Location field by the Sex field for the 400 employees and shows the count for each combination of location and gender.

ON the CD-ROM A workbook that demonstrates a pivot table created from non-numeric data is available on the companion CD-ROM. The file is named `employee list.xlsx`.

Following are the settings I used for this pivot table:

- The Sex field is used for the Column Labels.
- The Location field is used for the Row Labels.

IN THIS CHAPTER

How to create a pivot table from non-numeric data

How to group items in a pivot table

How to create a calculated field or a calculated item in a pivot table

How to create an attractive report using a pivot table

- Location is used for the Values and is summarized by Count (specified in the Data Field Settings dialog box).

- The pivot table has the field headers turned off (by choosing PivotTable Tools ⇨ Options ⇨ Show/Hide ⇨ Show Field headers).

FIGURE 35.1

This table doesn't have any numeric fields, but you can use it to generate a pivot table, shown next to the table.

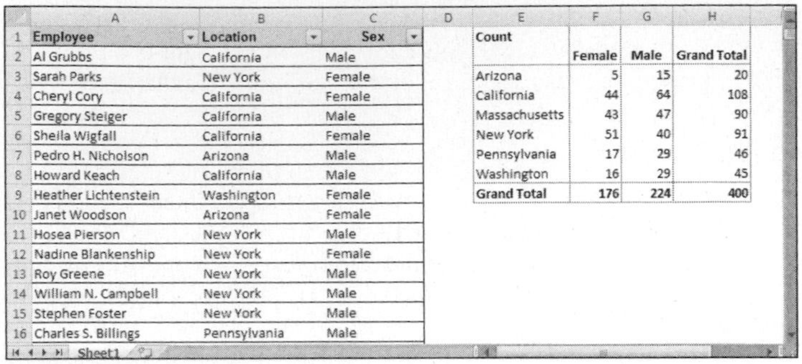

	A	B	C	D	E	F	G	H
1	Employee	Location	Sex		Count			
2	Al Grubbs	California	Male			Female	Male	Grand Total
3	Sarah Parks	New York	Female		Arizona	5	15	20
4	Cheryl Cory	California	Female		California	44	64	108
5	Gregory Steiger	California	Male		Massachusetts	43	47	90
6	Sheila Wigfall	California	Female		New York	51	40	91
7	Pedro H. Nicholson	Arizona	Male		Pennsylvania	17	29	46
8	Howard Keach	California	Male		Washington	16	29	45
9	Heather Lichtenstein	Washington	Female		Grand Total	176	224	400
10	Janet Woodson	Arizona	Female					
11	Hosea Pierson	New York	Male					
12	Nadine Blankenship	New York	Female					
13	Roy Greene	New York	Male					
14	William N. Campbell	New York	Male					
15	Stephen Foster	New York	Male					
16	Charles S. Billings	Pennsylvania	Male					

NOTE The Employee file is not used. This example uses the Location field for the Values section, but you can actually use any of the three fields because the pivot table is displaying a count.

Figure 35.2 shows the pivot table after making some additional changes:

- I added a second instance of the Location field to the Values section and used the Data Field Settings dialog box to display the values as Pct. Of Column.

- I changed the field names in the pivot table to Count and Pct.

- I selected a Pivot Table Style that uses Banded Columns, which makes it easier to distinguish the count columns from the percent columns.

FIGURE 35.2

The pivot table, after making a few changes.

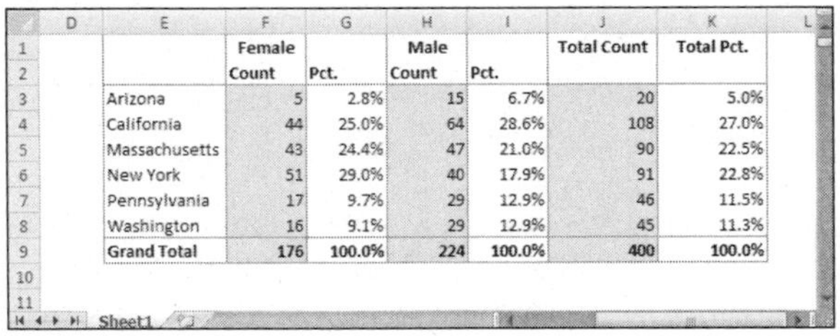

	D	E	F	G	H	I	J	K	L
1			Female		Male		Total Count	Total Pct.	
2			Count	Pct.	Count	Pct.			
3		Arizona	5	2.8%	15	6.7%	20	5.0%	
4		California	44	25.0%	64	28.6%	108	27.0%	
5		Massachusetts	43	24.4%	47	21.0%	90	22.5%	
6		New York	51	29.0%	40	17.9%	91	22.8%	
7		Pennsylvania	17	9.7%	29	12.9%	46	11.5%	
8		Washington	16	9.1%	29	12.9%	45	11.3%	
9		Grand Total	176	100.0%	224	100.0%	400	100.0%	
10									
11									

Grouping Pivot Table Items

One of the most useful features of a pivot table is the ability to combine items into groups. You can group items that appear as Row Labels or Column Labels. Excel offers two ways to group items:

- **Manually:** After creating the pivot table, select the items to be grouped and then choose PivotTable Tools ➪ Options ➪ Group ➪ Group Selection. Or, you can right-click and choose Group from the shortcut menu.
- **Automatically:** If the items are numeric (or dates), use the Grouping dialog box to specify how you would like to group the items. Select any item in the Row Labels or Column Labels and then choose PivotTable Tools ➪ Options ➪ Group ➪ Group Selection. Or, you can right-click and choose Group from the shortcut menu. In either case, Excel displays its Grouping dialog box.

A manual grouping example

Figure 35.3 shows the pivot table example from the previous sections, with two groups created from the Row Labels. To create the first group, I held the Ctrl key while I selected Arizona, California, and Washington. Then I right-clicked and chose Group from the shortcut menu. I repeated the operation to create the second group. Then I replaced the default group names (Group 1 and Group 2) with more meaningful names (Eastern Region and Western Region).

FIGURE 35.3

A pivot table with two groups.

	D	E	F	G	H	I
1		Count				
2			Female	Male	Grand Total	
3		⊟Western Region				
4		Arizona	5	15	20	
5		California	44	64	108	
6		Washington	16	29	45	
7		⊟Eastern Region				
8		Massachusetts	43	47	90	
9		New York	51	40	91	
10		Pennsylvania	17	29	46	
11		Grand Total	176	224	400	
12						

Sheet1

You can create any number of groups and even create groups of groups.

Viewing grouped data

Excel provides a number of options for displaying a pivot table, and you may want to experiment with these options when you use groups. These commands are on the PivotTable Tools ➪ Design tab of the Ribbon. There are no rules for these options. The key is to try a few and see which makes your pivot table look the best. In addition, try various PivotTable Styles, with options for banded rows or banded columns. Often, the style that you choose can greatly enhance readability.

Figure 35.4 shows pivot tables using various options for displaying subtotals, grand totals, and styles.

FIGURE 35.4

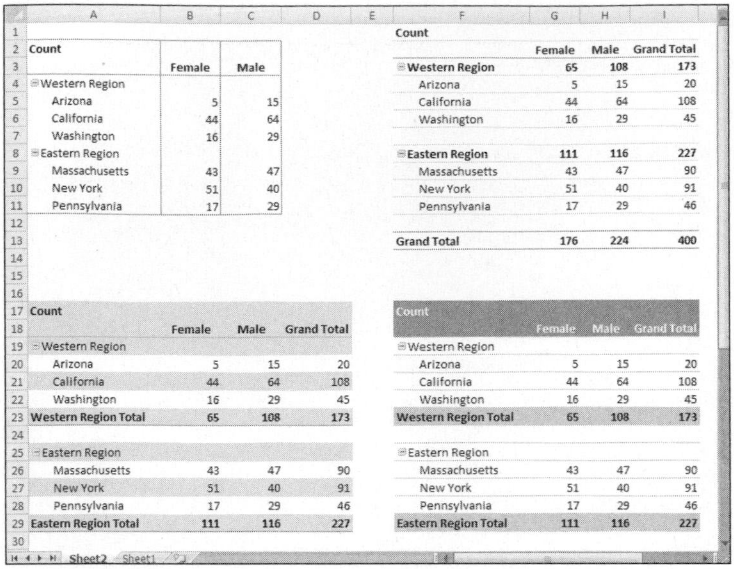

Count	Female	Male
Western Region		
Arizona	5	15
California	44	64
Washington	16	29
Eastern Region		
Massachusetts	43	47
New York	51	40
Pennsylvania	17	29

Count	Female	Male	Grand Total
Western Region	65	108	173
Arizona	5	15	20
California	44	64	108
Washington	16	29	45
Eastern Region	111	116	227
Massachusetts	43	47	90
New York	51	40	91
Pennsylvania	17	29	46
Grand Total	176	224	400

Count	Female	Male	Grand Total
Western Region			
Arizona	5	15	20
California	44	64	108
Washington	16	29	45
Western Region Total	65	108	173
Eastern Region			
Massachusetts	43	47	90
New York	51	40	91
Pennsylvania	17	29	46
Eastern Region Total	111	116	227

Count	Female	Male	Grand Total
Western Region			
Arizona	5	15	20
California	44	64	108
Washington	16	29	45
Western Region Total	65	108	173
Eastern Region			
Massachusetts	43	47	90
New York	51	40	91
Pennsylvania	17	29	46
Eastern Region Total	111	116	227

Pivot tables with options for subtotals and grand totals.

Automatic grouping examples

When a field contains numbers, dates, or times, Excel can create groups automatically. The two examples in this section demonstrate automatic grouping.

Grouping by date

Figure 35.5 shows a portion of a simple table with two fields: Date and Sales. This table has 730 rows and covers the dates between January 1, 2005, and December 31, 2006. The goal is to summarize the sales information by month.

ON the CD-ROM **A workbook demonstrating how to group pivot table items by date is available on the companion CD-ROM. The file is named sales by date.xlsx.**

Figure 35.6 shows part of a pivot table created from the data. The Date field is in the Row Labels section and the Sales field is in the Values section. Not surprisingly, the pivot table looks exactly like the input data because the dates have not been grouped.

To group the items by month, select any date and choose PivotTable Tools ➪ Options ➪ Group ➪ Group Field (or, right-click and choose Group from the shortcut menu). You see the Grouping dialog box, shown in Figure 35.7.

In the By list box, select Months and Years and verify that the starting and ending dates are correct. Click OK. The Date items in the pivot table are grouped by years and by months, as shown in Figure 35.8.

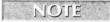

NOTE If you select only Months in the Grouping list box, months in different years combine together. For example, the January item would display sales for both 2005 and 2006.

FIGURE 35.5

You can use a pivot table to summarize the sales data by month.

	A	B	C
1	Date	Sales	
2	1/1/2005	1,277	
3	1/2/2005	1,255	
4	1/3/2005	1,454	
5	1/4/2005	1,223	
6	1/5/2005	1,314	
7	1/6/2005	1,496	
8	1/7/2005	1,472	
9	1/8/2005	1,124	
10	1/9/2005	1,210	
11	1/10/2005	1,516	
12	1/11/2005	1,831	
13	1/12/2005	1,902	
14	1/13/2005	2,193	
15	1/14/2005	2,111	
16	1/15/2005	2,034	
17	1/16/2005	1,763	
18	1/17/2005	1,783	
19	1/18/2005	1,938	
20	1/19/2005	2,167	
21	1/20/2005	2,171	
22	1/21/2005	1,990	

Sheet1 | data

FIGURE 35.6

The pivot table, before grouping by month.

	A	B	C
1			
2	Date	Sum of Sales	
3	1/1/2005	1,277	
4	1/2/2005	1,255	
5	1/3/2005	1,454	
6	1/4/2005	1,223	
7	1/5/2005	1,314	
8	1/6/2005	1,496	
9	1/7/2005	1,472	
10	1/8/2005	1,124	
11	1/9/2005	1,210	
12	1/10/2005	1,516	
13	1/11/2005	1,831	
14	1/12/2005	1,902	
15	1/13/2005	2,193	
16	1/14/2005	2,111	

Sheet1 | data

FIGURE 35.7

Use the Grouping dialog box to group pivot table items by dates.

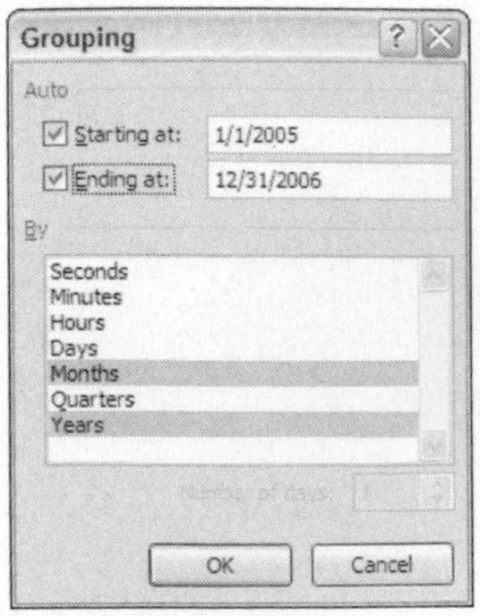

FIGURE 35.8

The pivot table, after grouping by month and year.

	Years	Date	Sum of Sales
2	**Years**	**Date**	**Sum of Sales**
3	⊟ **2005**	Jan	55,876
4		Feb	45,943
5		Mar	71,634
6		Apr	33,626
7		May	52,670
8		Jun	39,218
9		Jul	98,417
10		Aug	172,990
11		Sep	204,226
12		Oct	233,286
13		Nov	287,696
14		Dec	323,482
15	⊟ **2006**	Jan	324,877
16		Feb	323,233
17		Mar	360,533
18		Apr	327,771
19		May	348,109
20		Jun	310,027
21		Jul	320,520
22		Aug	312,812
23		Sep	325,169
24		Oct	316,041
25		Nov	316,832
26		Dec	302,131
27	**Grand Total**		**5,507,118**

Figure 35.9 shows another view of the data, grouped by quarter and by year.

FIGURE 35.9

This pivot table shows sales by quarter and by year.

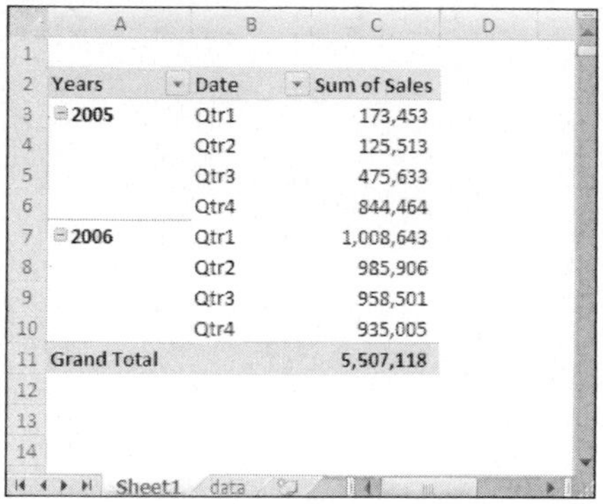

Years	Date	Sum of Sales
2005	Qtr1	173,453
	Qtr2	125,513
	Qtr3	475,633
	Qtr4	844,464
2006	Qtr1	1,008,643
	Qtr2	985,906
	Qtr3	958,501
	Qtr4	935,005
Grand Total		5,507,118

Grouping by time

Figure 35.10 shows a set of data in columns A:B. Each row is a reading from an instrument, taken at one-minute intervals throughout an entire day. The table has 1,440 rows, each representing one minute. The pivot table summarizes the data by hour.

ON the CD-ROM **This workbook, named hourly readings.xlsx, is available on the companion CD-ROM.**

Following are the settings I used for this pivot table:

- The values area has three instances of the Reading field. I used the Data Field Setting dialog box (Summarize By tab) to summarize the first instance by Average, the second instance by Min, and the third instance by Max.
- The Time field is in the Row Labels section, and I used the Grouping dialog box to group by Hours.

FIGURE 35.10

This pivot table is grouped by Hours.

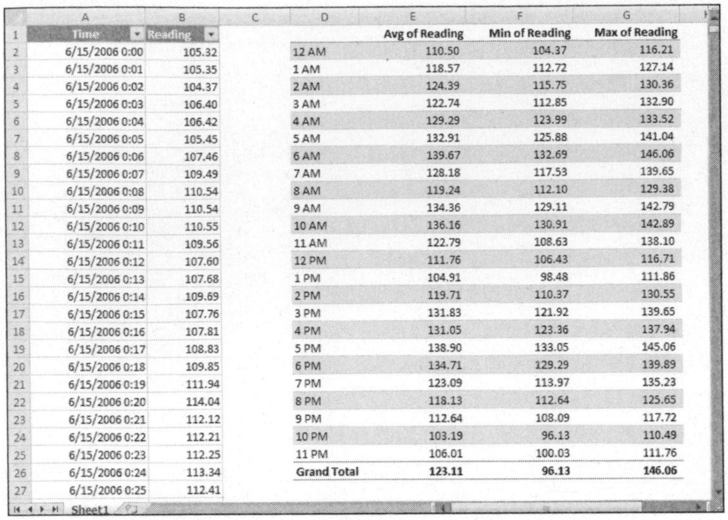

	A	B	C	D	E	F	G
1	Time	Reading			Avg of Reading	Min of Reading	Max of Reading
2	6/15/2006 0:00	105.32		12 AM	110.50	104.37	116.21
3	6/15/2006 0:01	105.35		1 AM	118.57	112.72	127.14
4	6/15/2006 0:02	104.37		2 AM	124.39	115.75	130.36
5	6/15/2006 0:03	106.40		3 AM	122.74	112.85	132.90
6	6/15/2006 0:04	106.42		4 AM	129.29	123.99	133.52
7	6/15/2006 0:05	105.45		5 AM	132.91	125.88	141.04
8	6/15/2006 0:06	107.46		6 AM	139.67	132.69	146.06
9	6/15/2006 0:07	109.49		7 AM	128.18	117.53	139.65
10	6/15/2006 0:08	110.54		8 AM	119.24	112.10	129.38
11	6/15/2006 0:09	110.54		9 AM	134.36	129.11	142.79
12	6/15/2006 0:10	110.55		10 AM	136.16	130.91	142.89
13	6/15/2006 0:11	109.56		11 AM	122.79	108.63	138.10
14	6/15/2006 0:12	107.60		12 PM	111.76	106.43	116.71
15	6/15/2006 0:13	107.68		1 PM	104.91	98.48	111.86
16	6/15/2006 0:14	109.69		2 PM	119.71	110.37	130.55
17	6/15/2006 0:15	107.76		3 PM	131.83	121.92	139.65
18	6/15/2006 0:16	107.81		4 PM	131.05	123.36	137.94
19	6/15/2006 0:17	108.83		5 PM	138.90	133.05	145.06
20	6/15/2006 0:18	109.85		6 PM	134.71	129.29	139.89
21	6/15/2006 0:19	111.94		7 PM	123.09	113.97	135.23
22	6/15/2006 0:20	114.04		8 PM	118.13	112.64	125.65
23	6/15/2006 0:21	112.12		9 PM	112.64	108.09	117.72
24	6/15/2006 0:22	112.21		10 PM	103.19	96.13	110.49
25	6/15/2006 0:23	112.25		11 PM	106.01	100.03	111.76
26	6/15/2006 0:24	113.34		Grand Total	123.11	96.13	146.06
27	6/15/2006 0:25	112.41					

Sheet1

Creating a Frequency Distribution

Excel provides a number of ways to create a frequency distribution (see Chapter 14). But none of these methods is easier than using a pivot table.

Figure 35.11 shows part of a table of 221 students and the test score for each. The goal is to determine how many students are in each 10-point range (1–10, 11–20, and so on).

ON the CD-ROM This workbook, named test scores.xlsx, is available on the companion CD-ROM.

The pivot table is simple:

- The Score field is in the Row Labels section (grouped).
- Another instance of the Score field is in the Values section (summarized by Count).

The Grouping dialog box that generated the bins specified that the groups start at 1, end at 100, and are incremented by 10.

NOTE By default, Excel does not display items with a zero value. In this example, no test scores are below 21, so the 1–10 and 11–20 items are hidden. To override this setting, access the PivotTable Options dialog box, click the Display tab, and put a check mark next to Display Item Labels When No Fields Are In The Values Area.

Figure 35.12 show the frequency distribution of the test scores, along with a pivot chart. (See "Creating Pivot Charts," later in this chapter).

FIGURE 35.11

Creating a frequency distribution for these test scores is simple.

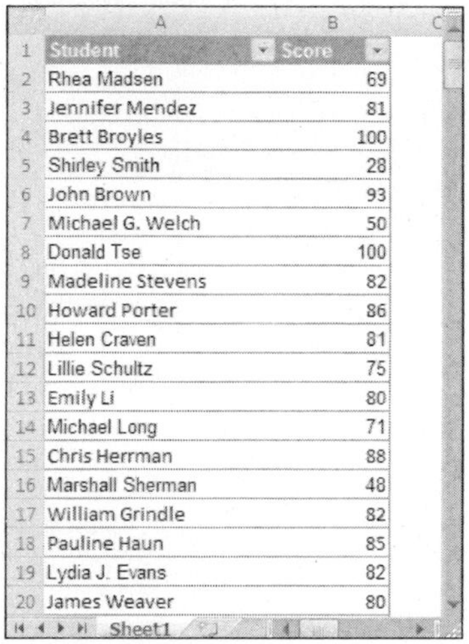

	A	B	C
1	**Student** ▾	**Score** ▾	
2	Rhea Madsen	69	
3	Jennifer Mendez	81	
4	Brett Broyles	100	
5	Shirley Smith	28	
6	John Brown	93	
7	Michael G. Welch	50	
8	Donald Tse	100	
9	Madeline Stevens	82	
10	Howard Porter	86	
11	Helen Craven	81	
12	Lillie Schultz	75	
13	Emily Li	80	
14	Michael Long	71	
15	Chris Herrman	88	
16	Marshall Sherman	48	
17	William Grindle	82	
18	Pauline Haun	85	
19	Lydia J. Evans	82	
20	James Weaver	80	

Sheet1

FIGURE 35.12

The pivot table and pivot chart shows the frequency distribution for the test scores.

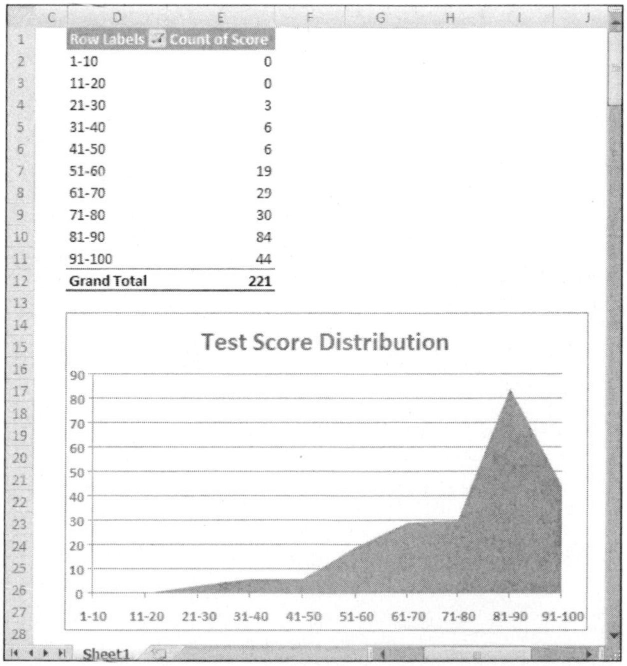

	C	D	E	F	G	H	I	J
1		**Row Labels** ▾	**Count of Score**					
2		1-10	0					
3		11-20	0					
4		21-30	3					
5		31-40	6					
6		41-50	6					
7		51-60	19					
8		61-70	29					
9		71-80	30					
10		81-90	84					
11		91-100	44					
12		**Grand Total**	**221**					

Test Score Distribution

Sheet1

617

NOTE   This example used Excel's Grouping dialog box to create the groups automatically. If you don't want to group in equal-sized bins, you can create your own groups. For example, you may want to assign letter grades based on the test score. Select the rows for the first group and then choose Group from the shortcut menu. Repeat these steps for each additional group. Then replace the default group names with more meaningful names.

Creating a Calculated Field or Calculated Item

Perhaps the most confusing aspect of pivot tables is calculated fields versus calculated items. Many pivot table users simply avoid dealing with calculated fields and items. However, these features can be useful, and they really aren't that complicated once you understand how they work.

First, some basic definitions:

- **A calculated field:** A new field created from other fields in the pivot table. If your pivot table source is a worksheet table, an alternative to using a calculated field is to add a new column to the table, and create a formula to perform the desired calculation. A calculated field must reside in the Values area of the pivot table. You can't use a calculated field in the Column Labels, Row Labels, or in a Report Filter.
- **A calculated item:** A calculated item uses the contents of other items within a field of the pivot table. If your pivot table source is a worksheet table, an alternative to using a calculated item is to insert one or more rows and write formulas that use values in other rows. A calculated item must reside in the Column Labels, Row Labels, or Report Filter area of a pivot table. You can't use a calculated item in the Values area.

The formulas used to create calculated fields and calculated items aren't standard Excel formulas. In other words, you don't enter the formulas into cells. Rather, you enter these formulas in a dialog box, and they're stored along with the pivot table data.

The examples in this section use the worksheet table shown in Figure 35.13. The table consists of five fields and 48 rows. Each row describes monthly sales information for a particular sales representative. For example, Amy is a sales rep for the North region, and she sold 239 units in January for total sales of $23,040.

ON the CD-ROM   A workbook demonstrating calculated fields and items is available on the companion CD-ROM. The file is named **calculated fields and items.xlsx**.

Figure 35.14 shows a pivot table created from the data. This pivot table shows Sales (Values area), cross-tabulated by Month (Row Labels) and by SalesRep (Column Labels).

The examples that follow create

- A calculated field, to compute average sales per unit
- Four calculated items, to compute the quarterly sales commission

FIGURE 35.13

This data demonstrates calculated fields and calculated items.

	A	B	C	D	E	F
1	SalesRep	Region	Month	Sales	Units Sold	
2	Amy	North	Jan	$23,040	239	
3	Amy	North	Feb	$24,131	79	
4	Amy	North	Mar	$24,646	71	
5	Amy	North	Apr	$22,047	71	
6	Amy	North	May	$24,971	157	
7	Amy	North	Jun	$24,218	92	
8	Amy	North	Jul	$25,735	175	
9	Amy	North	Aug	$23,638	87	
10	Amy	North	Sep	$25,749	557	
11	Amy	North	Oct	$24,437	95	
12	Amy	North	Nov	$25,355	706	
13	Amy	North	Dec	$25,899	180	
14	Bob	North	Jan	$20,024	103	
15	Bob	North	Feb	$23,822	267	
16	Bob	North	Mar	$24,854	96	
17	Bob	North	Apr	$22,838	74	
18	Bob	North	May	$25,320	231	
19	Bob	North	Jun	$24,733	164	
20	Bob	North	Jul	$21,184	68	
21	Bob	North	Aug	$23,174	114	

Sheet1 Data

FIGURE 35.14

This pivot table was created from the sales data.

	A	B	C	D	E	F
1						
2						
3	Tot Sales					
4		Amy	Bob	Chuck	Doug	
5	Jan	23,040	20,024	19,886	26,264	
6	Feb	24,131	23,822	23,494	29,953	
7	Mar	24,646	24,854	21,824	25,041	
8	Apr	22,047	22,838	22,058	29,338	
9	May	24,971	25,320	20,280	25,150	
10	Jun	24,218	24,733	23,965	27,371	
11	Jul	25,735	21,184	23,032	25,044	
12	Aug	23,638	23,174	21,273	29,506	
13	Sep	25,749	25,999	21,584	29,061	
14	Oct	24,437	22,639	19,625	27,113	
15	Nov	25,355	23,949	19,832	25,953	
16	Dec	25,899	23,179	20,583	28,670	
17	Grand Total	293,866	281,715	257,436	328,464	
18						
19						

Sheet1 Data

Creating a calculated field

Because a pivot table is a special type of range, you can't insert new rows or columns within the pivot table, which means that you can't insert formulas to perform calculations with the data in a pivot table. However, you can create calculated fields for a pivot table. A *calculated field* consists of a calculation that can involve other fields.

A calculated field is basically a way to display new information in a pivot table. It essentially presents an alternative to creating a new column field in your source data. In many cases, you may find it easier to insert a new column in the source range with a formula that performs the desired calculation. A calculated field is most useful when the data comes from a source that you can't easily manipulate — such as an external database.

In the sales example, for example, suppose that you want to calculate the average sales amount per unit. You can compute this value by dividing the Sales field by the Units Sold field. The result shows a new field (a calculated field) for the pivot table.

Use the following procedure to create a calculated field that consists of the Sales field divided by the Units Sold field:

1. **Select any cell within the pivot table.**
2. **Choose PivotTable Tools ⇨ Options ⇨ Tools ⇨ Formulas ⇨ Calculated Field.** Excel displays the Insert Calculated Field dialog box.
3. **Enter a descriptive name in the Name box and specify the formula in the Formula box (see Figure 35.15).** The formula can use worksheet functions and other fields from the data source. For this example, the calculated field name is **Avg Unit Price**, and the formula is

   ```
   =Sales/'Units Sold'
   ```
4. **Click Add to add this new field.**
5. **Click OK to close the Insert Calculated Field dialog box.**

FIGURE 35.15

The Insert Calculated Field dialog box.

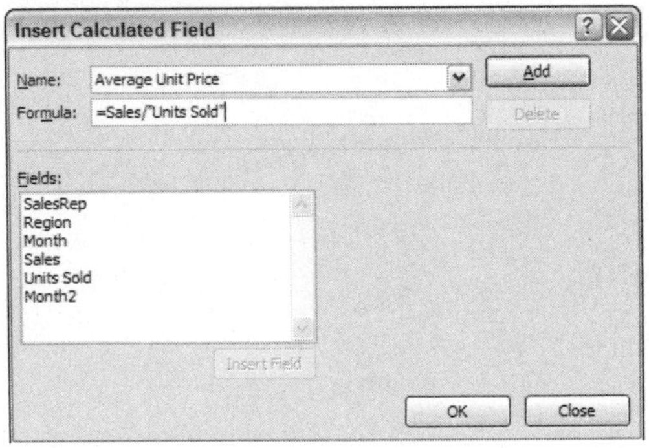

NOTE You can create the formula manually by typing it or by double-clicking items in the Fields list box. Double-clicking an item transfers it to the Formula field. Because the Units Sold field contains a space, Excel adds single quotes around the field name.

After you create the calculated field, Excel adds it to the Values area of the pivot table (and it also appears in the PivotTable Field List). You can treat it just like any other field, with one exception: You can't move it to the Row Labels, Column Labels, or Report Filter areas. It must remain in the Values area.

Figure 35.16 shows the pivot table after adding the calculated field. The new field displayed Sum of Avg Unit Price, but I changed this label to Avg Price. I also changed the style to display banded columns.

FIGURE 35.16

This pivot table uses a calculated field.

	Amy		Bob		Chuck		Doug	
	Tot Sales	Avg Price	Tot Sales	Avg Price	Tot Sales	Avg Price	Tot Sales	Avg Price
Jan	23,040	96	20,024	194	19,886	209	26,264	285
Feb	24,131	305	23,822	89	23,494	159	29,953	35
Mar	24,646	347	24,854	259	21,824	263	25,041	291
Apr	22,047	311	22,838	309	22,058	230	29,338	132
May	24,971	159	25,320	110	20,280	45	25,150	104
Jun	24,218	263	24,733	151	23,965	32	27,371	288
Jul	25,735	147	21,184	312	23,032	149	25,044	305
Aug	23,638	272	23,174	203	21,273	28	29,506	286
Sep	25,749	46	25,999	310	21,584	189	29,061	199
Oct	24,437	257	22,639	87	19,625	236	27,113	226
Nov	25,355	36	23,949	220	19,832	283	25,953	320
Dec	25,899	144	23,179	50	20,583	116	28,670	145
Grand Total	293,866	117	281,715	138	257,436	86	328,464	142

Sheet1 Data

TIP   The formulas that you develop can also use worksheet functions, but the functions can't refer to cells or named ranges.

Inserting a calculated item

The preceding section describes how to create a calculated field. Excel also enables you to create a *calculated item* for a pivot table field. Keep in mind that a calculated field can be an alternative to adding a new field to your data source. A calculated item, on the other hand, is an alternative to adding a new row to the data source — a row that contains a formula that refers to other rows.

In this example, you create four calculated items. Each item represents the commission earned on the quarter's sales, according to the following schedule:

- **Quarter 1:** 10% of January, February, and March sales
- **Quarter 2:** 11% of April, May, and June sales
- **Quarter 3:** 12% of July, August, and September sales
- **Quarter 4:** 12.5% of October, November, and December sales

NOTE   Modifying the source data to obtain this information would require inserting 16 new rows, each with formulas. So, for this example, creating four calculated items may be an easier task.

To create a calculated item to compute the commission for January, February, and March, follow these steps:

1. **Move the cell pointer to the Row Labels or Column Labels area of the pivot table and choose PivotTable Tools ⇨ Options ⇨ Tools ⇨ Formulas ⇨ Calculated Item.** Excel displays the Insert Calculated Item dialog box.

2. **Enter a name for the new item in the Name box and specify the formula in the Formula box (see Figure 35.17).** The formula can use items in other fields, but it can't use worksheet functions. For this example, the new item is named **Qtr1 Commission**, and the formula appears as follows:

   ```
   =10%*(Jan+Feb+Mar)
   ```

3. **Click Add.**

4. **Repeat Steps 2 and 3 to create three additional calculated items:**

   Qtr2 Commission: = 11%*(Apr+May+Jun)

   Qtr3 Commission: = 12%*(Jul+Aug+Sep)

   Qtr4 Commission: = 12.5%*(Oct+Nov+Dec)

5. **Click OK to close the dialog box.**

FIGURE 35.17

The Insert Calculated Item dialog box.

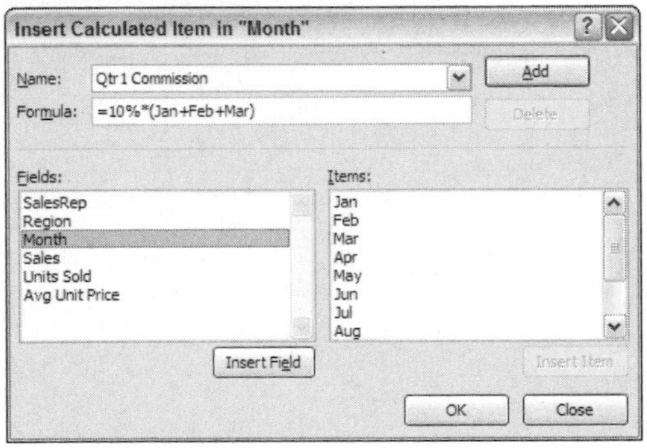

NOTE Note that a calculated item, unlike a calculated field, does not appear in the PivotTable Field List. Only fields appear in the field list.

CAUTION If you use a calculated item in your pivot table, you may need to turn off the Grand Total display for columns to avoid double counting. In this example the Grand Total includes the calculated items, so the commission amounts are included with the sales amounts. To turn off Grand Totals, choose PivotTable Tools ⇨ Design ⇨ Layout ⇨ Grand Totals.

After you create the calculated items, they appear in the pivot table. Figure 35.18 shows the pivot table after adding the four calculated items. Notice that the calculated items are added to the end of the Month items. You can rearrange the items by selecting the cell and dragging its border. Another option is to create two groups: One for the sales numbers and one for the commission calculations. Figure 35.19 shows the pivot table after creating the two groups and adding subtotals.

FIGURE 35.18

This pivot table uses calculated items for quarterly totals.

	A	B	C	D	E	F	G
2							
3	**Sum of Sales**						
4		Amy	Bob	Chuck	Doug	Grand Total	
5	Jan	23,040	20,024	19,886	26,264	89,214	
6	Feb	24,131	23,822	23,494	29,953	101,400	
7	Mar	24,646	24,854	21,824	25,041	96,365	
8	Apr	22,047	22,838	22,058	29,338	96,281	
9	May	24,971	25,320	20,280	25,150	95,721	
10	Jun	24,218	24,733	23,965	27,371	100,287	
11	Jul	25,735	21,184	23,032	25,044	94,995	
12	Aug	23,638	23,174	21,273	29,506	97,591	
13	Sep	25,749	25,999	21,584	29,061	102,393	
14	Oct	24,437	22,639	19,625	27,113	93,814	
15	Nov	25,355	23,949	19,832	25,953	95,089	
16	Dec	25,899	23,179	20,583	28,670	98,331	
17	**Qtr1 Commission**	**7,182**	**6,870**	**6,520**	**8,126**	**28,698**	
18	**Qtr2 Commission**	**7,836**	**8,018**	**7,293**	**9,004**	**32,152**	
19	**Qtr3 Commission**	**9,015**	**8,443**	**7,907**	**10,033**	**35,397**	
20	**Qtr4 Commission**	**9,461**	**8,721**	**7,505**	**10,217**	**35,904**	
21							
22							

Sheet1 / Data

FIGURE 35.19

The pivot table, after creating two groups and adding subtotals.

	A	B	C	D	E	F	G
2							
3	**Sum of Sales**						
4			Amy	Bob	Chuck	Doug	Grand Total
5	⊟Sales	Jan	23,040	20,024	19,886	26,264	89,214
6		Feb	24,131	23,822	23,494	29,953	101,400
7		Mar	24,646	24,854	21,824	25,041	96,365
8		Apr	22,047	22,838	22,058	29,338	96,281
9		May	24,971	25,320	20,280	25,150	95,721
10		Jun	24,218	24,733	23,965	27,371	100,287
11		Jul	25,735	21,184	23,032	25,044	94,995
12		Aug	23,638	23,174	21,273	29,506	97,591
13		Sep	25,749	25,999	21,584	29,061	102,393
14		Oct	24,437	22,639	19,625	27,113	93,814
15		Nov	25,355	23,949	19,832	25,953	95,089
16		Dec	25,899	23,179	20,583	28,670	98,331
17	**Sales Total**		**293,866**	**281,715**	**257,436**	**328,464**	**1,161,481**
18							
19	⊟Commission	Qtr1 Commission	7,182	6,870	6,520	8,126	28,698
20		Qtr2 Commission	7,836	8,018	7,293	9,004	32,152
21		Qtr3 Commission	9,015	8,443	7,907	10,033	35,397
22		Qtr4 Commission	9,461	8,721	7,505	10,217	35,904
23	**Commission Total**		**33,494**	**32,052**	**29,225**	**37,381**	**132,151**
24							
25							

Sheet1 / Data

A Reverse Pivot Table

Excel's Pivot Table feature creates a summary table from a list. But what if you want to perform the opposite operation? Often, you may have a two-way summary table, and it would be convenient if the data were in the form of a list.

In the figure, range A1:E13 contains a summary table with 48 data points. Notice that this summary table is similar to a pivot table. Column G:I shows part of a 48-row table that was derived from the summary table. In other words, every value in the original summary table gets converted to a row, which also contains the region name and month. This type of table is useful because it can be sorted and manipulated in other ways. And, you can create a pivot table from this transformed table.

	A	B	C	D	E	F	G	H	I
1		North	South	East	West		Month	Region	Sales
2	Jan	132	233	314	441		Jan	North	132
3	Feb	143	251	314	447		Jan	South	233
4	Mar	172	252	345	450		Jan	East	314
5	Apr	184	290	365	452		Jan	West	441
6	May	212	299	401	453		Feb	North	143
7	Jun	239	317	413	457		Feb	South	251
8	Jul	249	350	427	460		Feb	East	314
9	Aug	263	354	448	468		Feb	West	447
10	Sep	291	373	367	472		Mar	North	172
11	Oct	294	401	392	479		Mar	South	252
12	Nov	302	437	495	484		Mar	East	345
13	Dec	305	466	504	490		Mar	West	450
14							Apr	North	184
15							Apr	South	290
16							Apr	East	365
17							Apr	West	452
18							May	North	212
19							May	South	299
20							May	East	401
21							May	West	453

Sheet1

The companion CD-ROM contains a workbook, **reverse pivot.xlsm**, which has a macro that will convert any two-way summary table into a three-column normalized table.

Referencing Cells within a Pivot Table

In some cases, you may want to create a formula that references one or more cells within a pivot table. Figure 35.20 shows a simple pivot table that displays income and expense information for three years. In this pivot table, the Month field is hidden, so the pivot table shows the year totals.

ON the CD-ROM   This workbook, named income and expenses.xlsx, is available on the companion CD-ROM.

FIGURE 35.20

The formulas in column F reference cells in the pivot table.

	A	B	C	D	E	F
2						
3			Data			
4	Year ⌄	Month ⌄	Sum of Income	Sum of Expenses		Ratio
5	⊞2004		1,256,274	525,288		41.8%
6	⊞2005		1,357,068	533,893		39.3%
7	⊞2006		1,583,717	646,181		40.8%
8	Grand Total		4,197,059	1,705,362		40.6%
9						
10						

Sheet2 Sheet1

Column F contains formulas and this column is not part of the pivot table. These formulas calculate the expense-to-income ratio for each year. I created these formulas by pointing to the cells. You may expect to see this formula in cell F5:

    =D5/C5

In fact, the formula in cell F5 is

    =GETPIVOTDATA("Sum of Expenses",$A$3,"Year",2004)/GETPIVOTDATA("Sum of
    Income",$A$3,"Year",2004)

When you use the pointing technique to create a formula that references a cell in a pivot table, Excel replaces those simple cell references with a much more complicated GETPIVOTDATA function. If you type the cell references manually (rather than pointing to them), Excel does not use the GETPIVOTDATA function.

The reason? Using the GETPIVOTDATA function helps ensure that the formula will continue to reference the intended cells if the pivot table changed. Figure 35.21 shows the pivot table after expanding the years to show the month detail. As you can see, the formulas in column F still show the correct result, even though the references cells are in a different location. Had I used simple cell references, the formula would return incorrect results after expanding the years.

 Using the GETPIVOTDATA function has one caveat: the data that it retrieves must be visible. If you modify the pivot table so that the value returned by GETPIVOTDATA is no longer visible, the formula returns an error.

 If, for some reason, you want to prevent Excel from using the GETPIVOTDATA function when you point to pivot table cells when creating a formula, access the Excel Options dialog box, select the Formulas tab, and remove the check mark from Use GETPIVOTDATA Function For PivotTable References.

FIGURE 35.21

After expanding the pivot table, formulas that use the GETPIVOTDATA function continue to display the correct result.

	A	B	C	D	E	F
2						
3			Data			
4	Year	Month	Sum of Income	Sum of Expenses		Ratio
5	⊟2004	Jan	98,085	42,874		41.8%
6		Feb	98,698	44,167		39.3%
7		Mar	102,403	43,349		40.8%
8		Apr	106,044	43,102		40.6%
9		May	105,361	45,005		
10		Jun	105,729	44,216		
11		Jul	105,557	43,835		
12		Aug	109,669	41,952		
13		Sep	107,233	44,071		
14		Oct	105,048	43,185		
15		Nov	107,446	44,403		
16		Dec	105,001	45,129		
17	2004 Total		1,256,274	525,288		
18	⊟2005	Jan	109,699	46,245		
19		Feb	109,146	45,672		
20		Mar	106,576	44,143		
21		Apr	108,911	43,835		
22		May	108,011	44,114		
23		Jun	111,361	44,648		

Sheet2 Sheet1

Creating Pivot Charts

A *pivot chart* is a graphical representation of a data summary displayed in a pivot table. A pivot chart is always based on a pivot table. Although Excel lets you create a pivot table and a pivot chart at the same time, you can't create a pivot chart without a pivot table.

If you're familiar with creating charts in Excel, you'll have no problem creating and customizing pivot charts. All of Excel's charting features are available in a pivot chart.

 **I cover charting in Chapters 19 and 20.**

Excel provides two ways to create a pivot chart:

- Select any cell in an existing pivot table and choose PivotTable Tools ➪ Options ➪ Tools ➪ Pivot Chart.

- Choose Insert ➪ Tables ➪ Pivot Table ➪ Pivot Chart. Excel creates a pivot table and a pivot chart.

NOTE   If you've used pivot charts in a previous version of Excel — and were frustrated by their limitations — you'll be pleased to know that pivot charts are improved significantly in Excel 2007.

A pivot chart example

Figure 35.22 shows part of a table that tracks daily sales by region. The Date field contains dates for the entire year (excluding weekends), the Region field contains the region name (Eastern, Southern, or Western), and the Sales field contains the sales amount.

 This workbook, named sales by region.xlsx, is available on the companion CD-ROM.

FIGURE 35.22

This data will be used to create a pivot chart.

	A	B	C
1	**Date**	**Region**	**Sales**
2	1/2/2006	Eastern	10,909
3	1/3/2006	Eastern	11,126
4	1/4/2006	Eastern	11,224
5	1/5/2006	Eastern	11,299
6	1/6/2006	Eastern	11,265
7	1/9/2006	Eastern	11,328
8	1/10/2006	Eastern	11,494
9	1/11/2006	Eastern	11,328
10	1/12/2006	Eastern	11,598
11	1/13/2006	Eastern	11,868
12	1/16/2006	Eastern	11,702
13	1/17/2006	Eastern	11,846
14	1/18/2006	Eastern	11,898
15	1/19/2006	Eastern	11,871
16	1/20/2006	Eastern	12,053
17	1/23/2006	Eastern	12,073
18	1/24/2006	Eastern	12,153

The first step is to create a pivot table to summarize the data. Figure 35.23 shows the pivot table. The Date field is in the Row Labels area, and the daily dates have been grouped into months. The Region field is in the Column Labels area. The Sales field is in the Values area.

The pivot table is certainly easier to interpret than the raw data, but the trends would be easier to spot in a chart.

To create a pivot chart, select any cell in the pivot table and choose PivotTable Tools ➪ Options ➪ Tools ➪ Pivot Chart. Excel displays its Create Chart dialog box, from which you can choose a chart type. For this example, select a standard line chart and click OK. Excel creates the pivot chart and also displays the PivotChart Filter pane, shown in Figure 35.24.

The chart makes it easy to see an upward sales trend for the Western division, a downward trend for the Southern division, and relatively flat sales for the Eastern division.

When you select a pivot chart, the Ribbon displays a new tab: PivotChart Tools. The commands are virtually identical to those for a standard Excel chart, so you can manipulate the pivot chart any way you like.

FIGURE 35.23

This pivot table summarizes sales by region and by month.

	Eastern	Southern	Western	Grand Total
Sum of Sales				
Jan	259,416	171,897	99,833	531,146
Feb	255,487	135,497	100,333	491,317
Mar	296,958	147,425	107,884	552,267
Apr	248,956	131,401	110,628	490,985
May	293,192	132,165	144,889	570,246
Jun	281,641	122,156	133,153	536,950
Jul	263,899	110,844	147,484	522,227
Aug	283,917	107,935	176,325	568,177
Sep	252,049	101,233	181,518	534,800
Oct	273,592	104,542	212,932	591,066
Nov	292,585	98,041	232,032	622,658
Dec	288,378	95,986	239,514	623,878
Grand Total	3,290,070	1,459,122	1,886,525	6,635,717

FIGURE 35.24

The pivot chart uses the data displayed in the pivot table.

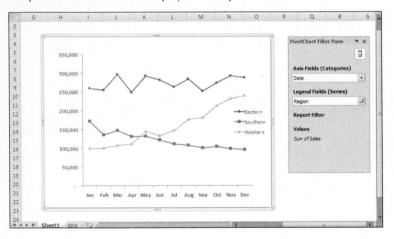

If you modify the underlying pivot table, the chart adjusts automatically to display the new summary data. Figure 35.25 shows the pivot chart after I changed the Date grouping to quarters.

FIGURE 35.25

If you modify the pivot table, the pivot chart is also changed.

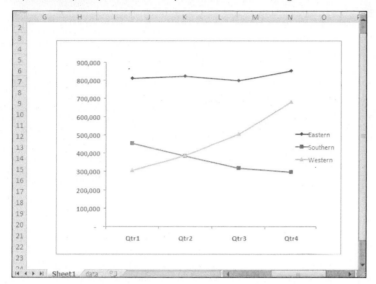

More about pivot charts

Following are a few points to keep in mind when using pivot charts:

- A pivot table and a pivot chart are joined in a two-way link. If you make structural or filtering changes to one, the other is also changed.

- The PivotChart Filter Pane, which is displayed when you select a pivot chart, contains the same controls as the pivot chart's field headers. These controls allow you to filter the data that's displayed in the pivot table (and pivot chart). If you make changes to the chart using the PivotChart Filter Pane, those changes are also reflected in the pivot table.

- If you find the PivotChart Filter Pane redundant or annoying, just click the X in its title bar to make it go away. To bring it back, choose PivotChart Tools ➪ Analyze ➪ Show/Hide ➪ PivotChart Filter.

- If you have a pivot chart and you delete the underlying pivot table, the pivot chart remains. The chart's Series formulas contain the original data, stored in arrays.

- By default, pivot charts are embedded in the sheet that contains the pivot table. To move the pivot chart to a different worksheet (or to a Chart sheet), choose PivotChart ➪ Tools ➪ Design ➪ Location ➪ Move Chart.

- You can create multiple pivot charts from a pivot table, and you can manipulate and format the charts separately. However, all the charts display the same data.

- Don't forget about themes. You can choose Page Layout ➪ Themes ➪ Themes to change the workbook theme, and your pivot table and pivot chart will both reflect the new theme.

Another Pivot Table Example

The pivot table example in this section demonstrates some useful ways to work with pivot tables.

Figure 35.26 shows a table with 3,144 data rows, one for each county in the U.S. The fields are

- **County:** The name of the county
- **State Name:** The state of the county
- **Region:** The region (Roman number ranging from I to XII)
- **Census 2000:** The population of the county, according to the 2000 Census
- **Census 1990:** The population of the county, according to the 1990 Census
- **Land Area:** The area, in square miles (excluding water-covered area)
- **Water Area:** The area, in square miles, covered by water

ON the CD-ROM **This workbook, named county data.xlsx, is available on the companion CD-ROM.**

FIGURE 35.26

This table contains data for each county in the U.S.

	A	B	C	D	E	F	G
1	County	State Name	Region	Census 2000	Census 1990	Land Area	WaterArea
2	Los Angeles	California	Region IX	9,519,338	8,863,164	4,060.87	691.45
3	Cook	Illinois	Region V	5,376,741	5,105,067	945.68	689.36
4	Harris	Texas	Region VI	3,400,578	2,818,199	1,728.83	48.87
5	San Diego	California	Region IX	2,813,833	2,498,016	4,199.89	325.62
6	Orange	California	Region IX	2,846,289	2,410,556	789.40	158.57
7	Kings	New York	Region II	2,465,326	2,300,664	70.61	26.29
8	Maricopa	Arizona	Region IX	3,072,149	2,122,101	9,203.14	21.13
9	Wayne	Michigan	Region V	2,061,162	2,111,687	614.15	58.05
10	Queens	New York	Region II	2,229,379	1,951,598	109.24	69.04
11	Dade	Florida	Region IV	2,253,362	1,937,094	1,946.21	77.85
12	Dallas	Texas	Region VI	2,218,899	1,852,810	879.60	28.96
13	Philadelphia	Pennsylvania	Region III	1,517,550	1,585,577	135.09	7.55
14	King	Washington	Region X	1,737,034	1,507,319	2,126.04	180.48
15	Santa Clara	California	Region IX	1,682,585	1,497,577	1,290.69	13.32
16	New York	New York	Region II	1,537,195	1,487,536	22.96	10.81
17	San Bernardino	California	Region IX	1,709,434	1,418,380	20,052.50	52.82
18	Cuyahoga	Ohio	Region V	1,393,978	1,412,140	458.49	787.07
19	Middlesex	Massachusetts	Region I	1,465,396	1,398,468	823.46	24.08
20	Allegheny	Pennsylvania	Region III	1,281,666	1,336,449	730.17	14.54
21	Suffolk	New York	Region II	1,419,369	1,321,864	912.20	1,460.87
22	Nassau	New York	Region II	1,334,544	1,287,348	286.69	166.39
23	Alameda	California	Region IX	1,443,741	1,279,182	737.57	83.57
24	Broward	Florida	Region IV	1,623,018	1,255,488	1,205.40	114.24

Sheet1 Sheet2

Figure 35.27 shows a pivot table created from the county data. The pivot table uses the Region and State Name fields for the Row Labels and uses Census 2000 and Census 1990 as the Column Labels.

I created three calculated fields to display additional information:

- Change (displayed as **Pop Change**): The difference between Census 2000 and Census 1990
- Pct Change (displayed as **Pct Pop Change**): The population change expressed as a percentage of the 1990 population
- Density (displayed as **Pop/Sq Mile**): The population per square mile of land.

A new feature in Excel 2007 lets you document your calculated fields and calculated items. Choose PivotTable Tools ⇨ Options ⇨ Tools ⇨ Formulas ⇨ List Formulas, and Excel inserts a new worksheet with information about your calculated fields and items. Figure 35.28 shows an example.

FIGURE 35.27

This pivot table was created from the county data.

	A	B	C	D	E	F	G
1			**Population Growth by State (1990 - 2000)**				
2							
3							
4			Census 1990 Population	Census 2000 Population	Pop Change	Pct Pop Change	Pop/Sq Mile
5	**Region I**		**13,206,943**	**13,922,517**	**715,574**	**5.4%**	**222**
6		Connecticut	3,287,116	3,405,565	118,449	3.6%	703
7		Maine	1,227,928	1,274,923	46,995	3.8%	41
8		Massachusetts	6,016,425	6,349,097	332,672	5.5%	810
9		New Hampshire	1,109,252	1,235,786	126,534	11.4%	138
10		Rhode Island	1,003,464	1,048,319	44,855	4.5%	1,003
11		Vermont	562,758	608,827	46,069	8.2%	66
12							
13	**Region II**		**25,720,643**	**27,390,807**	**1,670,164**	**6.5%**	**501**
14		New Jersey	7,730,188	8,414,350	684,162	8.9%	1,134
15		New York	17,990,455	18,976,457	986,002	5.5%	402
16							
17	**Region III**		**25,917,014**	**27,828,549**	**1,911,535**	**7.4%**	**231**
18		Delaware	666,168	783,600	117,432	17.6%	401
19		District of Columbia	606,900	572,059	(34,841)	-5.7%	9,316
20		Maryland	4,781,468	5,296,486	515,018	10.8%	542
21		Pennsylvania	11,881,643	12,281,054	399,411	3.4%	274
22		Virginia	6,187,358	7,087,006	899,648	14.5%	179
23		West Virginia	1,793,477	1,808,344	14,867	0.8%	75
24							
25	**Region IV**		**46,643,644**	**55,506,328**	**8,862,684**	**19.0%**	**150**
26		Alabama	4,040,587	4,447,100	406,513	10.1%	88
27		Florida	14,873,804	18,235,740	3,361,936	22.6%	326
28		Georgia	6,478,216	8,186,453	1,708,237	26.4%	141
29		Kentucky	3,685,296	4,041,769	356,473	9.7%	102
30		Mississippi	2,573,216	2,844,658	271,442	10.5%	61
31		North Carolina	6,628,637	8,049,313	1,420,676	21.4%	165
32		South Carolina	3,486,703	4,012,012	525,309	15.1%	133
33		Tennessee	4,877,185	5,689,283	812,098	16.7%	138
34							
35	**Region V**		**46,384,041**	**50,074,516**	**3,690,475**	**8.0%**	**155**
36		Illinois	11,430,602	12,419,293	988,691	8.6%	223
37		Indiana	5,544,159	6,080,485	536,326	9.7%	170

This pivot table is sorted on two columns. The main sort is by Region, and states within each region are sorted alphabetically. To sort, just select a cell that contains a data point to be included in the sort. Right-click and choose from the shortcut menu.

Sorting by Region requires some additional effort because Roman numerals are not in alphabetical order. Therefore, I had to create a custom list. To create a custom sort list, access the Excel Options dialog box, click the Personalize tab, and click Edit Custom Lists. Click New List, type your list entries, and click Add. Figure 35.29 shows the custom list I created for the region names.

FIGURE 35.28

This worksheet lists calculated fields and items for the pivot table.

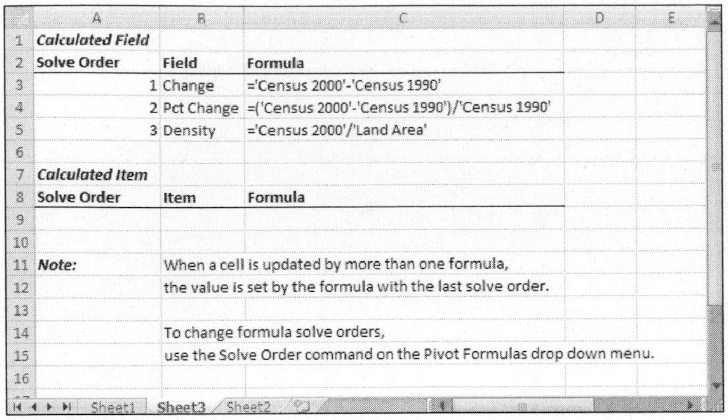

FIGURE 35.29

This custom list ensures that the Region names are sorted correctly.

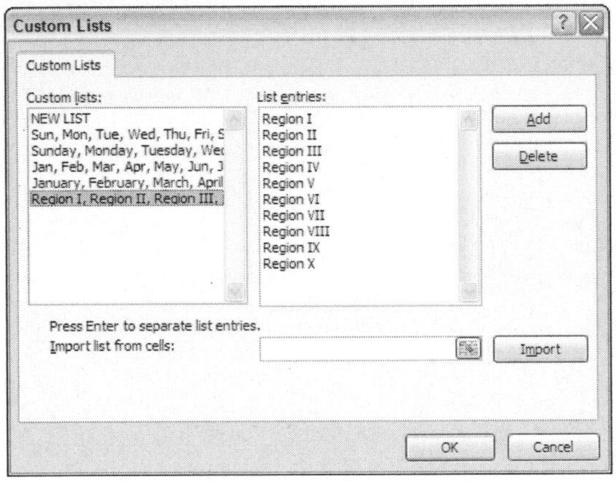

Producing a Report with a Pivot Table

By using a pivot table, you can convert a huge table of data into an attractive printed report. Figure 35.30 shows a small portion of a pivot table that I created from a table that has 25,664 rows of data. This data happens to be my digital music collection, and each row contains information about a single music file: The genre, the artist name, the album, the file name, the file size, and the duration.

The pivot table report created from this data is 119 pages long, and it took about five minutes to set up (and a little longer to fine-tune it).

ON the CD-ROM   This workbook, named music list .xlsx, is available on the companion CD-ROM.

Here's a quick summary of how I created this report:

1. I selected a cell in the table and chose Insert ➪ Tables ➪ PivotTable.
2. In the Create PivotTable dialog box, I clicked OK to accept the default settings.

FIGURE 35.30

A 119-page pivot table report.

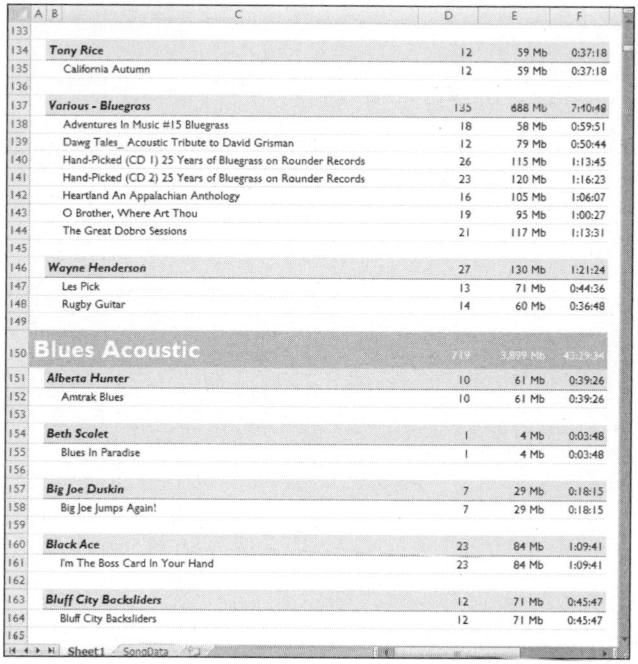

3. In the new worksheet, I used the PivotTable Field List and dragged the following fields to the Row Labels area: Genre, Artist, and Album.
4. I dragged these fields to the Values area: Song, Size, and Duration.
5. I used the Data Field Settings dialog box to summarize Song as Count, Size as Sum, and Duration as Sum.
6. I wanted the information in the Size column to display in megabytes, so I formatted the column using this custom number format:

   ###,###, "Mb";;

7. I wanted the information in the Duration column to display as hours, minutes, and seconds, so I formatted the column using this custom number format:

   [h]:mm:ss;;

8. **I edited the column headings.** For example, I replaced "Count of Song" with **No. Songs**.

9. **I changed the layout to outline format** by choosing PivotTable Tools ➪ Design ➪ Layout ➪ Report Layout.

10. **I turned off the field headers** by choosing PivotTable Tools ➪ Options ➪ Show/Hide ➪ Show Field Headers.

11. **I turned off the buttons** by choosing PivotTable Tools ➪ Options ➪ Show/Hide ➪ +/- Buttons.

12. **I displayed a blank row after each artist** by choosing PivotTable Tools ➪ Design ➪ Layout ➪ Blank Rows.

13. **I applied a built-in style** by choosing PivotTable Tools ➪ Design ➪ PivotTable Styles.

14. **I increased the font size for the Genre.**

15. **I went into Page Layout View, and I adjusted the column widths** so that the report would fit horizontally on the page.

> **NOTE** Step 14 was actually kind of tricky. I wanted to increase the size of the genre names, but leave the subtotals in the same font size. Therefore, I couldn't modify the style for the PivotTable Style I chose. I selected the entire column A and pressed Ctrl+G to bring up the Go To dialog box. I clicked Special to display the Go To Special dialog box. Then I selected the Constants option and clicked OK, which selected only the nonempty cells in column A. I then adjusted the font size for the selected cells.

Chapter 36

Performing Spreadsheet What-If Analysis

O ne of the most appealing aspects of Excel is its ability to create dynamic models. A *dynamic model* uses formulas that instantly recalculate when you change values in cells that are used by the formulas. When you change values in cells in a systematic manner and observe the effects on specific formula cells, you're performing a type of *what-if* analysis.

What-if analysis is the process of asking such questions as "What if the interest rate on the loan changes to 7.5 percent rather than 7.0 percent?" or "What if we raise our product prices by 5 percent?"

If you set up your worksheet properly, answering such questions is simply a matter of plugging in new values and observing the results of the recalculation. Excel provides useful tools to assist you in your what-if endeavors.

A What-If Example

Figure 36.1 shows a simple worksheet model that calculates information pertaining to a mortgage loan. The worksheet is divided into two sections: the input cells and the result cells (which contain formulas).

ON the CD-ROM **This workbook is available on the companion CD-ROM. The filename is mortgage loan.xlsx.**

With this worksheet, you can easily answer the following what-if questions:

- What if I can negotiate a lower purchase price on the property?
- What if the lender requires a 20-percent down payment?
- What if I can get a 40-year mortgage?
- What if the interest rate increases to 7.0 percent?

Avoid Hard-Coding Values in a Formula

The mortgage calculation example, simple as it is, demonstrates an important point about spreadsheet design: You should always set up your worksheet so that you have maximum flexibility to make changes. Perhaps the most fundamental rule of spreadsheet design is the following:

Do not hard-code values in a formula. Rather, store the values in separate cells and use cell references in the formula.

The term *hard-code* refers to the use of actual values, or *constants,* in a formula. In the mortgage loan example, all the formulas use references to cells, not actual values.

You *could* use the value 360, for example, for the loan term argument of the pmt function in cell C11. Using a cell reference has two advantages. First, you have no doubt about the values that the formula uses (they aren't buried in the formula). Second, you can easily change the value—which is easier than editing the formula.

Using values in formulas may not seem like much of an issue when only one formula is involved, but just imagine what would happen if this value were hard-coded into several hundred formulas that were scattered throughout a worksheet.

FIGURE 36.1

This simple worksheet model uses four input cells to produce the results.

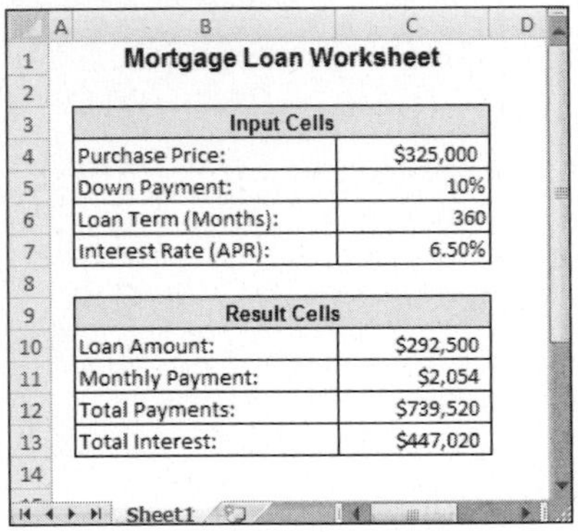

	A	B	C	D
1		**Mortgage Loan Worksheet**		
2				
3		**Input Cells**		
4		Purchase Price:	$325,000	
5		Down Payment:	10%	
6		Loan Term (Months):	360	
7		Interest Rate (APR):	6.50%	
8				
9		**Result Cells**		
10		Loan Amount:	$292,500	
11		Monthly Payment:	$2,054	
12		Total Payments:	$739,520	
13		Total Interest:	$447,020	
14				

H ◀ ▶ H   Sheet1

You can answer these questions by simply changing the values in the cells in range C4:C7 and observing the effects in the dependent cells (C10:C13). You can, of course, vary any number of input cells simultaneously.

Types of What-If Analyses

Not surprisingly, Excel can handle much more sophisticated models than the preceding example. To perform a what-if analysis using Excel, you have three basic options:

- **Manual what-if analysis:** Plug in new values and observe the effects on formula cells.
- **Data tables:** Create a table that displays the results of selected formula cells as you systematically change one or two input cells.
- **Scenario Manager:** Create named scenarios and generate reports that use outlines or pivot tables.

Manual What-If Analysis

This method doesn't require too much explanation. In fact, the example that opens this chapter demonstrates how it's done. Manual what-if analysis is based on the idea that you have one or more input cells that affect one or more key formula cells. You change the value in the input cells and see what happens to the formula cells. You may want to print the results or save each scenario to a new workbook. The term *scenario* refers to a specific set of values in one or more input cells.

Manual what-if analysis is very common, and people often use this technique without even realizing that they're doing a type of what-if analysis. This method of performing what-if analysis certainly has nothing wrong with it, but you should be aware of some other techniques.

> **TIP**   If your input cells are not located near the formula cells, consider using a Watch Window to monitor the formula results in a movable window. Chapter 4 discusses this feature.

Creating Data Tables

This section discusses one of Excel's most underutilized features: data tables. A *data table* is a dynamic range that summarizes formula cells for varying input cells. You can create a data table fairly easily, but data tables have some limitations. In particular, a data table can deal with only one or two input cells at a time. This limitation becomes clear as you view the examples.

> **NOTE**   Scenario Manager, discussed later in this chapter (see "Using Scenario Manager"), can produce a report that summarizes any number of input cells and result cells.

Don't confuse a data table with a standard table (which is created by choosing Insert ➪ Tables ➪ Table). These two features are completely independent of each other.

Creating a one-input data table

A *one-input data table* displays the results of one or more formulas for various values of a single input cell. Figure 36.2 shows the general layout for a one-input data table.

FIGURE 36.2

How a one-input data table is set up.

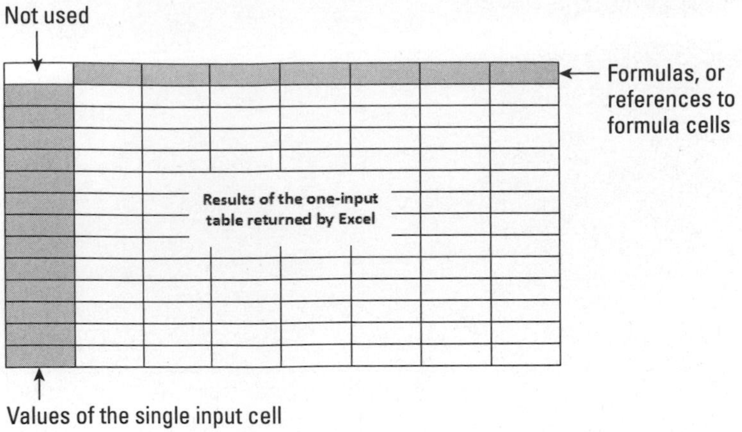

Not used

Formulas, or references to formula cells

Results of the one-input table returned by Excel

Values of the single input cell

You can place the data table anywhere in a worksheet. The left column contains various values for the single input cell. The top row contains references to formulas located elsewhere in the worksheet. You can use a single formula reference or any number of formula references. The upper-left cell of the table remains empty. Excel calculates the values that result from each value of the input cell and places them under each formula reference.

This example uses the mortgage loan worksheet from earlier in the chapter (see "A What-If Example"). The goal of this exercise is to create a data table that shows the values of the four formula cells (loan amount, monthly payment, total payments, and total interest) for various interest rates ranging from 6 to 8 percent, in 0.25-percent increments.

ON the CD-ROM   This workbook is available on the companion CD-ROM. The file is named **mortgage loan data table.xlsx.**

Figure 36.3 shows the setup for the data table area. Row 3 consists of references to the formulas in the worksheet. For example, cell F3 contains the formula =C10, and cell G3 contains the formula =C11. Column E contains the values of the single input cell (interest rate) that Excel will use in the table.

To create the table, select the data table range (in this case, E3:I12) and then choose Data ➪ Data Tools ➪ What-If Analysis ➪ Data Table. Excel displays the Data Table dialog box, shown in Figure 36.4.

FIGURE 36.3

Preparing to create a one-input data table.

Mortgage Loan Worksheet
Input Cells
Purchase Price: $325,900
Down Payment: 10%
Loan Term: 360
Interest Rate (Months): 6.50%
Result Cells
Loan Amount: $293,310
Monthly Payment: $2,060
Total Payments: $741,567
Total Interest: $448,257
Loan Amt
Mo Pmt
Total Pmts
Total Int
$293,310
$2,060
$741,567
$448,257
Interest rate
6.00%
6.25%
6.50%
6.75%
7.00%
7.25%
7.50%
7.75%
8.00%
data table

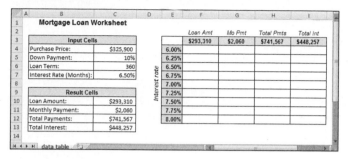

FIGURE 36.4

The Data Table dialog box.

Mortgage Loan Worksheet
Data Table
Row input cell:
Column input cell: $C$7
OK
Cancel
Input Cells
Purchase Price: $325,900
Down Payment: 10%
Loan Term: 360
Interest Rate (Months): 6.50%
Result Cells
Loan Amount: $293,310
Monthly Payment: $2,060
Total Payments: $741,567
Total Interest: $448,257
Total Pmts
Total Int
$741,567
$448,257
7.00%
7.25%
7.50%
7.75%
8.00%
data table

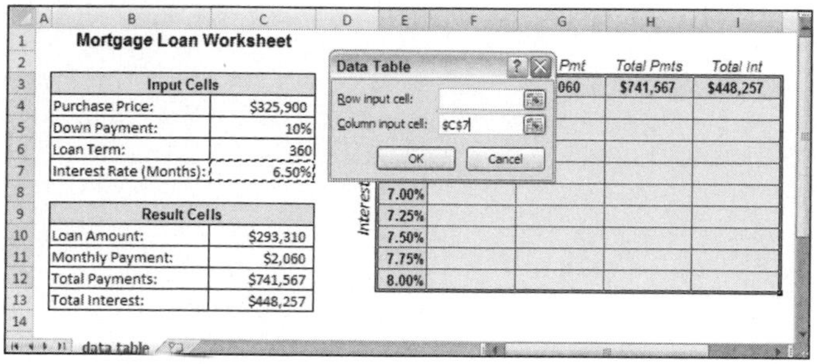

You must specify the worksheet cell that contains the input value. Because variables for the input cell appear in the left column in the data table, you place this cell reference in the text box labeled Column Input Cell. Enter **C7** or point to the cell in the worksheet. Leave the Row Input Cell field blank. Click OK, and Excel fills in the table with the calculated results (see Figure 36.5).

FIGURE 36.5

The result of the one-input data table.

Mortgage Loan Worksheet
Input Cells
Purchase Price: $325,900
Down Payment: 10%
Loan Term: 360
Interest Rate (Months): 6.50%
Result Cells
Loan Amount: $293,310
Monthly Payment: $2,060
Total Payments: $741,567
Total Interest: $448,257
Interest rate
Loan Amt | Mo Pmt | Total Pmts | Total Int
$293,310 | $2,060 | $741,567 | $448,257
6.00% | $293,310 | $1,954 | $703,417 | $410,107
6.25% | $293,310 | $2,007 | $722,384 | $429,074
6.50% | $293,310 | $2,060 | $741,567 | $448,257
6.75% | $293,310 | $2,114 | $760,961 | $467,651
7.00% | $293,310 | $2,168 | $780,559 | $487,249
7.25% | $293,310 | $2,223 | $800,356 | $507,046
7.50% | $293,310 | $2,279 | $820,346 | $527,036
7.75% | $293,310 | $2,335 | $840,524 | $547,214
8.00% | $293,310 | $2,391 | $860,882 | $567,572
data table

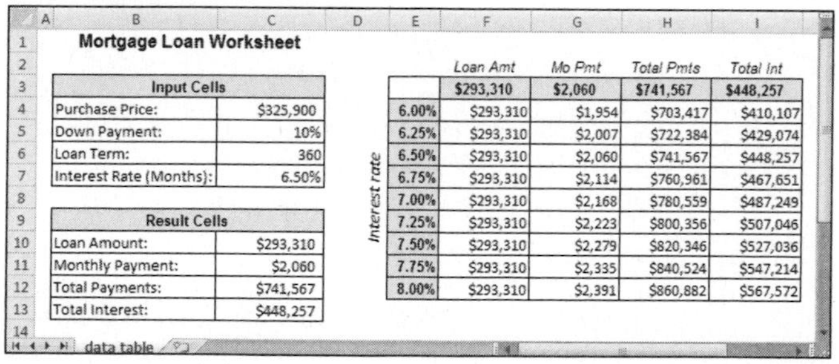

Using this table, you can now see the calculated loan values for varying interest rates. If you examine the contents of the cells that Excel entered as a result of this command, you'll see that the data is generated with a multicell array formula:

```
=TABLE(,C7)
```

As I discuss in Chapter 17, an *array formula* is a single formula that can produce results in multiple cells. Because the table uses formulas, Excel updates the table that you produce if you change the cell references in the first row or plug in different interest rates in the first column.

NOTE   You can arrange a one-input table vertically (as in this example) or horizontally. If you place the values of the input cell in a row, you enter the input cell reference in the text box labeled Row input cell in the Table dialog box.

Creating a two-input data table

As the name implies, a *two-input data table* lets you vary *two* input cells. You can see the setup for this type of table in Figure 36.6. Although it looks similar to a one-input table, the two-input table has one critical difference: It can show the results of only one formula at a time. With a one-input table, you can place any number of formulas, or references to formulas, across the top row of the table. In a two-input table, this top row holds the values for the second input cell. The upper-left cell of the table contains a reference to the single result formula.

FIGURE 36.6

The setup for a two-input data table.

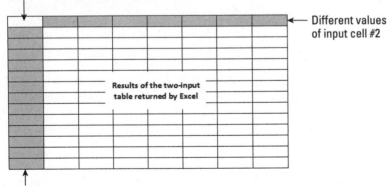

A formula, or a reference to a formula

Different values of input cell #2

Results of the two-input table returned by Excel

Different values of input cell #1

Using the mortgage loan worksheet, you could create a two-input data table that shows the results of a formula (say, monthly payment) for various combinations of two input cells (such as interest rate and down-payment percent). To see the effects on other formulas, you simply create multiple data tables — one for each formula cell that you want to summarize.

The example in this section uses the worksheet shown in Figure 36.7 to demonstrate a two-input data table. In this example, a company wants to conduct a direct-mail promotion to sell its product. The worksheet calculates the net profit from the promotion.

FIGURE 36.7

This worksheet calculates the net profit from a direct-mail promotion.

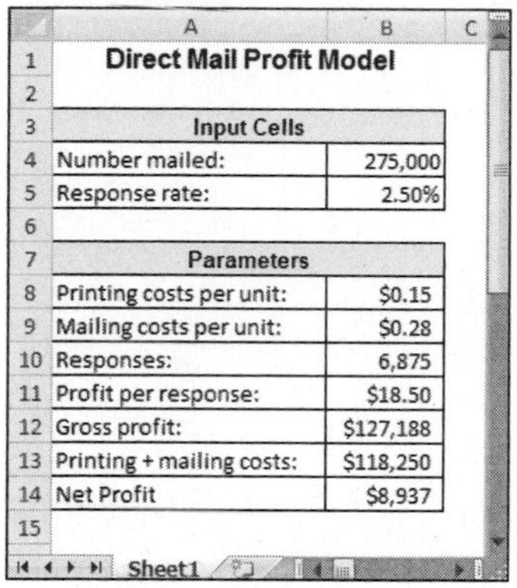

	A	B	C
1	**Direct Mail Profit Model**		
2			
3	**Input Cells**		
4	Number mailed:	275,000	
5	Response rate:	2.50%	
6			
7	**Parameters**		
8	Printing costs per unit:	$0.15	
9	Mailing costs per unit:	$0.28	
10	Responses:	6,875	
11	Profit per response:	$18.50	
12	Gross profit:	$127,188	
13	Printing + mailing costs:	$118,250	
14	Net Profit	$8,937	
15			

ON the CD-ROM   **This workbook, named direct mail.xlsx, is available on the companion CD-ROM.**

This model uses two input cells: the number of promotional pieces mailed and the anticipated response rate. The following items appear in the Parameters area:

- **Printing costs per unit:** The cost to print a single mailer. The unit cost varies with the quantity: $0.20 each for quantities less than 200,000; $0.15 each for quantities of 200,001 through 300,000; and $0.10 each for quantities of more than 300,000. The following formula is used:

  `=IF(B4<200000,0.2,IF(B4<300000,0.15,0.1))`

- **Mailing costs per unit:** A fixed cost, $0.28 per unit mailed.

- **Responses:** The number of responses, calculated from the response rate and the number mailed. The formula in this cell is the following:

  `=B4*B5`

- **Profit per response:** A fixed value. The company knows that it will realize an average profit of $18.50 per order.

- **Gross profit:** This is a simple formula that multiplies the profit-per-response by the number of responses:

  `=B10*B11`

- **Print + mailing costs:** This formula calculates the total cost of the promotion:

  `=B4*(B8+B9)`

- **Net Profit:** This formula calculates the bottom line — the gross profit minus the printing and mailing costs.

If you enter values for the two input cells, you see that the net profit varies quite a bit, often going negative to produce a net loss.

Figure 36.8 shows the setup of a two-input data table that summarizes the net profit at various combinations of quantity and response rate; the table appears in the range E4:M14. Cell E4 contains a formula that references the Net Profit cell:

  `=B15`

FIGURE 36.8

Preparing to create a two-input data table.

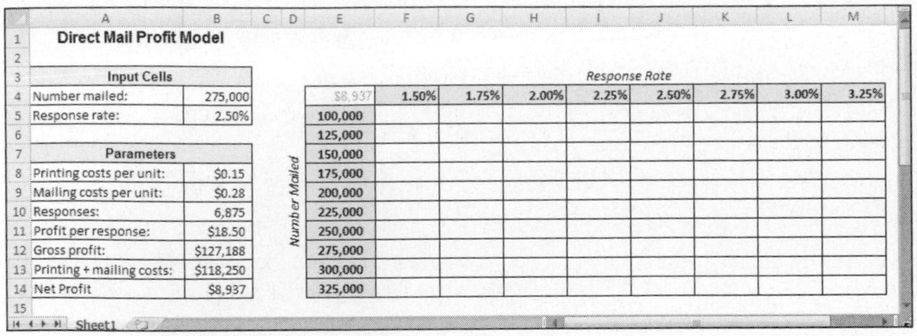

Direct Mail Profit Model

Input Cells	
Number mailed:	275,000
Response rate:	2.50%

Parameters	
Printing costs per unit:	$0.15
Mailing costs per unit:	$0.28
Responses:	6,875
Profit per response:	$18.50
Gross profit:	$127,188
Printing + mailing costs:	$118,250
Net Profit	$8,937

					Response Rate				
	$8,937	1.50%	1.75%	2.00%	2.25%	2.50%	2.75%	3.00%	3.25%
Number Mailed	100,000								
	125,000								
	150,000								
	175,000								
	200,000								
	225,000								
	250,000								
	275,000								
	300,000								
	325,000								

To create the data table:

1. **Enter the response rate values in F4:M4.**
2. **Enter the number mailed values in E5:E14.**
3. **Select the range E4:M14 and choose Data ➪ Data Tools ➪ What-If Analysis ➪ Data Table.**
4. **In the Data Table dialog box, specify B5 as the Row input cell (the response rate) and cell B4 as the Column input (the number mailed).**
5. **Click OK, and Excel fills in the data table.**

Figure 36.9 shows the result. As you see, quite a few of the combinations of response rate and quantity mailed result in a loss rather than a profit.

As with the one-input data table, this data table is dynamic. You can change the formula in cell E4 to refer to another cell (such a gross profit). Or, you can enter some different values for Response Rate and Number Mailed.

FIGURE 36.9

The result of the two-input data table.

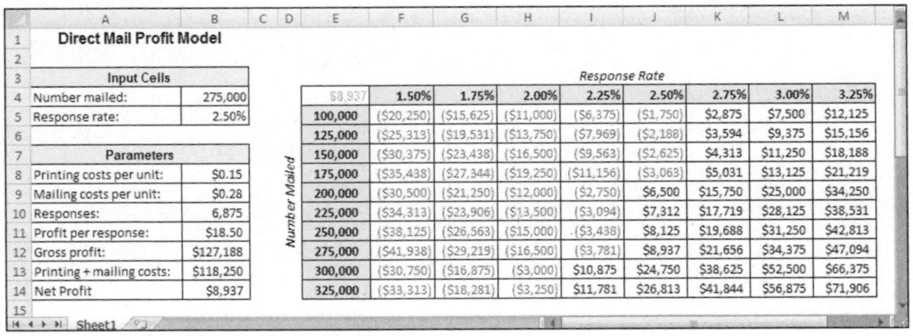

Direct Mail Profit Model

Input Cells	
Number mailed:	275,000
Response rate:	2.50%

Parameters	
Printing costs per unit:	$0.15
Mailing costs per unit:	$0.28
Responses:	6,875
Profit per response:	$18.50
Gross profit:	$127,188
Printing + mailing costs:	$118,250
Net Profit	$8,937

					Response Rate				
	$8,937	1.50%	1.75%	2.00%	2.25%	2.50%	2.75%	3.00%	3.25%
Number Mailed	100,000	($20,250)	($15,625)	($11,000)	($6,375)	($1,750)	$2,875	$7,500	$12,125
	125,000	($25,313)	($19,531)	($13,750)	($7,969)	($2,188)	$3,594	$9,375	$15,156
	150,000	($30,375)	($23,438)	($16,500)	($9,563)	($2,625)	$4,313	$11,250	$18,188
	175,000	($35,438)	($27,344)	($19,250)	($11,156)	($3,063)	$5,031	$13,125	$21,219
	200,000	($30,500)	($21,250)	($12,000)	($2,750)	$6,500	$15,750	$25,000	$34,250
	225,000	($34,313)	($23,906)	($13,500)	($3,094)	$7,312	$17,719	$28,125	$38,531
	250,000	($38,125)	($26,563)	($15,000)	($3,438)	$8,125	$19,688	$31,250	$42,813
	275,000	($41,938)	($29,219)	($16,500)	($3,781)	$8,937	$21,656	$34,375	$47,094
	300,000	($30,750)	($16,875)	($3,000)	$10,875	$24,750	$38,625	$52,500	$66,375
	325,000	($33,313)	($18,281)	($3,250)	$11,781	$26,813	$41,844	$56,875	$71,906

Using Scenario Manager

Data tables are useful, but they have a few limitations:

- You can vary only one or two input cells at a time.
- The process of setting up a data table is not all that intuitive.
- A two-input table shows the results of only one formula cell (although you can create additional tables for more formulas).
- In many situations, you're interested in a few select combinations, not an entire table that shows all possible combinations of two input cells.

Excel's Scenario Manager feature makes automating your what-if models easy. You can store different sets of input values (called *changing cells* in the terminology of Scenario Manager) for any number of variables and give a name to each set. You can then select a set of values by name, and Excel displays the worksheet by using those values. You can also generate a summary report that shows the effect of various combinations of values on any number of result cells. These summary reports can be an outline or a pivot table.

For example, your annual sales forecast may depend on several factors. Consequently, you can define three scenarios: best case, worst case, and most likely case. You then can switch to any of these scenarios by selecting the named scenario from a list. Excel substitutes the appropriate input values in your worksheet and recalculates the formulas.

Defining scenarios

To introduce you to Scenario Manager, this section starts with an example that uses a simplified production model, as shown in Figure 36.10.

ON the CD-ROM This workbook, named **production model.xlsx, is available on the companion CD-ROM.**

This worksheet contains two input cells: the hourly labor cost (cell B2) and the unit cost for materials (cell B3). The company produces three products, and each product requires a different number of hours and a different amount of materials to produce.

FIGURE 36.10

A simple production model to demonstrate Scenario Manager.

	A	B	C	D
1	Resource Cost Variables			
2	Hourly labor cost	30		
3	Material cost	57		
4				
5				
6		Product A	Product B	Product C
7	Hours per unit	12	14	24
8	Material per unit	6	9	14
9	Cost to produce	$702	$933	$1,518
10	Sales price	$795	$1,295	$2,195
11	Unit profit	$93	$362	$677
12	Units produced	36	18	12
13	Total profit per product	$3,348	$6,516	$8,124
14				
15	Total Profit	$17,988		
16				

Formulas calculate the total profit per product (row 13) and the total combined profit (cell B15). Management is trying to predict the total profit, but is uncertain what the hourly labor cost and material costs will be. They've identified three scenarios, listed in Table 36.1.

TABLE 36.1

Three Scenarios for the Production Model

Scenario	Hourly Cost	Materials Cost
Best Case	30	57
Worst Case	38	62
Most Likely	34	59

The Best Case scenario has the lowest hourly cost and lowest materials cost. The Worst Case scenario has high values for both the hourly cost and the materials cost. The third scenario, Most Likely Case, has intermediate values for both of these input cells. The managers need to be prepared for the worst case, however, and they're interested in what would happen under the Best Case scenario.

Choose Data ➪ Data Tools ➪ What-If Analysis ➪ Scenario Manger to display the Scenario Manager dialog box. When you first open this dialog box, it tells you that no scenarios are defined — which is not too surprising because you're just starting. As you add named scenarios, they appear in the Scenarios list in this dialog box.

TIP   I strongly suggest that you create names for the changing cells and all the result cells that you want to examine. Excel uses these names in the dialog boxes and in the reports that it generates. If you use names, keeping track of what's going on is much easier; names also make your reports more readable.

To add a scenario, click the Add button in the Scenario Manager dialog box. Excel displays its Add Scenario dialog box, shown in Figure 36.11.

FIGURE 36.11

The Add Scenario dialog box lets you create a named scenario.

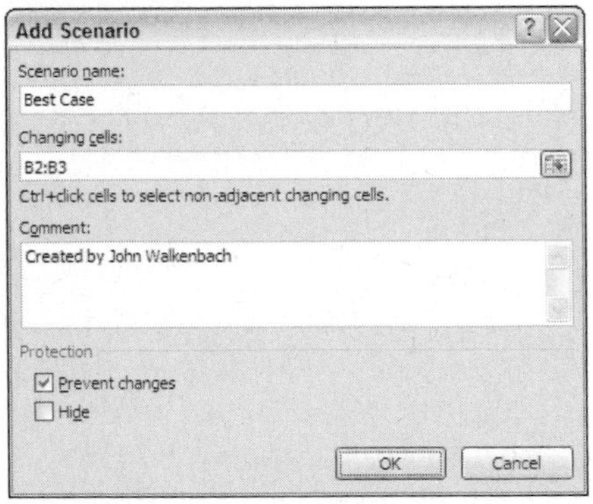

This dialog box consists of four parts:

- **Scenario Name:** The name for the scenario. You can give it any name that you like — preferably something meaningful.

- **Changing Cells:** The input cells for the scenario. You can enter the cell addresses directly or point to them. If you've created a name for the cells, type the name. Non-adjacent cells are allowed (if pointing to multiple cells, press Ctrl while you click the cells). Each named scenario can use the same set of changing cells or different changing cells. The number of changing cells for a scenario is limited to 32.

- **Comment:** By default, Excel displays the name of the person who created the scenario and the date that it was created. You can change this text, add new text to it, or delete it.

- **Protection:** The two Protection options (preventing changes and hiding a scenario) are in effect only when you protect the worksheet and choose the Scenario option in the Protect Sheet dialog box. Protecting a scenario prevents anyone from modifying it; a hidden scenario doesn't appear in the Scenario Manager dialog box.

In this example, define the three scenarios that are listed in Table 36.1. The changing cells are Hourly_Cost (B2) and Materials_Cost (B3).

After you enter the information in the Add Scenario dialog box, click OK. Excel then displays the Scenario Values dialog box, shown in Figure 36.12. This dialog box displays one field for each changing cell that you specified in the previous dialog box. Enter the values for each cell in the scenario. If you click OK, you return to the Scenario Manager dialog box, which then displays your named scenario in its list. If you have more scenarios to create, click the Add button to return to the Add Scenario dialog box.

FIGURE 36.12

You enter the values for the scenario in the Scenario Values dialog box.

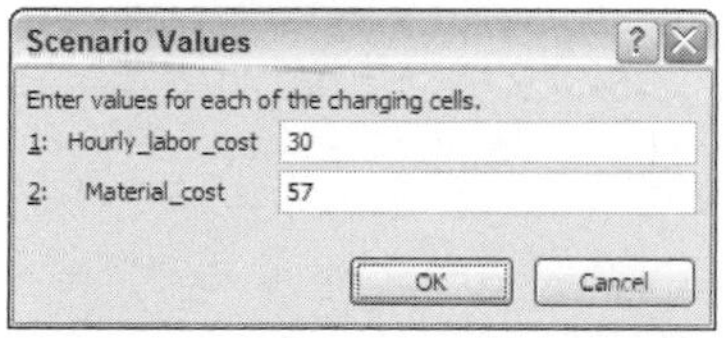

Displaying scenarios

After you define all the scenarios and return to the Scenario Manager dialog box, the dialog box displays the names of your defined scenarios. Select one of the scenarios and then click the Show button. Excel inserts the corresponding values into the changing cells and calculates the worksheet to show the results for that scenario.

Modifying scenarios

The Edit button in the Scenario Manager dialog box lets you change one or more of the values for the changing cells of a scenario. From the Scenarios list, select the scenario that you want to change and click the Edit button. In the Edit Scenario dialog box, click OK to access the Scenario Values dialog box. Make your changes and click OK to return to the Scenario Manager dialog box. Notice that Excel automatically updates the Comments box with new text that indicates when the scenario was modified.

Using the Scenarios Drop-Down List

Excel has a `Scenarios` control, which is a drop-down list that shows all the defined scenarios and enables you to quickly display a scenario. Oddly, this useful tool doesn't appear in the Ribbon. But, if you use Scenario Manager, you may want to add the `Scenarios` control to your Quick Access Toolbar (QAT), using the following procedure:

1. **Right-click your QAT and choose Customize Quick Access Toolbar.** Excel displays the Customization tab of the Excel Options dialog box.
2. **In the Choose Commands From drop-down list, select Commands Not In The Ribbon.**
3. **Scroll down the list and select Scenario.**
4. **Click the Add button.**
5. **Click OK to close the Excel Options dialog box.**

Refer to Chapter 23 for additional details on customizing your Quick Access Toolbar.

The accompanying figure shows this control, with three scenarios defined. Just click the scenario, and the worksheet is updated. Using the `Scenarios` control is more efficient than bringing up the Scenario Manager dialog box to view a different scenario.

Merging scenarios

In workgroup situations, you may have several people working on a spreadsheet model, and several people may have defined various scenarios. The marketing department, for example, may have its opinion of what the input cells should be, the finance department may have another opinion, and your CEO may have yet another opinion.

Excel makes it easy to merge these various scenarios into a single workbook by using the Merge button in the Scenario Manager dialog box. Clicking this button displays the Merge Scenarios dialog box.

Before you merge scenarios, make sure that the workbook from which you're merging is open. Then, click the Merge button in the Scenario Manager dialog box. Excel displays its Merge Scenarios dialog box. Choose the workbook that contains the scenarios you're merging in the Book drop-down list. Then, choose the sheet that contains the scenarios you want to merge from the Sheet list box. (Notice that the dialog box displays the number of scenarios in each sheet as you scroll through the Sheet list box.) Click OK, and you return to the previous dialog box, which now displays the scenario names that you merged from the other workbook.

Generating a scenario report

If you've created multiple scenarios, you may want to document your work by creating a scenario summary report. When you click the Summary button in the Scenario Manager dialog box, Excel displays the Scenario Summary dialog box.

You have a choice of report types:

- **Scenario Summary:** The summary report appears in the form of a worksheet outline.
- **Scenario PivotTable:** The summary report appears in the form of a pivot table.

CROSS-REF **Refer to Chapter 26 for more information about outlines, and Chapter 34 for more information about pivot tables.**

For simple cases of scenario management, a standard Scenario Summary report is usually sufficient. If you have many scenarios defined with multiple result cells, however, you may find that a Scenario Pivot Table provides more flexibility.

The Scenario Summary dialog box also asks you to specify the *result cells* (the cells that contain the formulas in which you're interested). For this example, select B13:D13 and B15 (a multiple selection) to make the report show the profit for each product, plus the total profit.

NOTE **As you work with Scenario Manager, you may discover its main limitation: A scenario can use no more than 32 changing cells. If you attempt to use more cells, you get an error message.**

Excel creates a new worksheet to store the summary table. Figure 36.13 shows the Scenario Summary form of the report. If you gave names to the changing cells and result cells, the table uses these names. Otherwise, it lists the cell references.

FIGURE 36.13

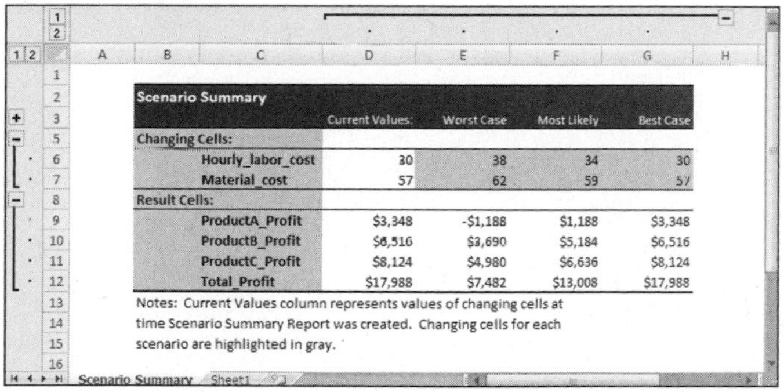

Scenario Summary	Current Values:	Worst Case	Most Likely	Best Case
Changing Cells:				
Hourly_labor_cost	30	38	34	30
Material_cost	57	62	59	57
Result Cells:				
ProductA_Profit	$3,348	-$1,188	$1,188	$3,348
ProductB_Profit	$6,516	$3,690	$5,184	$6,516
ProductC_Profit	$8,124	$4,980	$6,636	$8,124
Total_Profit	$17,988	$7,482	$13,008	$17,988

Notes: Current Values column represents values of changing cells at time Scenario Summary Report was created. Changing cells for each scenario are highlighted in gray.

Chapter 37

Analyzing Data Using Goal Seek and Solver

The preceding chapter discusses *what-if analysis* — the process of changing input cells to observe the results on other dependent cells. This chapter looks at that process from the opposite perspective: finding the value of one or more input cells that produces a desired result in a formula cell.

This chapter covers two tools: Goal Seeking and the Solver add-in.

What-If Analysis, in Reverse

Consider the following what-if question: "What is the total profit if sales increase by 20 percent?" If you set up your worksheet model properly, you can change the value in one cell to see what happens to the profit cell. The examples in this chapter take the opposite approach. If you know what a formula result should be, Excel can tell you the values that you need to enter in one or more input cells to produce that result. In other words, you can ask a question such as "How much do sales need to increase to produce a profit of $1.2 million?" Excel provides two tools that are relevant:

- **Goal Seeking:** Determines the value that you need to enter in a single input cell to produce a result that you want in a dependent (formula) cell.

- **Solver:** Determines the values that you need to enter in multiple input cells to produce a result that you want. Moreover, because you can specify certain constraints to the problem, you gain significant problem-solving ability.

Single-Cell Goal Seeking

Single-cell goal seeking is a rather simple concept. Excel determines what value in an input cell produces a desired result in a formula cell. The following example shows you how single-cell goal seeking works.

A goal-seeking example

Figure 37.1 shows the mortgage loan worksheet used in the preceding chapter. This worksheet has four input cells (C4:C7) and four formula cells (C10:C13). Originally, this worksheet was used for a what-if analysis example. This example demonstrates the opposite approach. Rather than supply different input cell values to look at the calculated formulas, this example lets Excel determine one of the input values that will produce the desired result.

ON the CD-ROM This workbook is available on the companion CD-ROM. The file is named **mortgage loan.xlsx**.

FIGURE 37.1

This worksheet is a good demonstration of goal seeking.

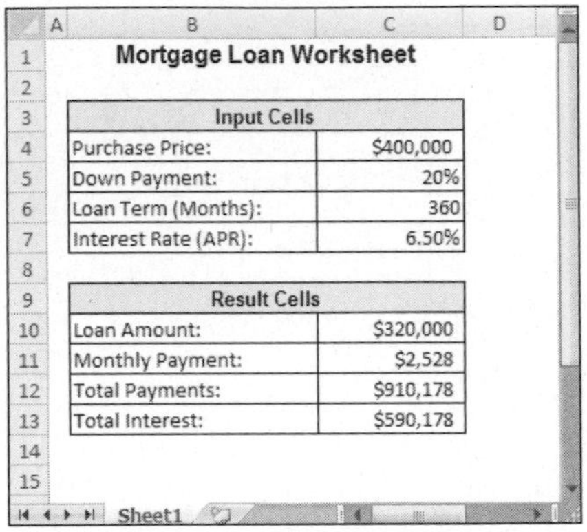

	A	B	C	D
1		Mortgage Loan Worksheet		
2				
3		Input Cells		
4		Purchase Price:	$400,000	
5		Down Payment:	20%	
6		Loan Term (Months):	360	
7		Interest Rate (APR):	6.50%	
8				
9		Result Cells		
10		Loan Amount:	$320,000	
11		Monthly Payment:	$2,528	
12		Total Payments:	$910,178	
13		Total Interest:	$590,178	
14				
15				

Assume that you're in the market for a new home and you know that you can afford an $1,800 monthly mortgage payment. You also know that a lender can issue a 30-year fixed-rate mortgage loan for 6.50 percent, based on an 80-percent *loan-to-value* (that is, a 20-percent *down payment*). The question is "What is the maximum purchase price I can handle?" In other words, what value in cell C4 causes the formula in cell C11 to result in $1,800? In this simple example, you could plug values into cell C4 until C11 displays $1,800. With more complex models, Excel can usually determine the answer much more efficiently.

To answer the question posed in the preceding paragraph, first set up the input cells to match what you already know. Specifically:

- Enter 20% in cell C5 (the down payment percent)
- Enter 360 in cell C6 (the loan term, in months)
- Enter 6.5% in cell C7, the annual interest rate

Next, choose Data ➪ Data Tools ➪ What-If Analysis ➪ Goal Seek. Excel displays the Goal Seek dialog box, shown in Figure 37.2. Completing this dialog box is similar to forming a sentence. You want to set cell C11 to 1800 by changing cell C4. Enter this information in the dialog box either by typing the cell references or by pointing with the mouse. Click OK to begin the goal-seeking process.

FIGURE 37.2

The Goal Seek dialog box.

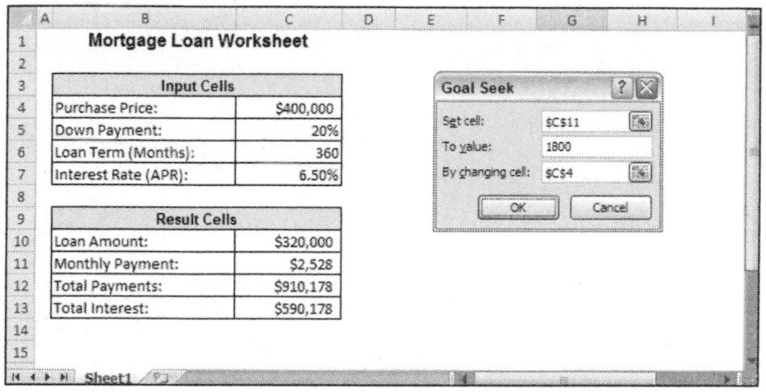

In less than a second, Excel displays the Goal Seek Status box, which shows the target value and the value that Excel calculated. In this case, Excel found an exact value. The worksheet now displays the found value in cell C4 ($284,779). As a result of this value, the monthly payment amount is $1,800. At this point, you have two options:

■ Click OK to replace the original value with the found value.

■ Click Cancel to restore your worksheet to the form that it had before you chose the **Goal Seek** command.

More about Goal Seeking

Excel can't always find a value that produces the result that you're seeking. Sometimes, a solution simply doesn't exist. In such a case, the Goal Seek Status box informs you of that fact.

Other times, however, Excel may report that it can't find a solution, but you're pretty sure that one exists. If that's the case, you can try the following options:

■ Change the current value of the By Changing Cell box in the Goal Seek dialog box to a value that is closer to the solution and then reissue the command.

■ Adjust the Maximum iterations setting in the Formulas tab of the Excel Options dialog box (choose Office ➪ Excel Options). Increasing the number of iterations (or calculations) makes Excel try more possible solutions.

■ Double-check your logic and make sure that the formula cell does, indeed, depend on the specified changing cell.

NOTE Like all computer programs, Excel has limited precision. To demonstrate this limitation, enter =A1^2 into cell A2. Then, use the Goal Seek dialog box to find the value in cell A1 (which is empty) that makes the formula return 16. Excel comes up with a value of 4.00002269010434 (you may need to widen the column to see the complete value), which is close to the square root of 16, but certainly not exact. You can adjust the precision in the Formulas tab of the Excel Options dialog box (make the Maximum Change value smaller).

> **NOTE** In some cases, multiple values of the input cell produce the same desired result. For example, the formula =A1^2 returns 16 if cell A1 contains either –4 or +4. If you use goal seeking when multiple solutions are possible, Excel gives you the solution that is closest to the current value.

Introducing Solver

The Excel Goal-Seek feature is a useful tool, but it clearly has limitations. It can solve for only one adjustable cell, and it returns only a single solution. Excel's powerful Solver tool extends this concept by enabling you to do the following:

- Specify multiple adjustable cells
- Specify constraints on the values that the adjustable cells can have
- Generate a solution that maximizes or minimizes a particular worksheet cell
- Generate multiple solutions to a problem

Although goal seeking is a relatively simple operation, using Solver can be much more complicated. In fact, Solver is probably one of the most difficult (and potentially frustrating) features in Excel. I'm the first to admit that Solver isn't for everyone. In fact, most Excel users have no use for this feature. However, many users find that having this much power is worth spending the extra time to learn about it.

Appropriate problems for Solver

Problems that are appropriate for Solver fall into a relatively narrow range. They typically involve situations that meet the following criteria:

- A target cell depends on other cells and formulas. Typically, you want to maximize or minimize this target cell or set it equal to some value.
- The target cell depends on a group of cells (called *changing cells*) that Solver can adjust to affect the target cell.
- The solution must adhere to certain limitations, or *constraints*.

After you set up your worksheet appropriately, you can use Solver to adjust the changing cells and produce the result that you want in your target cell—and simultaneously meet all the constraints that you've defined.

No Solver Command?

You access Solver by choosing Data ➪ Analysis ➪ Solver. If this command isn't available, you need to install the Solver add-in. It's a simple process:

1. **Choose File ➪ Excel Options.**
2. **In the Excel Options dialog box, click the Add-Ins tab.**
3. **At the bottom of the dialog box, select Excel Add-Ins from the Manage drop-down list and click Go.** Excel displays its Add-Ins dialog box.
4. **In the Add-Ins dialog box, place a check mark next to Solver Add-In and click OK.**

After performing these steps, the Solver add-in loads whenever you start Excel.

A simple Solver example

I start with a simple example to introduce Solver and then present some increasingly complex examples to demonstrate what this feature can do.

Figure 37.3 shows a worksheet that is set up to calculate the profit for three products. Column B shows the number of units of each product, Column C shows the profit per unit for each product, and Column D contains formulas that calculate the total profit for each product by multiplying the units by the profit per unit.

ON the CD-ROM **This workbook, named three products.xlsx, is available on this book's CD-ROM.**

FIGURE 37.3

Use Solver to determine the number of units to maximize the total profit.

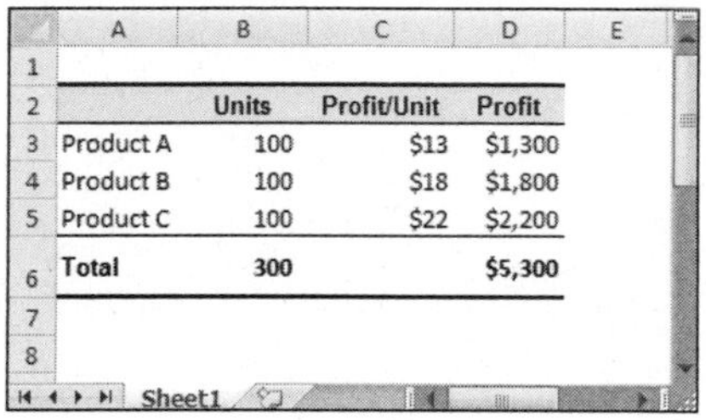

	A	B	C	D	E
1					
2		Units	Profit/Unit	Profit	
3	Product A	100	$13	$1,300	
4	Product B	100	$18	$1,800	
5	Product C	100	$22	$2,200	
6	Total	300		$5,300	
7					
8					

You don't need an MBA degree to realize that the greatest profit comes from Product C. Therefore, in order to maximize total profit, the logical solution is to produce only Product C. If things were really this simple, you wouldn't need tools such as Solver. As in most situations, this company has some constraints that must be met:

- The combined production capacity is 300 total units per day.
- The company needs 50 units of Product A to fill an existing order.
- The company needs 40 units of Product B to fill an anticipated order.
- Because the market for Product C is relatively limited, the company doesn't want to produce more than 40 units of this product.

These four constraints make the problem more realistic and a bit more challenging. In fact, it's a perfect problem for Solver.

I go into more detail in a moment, but here is the basic procedure for using Solver:

1. **Set up the worksheet with values and formulas.** Make sure that you format cells logically; for example, if you can't produce partial units of your products, format those cells to contain numbers with no decimal values.
2. **Choose Data ➪ Analysis ➪ Solver to bring up the Solver dialog box.**
3. **Specify the target cell.**
4. **Specify the range that contains the changing cells.**
5. **Specify the constraints.**
6. **Change the Solver options, if necessary.**
7. **Let Solver solve the problem.**

To start Solver to tackle this example, choose Data ⇨ Analysis ⇨ Solver. Excel displays its Solver Parameters dialog box, shown in Figure 37.4.

FIGURE 37.4

The Solver Parameters dialog box.

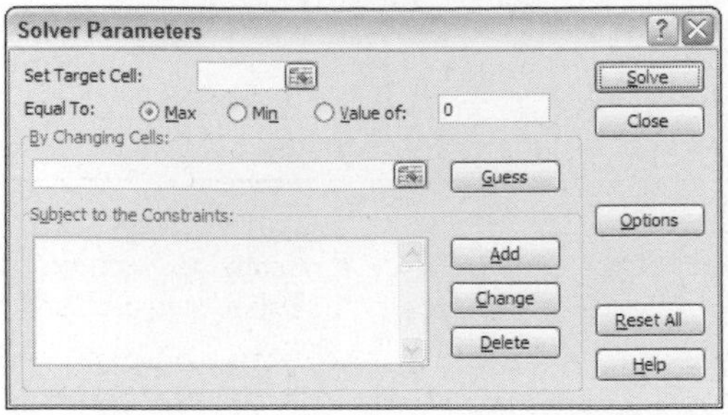

In this example, the target cell is D6 — the cell that calculates the total profit for three products.

1. **Enter (or point to) cell D6 in the Set Target Cell field of the Solver Parameters dialog box.**

2. **Because the objective is to maximize this cell, click the Max option.**

3. **Next, specify the changing cells (which are in the range B3:B5) in the By Changing Cells box.** The next step is to specify the constraints on the problem. The constraints are added one at a time and appear in the box labeled Subject To The Constraints.

4. **To add a constraint, click the Add button.** Excel displays the Add Constraint dialog box, shown in Figure 37.5. This dialog box has three parts: a Cell Reference, an operator, and a Constraint value.

5. **To set the first constraint (that the total production capacity is 300 units), enter** B6 **as the Cell Reference, choose equal (=) from the drop-down list of operators, and enter** 300 **as the Constraint value.**

6. **Click Add to add the remaining constraints.** Table 37.1 summarizes the constraints for this problem.

FIGURE 37.5

The Add Constraint dialog box.

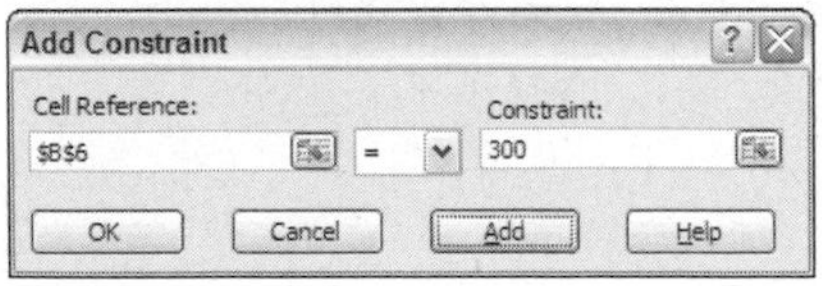

TABLE 37.1

Constraints Summary

Constraint	Expressed As
Capacity is 300 units	B6=300
At least 50 units of Product A	B3>=50
At least 40 units of Product B	B4>=40
No more than 40 units of Product C	B5<=40

7. **After you enter the last constraint, click OK to return to the Solver Parameters dialog box, which now lists the four constraints.** At this point, Solver knows everything about the problem.
8. **Click the Solve button to start the solution process.** You can watch the progress onscreen, and Excel soon announces that it has found a solution. The Solver Results dialog box is shown in Figure 37.6.

At this point, you have the following options:

- Replace the original changing cell values with the values that Solver found.
- Restore the original changing cell values.
- Create any or all three reports that describe what Solver did.
- Click the Save Scenario button to save the solution as a scenario, so that Scenario Manager can use it (see Chapter 36).

FIGURE 37.6

Solver displays this dialog box when it finds a solution to the problem.

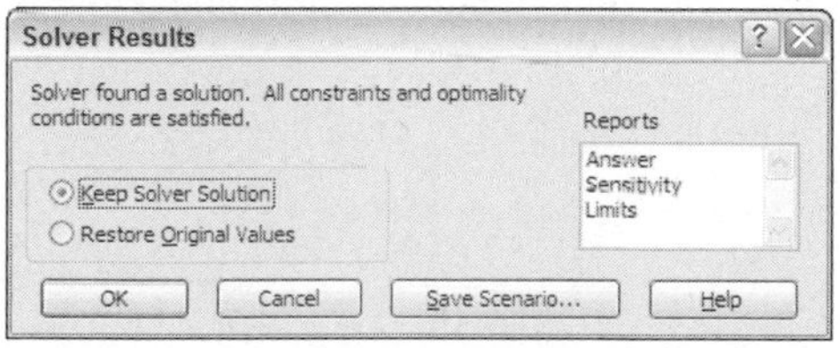

If you specify any report options, Excel creates each report on a new worksheet, with an appropriate name. Figure 37.7 shows an Answer Report. In the Constraints section of the report, two of the constraints are *binding,* which means that these constraints were satisfied at their limit with no more room to change.

This simple example illustrates how Solver works. The fact is, you could probably solve this particular problem manually just as quickly. That, of course, isn't always the case.

CAUTION If you select the option to replace the original changing cells, you can't restore your original values by using Undo.

FIGURE 37.7

One of three reports that Solver can produce.

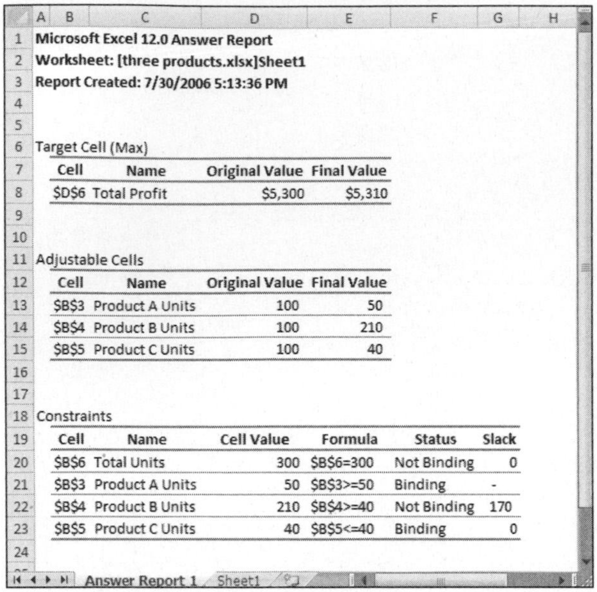

	A	B	C	D	E	F	G	H
1	**Microsoft Excel 12.0 Answer Report**							
2	**Worksheet: [three products.xlsx]Sheet1**							
3	**Report Created: 7/30/2006 5:13:36 PM**							
4								
5								
6	Target Cell (Max)							
7		**Cell**	**Name**	**Original Value**	**Final Value**			
8		$D$6	Total Profit	$5,300	$5,310			
9								
10								
11	Adjustable Cells							
12		**Cell**	**Name**	**Original Value**	**Final Value**			
13		$B$3	Product A Units	100	50			
14		$B$4	Product B Units	100	210			
15		$B$5	Product C Units	100	40			
16								
17								
18	Constraints							
19		**Cell**	**Name**	**Cell Value**	**Formula**	**Status**	**Slack**	
20		$B$6	Total Units	300	$B$6=300	Not Binding	0	
21		$B$3	Product A Units	50	$B$3>=50	Binding	-	
22		$B$4	Product B Units	210	$B$4>=40	Not Binding	170	
23		$B$5	Product C Units	40	$B$5<=40	Binding	0	
24								

Answer Report 1 / Sheet1

More about Solver

Before presenting more complex examples, this section discusses the Solver Options dialog box. From this dialog box, you control many aspects of the solution process, as well as load and save model specifications in a worksheet range.

It's not unusual for Solver to report that it can't find a solution, even when you know that one should exist. Often, you can change one or more of the Solver options and try again. When you choose the Options button in the Solver Parameters dialog box, Excel displays the Solver Options dialog box, shown in Figure 37.8.

FIGURE 37.8

You can control many aspects of how Solver solves a problem.

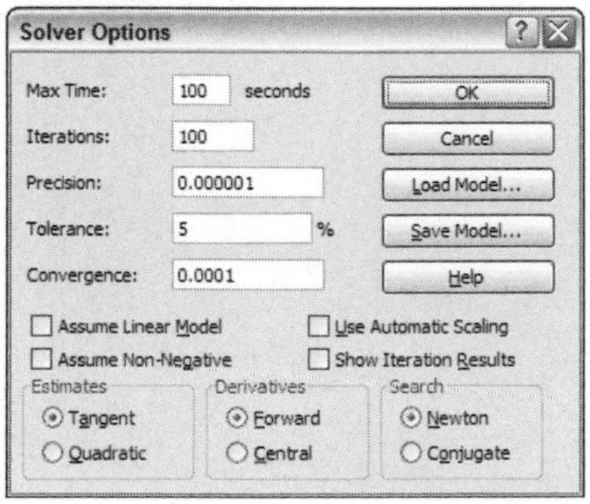

This list describes Solver's options:

- **Max Time:** Specify the maximum amount of time (in seconds) that you want Solver to spend on a problem. If Solver reports that it exceeded the time limit, you can increase the amount of time that it spends searching for a solution.

- **Iterations:** Enter the maximum number of trial solutions that you want Solver to perform.

- **Precision:** Specify how close the Cell Reference and Constraint formulas must be to satisfy a constraint. Excel may solve the problem more quickly if you specify less precision.

- **Tolerance:** Designate the maximum percentage of error allowed for integer solutions (relevant only if an integer constraint is used).

- **Convergence:** Enter a value between 0 and 1 that specifies the amount of change to allow before Solver stops. This setting is relevant only for nonlinear problems.

- **Assume Linear Model:** Choose this option to speed the solution process, but you can use it only if all the relationships in the model are linear. You can't use this option if the adjustable cells are multiplied or divided, or if the problem uses exponents.

- **Assume Non-Negative:** If checked, Solver assumes a lower limit of 0 for all adjustable cells that don't have a specified lower-limit constraint.

- **Use Automatic Scaling:** Use when the problem involves large differences in magnitude — when you attempt to maximize a percentage, for example, by varying cells that are very large.

- **Show Iteration Results:** Instruct Solver to pause and display the results after each iteration by checking this box.

- **Estimates, Derivatives, and Search group boxes:** Use these options to control some technical aspects of the solution. In most cases, you don't need to change these settings.

- **Load Model:** Click this button to make Excel display the Load Model dialog box, in which you specify a range containing the set of Solver parameters that you want to load.

- **Save Model:** Click this button to make Excel display the Save Model dialog box, in which you specify a range where Excel should save the model parameters.

Usually, you want to save a model only when you're using more than one set of Solver parameters with your worksheet. This is because Excel saves the first Solver model automatically with your worksheet (using hidden names). If you save additional models, Excel stores the information in the form of formulas that correspond to the specifications. (The last cell in the saved range is an Array formula that holds the options settings.)

Solver Examples

The remainder of this chapter consists of examples of using Solver for various types of problems.

Solving simultaneous linear equations

This example describes how to solve a set of three linear equations with three variables. Here's an example of a set of linear equations:

```
4x + 2y -2z =0
2x - 3y +3z =9
-6x -2y +z = 0
```

The question that Solver will answer is "What values of x, y, and z satisfy all three of these equations?"

Figure 37.9 shows a workbook set up to solve this problem. This workbook has three named cells, which makes the formulas more readable:

- x: C11
- y: C12
- z: C13

The three named cells are all initialized to 1 (which certainly doesn't solve the equations).

FIGURE 37.9

Solver will attempt to solve this series of linear equations.

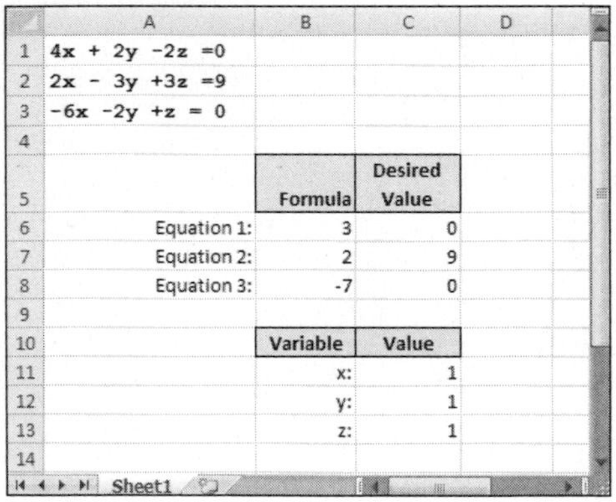

	A	B	C	D
1	4x + 2y -2z =0			
2	2x - 3y +3z =9			
3	-6x -2y +z = 0			
4				
5		Formula	Desired Value	
6	Equation 1:	3	0	
7	Equation 2:	2	9	
8	Equation 3:	-7	0	
9				
10		Variable	Value	
11		x:	1	
12		y:	1	
13		z:	1	
14				

 This workbook, named **linear equations.xlsx**, is available on the companion CD-ROM.

The three equations are represented by formulas in the range B6:B8:

- B6: =(4*x)+(y)-(2*z)
- B7: =(2*x)-(3*y)+(3*z)
- B8: =-(6*x)-(2*y)+(z)

These formulas use the values in the x, y, and z named cells. The range C6:C8 contains the "desired" result for these three formulas.

Solver will adjust the values in x, y, and z (that is, the changing cells in C11:C13), subject to these constraints:

- B6=C6
- B7=C7
- B8=C8

NOTE This problem doesn't have a target cell because it's not trying to maximize or minimize anything. However, the Solver Parameters dialog box insists that you specify a formula for the Set Target Cell field. Therefore, just enter a reference to any cell that has a formula.

Figure 37.10 shows the solution. The x (0.75), y (-2.0), and z (0.5) values satisfy all three equations.

FIGURE 37.10

Solver solved the simultaneous equations.

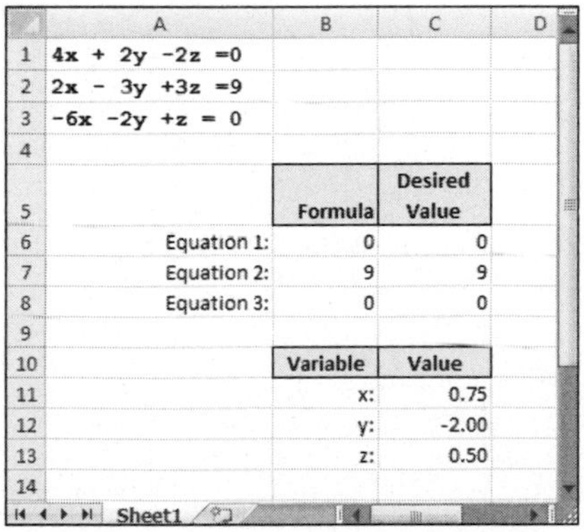

	A	B	C	D
1	4x + 2y -2z =0			
2	2x - 3y +3z =9			
3	-6x -2y +z = 0			
4				
5		Formula	Desired Value	
6	Equation 1:	0	0	
7	Equation 2:	9	9	
8	Equation 3:	0	0	
9				
10		Variable	Value	
11		x:	0.75	
12		y:	-2.00	
13		z:	0.50	
14				

Sheet1

NOTE Keep in mind that a set of linear equations may have one solution, no solution, or an infinite number of solutions.

Minimizing shipping costs

This example involves finding alternative options for shipping materials, while keeping total shipping costs at a minimum (see Figure 37.11). A company has warehouses in Los Angeles, St. Louis, and Boston. Retail outlets throughout the United States place orders, which the company then ships from one of the warehouses. The company wants to meet the product needs of all six retail outlets from available inventory and keep total shipping charges as low as possible.

ON the CD-ROM   This workbook, named **shipping costs.xlsx, is available on the companion CD-ROM.**

This workbook is rather complicated, so each part is explained individually:

- **Shipping Costs Table:** This table, in range B2:E8, is a matrix that contains per-unit shipping costs from each warehouse to each retail outlet. The cost to ship a unit from Los Angeles to Denver, for example, is $58.

- **Product needs of each retail store:** This information appears in C12:C17. For example, Denver needs 150 units, Houston needs 225, and so on. C18 contains a formula that calculates the total needed.

- **Number to ship from:** Range D12:F17 holds the adjustable cells that Solver varies. These cells are all initialized with a value of 25 to give Solver a starting value. Column G contains formulas that sum the number of units the company needs to ship to each retail outlet.

- **Warehouse inventory:** Row 21 contains the amount of inventory at each warehouse, and row 22 contains formulas that subtract the amount shipped (row 18) from the inventory.

- **Calculated shipping costs:** Row 24 contains formulas that calculate the shipping costs. Cell D24 contains the following formula, which is copied to the two cells to the right of Cell D24:

  `=SUMPRODUCT(C3:C8,D12:D17)`

Cell G24 is the bottom line, the total shipping costs for all orders.

Solver fills in values in the range D12:F17 in such a way that minimizes shipping costs while still supplying each retail outlet with the desired number of units. In other words, the solution minimizes the value in cell C24 by adjusting the cells in D12:F17, subject to the following constraints:

- The number of units needed by each retail outlet must equal the number shipped. (In other words, all the orders are filled.) These constraints are represented by the following specifications:

  ```
  C12=G12    C14=G14    C16=G16
  C13=G13    C15=G15    C17=G17
  ```

- The adjustable cells can't be negative because shipping a negative number of units makes no sense. These constraints are represented by the following specifications:

  ```
  D12>=0    E12>=0    F12>=0
  D13>=0    E13>=0    F13>=0
  D14>=0    E14>=0    F14>=0
  D15>=0    E15>=0    F15>=0
  D16>=0    E16>=0    F16>=0
  D17>=0    E17>=0    F17>=0
  ```

- The number of units remaining in each warehouse's inventory must not be negative (that is, they can't ship more than what is available). This is represented by the following constraint specifications:

  ```
  D22>=0    E22>=0    F22>=0
  ```

FIGURE 37.11

This worksheet determines the least expensive way to ship products from warehouses to retail outlets.

Shipping Costs Table

	L.A.	St. Louis	Boston
Denver	$58	$47	$108
Houston	$87	$46	$100
Atlanta	$121	$30	$57
Miami	$149	$66	$83
Seattle	$62	$115	$164
Detroit	$128	$28	$38

	Number	No. to ship from...			No. to be
Store	Needed	L.A.	St. Louis	Boston	Shipped
Denver	150	25	25	25	75
Houston	225	25	25	25	75
Atlanta	100	25	25	25	75
Miami	250	25	25	25	75
Seattle	120	25	25	25	75
Detroit	150	25	25	25	75
Total	**995**	**150**	**150**	**150**	**450**

Warehouse Inventory

Starting Inventory:	400	350	500	
No. Remaining:	250	200	350	
Shipping Costs:	$ 15,125	$ 8,300	$ 13,750	**$37,175**

Sheet1

NOTE Before you solve this problem with Solver, you may want to attempt to solve this problem manually, by entering values in D12:F17 that minimize the shipping costs. And, of course, you need to make sure that all the constraints are met. Doing so may help you better appreciate Solver.

Setting up the problem is the difficult part. For example, you must enter 27 constraints. When you have specified all the necessary information, click the Solve button to put Solver to work. Solver displays the solution shown in Figure 37.12.

The total shipping cost is $55,515, and all the constraints are met. Notice that shipments to Miami come from both St. Louis and Boston.

FIGURE 37.12

The solution that was created by Solver.

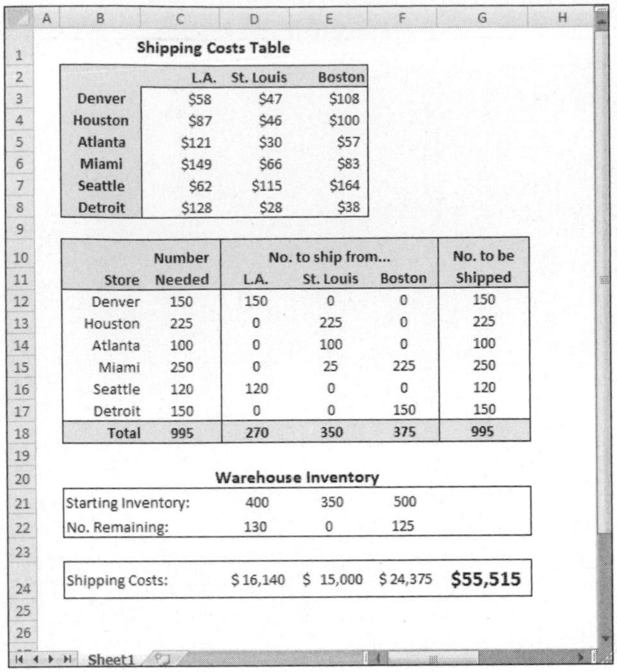

	Shipping Costs Table			
		L.A.	St. Louis	Boston
Denver		$58	$47	$108
Houston		$87	$46	$100
Atlanta		$121	$30	$57
Miami		$149	$66	$83
Seattle		$62	$115	$164
Detroit		$128	$28	$38

Store	Number Needed	No. to ship from...			No. to be Shipped
		L.A.	St. Louis	Boston	
Denver	150	150	0	0	150
Houston	225	0	225	0	225
Atlanta	100	0	100	0	100
Miami	250	0	25	225	250
Seattle	120	120	0	0	120
Detroit	150	0	0	150	150
Total	995	270	350	375	995

Warehouse Inventory			
Starting Inventory:	400	350	500
No. Remaining:	130	0	125

| Shipping Costs: | $ 16,140 | $ 15,000 | $ 24,375 | **$55,515** |

Allocating resources

The example in this section is a common type of problem that's ideal for Solver. Essentially, problems of this sort involve optimizing the volumes of individual production units that use varying amounts of fixed resources. Figure 37.13 shows an example for a toy company.

Learning More about Solver

Solver is a complex tool, and this chapter barely scratches the surface. If you'd like to learn more about Solver, I highly recommend the Web site for Frontline Systems:

www.solver.com

Frontline Systems is the company that developed Solver for Excel. Their Web site has several tutorials and lots of helpful information. They also sell additional Solver products for Excel that can handle much more complex problems.

 This workbook is available on the companion CD-ROM. The file is named **allocating resources.xlsx.**

FIGURE 37.13

Using Solver to maximize profit when resources are limited.

	A	B	C	D	E	F	G	H	I
1				XYZ Toys Inc.					
2				Materials Needed					
3	Material	Toy A	Toy B	Toy C	Toy D	Toy E	Amt. Avail.	Amt. Used	Amt. Left
4	Red Paint	0	1	0	1	3	625	250	375
5	Blue Paint	3	1	0	1	0	640	250	390
6	White Paint	2	1	2	0	2	1,100	350	750
7	Plastic	1	5	2	2	1	875	550	325
8	Wood	3	0	3	5	5	2,200	800	1,400
9	Glue	1	2	3	2	3	1,500	550	950
10	Unit Profit	$15	$30	$20	$25	$25			
11	No. to Make	50	50	50	50	50			
12	Profit	$750	$1,500	$1,000	$1,250	$1,250			
13	Total Profit	$5,750							
14									

Sheet1

This company makes five different toys, which use six different materials in varying amounts. For example, Toy A requires 3 units of blue paint, 2 units of white paint, 1 unit of plastic, 3 units of wood, and 1 unit of glue. Column G shows the current inventory of each type of material. Row 10 shows the unit profit for each toy.

The number of toys to make is shown in the range B11:F11. These are the values that Solver determines (the changing cells). The goal of this example is to determine how to allocate the resources to maximize the total profit (B13). In other words, Solver determines how many units of each toy to make. The constraints in this example are relatively simple:

- Ensure that production doesn't use more resources than are available. This can be accomplished by specifying that each cell in column F is greater than or equal to zero.

- Ensure that the quantities produced aren't negative. This can be accomplished by specifying that each cell in row 11 be greater than or equal to zero.

Figure 37.14 shows the results that are produced by Solver. It shows the product mix that generates $12,365 in profit and uses all resources in their entirety, except for glue.

FIGURE 37.14

Solver determined how to use the resources to maximize the total profit.

Material	Toy A	Toy B	Toy C	Toy D	Toy E	Amt. Avail.	Amt. Used	Amt. Left
			XYZ Toys Inc.					
			Materials Needed					
Red Paint	0	1	0	1	3	625	625	0
Blue Paint	3	1	0	1	0	640	640	0
White Paint	2	1	2	0	2	1,100	1,100	0
Plastic	1	5	2	2	1	875	875	0
Wood	3	0	3	5	5	2,200	2,200	0
Glue	1	2	3	2	3	1,500	1,353	147
Unit Profit	$15	$30	$20	$25	$25			
No. to Make	194	19	158	40	189			
Profit	$2,903	$573	$3,168	$1,008	$4,713			
Total Profit	$12,365							

Optimizing an investment portfolio

This example demonstrates how to use Solver to help maximize the return on an investment portfolio. A portfolio consist of several investments, each of which has a different yield. In addition, you may have some constraints that involve reducing risk and diversification goals. Without such constraints, a portfolio problem becomes a no-brainer: Put all of your money in the investment with the highest yield.

This example involves a credit union, a financial institution that takes members' deposits and invests them in loans to other members, bank CDs, and other types of investments. The credit union distributes part of the return on these investments to the members in the form of *dividends,* or interest on their deposits.

This hypothetical credit union must adhere to some regulations regarding its investments, and the board of directors has imposed some other restrictions. These regulations and restrictions comprise the problem's constraints. Figure 37.15 shows a workbook set up for this problem.

ON the CD-ROM This workbook is available on the companion CD-ROM. The file is named investment portfolio.xlsx.

The following constraints are the ones to which you must adhere in allocating the $5 million portfolio:

■ The amount that the credit union invests in new-car loans must be at least three times the amount that the credit union invests in used-car loans. (Used-car loans are riskier investments.) This constraint is represented as:

C5>=C6*3

■ Car loans should make up at least 15 percent of the portfolio. This constraint is represented as:

D14>=.15

FIGURE 37.15

This worksheet is set up to maximize a credit union's investments, given some constraints.

	A	B	C	D	E	F
1	Portfolio Amount:	$5,000,000				
2						
3						
4	Investment	Pct Yield	Amount Invested	Yield	Pct. of Portfolio	
5	New Car Loans	6.90%	1,000,000	69,000	20.00%	
6	Used Car Loans	8.25%	1,000,000	82,500	20.00%	
7	Real Estate Loans	8.90%	1,000,000	89,000	20.00%	
8	Unsecured Loans	13.00%	1,000,000	130,000	20.00%	
9	Bank CDs	4.60%	1,000,000	46,000	20.00%	
10	TOTAL		$5,000,000	$416,500	100.00%	
11						
12			Total Yield:	8.33%		
13						
14			Auto Loans	40.00%		
15						
16						

Sheet1

- Unsecured loans should make up no more than 25 percent of the portfolio. This constraint is represented as:

  E8<=.25

- At least 10 percent of the portfolio should be in bank CDs. This constraint is represented as:

  E9>=.10

- The total amount invested is $5,000,000.

- All investments should be positive or zero. In other words, the problem requires five additional constraints to ensure that none of the changing cells goes below zero.

The changing cells are C5:C9, and the goal is to maximize the total yield in cell D12. Starting values of 1,000,000 have been entered in the changing cells. When you run Solver with these parameters, it produces the solution shown in Figure 37.16, which has a total yield of 8.59 percent.

However, a total yield of 8.59 percent is *not* the optimal solution. If you select the Use Automatic Scaling option (in the Solver Options dialog box), Solver will arrive at a solution that has a total yield of 9.25 percent.

This demonstrates that you can't always trust Solver to arrive at the optimal solution with one try, even when the Solver Results dialog box tells you that *All constraints and optimality conditions are satisfied.* The best advice? Make sure that you understand Solver well before you entrust it with helping you make major decisions. Try different starting values and adjust the options to see whether Solver can do better.

FIGURE 37.16

The results of the portfolio optimization.

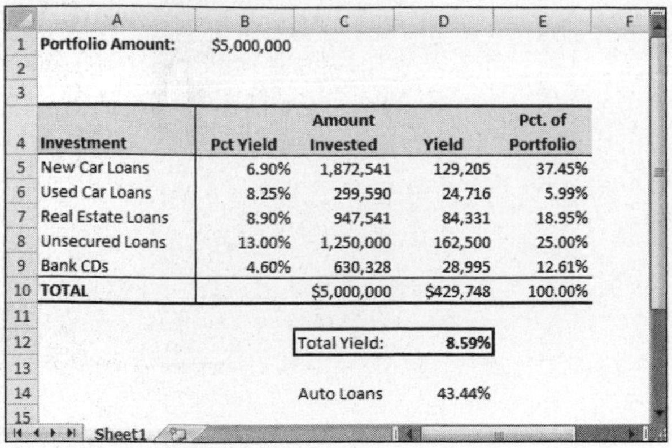

	A	B	C	D	E	F
1	**Portfolio Amount:**	$5,000,000				
2						
3						
4	**Investment**	**Pct Yield**	**Amount Invested**	**Yield**	**Pct. of Portfolio**	
5	New Car Loans	6.90%	1,872,541	129,205	37.45%	
6	Used Car Loans	8.25%	299,590	24,716	5.99%	
7	Real Estate Loans	8.90%	947,541	84,331	18.95%	
8	Unsecured Loans	13.00%	1,250,000	162,500	25.00%	
9	Bank CDs	4.60%	630,328	28,995	12.61%	
10	**TOTAL**		$5,000,000	$429,748	100.00%	
11						
12			Total Yield:	8.59%		
13						
14			Auto Loans	43.44%		
15						

Sheet1

Chapter 38

Analyzing Data with the Analysis ToolPak

Although Excel was designed primarily for business users, people in other disciplines, including education, research, statistics, and engineering, use it as well. One way that Excel addresses these nonbusiness users is with its Analysis ToolPak add-in. However, many features in the Analysis ToolPak are valuable for business applications as well.

The Analysis ToolPak: An Overview

The Analysis ToolPak is an add-in that provides analytical capability that normally isn't available.

NEW FEATURE In previous versions of Excel, the Analysis ToolPak add-in included many additional worksheet functions. In Excel 2007, these worksheet functions are built into Excel and no longer require the Analysis ToolPak add-in.

These analysis tools offer many features that may be useful to those in the scientific, engineering, and educational communities — not to mention business users whose needs extend beyond the normal spreadsheet fare.

This section provides a quick overview of the types of analyses that you can perform with the Analysis ToolPak. This chapter covers each of the following tools:

- Analysis of variance (three types)
- Correlation
- Covariance
- Descriptive statistics
- Exponential smoothing
- F-Test
- Fourier analysis
- Histogram

- Moving average
- Random number generation
- Rank and percentile
- Regression
- Sampling
- t-Test (three types)
- z-Test

As you see, the Analysis ToolPak add-in brings a great deal of functionality to Excel. These procedures have limitations, however, and in some cases, you may prefer to create your own formulas to do some calculations.

Installing the Analysis ToolPak Add-in

The Analysis ToolPak is implemented as an add-in. Before you can use it, you need to make sure that the add-in is installed. Click the Data tab. If you see an Analysis group, with a `Data Analysis` command, then the Analysis ToolPak is installed. If you can't access Data ➪ Analysis ➪ Data Analysis, install the add-in by following these steps:

1. **Choose Office ➪ Excel Options to display the Excel Options dialog box.**
2. **In the Excel Options dialog box, click the Add-Ins tab.**
3. **At the bottom of the dialog box, select Excel Add-Ins from the Manage drop-down list and click Go.** Excel displays the Add-Ins dialog box.
4. **In the Add-Ins dialog box, place a check mark next to Analysis ToolPak.**
5. **Click OK to close the Add-Ins dialog box.**

Using the Analysis Tools

Using the procedures in the Analysis ToolPak add-in is relatively straightforward, as long as you're familiar with the particular analysis type. To use any of these tools, you choose ➪ Data ➪ Analysis ➪ Data Analysis, which displays the dialog box shown in Figure 38.1. Scroll through the list until you find the analysis tool that you want to use and then click OK. Excel displays a new dialog box that's specific to the procedure that you select.

FIGURE 38.1

The Data Analysis dialog box enables you to select the tool in which you're interested.

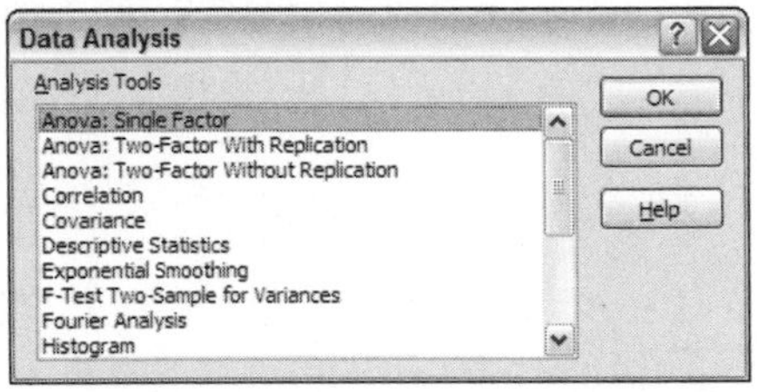

Usually, you need to specify one or more *Input* ranges, plus an *Output* range (one cell is sufficient). Alternatively, you can choose to place the results on a new worksheet or in a new workbook. The procedures vary in the amount of additional information required. In many dialog boxes, you may be able to indicate whether your *Data* range includes labels. If so, you can specify the entire range, including the labels, and indicate to Excel that the first column (or row) contains labels. Excel then uses these labels in the tables that it produces. Most tools also provide different output options that you can select, based on your needs.

> **CAUTION** The Analysis ToolPak isn't consistent in how it generates its output. In some cases, the procedures use formulas, so you can change your data, and the results update automatically. In other procedures, Excel stores the results as values, so if you change your data, the results don't reflect your changes. Make sure that you understand what Excel is doing.

Introducing the Analysis ToolPak Tools

This section describes each tool in the Analysis ToolPak and provides an example. Space limitations prevent a discussion of every available option in these procedures. However, if you need to use the advanced analysis tools, you probably already know how to use most of the options not covered here.

> **ON the CD-ROM** The companion CD-ROM contains a workbook that shows output from all the tools discussed in this section. The file is named atp examples.xlsx.

The Analysis of variance tool

Analysis of variance (sometimes abbreviated as Anova) is a statistical test that determines whether two or more samples were drawn from the same population. Using tools in the Analysis ToolPak, you can perform three types of analysis of variance:

- **Single-factor:** A one-way analysis of variance, with only one sample for each group of data.
- **Two-factor with replication:** A two-way analysis of variance, with multiple samples (or replications) for each group of data.
- **Two-factor without replication:** A two-way analysis of variance, with a single sample (or replication) for each group of data.

Figure 38.2 shows the dialog box for a single-factor analysis of variance. Alpha represents the statistical confidence level for the test.

FIGURE 38.2

Specifying parameters for a single-factor analysis of variance.

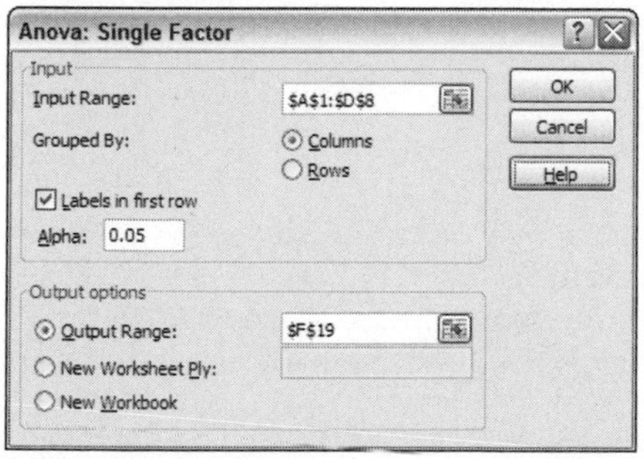

The output for this test consists of the means and variances for each of the samples, the value of F, the critical value of F, and the significance of F (P-value).

The Correlation tool

Correlation is a widely used statistic that measures the degree to which two sets of data vary together. For example, if higher values in one data set are typically associated with higher values in the second data set, the two data sets have a positive correlation. The degree of correlation is expressed as a coefficient that ranges from −1.0 (a perfect negative correlation) to +1.0 (a perfect positive correlation). A correlation coefficient of 0 indicates that the two variables aren't correlated.

Figure 38.3 shows the Correlation dialog box. Specify the input range, which can include any number of variables, arranged in rows or columns.

FIGURE 38.3

The Correlation dialog box.

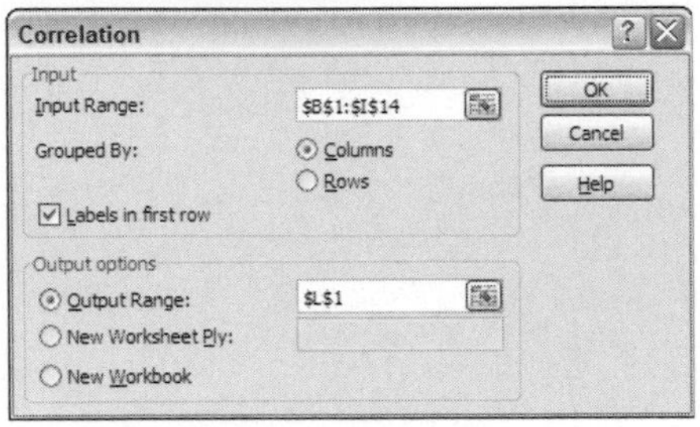

The output consists of a correlation matrix that shows the correlation coefficient for each variable paired with every other variable.

NOTE   Notice that the resulting correlation matrix doesn't use formulas to calculate the results. Therefore, if any data changes, the correlation matrix isn't valid. You can use Excel's CORREL function to create a correlation matrix that changes automatically when you change data.

The Covariance tool

The Covariance tool produces a matrix that is similar to the one generated by the Correlation tool. *Covariance*, like correlation, measures the degree to which two variables vary together. Specifically, *covariance* is the average of the product of the deviations of each data point pair from their respective means.

Because the Covariance tool does not generate formulas, you may prefer to calculate a covariance matrix using the COVAR function.

The Descriptive Statistics tool

The Descriptive Statistics tool produces a table that describes your data with some standard statistics. It uses the dialog box shown in Figure 38.4. The *K*th Largest option and *K*th Smallest option each displays the data value that corresponds to a rank that you specify. For example, if you check *K*th Largest and specify a value of 2, the output shows the second-largest value in the input range. (The standard output already includes the minimum and maximum values.)

FIGURE 38.4

The Descriptive Statistics dialog box.

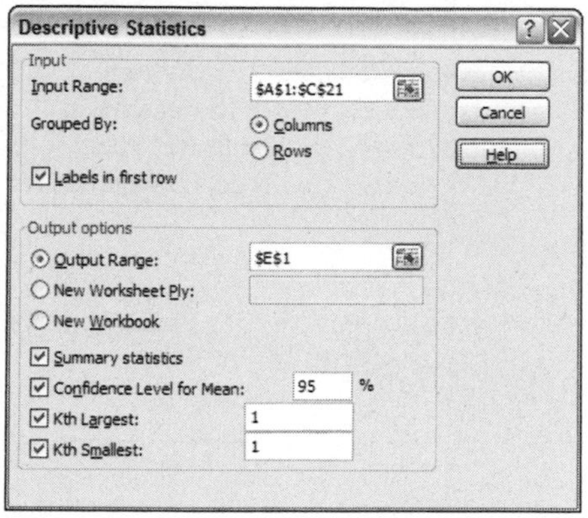

Because the output for this procedure consists of values (not formulas), you should use this procedure only when you're certain that your data isn't going to change; otherwise, you will need to re-execute the procedure. You can generate all these statistics by using formulas.

The Exponential Smoothing tool

Exponential smoothing is a technique for predicting data that is based on the previous data point and the previously predicted data point. You can specify the *damping factor* (also known as a *smoothing constant*), which can range from 0 to 1. This factor determines the relative weighting of the previous data point and the previously predicted data point. You also can request standard errors and a chart.

The exponential smoothing procedure generates formulas that use the damping factor that you specify. Therefore, if the data changes, Excel updates the formulas.

The F-Test (two-sample test for variance) tool

The *F-Test* is a commonly used statistical test that enables you to compare two population variances. Figure 38.5 shows the dialog box for this tool.

FIGURE 38.5

The F-Test dialog box.

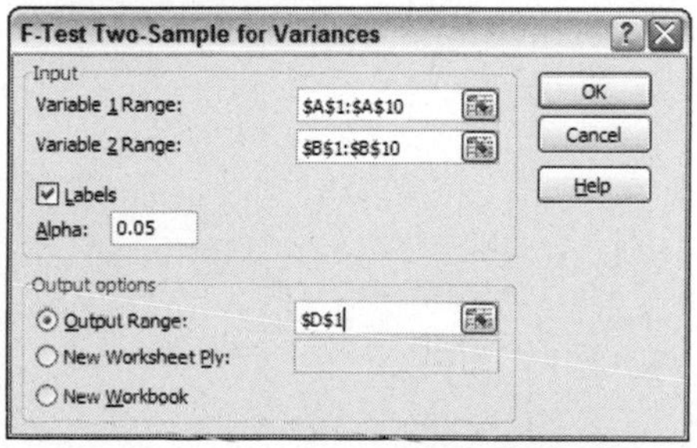

The output for this test consists of the means and variances for each of the two samples, the value of F, the critical value of F, and the significance of F.

The Fourier Analysis tool

The Fourier Analysis tool performs a "fast Fourier" transformation of a range of data. Using the Fourier Analysis tool, you can transform a range limited to the following sizes: 1, 2, 4, 8, 16, 32, 64, 128, 256, 512, or 1,024 data points. This procedure accepts and generates complex numbers, which are represented as text string (not numerical values).

The Histogram tool

The Histogram tool is useful for producing data distributions and histogram charts. It accepts an *Input* range and a *Bin* range. A *bin range* is a range of values that specifies the limits for each column of the histogram. If you omit the *bin* range, Excel creates 10 equal-interval bins for you. The size of each bin is determined by the following formula:

$$=(\text{MAX}(\texttt{input\_range})-\text{MIN}(\texttt{input\_range}))/10$$

The Histogram dialog box is shown in Figure 38.6. As an option, you can specify that the resulting histogram be sorted by frequency of occurrence in each bin.

FIGURE 38.6

The Histogram tool enables you to generate distributions and graphical output.

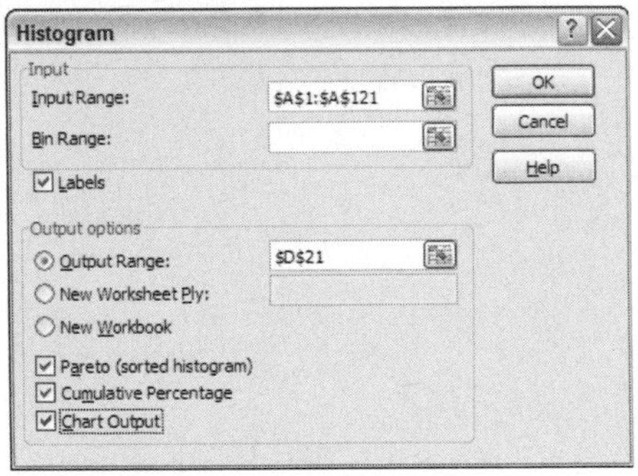

If you specify the Pareto (Sorted Histogram) option, the bin range must contain values and can't contain formulas. If formulas appear in the bin range, Excel doesn't sort properly, and your worksheet displays error values. The Histogram tool doesn't use formulas, so if you change any of the input data, you need to repeat the histogram procedure to update the results.

CROSS-REF For other ways of generating frequency distributions, refer to Chapter 14 and Chapter 35.

The Moving Average tool

The Moving Average tool helps you smooth out a data series that has a lot of variability. This procedure is best done in conjunction with a chart. Excel does the smoothing by computing a moving average of a specified number of values. In many cases, a moving average enables you to spot trends that otherwise would be obscured by noise in the data.

Figure 38.7 shows the Moving Average dialog box. You can, of course, specify the number of values that you want Excel to use for each average. If you place a check in the Standard Errors check box, Excel calculates standard errors and places formulas for these calculations next to the Moving Average formulas. The standard error values indicate the degree of variability between the actual values and the calculated moving averages. When you close this dialog box, Excel creates formulas that reference the input range that you specify.

FIGURE 38.7

The Moving Average dialog box.

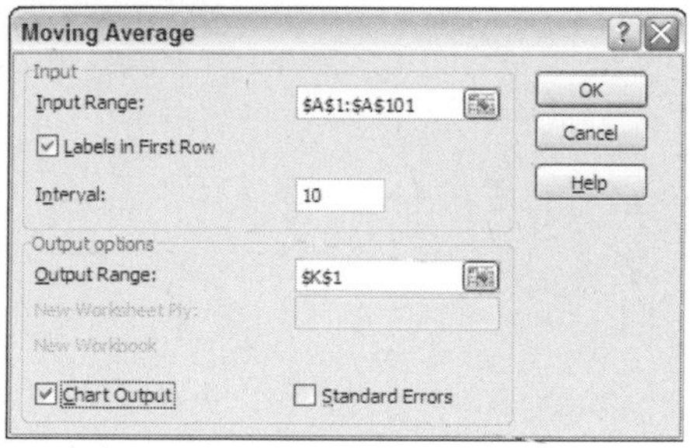

You'll notice that the first few cells in the output are #N/A because not enough data points exist to calculate the average for these initial values.

The Random Number Generation tool

Although Excel contains built-in functions to calculate random numbers, the Random Number Generation tool is much more flexible, because you can specify what type of distribution you want the random numbers to have. Figure 38.8 shows the Random Number Generation dialog box. The Parameters box varies, depending on the type of distribution that you select.

FIGURE 38.8

This dialog box enables you to generate a wide variety of random numbers.

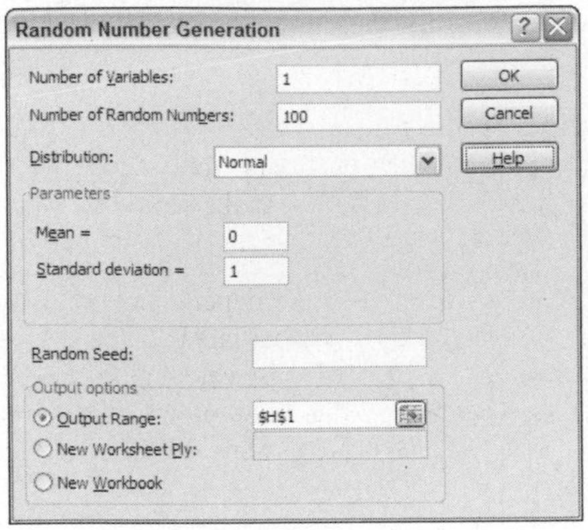

The Number of Variables refers to the number of columns that you want, and the Number of Random Numbers refers to the number of rows that you want. For example, if you want 200 random numbers arranged in 10 columns of 20 rows, you specify 10 and 20, respectively, in these text boxes.

The Random Seed box enables you to specify a starting value that Excel uses in its random number-generating algorithm. Usually, you leave this box blank. If you want to generate the same random number sequence, however, you can specify a seed between 1 and 32,767 (integer values only). You can create the following types of distributions by using the drop-down control in the Random Number Generation dialog box:

- **Uniform:** Every random number has an equal chance of being selected. You specify the upper and lower limits.

- **Normal:** The random numbers correspond to a normal distribution. You specify the mean and standard deviation of the distribution.

- **Bernoulli:** The random numbers are either 0 or 1, determined by the probability of success that you specify.

- **Binomial:** This option returns random numbers based on a Bernoulli distribution over a specific number of trials, given a probability of success that you specify.

- **Poisson:** This option generates values in a Poisson distribution. A Poisson distribution is characterized by discrete events that occur in an interval, where the probability of a single occurrence is proportional to the size of the interval. The lambda parameter is the expected number of occurrences in an interval. In a Poisson distribution, lambda is equal to the mean, which also is equal to the variance.

- **Patterned:** This option doesn't generate random numbers. Rather, it repeats a series of numbers in steps that you specify.

- **Discrete:** This option enables you to specify the probability that specific values are chosen. It requires a two-column input range; the first column holds the values, and the second column holds the probability of each value being chosen. The sum of the probabilities in the second column must equal 100 percent.

The Rank and Percentile tool

The Rank and Percentile tool creates a table that shows the ordinal and percentile ranking for each value in a range. You can also generate ranks and percentiles by using formulas that use the RANK, PERCENTILE, or PERCENTRANK functions.

The Regression tool

The Regression tool (see Figure 38.9) calculates a regression analysis from worksheet data. You can use regression to analyze trends, forecast the future, build predictive models, and, often, to make sense out of a series of seemingly unrelated numbers.

Regression analysis enables you to determine the extent to which one range of data (the dependent variable) varies as a function of the values of one or more other ranges of data (the independent variables). This relationship is expressed mathematically, using values that Excel calculates. You can use these calculations to create a mathematical model of the data and predict the dependent variable by using different values of one or more independent variables. This tool can perform simple and multiple linear regressions and calculate and standardize residuals automatically.

FIGURE 38.9

The Regression dialog box.

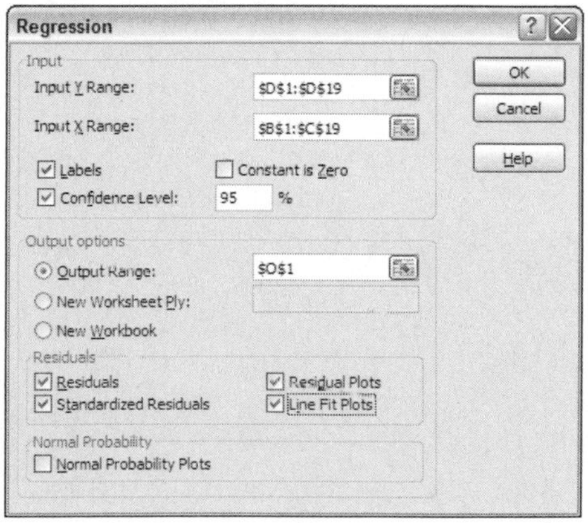

As you can see, the Regression dialog box offers many options:

- **Input Y Range:** The range that contains the dependent variable.
- **Input X Range:** One or more ranges that contain independent variables.
- **Confidence Level:** The confidence level for the regression.
- **Constant Is Zero:** If checked, forces the regression to have a constant of zero (which means that the regression line passes through the origin; when the X values are 0, the predicted Y value is 0).
- **Residuals:** Specify whether to include residuals in the output. *Residuals* are the differences between observed and predicted values.
- **Normal Probability:** Generates a chart for normal probability plots.

The Sampling tool

The Sampling tool generates a random sample from a range of input values. The Sampling tool can help you to work with a large database by creating a subset of it. The Sampling dialog box appears in Figure 38.10.

This procedure has two options: periodic and random. If you choose a periodic sample, Excel selects every *n*th value from the *Input* range, where *n* equals the period that you specify. With a random sample, you simply specify the size of the sample you want Excel to select, and every value has an equal probability of being chosen.

FIGURE 38.10

The Sampling dialog box is useful for selecting random samples.

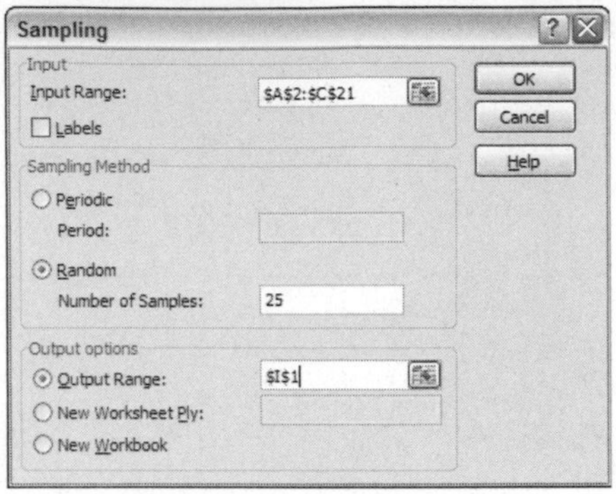

The t-Test tool

Use the *t-Test* to determine whether a statistically significant difference exists between two small samples. The Analysis ToolPak can perform three types of t-Tests:

- **Paired two-sample for means:** For paired samples in which you have two observations on each subject (such as a pretest and a post-test). The samples must be the same size.
- **Two-sample assuming equal variances:** For independent, rather than paired, samples. Excel assumes equal variances for the two samples.
- **Two-sample assuming unequal variances:** For independent, rather than paired, samples. Excel assumes unequal variances for the two samples.

Figure 38.11 shows the dialog box for the Paired Two Sample for Means t-Test. You specify the significance level (alpha) and the hypothesized difference between the two means (that is, the *null hypothesis*).

FIGURE 38.11

The paired t-Test dialog box.

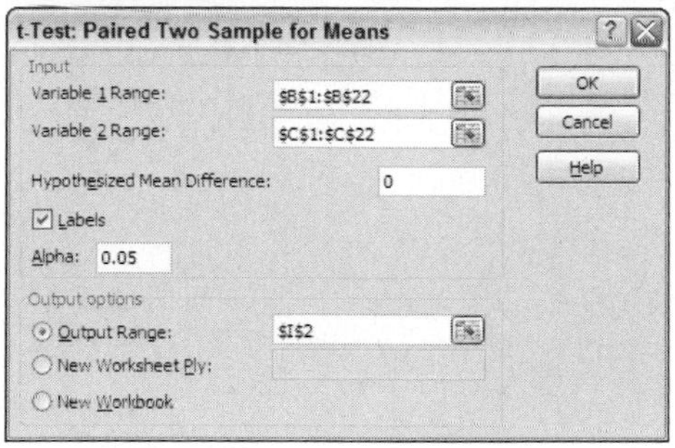

The z-Test (Two-Sample Test for Means) tool

The t-Test is used for small samples; the z-Test is used for larger samples or populations. You must know the variances for both input ranges.

Part VI

Programming Excel with VBA

If you've ever wanted to do a bit more or automate routine operations so that you don't always have to perform boring, repetitious tasks manually, this part is for you. This part is also aimed at those Excel users who want to develop Excel-based applications for other users. VBA — Visual Basic for Applications — is the powerful programming language that you can use for these tasks as well as for more esoteric purposes, such as developing that specialized worksheet function that you simply can't find in Excel.

Chapter 39

Introducing Visual Basic for Applications

This chapter is an introduction to the Visual Basic for Applications (VBA) macro language — a key component for users who want to customize Excel. This chapter teaches you how to record macros and create simple macro procedures. Subsequent chapters expand upon the topics in this chapter.

Introducing VBA Macros

In its broadest sense, a *macro* is a sequence of instructions that automates some aspect of Excel so that you can work more efficiently and with fewer errors. You may create a macro, for example, to format and print your month-end sales report. After the macro is developed, you can then execute the macro to perform many time-consuming procedures automatically.

You need not be a power user to create and use simple VBA macros. Casual users can simply turn on Excel's macro recorder: Excel records your actions and converts them into a VBA macro. When you execute this macro, Excel performs the actions again. More advanced users, though, can write code that tells Excel to perform tasks that can't be recorded. For example, you can write procedures that display custom dialog boxes, add new commands to Excel's menus, or process data in a series of workbooks.

Displaying the Developer tab

If you plan to work with VBA macros, you'll want to make sure that the Developer tab is present in Excel. To display this tab:

1. **Choose Office ⇨ Excel Options.**
2. **In the Excel Options dialog box, select Popular.**
3. **Place a check mark next to Show Developer tab in the Ribbon.**
4. **Click OK to return to Excel.**

What You Can Do with VBA

VBA is an extremely rich programming language with thousands of uses. The following list contains just a few things that you can do with VBA macros. (Not all of these tasks are covered in this book.)

- **Insert boilerplate text:** If you need to enter standard text into a range of cells, you can create a macro to do the typing for you.

- **Automate a procedure that you perform frequently:** For example, you may need to prepare a month-end summary. If the task is straightforward, you can develop a macro to do it for you.

- **Automate repetitive operations:** If you need to perform the same action in 12 different workbooks, you can record a macro while you perform the task once — and then let the macro repeat your action in the other workbooks.

- **Create a custom command:** For example, you can combine several of Excel's commands so that they're executed from a single keystroke or from a single mouse click.

- **Create a simplified "front end" for users who don't know much about Excel:** For example, you can set up a foolproof data-entry template.

- **Develop a new worksheet function:** Although Excel includes a wide assortment of built-in functions, you can create custom functions that greatly simplify your formulas.

- **Create complete macro-driven applications:** Excel macros can display custom dialog boxes and respond to new commands added to the Ribbon.

- **Create custom add-ins for Excel:** Most add-ins shipped with Excel were created with Excel macros. I used VBA exclusively to create my Power Utility Pak.

Figure 39.1 shows how the Ribbon looks when the Developer tab is selected.

FIGURE 39.1

The Developer tab, which does not appear by default, contains useful commands for VBA users.

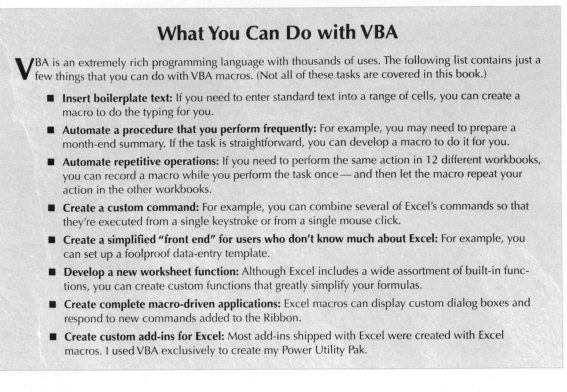

About Macro Security

Macro security was a key priority in developing Excel 2007. The reason is that macros are powerful — so powerful that they can do serious damage to your computer. The macro security features in Excel 2007 were created to help prevent macro-related problems.

Figure 39.2 shows the Macro Settings section of the Trust Center dialog box. To display this dialog box, choose Developer ➪ Macro Security.

FIGURE 39.2

The Macro Settings section of the Trust Center dialog box.

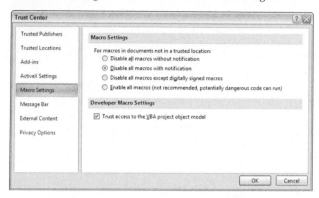

By default, Excel uses the Disable All Macros With Notification option. With this setting in effect, if you open a workbook that contains macros (and the file is not digitally "signed"), the macros will be disabled, and Excel displays a Security Warning above the Formula bar (see Figure 39.3). If you're certain that the workbook comes from a trusted source, click Enable Content (and verify your decision in the subsequent dialog box), and the macros will be enabled.

NOTE   If the Visual Basic Editor window is open when you open a workbook that contains macros, Excel does not display the Security Warning above the Formula bar. Rather, it displays a dialog box with two buttons: Enable Macros and Disable Macros.

FIGURE 39.3

Excel displays a Security Warning if a workbook contains macros.

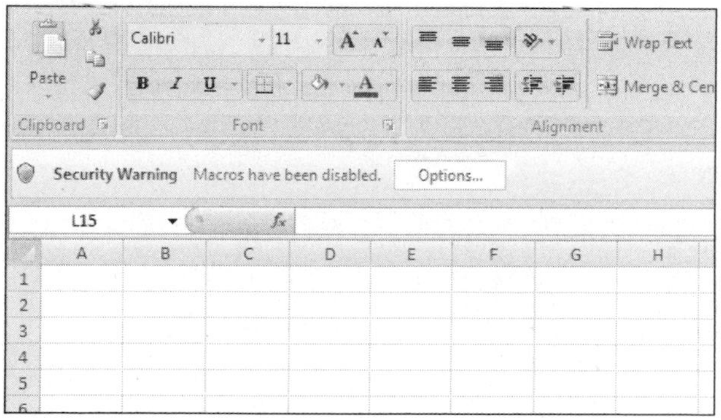

Perhaps the best way to handle macro security is to designate one or more folders as "trusted locations." All the workbooks in a trusted location are opened without a macro warning. You designate trusted folders in the Trusted Locations section of the Trust Center dialog box.

Saving Workbooks That Contain Macros

If you store one or more macros in a workbook, the file must be saved with macros enabled, which is a file with an XLSM extension.

The first time you save a workbook that contains macros, the file format defaults to XLSX — a format that can't contain macros. Unless you change the file format to XLSM, Excel displays the warning shown in Figure 39.4. You need to click No here and then choose Excel Macro-Enabled Workbook (*.xlsm) from the Save As Type drop-down.

Excel warns you if your workbook contains macros and you attempt to save it in a nonmacro file format.

Two Types of VBA Macros

Before getting into the details of creating macros, you need to understand a key distinction. A *VBA macro* (also known as a *procedure*) can be one of two types: a *Sub* or a *Function*. The next two sections discuss the difference.

VBA Sub procedures

You can think of a *Sub procedure* as a new command that either the user or another macro can execute. You can have any number of Sub procedures in an Excel workbook. Figure 39.5 shows a simple VBA Sub procedure. When this code is executed, VBA inserts the current date into the active cell, formats it, makes the cell bold, and then adjusts the column width.

A simple VBA procedure.

```
Sub CurrentDate()
    ' Inserts the current data into the active cell
    ActiveCell.Value = Date
    ActiveCell.NumberFormat = "mmmm d, yyyy"
    ActiveCell.Font.Bold = True
    ActiveCell.Columns.AutoFit
End Sub
```

What's New in the Visual Basic Editor?

Excel 2007 sports a brand new interface, but what about the Visual Basic Editor? If you used the Visual Basic Editor in a previous version of Excel, you'll be in familiar territory. In Office 2007, Microsoft left the VB Editor essentially untouched. The VBA language has been updated to accommodate the new Excel features, but the VB Editor has no new features, and the toolbars and menus work exactly like they always have.

ON the CD-ROM A workbook that contains this macro is available on the companion CD-ROM. The file is named current date.xlsm.

Sub procedures always start with the keyword Sub, the macro's name (every macro must have a unique name), and then a pair of parentheses. (The parentheses are required; they're empty unless the procedure uses one or more arguments.) The End Sub statement signals the end of the procedure. The lines in between comprise the procedure's code.

The macro shown in Figure 39.5 also includes a comment. *Comments* are simply notes to yourself, and they're ignored by VBA. A comment line begins with an apostrophe. You can also put a comment after a statement. In other words, when VBA encounters an apostrophe, it ignores the rest of the text in the line.

You execute a VBA Sub procedure in any of the following ways:

- Choose Developer ➪ Code ➪ Macros to display the Macro dialog box. Then select the procedure's name from the list and click Run.

  You can also access the Macro dialog box by pressing Alt+F8 or by clicking the Play Macro button in the left part of Excel's status bar.

- Press the procedure's shortcut key combination (if it has one).
- If the Visual Basic Editor is active, move the cursor anywhere within the code and press F5.
- Refer to the procedure in another VBA procedure.

VBA functions

The second type of VBA procedure is a function. A *function* always returns a single value (just as a worksheet function always returns a single value). A VBA function can be executed by other VBA procedures or used in worksheet formulas, just as you would use Excel's built-in worksheet functions.

Figure 39.6 shows the listing of a custom worksheet function and shows the function in use in a worksheet. This function is named CubeRoot, and it requires a single argument. CubeRoot calculates the cube root of its argument. A Function procedure looks much like a Sub procedure. Notice, however, that function procedures begin with the keyword Function and end with an End Function statement.

ON the CD-ROM A workbook that contains this function is available on the companion CD-ROM. The file is named cube root .xlsm.

FIGURE 39.6

This VBA function returns the cube root of its argument.

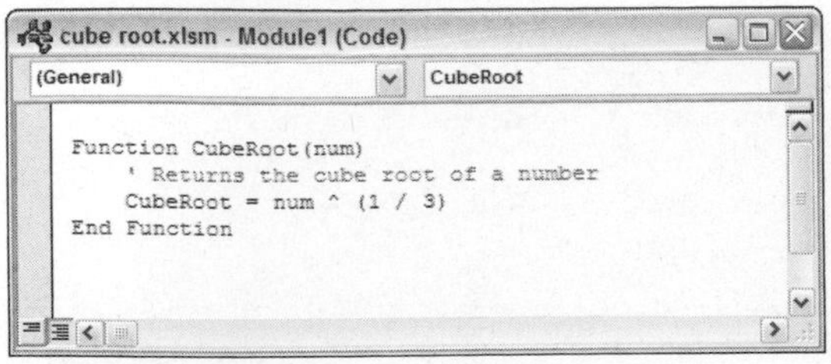

```
cube root.xlsm - Module1 (Code)
(General)                    CubeRoot

Function CubeRoot(num)
    ' Returns the cube root of a number
    CubeRoot = num ^ (1 / 3)
End Function
```

CROSS-REF Creating VBA functions that you use in worksheet formulas can simplify your formulas and enable you to perform calculations that otherwise may be impossible. Chapter 40 discusses VBA functions in greater detail.

Some Definitions

VBA newcomers are often overwhelmed by the terminology that is used in VBA. I've put together some key definitions to help you keep the terms straight. These terms cover VBA and UserForms (custom dialog boxes) — two important elements that are used to customize Excel:

- **Code:** VBA instructions that are produced in a module sheet when you record a macro. You also can enter VBA code manually.
- **Controls:** Objects on a UserForm (or in a worksheet) that you manipulate. Examples include buttons, check boxes, and list boxes.
- **Function:** One of two types of VBA macros that you can create. (The other is a Sub procedure.) A function returns a single value. You can use VBA functions in other VBA macros or in your worksheets.
- **Macro:** A set of VBA instructions performed automatically.
- **Method:** An action taken on an object. For example, applying the `Clear` method to a `Range` object erases the contents and formatting of the cells.
- **Module:** A container for VBA code.
- **Object:** An element that you manipulate with VBA. Examples include ranges, charts, drawing objects, and so on.
- **Procedure:** Another name for a macro. A VBA procedure can be a Sub procedure or a Function procedure.
- **Property:** A particular aspect of an object. For example, a `Range` object has properties, such as `Height`, `Style`, and `Name`.
- **Sub procedure:** One of two types of Visual Basic macros that you can create. The other is a function.
- **UserForm**: A container that holds controls for a custom dialog box and holds VBA code to manipulate the controls. (Chapters 41 and 42 explain UserForms in depth.)
- **VBA:** Visual Basic for Applications. The macro language that is available in Excel, as well as in the other applications in Microsoft Office.
- **VB Editor:** The window (separate from Excel) that you use to create VBA macros and UserForms.

Creating VBA Macros

Excel provides two ways to create macros:

- Turn on the macro recorder and record your actions.
- Enter the code directly into a VBA module.

The following sections describe these methods.

Recording VBA macros

In this section I describe the basic steps that you take to record a VBA macro. In most cases, you can record your actions as a macro and then simply replay the macro; you needn't look at the code that's automatically generated. If simply recording and playing back macros is as far as you go with VBA, you don't need to be concerned with the language itself (although a basic understanding of how things work doesn't do any harm).

Recording your actions to create VBA code: The basics

Excel's macro recorder translates your actions into VBA code. To start the macro recorder, choose Developer ➪ Code ➪ Record Macro (or, click the Record Macro icon in the status bar). Excel displays the Record Macro dialog box, shown in Figure 39.7.

FIGURE 39.7

The Record Macro dialog box.

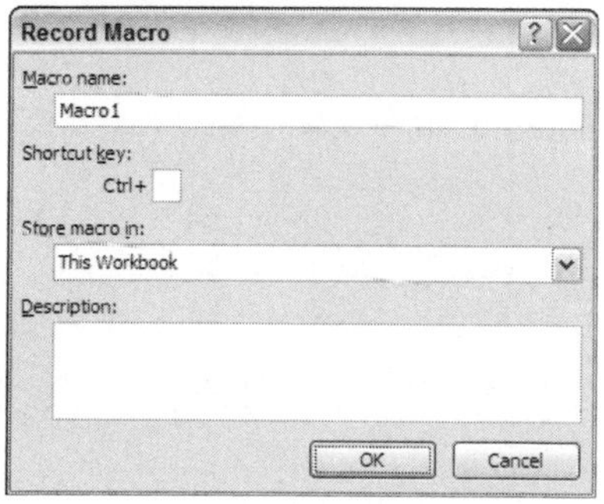

The Record Macro dialog box presents several options:

- **Macro Name:** The name of the macro. By default, Excel proposes names, such as Macro1, Macro2, and so on.
- **Shortcut Key:** You can specify a key combination that executes the macro. The key combination always uses the Ctrl key. You can also press Shift when you enter a letter. For example, pressing Shift while you enter the letter *H* makes the shortcut key combination Ctrl+Shift+H.
- **Store Macro In:** The location for the macro. Your choices are the current workbook, your Personal Macro Workbook (See "Storing macros in your Personal Macro Workbook," later in this chapter), or a new workbook.
- **Description:** A description of the macro (optional).

To begin recording your actions, click OK. When you finish recording the macro, choose Developer ➪ Code ➪ Stop Recording (or click the Stop Recording button in the status bar).

> **NOTE** Recording your actions always results in a new Sub procedure. You can't create a Function procedure by using the macro recorder. Function procedures must be created manually.

Recording a macro: A simple example

This example demonstrates how to record a very simple macro that inserts your name in the active cell.

To create the macro, follow these steps:

1. **Activate an empty cell.**
2. **Choose Developer ⇨ Code ⇨ Record Macro.** Excel displays the Record Macro dialog box.
3. **Enter a new single-word name for the macro, to replace the default** `Macro1` **name.** A good name is MyName.
4. **Assign this macro to the shortcut key Ctrl+Shift+N by entering uppercase N in the edit box labeled Shortcut Key.**
5. **Click OK to close the Record Macro dialog box.**
6. **Type your name into the selected cell.**
7. **The macro is finished, so choose Developer ⇨ Code ⇨ Stop Recording (or click the Stop Recording button in the status bar).**

Examining the macro

The macro was recorded in a new module named Module1. To view the code in this module, you must activate the Visual Basic Editor. You can activate the VB Editor in either of two ways:

- Press Alt+F11.
- Choose Developer ⇨ Code ⇨ Visual Basic.

In the VB Editor, the Project window displays a list of all open workbooks and add-ins. This list is displayed as a tree diagram, which you can expand or collapse. The code that you recorded previously is stored in Module1 in the current workbook. When you double-click Module1, the code in the module appears in the Code window.

Figure 39.8 shows the recorded macro, as displayed in the Code window.

FIGURE 39.8

The MyName procedure was generated by Excel's macro recorder.

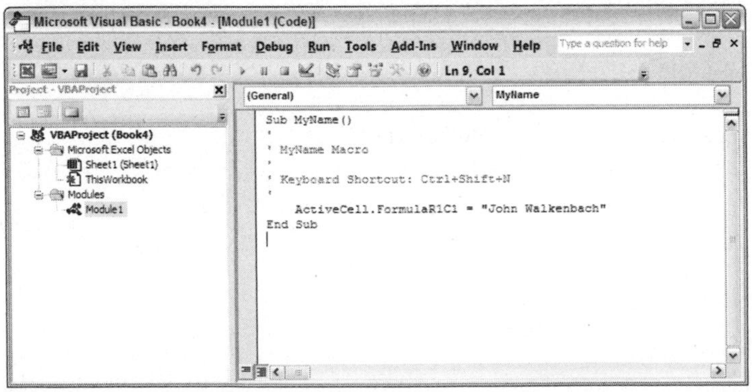

The macro should look something like this:

```
Sub MyName()
'
' MyName Macro
'
' Keyboard Shortcut: Ctrl+Shift+N
'
    ActiveCell.FormulaR1C1 = "John Walkenbach"
End Sub
```

The macro recorded is a Sub procedure that is named MyName. The statements tell Excel what to do when the macro is executed.

Notice that Excel inserted some comments at the top of the procedure. These comments are some of the information that appeared in the Record Macro dialog box. These comment lines (which begin with an apostrophe) aren't really necessary, and deleting them has no effect on how the macro runs. If you ignore the comments, you'll see that this procedure has only one VBA statement:

```
ActiveCell.FormulaR1C1 = "John Walkenbach"
```

This single statement causes the name to be inserted into the active cell. The FormulaR1C1 part is a property — but I'm getting ahead of myself.

Testing the macro

Before you recorded this macro, you set an option that assigned the macro to the Ctrl+Shift+N shortcut key combination. To test the macro, return to Excel by using either of the following methods:

- Press Alt+F11.
- Click the View Microsoft Excel button on the VB Editor toolbar.

When Excel is active, activate a worksheet. (It can be in the workbook that contains the VBA module or in any other workbook.) Select a cell and press Ctrl+Shift+N. The macro immediately enters your name into the cell.

NOTE In the preceding example, notice that you selected the cell to be formatted *before* you started recording your macro. This step is important. If you select a cell while the macro recorder is turned on, the actual cell that you selected will be recorded into the macro. In such a case, the macro would always format that particular cell, and it would not be a general-purpose macro.

Editing the macro

After you record a macro, you can make changes to it (although you must know what you're doing). For example, assume that you want your name to be bold. You could rerecord the macro, but this modification is simple, so editing the code is more efficient. Press Alt+F11 to activate the VB Editor window. Then activate Module1 and insert the following statement before the End Sub statement:

```
ActiveCell.Font.Bold = True
```

The edited macro appears as follows:

```
Sub MyName()
'
' MyName Macro
'
' Keyboard Shortcut: Ctrl+Shift+N
'
    ActiveCell.FormulaR1C1 = "John Walkenbach"
    ActiveCell.Font.Bold = True
End Sub
```

Test this new macro, and you see that it performs as it should.

Another example

This example demonstrates how to record a time-stamp macro that inserts the current date and time into the active cell. To create the macro, follow these steps:

1. **Activate an empty cell.**
2. **Choose Developer ⇨ Code ⇨ Record Macro.** Excel displays the Record Macro dialog box.
3. **Enter a new single-word name for the macro, to replace the default** `Macro1` **name.** A good name is TimeStamp.
4. **Assign this macro to the shortcut key Ctrl+Shift+T by entering uppercase** T **in the edit box labeled Shortcut Key.**
5. **Click OK to close the Record Macro dialog box.**
6. **Enter this formula into the selected cell:**
   `=NOW()`
7. **Click the Copy button (or press Ctrl+C) to copy the cell to the Clipboard.**
8. **Choose Home ⇨ Clipboard ⇨ Paste Values.** This step replaces the formula with static text, so the data and time do not update when the worksheet is calculated.
9. **Press Escape to cancel Copy mode.**
10. **The macro is finished, so choose Developer ⇨ Code ⇨ Stop Recording (or click the Stop Recording button in the status bar).**

Examining the macro

Activate the VB Editor and take a look at the recorded code. Figure 39.9 shows the recorded macro, as displayed in the Code window.

FIGURE 39.9

FIGURE 39.9

The TimeStamp procedure was generated by Excel's macro recorder.

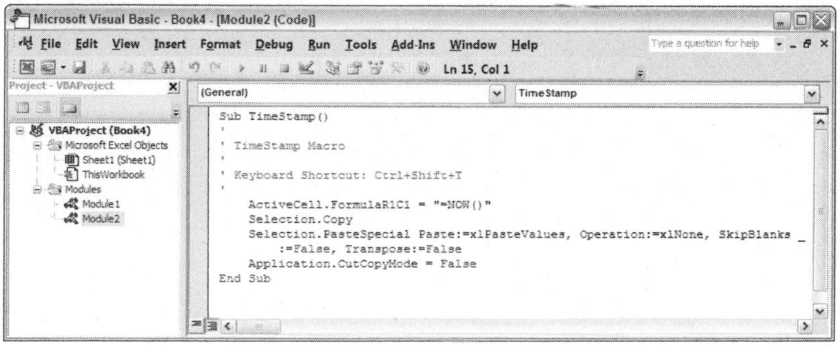

Double-click the module in the Projects window to activate the module so that you can examine the macro. It should consist of the following code:

```
Sub TimeStamp()
'
' TimeStamp Macro
' Keyboard Shortcut: Ctrl+Shift+T
'
    ActiveCell.FormulaR1C1 = "=NOW()"
    Selection.Copy
    Selection.PasteSpecial Paste:=xlPasteValues, _
        Operation:= xlNone, SkipBlanks _
        :=False, Transpose:=False
    Application.CutCopyMode = False
End Sub
```

The procedure has four statements. The first inserts the NOW() formula into the active cell. The second statement copies the cell. The third statement, which is displayed on three lines (the underscore character means that the statement continues on the next line), pastes the Clipboard contents (as a value) to the current selection. The fourth statement cancels the moving border around the selected range.

You may notice that the macro recorded some actions that you didn't take. For example, it specified several options for the PasteSpecial operation. Recording actions that you don't specifically make is just a byproduct of the method that Excel uses to translate actions into code.

Testing the macro

When Excel is active, activate a worksheet. (It can be in the workbook that contains the VBA module or in any other workbook.) Select a cell and press Ctrl+Shift+T. The macro immediately enters the current date and time into the cell. You may need to widen the column to see the date and time. To widen the column automatically, just add this statement to the end of the macro (before the End Sub statement):

```
ActiveCell.EntireColumn.AutoFit
```

More about recording VBA macros

If you followed along with the preceding examples, you should have a better feel for how to record macros. If you find the VBA code confusing, don't worry. You don't really have to be concerned with it as long as the macro that you record works correctly. If the macro doesn't work, rerecording the macro rather than editing the code often is easier.

A good way to learn about what gets recorded is to set up your screen so that you can see the code that is being generated in the Visual Basic Editor windows. To do so, make sure that Excel's Window isn't maximized; then arrange the Excel window and the VB Editor window so both are visible. While you're recording your actions, make sure that the VB Editor window is displaying the module in which the code is being recorded. (You may have to double-click the module name in the Project window.)

> **TIP**   If you do a lot of work with VBA, consider adding a second monitor to your system. Then you can display Excel on one monitor and the VB Editor on the other.

Absolute versus relative recording

If you're going to work with recorded macros, you need to understand the concept of *relative* versus *absolute* recording. Normally, when you record a macro, Excel stores exact references to the cells that you select. (That is, it performs *absolute* recording.) If you select the range B1:B10 while you're recording a macro, for example, Excel records this selection as

```
Range("B1:B10").Select
```

This statement means exactly what it says: "Select the cells in the range B1:B10." When you invoke the macro that contains this statement, the same cells are always selected, regardless of where the active cell is located.

You may have noticed that the Developer ⇨ Code section of the Ribbon has a control named Use Relative References. When you click this control, Excel changes its recording mode from absolute (the default) to relative. When recording in relative mode, selecting a range of cells is translated differently, depending on where the active cell is located. For example, if you're recording in relative mode and cell A1 is active, selecting the range B1:B10 generates the following statement:

```
ActiveCell.Offset(0, 1).Range("A1:A10").Select
```

This statement can be translated as "From the active cell, move 0 rows down and 1 column right, and then treat this new cell as if it were cell A1. Now select what would be A1:A10." In other words, a macro that is recorded in relative mode starts out by using the active cell as its base and then stores relative references to this cell. As a result, you get different results, depending on the location of the active cell. When you replay this macro, the cells that are selected depend on the active cell. This macro selects a range that is 10 rows by 1 column, offset from the active cell by 0 rows and 1 column.

When Excel is recording in relative mode, the Use Relative Reference control appears depressed. To return to absolute recording, click the Use Relative Reference control again (and it displays its normal, unde-pressed state).

> **NOTE**   The recording mode (either absolute or relative) can make a *major* difference in how your macro performs. Therefore, understanding the distinction is important.

Storing macros in your Personal Macro Workbook

Most user-created macros are designed for use in a specific workbook, but you may want to use some macros in all your work. You can store these general-purpose macros in the Personal Macro Workbook so that they're always available to you. The Personal Macro Workbook is loaded whenever you start Excel. This file, named **personal.xlsb**, doesn't exist until you record a macro, using Personal Macro Workbook as the destination.

NOTE The Personal Macro Workbook normally is in a hidden window (to keep it out of the way).

To record the macro in your Personal Macro Workbook, select the Personal Macro Workbook option in the Record Macro dialog box before you start recording. This option is in the Store Macro In drop-down box.

If you store macros in the Personal Macro Workbook, you don't have to remember to open the Personal Macro Workbook when you load a workbook that uses macros. When you want to exit, Excel asks whether you want to save changes to the Personal Macro Workbook.

Assigning a macro to a shortcut key

When you begin recording a macro, the Record Macro dialog box gives you an opportunity to provide a shortcut key for the macro. If you'd later like to change the shortcut key or provide a shortcut key for a macro that doesn't have one:

1. Press Alt+F8 to display the Macro dialog box.
2. In the Macro dialog box, select the macro name from the list.
3. Click the Options button, and Excel displays its Macro Options dialog box (see Figure 39.10).
4. Specify the shortcut key and click OK to return to the Macro dialog box.
5. Click Cancel to close the Macro dialog box.

FIGURE 39.10

Use the Macro Options dialog box to add or change a shortcut key for a macro.

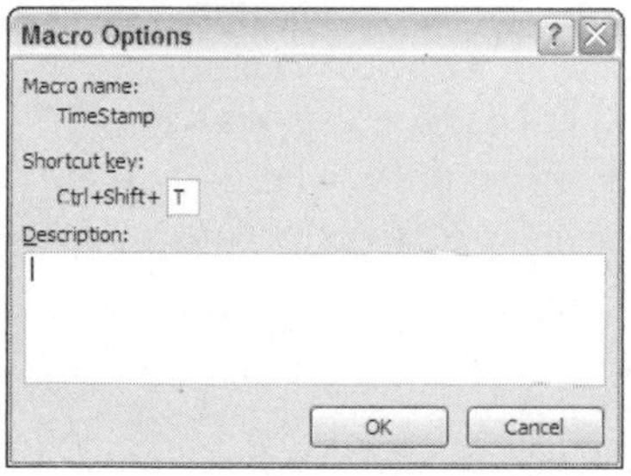

Assigning a macro to a button

After you record a macro and test it, you may want to assign the macro to a button placed in a worksheet. You can follow these steps to do so:

1. If the macro is a general-purpose macro that you plan to use in more than one workbook, make sure that the macro is stored in your Personal Macro Workbook.
2. Choose Developer ➪ Controls ➪ Insert and click the Button control from the Form Controls section (see Figure 39.11).
3. **Draw the button on the worksheet.** Excel displays the Assign Macro dialog box.
4. In the Assign Macro dialog box, select the macro from the list.
5. Click OK to close the Assign Macro dialog box.

6. You'll probably want to change the text that appears on the button to make it descriptive, so right-click the button, choose Edit Text from the shortcut menu, and make your changes.

After performing these steps, clicking the button executes the assigned macro.

FIGURE 39.11

Adding a button to a worksheet so that it can be used to execute a macro.

> **TIP**   You can also assign a macro to a button in your Quick Access Toolbar (QAT). Right-click your QAT and select Customize Quick Access Toolbar. In the Customize tab of the Excel Options dialog box, select Macros from the drop-down list on the left. Then select your macro and click the Add button. To change the icon, click the modify button.

Writing VBA code

As demonstrated in the preceding sections, the easiest way to create a simple macro is to record your actions. To develop more complex macros, however, you have to enter the VBA code manually — in other words, write a program. To save time, you can often combine recording with manual code entry.

Before you can begin writing VBA code, you must have a good understanding of such topics as objects, properties, and methods. And it doesn't hurt to be familiar with common programming constructs, such as looping and If-Then statements.

This section is an introduction to VBA programming, which is essential if you want to write (rather than record) VBA macros. It isn't intended to be a complete instructional guide. My book titled *Excel 2007 Power Programming with VBA* (Wiley Publishing, Inc.) covers all aspects of VBA and advanced spreadsheet application development.

The basics: Entering and editing code

Before you can enter code, you must insert a VBA module into the workbook. If the workbook already has a VBA module, you can use the existing module sheet for your new code.

Use the following steps to insert a new VBA module:

1. **Press Alt+F11 to activate the VB Editor window.** The VB Editor window is a separate application, although it works very closely with Excel.

VBA Coding Tips

When you enter code in a module sheet, you're free to use indenting and blank lines to make the code more readable. (In fact, this is an excellent habit.)

After you enter a line of code (by pressing Enter), it's evaluated for syntax errors. If none are found, the line of code is reformatted, and colors are added to keywords and identifiers. This automatic reformatting adds consistent spaces (before and after an equal sign, for example) and removes extra spaces that aren't needed. If a syntax error is found, you receive a pop-up message, and the line is displayed in a different color (red, by default). You need to correct your error before you can execute the macro.

A single statement can be as long as you need. However, you may want to break the statement into two or more lines. To do so, insert a space followed by an underscore(_). The following code, although written as two lines, is actually a single VBA statement:

```
Sheets("Sheet1").Range("B1").Value = _
  Sheets("Sheet1").Range("A1").Value
```

You can insert comments freely into your VBA code. The comment indicator is an apostrophe single quote character ('). Any text that follows a single quote is ignored. A comment can be a line by itself, or it can be inserted after a statement. The following examples show two comments:

```
' Assign the values to the variables
Rate = .085   'Rate as of November 16
```

2. The Project window displays a list of all open workbooks and add-ins. **Locate the workbook that you're currently working in and select it.**

3. **Choose Insert ➪ Module.** VBA inserts a new (empty) module into the workbook and displays it in the Code window.

A VBA module, which is displayed in a separate window, works like a text editor. You can move through the sheet, select text, insert, copy, cut, paste, and so on.

How VBA works

VBA is by far the most complex feature in Excel, and you can easily get overwhelmed. To set the stage for the details of VBA, here is a concise summary of how VBA works:

- **You perform actions in VBA by writing (or recording) code in a VBA module sheet and then executing the macro in any one of various ways.** VBA modules are stored in an Excel workbook, and a workbook can hold any number of VBA modules. To view or edit a VBA module, you must activate the Visual Basic Editor window. (Press Alt+F11 to toggle between Excel and the VB Editor window.)

- **A VBA module consists of procedures.** A *procedure* is basically computer code that performs some action. The following is an example of a simple Sub procedure called ShowSum (it adds 1 + 1 and displays the result):

```
Sub ShowSum()
   Sum = 1 + 1
   MsgBox "The answer is " & Sum
End Sub
```

■ **A VBA module also can store function procedures.** A *function procedure* performs calculations and returns a single value. A function can be called from another VBA procedure or can even be used in a worksheet formula. Here's an example of a function named AddTwo. (It adds two values, which are supplied as arguments.)

```
Function AddTwo(arg1, arg2)
   AddTwo = arg1 + arg2
End Function
```

■ **VBA manipulates objects.** Excel provides well over 100 classes of objects that you can manipulate. Examples of objects include a workbook, a worksheet, a range on a worksheet, a chart, and a rectangle shape.

■ **Objects are arranged in a hierarchy and can act as containers for other objects.** For example, Excel itself is an object called Application, and it contains other objects, such as Workbook objects. The Workbook object can contain other objects, such as Worksheet objects and Chart objects. A Worksheet object can contain objects such as Range objects, PivotTable objects, and so on. The arrangement of these objects is referred to as an *object model*.

■ **Objects that are alike form a** *collection*. For example, the Worksheets collection consists of all worksheets in a particular workbook. The ChartObjects collection consists of all ChartObjects on a worksheet. Collections are objects in themselves.

■ **You refer to an object in your VBA code by specifying its position in the object hierarchy, using a period as a separator.**

For example, you can refer to a workbook named Book1.xlsx as

```
Application.Workbooks("Book1.xlsx")
```

This expression refers to the Book1.xlsx workbook in the Workbooks collection. The Workbooks collection is contained in the Application object (that is, Excel). Extending this to another level, you can refer to Sheet1 in Book1 as follows:

```
Application.Workbooks("Book1.xlsx").Worksheets("Sheet1")
```

You can take it to still another level and refer to a specific cell as follows:

```
Application.Workbooks("Book1.xlsx").Worksheets("Sheet1").Range("A1")
```

■ **If you omit specific references, Excel uses the** *active* **objects.** If Book1.xlsx is the active workbook, the preceding reference can be simplified as follows:

```
Worksheets("Sheet1").Range("A1")
```

If you know that Sheet1 is the active sheet, you can simplify the reference even more:

```
Range("A1")
```

■ **Objects have properties.** A *property* can be thought of as a setting for an object. For example, a Range object has properties, such as Value and Address. A Chart object has properties such as HasTitle and Type. You can use VBA both to determine object properties and to change them.

■ **You refer to properties by combining the object with the property, separated by a period.** For example, you can refer to the value in cell A1 on Sheet1 as follows:

```
Worksheets("Sheet1").Range("A1").Value
```

■ **You can assign values to variables.** To assign the value in cell A1 on Sheet1 to a variable called Interest, use the following VBA statement:

```
Interest = Worksheets("Sheet1").Range("A1").Value
```

■ **Objects have methods.** A *method* is an action that is performed with the object. For example, one of the methods for a Range object is ClearContents. This method clears the contents of the range.

■ **You specify methods by combining the object with the method, separated by a period.** For example, to clear the contents of cell A1, use the following statement:

```
Worksheets("Sheet1").Range("A1:C12").ClearContents
```

■ **VBA also includes all the constructs of modern programming languages, including variables, arrays, looping, and so on.**

The preceding describes VBA in a nutshell. Now you just have to learn the details, some of which are covered in the rest of this chapter.

Objects and collections

VBA is an *object-oriented language,* which means that it manipulates *objects,* such as Ranges, Charts, AutoShapes, and so on. These objects are arranged in a hierarchy. The Application object (which is Excel) contains other objects. For example, the Application object contains a number of objects, including the following:

■ AddIns (a collection of AddIn objects)

■ Windows (a collection of Window objects)

■ Workbooks (a collection of Workbook objects)

Most of these objects can contain other objects. For example, a Workbook object can contain the following objects:

■ Charts (a collection of Chart sheet objects)

■ Names (a collection of Name objects)

■ Styles (a collection of Style objects)

■ Windows (a collection of Window objects in the workbook)

■ Worksheets (a collection of Worksheet objects)

Each of these objects, in turn, can contain other objects. A Worksheet object, for example, can contain the following objects:

■ ChartObjects (a collection of all ChartObject objects)

■ PageSetup (an object that stores printing information)

■ PivotTables (a collection of all PivotTable objects)

A *collection* consists of all like objects. For example, the collection of all Workbook objects is known as the Workbooks collection. You can refer to an individual object in a collection by using an index number or a name. For example, if a workbook has three worksheets (named Sheet1, Sheet2, and Sheet3), you can refer to the first object in the Worksheets collection in either of these ways:

```
Worksheets(1)
Worksheets("Sheet1")
```

Properties

The objects that you work with have *properties,* which you can think of as attributes of the objects. For example, a Range object has properties, such as Column, Row, Width, and Value. A Chart object has properties, such as Legend, ChartTitle, and so on. ChartTitle is also an object, with properties such as Font, Orientation, and Text. Excel has many objects, and each has its own set of properties. You can write VBA code to do the following:

■ Examine an object's current property setting and take some action based on it.

■ Change an object's property setting.

You refer to a property in your VBA code by placing a period (a dot) and the property name after the object's name. For example, the following VBA statement sets the `Value` property of a range named *frequency* to 15. (That is, the statement causes the number *15* to appear in the range's cells.)

```
Range("frequency").Value = 15
```

Some properties are *read-only,* which means that you can examine the property, but you can't change the property. For a single-cell `Range` object, the `Row` and `Column` properties are read-only properties: You can determine where a cell is located (in which row and column), but you can't change the cell's location by changing these properties.

A `Range` object also has a `Formula` property, which is *not* read-only; that is, you can insert a formula into a cell by changing its `Formula` property. The following statement inserts a formula into cell A1 by changing the cell's `Formula` property:

```
Range("A11").Formula = "=SUM(A1:A10)"
```

> **NOTE** Contrary to what you may think, Excel doesn't have a `Cell` object. When you want to manipulate a single cell, you use the `Range` object (with only one cell in it).

At the top of the object hierarchy is the `Application` object, which is actually Excel, the program. The `Application` object has several useful properties:

■ `Application.ActiveWorkbook`: Returns the active workbook (a `Workbook` object) in Excel.

■ `Application.ActiveSheet`: Returns the active sheet (a `Sheet` object) of the active workbook.

■ `Application.ActiveCell`: Returns the active cell (a `Range` object) object of the active window.

■ `Application.Selection`: Returns the object that is currently selected in the active window of the `Application` object. This can be a `Range`, a `Chart`, a `Shape`, or some other selectable object.

You also should understand that properties can return objects. In fact, that's exactly what the preceding examples do. The result of `Application.ActiveCell`, for example, is a `Range` object. Therefore, you can access properties by using a statement such as the following:

```
Application.ActiveCell.Font.Size = 15
```

In this case, the `ActiveCell` property returns a `Range` object. The `Font` property returns a `Font` object, which is contained in the `Range` object. `Size` is a property of the `Font` object. The preceding statement sets the `Size` property to 15 — that is, it causes the font in the currently selected cell to have a size of 15 points.

> **TIP** Because `Application` properties are so commonly used, you can omit the object qualifier (`Application`). For example, to get the row of the active cell, you can use a statement such as the following:

```
ActiveCell.Row
```

In many cases, you can refer to the same object in a number of different ways. Assume that you have a workbook named Sales.xlsx and it's the only workbook open. Furthermore, assume that this workbook has one worksheet, named Summary. Your VBA code can refer to the Summary sheet in any of the following ways:

```
Workbooks("Sales.xlsx").Worksheets("Summary")
Workbooks(1).Worksheets(1)
Workbooks(1).Sheets(1)
Application.ActiveWorkbook.ActiveSheet
ActiveWorkbook.ActiveSheet
ActiveSheet
```

The method that you use is determined by how much you know about the workspace. For example, if more than one workbook is open, the second or third method is not reliable. If you want to work with the active sheet (whatever it may be), any of the last three methods would work. To be absolutely sure that you're referring to a specific sheet on a specific workbook, the first method is your best choice.

Methods

Objects also have *methods*. You can think of a method as an action taken with an object. For example, Range objects have a Clear method. The following VBA statement clears a Range, an action that is equivalent to selecting the Range and then choosing Home ➪ Editing ➪ Clear ➪ Clear All:

```
Range("A1:C12").Clear
```

In VBA code, methods *look* like properties because they are connected to the object with a "dot." However, methods and properties are different concepts.

Variables

Like all programming languages, VBA enables you to work with variables. In VBA (unlike in some languages), you don't need to declare variables explicitly before you use them in your code (although doing so is definitely a good practice).

> **NOTE** If your VBA module contains an Option Explicit statement at the top of the module, then you *must* declare all variables in the module. Undeclared variables will result in a compile error, and your procedures will not run.

In the following example, the value in cell A1 on Sheet1 is assigned to a variable named Rate:

```
rate = Worksheets("Sheet1").Range("A1").Value
```

You then can work with the variable Rate in other parts of your VBA code. Note that the variable Rate is not a named range, which means that you can't use it as such in a worksheet formula.

Controlling execution

VBA uses many constructs that are found in most other programming languages. These constructs are used to control the flow of execution. This section introduces a few of the more common programming constructs.

The If-Then construct

One of the most important control structures in VBA is the If-Then construct, which gives your applications decision-making capability. The basic syntax of the If-Then structure is as follows:

```
If condition Then statements [Else elsestatements]
```

In plain English, if a condition is true, then a group of statement will be executed. If you include the `Else` clause, then another group of statements will be executed if the condition is not true.

The following is an example (which doesn't use the optional `Else` clause). This procedure checks the active cell. If it contains a negative value, the cell's color is changed to red. Otherwise, nothing happens.

```
Sub CheckCell()
    If ActiveCell.Value < 0 Then ActiveCell.Font.ColorIndex = 3
End Sub
```

For-Next loops

You can use a `For-Next` loop to execute one or more statements a number of times. Here's an example of a `For-Next` loop:

```
Sub SumSquared()
   Total = 0
   For Num = 1 To 10
     Total = Total + (Num ^ 2)
   Next Num
   MsgBox Total
End Sub
```

This example has one statement between the `For` statement and the `Next` statement. This single statement is executed 10 times. The variable `Num` takes on successive values of 1, 2, 3, and so on, up to 10. The variable `Total` stores the sum of `Num` squared, added to the previous value of `Total`. The result is a value that represents the sum of the first 10 integers squared. This result is displayed in a message box.

The With-End With construct

Another construct that you encounter if you record macros is the `With-End With` construct. This is a shortcut way of dealing with several properties or methods of the same object. The following is an example:

```
Sub AlignCells()
   With Selection
     .HorizontalAlignment = xlCenter
     .VerticalAlignment = xlCenter
     .WrapText = False
     .Orientation = xlHorizontal
   End With
End Sub
```

The following macro performs exactly the same operations but doesn't use the `With-End With` construct:

```
Sub AlignCells()
   Selection.HorizontalAlignment = xlCenter
   Selection.VerticalAlignment = xlCenter
   Selection.WrapText = False
   Selection.Orientation = xlHorizontal
End Sub
```

The Select Case construct

The Select Case construct is useful for choosing among two or more options. The following example demonstrates the use of a Select Case construct. In this example, the active cell is checked. If its value is less than 0, it's colored red. If it's equal to 0, it's colored blue. If the value is greater than 0, it's colored black.

```
Sub CheckCell()
  Select Case ActiveCell.Value
    Case Is < 0
      ActiveCell.Font.Color = vbRed
    Case 0
      ActiveCell.Font.Color = vbBlue
    Case Is > 0
      ActiveCell.Font.Color = vbBlack
  End Select

End Sub
```

Any number of statements can go below each Case statement, and they all get executed if the case is true.

A macro that can't be recorded

The following is a VBA macro that can't be recorded because it uses programming concepts that must be entered manually. This macro creates a list of all formulas on the active sheet. The list is stored on a new worksheet.

```
Sub ListFormulas()
' Create a range object
  Set InputRange = ActiveSheet.UsedRange
' Add a new sheet
  Set OutputSheet = Worksheets.Add
' Variable for the output row
  OutputRow = 1
' Loop through the range
  For Each cell In InputRange
    If cell.HasFormula Then
      OutputSheet.Cells(OutputRow, 1) = "'" & cell.Address
      OutputSheet.Cells(OutputRow, 2) = "'" & cell.Formula
      OutputRow = OutputRow + 1
    End If
  Next cell
End Sub
```

ON the CD-ROM A workbook that contains this example is available on the companion CD-ROM. The file is named list formulas.xlsm.

Although this macro may look complicated, it's fairly simple when you break it down.

First, the macro creates an object variable named InputRange. This variable corresponds to the used range on the active sheet (avoiding the need to check every cell). It then adds a new worksheet and assigns the worksheet to an object variable named OutputSheet. The OutputRow variable is set to 1. This variable is incremented later on.

The For-Next loop examines each cell in the `InputRange`. If the cell has a formula, then the cell's address and formula are written to the `OutputSheet`. The `OutputRow` variable is also incremented.

Figure 39.12 shows the result of running this macro—a handy list of all formulas in the worksheet.

FIGURE 39.12

The ListFormulas macro creates a list of all formulas in a worksheet.

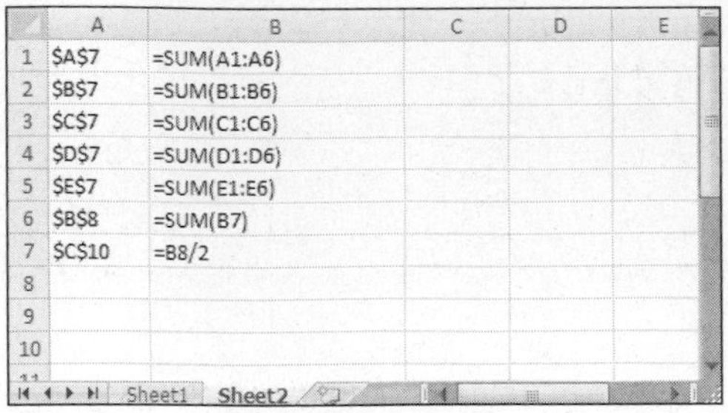

	A	B	C	D	E
1	$A$7	=SUM(A1:A6)			
2	$B$7	=SUM(B1:B6)			
3	$C$7	=SUM(C1:C6)			
4	$D$7	=SUM(D1:D6)			
5	$E$7	=SUM(E1:E6)			
6	$B$8	=SUM(B7)			
7	$C$10	=B8/2			
8					
9					
10					
11					

Sheet1 **Sheet2**

As macros go, this example is okay, but it's certainly not perfect. It's not very flexible, and it doesn't include any error handling. For example, if the workbook structure is protected, trying to add a new sheet will cause an error.

Learning More

This chapter barely scratches the surface of what you can do with VBA. If this is your first exposure to VBA, you're probably a bit overwhelmed by objects, properties, and methods. I don't blame you. If you try to access a property that an object doesn't have, you get a run-time error, and your VBA code grinds to a screeching halt until you correct the problem. Fortunately, several good ways are available to learn about objects, properties, and methods.

- **Read the rest of the book.** Subsequent chapters in this section contain additional information and many more examples.

- **Record your actions.** The best way to become familiar with VBA is to turn on the macro recorder and record actions that you make in Excel. You can then examine the code to gain some insights regarding the objects, properties, and methods.

- **Use the Help system.** The main source of detailed information about Excel's objects, methods, and procedures is the VBA Help system. Help is very thorough and easy to access. When you're in a VBA module, just move the cursor to a property or method and press F1. You get help that describes the word that is under the cursor.

- **Get another book.** Several books are devoted exclusively to using VBA with Excel. My book, *Excel 2007 Power Programming with VBA* (Wiley Publishing, Inc.), is one of them.

Chapter 40

Creating Custom Worksheet Functions

A s mentioned in the preceding chapter, you can create two types of VBA procedures: Sub procedures and Function procedures. This chapter focuses on Function procedures.

Overview of VBA Functions

Function procedures that you write in VBA are quite versatile. You can use these functions in two situations:

- You can call the function from a different VBA procedure.
- You can use the function in formulas that you create in a worksheet.

This chapter focuses on creating functions for use in your formulas.

Excel contains hundreds of predefined worksheet functions. With so many from which to choose, you may be curious as to why anyone would need to develop additional functions. The main reason is that creating a custom function can greatly simplify your formulas by making them shorter, and shorter formulas are more readable and easier to work with. For example, you can often replace a complex formula with a single function. Another reason is that you can write functions to perform operations that would otherwise be impossible.

> **NOTE** This chapter assumes that you're familiar with entering and editing VBA code in the Visual Basic Editor (VB Editor). Refer to Chapter 39 for an overview of the VB Editor.

An Introductory Example

The process of creating custom functions is relatively easy, once you understand VBA. Without further ado, here's an example of a VBA function procedure. This function is stored in a VBA module, which is accessible from the VB Editor.

A custom function

This example function, named NumSign, uses one argument. The function returns a text string of Positive if its argument is greater than zero, Negative if the argument is less than zero, and Zero if the argument is equal to zero. The function is shown in Figure 40.1.

A simple custom worksheet function.

You can, of course, accomplish the same effect with the following worksheet formula, which uses a nested IF function:

```
=IF(A1=0,"Zero",IF(A1>0,"Positive","Negative"))
```

Many would agree that the custom function solution is easier to understand and to edit than the worksheet formula.

Using the function in a worksheet

When you enter a formula that uses the NumSign function, Excel executes the function to get the result. This custom function works just like any built-in worksheet function. You can insert it in a formula by choosing Formulas ➪ Function Library ➪ Function Wizard, which displays the Insert Function dialog box. (Custom functions are listed in the User Defined category.) When you select the function from the list, you can then use the Function Arguments dialog box to specify the arguments for the function, as shown in Figure 40.2. You also can nest custom functions and combine them with other elements in your formulas.

FIGURE 40.2

Creating a worksheet formula that uses a custom function.

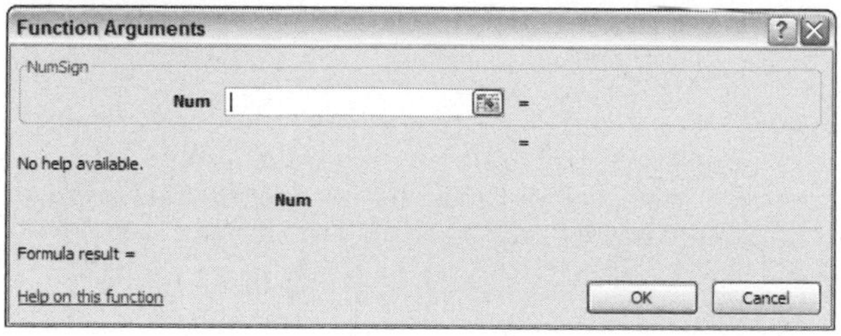

Analyzing the custom function

This section describes the NumSign function. Here again is the code:

```
Function NumSign(num)
    Select Case num
        Case Is < 0
            NumSign = "Negative"
        Case 0
            NumSign = "Zero"
        Case Is > 0
            NumSign = "Positive"
    End Select
End Function
```

Notice that the procedure starts with the keyword Function, followed by the name of the function (NumSign). This custom function uses one argument (num), and the argument's name is enclosed in parentheses. The num argument represents the cell or variable that is to be processed. When the function is used in a worksheet, the argument can be a cell reference (such as A1) or a literal value (such as –123). When the function is used in another procedure, the argument can be a numeric variable, a literal number, or a value that is obtained from a cell.

The NumSign function uses the Select Case construct (described in Chapter 39) to take a different action, depending on the value of num. If num is less than zero, NumSign is assigned the text "Negative". If num is equal to zero, NumSign is "Zero". If num is greater than zero, NumSign is "Positive". The value returned by a function is always assigned to the function's name.

About Function Procedures

A custom Function procedure has a lot in common with a Sub procedure. Function procedures have some important differences, however. Perhaps the key difference is that a function returns a *value*. When writing a Function procedure, the value that's returned is the value that has been assigned to the function's name when a function is finished executing.

What a Function Can't Do

Almost everyone who starts creating custom worksheet functions using VBA makes a fatal mistake: They try to get the function to do more than is possible.

A worksheet function returns a value, and the function must be completely "passive." In other words, the function can't change anything on the worksheet. For example, you can't develop a worksheet function that changes the formatting of a cell. (Every VBA programmer has tried, and not one of them has been successful!) If your function attempts to perform an action that isn't allowed, the function simply returns an error.

VBA functions that aren't used in worksheet formulas can do anything that a regular Sub procedure can do — including changing cell formatting.

To create a custom function, follow these steps:

1. **Activate the VB Editor (press Alt+F11).**
2. **Select the workbook in the Project window.**
3. **Choose Insert ⇨ Module to insert a VBA module.** (Or you can use an existing module.)
4. **Enter the keyword Function followed by the function's name and a list of the arguments (if any) in parentheses.**
5. **Insert the VBA code that performs the work — and make sure that the variable corresponding to the function's name has the appropriate value when the function ends.** (This is the value that the function returns.)
6. **End the function with an End Function statement.**

Function names that are used in worksheet formulas must adhere to the same rules as variable names.

Executing Function Procedures

You can execute a Sub procedure in many ways, but you can execute a Function procedure in just two ways:

- Call it from another VBA procedure.
- Use it in a worksheet formula.

Calling custom functions from a procedure

You can call custom functions from a procedure just as you call built-in VBA functions. For example, after you define a function called CalcTax, you can enter a statement such as the following:

```
Tax = CalcTax(Amount, Rate)
```

This statement executes the CalcTax custom function with Amount and Rate as its arguments. The function's result is assigned to the Tax variable.

Using custom functions in a worksheet formula

You use a custom function in a worksheet formula just like you use built-in functions. However, you must ensure that Excel can locate the function. If the function procedure is in the same workbook, you don't have to do anything special. If the function is defined in a different workbook, you may have to tell Excel where to find the function. The following are the three ways in which you can do this:

- **Precede the function's name with a file reference.** For example, if you want to use a function called `CountNames` that's defined in a workbook named `MyFunctions`, you can use a reference such as the following:

  `=MyFunctions.xlsm!CountNames(A1:A1000)`

  If the workbook name contains a space, you need to add single quotes around the workbook name. For example:

  `='My Functions.xlsm'!CountNames(A1:A1000)`

  If you insert the function with the Insert Function dialog box, the workbook reference is inserted automatically.

- **Set up a reference to the workbook.** If the custom function is defined in a referenced workbook, you don't need to precede the function name with the workbook name. You establish a reference to another workbook with the Tools ➪ References command (in the VB Editor). You are presented with a list of references that includes all open workbooks. Place a check mark in the item that refers to the workbook that contains the custom function. (Use the Browse button if the workbook isn't open.)

- **Create an add-in.** When you create an add-in from a workbook that has function procedures, you don't need to use the file reference when you use one of the functions in a formula; the add-in must be installed, however. Chapter 45 discusses add-ins.

NOTE Your Function procedures don't appear in the Macro dialog box because you can't execute a function directly. As a result, you need to do extra, up-front work to test your functions as you're developing them. One approach is to set up a simple Sub procedure that calls the function. If the function is designed to be used in worksheet formulas, you can enter a simple formula to test it as you're developing the function.

Function Procedure Arguments

Keep in mind the following about function procedure arguments:

- Arguments can be variables (including arrays), constants, literals, or expressions.
- Some functions do not have arguments.
- Some functions have a fixed number of required arguments (from 1 to 60).
- Some functions have a combination of required and optional arguments.

The following sections present a series of examples that demonstrate how to use arguments effectively with functions. Coverage of optional arguments is beyond the scope of this book.

ON the CD-ROM The examples in this chapter are available on the companion CD-ROM. The file is named VBA functions.xlsm.

A function with no argument

Functions don't necessarily use arguments. Excel, for example, has a few built-in worksheet functions that don't use arguments, such as RAND, TODAY, and NOW.

The following is a simple example of a function that has no arguments. This function returns the UserName property of the Application object, which is the name that appears in the Personalize section of the Excel Options dialog box. This function is very simple, but it can be useful, because no other way is available to get the user's name to appear in a worksheet formula.

```
Function User()
' Returns the name of the current user
   User = Application.UserName
End Function
```

When you enter the following formula into a worksheet cell, the cell displays the name of the current user:

```
=User()
```

As with Excel's built-in functions, when you use a function with no arguments, you must include a set of empty parentheses.

A function with one argument

The function that follows takes a single argument and uses Excel's text-to-speech generator to "speak" the argument.

```
Function SayIt(txt)
   Application.Speech.Speak (txt)
End Function
```

For example, if you enter this formula, you will hear the contents of cell A1 whenever the worksheet is recalculated:

```
=SayIt(A1)
```

You can use this function in a slightly more complex formula, as shown here. In this example, the argument is a text string rather than a cell reference.

```
=IF(SUM(A:A)>1000,SayIt("Goal reached"),)
```

This formula calculates the sum of the values in Column A. If that sum exceeds 1,000, you will hear "Goal reached."

When you use the SayIt function in a worksheet formula, the function always returns 0 because a value is not assigned to the function's name.

NOTE   In order to hear the synthesized voice, your system must be set up to play sound.

Another function with one argument

This section contains a more complex function that is designed for a sales manager who needs to calculate the commissions earned by the sales force. The commission rate is based on the amount sold — those who sell more earn a higher commission rate. The function returns the commission amount, based on the sales made (which is the function's only argument — a required argument). The calculations in this example are based on the following table:

Monthly Sales	Commission Rate
0–$9,999	8.0%
$10,000–$19,999	10.5%
$20,000–$39,999	12.0%
$40,000+	14.0%

You can use any of several different methods to calculate commissions for various sales amounts that are entered into a worksheet. You could write a formula such as the following:

```
=IF(AND(A1>=0,A1<=9999.99),A1*0.08,IF(AND(A1>=10000,
A1<=19999.99), A1*0.105,IF(AND(A1>=20000,
A1<=39999.99),A1*0.12,IF(A1>=40000,A1*0.14,0))))
```

This approach isn't the best for a couple of reasons. First, the formula is overly complex and difficult to understand. Second, the values are hard-coded into the formula, making the formula difficult to modify if the commission structure changes.

A better solution is to use a lookup table function to compute the commissions; for example:

```
=VLOOKUP(A1,Table,2)*A1
```

Using the VLOOKUP function requires that you have a table of commission rates set up in your worksheet.

Another option is to create a custom function, such as the following:

```
Function Commission(Sales)
'   Calculates sales commissions
    Tier1 = 0.08
    Tier2 = 0.105
    Tier3 = 0.12
    Tier4 = 0.14
    Select Case Sales
        Case 0 To 9999.99
            Commission = Sales * Tier1
        Case 1000 To 19999.99
            Commission = Sales * Tier2
        Case 20000 To 39999.99
            Commission = Sales * Tier3
        Case Is >= 40000
            Commission = Sales * Tier4
    End Select
End Function
```

After you define the Commission function in a VBA module, you can use it in a worksheet formula. Entering the following formula into a cell produces a result of 3,000. (The amount, 25,000, qualifies for a commission rate of 12 percent.)

```
=Commission(25000)
```

If the sales amount is in cell D23, the function's argument would be a cell reference, like this:

```
=Commission(D23)
```

A function with two arguments

This example builds on the previous one. Imagine that the sales manager implements a new policy: The total commission paid is increased by 1 percent for every year that the salesperson has been with the company. For this example, the custom `Commission` function (defined in the preceding section) has been modified so that it takes two arguments, both of which are required arguments. Call this new function `Commission2`:

```
Function Commission2(Sales, Years)
'     Calculates sales commissions based on years in service
      Tier1 = 0.08
      Tier2 = 0.105
      Tier3 = 0.12
      Tier4 = 0.14
      Select Case Sales
          Case 0 To 9999.99
            Commission2 = Sales * Tier1
          Case 1000 To 19999.99
            Commission2 = Sales * Tier2
          Case 20000 To 39999.99
            Commission2 = Sales * Tier3
          Case Is >= 40000
            Commission2 = Sales * Tier4
      End Select
      Commission2 = Commission2 + (Commission2 * Years / 100)
End Function
```

The modification was quite simple. The second argument (`Years`) was added to the `Function` statement, and an additional computation was included that adjusts the commission before exiting the function.

The following is an example of how you write a formula by using this function. It assumes that the sales amount is in cell A1, and that the number of years that the salesperson has worked is in cell B1.

```
=Commission2(A1,B1)
```

A function with a range argument

The example in this section demonstrates how to use a worksheet range as an argument. Actually, it's not at all tricky; Excel takes care of the details behind the scenes.

Assume that you want to calculate the average of the five largest values in a range named `Data`. Excel doesn't have a function that can do this calculation, so you can write the following formula:

```
=(LARGE(Data,1)+LARGE(Data,2)+LARGE(Data,3)+
LARGE(Data,4)+LARGE(Data,5))/5
```

This formula uses Excel's `LARGE` function, which returns the *n*th largest value in a range. The preceding formula adds the five largest values in the range named `Data` and then divides the result by 5. The formula works fine, but it's rather unwieldy. And, what if you need to compute the average of the top *six* values? You'd need to rewrite the formula and make sure that all copies of the formula also get updated.

Wouldn't it be easier if Excel had a function named TopAvg? For example, you could use the following (nonexistent) function to compute the average:

    =TopAvg (Data,5)

This situation is an example of when a custom function can make things much easier for you. The following is a custom VBA function, named TopAvg, which returns the average of the top *n* values in a range:

```
Function TopAvg(Data, Num)
' Returns the average of the highest Num values in Data
  Sum = 0
  For i = 1 To Num
    Sum = Sum + WorksheetFunction.Large(Data, i)
  Next i
  TopAvg = Sum / Num
End Function
```

This function takes two arguments: Data (which represents a range in a worksheet) and Num (the number of values to average). The code starts by initializing the Sum variable to 0. It then uses a For-Next loop to calculate the sum of the *n*th largest values in the range. (Note that Excel's LARGE function is used within the loop.) You can use an Excel worksheet function in VBA if you precede the function with WorksheetFunction and a dot. Finally, TopAvg is assigned the value of Sum divided by Num.

You can use all of Excel's worksheet functions in your VBA procedures *except* those that have equivalents in VBA. For example, VBA has a Rnd function that returns a random number. Therefore, you can't use Excel's RAND function in a VBA procedure.

Debugging Custom Functions

Debugging a Function procedure can be a bit more challenging than debugging a Sub procedure. If you develop a function to use in worksheet formulas, an error in the Function procedure simply results in an error display in the formula cell (usually #VALUE!). In other words, you don't receive the normal run-time error message that helps you to locate the offending statement.

When you're debugging a worksheet formula, using only one instance of the function in your worksheet is the best technique. The following are three methods that you may want to use in your debugging:

- **Place MsgBox functions at strategic locations to monitor the value of specific variables.** Fortunately, message boxes in function procedures pop up when the procedure is executed. But make sure that you have only one formula in the worksheet that uses your function; otherwise, the message boxes appear for each formula that's evaluated.

- **Test the procedure by calling it from a Sub procedure.** Run-time errors display normally, and you can either fix the problem (if you know what it is) or jump right into the debugger.

- **Set a breakpoint in the function and then use Excel's debugger to step through the function.** Press F9, and the statement at the cursor becomes a breakpoint. The code will stop executing, and you can step through the code line-by-line (by pressing F8). Consult the Help system for more information about using VBA's debugging tools.

Inserting Custom Functions

Excel's Insert Function dialog box is a handy tool that enables you to choose a worksheet function; you even can choose one of your custom worksheet functions. After you select a function, the Function Arguments dialog box prompts you for the function's arguments.

> **NOTE** Function procedures that are defined with the `Private` keyword do not appear in the Insert Function dialog box. So if you create a function that will be used only by other VBA procedures, you should declare the function using the `Private` keyword.

You also can display a description of your custom function in the Insert Function dialog box. To do so, follow these steps:

1. **Create the function in a module by using the VB Editor.**
2. **Activate Excel.**
3. **Choose Developer ➪ Code ➪ Macros.**
   Excel displays its Macro dialog box.
4. **In the Macro dialog box, type the name of the function in the box labeled Macro Name.** Notice that functions don't normally appear in this dialog box, so you must enter the function name yourself.
5. **Click the Options button.** Excel displays its Macro Options dialog box. (See Figure 40.3.)
6. **Enter a description of the function and then click OK.** The Shortcut key field is irrelevant for functions.

The description that you enter appears in the Insert Function dialog box.

FIGURE 40.3

Entering a description for a custom function. This description appears in the Insert Function dialog box.

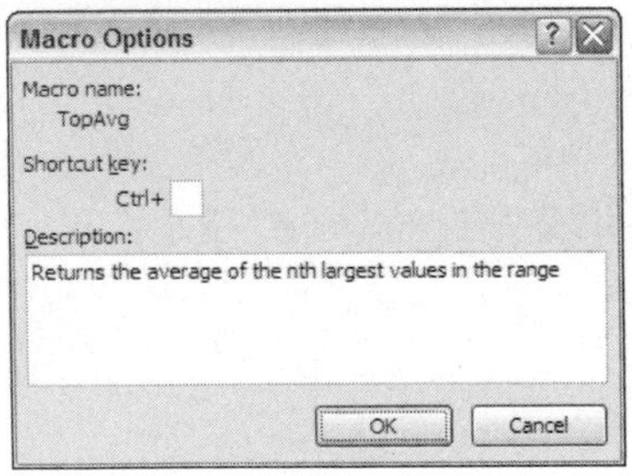

Custom functions are listed under the User Defined category.

Figure 40.4 shows the Function Arguments dialog box, which prompts the user to enter arguments for a custom function.

FIGURE 40.4

Using the Function Arguments dialog box to insert a custom function.

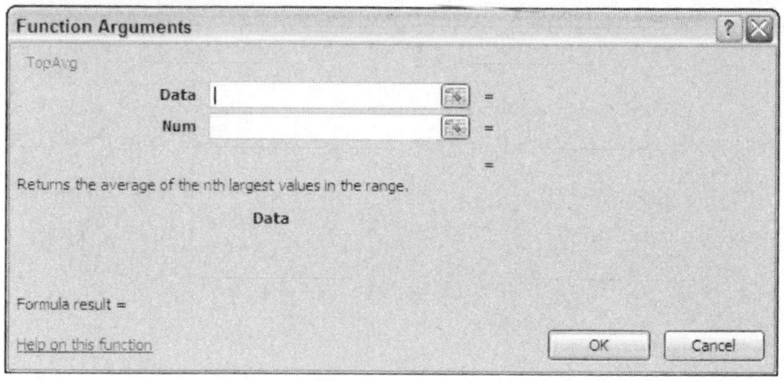

When you access a *built-in* function from the Insert Function dialog box, the Function Arguments dialog box displays a description of each argument. Unfortunately, you can't provide such descriptions for custom functions.

Learning More

The information in this chapter only scratches the surface when it comes to creating custom functions. It should be enough to get you started, however, if you're interested in this topic. Refer to Chapter 44 for more examples of useful VBA functions. You may be able to use the examples directly or adapt them for your needs.

Chapter 41

Creating UserForms

Y ou can't use Excel very long without being exposed to dialog boxes. Excel, like most Windows programs, uses dialog boxes to obtain information, clarify commands, and display messages. If you develop VBA macros, you can create your own dialog boxes that work very much like those that are built into Excel. These dialog boxes are known as UserForms.

Why Create UserForms?

Some macros that you create behave exactly the same every time that you execute them. For example, you may develop a macro that enters a list of your sales regions into a worksheet range. This macro always produces the same result and requires no additional user input. You may develop other macros, however, that perform differently under different circumstances or that offer options for the user. In such cases, the macro may benefit from a custom dialog box.

The following is an example of a simple macro that makes each cell in the selected range uppercase (but it skips cells that have a formula). The procedure uses VBA's built-in StrConv function.

```
Sub ChangeCase()
  For Each cell In Selection
    If Not cell.HasFormula Then
      cell.Value = StrConv(cell.Value, vbUpperCase)
    End If
  Next cell
End Sub
```

This macro is useful, but it can be improved. For example, the macro would be more helpful if it could also change the cells to *lowercase* or *proper case* (only the first letter of each word is uppercase). This modification is not difficult to make, but if you make this change to the macro, you need some method of asking the user what type of change to make to the cells. The solution is to present a dialog box like the one shown in Figure 41.1. This dialog box is a UserForm that was created by using the Visual Basic Editor, and it is displayed by a VBA macro.

FIGURE 41.1

A UserForm that asks the user for an option.

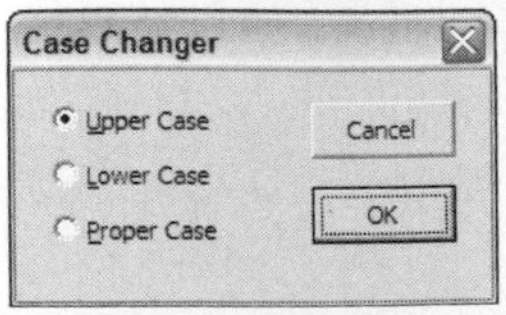

Another solution is to develop three macros, one for each type of text case change. Combining these three operations into a single macro and using a UserForm is a more efficient approach, however. I discuss this example, including how to create the UserForm, in "Another UserForm Example," later in the chapter.

UserForm Alternatives

Once you get the hang of it, developing UserForms isn't difficult. But sometimes using the tools that are built into VBA is easier. For example, VBA includes two functions (InputBox and MsgBox) that enable you to display simple dialog boxes without having to create a UserForm in the VB Editor. You can customize these dialog boxes in some ways, but they certainly don't offer the number of options that are available in a UserForm.

The InputBox function

The InputBox function is useful for obtaining a single input from the user. A simplified version of the function's syntax follows:

```
InputBox(prompt[,title][,default])
```

The elements are defined as follows:

- prompt: Text that is displayed in the input box. (Required)
- title: Text that appears in the input box's title bar. (Optional)
- default: The default value. (Optional)

The following is an example of how you can use the InputBox function:

```
CName = InputBox("Customer name?","Customer Data")
```

When this VBA statement is executed, Excel displays the dialog box shown in Figure 41.2. Notice that this example uses only the first two arguments for the InputBox function and does not supply a default value. When the user enters a value and clicks OK, the value is assigned to the variable CName. Your VBA code can then use that variable.

FIGURE 41.2

This dialog box is displayed by VBA's `InputBox` function.

The MsgBox function

VBA's `MsgBox` function is a handy way to display information and to solicit simple input from users. I use VBA's `MsgBox` function in many of this book's examples to display a variable's value. A simplified version of the `MsgBox` syntax is as follows:

```
MsgBox(prompt[,buttons][,title])
```

The elements are defined as follows:

- `prompt`: Text that is displayed in the message box. (Required)
- `buttons`: The code for the buttons that are to appear in the message box. (Optional)
- `title`: Text that appears in the message box's title bar. (Optional)

You can use the `MsgBox` function by itself or assign its result to a variable. If you use it by itself, don't include parentheses around the arguments. The following example displays a message and does not return a result:

```
Sub MsgBoxDemo()
    MsgBox "Click OK to continue"
End Sub
```

Figure 41.3 shows how this message box appears.

FIGURE 41.3

A simple message box, displayed with VBA's `MsgBox` function.

To get a response from a message box, you can assign the result of the MsgBox function to a variable. The following code uses some built-in constants (described in the "Constants That Are Used in the MsgBox Function" sidebar) to make it easier to work with the values that are returned by MsgBox:

```
Sub GetAnswer()
  Ans = MsgBox("Continue?", vbYesNo)
  Select Case Ans
   Case vbYes
' ...[code if Ans is Yes]...
   Case vbNo
' ...[code if Ans is No]...
  End Select
End Sub
```

When this procedure is executed, the Ans variable contains a value that corresponds to vbYes or vbNo. The Select Case statement determines the action to take based on the value of Ans.

You can easily customize your message boxes because of the flexibility of the button argument. Table 41.1 lists the built-in constants that you can use for the button argument. You can specify which buttons to display, whether an icon appears, and which button is the default.

TABLE 41.1

Constants That Are Used in the MsgBox Function

Constant	Value	Description
vbOKOnly	0	Display OK button.
vbOKCancel	1	Display OK and Cancel buttons.
vbAbortRetryIgnore	2	Display Abort, Retry, and Ignore buttons.
vbYesNoCancel	3	Display Yes, No, and Cancel buttons.
vbYesNo	4	Display Yes and No buttons.
vbRetryCancel	5	Display Retry and Cancel buttons.
vbCritical	16	Display Critical Message icon.
vbQuestion	32	Display Warning Query icon.
VBExclamation	48	Display Warning Message icon.
vbInformation	64	Display Information Message icon.
vbDefaultButton1	0	First button is default.
vbDefaultButton2	256	Second button is default.
vbDefaultButton3	512	Third button is default.

The following example uses a combination of constants to display a message box with a Yes button, a No button (vbYesNo), and a question mark icon (vbQuestion); the second button is designated as the default button (vbDefaultButton2) — which is the button that is executed if the user presses Enter. For simplicity, these constants are assigned to the Config variable, and Config is then used as the second argument in the MsgBox function.

```
Sub GetAnswer()
   Config = vbYesNo + vbQuestion + vbDefaultButton2
   Ans = MsgBox("Process the monthly report?", Config)
   If Ans = vbYes Then RunReport
   If Ans = vbNo Then Exit Sub
End Sub
```

Figure 41.4 shows how this message box appears when the GetAnswer Sub is executed. If the user clicks the Yes button (or presses Enter), the routine executes the procedure named RunReport (which is not shown). If the user clicks the No button, the procedure is ended with no action. Because the title argument was omitted in the MsgBox function, Excel uses the default title ("Microsoft Excel").

FIGURE 41.4

The second argument of the MsgBox function determines what appears in the message box.

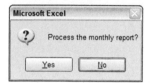

The Sub procedure that follows is another example of using the MsgBox function:

```
Sub GetAnswer2()
   Msg = "Do you want to process the monthly report?"
   Msg = Msg & vbNewLine & vbNewLine
   Msg = Msg & "Processing the monthly report will take approximately "
   Msg = Msg & "15 minutes. It will generate a 30-page report for all "
   Msg = Msg & "sales offices for the current month."
   Title = "XYZ Marketing Company"
   Config = vbYesNo + vbQuestion
   Ans = MsgBox(Msg, Config, Title)
   If Ans = vbYes Then RunReport
   If Ans = vbNo Then Exit Sub
End Sub
```

This example demonstrates an efficient way to specify a longer message in a message box. A variable (Msg) and the concatenation operator (&) are used to build the message in a series of statements. vbNewLine is a constant that represents a break character. (Using two line breaks inserts a blank line.) The title argument is also used to display a different title in the message box. Figure 41.5 shows how this message box appears when the procedure is executed.

A message box with a longer message and a title.

Creating UserForms: An Overview

The `InputBox` and `MsgBox` functions do just fine for many cases, but if you need to obtain more information, you need to create a UserForm.

Following is a list of the general steps that you typically take to create a UserForm:

1. **Determine exactly how the dialog box is going to be used and where it is to fit into your VBA macro.**
2. **Activate the VB Editor and insert a new UserForm.**
3. **Add the appropriate controls to the UserForm.**
4. **Create a VBA macro to display the UserForm.** This macro goes in a normal VBA module.
5. **Create event handler VBA procedures that are executed when the user manipulates the controls (for example, clicks the OK button).** These procedures go in the code module for the UserForm.

The following sections provide more details on creating a UserForm.

Working with UserForms

To create a dialog box, you must first insert a new UserForm in the VB Editor window. To activate the VB Editor, choose Developer ➪ Visual Basic (or press Alt+F11). Make sure that the correct workbook is selected in the Project window and then choose Insert ➪ UserForm. The VB Editor displays an empty UserForm, shown in Figure 41.6. When you activate a UserForm, the VB editor displays the Toolbox, which is used to add controls to the UserForm.

FIGURE 41.6

An empty UserForm.

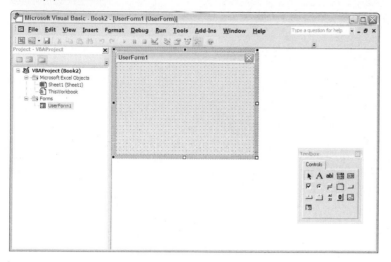

Adding controls

The Toolbox, also shown in Figure 41.6, contains various ActiveX controls that you can add to your UserForm.

When you move the mouse pointer over a control in the Toolbox, the control's name appears. To add a control, click and drag it in the form. After adding a control, you can move it or change its size.

Table 41.2 lists the Toolbox controls.

TABLE 41.2

Toolbox Controls

Control	Description
Select Objects	Lets you select other controls by dragging.
Label	Adds a label (a container for text).
TextBox	Adds a text box (allows the user to type text).
ComboBox	Adds a combo box (a drop-down list).
ListBox	Adds a list box (to allow the user to select an item from a list).
CheckBox	Adds a check box (to control Boolean options).

continued

TABLE 41.2 *(continued)*

Control	Description
OptionButton	Adds an option button (to allow a user to select from multiple options).
ToggleButton	Adds a toggle button (to control Boolean options).
Frame	Adds a frame (a container for other objects).
CommandButton	Adds a command button (a clickable button).
TabStrip	Adds a tab strip (a container for other objects).
MultiPage	Adds a multipage control (a container for other objects).
ScrollBar	Adds a scroll bar (to specify a value by dragging a bar).
SpinButton	Adds a spin button (to specify a value by clicking up or down).
Image	Adds a control that can contain an image.
RefEdit	Adds a reference edit control (lets the user select a range).

CROSS-REF   You can also place some of these controls directly on your worksheet. Refer to Chapter 42 for details.

Changing the properties of a control

Every control that you add to a UserForm has several properties that determine how the control looks and behaves. You can change some of these properties (such as Height and Width) by clicking and dragging the control's border. To change other properties, use the Properties window.

To display the Properties window, choose View ⇨ Properties Window (or press F4). The Properties window displays a list of properties for the selected control. (Each control has a different set of properties.) If you click the UserForm itself, the Properties window displays properties for the form. Figure 41.7 shows the Properties window for a CommandButton control.

To change a property, select the property in the Property window and then enter a new value. Some properties (such as BackColor) enable you to select a property from a list. The top of the Properties window contains a drop-down list that enables you to select a control to work with. You can also click a control to select it and display its properties.

The Properties window for a `CommandButton` control.

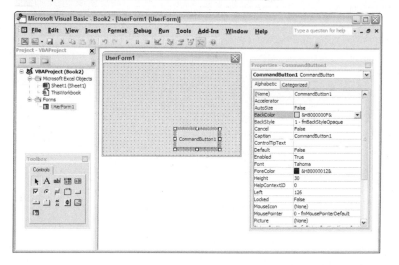

When you set properties by using the Property window, you're setting properties at *design time*. You can also use VBA to change the properties of controls while the UserForm is displayed (that is, at *run time*).

A complete discussion of all the properties is well beyond the scope of this book — and it would indeed be very dull reading. To find out about a particular property, select it in the Property window and press F1. The Help for UserForm controls is extremely thorough.

Handling events

When you insert a UserForm, that form can also hold VBA Sub procedures to handle the events that are generated by the UserForm. An *event* is something that occurs when the user manipulates a control. For example, clicking a button causes an event. Selecting an item in a list box control also triggers an event. To make a UserForm useful, you must write VBA code to do something when an event occurs.

Event-handler procedures have names that combine the control with the event. The general form is the control's name, followed by an underscore, and then the event name. For example, the procedure that is executed when the user clicks a button named MyButton is `MyButton_Click`.

Displaying a UserForm

You also need to write a procedure to display the UserForm. You use the Show method of the UserForm object. The following procedure displays the UserForm named UserForm1:

```
Sub ShowDialog()
    UserForm1.Show
End Sub
```

This procedure should be stored in a regular VBA module (not the code module for the UserForm). If your VB project doesn't have a normal VBA module, choose Insert ➪ Module to add one.

When the ShowDialog procedure is executed, the UserForm is displayed. What happens next depends on the event-handler procedures that you create.

A UserForm Example

The preceding section is, admittedly, rudimentary. This section demonstrates how to develop a UserForm. This example is rather simple. The UserForm displays a message to the user — something that can be accomplished more easily by using the MsgBox function. However, a UserForm gives you a lot more flexibility in terms of formatting and layout of the message.

ON the CD-ROM This workbook is available on the companion CD-ROM. The file is named show message.xlsm.

Creating the UserForm

If you're following along on your computer, start with a new workbook. Then follow these steps:

1. **Choose Developer ➪ Visual Basic (or press Alt+F11) to activate the VB Editor window.**

2. **In the VB Editor Project window, double-click your workbook's name to activate it.**

3. **Choose Insert ➪ UserForm.** The VB Editor adds an empty form named UserForm1 and displays the Toolbox.

4. **Press F4 to display the Properties window and then change the following properties of the UserForm object:**

Property	Change To
Name	AboutBox
Caption	About This Workbook

5. **Use the Toolbox to add a Label object to the UserForm.**

6. **Select the Label object. In the Properties window, enter any text that you want for the label's Caption.**

7. **In the Properties window, click the Font property and adjust the font.** You can change the typeface, size, and so on. The changes then appear in the form. Figure 41.8 shows an example of a formatted Label control.

8. Add a `CommandButton` object to the UserForm and change the following properties for the CommandButton:

Property	Change To
Name	OKButton
Caption	OK
Default	True

9. **Make other adjustments so that the form looks good to you.** You can change the size of the form or move or resize the controls.

A `Label` control, after changing its `Font` properties.

Testing the UserForm

At this point, the UserForm has all the necessary controls. But what's missing is a way to display the UserForm. While you're developing the UserForm, you can press F5 to display it and see how it looks.

This section explains how to write a VBA Sub procedure to display the UserForm when Excel is active.

1. **Insert a VBA module by choosing Insert ➪ Module.**

2. **In the empty module, enter the following code:**

```
Sub ShowAboutBox()
  AboutBox.Show
End Sub
```

3. **Activate Excel (Alt+F11 is one way).**

4. **Choose Developer ➪ Code ➪ Macros to display the Macros dialog box.** Or you can press Alt+F8 or click the Play Macro button in the status bar.

5. **In the Macros dialog box, select ShowAboutBox from the list of macros and click Run.** The UserForm then appears.

If you click the OK button, notice that it doesn't close the UserForm as you may expect. This button needs to have an event-handler procedure in order for it to do anything when it's clicked. To dismiss the UserForm, click the close button in its title box.

CROSS-REF You may prefer to display the UserForm by clicking a CommandButton on your worksheet. See Chapter 42 for details on attaching a macro to a Worksheet CommandButton.

Creating an event-handler procedure

An event-handler procedure is executed when an event occurs. In this case, you need a procedure to handle the Click event that's generated when the user clicks the OK button.

1. **Activate the VB Editor.** (Pressing Alt+F11 is the fastest way.)

2. **Activate the AboutBox UserForm by double-clicking its name in the Project window.**

3. **Double-click the CommandButton control.** The VB Editor activates the code module for the UserForm and inserts some boilerplate code, as shown in Figure 41.9.

4. **Insert the following statement before the End Sub statement:**

   Unload AboutBox

FIGURE 41.9

The code module for the UserForm.

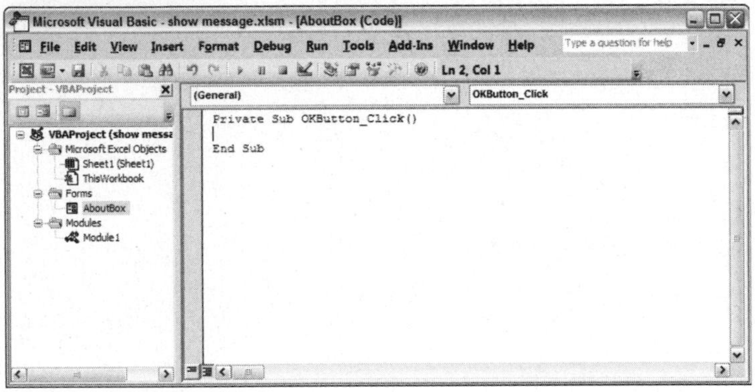

This statement simply dismisses the UserForm. The complete event-handler procedure is

```
Private Sub OKButton_Click()
 Unload AboutBox
End Sub
```

Another UserForm Example

The example in this section is an enhanced version of the ChangeCase procedure presented at the beginning of the chapter. Recall that the original version of this macro changes the text in the selected cells to uppercase characters. This modified version asks the user what type of case change to make: uppercase, lowercase, or proper case (initial capitals).

This workbook is available on the companion CD-ROM. The file is change case.xlsm.

Creating the UserForm

This UserForm needs one piece of information from the user: the type of change to make to the text. Because only one option can be selected, `OptionButton` controls are appropriate. Start with an empty workbook and follow these steps to create the UserForm:

1. **Press Alt+F11 to activate the VB Editor window.**

2. **In the VB Editor, choose Insert ⇨ UserForm.** The VB Editor adds an empty form named `UserForm1` and displays the Toolbox.

3. **Press F4 to display the Properties window and then change the following property of the `UserForm` object:**

Property	Change To
Caption	Case Changer

4. **Add a `CommandButton` object to the UserForm and then change the following properties for the CommandButton:**

Property	Change To
Name	OKButton
Caption	OK
Default	True

5. **Add another `CommandButton` object and then change the following properties:**

Property	Change To
Name	CancelButton
Caption	Cancel
Cancel	True

6. **Add an `OptionButton` control and then change the following properties.** (This option is the default, so its `Value` property should be set to `True`.)

Property	Change To
Name	OptionUpper
Caption	Upper Case
Value	True

7. **Add a second `OptionButton` control and then change the following properties:**

Property	Change To
Name	OptionLower
Caption	Lower Case

8. **Add a third `OptionButton` control and then change the following properties:**

Property	Change To
Name	OptionProper
Caption	Proper Case

9. **Adjust the size and position of the controls and the form until your UserForm resembles the UserForm shown in Figure 41.10.** Make sure that the controls do not overlap.

FIGURE 41.10

The UserForm after adding controls and adjusting some properties.

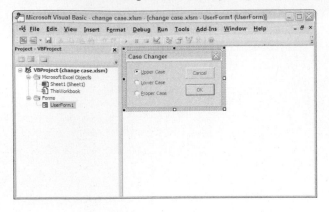

> **TIP** The VB Editor provides several useful commands to help you size and align the controls. Select the controls that you want to work with and then choose a command from the Format menu. These commands are fairly self-explanatory, and the Help system has complete details.

Testing the UserForm

At this point, the UserForm has all the necessary controls. What's missing is a way to display the form. This section explains how to write a VBA procedure to display the UserForm.

1. **Make sure that the VB Editor window is activated.**

2. **Insert a module by choosing Insert ⇨ Module.**

3. **In the empty module, enter the following code:**

```
Sub ShowUserForm()
 UserForm1.Show
End Sub
```

4. **Choose Run ⇨ Sub/UserForm (or press F5).**

The Excel window is then activated, and the new UserForm is displayed, as shown in Figure 41.11. The `OptionButton` controls work, but clicking the OK and Cancel buttons has no effect. These two buttons need to have event-handler procedures. Click the Close button in the title bar to dismiss the UserForm.

FIGURE 41.11

Displaying the UserForm.

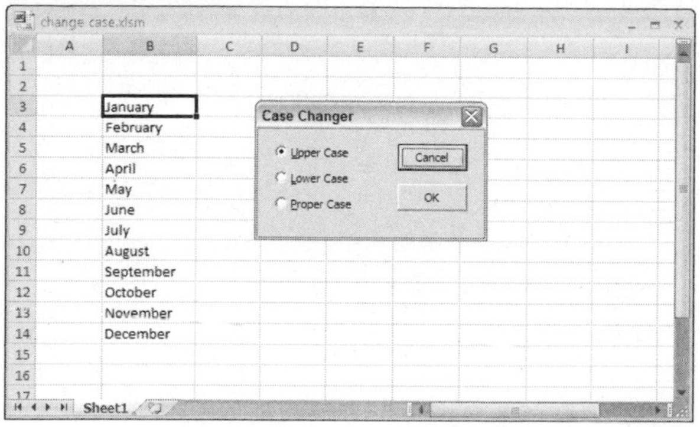

Creating event-handler procedures

This section explains how to create two event-handler procedures: one to handle the `Click` event for the CancelButton `CommandButton` and the other to handle the `Click` event for the OKButton `CommandButton`. Event handlers for the `OptionButton` controls are not necessary. The VBA code can determine which of the three `OptionButton` controls is selected.

Event-handler procedures are stored in the UserForm code module. To create the procedure to handle the `Click` event for the CancelButton, follow these steps:

1. **Activate the UserForm1 form by double-clicking its name in the Project window.**
2. **Double-click the `CancelButton` control.** The VB Editor activates the code module for the UserForm and inserts an empty procedure.
3. **Insert the following statement before the `End Sub` statement:**

   ```
   Unload UserForm1
   ```

That's all there is to it. The following is a listing of the entire procedure that's attached to the `Click` event for the CancelButton:

```
Private Sub CancelButton_Click()
   Unload UserForm1
End Sub
```

This procedure is executed when the CancelButton is clicked. It consists of a single statement that unloads the UserForm1 form.

The next step is to add the code to handle the Click event for the OKButton control. Follow these steps:

1. **Select OKButton from the drop-down list at the top of the module.** The VB Editor begins a new procedure called OKButton_Click.

2. **Enter the following code.** (The first and last statements have already been entered for you by the VB Editor.)

```
Private Sub OKButton_Click()
    Application.ScreenUpdating = False
'   Exit if a range is not selected
    If TypeName(Selection) <> "Range" Then Exit Sub
'     Upper case
    If OptionUpper Then
        For Each cell In Selection
        If Not cell.HasFormula Then
            cell.Value = StrConv(cell.Value, vbUpperCase)
        End If
        Next cell
    End If
'   Lower case
    If OptionLower Then
        For Each cell In Selection
        If Not cell.HasFormula Then
            cell.Value = StrConv(cell.Value, vbLowerCase)
        End If
        Next cell
    End If
'   Proper case
    If OptionProper Then
        For Each cell In Selection
        If Not cell.HasFormula Then
            cell.Value = StrConv(cell.Value, bProperCase)
        End If
        Next cell
    End If
    Unload UserForm1
End Sub
```

The macro starts by turning off screen updating, which makes the macro run a bit faster. Next, the code checks the type of the selection. If a range is not selected, the procedure ends. The remainder of the procedure consists of three separate blocks. Only one block is executed, determined by which OptionButton is selected. The selected OptionButton has a value of True. Finally, the UserForm is unloaded (dismissed).

Testing the UserForm

To try out the UserForm from Excel, follow these steps:

1. **Activate Excel.**

2. **Enter some text into some cells.**

3. **Select the range with the text.**

4. **Choose Developer ⇨ Code ⇨ Macros (or press Alt+F8).**

5. In the Macros dialog box, select ShowUserForm from the list of macros and then click OK. The UserForm appears.

6. **Make your choice and click OK.**

Try it with a few more selections. Notice that if you click Cancel, the UserForm is dismissed, and no changes are made.

Making the macro available from a worksheet button

At this point, everything should be working properly. However, you have no quick and easy way to execute the macro. A good way to execute this macro would be from a button on the worksheet. You can use the following steps:

1. **Choose Developer ⇨ Controls ⇨ Insert and click the Button control in the Form Controls group.**

2. **Click and drag in the worksheet to create the button.**

3. **Excel display the Assign Macro dialog box.**

4. **In the Assign Macro dialog box, select ShowUserForm and click OK.**

   At this point, the button is still selected, so you can change the text to make it more descriptive. You can also right-click the button at any time to change the text.

After performing the preceding steps, clicking the button executes the macro and displays the UserForm.

CROSS-REF The button in this example is from the Form Controls group. Excel also provides a button in the ActiveX Controls group. See Chapter 42 for more information about the ActiveX Controls group.

Making the macro available on your Quick Access Toolbar

You can also add a button to your Quick Access Toolbar (QAT) that, when clicked, executes your macro. Unfortunately, the button works only when the workbook that contains the macro is active. To add a macro button to your QAT, use the following steps:

1. **Make sure that the workbook containing the macro is open.**

2. **Right-click anywhere in the Ribbon and then select Customize Quick Access Toolbar.** The Excel Options dialog box appears, with the Customization setting selected.

3. **Choose Macros from the drop-down menu on the left (labeled Choose Commands From).** You'll see your macro listed.

4. **Select the macro's name and click Add to adds the item to the list on the right.**

5. **If you'd like to change the icon, click Modify and choose a new image.** You can also change the Display Name.

6. **Click OK to close the Excel Options dialog box.** After performing these steps, your QAT will have a new icon.

More on Creating UserForms

Creating UserForms can make your macros much more versatile. You can create custom commands that display dialog boxes that look exactly like those that Excel uses. This section contains some additional information to help you develop custom dialog boxes that work like those that are built into Excel.

Adding accelerator keys

Custom dialog boxes should not discriminate against those who prefer to use the keyboard rather than a mouse. All of Excel's dialog boxes work equally well with a mouse and a keyboard because each control has an associated accelerator key. The user can press Alt plus the accelerator key to work with a specific dialog box control.

Adding accelerator keys to your UserForms is a good idea. You do this in the Properties window by entering a character for the `Accelerator` property.

The letter that you enter as the accelerator key must be a letter that is contained in the caption of the object. It can be any letter in the text (not necessarily the first letter). You should make sure that an accelerator key is not duplicated in a UserForm. If you have duplicate accelerator keys, the accelerator key acts on the first control in the tab order of the UserForm. Then, pressing the accelerator key again takes you to the next control.

Some controls (such as edit boxes) don't have a caption property. You can assign an accelerator key to a label that describes the control. Pressing the accelerator key then activates the next control in the tab order (which you should ensure is the edit box).

Controlling tab order

The previous section refers to a UserForm's *tab order*. When you're working with a UserForm, pressing Tab and Shift+Tab cycles through the dialog box's controls. When you create a UserForm, you should make sure that the tab order is correct. Usually, it means that tabbing should move through the controls in a logical sequence.

To view or change the tab order in a UserForm, choose View ➪ Tab Order to display the Tab Order dialog box. You can then select a control from the list; use the Move Up and Move Down buttons to change the tab order for the selected control.

Learning More

Mastering UserForms takes practice. You should closely examine the dialog boxes that Excel uses to get a feeling for how dialog boxes are designed. You can duplicate many of the dialog boxes that Excel uses.

The best way to learn more about creating dialog boxes is by using the VBA Help system.

Chapter 42

Using UserForm Controls in a Worksheet

C hapter 41 presented an introduction to UserForms. If you like the idea of using dialog box controls — but don't like the idea of creating a custom dialog box — this chapter is for you. It explains how to enhance your worksheet with a variety of interactive controls, such as buttons, ListBoxes, and OptionButtons.

Why Use Controls on a Worksheet?

The main reason to use controls on a worksheet is to make it easier for the user to provide input. For example, if you create a model that uses one or more input cells, you can create controls to allow the user to select values for the input cells.

Adding controls to a worksheet requires much less effort than creating a dialog box. In addition, you may not have to create any macros because you can link a control to a worksheet cell. For example, if you insert a CheckBox control on a worksheet, you can link it to a particular cell. When the CheckBox is checked, the linked cell displays TRUE. When the CheckBox is not checked, the linked cell displays FALSE.

Figure 42.1 shows a simple example that uses three types of controls: a Checkbox, OptionButtons, and a ScrollBar.

ON the CD-ROM This workbook is available on the companion CD-ROM. The file is named mortgage loan.xlsm.

FIGURE 42.1

This worksheet uses UserForm controls.

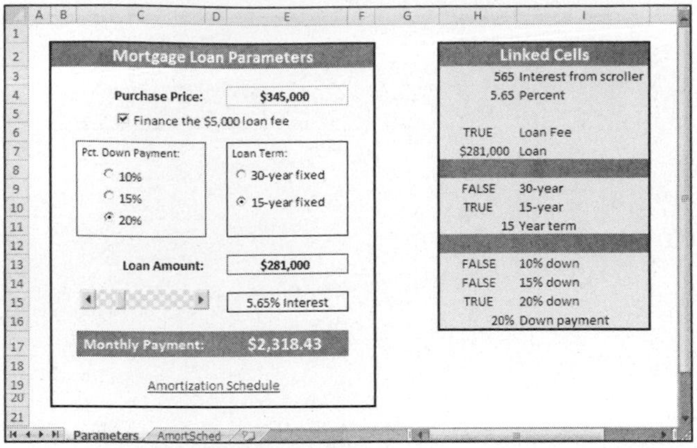

Adding controls to a worksheet can be a bit confusing because Excel offers two different sets of controls, both of which you access by choosing Developer ➪ Controls ➪ Insert.

- **Form controls:** These controls are unique to Excel.
- **ActiveX controls:** These controls are a subset of those that are available for use on UserForms.

Figure 42.2 shows the controls that appear when you choose Developer ➪ Controls ➪ Insert.

To add to the confusion, many controls are available from both sources. For example, a control named ListBox is listed in both the Forms controls and the ActiveX controls. However, they are two entirely different controls. In general, the Forms controls are easier to use, but the ActiveX controls provide more flexibility.

NOTE   This chapter focuses exclusively on the ActiveX controls.

FIGURE 42.2

Excel's two sets of worksheet controls.

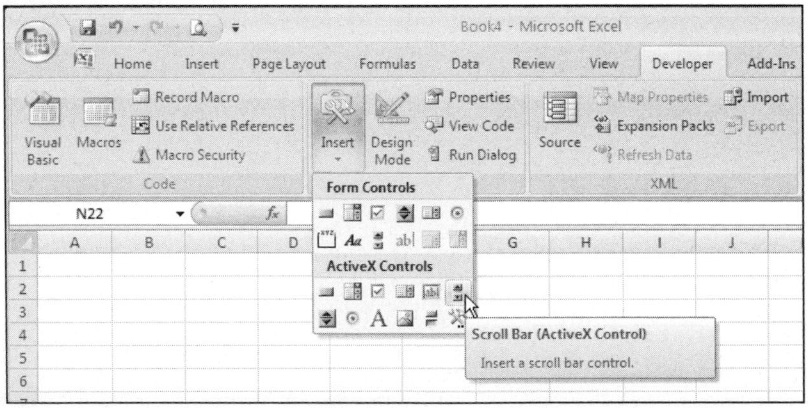

A description of the ActiveX controls appears in Table 42.1.

TABLE 42.1

ActiveX Controls

Button	What It Does
CommandButton	Inserts a `CommandButton` control (a clickable button)
ComboBox	Inserts a `ComboBox` control (a drop-down list)
CheckBox	Inserts a `CheckBox` control (to control Boolean options)
ListBox	Inserts a `ListBox` control (to allow the user to select an item from a list)
TextBox	Inserts a `TextBox` control (allows the user to type text)
ScrollBar	Inserts a `ScrollBar` control (to specify a value by dragging a bar)
SpinButton	Inserts a `SpinButton` control (to specify a value by clicking up or down)
OptionButton	Inserts an `OptionButton` control (to allow a user to select from multiple options)
Label	Inserts a `Label` control (a container for text)
Image	Inserts an `Image` control (to hold an image)
ToggleButton	Inserts a `ToggleButton` control (to control Boolean options)
More Controls	Displays a list of other ActiveX controls that are installed on your system

Using Controls

Adding ActiveX controls in a worksheet is easy. After you add a control, you can adjust its properties to modify the way that the control looks and works.

Adding a control

To add a control to a worksheet, choose Developer ➪ Controls and click the Insert drop-down control. Then, click and drag the control that you want to use into the worksheet to create the control. You don't need to be too concerned about the exact size or position because you can modify these properties at any time.

WARNING Make sure that you select a control from the ActiveX controls — not from the Forms controls. If you insert a Forms control, the instructions in this chapter will not apply.

About design mode

When you add a control to a worksheet, Excel goes into *design mode*. In this mode, you can adjust the properties of any controls on your worksheet, add or edit macros for the control, or change the control's size or position.

 When Excel is in design mode, the Design Mode icon in the Developer ➪ Controls section appears highlighted. You can click this icon to toggle design mode on and off.

When Excel is in design mode, the controls aren't activated. In order to test the controls, you must exit design mode by clicking the Design Mode icon. When you're working with controls, you'll probably need to need to switch in and out of design mode frequently.

Adjusting properties

Every control that you add has various properties that determine how it looks and behaves. You can adjust these properties only when Excel is in design mode. When you add a control to a worksheet, Excel enters design mode automatically. If you need to change a control after you exit design mode, simply click the Design Mode icon in the Controls section of the Developer tab.

To change the properties for a control:

1. **Make sure that Excel is in design mode**
2. **Click the control to select it**
3. **If the Properties window is not visible, click the Properties icon in the Controls section of the Developer tab.**

   The Properties window appears, as shown in Figure 42.3.
4. **Select the property and make the change.**

The manner in which you change a property depends on the property. Some properties display a drop-down list that enables you to select from a list of options. Others (such as Font) provide a button that, when clicked, displays a dialog box. Other properties require you to type the property value. When you change a property, the change takes effect immediately.

TIP To find out about a particular property, select the property in the Properties window and press F1.

The Properties window has two tabs. The Alphabetic tab displays the properties in alphabetical order. The Categorized tab displays the properties by category. Both tabs show the same properties; only the order is different.

FIGURE 42.3

The Properties window lets you adjust the properties of a control.

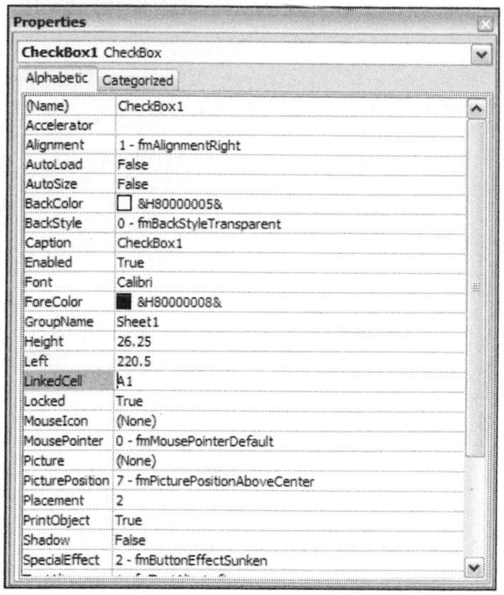

Common properties

Each control has its own unique set of properties. However, many controls share properties. This section describes some properties that are common to all or many controls, as set forth in Table 42.2.

NOTE Some ActiveX control properties are required (for example, the Name property). In other words, you can't leave the property empty. Excel will always tell you if a required property is missing, by displaying an error message.

TABLE 42.2

Properties Shared by Multiple Controls

Property	Description
AutoSize	If True, the control resizes itself automatically, based on the text in its caption.
BackColor	The background color of the control.
BackStyle	The style of the background (either transparent or opaque).
Caption	The text that appears on the control.
LinkedCell	A worksheet cell that contains the current value of a control.
ListFillRange	A worksheet range that contains items displayed in a ListBox or ComboBox control.

continued

TABLE 44.2	*(continued)*
Property	**Description**
Value	The control's value.
Left and Top	Values that determine the control's position.
Width and Height	Values that determine the control's width and height.
Visible	If False, the control is hidden.
Name	The name of the control. By default, a control's name is based on the control type. You can change the name to any valid name. However, each control's name must be unique on the worksheet.
Picture	Enables you to specify a graphic image to display.

Linking controls to cells

Often, you can use ActiveX controls in a worksheet without using any macros. Many controls have a LinkedCell property, which specifies a worksheet cell that is "linked" to the control.

For example, you may add a SpinButton control and specify cell B1 as its LinkedCell property. After doing so, cell B1 contains the value of the SpinButton, and clicking the SpinButton changes the value in cell B1. You can, of course, use the value contained in the linked cell in your formulas.

> **NOTE** When specifying the LinkedCell property in the Properties window, you can't "point" to the linked cell. You must type the cell address. Also, cell and range names aren't allowed.

Creating macros for controls

To create a macro for a control, you must use the Visual Basic Editor (VB Editor). The macros are stored in the code module for the sheet that contains the control. For example, if you place a control on Sheet2, the VBA code for that control is stored in the Sheet2 code module. Each control can have a macro to handle any of its events. For example, a CommandButton control can have a macro for its Click event, its DblClick event, and various other events.

> **TIP** The easiest way to access the code module for a control is to double-click the control while in design mode. Excel displays the VB Editor and creates an empty procedure for the control's default event. For example, the default event for a CommandButton control is the Click event. Figure 42.4 shows the autogenerated code for a control named CheckBox1, located on Sheet1.

The control's name appears in the upper-left portion of the code window, and the event appears in the upper-right area. If you want to create a macro that executes when a different event occurs, select the event from the list in the upper-right area.

The following steps demonstrate how to insert a CommandButton and create a simple macro that displays a message when the button is clicked:

1. **Choose Developer ⇨ Controls and click the Insert drop-down control.**
2. **Click the CommandButton tool in the ActiveX Controls section.**
3. **Click and drag in the worksheet to create the button.** Excel automatically enters design mode.

FIGURE 42.4

Double-clicking a control in design mode activates the Visual Basic Editor and enters an empty event-handler procedure.

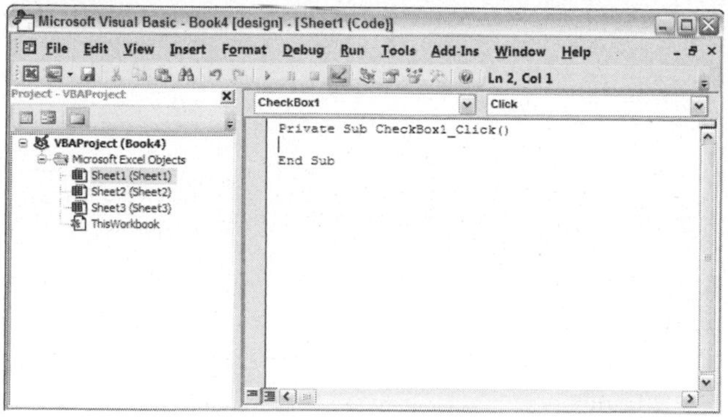

4. **Double-click the button.**

   The VB Editor window is activated, and an empty Sub procedure is created.

5. **Enter the following VBA statement before the** `End Sub` **statement:**

   `MsgBox "Hello. You clicked the command button."`

6. **Press Alt+F11 to return to Excel.**

7. **If you want, adjust any other properties for the CommandButton using the Properties window.** (Click Developer ➪ Controls ➪ Properties if the Properties window doesn't appear.)

8. **Click the Design Mode button in the Developer ➪ Controls section to exit design mode.**

After performing the preceding steps, click the `CommandButton` to display the message box.

> **NOTE**
> You must enter the VBA code manually. You can't create macros for controls using the VBA macro recorder.

Reviewing the Available ActiveX Controls

The sections that follow describe the ActiveX controls that are available for use in your worksheets.

> **ON the CD-ROM**
> The companion CD-ROM contains a file that includes examples of all the ActiveX controls. This file is named **worksheet controls.xlsm**.

CheckBox control

A `CheckBox` control is useful for getting a binary choice: `yes` or `no`, `true` or `false`, `on` or `off`, and so on.

The following is a description of the most useful properties of a `CheckBox` control:

- **Accelerator:** A letter that enables the user to change the value of the control by using the keyboard. For example, if the accelerator is A, pressing Alt+A changes the value of the `CheckBox` control. The accelerator letter is underlined in the Caption of the control.

- **LinkedCell:** The worksheet cell that's linked to the CheckBox. The cell displays `TRUE` if the control is checked or `FALSE` if the control is not checked.

ComboBox control

A `ComboBox` control is similar to a `ListBox` control. A ComboBox, however, is a drop-down box, and it displays only one item at a time. Another difference is that the user may be allowed to enter a value that does not appear in the list of items.

Figure 42.5 shows a `ComboBox` control that uses the range D1:D12 for the ListFillRange and cell A1 for the LinkedCell.

FIGURE 42.5

A `ComboBox` control.

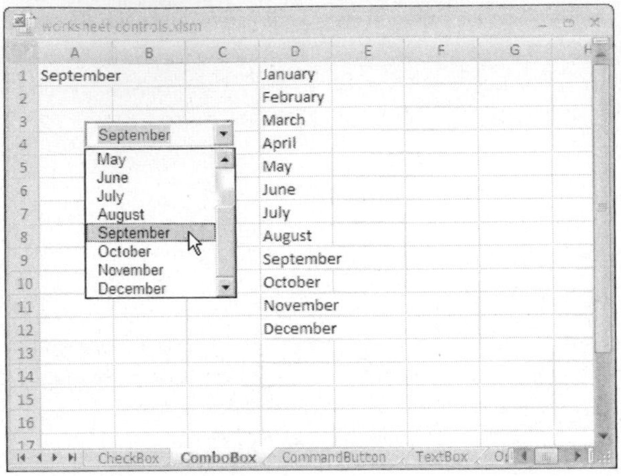

The following is a description of the most useful properties of a `ComboBox` control:

- **`BoundColumn`**: If the ListFillRange contains multiple columns, this property determines which column contains the returned value.
- **`ColumnCount`**: The number of columns in the list.
- **`LinkedCell`**: The worksheet cell that displays the selected item.
- **`ListFillRange`**: The worksheet range that contains the list items.
- **`ListRows`**: The number of items to display when the list drops down.
- **`ListStyle`**: Determines the appearance of the list items.
- **`Style`**: Determines whether the control acts like a drop-down list or a ComboBox. A drop-down list doesn't allow the user to enter a new value.

CommandButton control

A `CommandButton` is most commonly used to execute a macro. When a `CommandButton` is clicked, it executes a macro with a name that is made up of the `CommandButton`'s name, an underscore, and the word *Click*. For example, if a `CommandButton` is named `MyButton`, clicking it executes the macro named `MyButton_Click`. This macro is stored in the code module for the sheet that contains the CommandButton.

Image control

An Image control is used to display an image.

The following is a description of the most useful properties of an Image control:

- **AutoSize:** If True, the Image control is resized automatically to fit the image.
- **Picture:** The path to the image file. Click the button in the Properties window, and Excel displays a dialog box so you can locate the image.

> **TIP**
> Another way to display the image is to copy it to the Clipboard. Then, select the Picture property in the Properties window and press Ctrl+V. The advantage is that the image is stored with the workbook.

Label control

A Label control simply displays text. This control isn't a very useful for use on worksheets, and a TextBox control (described later in this list) gives you more versatility.

ListBox control

The ListBox control presents a list of items, and the user can select an item (or multiple items). It's similar to a ComboBox. The main difference is that a ListBox displays more than one item at a time.

The following is a description of the most useful properties of a ListBox control:

- **BoundColumn:** If the list contains multiple columns, this property determines which column contains the returned value.
- **ColumnCount:** The number of columns in the list.
- **IntegralHeight:** This is True if the height of the ListBox adjusts automatically to display full lines of text when the list is scrolled vertically. If False, the ListBox may display partial lines of text when it is scrolled vertically.
- **LinkedCell:** The worksheet cell that displays the selected item.
- **ListFillRange:** The worksheet range that contains the list items.
- **ListStyle:** Determines the appearance of the list items.
- **MultiSelect:** Determines whether the user can select multiple items from the list.

> **NOTE**
> If you use a MultiSelect ListBox, you can't specify a LinkedCell; you need to write a macro to determine which items are selected.

OptionButton control

OptionButton controls are useful when the user needs to select from a small number of items. OptionButtons are always used in groups of at least two.

The following is a description of the most useful properties of an OptionButton control:

- **Accelerator:** A letter that lets the user select the option by using the keyboard. For example, if the accelerator for an OptionButton is C, pressing Alt+C selects the control.
- **GroupName:** A name that identifies an OptionButton as being associated with other OptionButtons with the same GroupName property.
- **LinkedCell:** The worksheet cell that's linked to the OptionButton. The cell displays TRUE if the control is selected or FALSE if the control isn't selected.

> **NOTE** If your worksheet contains more than one set of OptionButton controls, you *must* ensure that each set of OptionButtons has a different GroupName property. Otherwise, all OptionButtons become part of the same set.

ScrollBar control

The ScrollBar control is useful for specifying a cell value. Figure 42.6 shows a worksheet with three ScrollBar controls. These ScrollBars are used to change the color in the rectangle shape. The value of the ScrollBars determines the red, green, or blue component of the rectangle's color. This example uses a few simple macros to change the colors.

FIGURE 42.6

This worksheet has several ScrollBar controls.

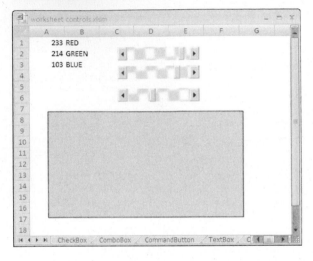

The following is a description of the most useful properties of a ScrollBar control:

- Value: The current value of the control.
- Min: The minimum value for the control.
- Max: The maximum value for the control.
- LinkedCell: The worksheet cell that displays the value of the control.
- SmallChange: The amount that the control's value is changed by a click.
- LargeChange: The amount that the control's value is changed by clicking either side of the button.

The ScrollBar control is most useful for selecting a value that extends across a wide range of possible values.

SpinButton control

The SpinButton control lets the user select a value by clicking the control, which has two arrows (one to increase the value and the other to decrease the value). A SpinButton can display either horizontally or vertically.

The following is a description of the most useful properties of a SpinButton control:

- Value: The current value of the control.
- Min: The minimum value of the control.
- Max: The maximum value of the control.
- LinkedCell: The worksheet cell that displays the value of the control.
- SmallChange: The amount that the control's value is changed by a click. Usually, this property is set to 1, but you can make it any value.

TextBox controls

On the surface, a TextBox control may not seem useful. After all, it simply contains text — you can usually use worksheet cells to get text input. In fact, TextBox controls are useful not so much for input control but for output control. Because a TextBox can have scroll bars, you can use a TextBox to display a great deal of information in a small area.

Figure 42.7 shows a TextBox control that contains Lincoln's Gettysburg Address. Notice the vertical scroll bar, displayed using the ScrollBars property.

FIGURE 42.7

A TextBox control with a vertical scroll bar.

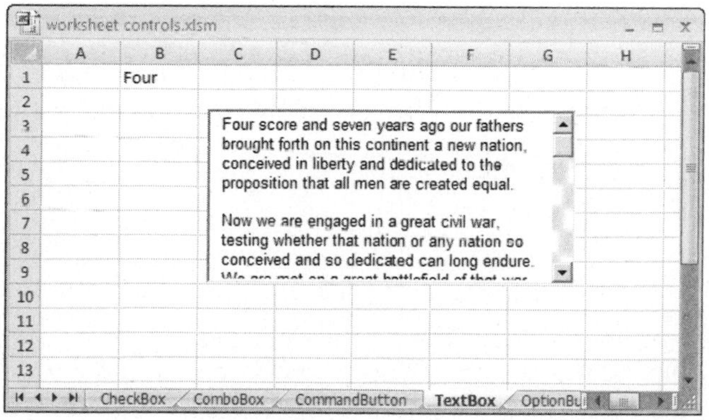

The following is a description of the most useful properties of a TextBox control:

- AutoSize: Determines whether the control adjusts its size automatically, based on the amount of text.
- IntegralHeight: If True, the height of the TextBox adjusts automatically to display full lines of text when the list is scrolled vertically. If False, the ListBox may display partial lines of text when it is scrolled vertically.

- **MaxLength**: The maximum number of characters allowed in the TextBox. If 0, no limit exists on the number of characters.
- **MultiLine**: If True, the TextBox can display more than one line of text.
- **TextAlign**: Determines how the text is aligned in the TextBox.
- **WordWrap**: Determines whether the control allows word wrap.
- **ScrollBars**: Determines the type of ScrollBars for the control: horizontal, vertical, both, or none.

ToggleButton control

A ToggleButton control has two states: on or off. Clicking the button toggles between these two states, and the button changes its appearance. Its value is either True (pressed) or False (not pressed). You can often use a ToggleButton in place of a CheckBox control.

Chapter 43

Working with Excel Events

I n the preceding chapters, you've seen some examples of VBA event-handler procedures. These procedures are the keys to making your Excel applications interactive. This chapter provides an introduction to the concept of Excel events and includes many examples that you can adapt to meet your own needs.

Understanding Events

Excel is capable of monitoring a wide variety of events and executing your VBA code when a particular event occurs. This chapter covers the following types of events.

- **Workbook events:** These occur for a particular workbook. Examples include Open (the workbook is opened or created), BeforeSave (the workbook is about to be saved), and NewSheet (a new sheet is added). VBA code for workbook events must be stored in the ThisWorkbook code module.

- **Worksheet events:** These occur for a particular worksheet. Examples include Change (a cell on the sheet is changed), SelectionChange (the cell pointer is moved), and Calculate (the worksheet is recalculated). VBA code for worksheet events must be stored in the code module for the worksheet (for example, the module named Sheet1).

- **Events not associated with objects:** The final category consists of two useful application-level events: OnTime and OnKey. These work differently from other events.

Entering event-handler VBA code

Every event-handler procedure must go into a specific type of code module. Code for workbook-level events goes into the ThisWorkbook code module. Code for worksheet-level events goes into the code module for the particular sheet (for example, the code module named Sheet1).

IN THIS CHAPTER

Understanding events

Using workbook-level events

Working with worksheet events

Using non-object events

In addition, every event-handler procedure has a predetermined name. You can declare the procedure by typing it, but a much better approach is to let the VB Editor do it for you. Figure 43.1 shows the code module for the `ThisWorkbook` object. To insert a procedure declaration, select `Workbook` from the objects list on the left. Then select the event from the procedures list on the right. When you do, you get a procedure "shell" that contains the procedure declaration line and an `End Sub` statement.

The best way to create an event procedure is to let the VBE do it for you.

For example, if you select `Workbook` from the objects list and `Open` from the procedures list, the VB Editor inserts the following (empty) procedure:

```
Private Sub Workbook_Open()

End Sub
```

Your event-handler VBA code goes between these two lines.

Some event-handler procedures contain an argument list. For example, you may need to create an event-handler procedure to monitor the `SheetActivate` event for a workbook. If you use the technique described in the previous section, the VB Editor creates the following procedure:

```
Private Sub Workbook_SheetActivate(ByVal Sh As Object)

End Sub
```

This procedure uses one argument (`Sh`), which represents the activated sheet. In this case, `Sh` is declared as an `Object` data type rather than a `Worksheet` data type because the activated sheet also can be a chart sheet.

Your code can, of course, make use of information passed as an argument. The following example displays the name of the activated sheet by accessing the argument's Name property. The argument becomes either a Worksheet object or a Chart object.

```
Private Sub Workbook_SheetActivate(ByVal Sh As Object)
    MsgBox Sh.Name & " was activated."
End Sub
```

Several event-handler procedures use a Boolean argument named Cancel. For example, the declaration for a workbook's BeforePrint event is

```
Private Sub Workbook_BeforePrint(Cancel As Boolean)
```

The value of Cancel passed to the procedure is False. However, your code can set Cancel to True, which cancels the printing. The following example demonstrates this:

```
Private Sub Workbook_BeforePrint(Cancel As Boolean)
    Msg = "Have you loaded the 5164 label stock? "
    Ans = MsgBox(Msg, vbYesNo, "About to print... ")
    If Ans = vbNo Then Cancel = True
End Sub
```

The Workbook_BeforePrint procedure executes before the workbook prints. This procedure displays a message box asking the user to verify that the correct label stock is loaded. If the user clicks the No button, Cancel is set to True, and nothing prints.

Using Workbook-Level Events

Workbook-level events occur for a particular workbook. Table 43.1 lists the most commonly used workbook events, along with a brief description of each. Keep in mind that workbook event-handler procedures must be stored in the code module for the ThisWorkbook object.

TABLE 43.1

Workbook Events

Event	Action That Triggers the Event
Activate	The workbook is activated.
AddinInstall	The workbook is installed as an add-in.
AddinUninstall	The workbook is uninstalled as an add-in.
BeforeClose	The workbook is about to be closed.
BeforePrint	The workbook (or anything in it) is about to be printed.
BeforeSave	The workbook is about to be saved.
Deactivate	The workbook is deactivated.
NewSheet	A new sheet is created in the workbook.

continued

TABLE 43.1   *(continued)*

Event	Action That Triggers the Event
Open	The workbook is opened.
SheetActivate	Any sheet in the workbook is activated.
SheetBeforeDoubleClick	Any worksheet in the workbook is double-clicked. This event occurs before the default double-click action.
SheetBeforeRightClick	Any worksheet in the workbook is right-clicked. This event occurs before the default right-click action.
SheetCalculate	Any worksheet in the workbook is calculated (or recalculated).
SheetChange	Any worksheet in the workbook is changed by the user.
SheetDeactivate	Any sheet in the workbook is deactivated.
SheetFollowHyperlink	Any hyperlink in the workbook is clicked.
SheetSelectionChange	The selection on any worksheet in the workbook is changed.
WindowActivate	Any window of the workbook is activated.
WindowDeactivate	Any workbook window is deactivated.
WindowResize	Any workbook window is resized.

The remainder of this section presents examples of using workbook-level events. All the example procedures that follow must be located in the code module for the ThisWorkbook object. If you put them into any other type of code module, they will not work.

Using the Open event

One of the most common monitored events is a workbook's Open event. This event is triggered when the workbook (or add-in) opens and executes the Workbook_Open procedure. A Workbook_Open procedure is very versatile and is often used for the following tasks:

- Displaying welcome messages.
- Opening other workbooks.
- Activating a specific sheet.
- Ensuring that certain conditions are met; for example, a workbook may require that a particular add-in is installed.

CAUTION Be aware that there is no guarantee that your Workbook_Open procedure will be executed. For example, the user may choose to disable macros. And if the user holds down the Shift key while opening a workbook, the workbook's Workbook_Open procedure will not execute.

The following is a simple example of a Workbook_Open procedure. It uses VBA's Weekday function to determine the day of the week. If it's Friday, a message box appears to remind the user to perform a file backup. If it's not Friday, nothing happens.

```
Private Sub Workbook_Open()
    If Weekday(Now) = 6 Then
        Msg = "Make sure you do your weekly backup!"
```

```
        MsgBox Msg, vbInformation
      End If
  End Sub
```

Unfortunately, VBA can't do much at all with Excel 2007's ribbon. For example, there is no direct way to activate a particular ribbon tab. The next example uses the `SendKeys` statement to simulate keystrokes. In this case, it sends Alt+H, which is the Excel 2007 "keytip" equivalent of activating the Home tab in the ribbon. Sending the F6 keystroke removes the keytip letters from the ribbon.

```
    Private Sub Workbook_Open()
        Application.SendKeys ("%h{F6}")
    End Sub
```

The following example performs a number of actions when the workbook is opened. It maximizes Excel's window, maximizes the workbook window, activates the sheet named DataEntry, and selects the first empty cell in column A. If a sheet named DataEntry does not exist, the code generates an error.

```
    Private Sub Workbook_Open()
        Application.WindowState = xlMaximized
        ActiveWindow.WindowState = xlMaximized
        Worksheets("DataEntry").Activate
        Range("A1").End(xlDown).offset(1,0).Select
    End Sub
```

Using the SheetActivate event

The following procedure executes whenever the user activates any sheet in the workbook. The code simply selects cell A1. Including the `On Error Resume Next` statement causes the procedure to ignore the error that occurs if the activated sheet is a chart sheet.

```
    Private Sub Workbook_SheetActivate(ByVal Sh As Object)
        On Error Resume Next
        Range("A1").Select
    End Sub
```

An alternative method to handle the case of a chart sheet is to check the sheet type. Use the Sh argument, which is passed to the procedure.

```
    Private Sub Workbook_SheetActivate(ByVal Sh As Object)
        If TypeName(Sh) = "Worksheet" Then Range("A1").Select
    End Sub
```

Using the NewSheet event

The following procedure executes whenever a new sheet is added to the workbook. The sheet is passed to the procedure as an argument. Because a new sheet can be either a worksheet or a chart sheet, this procedure determines the sheet type. If it's a worksheet, it inserts a date and time stamp in cell A1.

```
    Private Sub Workbook_NewSheet(ByVal Sh As Object)
      If TypeName(Sh) = "Worksheet" Then _
        Range("A1") = "Sheet added " & Now()
    End Sub
```

Using the BeforeSave event

The BeforeSave event occurs before the workbook is actually saved. As you know, choosing Office ⇨ Save sometimes brings up the Save As dialog box — for example, when the file has never been saved or was opened in read-only mode.

When the Workbook_BeforeSave procedure executes, it receives an argument that enables you to identify whether the Save As dialog box will appear. The following example demonstrates this:

```
Private Sub Workbook_BeforeSave _
  (ByVal SaveAsUI As Boolean, Cancel As Boolean)
    If SaveAsUI Then
        MsgBox "Use the new file-naming convention."
    End If
End Sub
```

When the user attempts to save the workbook, the Workbook_BeforeSave procedure executes. If the save operation brings up the Save As dialog box, the SaveAsUI variable is True. The preceding procedure checks this variable and displays a message only if the Save As dialog box is displayed. In this case, the message is a reminder about how to name the file.

The BeforeSave event procedure also has a Cancel variable in its argument list. If the procedure sets the Cancel argument to True, then the file is not saved.

Using the BeforeClose event

The BeforeClose event occurs before a workbook is closed. This event often is used in conjunction with a Workbook_Open event handler. For example, use the Workbook_Open procedure to initialize items in your workbook and use the Workbook_BeforeClose procedure to clean up or restore settings to normal before the workbook closes.

If you attempt to close a workbook that hasn't been saved, Excel displays a prompt that asks whether you want to save the workbook before it closes.

CAUTION **A problem can arise from this event. By the time the user sees this message, the** BeforeClose **event has already occurred. This means that the** Workbook_BeforeClose **procedure has already executed.**

Working with Worksheet Events

The events for a Worksheet object are some of the most useful. As you'll see, monitoring these events can make your applications perform feats that otherwise would be impossible.

Table 43.2 lists the worksheet events, with a brief description of each. Remember that these event procedures must be entered into the code module for the sheet. These code modules have default names like Sheet1, Sheet2, and so on.

TABLE 43.2

Worksheet Events

Event	Action That Triggers the Event
Activate	The worksheet is activated.
BeforeDoubleClick	The worksheet is double-clicked.
BeforeRightClick	The worksheet is right-clicked.
Calculate	The worksheet is calculated (or recalculated).
Change	Cells on the worksheet are changed by the user.
Deactivate	The worksheet is deactivated.
FollowHyperlink	A hyperlink on the worksheet is clicked.
PivotTableUpdate	A PivotTable on the worksheet has been updated.
SelectionChange	The selection on the worksheet is changed.

Using the Change event

The Change event is triggered when any cell in the worksheet is changed by the user. The Change event is not triggered when a calculation generates a different value for a formula or when an object (such as a chart or SmartArt) is added to the sheet.

When the Worksheet_Change procedure executes, it receives a Range object as its Target argument. This Range object corresponds to the changed cell or range that triggered the event. The following example displays a message box that shows the address of the Target range:

```
Private Sub Worksheet_Change(ByVal Target As Excel.Range)
    MsgBox "Range " & Target.Address & " was changed."
End Sub
```

To get a feel for the types of actions that generate the Change event for a worksheet, enter the preceding procedure into the code module for a Worksheet object. After entering this procedure, activate Excel and, using various techniques, make changes to the worksheet. Every time that the Change event occurs, a message box displays the address of the range that changed.

Unfortunately, the Change event doesn't always work as expected. For example:

- Changing the formatting of a cell does not trigger the Change event (as expected), but choosing Home ➪ Editing ➪ Clear ➪ Clear Formats *does*.
- Pressing Delete generates an event even if the cell is empty at the start.
- Cells changed via Excel commands may or may not trigger the Change event. For example, the following operations do not trigger the Change event: sorting and goal seeking. However, operations such as find and replace, using the AutoSum button, or adding a Totals row to a table *do* trigger the event.
- If your VBA procedure changes a cell, it *does* trigger the Change event.

Monitoring a specific range for changes

The Change event occurs when any cell on the worksheet changes. In most cases, you'll only be concerned with changes that are made to a specific cell or range. When the Worksheet_Change event-handler procedure is called, it receives a Range object as its argument. This Range object corresponds to the cell or cells that changed.

Assume that your worksheet has a range named InputRange, and you want to monitor changes to this range only. No Change event exists for a Range object, but you can perform a quick check within the Worksheet_Change procedure. The following procedure demonstrates this:

```
Private Sub Worksheet_Change(ByVal Target As Excel.Range)
    Dim VRange As Range
    Set VRange = Range("InputRange")
    If Union(Target, VRange).Address = VRange.Address Then
        Msgbox "The changed cell is in the input range."
    End if
End Sub
```

This example creates a Range object variable named VRange, which represents the worksheet range that you want to monitor for changes. The procedure uses VBA's Union function to determine whether VRange contains the Target range (passed to the procedure in its argument). The Union function returns an object that consists of all the cells in both of its arguments. If the range address is the same as the VRange address, Vrange contains Target, and a message box appears. Otherwise, the procedure ends, and nothing happens.

The preceding procedure has a flaw. Target may consist of a single cell or a range. For example, if the user changes more than one cell at a time, Target becomes a multicell range. Therefore, the procedure requires modification to loop through all the cells in Target. The following procedure checks each changed cell and displays a message box if the cell is within the desired range:

```
Private Sub Worksheet_Change(ByVal Target As Excel.Range)
    Set VRange = Range("InputRange")
    For Each cell In Target
      If Union(cell, VRange).Address = VRange.Address Then
          Msgbox "The changed cell is in the input range."
      End if
    Next cell
End Sub
```

ON the CD-ROM   A workbook with this example is available on the CD-ROM the file is named **monitor a range.xlsm.**

Using the SelectionChange event

The following procedure demonstrates the SelectionChange event. It executes whenever the user makes a new selection on the worksheet.

```
Private Sub Worksheet_SelectionChange(ByVal Target _
  As Excel.Range)
    Cells.Interior.ColorIndex = xlNone
    With ActiveCell
      .EntireRow.Interior.ColorIndex = 35
```

```
                    .EntireColumn.Interior.ColorIndex = 35
                End With
            End Sub
```

This procedure shades the row and column of an active cell, making it easy to identify. The first statement removes the background color of all cells. Next, the entire row and column of the active cell is shaded light yellow. Figure 43.2 shows the shading.

ON the CD-ROM A workbook with this example is available on the CD-ROM. The file is named selection change event.xlsm.

FIGURE 43.2

Moving the cell cursor causes the active cell's row and column to become shaded.

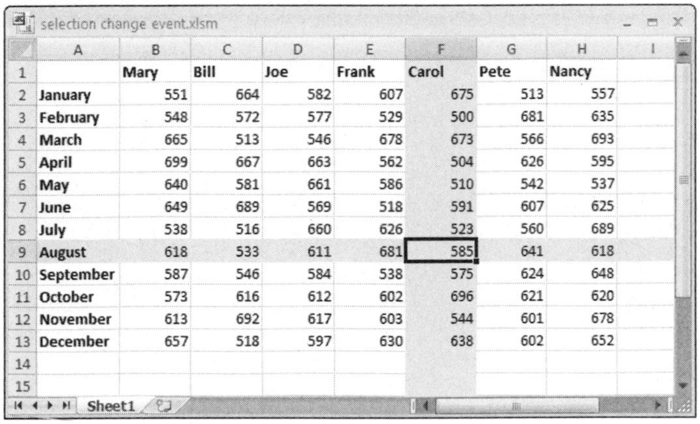

	A	B	C	D	E	F	G	H	I
1		Mary	Bill	Joe	Frank	Carol	Pete	Nancy	
2	January	551	664	582	607	675	513	557	
3	February	548	572	577	529	500	681	635	
4	March	665	513	546	678	673	566	693	
5	April	699	667	663	562	504	626	595	
6	May	640	581	661	586	510	542	537	
7	June	649	689	569	518	591	607	625	
8	July	538	516	660	626	523	560	689	
9	August	618	533	611	681	585	641	618	
10	September	587	546	584	538	575	624	648	
11	October	573	616	612	602	696	621	620	
12	November	613	692	617	603	544	601	678	
13	December	657	518	597	630	638	602	652	
14									
15									

Sheet1

CAUTION You won't want to use this procedure if your worksheet contains background shading because the macro will erase it.

Using the BeforeRightClick event

Normally, when the user right-clicks in a worksheet, a shortcut menu appears. If, for some reason, you want to prevent the shortcut menu from appearing, you can trap the RightClick event. The following procedure sets the Cancel argument to True, which cancels the RightClick event and, thus, the shortcut menu. Instead, a message box appears.

```
Private Sub Worksheet_BeforeRightClick _
  (ByVal Target As Excel.Range, Cancel As Boolean)
    Cancel = True
    MsgBox "The shortcut menu is not available."
End Sub
```

Using Non-Object Events

So far, the events discussed in this chapter are associated with an object (`Application`, `Workbook`, `Sheet`, and so on). This section discusses two additional events: `OnTime` and `OnKey`. These events are not associated with an object. Rather, you access them by using methods of the `Application` object.

> **NOTE**   Unlike the other events discussed in this chapter, you use a general VBA module to program the "On" events in this section.

Using the OnTime event

The `OnTime` event occurs at a specified time. The following example demonstrates how to program Excel to beep and then display a message at 3 p.m.:

```
Sub SetAlarm()
  Application.OnTime 0.625, "DisplayAlarm"
End Sub

Sub DisplayAlarm()
  Beep
  MsgBox "Wake up. It's time for your afternoon break!"
End Sub
```

In this example, the `SetAlarm` procedure uses the `OnTime` method of the `Application` object to set up the `OnTime` event. This method takes two arguments: the time (`0.625`, or 3 p.m., in the example) and the procedure to execute when the time occurs (`DisplayAlarm` in the example). In the example, after `SetAlarm` executes, the `DisplayAlarm` procedure is called at 3 p.m., bringing up the message.

Most people find it difficult to think of time in terms of Excel's time numbering system. Therefore, you may want to use VBA's `TimeValue` function to represent the time. `TimeValue` converts a string that looks like a time into a value that Excel can handle. The following statement shows an easier way to program an event for 3 p.m.:

```
Application.OnTime TimeValue("3:00:00 pm"), "DisplayAlarm"
```

If you want to schedule an event that's relative to the current time — for example, 20 minutes from now — you can write an instruction like this:

```
Application.OnTime Now + TimeValue("00:20:00"), "DisplayAlarm"
```

You also can use the `OnTime` method to schedule a procedure on a particular day. Of course, you must keep your computer turned on, and Excel must be running.

Using the OnKey event

While you work, Excel constantly monitors what you type. As a result, you can set up a keystroke or a key combination that — when pressed — executes a particular procedure.

The following example uses the `OnKey` method to set up an `OnKey` event. This event essentially reassigns the PgDn and PgUp keys. After the `Setup_OnKey` procedure executes, pressing PgDn executes the `PgDn_Sub` procedure, and pressing PgUp executes the `PgUp_Sub` procedure. The next effect is that pressing PgDn moves down one row, and pressing PgUp moves up one row.

```
Sub Setup_OnKey()
  Application.OnKey "{PgDn}", "PgDn_Sub"
  Application.OnKey "{PgUp}", "PgUp_Sub"
End Sub

Sub PgDn_Sub()
  On Error Resume Next
  ActiveCell.Offset(1, 0).Activate
End Sub

Sub PgUp_Sub()
  On Error Resume Next
  ActiveCell.Offset(-1, 0).Activate
End Sub
```

NOTE Notice that the key codes are enclosed in brackets, not parentheses. For a complete list of the keyboard codes, consult the VBA Help. Search for OnKey.

TIP The preceding examples used `On Error Resume Next` to ignore any errors generated. For example, if the active cell is in the first row, trying to move up one row causes an error. Furthermore, if the active sheet is a chart sheet, an error occurs because no such thing as an active cell exists in a chart sheet.

By executing the following procedure, you cancel the OnKey events, and the keys return to their normal functions.

```
Sub Cancel_OnKey()
    Application.OnKey "{PgDn}"
    Application.OnKey "{PgUp}"
End Sub
```

CAUTION Contrary to what you may expect, using an empty string as the second argument for the OnKey method does *not* cancel the OnKey event. Rather, it causes Excel to ignore the keystroke and do nothing. For example, the following instruction tells Excel to ignore Alt+F4 (the percent sign represents the Alt key):

```
Application.OnKey "%{F4}", ""
```

Chapter 44

VBA Examples

y philosophy about learning to write Excel macros places heavy emphasis on examples. I've found that a well-thought-out example often communicates a concept much better than a lengthy description of the underlying theory. In this book, space limitations don't allow describing every nuance of VBA, so I've prepared many examples. Don't overlook VBA's Help system for specific details. To get help while working in the VB Editor window, press F1 or type your search terms into the Type A Question For Help box in the menu bar.

This chapter consists of several examples that demonstrate common VBA techniques. You may be able to use some examples directly, but in most cases, you must adapt them to your own needs. These examples are organized into the following categories:

- Working with ranges
- Working with workbooks
- Working with charts
- Programming techniques to speed up your VBA code

Working with Ranges

Most of what you do in VBA probably involves worksheet ranges. When you work with range objects, keep the following points in mind:

- Your VBA code doesn't need to select a range to do something with the range.
- If your code does select a range, its worksheet must be active.
- The macro recorder doesn't always generate the most efficient code. Often, you can use the recorder to create your macro and then edit the code to make it more efficient.

■ I recommend that you use named ranges in your VBA code. For example, a reference such as Range ("Total") is better than Range ("D45"). In the latter case, you need to modify the macro if you add a row above row 45.

■ When you record macros that select ranges, pay close attention to relative versus absolute recording mode (see Chapter 39). The recording mode that you choose can drastically affect the way the macro operates.

■ If you create a macro that loops through each cell in the current range selection, be aware that the user can select entire columns or rows. For example, you may want to eliminate empty cells. In such a case, you need to create a subset of the selection that consists only of nonblank cells. Or, you can work with cells in the worksheet's used range (by using the UsedRange property).

■ Be aware that Excel allows you to select multiple ranges in a worksheet. For example, you can select a range, press Ctrl, and then select another range. You can test for this in your macro and take appropriate actions.

The examples in the following sections demonstrate these points.

Copying a range

Copying a range is a frequent activity in macros. When you turn on the macro recorder (using absolute recording mode) and copy a range from A1:A5 to B1:B5, you get a VBA macro like this:

```
Sub CopyRange()
  Range("A1:A5").Select
  Selection.Copy
  Range("B1").Select
  ActiveSheet.Paste
  Application.CutCopyMode = False
End Sub
```

This macro works, but it's not the most efficient way to copy a range. You can accomplish exactly the same result with the following one-line macro:

```
Sub CopyRange2()
  Range("A1:A5").Copy Range("B1")
End Sub
```

This code takes advantage of the fact that the Copy method can use an argument that specifies the destination. Useful information about properties and methods is available in the Help system.

The example demonstrates that the macro recorder doesn't always generate the most efficient code. As you see, you don't have to select an object to work with it. Note that CopyRange2 doesn't select a range; therefore, the active cell doesn't change when this macro is executed.

Copying a variable-size range

Often, you want to copy a range of cells in which the exact row and column dimensions are unknown.

Figure 44.1 shows a range on a worksheet. This range contains data that is updated weekly. Therefore, the number of rows changes. Because the exact range address is unknown at any given time, writing a macro to copy the range can be challenging.

FIGURE 44.1

This range can consist of any number of rows.

	A	B	C	D	E
1	Week Ending	Calls	Orders		
2	1/5/2007	452	89		
3	1/12/2007	546	102		
4	1/19/2007	587	132		
5	1/26/2007	443	65		
6	2/2/2007	609	156		
7	2/9/2007	592	92		
8	2/16/2007	487	95		
9	2/23/2007	601	105		
10	3/2/2007	515	133		
11	3/9/2007	540	122		
12					

Copying a variable-sized range

The macro that follows demonstrates how to copy this range from Sheet1 to Sheet2 (beginning at cell A1). It uses the `CurrentRegion` property, which returns a `Range` object that corresponds to the block of used cells surrounding a particular cell. This is equivalent to choosing Home ⇨ Editing ⇨ Find & Select ⇨ Go To, clicking the Special button, and then selecting the Current Region option.

```
Sub CopyCurrentRegion()
    Range("A1").CurrentRegion.Copy  Sheets("Sheet2").Range("A1")
End Sub
```

ON the CD-ROM   A workbook that contains this macro is available on the companion CD-ROM. The file is named range copy.xlsm.

Selecting to the end of a row or column

You probably are in the habit of using key combinations, such as pressing Ctrl+Shift+right-arrow key and Ctrl+Shift+down-arrow key, to select from the active cell to the end of a row or column. When you record these actions in Excel (using relative recording mode), you'll find that the resulting code works as you would expect it to.

The following VBA procedure selects the range that begins at the active cell and extends down to the last cell in the column (or to the first empty cell, whichever comes first). When the range is selected, you can do whatever you want with it — copy it, move it, format it, and so on.

```
Sub SelectDown()
    Range(ActiveCell, ActiveCell.End(xlDown)).Select
End Sub
```

Notice that the `Range` property has two arguments. These arguments represent the upper-left and lower-right cells in a range.

This example uses the `End` method of the `Range` object, which returns a `Range` object. The `End` method takes one argument, which can be any of the following constants: `xlUp`, `xlDown`, `xlToLeft`, or `xlToRight`.

Selecting a row or column

The macro that follows demonstrates how to select the column of the active cell. It uses the EntireColumn property, which returns a range that consists of a column.

```
Sub SelectColumn()
   ActiveCell.EntireColumn.Select
End Sub
```

As you may suspect, an EntireRow property also is available, which returns a range that consists of a row.

If you want to perform an operation on all cells in the selected column, you don't need to select the column. For example, when the following procedure is executed, all cells in the row that contains the active cell are made bold:

```
Sub MakeRowBold()
   ActiveCell.EntireRow.Font.Bold = True
End Sub
```

Moving a range

Moving a range consists of cutting it to the Clipboard and then pasting it to another area. If you record your actions while performing a move operation, the macro recorder generates code as follows:

```
Sub MoveRange()
   Range("A1:C6").Select
   Selection.Cut
   Range("A10").Select
   ActiveSheet.Paste
End Sub
```

As demonstrated with copying earlier in this chapter (see "Copying a range"), this method is not the most efficient way to move a range of cells. In fact, you can do it with a single VBA statement, as follows:

```
Sub MoveRange2()
   Range("A1:C6").Cut Range("A10")
End Sub
```

This statement takes advantage of the fact that the Cut method can use an argument that specifies the destination.

Looping through a range efficiently

Many macros perform an operation on each cell in a range, or they may perform selective actions based on the content of each cell. These operations usually involve a For-Next loop that processes each cell in the range.

The following example demonstrates how to loop through all the cells in a range. In this case, the range is the current selection. In this example, Cell is a variable name that refers to the cell being processed. (Notice that this variable is declared as a Range object.) Within the For-Next loop, the single statement evaluates the cell. If the cell is negative, it's converted to a positive value.

```
Sub ProcessCells()
  Dim Cell As Range
  For Each Cell In Selection
    If Cell.Value < 0 Then Cell.Value = Cell.Value * -1
  Next Cell
End Sub
```

The preceding example works, but what if the selection consists of an entire column or an entire range? This is not uncommon because Excel lets you perform operations on entire columns or rows. But in this case, the macro seems to take forever because it loops through each cell — even those that are blank. What's needed is a way to process only the nonblank cells.

You can accomplish this task by using the SelectSpecial method. In the following example, the SelectSpecial method is used to create a new object: the subset of the selection that consists of cells with constants (as opposed to formulas). This subset is processed, with the net effect of skipping all blank cells and all formula cells.

```
Sub ProcessCells2()
    Dim ConstantCells As Range
    Dim Cell As Range
'   Ignore errors
    On Error Resume Next

'   Process the constants
    Set ConstantCells = Selection.SpecialCells(xlConstants, xlNumbers)
    For Each Cell In ConstantCells
        If Cell.Value < 0 Then Cell.Value = Cell.Value * -1
    Next Cell
End Sub
```

The ProcessCells2 procedure works fast, regardless of what is selected. For example, you can select the range, select all columns in the range, select all rows in the range, or even select the entire worksheet. In all these cases, only the cells that contain constants are processed inside of the loop. This procedure is a vast improvement over the ProcessCells procedure presented earlier in this section.

Notice that the following statement is used in the procedure:

```
On Error Resume Next
```

This statement causes Excel to ignore any errors that occur and simply to process the next statement. This statement is necessary because the SpecialCells method produces an error if no cells qualify and because the numerical comparison will fail if a cell contains an error value. Normal error checking is resumed when the procedure ends. To tell Excel explicitly to return to normal error-checking mode, use the following statement:

```
On Error GoTo 0
```

761

This macro is available on the companion CD-ROM. The file is named **skip blanks while loop-ing.xlsm.**

Prompting for a cell value

As discussed in Chapter 41, you can take advantage of VBA's `InputBox` function to ask the user to enter a value. Figure 44.2 shows an example.

FIGURE 44.2

Using VBA's `InputBox` function to get a value from the user.

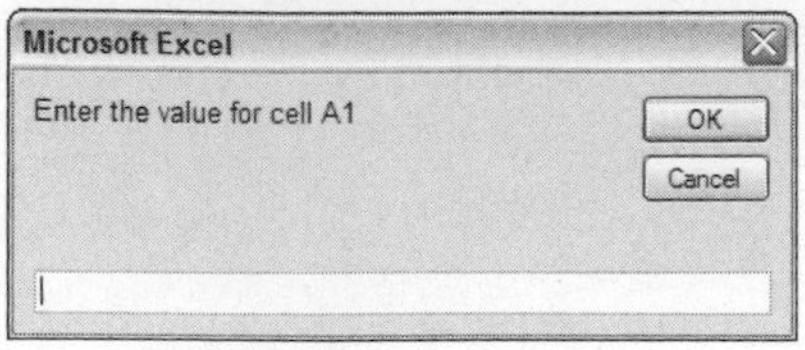

You can assign this value to a variable and use it in your procedure. Often, however, you want to place the value into a cell. The following procedure demonstrates how to ask the user for a value and place it into cell A1 of the active worksheet, using only one statement:

```
Sub GetValue()
    Range("A1").Value = InputBox("Enter the value for cell A1")
End Sub
```

Determining the type of selection

If your macro is designed to work with a range selection, you need to determine that a range is actually selected. Otherwise, the macro most likely fails. The following procedure identifies the type of object that is currently selected:

```
Sub SelectionType()
    MsgBox TypeName(Selection)
End Sub
```

A workbook that contains this macro is available on the companion CD-ROM. The file is named **selection type.xlsm.**

If a cell or a range is selected, the `MsgBox` displays `Range`. If your macro is designed to work only with ranges, you can use an `If` statement to ensure that a range is actually selected. The following is an example that displays a message and exits the procedure if the current selection is not a `Range` object:

```
Sub CheckSelection()
    If TypeName(Selection) <> "Range" Then
        MsgBox "Select a range."
        Exit Sub
    End If
' ... [Other statements go here]
End Sub
```

Another way to approach this task is to define a custom function that returns True if the selection is a Range object, and False otherwise. The following function does just that:

```
Function IsRange(sel) As Boolean
 IsRange = False
 If TypeName(sel) = "Range" Then IsRange = True
End Function
```

If you enter the IsRange function in your module, you can rewrite the CheckSelection procedure as follows:

```
Sub CheckSelection()
 If IsRange(Selection) Then
' ... [Other statements go here]
 Else
  MsgBox "Select a range."
  Exit Sub
 End If
End Sub
```

Identifying a multiple selection

As you know, Excel enables you to make a multiple selection by pressing Ctrl while you select objects or ranges. This method can cause problems with some macros; for example, you can't copy a multiple selection that consists of nonadjacent ranges. The following macro demonstrates how to determine whether the user has made a multiple selection:

```
Sub MultipleSelection()
   If Selection.Areas.Count > 1 Then
     MsgBox "Multiple selections not allowed."
     Exit Sub
   End If
' ... [Other statements go here]
End Sub
```

This example uses the Areas method, which returns a collection of all Range objects in the selection. The Count property returns the number of objects that are in the collection.

The following is a VBA function that returns True if the selection is a multiple selection:

```
Function IsMultiple(sel) As Boolean
   IsMultiple = Selection.Areas.Count > 1
End Function
```

Counting selected cells

You can create a macro that works with the selected range of cells. Use the Count property of the Range object to determine how many cells are contained in a range selection (or any range, for that matter). For example, the following statement displays a message box that contains the number of cells in the current selection:

```
MsgBox Selection.Count
```

CAUTION With the larger worksheet size in Excel 2007, the Count property can generate an error. The Count property uses the Long data type, so the largest value that it can store is 2,147,483,647. For example, if the user selects 2,048 complete columns (2,147,483,648 cells), the Count property generates an error. Fortunately, Microsoft added a new property: CountLarge. CountLarge uses the Double data type, which can handle values up to 1.79+E^308.

Bottom line? In the vast majority of situations, the Count property will work fine. If there's a chance that you may need to count more cells (such as all cells in a worksheet), use CountLarge instead of Count.

If the active sheet contains a range named data, the following statement assigns the number of cells in the data range to a variable named CellCount:

```
CellCount = Range("data").Count
```

You can also determine how many rows or columns are contained in a range. The following expression calculates the number of columns in the currently selected range:

```
Selection.Columns.Count
```

And, of course, you can also use the Rows property to determine the number of rows in a range. The following statement counts the number of rows in a range named data and assigns the number to a variable named RowCount:

```
RowCount = Range("data").Rows.Count
```

Working with Workbooks

The examples in this section demonstrate various ways to use VBA to work with workbooks.

Saving all workbooks

The following procedure loops through all workbooks in the Workbooks collection and saves each file that has been saved previously:

```
Public Sub SaveAllWorkbooks()
    Dim Book As Workbook
    For Each Book In Workbooks
        If Book.Path <> "" Then Book.Save
    Next Book
End Sub
```

Notice the use of the Path property. If a workbook's Path property is empty, the file has never been saved (it's a new workbook). This procedure ignores such workbooks and saves only the workbooks that have a nonempty Path property.

Saving and closing all workbooks

The following procedure loops through the Workbooks collection. The code saves and closes all workbooks.

```
Sub CloseAllWorkbooks()
    Dim Book As Workbook
    For Each Book In Workbooks
```

```
        If Book.Name <> ThisWorkbook.Name Then
            Book.Close savechanges:=True
        End If
    Next Book
    ThisWorkbook.Close savechanges:=True
End Sub
```

The procedure uses an `If` statement within the `For-Next` loop to determine whether the workbook is the workbook that contains the code. This is necessary because closing the workbook that contains the procedure would end the code, and subsequent workbooks would not be affected.

Working with Charts

Manipulating charts with VBA can be confusing, mainly because of the large number of objects involved. To get a feel for working with charts, turn on the macro recorder, create a chart, and perform some routine chart editing. You may be surprised by the amount of code that's generated.

When you understand how objects function within in a chart, however, you can create some useful macros. This section presents a few macros that deal with charts. When you write macros that manipulate charts, you need to understand some terminology. An embedded chart on a worksheet is a `ChartObject` object, and the `ChartObject` contains the actual `Chart` object. A chart on a chart sheet, on the other hand, does not have a `ChartObject` container.

It's often useful to create an object reference to a chart (see "Simplifying object references," later in this chapter). For example, the following statement creates an object variable (`MyChart`) for the embedded chart named Chart 1 on the active sheet.

```
Dim MyChart As Chart
Set MyChart = ActiveSheet.ChartObjects("Chart 1")
```

The following sections contain examples of macros that work with charts.

ON the CD-ROM These macros are available on the companion CD-ROM. The file is named **chart macros.xlsm.**

Modifying the chart type

The following example changes the chart type of every embedded chart on the active sheet. It makes each chart an area chart by adjusting the `ChartType` property of the `Chart` object. A built-in constant, `xlColumnClustered`, represents a standard column chart.

```
Sub ChartType()
    Dim ChtObj As ChartObject
    For Each ChtObj In ActiveSheet.ChartObjects
        ChtObj.Chart.ChartType = xlColumnClustered
    Next ChtObj
End Sub
```

The preceding example uses a `For-Next` loop to cycle through all the `ChartObject` objects on the active sheet. Within the loop, the chart type is assigned a new value, making it an area chart.

The following macro performs the same function but works on all chart sheets in the active workbook:

```
Sub ChartType2()
    Dim Cht As Chart
    For Each Cht In ActiveWorkbook.Charts
        Cht.ChartType = xlColumnClustered
    Next Cht
End Sub
```

Modifying chart properties

The following example changes the legend font for all charts that are on the active sheet. It uses a For-Next loop to process all ChartObject objects and uses the HasLegend property to ensure that the chart has a legend. The code then adjusts the properties of the Font object contained in the Legend object.

```
Sub LegendMod()
    Dim ChtObj As ChartObject
    For Each ChtObj In ActiveSheet.ChartObjects
        ChtObj.Chart.HasLegend = True
        With ChtObj.Chart.Legend.Font
            .Name = "Arial"
            .FontStyle = "Bold"
            .Size = 8
        End With
    Next ChtObj
End Sub
```

Applying chart formatting

This example applies several different formatting types to the specified chart (in this case, Chart 1 on the active sheet).

```
Sub ChartMods()
    With ActiveSheet.ChartObjects("Chart 1").Chart
        .ChartType = xlArea
        .ChartArea.Font.Name = "Arial"
        .ChartArea.Font.FontStyle = "Regular"
        .ChartArea.Font.Size = 9
        .PlotArea.Interior.ColorIndex = 6
        .Axes(xlValue).TickLabels.Font.Bold = True
        .Axes(xlCategory).TickLabels.Font.Bold = True
    End With
End Sub
```

One way to learn about these properties is to record a macro while you apply various changes to a chart.

VBA Speed Tips

VBA is fast, but it's often not fast enough. This section presents programming examples that you can use to help speed your macros.

Turning off screen updating

You've probably noticed that when you execute a macro, you can watch everything that occurs in the macro. Sometimes, this view is instructive; but after you get the macro working properly, it can be annoying and slow things considerably.

Fortunately, you can disable the normal screen updating that occurs when you execute a macro. Insert the following statement to turn off screen updating:

```
Application.ScreenUpdating = False
```

If, at any point during the macro, you want the user to see the results of the macro, use the following statement to turn screen updating back on:

```
Application.ScreenUpdating = True
```

Preventing alert messages

One benefit of using a macro is that you can perform a series of actions automatically. You can start a macro and then get a cup of coffee while Excel does its thing. Some operations cause Excel to display messages that must be attended to, however. For example, if your macro deletes a sheet, you see the message that is shown in the dialog box in Figure 44.3. These types of messages mean that you can't execute your macro unattended.

You can instruct Excel not to display these types of alerts while a macro is running.

To avoid these alert messages, insert the following VBA statement:

```
Application.DisplayAlerts = False
```

To turn alerts back on, use this statement:

```
Application.DisplayAlerts = True
```

Simplifying object references

As you may have discovered, references to objects can get very lengthy — especially if your code refers to an object that's not on the active sheet or in the active workbook. For example, a fully qualified reference to a Range object may look like this:

```
Workbooks("MyBook.xlsx").Worksheets("Sheet1").Range("IntRate")
```

If your macro uses this range frequently, you may want to use the Set command to create an object variable. For example, to assign this Range object to an object variable named Rate, use the following statement:

```
Set Rate= Workbooks("MyBook.xlsx").Worksheets("Sheet1").Range("IntRate")
```

After this variable is defined, you can use the variable `Rate` instead of the lengthy reference. For example:

```
Rate.Value = .0725
```

Besides simplifying your coding, using object variables also speeds your macros quite a bit. I've seen macros execute twice as fast after creating object variables.

Declaring variable types

Usually, you don't have to worry about the type of data that's assigned to a variable. Excel handles all these details behind the scenes. For example, if you have a variable named `MyVar`, you can assign a number of any type to it. You can even assign a text string to it later in the procedure.

But if you want your procedures to execute as fast as possible, you should tell Excel in advance what type of data is going be assigned to each of your variables. Providing this information in your VBA procedure is known as *declaring* a variable's type.

Table 44.1 lists all the data types that are supported by VBA. This table also lists the number of bytes that each type uses and the approximate range of possible values.

TABLE 44.1

Data Types

Data Type	Bytes Used	Approximate Range of Values
Byte	1	0 to 255
Boolean	2	True or False
Integer	2	–32,768 to 32,767
Long (long integer)	4	–2,147,483,648 to 2,147,483,647
Single (single-precision floating-point)	4	–3.4E38 to –1.4E–45 for negative values
	3	1.4E–45 to 4E38 for positive values
Double (double-precision floating-point)	8	–1.7E308 to –4.9E–324 for negative values
	1	4.9E–324 to .7E308 for positive values
Currency (scaled integer)	8	–9.2E14 to 9.2E14
Decimal	14	+/–7.9E28 with no decimal point
Date	8	January 1, 100 to December 31, 9999
Object	4	Any object reference
String (variable-length)	10 + string length	0 to approximately 2 billion
String (fixed-length)	Length of string	1 to approximately 65,400
Variant (with numbers)	16	Any numeric value up to the range of a Double
Variant (with characters)	22 + string length	Same range as for variable-length String
User-defined (using Type)	Number required by elements	Range of each element is the same as the range of its data type

If you don't declare a variable, Excel uses the `Variant` data type. In general, the best technique is to use the data type that uses the smallest number of bytes yet can still handle all the data assigned to it. An exception is when you're performing floating-point calculations. In such a case, it is always best to use the `Double` data type (rather than the `Single` data type) to maintain maximum precision.

When VBA works with data, execution speed is a function of the number of bytes that VBA has at its disposal. In other words, the fewer bytes that are used by data, the faster VBA can access and manipulate the data.

To declare a variable, use the `Dim` statement before you use the variable for the first time. For example, to declare the variable `Units` as an integer, use the following statement:

```
Dim Units as Integer
```

To declare the variable `UserName` as a string, use the following statement:

```
Dim UserName as String
```

If you declare a variable within a procedure, the declaration is valid only within that procedure. If you declare a variable outside of any procedures (but before the first procedure), the variable is valid in all procedures in the module.

If you use an object variable (as described in "Simplifying object references," earlier in this chapter), you can declare the variable as the appropriate object data type. The following is an example:

```
Dim Rate as Range
Set Rate = Workbooks("MyBook.xlsx").Worksheets("Sheet1").Range("IntRate")
```

To force yourself to declare all the variables that you use, insert the following statement at the top of your module:

```
Option Explicit
```

If you use this statement, Excel displays an error message if it encounters a variable that hasn't been declared. After you get into the habit of correctly declaring all your variables, you will find that it helps eliminate errors and makes spotting errors easier.

Chapter 45

Creating Custom Excel Add-Ins

IN THIS CHAPTER

Understanding add-ins

Converting a workbook to an add-in

For developers, one of the most useful features in Excel is the capability to create add-ins. This chapter discusses this concept and provides a practical example of creating an add-in.

What Is an Add-In?

Generally speaking, an *add-in* is something that's added to software to give it additional functionality. Excel includes several add-ins, including the Analysis ToolPak and Solver. Some add-ins (the Analysis ToolPak, discussed in Chapter 38, is one example) provide new worksheet functions that you can use in formulas. Ideally, the new features blend in well with the original interface so that they appear to be part of the program.

Excel's approach to add-ins is quite powerful because any knowledgeable Excel user can create add-ins from workbooks. An Excel add-in is basically a different form of a workbook file. Any Excel workbook can be converted into an add-in, but not every workbook is a good candidate for an add-in.

What distinguishes an add-in form a normal workbook? Add-ins, by default, have an .xlam extension In addition, add-ins are always hidden, so you can't display worksheets or chart sheets that are contained in an add-in. But, you can access its VBA procedures and display dialog boxes that are contained on UserForms.

The following are some typical uses for Excel add-ins:

- **To store one or more custom worksheet functions.** When the add-in is loaded, you can use the functions like any built-in worksheet function.

- **To store Excel utilities.** VBA is ideal for creating general-purpose utilities that extend the power of Excel. The Power Utility Pak that I created is an example.

■ **To store proprietary macros.** If you don't want end users to see (or modify) your macros, store the macros in an add-in and protect the VBA project with a password. A user can use the macros, but they can't view or change them unless the user knows the password. An additional benefit is that the add-in doesn't display a workbook window, which can be distracting.

As previously noted, Excel ships with several useful add-ins (see the sidebar "Add-Ins Included with Excel"), and you can acquire other add-ins from third-party vendors or the Internet. In addition, Excel includes the tools that enable you to create your own add-ins. I explain this process later in the chapter (see "Creating Add-Ins").

Working with Add-Ins

The best way to work with add-ins is to use Excel's Add-In Manager. To display the Add-In Manager:

1. Choose Office ➪ Excel Options
2. In the Excel Options dialog box, select the Add-Ins category
3. At the bottom of the dialog box, select Excel Add-Ins from the Manage list and click Go.

Excel displays its Add-Ins dialog box, shown in Figure 45.1. The list box contains all the add-ins that Excel knows about. Those checked are currently open. You can open and close add-ins from this dialog box by selecting or deselecting the check boxes.

FIGURE 45.1

The Add-Ins dialog box.

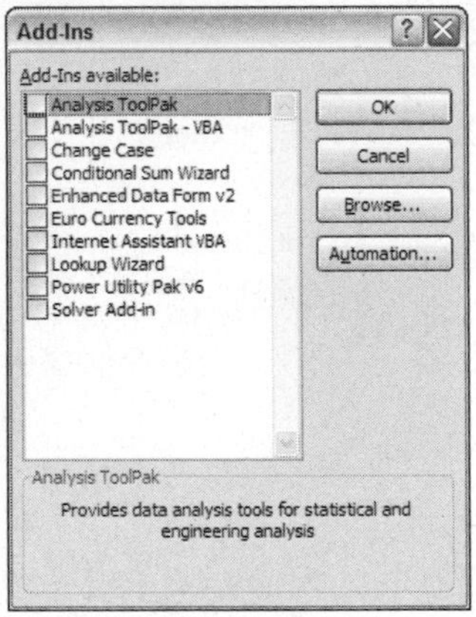

You can also open most add-in files can by choosng Office ➪ Open. After an add-in is opened, however, you can't choose Office ➪ Close to close it. The only way to remove the add-in is to exit and restart Excel or to write a macro to close the add-in. Therefore, you're usually better off opening the add-ins by using the Add-Ins dialog box.

Add-Ins Included with Excel

The following is a list of the add-ins included with Excel 2007. Some add-ins may not have been installed. If you try to use one of these add-ins and it's not installed, you receive a prompt asking whether you want to install it.

- **Analysis ToolPak:** Statistical and engineering tools, plus new worksheet functions. Access the Analysis ToolPak by choosing Formulas ➪ Solutions ➪ Data Analysis.

- **Analysis ToolPak — VBA:** VBA functions for the Analysis ToolPak. The functions in this add-in are used by VBA programmers, and they are not accessible from Excel.

- **Conditional Sum Wizard:** Helps you to create formulas that add values based on a condition. Access the Conditional Sum Wizard by choosing Formulas ➪ Solutions ➪ Conditional Sum.

- **Euro Currency Tools:** Tools for converting and formatting the euro currency. Access the Euro Currency Tools by choosing Formulas ➪ Solutions ➪ Euro Conversion And Formulas ➪ Solutions ➪ Euro Formatting.

- **Internet Assistant VBA:** A tool for programmers that enables them to publish data to the Web. This add-in is for VBA programmers and is not accessible from Excel.

- **Lookup Wizard:** Helps you to create formulas that look up data in a list. Access the Lookup wizard by choosing Formulas ➪ Solutions ➪ Lookup.

- **Solver Add-In:** A tool that helps you to use a variety of numeric methods for equation solving and optimization. Access the Solver add-in by choosing Formulas ➪ Solutions ➪ Solver.

In addition, you can download additional Excel add-ins from http://office.microsoft.com/.

The user interface for some Add-ins (including those included with Excel) may be integrated into the Ribbon. For example, when you open the Analysis ToolPak add-in, you access these tools by choosing Formulas ➪ Solutions ➪ Data Analysis.

NEW FEATURE If you open an add-in created in a previous version of Excel, any user interface modifications made by the add-in will not appear as they were intended to appear. Rather, you must access the user interface items (menus and toolbars) by choosing Add-Ins ➪ Menu Commands or Add-Ins ➪ Custom Toolbars. It's likely that most add-in developers will create a new version of their add-in that uses the new Ribbon interface.

Why Create Add-Ins?

Most Excel users have no need to create add-ins. But if you develop spreadsheets for others — or if you simply want to get the most out of Excel — you may be interested in pursuing this topic further.

The following are several reasons why you may want to convert your Excel workbook application to an add-in:

- **To avoid confusion.** If an end user loads your application as an add-in, the file isn't visible in the Excel window — and, therefore, is less likely to confuse novice users or get in the way. Unlike a hidden workbook, an add-in can't be unhidden.

- **To simplify access to worksheet functions.** Custom worksheet functions stored in an add-in don't require the workbook name qualifier. For example, if you have a custom function named MOVAVG stored in a workbook named `Newfuncs.xlsm`, you have to use a syntax such as the following to use this function in a different workbook:

```
=NEWFUNC.XLSM!MOVAVG(A1:A50)
```

But if this function is stored in an add-in file that's open, the syntax is much simpler because you don't need to include the file reference:

```
=MOVAVG(A1:A50)
```

- **To provide easier access.** After you identify the location of your add-in, it appears in the Add-Ins dialog box and can display a friendly name and a description of what it does.
- **To permit better control over loading.** You can automatically open add-ins when Excel starts, regardless of the directory in which they're stored.
- **To omit prompts when unloading.** When an add-in is closed, the user never sees the Save Change In prompt because changes to add-ins aren't saved unless you specifically do so from the VB Editor window.

Creating Add-Ins

Technically, you can convert any workbook to an add-in. But not all workbooks benefit from this conversion. In fact, workbooks that consist only of worksheets (that is, not macros or custom dialog boxes) become unusable because add-ins are hidden.

Workbooks that benefit from conversion to an add-in are those with macros. For example, you may have a workbook that consists of general-purpose macros and functions. This type of workbook makes an ideal add-in.

These steps describe how to create an add-in from a workbook.

1. **Develop your application and make sure that everything works properly.**
2. **Choose Office ⇨ Prepare ⇨ Properties to display the Properties panel above your worksheet, enter a brief descriptive title in the Title field, and then enter a longer description in the Comments field.** This step isn't required, but it makes installing and identifying the add-in easier. To close the Properties panel, click its close button (X).
3. **Lock the VBA project.** This optional step protects the VBA code and UserForms from being viewed. You do this in the VB Editor, using the Tools ⇨ *projectname* Properties command (where *projectname* corresponds to your VB project name). In the dialog box, click the Protection tab and select Lock Project For Viewing. If you like, you can specify a password to prevent others from viewing your code.
4. **Save the workbook as an add-in file by choosing Office ⇨ Save As and selecting Excel Add-In (*.xlam) from the Save As Type drop-down list.** By default, Excel saves your add-in in your AddIns directory. But you can override this location and choose any directory you like.

NOTE After you save the workbook as an add-in, the original (non-add-in) workbook remains active. You should close this file to avoid having two macros with the same name.

After you create the add-in, you need to install it:

1. **Choose Office ⇨ Excel Options ⇨ Add-Ins.**
2. **Select Excel Add-Ins from the Manage drop-down list and click Go to display the Add-Ins dialog box.**
3. **In the Add-Ins dialog box, click the Browse button to locate the XLAM file that you created, which installs the add-in.** The Add-Ins dialog box uses the descriptive title that you provided in the Properties panel.

> **NOTE** You can continue to modify the macros and UserForms in the XLAM version of your file. Because the add-in doesn't appear in the Excel window, you save your changes in the VB Editor by choosing Office ⇨ Save.

An Add-In Example

This section discusses the steps to create a useful add-in from the **change case.xlsm** workbook I covered in Chapter 41. This workbook contains a UserForm that displays options that change the text case of selected cells (uppercase, lowercase, or proper case). Figure 45.2 shows the add-in in action.

FIGURE 45.2

This dialog box enables the user to change the case of text in the selected cells.

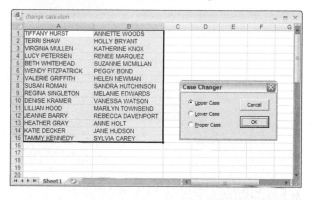

> **ON the CD-ROM** This file is available on the companion CD-ROM and is named change case.xlam. The file is not locked, so you have full access to the VBA code and UserForm.

Setting up the workbook

This workbook contains one worksheet, which is empty. Although the worksheet is not used, it must be present because every workbook must have at least one sheet.

Choose Insert ⇨ Module in the VB Editor to insert a VBA module (named Module1). Choose Insert ⇨ UserForm to insert a UserForm (named UserForm1).

Procedures in Module1

The two macro that follow are contained in the Module1 code module. The ShowUserForm procedure checks the type of selection. If a range is selected, the dialog box in UserForm1 appears. If anything other than a range is selected, a message box is displayed.

The ChangeCaseOfText procedure is a special callback procedure, with one argument, that is executed from a control on the Ribbon. See "Creating the user interface for your add-in macro," later in this chapter. This procedure simply executes the ShowUserForm procedure.

```
Sub ShowUserForm()
    If TypeName(Selection) = "Range" Then
        UserForm1.Show
    Else
        MsgBox "Select some cells."
    End If
End Sub

Sub ChangeCaseOfText(ByVal control As IRibbonControl)
    Call ShowUserForm
End Sub
```

About the UserForm

Figure 45.3 shows the UserForm1 form, which has five controls: three OptionButton controls and two CommandButton controls. The controls have descriptive names, and the Accelerator property is set so that the controls display an accelerator key (for keyboard users). The option button with the Upper Case caption has its Value property set to True, which makes it the default option.

The UserForm1 object contains the event-handler procedures for the two CommandButton objects that are on the form. The following procedure is executed when the OK button is clicked. This procedure does all the work:

FIGURE 45.3

The custom dialog box.

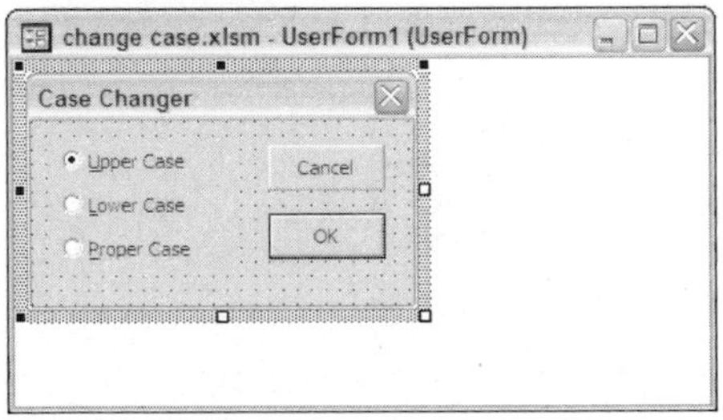

```
Private Sub OKButton_Click()
    CaseChangerDialog.Hide
    Application.ScreenUpdating = False

'   Upper case
    If OptionUpper Then
        For Each cell In Selection
        If Not cell.HasFormula Then
            cell.Value = StrConv(cell.Value, vbUpperCase)
        End If
        Next cell
    End If
'   Lower case
    If OptionLower Then
        For Each cell In Selection
        If Not cell.HasFormula Then
            cell.Value = StrConv(cell.Value, vbLowerCase)
        End If
        Next cell
    End If
'   Proper case
    If OptionProper Then
        For Each cell In Selection
        If Not cell.HasFormula Then
            cell.Value = StrConv(cell.Value, vbProperCase)
        End If
        Next cell
    End If
    Unload UserForm1
End Sub
```

The following procedure is executed if the user clicks the Cancel button.

```
Private Sub CancelButton_Click()
    Unload UserForm1
End Sub
```

Testing the workbook

Before you convert this workbook to an add-in, it's a good idea to test it. You should test it when a different workbook is active in order to simulate what happens when the workbook is an add-in. Remember that an add-in is never the active workbook, and it never displays any of its worksheets.

To test it, I saved the workbook, closed it, and then reopened it. With the workbook open, I then activated a different workbook, selected some cells that contained text and then pressed Alt+F8 to display the Macros dialog box. I executed the ShowUserForm macro and tried all of the options.

Adding descriptive information

Adding descriptive information is recommended but not necessary. Choose Office ➪ Prepare ➪ Properties to display the Properties panel below the Ribbon. Enter a title for the add-in in the Title field. This text appears in the Add-Ins dialog box. In the Comments field, enter a description. This information appears at the bottom of the Add-Ins dialog box when the add-in is selected. See Figure 45.4.

FIGURE 45.4

Use the Properties panel to enter descriptive information about your add-in.

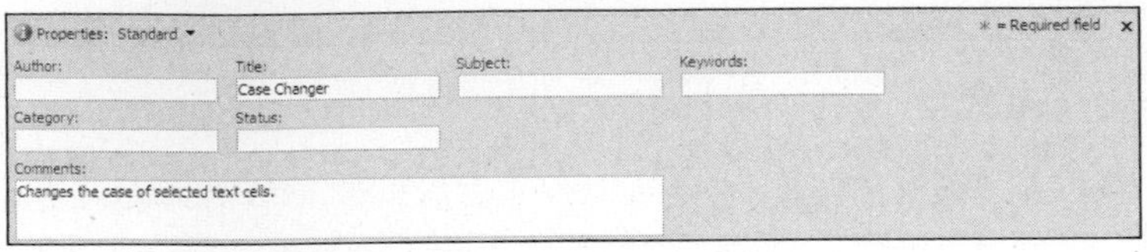

Protecting the project

In some situations (such as a commercial product), you may want to protect your project so that others can't see the source code. To protect the project, follow these steps:

1. **Activate the Visual Basic Editor.**
2. **In the Project window, click the project.**
3. **Choose Tools ➪ *project name* Properties.** The VB Editor displays its Project Properties dialog box.
4. **Click the Protection tab (as shown in Figure 45.5).**

FIGURE 45.5

The Project Properties dialog box.

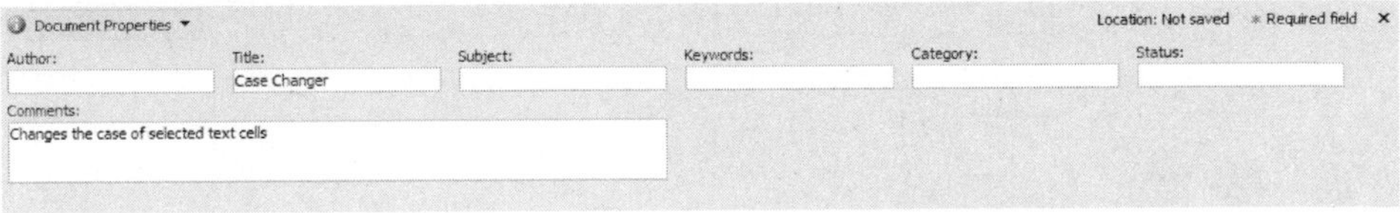

5. Select the Lock Project For Viewing check box.

6. Enter a password (twice) for the project.

7. Click OK.

Creating the add-in

To save the workbook as an add-in, switch to the Excel window and activate your workbook. Then choose Office ➪ Save As. Select Microsoft Excel Add-In (*.xlam) from the Save As Type drop-down list. Enter a name for the add-in file and then click OK. By default, Excel saves the add-in in your AddIns directory, but you can choose a different directory if you like.

Creating the user interface for your add-in macro

At this point, the add-in is created, but it's missing one key component: A way to execute the macro that displays the UserForm. This section describes how to modify your add-in file so that it adds a new button to the Ribbon. It uses a technique known as RibbonX, which involves XML.

> **NOTE** In previous versions, Excel's user interface was very easy to modify. Even a relatively inexperienced user could add a new toolbar button and attach a macro to it. Things have changed with Excel 2007. Modifying Excel's user interface is much more complicated. The following example is, admittedly, a very simple one. A complete discussion of RibbonX is well beyond the scope of this book. In fact, entire books are devoted to this topic.

Specifically, we'll add a new group that's displayed when the Home tab is clicked. This group will contain one button, and clicking this button will execute the ChangeCaseofText macro.

The changes you need to make are done outside of Excel. Make sure that the add-in file is not open in Excel. You'll need to use a text editor. such as Notepad.

1. Create a folder named customUI.

2. Inside of that folder, create a text file named customUI.xml, with the following XML code:

```
<customUI xmlns="http://schemas.microsoft.com/office/2006/01/customui">
<ribbon>
<tabs>
<tab idMso="TabHome">
<group id="myAddins"
label="My Add-Ins"
insertAfterMso="GroupEditingExcel">
<button id="myButton"
label="Change Case of Text"
onAction="ChangeCaseofText"/>
</group>
</tab>
</tabs>
</ribbon>
</customUI>
```

Note that this XML code refers to the macro, ChangeCaseofText. That explains the argument that's required in the Sub procedure declaration, listed earlier in this chapter (see "Procedures in Module1").

3. **Locate and select your XLAM file in Windows Explorer.** This example assumes that the file is named change case.xlam.

4. **Add a .zip extension to the file by pressing F2 and then changing the filename to** change-case.xlam.zip.

5. **Drag the customUI folder you created in Step 1 into the change case.xlam.zip file.** (Windows treats ZIP files as if they were folders.) Figure 45.6 shows the contents of the change case.xlam.zip file.

FIGURE 45.6

The change case.xlam.zip file contains subfolders, including the customUI folder you created.

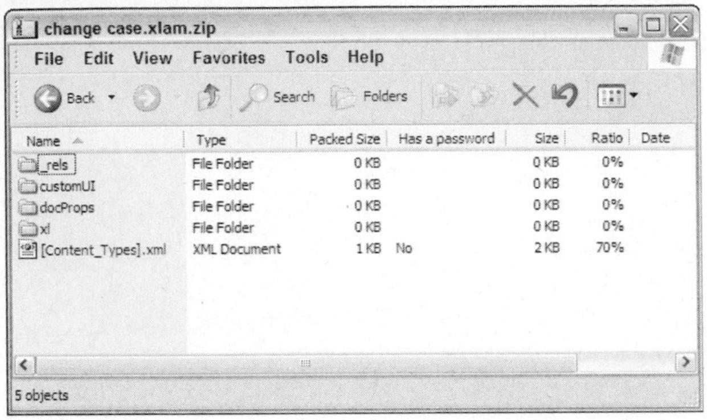

6. **Double-click the rels folder within the ZIP file.** This folder contains one file, .rels.

7. **Drag the .rels file to a location outside of the ZIP file (your Desktop, for example).**

8. **Open the .rels file (which is an XML file) with a text editor, such as Notepad.**

9. **Add the following line to the .rels file, before the </Relationships> tag:**

```
<Relationship Type="http://schemas.microsoft.com/office/2006/
relationships/ui/extensibility" Target="/customUI/customUI.xml"/>
```

10. **Drag the .rels file back into the ZIP file, overwriting the original version.**

11. **Remove the .zip extension so that the file is back to its original name: change case.xlam.**

> **NOTE** Yes, these steps represent an absurd amount of error-prone manual effort. Remember, this book was published when Excel 2007 was just released. By the time you read this book, tools should be available to simplify this task. Try searching the Web for *office custom UI editor*.

Installing the add-in

Now it's time to try the add-in. Choose Office ➪ Excel Options ➪ Add-Ins. Select Excel Add-ins from the Manage drop-down list, and click Go.

Excel displays its Add-Ins dialog box. Click the Browse button and locate the change case.xlam add-in that you just created. After you do so, the Add-Ins dialog box displays the add-in in its list. Notice that the information that you provided in the Properties panel appears here. Click OK to close the dialog box and open the add-in.

Modify the User Interface the Old Way

Before Excel 2007, it was much simpler to provide a way to execute a macro in an add-in. It was done using a CommandBar objects, which display menus and toolbars. Excel 2007 still supports CommandBars for compatibility. All changes made to a CommandBar object are displayed in the Menu Commands or Custom Toolbars groups in the Add-Ins tab.

If you would like to modify change case.xlsm to use CommandBars, add these two procedures to the ThisWorkbook code module:

```
Private Sub Workbook_Open()
    Set NewMenuItem = Application.CommandBars("Worksheet Menu Bar") _
        .Controls("Tools").Controls.Add
    With NewMenuItem
        .Caption = "Change Case of Text..."
        .BeginGroup = True
        .OnAction = "ChangeCaseofText"
    End With
End Sub

Private Sub Workbook_BeforeClose(Cancel As Boolean)
    On Error Resume Next
    Application.CommandBars("Worksheet Menu Bar").Controls("Tools"). _
        Controls("Change Case of Text...").Delete
End Sub
```

When the add-in is opened, this code adds a new control to the Menu Commands group of the Add-Ins tab. When it's closed, the new control is removed. Simple and easy. It's too bad Microsoft couldn't use such a simple approach for customizing the Ribbon.

Figure 45.7 shows the new command in the Ribbon. Click this button, and the ChangeCaseofText macro executes.

FIGURE 45.7

The new user interface control in the Ribbon.

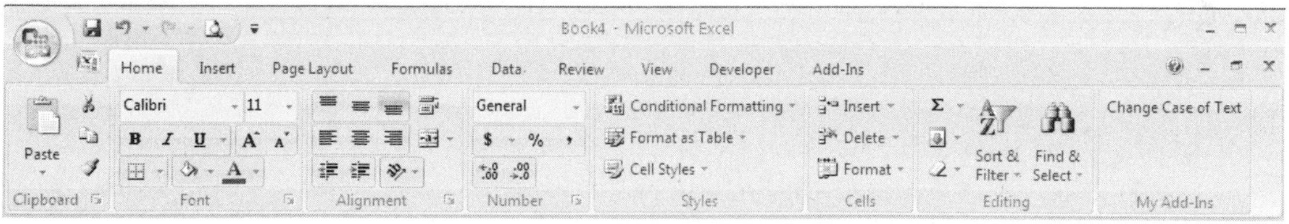

Part VII

Appendixes

This part contains some very useful appendixes. Appendix A provides a complete reference of all the worksheet functions. Appendix B gives you the run-down on all the great sample files on the CD-ROM that accompanies this book. Appendix C contains some great additional Excel resources; discover Excel shortcut keys in Appendix D.

IN THIS PART

Appendix A
Worksheet Function Reference

Appendix B
What's On the CD-ROM

Appendix C
Additional Excel Resources

Appendix D
Excel Shortcut Keys

Appendix A

Worksheet Function Reference

This appendix contains a complete listing of Excel's worksheet functions. The functions are arranged alphabetically by the categories displayed in the Insert Function dialog box.

For more information about a particular function, including its arguments, select the function in the Insert Function dialog box and click Help On This Function.

ON the CD-ROM A workbook that contains this information is available on the companion CD-ROM. The filename is worksheet functions.xlsx.

TABLE A.1

Cube Category Functions

Function	What It Does
CUBEKPIMEMBER*	Returns a key performance indicator name, property, and measure, and displays the name and property in the cell.
CUBEMEMBER*	Returns a member or tuple in a cube hierarchy.
CUBEMEMBERPROPERTY*	Returns the value of a member property in the cube.
CUBERANKEDMEMBER*	Returns the nth, or ranked, member in a set.
CUBESET*	Defines a calculated set of members or tuples by sending a set expression to the cube on the server.
CUBESETCOUNT*	Returns the number of items in a set.
CUBEVALUE*	Returns an aggregated value from a cube.

* Indicates a new function in Excel 2007.

TABLE A.2

Database Category Functions

Function	What It Does
DAVERAGE	Averages the values in a column of a list or database that match conditions you specify.
DCOUNT	Counts the cells that contain numbers in a column of a list or database that match conditions you specify.
DCOUNTA	Counts the nonblank cells in a column of a list or database that match conditions you specify.
DGET	Extracts a single value from a column of a list or database that matches conditions you specify.
DMAX	Returns the largest number in a column of a list or database that matches conditions you specify.
DMIN	Returns the smallest number in a column of a list or database that matches conditions you specify.
DPRODUCT	Multiplies the values in a column of a list or database that match conditions you specify.
DSTDEV	Estimates the standard deviation of a population based on a sample by using the numbers in a column of a list or database that match conditions you specify.
DSTDEVP	Calculates the standard deviation of a population based on the entire population, using the numbers in a column of a list or database that match conditions you specify.
DSUM	Adds the numbers in a column of a list or database that match conditions you specify.
DVAR	Estimates the variance of a population based on a sample by using the numbers in a column of a list or database that match conditions you specify.
DVARP	Calculates the variance of a population based on the entire population by using the numbers in a column of a list or database that match conditions you specify.

TABLE A.3

Date & Time Category Functions

Function	What It Does
DATE	Returns the serial number of a particular date.
DATEVALUE	Converts a date in the form of text to a serial number.
DAY	Converts a serial number to a day of the month.
DAYS360	Calculates the number of days between two dates, based on a 360-day year.
EDATE	Returns the serial number of the date that is the indicated number of months before or after the start date.
EOMONTH	Returns the serial number of the last day of the month before or after a specified number of months.
HOUR	Converts a serial number to an hour.
MINUTE	Converts a serial number to a minute.
MONTH	Converts a serial number to a month.
NETWORKDAYS	Returns the number of whole workdays between two dates.
NOW	Returns the serial number of the current date and time.
SECOND	Converts a serial number to a second.
TIME	Returns the serial number of a particular time.
TIMEVALUE	Converts a time in the form of text to a serial number.
TODAY	Returns the serial number of today's date.
WEEKDAY	Converts a serial number to a day of the week.
WEEKNUM	Returns the week number in the year.
WORKDAY	Returns the serial number of the date before or after a specified number of work days.
YEAR	Converts a serial number to a year.
YEARFRAC	Returns the year fraction representing the number of whole days between *start_date* and *end_date.*

TABLE A.4

Engineering Category Functions

Function	What It Does
BESSELI	Returns the modified Bessel function In(x).
BESSELJ	Returns the Bessel function Jn(x).
BESSELK	Returns the modified Bessel function Kn(x).
BESSELY	Returns the Bessel function Yn(x).
BIN2DEC	Converts a binary number to decimal.
BIN2HEX	Converts a binary number to hexadecimal.

continued

TABLE A.4	*(continued)*
Function	**What It Does**
BIN2OCT	Converts a binary number to octal.
COMPLEX	Converts real and imaginary coefficients into a complex number.
CONVERT	Converts a number from one measurement system to another.
DEC2BIN	Converts a decimal number to binary.
DEC2HEX	Converts a decimal number to hexadecimal.
DEC2OCT	Converts a decimal number to octal.
DELTA	Tests whether two values are equal.
ERF	Returns the error function.
ERFC	Returns the complementary error function.
GESTEP	Tests whether a number is greater than a threshold value.
HEX2BIN	Converts a hexadecimal number to binary.
HEX2DEC	Converts a hexadecimal number to decimal.
HEX2OCT	Converts a hexadecimal number to octal.
IMABS	Returns the absolute value (modulus) of a complex number.
IMAGINARY	Returns the imaginary coefficient of a complex number.
IMARGUMENT	Returns the argument *theta*, an angle expressed in radians.
IMCONJUGATE	Returns the complex conjugate of a complex number.
IMCOS	Returns the cosine of a complex number.
IMDIV	Returns the quotient of two complex numbers.
IMEXP	Returns the exponential of a complex number.
IMLN	Returns the natural logarithm of a complex number.
IMLOG10	Returns the base-10 logarithm of a complex number.
IMLOG2	Returns the base-2 logarithm of a complex number.
IMPOWER	Returns a complex number raised to an integer power.
IMPRODUCT	Returns the product of complex numbers.
IMREAL	Returns the real coefficient of a complex number.
IMSIN	Returns the sine of a complex number.
IMSQRT	Returns the square root of a complex number.
IMSUB	Returns the difference of two complex numbers.
IMSUM	Returns the sum of complex numbers.
OCT2BIN	Converts an octal number to binary.
OCT2DEC	Converts an octal number to decimal.
OCT2HEX	Converts an octal number to hexadecimal.

Financial Category Functions

Function	What It Does
ACCRINT	Returns the accrued interest for a security that pays periodic interest.
ACCRINTM	Returns the accrued interest for a security that pays interest at maturity.
AMORDEGRC	Returns the depreciation for each accounting period.
AMORLINC	Returns the depreciation for each accounting period (the depreciation coefficient depends on the life of the assets).
COUPDAYBS	Returns the number of days from the beginning of the coupon period to the settlement date.
COUPDAYS	Returns the number of days in the coupon period that contains the settlement date.
COUPDAYSNC	Returns the number of days from the settlement date to the next coupon date.
COUPNCD	Returns the next coupon date after the settlement date.
COUPNUM	Returns the number of coupons payable between the settlement date and maturity date.
COUPPCD	Returns the previous coupon date before the settlement date.
CUMIPMT	Returns the cumulative interest paid between two periods.
CUMPRINC	Returns the cumulative principal paid on a loan between two periods.
DB	Returns the depreciation of an asset for a specified period, using the fixed-declining-balance method.
DDB	Returns the depreciation of an asset for a specified period, using the double-declining-balance method or some other method that you specify.
DISC	Returns the discount rate for a security.
DOLLARDE	Converts a dollar price, expressed as a fraction, into a dollar price expressed as a decimal number.
DOLLARFR	Converts a dollar price, expressed as a decimal number, into a dollar price expressed as a fraction.
DURATION	Returns the annual duration of a security with periodic interest payments.
EFFECT	Returns the effective annual interest rate.
FV	Returns the future value of an investment.
FVSCHEDULE	Returns the future value of an initial principal after applying a series of compound interest rates.
INTRATE	Returns the interest rate for a fully invested security.
IPMT	Returns the interest payment for an investment for a given period.
IRR	Returns the internal rate of return for a series of cash flows.
ISPMT	Returns the interest associated with a specific loan payment.
MDURATION	Returns the Macauley modified duration for a security with an assumed par value of $100.

continued

TABLE A.5 (continued)	
Function	**What It Does**
MIRR	Returns the internal rate of return where positive and negative cash flows are financed at different rates.
NOMINAL	Returns the annual nominal interest rate.
NPER	Returns the number of periods for an investment.
NPV	Returns the net present value of an investment based on a series of periodic cash flows and a discount rate.
ODDFPRICE	Returns the price per $100 face value of a security with an odd first period.
ODDFYIELD	Returns the yield of a security with an odd first period.
ODDLPRICE	Returns the price per $100 face value of a security with an odd last period.
ODDLYIELD	Returns the yield of a security with an odd last period.
PMT	Returns the periodic payment for an annuity.
PPMT	Returns the payment on the principal for an investment for a given period.
PRICE	Returns the price per $100 face value of a security that pays periodic interest.
PRICEDISC	Returns the price per $100 face value of a discounted security.
PRICEMAT	Returns the price per $100 face value of a security that pays interest at maturity.
PV	Returns the present value of an investment.
RATE	Returns the interest rate per period of an annuity.
RECEIVED	Returns the amount received at maturity for a fully invested security.
SLN	Returns the straight-line depreciation of an asset for one period.
SYD	Returns the sum-of-years' digits depreciation of an asset for a specified period.
TBILLEQ	Returns the bond-equivalent yield for a Treasury bill.
TBILLPRICE	Returns the price per $100 face value for a Treasury bill.
TBILLYIELD	Returns the yield for a Treasury bill.
VDB	Returns the depreciation of an asset for a specified or partial period using a declining-balance method.
XIRR	Returns the internal rate of return for a schedule of cash flows that is not necessarily periodic.
XNPV	Returns the net present value for a schedule of cash flows that is not necessarily periodic.
YIELD	Returns the yield on a security that pays periodic interest.
YIELDDISC	Returns the annual yield for a discounted security, for example, a Treasury bill.
YIELDMAT	Returns the annual yield of a security that pays interest at maturity.

TABLE A.6

Information Category Functions

Function	What It Does
CELL	Returns information about the formatting, location, or contents of a cell.
ERROR.TYPE	Returns a number corresponding to an error type.
INFO	Returns information about the current operating environment.
ISBLANK	Returns TRUE if the value is blank.
ISERR	Returns TRUE if the value is any error value except #N/A.
ISERROR	Returns TRUE if the value is any error value.
ISEVEN	Returns TRUE if the number is even.
ISLOGICAL	Returns TRUE if the value is a logical value.
ISNA	Returns TRUE if the value is the #N/A error value.
ISNONTEXT	Returns TRUE if the value is not text.
ISNUMBER	Returns TRUE if the value is a number.
ISODD	Returns TRUE if the number is odd.
ISREF	Returns TRUE if the value is a reference.
ISTEXT	Returns TRUE if the value is text.
N	Returns a value converted to a number.
NA	Returns the error value #N/A.
TYPE	Returns a number indicating the data type of a value.

TABLE A.7

Logical Category Functions

Function	What It Does
AND	Returns TRUE if all its arguments are TRUE.
FALSE	Returns the logical value FALSE.
IF	Specifies a logical test to perform.
IFERROR*	Returns a different result if the first argument evaluates to an error.
NOT	Reverses the logic of its argument.
OR	Returns TRUE if any argument is TRUE.
TRUE	Returns the logical value TRUE.

* Indicates a new function in Excel 2007.

TABLE A.8

Lookup & Reference Category Functions

Function	What It Does
ADDRESS	Returns a reference as text to a single cell in a worksheet.
AREAS	Returns the number of areas in a reference.
CHOOSE	Chooses a value from a list of values.
COLUMN	Returns the column number of a reference.
COLUMNS	Returns the number of columns in a reference
GETPIVOTDATA	Returns data stored in a PivotTable.
HLOOKUP	Searches for a value in the top column of a table and then returns a value in the same column from a row you specify in the table.
HYPERLINK	Creates a shortcut that opens a document on your hard drive, a server, or the Internet.
INDEX	Uses an index to choose a value from a reference or array.
INDIRECT	Returns a reference indicated by a text value.
LOOKUP	Returns a value from either a one-row or one-column range or from an array.
MATCH	Returns the relative position of an item in an array.
OFFSET	Returns a reference offset from a given reference.
ROW	Returns the row number of a reference.
ROWS	Returns the number of rows in a reference.
RTD	Returns real-time data from a program that supports COM automation.
TRANSPOSE	Returns the transpose of an array.
VLOOKUP	Searches for a value in the leftmost column of a table and then returns a value in the same row from a column you specify in the table.

TABLE A.9

Math & Trig Category Functions

Function	What It Does
ABS	Returns the absolute value of a number.
ACOS	Returns the arccosine of a number.
ACOSH	Returns the inverse hyperbolic cosine of a number.
ASIN	Returns the arcsine of a number.
ASINH	Returns the inverse hyperbolic sine of a number.
ATAN	Returns the arctangent of a number.
ATAN2	Returns the arctangent from x and y coordinates.
ATANH	Returns the inverse hyperbolic tangent of a number.
CEILING	Rounds a number to the nearest integer or to the nearest multiple of significance.

Function	What It Does
COMBIN	Returns the number of combinations for a given number of objects.
COS	Returns the cosine of a number.
COSH	Returns the hyperbolic cosine of a number.
DEGREES	Converts radians to degrees.
EVEN	Rounds a number up to the nearest even integer.
EXP	Returns e raised to the power of a given number.
FACT	Returns the factorial of a number.
FACTDOUBLE	Returns the double factorial of a number.
FLOOR	Rounds a number down, toward 0.
GCD	Returns the greatest common divisor.
INT	Rounds a number down to the nearest integer.
LCM	Returns the least common multiple.
LN	Returns the natural logarithm of a number.
LOG	Returns the logarithm of a number to a specified base.
LOG10	Returns the base-10 logarithm of a number.
MDETERM	Returns the matrix determinant of an array.
MINVERSE	Returns the matrix inverse of an array.
MMULT	Returns the matrix product of two arrays.
MOD	Returns the remainder from division.
MROUND	Returns a number rounded to the desired multiple.
MULTINOMIAL	Returns the multinomial of a set of numbers.
ODD	Rounds a number up to the nearest odd integer.
PI	Returns the value of pi.
POWER	Returns the result of a number raised to a power.
PRODUCT	Multiplies its arguments.
QUOTIENT	Returns the integer portion of a division.
RADIANS	Converts degrees to radians.
RAND	Returns a random number between 0 and 1.
RANDBETWEEN	Returns a random number between the numbers that you specify.
ROMAN	Converts an Arabic numeral to Roman, as text.
ROUND	Rounds a number to a specified number of digits.
ROUNDDOWN	Rounds a number down, toward 0.
ROUNDUP	Rounds a number up, away from 0.
SERIESSUM	Returns the sum of a power series based on the formula.
SIGN	Returns the sign of a number.

continued

TABLE A.9   (continued)

Function	What It Does
SIN	Returns the sine of the given angle.
SINH	Returns the hyperbolic sine of a number.
SQRT	Returns a positive square root.
SQRTPI	Returns the square root of pi.
SUBTOTAL	Returns a subtotal in a list or database.
SUM	Adds its arguments.
SUMIF	Adds the cells specified by a given criteria.
SUMIFS*	Adds the cells specified by a multiple criteria.
SUMPRODUCT	Returns the sum of the products of corresponding array components.
SUMSQ	Returns the sum of the squares of the arguments.
SUMX2MY2	Returns the sum of the difference of squares of corresponding values in two arrays.
SUMX2PY2	Returns the sum of the sum of squares of corresponding values in two arrays.
SUMXMY2	Returns the sum of squares of differences of corresponding values in two arrays.
TAN	Returns the tangent of a number.
TANH	Returns the hyperbolic tangent of a number.
TRUNC	Truncates a number (you specify the precision of the truncation).

* Indicates a new function in Excel 2007.

TABLE A.10

Statistical Category Functions

Function	What It Does
AVEDEV	Returns the average of the absolute deviations of data points from their mean.
AVERAGE	Returns the average of its arguments.
AVERAGEA	Returns the average of its arguments and includes evaluation of text and logical values.
AVERAGEIF*	Returns the average for the cells specified by a given criterion.
AVERAGEIFS*	Returns the average for the cells specified by multiple criteria.
BETADIST	Returns the cumulative beta probability density function.
BETAINV	Returns the inverse of the cumulative beta probability density function.
BINOMDIST	Returns the individual term binomial distribution probability.
CHIDIST	Returns the one-tailed probability of the chi-squared distribution.
CHIINV	Returns the inverse of the one-tailed probability of the chi-squared distribution.
CHITEST	Returns the test for independence.

Function	What It Does
CONFIDENCE	Returns the confidence interval for a population mean.
CORREL	Returns the correlation coefficient between two data sets.
COUNT	Counts how many numbers are in the list of arguments.
COUNTA	Counts how many values are in the list of arguments.
COUNTBLANK	Counts the number of blank cells in the argument range.
COUNTIF	Counts the number of cells that meet the criteria you specify in the argument.
COUNTIFS*	Counts the number of cells that meet multiple criteria.
COVAR	Returns covariance, the average of the products of paired deviations.
CRITBINOM	Returns the smallest value for which the cumulative binomial distribution is less than or equal to a criterion value.
DEVSQ	Returns the sum of squares of deviations.
EXPONDIST	Returns the exponential distribution.
FDIST	Returns the F probability distribution.
FINV	Returns the inverse of the F probability distribution.
FISHER	Returns the Fisher transformation.
FISHERINV	Returns the inverse of the Fisher transformation.
FORECAST	Returns a value along a linear trend.
FREQUENCY	Returns a frequency distribution as a vertical array.
FTEST	Returns the result of an F-Test.
GAMMADIST	Returns the gamma distribution.
GAMMAINV	Returns the inverse of the gamma cumulative distribution.
GAMMALN	Returns the natural logarithm of the gamma function, $G(x)$.
GEOMEAN	Returns the geometric mean.
GROWTH	Returns values along an exponential trend.
HARMEAN	Returns the harmonic mean.
HYPGEOMDIST	Returns the hypergeometric distribution.
INTERCEPT	Returns the intercept of the linear regression line.
KURT	Returns the kurtosis of a data set.
LARGE	Returns the kth largest value in a data set.
LINEST	Returns the parameters of a linear trend.
LOGEST	Returns the parameters of an exponential trend.
LOGINV	Returns the inverse of the lognormal distribution.
LOGNORMDIST	Returns the cumulative lognormal distribution.
MAX	Returns the maximum value in a list of arguments, ignoring logical values and text.
MAXA	Returns the maximum value in a list of arguments, including logical values and text.

continued

TABLE A.10   *(continued)*

Function	What It Does
MEDIAN	Returns the median of the given numbers.
MIN	Returns the minimum value in a list of arguments, ignoring logical values and text.
MINA	Returns the minimum value in a list of arguments, including logical values and text.
MODE	Returns the most common value in a data set.
NEGBINOMDIST	Returns the negative binomial distribution.
NORMDIST	Returns the normal cumulative distribution.
NORMINV	Returns the inverse of the normal cumulative distribution.
NORMSDIST	Returns the standard normal cumulative distribution.
NORMSINV	Returns the inverse of the standard normal cumulative distribution.
PEARSON	Returns the Pearson product moment correlation coefficient.
PERCENTILE	Returns the *k*th percentile of values in a range.
PERCENTRANK	Returns the percentage rank of a value in a data set.
PERMUT	Returns the number of permutations for a given number of objects.
POISSON	Returns the Poisson distribution.
PROB	Returns the probability that values in a range are between two limits.
QUARTILE	Returns the quartile of a data set.
RANK	Returns the rank of a number in a list of numbers.
RSQ	Returns the square of the Pearson product moment correlation coefficient.
SKEW	Returns the skewness of a distribution.
SLOPE	Returns the slope of the linear regression line.
SMALL	Returns the *k*th smallest value in a data set.
STANDARDIZE	Returns a normalized value.
STDEV	Estimates standard deviation based on a sample, ignoring text and logical values.
STDEVA	Estimates standard deviation based on a sample, including text and logical values.
STDEVP	Calculates standard deviation based on the entire population, ignoring text and logical values.
STDEVPA	Calculates standard deviation based on the entire population, including text and logical values.
STEYX	Returns the standard error of the predicted y-value for each x in the regression.
TDIST	Returns the student's t-distribution.
TINV	Returns the inverse of the student's t-distribution.
TREND	Returns values along a linear trend.
TRIMMEAN	Returns the mean of the interior of a data set.
TTEST	Returns the probability associated with a student's t-Test.
VAR	Estimates variance based on a sample, ignoring logical values and text.

Function	What It Does
VARA	Estimates variance based on a sample, including logical values and text.
VARP	Calculates variance based on the entire population, ignoring logical values and text.
VARPA	Calculates variance based on the entire population, including logical values and text.
WEIBULL	Returns the Weibull distribution.
ZTEST	Returns the two-tailed P-value of a z-test.

* Indicates a new function in Excel 2007.

TABLE A.11

Text Category Functions

Function	What It Does
BAHTTEXT	Converts a number to Baht text.
CHAR	Returns the character specified by the code number.
CLEAN	Removes all nonprintable characters from text.
CODE	Returns a numeric code for the first character in a text string.
CONCATENATE	Joins several text items into one text item.
DOLLAR	Converts a number to text, using currency format.
EXACT	Checks to see whether two text values are identical.
FIND	Finds one text value within another (case sensitive).
FIXED	Formats a number as text with a fixed number of decimals.
LEFT	Returns the leftmost characters from a text value.
LEN	Returns the number of characters in a text string.
LOWER	Converts text to lowercase.
MID	Returns a specific number of characters from a text string, starting at the position you specify.
PROPER	Capitalizes the first letter in each word of a text value.
REPLACE	Replaces characters within text.
REPT	Repeats text a given number of times.
RIGHT	Returns the rightmost characters from a text value.
SEARCH	Finds one text value within another (not case-sensitive).
SUBSTITUTE	Substitutes new text for old text in a text string.
T	Returns the text referred to by value.
TEXT	Formats a number and converts it to text.
TRIM	Removes excess spaces from text.
UPPER	Converts text to uppercase.
VALUE	Converts a text argument to a number.

Appendix B

What's on the CD-ROM

This appendix describes the contents of the CD that accompanies this book. For any last minute changes, please refer to the ReadMe file located at the root of the CD.

This appendix provides information on the following topics:

- System Requirements
- Using the CD
- Files and software on the CD
- Troubleshooting

System Requirements

Make sure that your computer meets the minimum system requirements listed in this section. If your computer doesn't match up to most of these requirements, you may have a problem using the contents of the CD.

- A Windows PC with Microsoft Excel 2007.
- A CD-ROM drive.

Using the CD

To install the items from the CD to your hard drive, follow these steps:

1. **Insert the CD into your computer's CD drive.** The license agreement appears.

NOTE The interface won't launch if you have autorun disabled. In that case, click Start ⇨ Run. In the dialog box that appears, type D:\start.exe. (Replace D with the proper letter if your CD drive uses a different letter. If you don't know the letter, see how your CD drive is listed under My Computer.) Click OK.

2. **Read through the license agreement and then click the Accept button if you want to use the CD.** After you click Accept, the License Agreement window won't appear again.

   The CD interface appears. The interface allows you to install the programs and run the demos with just a click of a button (or two).

What's on the CD

The following sections provide more details about the software and other materials available on the CD.

eBook version of *Excel 2007 Bible*

The complete text of the book you hold in your hands is provided on the CD in Adobe's Portable Document Format (PDF). You can read and quickly search the content of this PDF file by using Adobe's Acrobat Reader, also included on the CD.

Sample files for the *Excel 2007 Bible*

The files discussed in the book are organized by chapter. With a few exceptions, the files are all Excel 2007 files that have either of the following extensions:

- XLSX: An Excel workbook file
- XLSM: An Excel workbook file that contains VBA macros

When you open an XLSM file, Excel may display a Security Warning and tells you that macros have been disabled. To enable macros, click the Options button in the Security Warning panel and then select the option labeled Enable This Content.

Because the files on this CD are from a trusted source, you may want to copy the files to your hard drive and then designate the folder as a trusted location. To do so, follow these steps:

1. **Open an Explorer window, and select the CD-ROM drive that contains the companion CD-ROM.**
2. **Right-click the folder that corresponds to the root folder for the samples files, and choose Copy from the shortcut menu.**
3. **Activate the folder on your hard drive where you'd like to copy the files.** Right-click the directory, and choose Paste from the shortcut menu.

The CD-ROM files will be copied to a subfolder in the folder you specified in Step 3. To designate this new folder as a trusted location:

1. **Start Excel and choose Office ⇨ Excel Options to display the Excel Options dialog box.**
2. **In the Excel Options dialog box, click the Trust Center tab.**
3. **Click the Trust Center Settings button.**
4. **In the Trust Center dialog box, click the Trusted Locations tab.**

5. Click the Add New Location button to display the Microsoft Office Trusted Location dialog box.

6. In the Microsoft Office Trusted Location dialog box, click the Browse button and locate the folder that contains the files copied from the CD-ROM.

7. Make sure that you select the option labeled Subfolders Of This Location Are Also Trusted.

After performing these steps, when you open XLSM files from this location, the macros are enabled and you don't see the security warning.

Following is a list of the sample files, along with a brief description.

NOTE Some chapters don't use any sample file.

Chapter 01

- **table and chart.xlsx:** An introductory hands-on example that creates a table and a chart.

Chapter 03

- **loan payment calculator.xlsx:** A workbook that demonstrates some formulas.
- **number formatting.xlsx:** A workbook that contains a few examples of built-in number formats.

Chapter 05

- **budget.xlsx:** A simple multisheet budget workbook to demonstrate formatting across worksheets.

Chapter 06

- **real estate table.xlsx:** A workbook that contains a table of real estate listings for practice working with tables.

Chapter 07

- **loan payments.xlsx:** A workbook that contains a range of data and formulas to demonstrate the effect of applying simple formatting
- **theme examples.xlsx:** A workbook that contains a table, SmartArt, and a chart to demonstrate the effect of applying different document themes

Chapter 11

- **cell references.xlsx:** A workbook used to demonstrate the effect of using different types of cell references when copying formulas.
- **circular reference.xlsx:** A workbook that demonstrates an intentional circular reference. When you open this workbook, you see a message informing you of the circular reference.
- **worksheet functions.xlsx:** A workbook that contains a table that lists and describes every worksheet function.
- **table formulas.xlsx:** A workbook used to demonstrate the use of formulas within a table.

Chapter 12

- **character set.xlsm:** A workbook that displays the characters available in any font installed on your system.

- **text formula examples.xlsx:** A workbook that contains examples of advanced text formulas.
- **text histogram.xlsx:** A workbook that contains two examples of creating a histogram directly in a range.

Chapter 13

- **holidays.xlsx:** A workbook that demonstrates how to calculate the date for 10 U.S. holidays.
- **jogging log.xlsx:** A workbook that tracks time and distanced jogged. Demonstrates the use of times not associated with a time of day.
- **time sheet.xlsm:** A workbook that tracks hours worked during a week.
- **work days.xlsx:** A workbook that demonstrates how to calculate the number of work days between two dates (excluding weekends and holidays).

Chapter 14

- **basic counting.xlsx:** A workbook that demonstrates basic counting formulas.
- **conditional sum.xlsx:** A workbook that demonstrates how to calculate conditional sums, using single and multiple criteria.
- **count unique.xlsx:** A workbook that demonstrates how to count unique (nonduplicated) items in a range.
- **counting text in a range.xlsx:** A workbook that demonstrates various ways to count text in a range.
- **cumulative sum.xlsx:** A workbook that demonstrates how to display a cumulative sum.
- **frequency distribution.xlsx:** A workbook that demonstrates four methods to create a frequency distribution.
- **multiple criteria counting.xlsx:** A workbook that demonstrates counting formulas that use multiple criteria

Chapter 15

- **basic lookup examples.xlsx:** A workbook that demonstrates a variety of common lookup techniques.
- **specialized lookup examples.xlsx:** A workbook that demonstrates a variety of specialized lookup techniques.

Chapter 16

- **annuity calculator.xlsx:** A workbook that calculates interest on annuities.
- **credit card payments.xlsx:** A workbook that contains formulas to calculate credit card payments.
- **depreciation calculations.xlsx:** A workbook that demonstrates methods to calculate depreciation of an asset.
- **investment calculations.xlsx:** A workbook that demonstrates formulas to calculate interest on investments.
- **irregular payments.xlsx:** A workbook that calculates a loan with irregular payments.

- **loan amortization schedule.xlsx:** A workbook that calculates a loan amortization schedule.
- **loan data tables.xlsx:** A workbook that demonstrates how to use 1-way and 2-way data tables to calculate loan information.
- **loan payment.xlsx:** A workbook that contains formulas to calculate loan payments.

Chapter 18

- **array formula calendar.xlsx:** A workbook that displays a calendar for any month by using a complex array formula.
- **multi-cell array formulas.xlsx:** A workbook that demonstrates a variety of multicell array formulas.
- **single-cell array formulas.xlsx:** A workbook that demonstrates a variety of single-cell array formulas.

Chapter 19

- **area charts.xlsx:** A workbook that contains an area chart example.
- **bar charts.xlsx:** A workbook that contains bar chart examples.
- **bubble charts.xlsx:** A workbook that contains bubble chart examples.
- **column charts.xlsx:** A workbook that contains various types of column charts.
- **doughnut charts.xlsx:** A workbook that contains a doughnut chart example
- **hands-on example.xlsx:** A workbook that contains data used in the hands-on charting example.
- **line charts.xlsx:** A workbook that contains bar chart examples.
- **pie charts.xlsx:** A workbook that contains pie chart examples.
- **radar charts.xlsx:** A workbook that contains radar chart examples.
- **six chart types.xlsx:** A workbook that shows a single range, displayed using six chart types.
- **stock charts.xlsx:** A workbook that contains stock chart examples.
- **surface charts.xlsx:** A workbook that contains a surface chart example.
- **xy charts.xlsx:** A workbook that contains XY chart examples.

Chapter 20

- **comparative histogram.xlsx:** A workbook that demonstrates how to create a comparative histogram chart.
- **conditional colors.xlsx:** A workbook that contains a chart that displays different color columns, based on the value.
- **function plot 2D.xlsx:** A workbook that demonstrates how to plot a function that uses one variable.
- **function plot 3D.xlsm:** A workbook that demonstrates how to plot a function that uses two variables.
- **gantt chart.xlsx:** A workbook that demonstrates how to create a simple Gantt chart for project planning.
- **gauge chart.xlsx:** A workbook that contains a chart that plots a single data point as a gauge.

- **log scale.xlsx:** A workbook that demonstrates a logarithmic scale on a chart.
- **picture charts.xlsx:** A workbook that demonstrates the use of pictures in charts.
- **thermometer chart.xlsx:** A workbook that contains a chart that plots a single data point as a thermometer.
- **weather combination chart.xlsx:** A workbook that demonstrates a combination chart with two value axes.

Chapter 21

- **daily staffing levels.xlsx:** A workbook that demonstrates a conditional formatting color scale.
- **conditional formatting formulas.xlsx:** A workbook that demonstrates a variety of conditional formatting formulas.
- **data bars examples.xlsx:** A workbook that demonstrates conditional formatting data bars.
- **extreme color scale.xlsx:** A workbook that demonstrates a conditional formatting color scale in a large range.
- **icon set examples.xlsx:** A workbook that demonstrates a conditional formatting icon sets.

Chapter 24

- **number formats.xlsx:** A workbook that contains examples of many custom number formats.

Chapter 25

- **data validation examples.xlsx:** A workbook that contains examples that demonstrate data validation.

Chapter 26

- **outline example.xlsx:** A workbook that contains data suitable for an outline.

Chapter 27

- **region1.xlsx:** One of three workbooks used to demonstrate data consolidation.
- **region2.xlsx:** One of three workbooks used to demonstrate data consolidation.
- **region3.xlsx:** One of three workbooks used to demonstrate data consolidation.

Chapter 28

- **webpage.xlsx:** A workbook used to demonstrate HTML exporting.

Chapter 33

- **budget data.accdb:** A single-table Microsoft Access 2007 file, used to demonstrate Microsoft Query.

Chapter 34

- **bank accounts.xlsx:** A workbook that contains data suitable for a pivot table.

Chapter 35

- **calculated fields and items.xlsx:** A workbook that contains a pivot table that demonstrates calculated fields and calculated items.
- **county data.xlsx:** A workbook that contains a large table and a pivot table created from the table.

- **employee list.xlsx:** A workbook that contains a table to demonstrate the use of non-numeric data in a pivot table.

- **hourly readings.xlsx:** A workbook that contains time-based information to demonstrate grouping item by time.

- **income and expense.xlsx:** A workbook that contains a pivot table to demonstrate how to reference cells within a pivot table.

- **music list.xlsx:** A workbook that demonstrates how to create and format a pivot table report.

- **reverse pivot.xlsm:** A workbook that contains a VBA macro that converts a summary table into a 3-column database table.

- **sales by date.xlsx:** A workbook that contains time-based information to demonstrate grouping item by date.

- **sales by region.xlsx:** A workbook that demonstrates how to create a pivot chart from a pivot table.

- **test scores.xlsx:** A workbook that demonstrates how to use a pivot table to create a frequency distribution.

Chapter 36

- **direct mail.xlsx:** A workbook that contains a profit model to demonstrate how to create a 2-way data table for what-if analysis.

- **mortgage loan data table.xlsx:** A workbook that demonstrate how to create a data 1-way data table for what-if analysis.

- **mortgage loan.xlsx:** A workbook with input cells and formula cells to demonstrate what-if analysis.

- **production model.xlsx:** A workbook to demonstrate the Scenario Manager.

Chapter 37

- **allocating resources.xlsx:** A workbook that contains a model to demonstrate how to allocate resources and maximize profit using Solver.

- **investment portfolio.xlsx:** A workbook that contains a model to demonstrate how to maximize the return on an investment portfolio using Solver.

- **linear equations.xlsx:** A workbook that demonstrates how to use Solver to solve a set of linear equations.

- **mortgage loan.xlsx:** A workbook with input cells and formula cells to demonstrate goal seeking.

- **shipping costs.xlsx:** A workbook that contains a model to demonstrate how to minimize shipping costs using Solver.

- **three products.xlsx:** A workbook that contains a simple profit model to demonstrate Solver.

Chapter 38

- **atp examples.xlsx:** A workbook that demonstrates the tools in the Analysis ToolPak add-in.

Chapter 39

- **cube root.xlsm:** A workbook that contains a VBA function to calculate the cube root.

- **current date.xlsm:** A workbook that contains a simple VBA macro to insert the current date into the active cell.

- **list formulas.xlsm:** A workbook that contains a VBA macro to generate a list of all formulas in a worksheet.

Chapter 40
- **vba functions.xlsm:** A workbook that contains examples of VBA functions used in worksheet formulas.

Chapter 41
- **change case.xlsm:** A VBA macro that uses a UserForm to enable the user to make a choice.
- **show message.xlsm:** A workbook that contains a UserForm that displays a message.

Chapter 42
- **mortgage loan.xlsx:** A workbook that demonstrate how to use ActiveX controls on a worksheet, with no macros.
- **worksheet controls.xlsm:** A workbook that contains examples of all ActiveX controls that can be used on a worksheet.

Chapter 43
- **monitor a range.xlsm:** A workbook that contains a VBA `Worksheet_Change` macro that monitors all changes made to a specific range.
- **selection change event.xlsm:** A workbook that contains a VBA `Selection_Change` macro that changes the color of the row and column of the active cell.

Chapter 44
- **chart macros.xlsm:** A workbook that contains VBA macros that manipulate charts.
- **range copy.xlsm:** A workbook that contains a VBA macro that copies a variable-sized range.
- **range move.xlsm:** A workbook that contains a VBA macro that moves a range of cells.
- **select cells.xlsm:** A workbook that contains VBA macros that demonstrate range selection techniques.
- **selection type.xlsm:** A workbook that contains a VBA macro that demonstrates how to identify the object type of the current selection.
- **skip blanks while looping.xlsm:** A workbook that contains a VBA macro that demonstrates how to loop through a range of cells efficiently.

Chapter 45
- **change case.xlam:** An add-in file, created from the change case.xlsm example in Chapter 41.

Troubleshooting

If you have difficulty installing or using any of the materials on the companion CD, try the following solutions:

- **Turn off any antivirus software that you may have running.** Installers sometimes mimic virus activity and can make your computer incorrectly believe that it is being infected by a virus. (Be sure to turn the antivirus software back on later.)

- **Close all running programs.** The more programs you're running, the less memory is available to other programs. Installers also typically update files and programs; if you keep other programs running, installation may not work properly.
- **Reference the ReadMe:** Refer to the ReadMe file located at the root of the CD-ROM for the latest product information (if any) at the time of publication.

Customer Care

If you have trouble with the CD-ROM, please call the Wiley Product Technical Support phone number at (800) 762-2974. Outside the United States, call 1(317) 572-3994. You can also contact Wiley Product Technical Support at **http://support.wiley.com**. John Wiley & Sons will provide technical support only for installation and other general quality control items. For technical support on the applications themselves, consult the program's vendor or author.

To place additional orders or to request information about other Wiley products, please call (877) 762-2974.

Appendix C

Additional Excel Resources

I f I've done my job, the information provided in this book will be very useful to you. The book, however, can't cover every conceivable topic about Excel. Therefore, I've compiled a list of additional resources that you may find helpful.

I classify these resources into four categories: Excel's Help System, Microsoft technical support, Internet newsgroups, and Internet Web sites.

The Excel Help System

Many users tend to forget about an excellent source of information: the Excel Help system. This Help information is available by clicking the question mark icon in the upper-right corner of Excel's window. Or, just press F1. Either of these methods displays Excel Help in a new window. Then, type your search query and click Search.

> **NOTE** The Search button is a drop-down control that lets you specify what and where to search. See Figure C.1.

FIGURE C.1

Use the Search control to help target your search.

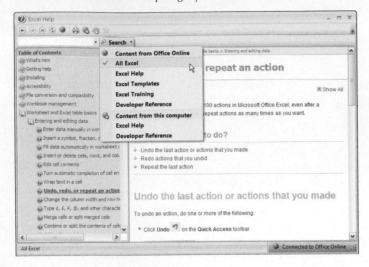

The Excel Help system isn't perfect — it often provides only superficial help and ignores some topics altogether. But if you're stuck, a quick search of the Help system may be worth a try.

Microsoft Technical Support

Technical support is the common term for assistance provided by a software vendor. In this case, I'm talking about assistance that comes directly from Microsoft. Microsoft's technical support is available in several different forms.

Support options

Microsoft's support options are constantly changing. To find out what options are available (both free and fee-based), go to

```
http://support.microsoft.com
```

Microsoft Knowledge Base

Perhaps your best bet for solving a problem may be the Microsoft Knowledge Base, which is the primary Microsoft product information source. It's an extensive, searchable database that consists of tens of thousands of detailed articles containing technical information, bug lists, fix lists, and more.

You have free and unlimited access to the Knowledge Base via the Internet. To access the Knowledge Base, use the following URL and then click Search The Knowledge Base:

```
http://support.microsoft.com/search
```

Microsoft Excel Home Page

The official home page of Excel is at

```
http://www.microsoft.com/office/excel
```

This site contains a variety of material, such as tips, templates, answers to questions, training materials, and links to companion products.

Microsoft Office Home Page

For information about Office 2007 (including Excel), try this site:

```
http://office.microsoft.com
```

You'll find product updates, add-ins, examples, and lots of other useful information.

> **NOTE** As you know, the Internet is a dynamic entity that changes rapidly. Web sites are often reorganized, so a particular URL listed in this appendix may not be available when you try to access it.

Internet Newsgroups

Usenet is an Internet service that provides access to several thousand special interest groups that enable you to communicate with people who share common interests. A newsgroup works like a public bulletin board. You can post a message or questions, and (usually) others reply to your message.

Thousands of newsgroups cover virtually every topic you can think of (and many that you haven't thought of). Typically, questions posed on a newsgroup are answered within 24 hours — assuming, of course, that you ask the questions in a manner that makes others want to reply.

Accessing newsgroups by using a newsreader

You can use newsreader software to access the Usenet newsgroups. Many such programs are available, but you probably already have one installed: Microsoft Outlook Express, which is installed with Internet Explorer.

Microsoft maintains an extensive list of newsgroups, including quite a few devoted to Excel. If your Internet Service Provider doesn't carry the Microsoft newsgroups, you can access them directly from Microsoft's news server. (In fact, that's the preferred method.) You need to configure your newsreader software (not your Web browser) to access Microsoft's news server at this address:

```
msnews.microsoft.com
```

Accessing newsgroups by using a Web browser

As an alternative to using newsreader software, you can read and post to the Microsoft newsgroups directly from your Web browser. This option is often significantly slower than using standard newsgroup software and is best suited for situations in which newsgroup access is prohibited by network policies.

- Access thousands of newsgroups at Google Groups. The URL is
  ```
  http://groups.google.com
  ```
- Access the Microsoft newsgroups (including Excel newsgroups) from this URL:
  ```
  www.microsoft.com/communities/newsgroups/default.mspx
  ```

Table C.1 lists the most popular English-language Excel newsgroups found on Microsoft's news server (and also available at Google Groups).

TABLE C.1

The Microsoft.com Excel-Related Newsgroups

Newsgroup	Topic
microsoft.public.excel	General Excel topics
microsoft.public.excel.charting	Building charts with Excel
microsoft.public.excel.interopoledde	OLE, DDE, and other cross-application issues
microsoft.public.excel.macintosh	Excel issues on the Macintosh operating system
microsoft.public.excel.misc	General topics that don't fit one of the other categories
microsoft.public.excel.newusers	Help for newcomers to Excel
microsoft.public.excel.printing	Printing with Excel
microsoft.public.excel.programming	Programming Excel with VBA macros
microsoft.public.excel.templates	Spreadsheet Solutions templates and other XLT files
microsoft.public.excel.worksheet.functions	Worksheet functions

Searching newsgroups

The fastest way to find a quick answer to a question is to search the past newsgroup postings. Often, searching past newsgroup postings is an excellent alternative to posting a question to the newsgroup because you can get the answer immediately. Unless your question is very obscure, there's an excellent chance that your question has already been asked and answered. The best source for searching newsgroup postings is Google Groups, at the following Web address:

```
http://groups.google.com
```

How does searching work? Suppose that you have a problem identifying unique values in a range of cells. You can perform a search using the following keywords: **Excel**, **Range**, and **Unique**. The Google search engine probably will find dozens of newsgroup postings that deal with these topics.

If the number of results is too large, refine your search by adding search terms. Sifting through the messages may take a while, but you have an excellent chance of finding an answer to your question. In fact, I estimate that at least 90 percent of the questions posted in the Excel newsgroups can be answered by searching Google.

Tips for Posting to a Newsgroup

If you're new to online newsgroups, here are some pointers:

- Make sure that your question has not already been answered by conducting a search.
- Make the subject line descriptive. Postings with a subject line such as "Help me!" and "Another Question" are less likely to be answered than postings with a more specific subject, such as "Sizing a Chart's Plot Area."
- Specify the Excel version that you use. In many cases, the answer to your question depends on your version of Excel.
- For best results, ask only one question per message.
- Make your question as specific as possible.
- Keep your question brief and to the point but provide enough information so that someone can answer it adequately.
- Indicate what you've done to try to answer your own question.
- Post in the appropriate newsgroup, and don't cross-post to other groups unless the question applies to multiple groups.
- Don't type in all uppercase or all lowercase; check your grammar and spelling.
- Don't include a file attachment.
- Avoid posting in HTML format. Plain text is the preferred format.
- If you request an e-mail reply in addition to a newsgroup reply, don't use an "anti-spam" e-mail address that requires the responder to modify your address. Why cause extra work for someone doing you a favor?

Internet Web Sites

The World Wide Web (WWW) has dozens of excellent sites devoted to Excel. I list a few of my favorites here.

The Spreadsheet Page

This is my own Web site, which contains files to download, developer tips, instructions for accessing Excel Easter eggs, spreadsheet jokes, an extensive list of links to other Excel sites, and information about my books. The URL is

```
http://www.j-walk.com/ss
```

Daily Dose of Excel

This is a frequently updated weblog created by Dick Kusleika, with about a dozen contributors (including me). It covers a variety of topics, and readers can leave comments. The URL is

```
http://dailydoseofexcel.com
```

Jon Peltier's Excel Page

Those who frequent the microsoft.public.excel.charting newsgroup are familiar with Jon Peltier. Jon has an uncanny ability to solve practically any chart-related problem. His Web site contains many Excel tips and an extensive collection of charting examples. The URL is

```
http://peltiertech.com/Excel
```

Pearson Software Consulting

This site, maintained by Chip Pearson, contains dozens of useful examples of VBA and clever formula techniques. The URL is

```
www.cpearson.com/excel.htm
```

Stephen Bullen's Excel Page

Stephen's Web site contains some fascinating examples of Excel code, including a section titled "They Said It Couldn't Be Done." The URL is

```
www.bmsltd.co.uk/excel
```

David McRitchie's Excel Pages

David's site is jam-packed with useful Excel information and is updated frequently. The URL is

```
www.mvps.org/dmcritchie/excel/excel.htm
```

Mr. Excel

Mr. Excel, also known as Bill Jelen, maintains an extensive site devoted to Excel. The site also features a message board. The URL is

```
www.mrexcel.com/
```

Appendix D

Excel Shortcut Keys

Many users have discovered that using their keyboard can often be much more efficient than using their mouse. This appendix lists the most useful shortcut keys available in Excel. The shortcuts are arranged by context.

The keys listed assume that you're not using the Transition Navigation Keys, which are designed to emulate Lotus 1-2-3. You can select the Transition Navigation Keys option in the Advanced tab of the Excel Options dialog box. This option is in the Lotus Compatibility section.

NEW FEATURE On the surface, the new Ribbon interface in Excel 2007 appears to be designed for a mouse. However, you can access nearly all the Ribbon commands by using the keyboard. Press the Alt key, and Excel displays "key tips" next to each command. Just press the key that corresponds to the command you need. For example, the command to toggle worksheet gridlines is View ⇨ Show/Hide ⇨ Gridlines. The keyboard equivalent is Alt, followed by WVG. Note that you don't need to keep the Alt key depressed while you type the subsequent letters.

TABLE D.1

Moving Through a Worksheet

Key(s)	What It Does
Arrow keys	Moves left, right, up, or down one cell
Home	Moves to the beginning of the row
Home*	Moves to the upper-left cell displayed in the window
End*	Moves to the lower-left cell displayed in the window
Arrow keys*	Scrolls left, right, up, or down one cell
PgUp	Moves up one screen
PgDn	Moves down one screen
Ctrl+PgUp	Moves to the previous sheet
Ctrl+PgDn	Moves to the next sheet
Alt+PgUp	Moves one screen to the left
Alt+PgDn	Moves one screen to the right
Ctrl+Home	Moves to the first cell in the worksheet (A1)
Ctrl+End	Moves to the last nonempty cell of the worksheet
Ctrl+arrow key	Moves to the edge of a data block; if the cell is blank, moves to the first nonblank cell
Ctrl+Backspace	Scrolls to display the active cell
End, followed by Home	Moves to the last nonempty cell on the worksheet
F5	Prompts for a cell address to go to
F6	Moves to the next pane of a window that has been split
Shift+F6	Moves to the previous pane of a window that has been split
Ctrl+Tab	Moves to the next window
Ctrl+Shift+Tab	Moves to the previous window
Ctrl+F6	Moves to the next window
Ctrl+Shift+F6	Moves to the previous window

* With Scroll Lock on

TABLE D.2

Selecting Cells in the Worksheet

Key(s)	What It Does
Shift+arrow key	Expands the selection in the direction indicated
Shift+spacebar	Selects the entire row(s) in the selected range
Ctrl+spacebar	Selects the entire column(s) in the selected range
Ctrl+Shift+ spacebar	Selects the entire worksheet.

816

Key(s)	What It Does
Ctrl+Shift+ spacebar*	Selects the table without the header row and totals row. Ctrl+Shift+ spacebar again selects the complete table. Ctrl+Shift+ spacebar again selects the entire worksheet
Shift+Home	Expands the selection to the beginning of the current row
Ctrl+*	Selects the block of data surrounding the active cell
F8	Extends the selection as you use navigation keys. Press F8 again to return to normal selection mode
Shift+F8	Adds other nonadjacent cells or ranges to the selection; pressing Shift+F8 again ends Add mode
F5	Prompts for a range or range name to select
Ctrl+G	Prompts for a range or range name to select
Ctrl+A	Selects the entire worksheet
Ctrl+A*	Selects the table without the header row and totals row. Ctrl+Shift+ spacebar again selects the complete table. Ctrl+Shift+ spacebar again selects the entire worksheet.
Shift+Backspace	Cancels a range selection and selects only the active cell

* If the active cell is within a multicell range

TABLE D.3

Moving within a Range Selection

Key(s)	What It Does
Enter	Moves the cell pointer. The direction depends on the setting in the Edit tab of the Options dialog box.
Shift+Enter	Moves the cell pointer up to the preceding cell in the selection
Tab	Moves the cell pointer right to the next cell in the selection
Shift+Tab	Moves the cell pointer left to the preceding cell in the selection
Ctrl+period (.)	Moves the cell pointer to the next corner of the current cell range
Shift+Backspace	Collapses the cell selection to just the active cell

TABLE D.4

Editing Keys in the Formula Bar

Key(s)	What It Does
F2	Begins editing the active cell
Arrow keys	Moves the cursor one character in the direction of the arrow
Home	Moves the cursor to the beginning of the line

continued

TABLE D.4 *(continued)*

Key(s)	What It Does
End	Moves the cursor to the end of the line
Ctrl+right arrow	Moves the cursor one word to the right
Ctrl+left arrow	Moves the cursor one word to the left
F3	Displays the Paste Name dialog box when you're creating a formula
Ctrl+A	Displays the Function Arguments dialog box (after you type a function name in a formula)
Del	Deletes the character to the right of the cursor
Ctrl+Del	Deletes all characters from the cursor to the end of the line
Backspace	Deletes the character to the left of the cursor
Esc	Cancels the editing

TABLE D.5

Formatting Keys

Key(s)	What It Does
Ctrl+1	Displays the Format dialog box for the selected object
Ctrl+B	Sets or removes boldface
Ctrl+I	Sets or removes italic
Ctrl+U	Sets or removes underlining
Ctrl+5	Sets or removes strikethrough
Ctrl+Shift+~	Applies the general number format
Ctrl+Shift+!	Applies the comma format with two decimal places
Ctrl+Shift+#	Applies the date format (day, month, year)
Ctrl+Shift+@	Applies the time format (hour, minute, a.m./p.m.)
Ctrl+Shift+$	Applies the currency format with two decimal places
Ctrl+Shift+%	Applies the percent format with no decimal places
Ctrl+Shift+&	Applies border to outline
Ctrl+Shift+_	Removes all borders

TABLE D.6

Other Shortcut Keys

Key(s)	What It Does
Ctrl+F1	Toggles the display of the Ribbon
Alt+=	Inserts the AutoSum formula
Alt+Backspace	Equivalent to Undo
Alt+Enter	Starts a new line in the current cell
Ctrl+;	Enters the current date
Ctrl+:	Enters the current time
Ctrl+0 (zero)	Hides columns
Ctrl+6	Cycles among various ways of displaying objects on a worksheet
Ctrl+8	Toggles the display of outline symbols
Ctrl+9	Hides rows
Ctrl+[	Selects direct precedent cells
Ctrl+]	Selects directly dependent cells
Ctrl+C	Equivalent to Home ⇨ Clipboard ⇨ Copy
Ctrl+D	Equivalent to Home ⇨ Editing ⇨ Fill ⇨ Down
Ctrl+F	Equivalent to Home ⇨ Editing ⇨ Find & Select ⇨ Find
Ctrl+H	Equivalent to Home ⇨ Editing ⇨ Find & Select ⇨ Replace
Ctrl+K	Equivalent to Insert ⇨ Links ⇨ Hyperlink
Ctrl+N	Creates a new workbook
Ctrl+O	Equivalent to Office ⇨ Open
Ctrl+P	Equivalent to Office ⇨ Print
Ctrl+R	Equivalent to Home ⇨ Editing ⇨ Fill ⇨ Fill Right
Ctrl+T	Equivalent to Insert ⇨ Tables ⇨ Table
Ctrl+Shift+T	Toggles the Total row in a table
Ctrl+Shift+L	Toggles the Autofilter controls in a table
Ctrl+S	Equivalent to Office ⇨ Save
Ctlr+Alt+V	Equivalent to Home ⇨ Clipboard ⇨ Paste ⇨ Paste Special
Ctrl+Shift+(	Unhides rows in the selection
Ctrl+Shift+)	Unhides columns in the selection
Ctrl+Shift+A	Inserts the argument names and parentheses for the function (after you type a valid function name in a formula)
Ctrl+V	Equivalent to Home ⇨ Clipboard ⇨ Paste
Ctrl+X	Equivalent to Home ⇨ Clipboard ⇨ Cut
Ctrl+Z	Undo

TABLE D.7

Function Keys

Key(s)	What It Does
F1	Displays Help
Alt+F1	Inserts default chart object that uses the selected range
Alt+Shift+ F1	Inserts a new worksheet
F2	Edits the active cell
Shift+F2	Edits a cell comment
Alt+F2	Equivalent to Office ➪ Save As
Alt+Shift+F2	Equivalent to Office ➪ Save
F3	Pastes a name into a formula
Shift+F3	Pastes a function into a formula
Ctrl+F3	Equivalent to Formulas ➪ Defined Names ➪ Name Manager
Ctrl+Shift+F3	Equivalent to Formulas ➪ Defined Names@>Create From Selection
F4	Repeats the last action
Shift+F4	Repeats the last Find (Find Next)
Ctrl+F4	Closes the window
Alt+F4	Equivalent to Office ➪ Exit Excel
F5	Equivalent to Home ➪ Editing ➪ Find & Select ➪ Go To
Shift+F5	Equivalent to Home ➪ Editing ➪ Find & Select ➪ Find
Ctrl+F5	Restores a minimized or maximized workbook window
Alt+F5	Refreshes active query or pivot table
F6	Moves to the next pane
Shift+F6	Moves to the previous pane
Ctrl+F6	Activates to the next window
Ctrl+Shift+F6	Activates the previous workbook window
F7	Equivalent to Review ➪ Proofing ➪ Spelling
Ctrl+F7	Allows moving the window with the arrow keys
F8	Extends a selection (toggle)
Shift+F8	Adds to the selection (toggle)
Ctrl+F8	Allows resizing the window with the arrow keys
Alt+F8	Equivalent to Developer ➪ Code ➪ Macros
F9	Calculates all sheets in all open workbooks
Shift+F9	Calculates the active worksheet
Ctrl+Alt+F9	Global calculation

Key(s)	What It Does
Ctrl+F9	Minimizes the workbook
F10	Displays keytips for the Ribbon
Shift+F10	Displays a shortcut menu for the selected object (equivalent to right-clicking)
Ctrl+F10	Maximizes or restores the workbook window
F11	Creates a chart in a chart sheet
Shift+F11	Inserts a new worksheet
Ctrl+F11	Inserts an Excel 4.0 macro sheet
Alt+F11	Equivalent to Developer ➪ Code ➪ Visual Basic
F12	Equivalent to Office ➪ Save
Shift+F12	Equivalent to Office ➪ Save
Ctrl+F12	Equivalent to Office ➪ Open
Ctrl+Shift+F12	Equivalent to Office ➪ Print

Index

Symbols and Numerics

+ (addition) operator, 176
: (colon) range reference operator, 201
, (comma) union operator, 201
& (concatenation) operator, 176, 210
/ (division) operator, 176
#DIV/0! error value, 554–555
= (equal to) operator, 176
^ (exponentiation) operator, 176
> (greater than) operator, 176
>= (greater than or equal to) operator, 176
(hash mark), denoting error values, 195, 552
< (less than) operator, 176
<= (less than or equal to) operator, 176
* (multiplication) operator, 176
#N/A error value, 555
#NAME? error value, 555- (negative sign), 476–477
<> (not equal to) operator, 176
#NULL! error value, 555–556
#NUM! error value, 556
#REF! error value, 556
- (subtraction) operator, 176
3-D charts, 406–407
#VALUE! error value, 556
1900 date system, 224
1904 date system, 224

A

ABS function, 792
absolute cell references, 187–191, 556–557
absolute macro recording, 692
accelerator keys
    dialog boxes, 16
    UserForms, 732
accepting changes, 538
Access databases, importing, 576–578
accessing
    CD-ROM, 800
    external database files, 575
    help system, 809
    newsgroups, 811
    Ribbon with keyboard, 12
    worksheets, 4
Accounting format, 50
ACCRINT function, 789
ACCRINTM function, 789

accuracy of large values, 36
ACOS function, 792
ACOSH function, 792
actions
    repeating, 13
    undoing, 13
Activate event
    workbooks, 747
    worksheets, 751
activating
    charts, 360
    dialog box controls, 16
    worksheets, 56–57
active area (of worksheets), 156
active cell, 7
active cell indicator, 6
ActiveX controls
    CheckBox, 735, 739
    ComboBox, 735, 740
    CommandButton, 735, 740
    defined, 734
    design mode, 736
    Image, 735, 741
    inserting, 733–736
    Label, 735, 741
    linking to cells, 738
    ListBox, 735, 741
    listing, 735
    macros, 738–739
    OptionButton, 735, 741–742
    properties, 736–738
    ScrollBar, 735, 742
    SpinButton, 735, 743
    testing, 736
    TextBox, 735, 743–744
    ToggleButton, 735, 744
    UserForms, 721–723
actual versus displayed values, 558
Add Constraint dialog box, 654–655
Add Scenario dialog box, 644–645
Add View dialog box, 172
adding
    background images, 121
    chart elements, 361
    chart titles, 388
    columns to tables, 101
    columns to worksheets, 66–67

B

G

S

T

Wiley Publishing, Inc.
End-User License Agreement

READ THIS. You should carefully read these terms and conditions before opening the software packet(s) included with this book "Book". This is a license agreement "Agreement" between you and Wiley Publishing, Inc. "WPI". By opening the accompanying software packet(s), you acknowledge that you have read and accept the following terms and conditions. If you do not agree and do not want to be bound by such terms and conditions, promptly return the Book and the unopened software packet(s) to the place you obtained them for a full refund.

1. **License Grant.** WPI grants to you (either an individual or entity) a nonexclusive license to use one copy of the enclosed software program(s) (collectively, the "Software") solely for your own personal or business purposes on a single computer (whether a standard computer or a workstation component of a multi-user network). The Software is in use on a computer when it is loaded into temporary memory (RAM) or installed into permanent memory (hard disk, CD-ROM, or other storage device). WPI reserves all rights not expressly granted herein.

2. **Ownership.** WPI is the owner of all right, title, and interest, including copyright, in and to the compilation of the Software recorded on the physical packet included with this Book "Software Media". Copyright to the individual programs recorded on the Software Media is owned by the author or other authorized copyright owner of each program. Ownership of the Software and all proprietary rights relating thereto remain with WPI and its licensers.

3. **Restrictions on Use and Transfer.**

    (a) You may only (i) make one copy of the Software for backup or archival purposes, or (ii) transfer the Software to a single hard disk, provided that you keep the original for backup or archival purposes. You may not (i) rent or lease the Software, (ii) copy or reproduce the Software through a LAN or other network system or through any computer subscriber system or bulletin-board system, or (iii) modify, adapt, or create derivative works based on the Software.

    (b) You may not reverse engineer, decompile, or disassemble the Software. You may transfer the Software and user documentation on a permanent basis, provided that the transferee agrees to accept the terms and conditions of this Agreement and you retain no copies. If the Software is an update or has been updated, any transfer must include the most recent update and all prior versions.

4. **Restrictions on Use of Individual Programs.** You must follow the individual requirements and restrictions detailed for each individual program in Appendix B of this Book or on the Software Media. These limitations are also contained in the individual license agreements recorded on the Software Media. These limitations may include a requirement that after using the program for a specified period of time, the user must pay a registration fee or discontinue use. By opening the Software packet(s), you agree to abide by the licenses and restrictions for these individual programs that are detailed in Appendix B and/or on the Software Media. None of the material on this Software Media or listed in this Book may ever be redistributed, in original or modified form, for commercial purposes.

5. **Limited Warranty.**

    (a) WPI warrants that the Software and Software Media are free from defects in materials and workmanship under normal use for a period of sixty (60) days from the date of purchase of this Book. If WPI receives notification within the warranty period of defects in materials or workmanship, WPI will replace the defective Software Media.

(b) WPI AND THE AUTHOR(S) OF THE BOOK DISCLAIM ALL OTHER WARRANTIES, EXPRESS OR IMPLIED, INCLUDING WITHOUT LIMITATION IMPLIED WARRANTIES OF MERCHANTABILITY AND FITNESS FOR A PARTICULAR PURPOSE, WITH RESPECT TO THE SOFTWARE, THE PROGRAMS, THE SOURCE CODE CONTAINED THEREIN, AND/OR THE TECHNIQUES DESCRIBED IN THIS BOOK. WPI DOES NOT WARRANT THAT THE FUNCTIONS CONTAINED IN THE SOFTWARE WILL MEET YOUR REQUIREMENTS OR THAT THE OPERATION OF THE SOFTWARE WILL BE ERROR FREE.

(c) This limited warranty gives you specific legal rights, and you may have other rights that vary from jurisdiction to jurisdiction.

6. **Remedies.**

(a) WPI's entire liability and your exclusive remedy for defects in materials and workmanship shall be limited to replacement of the Software Media, which may be returned to WPI with a copy of your receipt at the following address: Software Media Fulfillment Department, Attn.: *Excel 2007 Bible*, Wiley Publishing, Inc., 10475 Crosspoint Blvd., Indianapolis, IN 46256, or call 1-800-762-2974. Please allow four to six weeks for delivery. This Limited Warranty is void if failure of the Software Media has resulted from accident, abuse, or mis-application. Any replacement Software Media will be warranted for the remainder of the original warranty period or thirty (30) days, whichever is longer.

(b) In no event shall WPI or the author be liable for any damages whatsoever (including without limitation damages for loss of business profits, business interruption, loss of business information, or any other pecuniary loss) arising from the use of or inability to use the Book or the Software, even if WPI has been advised of the possibility of such damages.

(c) Because some jurisdictions do not allow the exclusion or limitation of liability for consequential or incidental damages, the above limitation or exclusion may not apply to you.

7. **U.S. Government Restricted Rights.** Use, duplication, or disclosure of the Software for or on behalf of the United States of America, its agencies and/or instrumentalities "U.S. Government" is subject to restrictions as stated in paragraph (c)(1)(ii) of the Rights in Technical Data and Computer Software clause of DFARS 252.227-7013, or subparagraphs (c) (1) and (2) of the Commercial Computer Software - Restricted Rights clause at FAR 52.227-19, and in similar clauses in the NASA FAR supplement, as applicable.

8. **General.** This Agreement constitutes the entire understanding of the parties and revokes and supersedes all prior agreements, oral or written, between them and may not be modified or amended except in a writing signed by both parties hereto that specifically refers to this Agreement. This Agreement shall take precedence over any other documents that may be in conflict herewith. If any one or more provisions contained in this Agreement are held by any court or tribunal to be invalid, illegal, or otherwise unenforceable, each and every other provision shall remain in full force and effect.